Living Liturgy

Using this book for small group sharing

Groups using *Living Liturgy*™ for prayer and faith-sharing might begin with the following general format and then adjust it to fit different needs.

OPENING PRAYER
- Begin with a hymn
- Pray the opening prayer for the Sunday or solemnity

GOD'S WORD
- Proclaim the gospel
- Observe a brief period of silence

INDIVIDUAL STUDY, REFLECTION, PRAYER
- Read and consider "Reflecting on the Gospel" or "Living the Paschal Mystery"
- Spend some time in reflection and prayer

FAITH-SHARING
- Use the "Assembly & Faith-sharing Groups" spirituality statements (and the specific liturgical ministry statements if they apply)
- Consider what ways the gospel is challenging you to *live* the liturgy you will celebrate on Sunday

CONCLUDING PRAYER
- Pray the "Model Prayer of the Faithful"
- Pray the Our Father at the end of the intercessions
- Conclude with a hymn

BOOKMARK

Living Liturgy™

Using this book for personal prayer

The best preparation for Sunday celebration of Eucharist is prayer. Here are two suggested approaches for an individual to use this book for personal prayer.

Daily Prayer

MONDAY
- Read the gospel prayerfully

TUESDAY
- Read the gospel again
- Reflect on the statements from "Assembly and Faith-sharing Groups" and let your reflection lead you to prayer

WEDNESDAY
- Read again the gospel
- Read "Reflecting on the Gospel" and let it lead you to prayer

THURSDAY
- Read and study "Living the Paschal Mystery"
- Pray the "Model Prayer of the Faithful"

FRIDAY
- Pray the responsorial psalm
- Read "Connecting the Responsorial Psalm to the readings"

SATURDAY
- Read the gospel and first reading
- Read and study "Focusing the Gospel"
- Reflect on how you have been able to live this gospel during the week

SUNDAY
- Enter fully into the celebration of Eucharist
- Enjoy a day of rest

Prayer as Time and Opportunity Permit

A daily routine of study and prayer is not always possible. As time and opportunity permit:
- Read the gospel prayerfully
- Reflect on "Living the Paschal Mystery"
- Pray the "Model Prayer of the Faithful"

Living Liturgy™

Living Liturgy™

Spirituality, Celebration, and Catechesis for Sundays and Solemnities

Year B • 2009

Joyce Ann Zimmerman, C.PP.S.
Kathleen Harmon, S.N.D. de N.
Christopher W. Conlon, S.M.

LITURGICAL PRESS
Collegeville, Minnesota

www.litpress.org

Design by Ann Blattner. Art by Annika Nelson.

ISSN 1547-089X

ISBN 978-0-8146-2746-4

✠ CONTENTS

Joyce Ann Zimmerman, C.PP.S. is the director of the Institute for Liturgical Ministry in Dayton, Ohio, and is the founding editor and columnist for *Liturgical Ministry*. She is also an adjunct professor of liturgy, liturgical consultant, and frequent facilitator of workshops on liturgy. She has published numerous scholarly and pastoral liturgical works. She holds civil and pontifical doctorates of theology.

Kathleen Harmon, S.N.D. de N. is the music director for programs of the Institute for Liturgical Ministry in Dayton, Ohio, and is the author of the *Music Notes* column for *Liturgical Ministry*. An educator and musician, she facilitates liturgical music workshops and cantor formation programs, and is a parish director of music. She holds a graduate degree in music and a doctorate in liturgy.

Christopher W. Conlon, S.M. is a Marianist priest who works with faculty and staff as well as teaches Scripture at the University of Dayton. He has been an educator for over a half century and is a highly respected homilist, a frequent workshop presenter, and a spiritual director. He holds a graduate degree in religious education and the licentiate in theology.

USING THIS RESOURCE

This is the tenth volume of *Living Liturgy™: Spirituality, Celebration, and Catechesis for Sundays and Solemnities*. A decade! Some people other than the writers themselves even have all ten volumes on their bookshelf. Rather than a monument to the team's perseverance, this mark of accomplishment is a testimony to the Spirit's working within all of us—writers and readers alike. It is a testimony that the Scriptures (and especially the gospels) are ever fresh, bringing God's challenging and comforting word.

TENTH VOLUME

As with each year, there are some new things in this volume. First, we have a change in team membership. Replacing Fr. Tom Greisen and Fr. Tom Leclerc (whose excellent contribution to previous volumes is much appreciated) is Fr. Christopher Conlon, a Marianist educator who brings a wealth of knowledge, experience, and wit to our team meetings. Second, we now have a section on the Celebration page suggesting homily points; this is a response to repeated requests for more help for homilists. Introducing this section necessarily meant eliminating something; regular subscribers to *Living Liturgy™* will notice that the section entitled "Understanding Scripture" is missing (we hope some day to publish these more than 500 entries from the past nine years as a separate volume). Third, we have retitled and moved to the Spirituality pages the sections on the responsorial psalm and cantor preparation. Finally, we've changed the layout of the liturgical ministry questions (unshaded, but in a box) so they more clearly stand out from the shaded areas where the Scripture texts are printed.

NEW TEAM, NEW FEATURES, NEW LOOK

Living Liturgy™ continues its original purpose: to help people prepare for liturgy and live a liturgical spirituality (that is, a way of living that is rooted in liturgy) that opens their vision to their baptismal identity as the Body of Christ and shapes their living according to the rhythm of paschal mystery dying and rising. The paschal mystery is the central focus of liturgy, of the gospels, and of this volume.

PASCHAL MYSTERY STILL CENTRAL FOCUS

A threefold dynamic of daily living, prayer, and study continues to determine the basic structure of *Living Liturgy™*, captured in the layout under the headings "Spirituality," "Celebration," and "Catechesis." So, there is much that is new, and much with which regular readers will recognize and be familiar.

SPIRITUALITY, CELEBRATION, AND CATECHESIS

A note about music suggestions on the Catechesis page: because a number of the music suggestions made in *Living Liturgy™* are drawn from resources published annually, some suggestions made at the time a volume of *Living Liturgy™* was being written and published may no longer appear in the resources cited. Also, our intention here is not to provide a complete list of music suggestions for each Sunday or solemnity (these are readily available in other publications), but to make a few suggestions with accompanying catechesis; thus, we hope this is a learning process.

A NOTE ABOUT MUSIC SUGGESTIONS

During Ordinary Time of the 2009 liturgical year, we read from Mark's gospel where one recurring theme is discipleship. Faithful discipleship means uniting ourselves with Christ in his paschal mystery. It means acknowledging him as Son of God and Messiah. It means conforming our lives to his.

FAITHFUL DISCIPLESHIP

INTRODUCTION TO THE GOSPEL OF MARK

The Gospel of Mark, generally recognized as the first of the four canonical gospels, was written around the year seventy—the year the Romans destroyed the city of Jerusalem. This gospel addresses both Gentiles and Jews and "invites" them to follow Jesus of Nazareth. It is sometimes called the "gospel of surprises." For example, the relationship of Jesus with his family and particularly with his disciples shows more conflict than we encounter in the later Evangelists. Likewise the Markan Jesus seems to show more "human" reactions—anger, frustration, disappointment—than he does in the other three gospels. Another surprise, again in comparison to the other three canonical gospels, is that in Mark's original version there was almost exclusive emphasis on the suffering entailed in being a disciple of the Messiah; the stories of the resurrection were added later after the appearance of the other three gospels.

The first eight chapters of Mark's gospel address the question, Who is Jesus? and they climax in the answer given by Peter at the end of Chapter Eight: "You are the Christ," the Anointed, the Messiah. This first half of Mark's gospel portrays Jesus going up and down Galilee healing and forgiving, eating with sinners, and in amazing ways nourishing people through word and deed. He invites people to follow him not because they are spellbound by his teaching and deeds (more miracles are recorded in Mark than in any other gospel), but because they are willing to live in such ways as to announce to all people the Good News that God loves them.

The second half of the gospel asks the follow-up question, What does it mean to be the Messiah? Jesus' answer is contrary to popular opinion; the Messiah would not come as a great and successful military leader, but as One who must suffer and die. This very answer, revealed in the reaction of Peter to Jesus, is not only surprising, but is also disturbingly challenging to his disciples. Mark intertwines predictions of his suffering and death (which the disciples don't understand and even seem to ignore) with stories of healing those who are blind, including his disciples who cannot "see" what Jesus is saying. Yet the Messiah is the One who gives his life for the people—first in smaller things, for example, by staying with them when they misunderstand and even disappoint him; then in the greatest act of all time, by giving his very life on the cross. This second half of the gospel climaxes not in the disciples acknowledging Jesus as the suffering Messiah, but in the confession of the centurion who gazes on the crucified Jesus: "Truly this man was the Son of God!"

The Markan call to discipleship entails the same difficulties, frustrations, and annoyances as Jesus endured. But it is precisely by continuing the paschal journey through suffering and death that new life can be experienced and come to fullness. Mark's Good News is that the Word continues to be made flesh first in Jesus himself, and then through his followers. Jesus continues to dwell among us.

LITURGICAL RESOURCES

BofB	*Book of Blessings.* International Commission on English in the Liturgy. Collegeville: Liturgical Press, 1989.
BLS	*Built of Living Stones: Art, Architecture, and Worship.* Guidelines of the National Conference of Catholic Bishops, 2000.
CCC	*Catechism of the Catholic Church.* USCCB, 2004.
GIRM	*General Instruction of the Roman Missal* (2002).
GNLYC	General Norms for the Liturgical Year and the Calendar
ILM	Introduction to the Lectionary for Mass
L	*Lectionary*
NT	New Testament
OT	Old Testament
SC	*Sacrosanctum Concilium.* The Constitution on the Sacred Liturgy. Vatican II.

MUSICAL RESOURCES

BB	*Breaking Bread.* Portland, OR: Oregon Catholic Press, annual.
CBW3	*Catholic Book of Worship III.* Ottawa, Ontario: Canadian Conference of Catholic Bishops, 1994.
CH	*The Collegeville Hymnal.* Collegeville: Liturgical Press, 1990.
G2	*Gather.* 2nd edition. Chicago: GIA Publications, Inc., 1994.
GC	*Gather Comprehensive.* Chicago: GIA Publications, Inc., 1994.
GC2	*Gather Comprehensive.* 2nd edition. Chicago: GIA Publications, Inc., 2004.
HG	*Hymns for the Gospels.* Chicago: GIA Publications, Inc., 2001.
JS2	*Journeysongs.* 2nd edition. Portland, OR: Oregon Catholic Press, 2003.
LMGM	*Lead Me, Guide Me.* Chicago: GIA Publications, Inc., 1987.
OFUV	*One Faith/Una Voz.* Portland, OR: Oregon Catholic Press, 2005.
PMB	*People's Mass Book.* Schiller Park, IL: World Library Publications, 2003.
RS	*Ritual Song.* Chicago: GIA Publications, Inc., 1996.
SS	*Sacred Song.* Collegeville: Liturgical Press, annual.
VO	*Voices As One.* Schiller Park, IL: World Library Publications, 1998.
VO2	*Voices As One,* vol. 2. Schiller Park, IL: World Library Publications, 2005.
W3	*Worship.* 3rd edition. Chicago: GIA Publications, Inc., 1986.
WC	*We Celebrate.* Schiller Park, IL: World Library Publications, 2008.
WS	*Word and Song.* Schiller Park, IL: World Library Publications, annual.
GIA	GIA Publications, Inc.
LTP	Liturgy Training Publications, Inc.
OCP	Oregon Catholic Press
WLP	World Library Publications

Focusing the Gospel

Key words and phrases: Be watchful! Be alert! the lord . . . is coming, find you sleeping, Watch!

To the point: The gospel admonishes us, "Be watchful! Be alert!" Yet how often we find ourselves not alert but sleepy. We are worn out, worn down—even the good we do sometimes seems worthless (see first reading). The Advent season calls us to overcome our drowsiness by calling out to God for help (see first reading) and watching for the One who comes to renew us (see second reading).

Connecting the Gospel

to the first two readings: God's just judgment is tempered when we remember God's mighty deeds and call upon God for mercy. The first reading faces us with our infidelity to God and with the futility of our own work. But it also reminds us who God is for us: our Father who is always faithful. God's fidelity to us is fully revealed in the gift of Jesus whom God sends to "keep [us] firm to the end" (second reading).

to daily Christian living: Our lives often seem to bog down with the endless "sameness" of things. The work of Christian living is to constantly watch for the redeeming possibility of every moment.

Connecting the Responsorial Psalm

to the readings: Psalm 80 was written at a time when Israel had suffered devastating defeat at the hands of an enemy. Their homeland lay in ruins and their way of life had been destroyed. In their anguish they cried out for restoration to the One who had called them into existence as a people and given them a homeland. Part of their cry centers on the person of the king—the "man of your right hand" of verse 18—who embodies both God's presence among them and their responding fidelity. To restore the king's strength would be to restore their identity and way of life as God's chosen people.

The psalm text indicates Israel's sense of complicity in their own destruction. In numerous ways they have chosen to withdraw from God; God has merely "delivered them up to their guilt" (first reading). Yet Israel confronts God with the fact that fidelity and salvation are ultimately divine work: "make us turn to you," they cry, that we may be saved. As we pray these verses this Sunday, we need to reflect on how this psalm is a call from our present time and situation. What needs God's restoration? Where are we wandering (first reading)? How is Christ the promise which will "keep us firm to the end" (second reading)?

to cantor preparation: Notice that when you sing these verses from Psalm 80 you beg God to act to save us, and you also promise that we will respond to whatever God does. How during this week can you prepare yourself to be such a mediator?

**ASSEMBLY &
FAITH-SHARING GROUPS**
- I experience fatigue and weariness because . . .
- Christian living seems too demanding when . . .
- At times like these, Jesus comes to renew my discipleship by . . .

PRESIDERS
- I am most aware of my weariness when . . .
- I find in Jesus the response to my weariness when . . .

DEACONS
- My service brings others to Jesus and helps lift their weariness whenever . . .

HOSPITALITY MINISTERS
- My greeting helps those who come to liturgy be watchful and alert for Jesus among us when . . .

MUSIC MINISTERS
- My music ministry lifts the assembly from weariness when . . . their singing lifts me from weariness when . . .

ALTAR MINISTERS
- The manner in which I do my service embodies the attitude of Jesus when . . .

LECTORS
- My proclamation alerts the assembly to the coming of the Lord when . . .

**EXTRAORDINARY MINISTERS
OF HOLY COMMUNION**
- The face of each communicant renews my hope in the coming of the Lord by . . .

Model Act of Penitence

Presider: On this first Sunday of Advent we are reminded to be watchful and alert for Christ's coming. Let us reflect on how aware we are of God's presence in our lives and open ourselves to God's coming in Word and sacrament during this Mass . . . [pause]

Lord Jesus, you enrich us in every way: Lord . . .

Christ Jesus, you are the revelation of God's glory and peace: Christ . . .

Lord Jesus, you call us to be watchful and alert until your coming: Lord . . .

Homily Points

• At this time of year, many of us are feeling worn out and we are faced with a lot more work (preparations for Christmas: baking cookies, buying gifts, decorating the house, etc.). In the North, this is also a season of increasing darkness and cold; in the warm South there is an influx of visitors. In general, life is more congested and frantic.

• In the first reading, we are reminded that God is *always* faithful, always watching out for us. The Israelites realized this whenever they remembered God's marvelous deeds on their behalf. Advent is a particular time of the liturgical year when we are mindful of God's saving deeds on our behalf, both in history and in our own daily living.

• God's most stunning intervention on our behalf was to send Jesus to live among us. Jesus taught us how to live as God's chosen people. Advent calls us, then, not only to watch *for* Jesus, but also to *watch Jesus* (see second reading) and so continue to see the Word being made flesh today.

Model Prayer of the Faithful

Presider: Our God is ever faithful, and so will hear and answer our every prayer.

Response: Lord, ——— hear our prayer.

Cantor: we pray to the Lord,

That the church be firm and constant in making known God's marvelous deeds on our behalf . . . [pause]

That all world leaders be alert and responsive to the well-being of their people . . . [pause]

That the sick, the dying, and all those in need keep watch and wait patiently for Christ's presence and care . . . [pause]

That all of us gathered here spend Advent carefully waiting and watching for the many ways Christ comes into our lives . . . [pause]

Presider: Gracious God, you come to heal us and save us: hear these our prayers that we might be found alert and watchful on the day of Christ's coming. We ask this through that same Christ our Lord. **Amen.**

ALTERNATIVE OPENING PRAYER
Let us pray
[in Advent time with longing and
waiting for the coming of the Lord]

Pause for silent prayer

Father in heaven,
our hearts desire the warmth of your love
and our minds are searching for the light
of your Word.
Increase our longing for Christ our Savior
and give us the strength to grow in love,
that the dawn of his coming
may find us rejoicing in his presence
and welcoming the light of his truth.

We ask this in the name of Jesus the Lord.
Amen.

FIRST READING
Isa 63:16b-17, 19b; 64:2-7

You, LORD, are our father,
      our redeemer you are named forever.
Why do you let us wander, O LORD, from
      your ways,
      and harden our hearts so that we fear
      you not?
Return for the sake of your servants,
      the tribes of your heritage.
Oh, that you would rend the heavens and
      come down,
      with the mountains quaking before you,
while you wrought awesome deeds we
      could not hope for,
      such as they had not heard of from of
      old.
No ear has ever heard, no eye ever seen,
      any God but you
      doing such deeds for those who wait
      for him.
Would that you might meet us doing right,
      that we were mindful of you in our
      ways!
Behold, you are angry, and we are sinful;
      all of us have become like unclean
      people,
      all our good deeds are like polluted rags;
we have all withered like leaves,
      and our guilt carries us away like the
      wind.
There is none who calls upon your name,
      who rouses himself to cling to you;
for you have hidden your face from us
      and have delivered us up to our guilt.
Yet, O LORD, you are our father;
      we are the clay and you the potter:
      we are all the work of your hands.

✠ CATECHESIS

RESPONSORIAL PSALM

Ps 80:2-3, 15-16, 18-19

R̸. (4) Lord, make us turn to you; let us see
your face and we shall be saved.

O shepherd of Israel, hearken,
    from your throne upon the cherubim,
        shine forth.
Rouse your power,
    and come to save us.

R̸. Lord, make us turn to you; let us see
your face and we shall be saved.

Once again, O LORD of hosts,
    look down from heaven, and see;
take care of this vine,
    and protect what your right hand has
        planted,
    the son of man whom you yourself
        made strong.

R̸. Lord, make us turn to you; let us see
your face and we shall be saved.

May your help be with the man of your
        right hand,
    with the son of man whom you yourself
        made strong.
Then we will no more withdraw from you;
    give us new life, and we will call upon
        your name.

R̸. Lord, make us turn to you; let us see
your face and we shall be saved.

SECOND READING

1 Cor 1:3-9

Brothers and sisters:
Grace to you and peace from God our
        Father
    and the Lord Jesus Christ.

I give thanks to my God always on your
        account
    for the grace of God bestowed on you in
        Christ Jesus,
    that in him you were enriched in every
        way,
    with all discourse and all knowledge,
    as the testimony to Christ was
        confirmed among you,
    so that you are not lacking in any
        spiritual gift
    as you wait for the revelation of our
        Lord Jesus Christ.
He will keep you firm to the end,
    irreproachable on the day of our Lord
        Jesus Christ.
God is faithful,
    and by him you were called to
        fellowship with his Son,
        Jesus Christ our Lord.

About Liturgy

Advent penance: Advent has become a time for joyful expectation and waiting for the coming of Christ; and this is true and appropriate. This Sunday's first reading from Isaiah, however, also reminds us that we might not want to do away altogether with the penance that has always been traditionally associated with Advent. This reading gives us a context for such penance: Christ's judgment that will accompany his coming at the end of time. We are judged according to how "mindful of [God] in our ways" we are. We are sinners and we must turn our faces to God.

Penance helps us be mindful of God in our lives and helps us become more pliable so that God, the potter, can truly mold us into God's image and likeness. Advent's penance, then, might be directed toward the discipline of watching for God and being mindful of God at the center of our lives. For example, we might consciously look at the face of others and see an image of Jesus. Or we might take five minutes each day and just *stop* all our activity to be aware of God's presence to us. Or we might take the time to read each day the gospel for the next Sunday and begin to see how it motivates our actions during each day.

Environment for the Advent sacred space: It has become popular to mark the passing weeks of Advent either by adding more plain fabric banners to the sacred space or by adding deeper colors of royal purple to those banners already in place. Another approach to the Advent environment might be to mark the two Advent comings of Christ: during the first two weeks draw attention to Christ's coming at the end of time and only during the last two weeks begin to focus on Christ's coming at the Incarnation. For example, at the beginning of Advent the banners might suggest the chaos of the end times and judgment; during the last two weeks of Advent the chaos might give way to the peace and warmth of the Sun of Righteousness or the starry night of a Light coming constantly in our lives to guide us on our way.

About Liturgical Music

Music suggestions: The songs we sing for the first two Sundays of Advent need to focus on Christ's coming as King and Judge at the end of time rather than on his coming in the Incarnation, which is the focus of the last two Sundays of Advent. Some well-known songs that carry this focus include "The King Shall Come," "City of God, Jerusalem," "When the Lord in Glory Comes," "Soon and Very Soon," "Lift Up Your Heads, Ye Mighty Gates," "Wake, Awake and Sleep No Longer," and "Comfort, Comfort, O My People." The texts of these hymns provide a good guideline for assessing the appropriateness of other songs to sing during these first two weeks of the season.

NOVEMBER 30, 2008

FIRST SUNDAY OF ADVENT

SPIRITUALITY

R⁊. Alleluia, alleluia.
Prepare the way of the Lord, make straight his
    paths:
all flesh shall see the salvation of God.
R⁊. Alleluia, alleluia.

Gospel

Mark 1:1-8; L5B

The beginning of the gospel
    of Jesus Christ the Son of
    God.

As it is written in Isaiah the
    prophet:
*Behold, I am sending my
    messenger ahead of you;
he will prepare your way.
A voice of one crying out in
    the desert:
"Prepare the way of the
    Lord,
make straight his paths."*
John the Baptist appeared in the desert
    proclaiming a baptism of repentance
    for the forgiveness of sins.
People of the whole Judean countryside
    and all the inhabitants of Jerusalem
    were going out to him
    and were being baptized by him in
        the Jordan River
    as they acknowledged their sins.
John was clothed in camel's hair,
    with a leather belt around his waist.
He fed on locusts and wild honey.
And this is what he proclaimed:
    "One mightier than I is coming after
        me.
I am not worthy to stoop and loosen the
    thongs of his sandals.
I have baptized you with water;
    he will baptize you with the Holy
        Spirit."

Reflecting on the Gospel

Each day all of us are faced with countless tasks. Some of them we do without even a first thought—we brush our teeth, get dressed, go to work or school. Other tasks can require some motivation for us to begin tackling them. Grocery shopping might be put off until there isn't a crumb of bread or a speck of milk left in the house and we're hungry. Studying for an exam might be put off until the final hours that are spent madly cramming. Paying bills might be ignored until we face late charges. Still other tasks may be put off because there is no immediate pressure or no beneficial consequence. In all but the most routine of our tasks, sometimes it's the *beginning* which is the hardest of all. Once we plunge in, energy and motivation for completion seem to emerge.

This Sunday's gospel opens with the words, "The beginning of the gospel of Jesus Christ the Son of God." *What*, really, is the "beginning of the gospel"? Mark's gospel (the one we read this year) begins with an announcement: a messenger is coming. That messenger is John the Baptist who preached repentance, but more important he announced the coming of One who would "baptize . . . with the Holy Spirit." Yet, the real beginning of the gospel does not come with a mere announcement, but with an *encounter*. "[A]ll the inhabitants of Jerusalem" were going out to meet John. Yes, there is a beginning with John, the messenger. There is also a beginning with Jesus, as the unfolding of the gospel shows time and again how people went out to meet him. And there is a beginning with *each of us*, those who prepare for and await the coming of the Lord, who encounter him in our daily lives, and who hasten his coming as we "conduct [. . .] ourselves in holiness and devotion" (second reading).

The first reading and gospel summon us to "prepare the way of the LORD." Our preparation, however, is not primarily for Christmas. The vision of Isaiah and the promise of the second reading point us toward a *final* day of glory, a day of peace. Furthermore, the gospel reminds us that we are at the "*beginning* of the gospel." And it is just that: a beginning. From Isaiah to John the Baptist through Jesus to us, the "beginning" continues until the valleys are filled and the mountains are laid low, until the paths are finally made straight to "a new heavens and a new earth" (second reading).

Living the Paschal Mystery

John the Baptist diverted attention from himself to Jesus. His ministry was not about himself but about the "One mightier than I [who] is coming after me." He proclaimed repentance, prepared for Jesus, died—this is the pattern of John's life. Actually, it's the pattern of Jesus' life, too: he proclaimed the Good News, prepared the way to the Father, died. Further, it's the pattern of our own paschal mystery living: proclaim the gospel of repentance, prepare for Christ's many comings, die to ourselves.

Our being baptized "with the Holy Spirit" enables us to do the work of God, for in baptism our lives are grafted onto Christ. In baptism we become heralds, like John, of Christ's redeeming presence in our world. By our Christian living (blamelessly and with righteousness) we not only point to Christ, but we also make present the Christ who dwells in us! The challenge of gospel living is the *beginning*—get started, encounter Christ, surrender ourselves to the Holy Spirit.

Focusing the Gospel

Key words and phrases: The beginning of the gospel, Prepare the way of the Lord, make straight his paths

To the point: The first reading and gospel summon us to "prepare the way of the LORD." Our preparation, however, is not primarily for Christmas. The vision of Isaiah and the promise of the second reading point us toward a *final* day of glory, a day of peace. Furthermore, the gospel reminds us that we are at the "*beginning* of the gospel." And it is just that: a beginning. From Isaiah to John the Baptist through Jesus to us, the "beginning" continues until the valleys are filled and the mountains are laid low, until the paths are finally made straight to "a new heavens and a new earth" (second reading).

Connecting the Gospel

to the first and second reading: The poetic vision of Isaiah proclaimed an Old Testament "gospel" ("glad tidings," "good news"): our service is ended, our guilt is expiated. This good news is fulfilled in Jesus who comes to save us and whose Spirit leads us to "a new heavens and a new earth."

to our Advent experience: We spend Advent preparing for Christmas and this is appropriate. These readings, however, broaden our understanding of Advent to include the ways Jesus comes to us every day and the way he will come in final glory.

Connecting the Responsorial Psalm

to the readings: In these readings and psalm God promises to come in power and glory, tenderness and mercy, to free us from sin and lead us with care to a "new heavens and a new earth" (second reading) characterized by righteousness, compassion, justice, and peace (psalm). In the psalm we both listen to what God is proclaiming and proclaim our trust in what we are hearing. God *will* bring kindness together with truth, we say. God *will* bring justice to the earth, we sing. We also beg God in this psalm to support our trust by letting us see the kindness and salvation we have been promised (refrain). It is John in the gospel who turns our eyes in the direction of God's answer: toward the One who comes to baptize us with the Holy Spirit. This Jesus will be our shepherd, divine kindness and truth, justice and peace, mercy and forgiveness in human flesh, the cornerstone of God's new creation. As we sing this psalm, let us pray that we may see what God has begun in Christ and believe what God will complete in us through him.

to cantor preparation: In this responsorial psalm you both declare your trust in God's promise of salvation and beg God to show you this salvation here and now. You have an eye on the future but a foot in the present. What keeps your hope for the ultimate salvation of the world alive? Where in the world do you see God acting now to bring salvation?

**ASSEMBLY &
FAITH-SHARING GROUPS**

· What I need to make straight in my life to prepare the way of the Lord is . . .

· I have already experienced "a new heavens and a new earth" in . . .

· One example of the ongoing promise of the Gospel in my life is . . .

PRESIDERS

· I see signs of "a new heavens and a new earth" in the people I serve when I . . . I am an obstacle to the vision of Isaiah when I . . .

DEACONS

· My service witnesses to the fulfillment of the Gospel when . . .

HOSPITALITY MINISTERS

· My ministry helps prepare the way of the Lord for the people when . . .

MUSIC MINISTERS

· My music is a pathway to the Lord when . . .

ALTAR MINISTERS

· The kind of attentiveness on my part that helps smooth the valleys and mountains of liturgy is . . .

LECTORS

· I find my proclamation "make[s] straight" the way for the assembly to encounter the Word when I . . .

**EXTRAORDINARY MINISTERS
OF HOLY COMMUNION**

· My distribution of Holy Communion participates in the coming of "a new heavens and a new earth" because . . .

Model Act of Penitence

Presider: Let us prepare the way of the Lord by opening ourselves to his coming in word and sacrament during this liturgy . . . [pause]

Lord Jesus, you are the way, the truth, and the life: Lord . . .

Christ Jesus, you came to baptize us with the Spirit: Christ . . .

Lord Jesus, you will come in glory to lead us to "a new heavens and a new earth": Lord . . .

Homily Points

• Valleys and mountains are not simply topographic features, but they are metaphors for the gaps and blocks in our lives that impede our relationships with God and one another. Fears, negative past experiences, prejudices, mistrust, judgments all can hinder and hurt our relationships. Preparing the way of the Lord means coming to grips in our daily living with these gaps and blocks and recognizing how growth has already happened in our lives.

• We know from experience that the "beginning" is often the hardest part, but it is also the most important. In this Sunday's gospel God gives us the beginning, opening a new path for us in the person of Jesus. This is what Jesus constantly did: gave people a *new beginning*.

• Our whole Christian living is one new beginning after another, all leading to God's final gift of "a new heavens and a new earth."

Model Prayer of the Faithful

Presider: Let us turn to our saving God and ask for what we need.

Response: Lord, hear our prayer.

Cantor: we pray to the Lord,

That all members of the Body of Christ proclaim a new heavens and a new earth by the way they live with each other . . . [pause]

That all peoples of the world might make straight the paths of their lives . . . [pause]

That those suffering from the ravages of war or disease experience the tender care of God through the ministry of others . . . [pause]

That all of us here hurry the coming of the Lord by courageously living the Gospel . . . [pause]

Presider: O God who comes, you shepherd us with care: hear these our prayers that we might enjoy everlasting life with you. We ask this through your Son Jesus Christ. **Amen.**

OPENING PRAYER

Let us pray

Pause for silent prayer

God of power and mercy,
open our hearts in welcome.
Remove the things that hinder us from
    receiving Christ with joy,
so that we may share his wisdom
and become one with him
when he comes in glory,
for he lives and reigns with you and the
    Holy Spirit,
one God, for ever and ever. **Amen.**

FIRST READING

Is 40:1-5, 9-11

Comfort, give comfort to my people,
    says your God.
Speak tenderly to Jerusalem, and proclaim
        to her
    that her service is at an end,
    her guilt is expiated;
indeed, she has received from the hand of
        the Lord
    double for all her sins.

        A voice cries out:
In the desert prepare the way of the Lord!
    Make straight in the wasteland a
        highway for our God!
Every valley shall be filled in,
    every mountain and hill shall be made
        low;
the rugged land shall be made a plain,
    the rough country, a broad valley.
Then the glory of the Lord shall be revealed,
    and all people shall see it together;
    for the mouth of the Lord has spoken.

Go up onto a high mountain,
    Zion, herald of glad tidings;
cry out at the top of your voice,
    Jerusalem, herald of good news!
Fear not to cry out
    and say to the cities of Judah:
    Here is your God!
Here comes with power
    the Lord God,
    who rules by his strong arm;
here is his reward with him,
    his recompense before him.
Like a shepherd he feeds his flock;
    in his arms he gathers the lambs,
carrying them in his bosom,
    and leading the ewes with care.

RESPONSORIAL PSALM

Ps 85:9-10, 11-12, 13-14

R̞. (8) Lord, let us see your kindness, and grant us your salvation.

I will hear what God proclaims;
   the LORD—for he proclaims peace to his
      people.
Near indeed is his salvation to those who
      fear him,
   glory dwelling in our land.

R̞. Lord, let us see your kindness, and grant us your salvation.

Kindness and truth shall meet;
   justice and peace shall kiss.
Truth shall spring out of the earth,
   and justice shall look down from heaven.

R̞. Lord, let us see your kindness, and grant us your salvation.

The LORD himself will give his benefits;
   our land shall yield its increase.
Justice shall walk before him,
   and prepare the way of his steps.

R̞. Lord, let us see your kindness, and grant us your salvation.

SECOND READING

2 Pet 3:8-14

Do not ignore this one fact, beloved,
   that with the Lord one day is like a
      thousand years
   and a thousand years like one day.
The Lord does not delay his promise, as
      some regard "delay,"
   but he is patient with you,
   not wishing that any should perish
   but that all should come to repentance.
But the day of the Lord will come like a
      thief,
   and then the heavens will pass away
      with a mighty roar
   and the elements will be dissolved by fire,
   and the earth and everything done on it
      will be found out.

Since everything is to be dissolved in this
      way,
   what sort of persons ought you to be,
   conducting yourselves in holiness and
      devotion,
   waiting for and hastening the coming
      of the day of God,
   because of which the heavens will be
      dissolved in flames
   and the elements melted by fire.
But according to his promise
   we await new heavens and a new earth
   in which righteousness dwells.
Therefore, beloved, since you await these
      things,
   be eager to be found without spot or
      blemish before him, at peace.

About Liturgy

The structure of the Lectionary: The Lectionary selections this Sunday offer a good opportunity to reflect on how this important liturgical book was put together. The gospels were selected first, arranged in a three-year cycle with each year focusing on either Matthew, Mark, or Luke (especially evident during Ordinary Time when one of these gospels is read semi-continuously; this year we read from Mark). Rather than having its own year, the Gospel of John is read during key times such as during the Easter season and in Ordinary Time from the 17th to 21st Sundays in year B (this year).

Once the gospels were assigned, then the first readings were chosen to relate to the gospel and they are mostly taken from the Old Testament (a notable exception is during the Sundays of Easter when the first reading is taken from the Acts of the Apostles). During the festal seasons (such as now, during Advent) the second reading is also specially selected to relate to the other two readings, but during Ordinary Time the second reading stands on its own as a semi-continuous reading of one of the New Testament letters over several Sundays. The second reading for this second Sunday of Advent is especially important because it gives the eschatological context that is notable during the first two weeks of Advent.

Advent and Christ's comings: "Eschatological" is a term that derives from two Greek terms meaning the word of (or science of) the end times. Specifically, it refers to the final fulfillment of all things that will take place at Christ's coming at the end of time, a motif during the last part of the liturgical year and during the first part of Advent. Advent actually celebrates three comings of Christ. Christ's first coming took place in the past (over two thousand years ago!) and celebrates his coming in history. Christ's second coming will take place only in the future and celebrates his coming in final glory (this is the eschatological coming we mentioned above). And, finally, Christ's coming in sacraments takes place in the present and celebrates his coming in mystery.

About Liturgical Music

Music suggestions: "Comfort, Comfort, O My People" is based on this Sunday's first reading from Isaiah. The hymn was written for the solemnity of the Nativity of John the Baptist and first published in 1671. Despite its tender words, the hymn is meant to move at a dance-like pace. It would work well for the preparation of the gifts. Bob Dufford's "Like A Shepherd" is also drawn from this Sunday's first reading and would work well either during preparation of the gifts or as a choral prelude. Michael Joncas' "A Voice Cries Out" would also be an appropriate prelude, or could be used for the entrance or Communion song. An SATB setting of the refrain can be found in *Choral Praise Comprehensive Edition* [OCP #10317] and in *Choral Praise Comprehensive,* second edition [OCP #11450 or 12035]. The full SATB arrangement with instrumental parts is available in octavo form [OCP #10000].

DECEMBER 7, 2008
SECOND SUNDAY OF ADVENT

✦ SPIRITUALITY

GOSPEL ACCLAMATION
cf. Luke 1:28

℟. Alleluia, alleluia.
Hail, Mary, full of grace, the Lord is with you;
blessed are you among women.
℟. Alleluia, alleluia.

Gospel   Luke 1:26-38; L689

The angel Gabriel was sent from God
  to a town of Galilee called Nazareth,
  to a virgin betrothed to a man named
    Joseph,
  of the house of David,
  and the virgin's name was Mary.
And coming to her, he said,
  "Hail, full of grace! The Lord is with
    you."
But she was greatly troubled at what was
    said
  and pondered what sort of greeting this
    might be.
Then the angel said to her,
  "Do not be afraid, Mary,
  for you have found favor with God.
Behold, you will conceive in your womb and
    bear a son,
  and you shall name him Jesus.
He will be great and will be called Son of
    the Most High,
  and the Lord God will give him the throne
    of David his father,
  and he will rule over the house of Jacob
    forever,
  and of his Kingdom there will be no end."

Continued in Appendix A, p. 261.

See Appendix A, p. 261, for the other readings.

Reflecting on the Gospel

Causality is a branch of logic (philosophy) that few of us have studied but we think in this way all the time. Basically it means that if this happens that will happen. One thing is the cause (reason for or why, impetus, or producer or generator) of another thing. Even some of our common sayings bear out a cause/effect relationship; for example, "familiarity breeds contempt" or "absence makes the heart grow fonder." The first reading and gospel might lead us to cause/effect thinking: Adam and Eve sinned so we, their offspring, share in their punishment; Mary was conceived sinless so she was worthy to bear Christ. While these causalities are true, much more can and needs to be said about this mystery of our salvation. The readings recall for us not only how graced Mary was, but also how graced we are.

In a sense we might look at the first reading and gospel as exact opposites. In the first reading Adam and Eve enjoyed a singular presence with God who would come to them in the garden during the cool breeze of the evening (see Gen 3:8). The picture here is one of easy relationship and personal intimacy: God and Adam and Eve were friends. Yet Adam and Eve walked away from God's presence—they hid themselves from God. By contrast, Mary is full of grace and to her, too, God comes. Rather than shy from God's presence, Mary welcomes it with her yes. Her emptiness as a virgin is filled by her acceptance of the Lord's coming to her, and a whole new in-breaking of God's presence happens—of which we are benefactors.

In the first reading, Adam and Eve are afraid to be in God's presence because they have sinned. In the gospel, Gabriel reassures Mary, "Do not be afraid," because she was "full of grace." Like Mary, we need not be afraid. Though sinners, we have been adopted by God and filled with God's grace (see second reading). Surely "nothing [is] impossible with God"! God is present to us and within us just as surely as God was present to and within Mary. No wonder we join with the psalmist and "sing to the Lord a new song, for he has done marvelous deeds."

Living the Paschal Mystery

This is what it looks like when God comes: like Mary, we are surprised; our emptiness (barrenness) is filled; the Holy Spirit overshadows us; our questioning, probing, pondering help us discern God's presence, which isn't always immediately grasped. Like Mary, too, God's coming and our yes to it changes us for life.

The gospels say little about Mary: she bore and gave birth to the Messiah, she was the mother who helped him grow in wisdom and grace, she was with him during his ministry, she stood at the foot of the cross when he was dying. Yet this is enough to know that Mary's yes to God carried far beyond the initial Christmas events of conception and birth. Her own everyday living bore out her continual living in and openness to God's presence. So it is with us. Our everyday living must proclaim that God is present to us and fills us. "How can this be?" Because we are blessed in Christ, adopted as God's own children, chosen, and destined to exist "for the praise of his glory" (second reading). The results of God's presence to us are just as astounding as God's coming to Mary. All we need do is *believe* that we, too, are extended God's grace and we are faithful to that grace as we say yes to God's will in our everyday lives.

Focusing the Gospel

Key words and phrases: full of grace, Do not be afraid

To the point: In the first reading, Adam and Eve are afraid to be in God's presence because they have sinned. In the gospel, Gabriel reassures Mary, "Do not be afraid," because she was "full of grace." Like Mary, we need not be afraid. Though sinners, we have been adopted by God and filled with God's grace (see second reading).

Model Act of Penitence

Presider: Mary was conceived without sin, remained sinless her whole life, and bore Christ our Lord within her. Let us open ourselves to God who forgives our sins and invites us to celebrate these mysteries of our salvation . . . [pause]

 Lord Jesus, you are the holy One, the Son of God: Lord . . .

 Christ Jesus, you call us to be holy and without blemish before God: Christ . . .

 Lord Jesus, you gave us your mother as our pattern of holiness: Lord . . .

Model Prayer of the Faithful

Presider: The God who makes us holy will surely give us what we need. And so we pray.

 Response:

Lord, hear our prayer.

Cantor:

we pray to the Lord,

That all members of the church witness by the holiness of their lives their adoption as sons and daughters of God . . . [pause]

That all people in the world see themselves worthy to walk in God's presence . . . [pause]

That the sick and dying and anyone who feels alienated from God's presence be comforted by God's nearness . . . [pause]

That all of us gathered here recognize we, too, have found favor with God and respond with fidelity . . . [pause]

Presider: Loving God, you called us from the foundation of the world to be holy and blameless in your sight: hear these our prayers that one day we might enjoy everlasting peace in your presence. We pray through Christ our Lord. **Amen.**

FOR REFLECTION

· Adam and Eve hid from God's presence, while Mary made herself available to God. I am like Adam and Eve when . . . I am like Mary when . . .

· I look to Mary as a model in my daily Christian living because . . .

· I am aware of God's grace working in me when . . .

Homily Points

• Full of grace, Mary is not afraid to venture into the impossible. Full of grace, Mary is not afraid to say a courageous yes to God, in spite of her being "greatly troubled." Full of grace, Mary is not afraid to believe in the God for whom nothing is impossible. God fills us with the same grace.

• Being filled with God's grace makes a difference in our everyday lives. First, we are challenged truly to *believe* that God's grace dwells with us. And, second, we are encouraged by this belief to say yes to God's will in our lives.

+ SPIRITUALITY

GOSPEL ACCLAMATION
Isa 61:1 (cited in Luke 4:18)

℟. Alleluia, alleluia.
The Spirit of the Lord is upon me,
because he has anointed me
to bring glad tidings to the poor.
℟. Alleluia, alleluia.

Gospel   John 1:6-8, 19-28; L8B

A man named John was sent from God.
He came for testimony, to testify to
   the light,
   so that all might believe through
      him.
He was not the light,
   but came to testify to the light.

And this is the testimony of John.
When the Jews from Jerusalem sent
      priests and Levites to him
   to ask him, "Who are you?"
   he admitted and did not deny it,
   but admitted, "I am not the Christ."
So they asked him,
   "What are you then? Are you Elijah?"
And he said, "I am not."
"Are you the Prophet?"
He answered, "No."
So they said to him,
   "Who are you, so we can give an answer
      to those who sent us?
What do you have to say for yourself?"
He said:
   "I am *the voice of one crying out in the
      desert,*
   make straight the way of the Lord,
   as Isaiah the prophet said."
Some Pharisees were also sent.
They asked him,
   "Why then do you baptize
   if you are not the Christ or Elijah or the
      Prophet?"
John answered them,
   "I baptize with water;
   but there is one among you whom you do
      not recognize,
   the one who is coming after me,
   whose sandal strap I am not worthy to
      untie."
This happened in Bethany across the Jordan,
   where John was baptizing.

Reflecting on the Gospel

Two-year-old Patrick was pushing on the kitchen table that had a fragile vase on it. His older sister Carrie told him to stop pushing on the table because he might break the vase. True to his being two, his sister's bidding only made him push all the harder. And, yes, the vase tipped over and broke into a thousand pieces. As his mother came into the kitchen, he ran to his room in tears and fear. Soon Mother came in, took him on her lap, and told the little fellow she was angry with him because he didn't obey, but she still loved him. With that, Patrick tearfully said he was sorry and wouldn't do it again.

This simple act of reconciliation is replayed thousands of times each day across our families. It is a reminder that we are called to "heal the brokenhearted" (first reading) and pave the way for loving encounter. This story is a reminder of our own relationship to Jesus (as those who are poor and brokenhearted) and to each other (as those who are to reach out to all those in need). This is a message of the gospel this Sunday: we are to be like John the Baptist in the gospel, whose mission was to "testify to the light"—Christ's presence among the people. Testimony to the light implies two things. First, it means to do good works ("bring glad tidings to the poor," "heal the brokenhearted," etc.; first reading). By these good works we, too, bring the presence of Christ to others. Second, "testify to the light" means to grow in relationship to Christ and with others. Yes, sometimes we are like the people in the gospel in that we seek the Messiah but often do not recognize his presence in our midst. The work of Advent is to intensify our good works so that we can recognize Christ in our midst; even more, it is the work of our whole Christian lives.

Living the Paschal Mystery

It's easy and comfortable to recognize Christ in the expected places and ways. When we enter the peace of a church, for example, we expect to find God. When we sit and pray in our homes, we expect to find God and have our prayers answered. All this is good. However, living the paschal mystery means that we take up the mission of Christ ourselves, that we ourselves are to be Christ for others. Especially during these final days before Christmas when everyone is so busy, we can forget that our mission is like John's: to testify to the light. We do this by how we respond to those around us: take time to listen to the one hurting, visit those who might be forgotten, do with a little less ourselves so others might have more, take time to pray, remember to give thanks, offer a helping hand, reorganize our priorities, praise the God in others.

John's mission was to testify to the light, the Mighty One who had come. Like John, our mission is also to testify to the light. To do this we must first recognize Christ's presence among us. But more: when we ourselves perform good works, we make present the Savior in our world. Conversely, when we lack charity and justice we fail to witness to the light or make Christ present. The way we live does make a difference both for ourselves and for others. Thus, testimony to the light is not a matter of mere words—it requires the witness of good works (first reading) and choosing what is good and avoiding evil (second reading). This is the kind of testimony that reveals Christ among us. For this we rejoice (see both first and second readings).

Focusing the Gospel

Key words and phrases: testimony, light, one among you

To the point: John's mission was to "testify to the light"—Christ's presence among the people. Testimony to the light implies two things. First, it means to do good works ("bring glad tidings to the poor," "heal the brokenhearted," etc.; first reading). And, second, it means to grow in relationship to Christ and with others. Such testimony is the work of Advent; even more, it is the work of our whole Christian lives.

Connecting the Gospel

to the first two readings: The gospel highlights our work: testifying to Christ. The first two readings highlight what God does for and in us so that we might testify faithfully: anoints us, clothes us, adorns us, bedecks us, and makes us holy and blameless.

to religious culture: We tend to think of only extraordinary manifestations as the work of God. In fact, the gifts of God are manifested through the simple, faithful, human activity of doing good for others.

Connecting the Responsorial Psalm

to the readings: This Sunday's responsorial psalm is taken from the *Magnificat*, the hymn of praise through which Mary applauds what God is doing for her and for all people. Through her song Mary testifies to the presence and activity of God within her and within the world. What she sees God doing is concrete: the lowly are being lifted up, the hungry are being filled, mercy is being granted. And what she sees is here and now.

This Sunday's readings call us, like Mary, to recognize the Messiah among us and to rejoice in what we see. In the responsorial psalm for the first Sunday of Advent we cried out to God for restoration. In the psalm for the second Sunday of Advent we begged God to show us the salvation promised us. This Sunday we sing with Mary that we see God's salvation at work here and now, in ways both personal and universal, both timely and for all generations to come.

to cantor preparation: How can you make Mary's words in the *Magnificat* your own? What do you see God doing in the world? In your own life? Where do you see justice happening and mercy being granted? Even more, how do you, like Mary, testify to what you see?

**ASSEMBLY &
FAITH-SHARING GROUPS**
- My good works testifying to the presence of Christ include . . .
- I have experienced the presence of Christ in . . . through . . . with . . .
- One way I have grown in my relationship with Christ and others is . . . One area where I need to do more growing is . . .

PRESIDERS
- When I am leading the community in prayer, I most effectively mediate Christ's presence when . . .

DEACONS
- My ministry of service most effectively testifies to Christ's presence when . . .

HOSPITALITY MINISTERS
- The kind of greeting that gives testimony to Christ's presence among us is . . .

MUSIC MINISTERS
- We sing the presence of Christ when . . .

ALTAR MINISTERS
- My quiet ministry of service helps the assembly grow in their relationship to Christ because . . .

LECTORS
- Like John the Baptist, I proclaim Christ through public proclamation; what helps me internalize this proclamation is . . .

**EXTRAORDINARY MINISTERS
OF HOLY COMMUNION**
- My ministry of giving the Sacramental Christ to others brings glad tidings to the poor when . . .

Model Act of Penitence

Presider: We hear in today's gospel about John's mission to testify to Christ, the light. Let us reflect on how our living out of charity and justice also testifies to the presence of Christ in our midst . . . [pause]

Lord Jesus, you are the Light come into our midst: Lord . . .

Christ Jesus, you are the One we seek to recognize in our midst: Christ . . .

Lord Jesus, you are the One to whom our lives testify: Lord . . .

Homily Points

• The poor and the brokenhearted have many faces: family members, neighbors, even the stranger in the grocery line. Our challenge is not only to recognize them, but also to have the courage and compassion to reach out to them. In this way we testify to the presence of Christ.

• In his own ministry, Jesus manifested his good works to both the deserving and undeserving, to the poor and brokenhearted, and to the powerful and wealthy. By doing so he drew many—even outcasts—to his presence.

• In our lives, we are at times the minister, and at other times we receive the ministry of others. In this exchange, the presence of Christ is strengthened in us as a community of believers testifying to the One who comes and dwells among us.

Model Prayer of the Faithful

Presider: Let us pray that we might reach out in charity and justice toward others and thus testify to the presence of Christ in our midst.

Response: Lord, hear our prayer.

Cantor: we pray to the Lord,

For all members of the church to witness to Christ's presence in the world by their charity and justice . . . [pause]

For all peoples of the world to live in the peace that only comes from loving their neighbor . . . [pause]

For those suffering injustices to be comforted and encouraged by the ministry of others . . . [pause]

For all of us to prepare for Christmas by already recognizing the Christ in each other . . . [pause]

Presider: O God, you hear the prayers of those who cry out to you: make us more just and charitable toward one another that we might celebrate Christmas with a deeper recognition of your messiah Son in our midst. We ask this through that same Jesus Christ our Lord. **Amen.**

OPENING PRAYER

Let us pray

Pause for silent prayer

Lord God,
may we, your people,
who look forward to the birthday of Christ
experience the joy of salvation
and celebrate that feast with love and
    thanksgiving.

We ask this through our Lord Jesus Christ,
    your Son,
who lives and reigns with you and the
    Holy Spirit,
one God, for ever and ever. **Amen.**

FIRST READING
Isa 61:1-2a, 10-11

The spirit of the Lord God is upon me,
    because the Lord has anointed me;
he has sent me to bring glad tidings to the
    poor,
    to heal the brokenhearted,
to proclaim liberty to the captives
    and release to the prisoners,
to announce a year of favor from the Lord
    and a day of vindication by our God.

I rejoice heartily in the Lord,
    in my God is the joy of my soul;
for he has clothed me with a robe of
    salvation
    and wrapped me in a mantle of justice,
like a bridegroom adorned with a diadem,
    like a bride bedecked with her jewels.
As the earth brings forth its plants,
    and a garden makes its growth spring
        up,
so will the Lord God make justice and
    praise
        spring up before all the nations.

RESPONSORIAL PSALM
Luke 1:46-48, 49-50, 53-54

R7. (Isa 61:10b) My soul rejoices in my God.

My soul proclaims the greatness of the
   Lord;
   my spirit rejoices in God my Savior,
for he has looked upon his lowly servant.
   From this day all generations will call
      me blessed:

R7. My soul rejoices in my God.

The Almighty has done great things for
   me,
   and holy is his Name.
He has mercy on those who fear him
   in every generation.

R7. My soul rejoices in my God.

He has filled the hungry with good things,
   and the rich he has sent away empty.
He has come to the help of his servant
   Israel
   for he has remembered his promise of
      mercy.

R7. My soul rejoices in my God.

SECOND READING
1 Thess 5:16-24

Brothers and sisters:
Rejoice always. Pray without ceasing.
In all circumstances give thanks,
   for this is the will of God for you in
      Christ Jesus.
Do not quench the Spirit.
Do not despise prophetic utterances.
Test everything; retain what is good.
Refrain from every kind of evil.

May the God of peace make you perfectly
   holy
   and may you entirely, spirit, soul, and
      body,
   be preserved blameless for the coming
      of our Lord Jesus Christ.
The one who calls you is faithful,
   and he will also accomplish it.

About Liturgy

Liturgy's link with right living: Christmas is one time of the year when charitable giving is very high. Many families, for example, limit or eliminate altogether their gift exchange and collect the saved money to give to a family in need or to some worthy cause. All of this is very good and laudable, but the first reading challenges us further and reminds us particularly of two things.

First, our charity isn't something that might happen once a year. Charity—genuine caring for others—aptly describes our Christian living. It is something that we must pay attention to every day; we are "anointed" to do good works. Second, our just acts on behalf of others less fortunate than ourselves are clearly linked both to being "clothed . . . with . . . salvation" and to the praise of God.

To state this liturgically: liturgy and right living are inextricably linked. The reason for this link rests not only in our intimate relationship with God—which liturgy celebrates in praise and thanksgiving—but also because of our intimate relationship with each other. In liturgy we come together and manifest the Body of Christ; as members we are joined one to another. When one part of the Body hurts, the whole Body hurts. Thus it is only right and just that we do whatever we can to "bring glad tidings to the poor, to heal the brokenhearted, to proclaim liberty to the captives and release to the prisoners . . . ."

Gaudete Sunday: Traditionally the third Sunday of Advent is called *gaudete* (rejoice) Sunday. The rose vestments for this day are still an option, but since we have a different understanding of Advent (it is not simply about penance and today we rejoice because we are almost through the season) it is probably best to retain the royal purple color of Advent for this Sunday. True, penance is appropriate for Advent, but it has a different meaning from the penance of Lent; during Advent the reason for penance is as preparation for the final judgment (especially prominent during the first two weeks of Advent).

About Liturgical Music

Music suggestions: With this Sunday's liturgy we shift from awaiting the triumphant Christ who will come at the end of time to recognizing the incarnate Christ already close at hand. Well-known songs such as "O Come, O Come, Emmanuel"; "Savior of the Nations, Come"; "Come, O Long Expected Jesus"; "Creator of the Stars of Night"; "The Coming of Our God"; " People, Look East"; and "O Come, Divine Messiah" are good choices because they help us make this shift.

Howard S. Olson's "Good News" [G2, CG, RS, LMGM] is specific to both this Sunday's gospel and first reading. Set to an Ethiopian verse-refrain tune, the song would work well for the Communion procession with choir or cantor singing the verses. Both text and tune capture the joyful sense of this Sunday's celebration. Dan Schutte's "Christ, Circle Round Us" [BB] combines words adapted from the O Antiphons with music based on the *Salve Regina* to create a lovely verse-refrain song suitable for Communion. An SAB arrangement with handbells is available in octavo form [OCP #10782].

✠ SPIRITUALITY

GOSPEL ACCLAMATION
Luke 1:38

℟. Alleluia, alleluia.
Behold, I am the handmaid of the Lord.
May it be done to me according to your word.
℟. Alleluia, alleluia.

Gospel   Luke 1:26-38; L11B

The angel Gabriel was sent from God
  to a town of Galilee called Nazareth,
  to a virgin betrothed to a man named
    Joseph,
  of the house of David,
  and the virgin's name was Mary.
And coming to her, he said,
  "Hail, full of grace! The Lord is with
    you."
But she was greatly troubled at what
    was said
  and pondered what sort of greeting this
    might be.
Then the angel said to her,
  "Do not be afraid, Mary,
  for you have found favor with God.

"Behold, you will conceive in your womb
    and bear a son,
  and you shall name him Jesus.
He will be great and will be called Son of
    the Most High,
  and the Lord God will give him the throne
    of David his father,
  and he will rule over the house of Jacob
    forever,
  and of his kingdom there will be no end."
But Mary said to the angel,
  "How can this be,
  since I have no relations with a man?"
And the angel said to her in reply,
  "The Holy Spirit will come upon you,
  and the power of the Most High will
    overshadow you.
Therefore the child to be born
  will be called holy, the Son of God.
  And behold, Elizabeth, your relative,
  has also conceived a son in her old age,
  and this is the sixth month for her who
    was called barren;
  for nothing will be impossible for God."
Mary said, "Behold, I am the handmaid of
    the Lord.
May it be done to me according to your word."
Then the angel departed from her.

Reflecting on the Gospel

"Words! Words! Words! I'm so sick of words!" Eliza Doolittle sings in "My Fair Lady." We ourselves often say, "Talk is cheap." In this Sunday's gospel and first reading, God speaks: first through Nathan the prophet to King David, then through Gabriel to the Virgin Mary. We also say, "Actions speak louder than words." Unlike so many of our own words, God's word always bears meaning and power—words and actions fuse for the good of humankind. God's word (Hebrew: *dabar*) is always active and effective, bringing about our salvation. God's whole plan of salvation is an ongoing annunciation.

In this Sunday's first reading, God speaks and David's throne is assured—his offspring becomes the lineage from which the Savior of the world will be born. God does more for David than simply promise that his kingdom will last forever; God also promises that David's heir will "be a son to me" (first reading). Little could David have imagined that God meant this literally! The heir to David's throne who changes the course of history and establishes God's reign forever is none other than the "Son of the Most High" (gospel). God's reign is no longer measured by the usual standards of kingdoms (possession of land and kings living in cedar palaces) but by "the obedience of faith" (second reading) that is captured in a simple yes ("May it be done to me according to your word"). In the gospel, God speaks and Mary conceives the Savior in her womb. From the beginning of salvation history, God has been acting so the Word becomes flesh and dwells among us.

While the saving plan and work is always God's, it is not without the invitation for human response. What both David and Mary planned for their lives didn't quite happen the way they envisioned. But when David and Mary trust and cooperate with God, a whole new in-breaking of God takes place. God's announcements through Nathan and Gabriel, which we remember this Sunday, prepare us well for Christmas, when God's announcement of salvation is a Child born and called "the Son of God."

Living the Paschal Mystery

This mystery made known in Christ is none other than our own participation in divine life. We are first plunged into this life at our baptism, and through our faithful obedience (our yes to God's will) we further the word-action of God on our own behalf. Our lives must declare that the Christmas mystery isn't limited to a day or season, or even to a Person. The Christmas mystery includes our own share in the divine life and our taking up Christ's mission to announce the Good News of salvation for all. But remember: our yes is no less demanding than Mary's. Bearing Christ has its cost: dying to self. But the fruit is unimaginable: God is with us and within us.

We have only a few days left before we celebrate Christmas, the mystery of God becoming man. Now is the time to rehearse our own yes to God by imitating God's word-action. Perhaps we could consciously make our holiday greeting to others a way to make concrete our generosity and joy. Perhaps we could take a few minutes out of our busy days to listen for God's word to us, say yes, and then put it into action, "en-flesh" God's presence in the goodness of our own lives.

Focusing the Gospel

Key words and phrases: throne of David his father, you will conceive in your womb, Son of God

To the point: God's whole plan of salvation is an ongoing annunciation. God speaks and David's offspring becomes the lineage from which the Savior of the world will be born. God speaks and Mary conceives the Savior in her womb. From the beginning of salvation history, God has been acting so the Word becomes flesh and dwells among us.

Connecting the Gospel

to the second reading: The gospel as well as the second reading make explicit the "revelation of the mystery kept secret for long ages": the Son of God comes as our Savior.

to Christian experience: Advent is both waiting and preparing. Waiting focuses on what God does; preparing focuses on what we do. These divine and human activities come together in Christ.

Connecting the Responsorial Psalm

to the readings: The verses from Psalm 89 used for this Sunday's responsorial psalm are the sung version of the story related in the first reading. God establishes a covenant with David and promises him a kingdom that will last forever. Missing from the Lectionary selection, however, is the part of the story in which God seems to renege on this promise, for David's kingdom is eventually destroyed by enemies. Indeed, by the time of Mary and Joseph no king has been sitting on the throne of David for over five centuries.

The gospel reveals, however, that despite appearances God has been neither absent nor inactive. Instead, God has continued to work relentlessly behind the scenes to prepare the ground for the full flowering of redemption. When that ground is ready in Mary, God plants his seed. May we, like Mary, be open to God's unexpected movements and sing forever of God's saving goodness (psalm refrain).

to cantor preparation: In preparing to sing this responsorial psalm you need to pay careful attention to the shifts in direct address that the verses contain. When are you speaking *to* God? When are you speaking *for* God? Your task is to communicate to the assembly both God's love for us and our love for God. How might Christ, who is fully human and fully God, help you do this?

ASSEMBLY & FAITH-SHARING GROUPS
· God acts in the lives of David and Mary. I experience God acting in my life when . . . through . . . by . . .
· God is acting to make the Word flesh in my life today by . . .
· Like Mary, I bear the Word for others when . . .

PRESIDERS
· My presiding announces God's plan of salvation to the people when I . . .

DEACONS
· My service enables others to carry out the plan of God because . . .

HOSPITALITY MINISTERS
· My hospitality (both at home and at liturgy) announces the "Lord is with you" when . . .

MUSIC MINISTERS
· My music making is an announcement of salvation in that . . .

ALTAR MINISTERS
· As I serve, Christ is conceived in me because . . .

LECTORS
· My proclamation of the word reveals "the mystery kept secret for long ages" when . . .

EXTRAORDINARY MINISTERS OF HOLY COMMUNION
· Like Mary, I am a Christ-bearer most effectively when . . .

17

✠ CELEBRATION

Model Act of Penitence

Presider: God continually announces new possibilities of life for us. Let us call on the Spirit of Jesus to quiet our hearts and minds so that we can hear what God is saying to us through this liturgy . . . [pause]

Lord Jesus, you were conceived in the womb of the virgin Mary: Lord . . .

Christ Jesus, you are God's Word of new life: Christ . . .

Lord Jesus, you are the Word made flesh among us: Lord . . .

Homily Points

• "Words! Words! Words! I'm so sick of words!" Eliza Doolittle sings in "My Fair Lady." We ourselves often say, "Talk is cheap." God's word, however, always bears meaning and power. God's word (Hebrew: *dabar*) is always active and effective: God speaks, and David is promised a kingdom that is to endure forever; God speaks, and the Word is made flesh.

• God's word surprised both David and Mary, announcing a much greater future than they envisioned not only for themselves but for the whole world. God announces to David through the prophet Nathan that God's house is to be a holy people who will "endure forever" rather than a temple. God announces to Mary through Gabriel that the Infant she will conceive will be no ordinary Child, but "the Son of God." God's word always calls *us* to new possibilities and new life.

• A word about new possibilities for our lives raises two challenges for us: first, discerning whether the word we hear is in fact from God and God's will for us; second, having the courage to say Yes, if it is.

Model Prayer of the Faithful

Presider: God is always faithful to the divine plan for our salvation and so we are encouraged to make our needs known.

Response:

Lord,   hear our prayer.

Cantor:

we pray to the Lord,

May all members of the church announce faithfully God's word of new life . . . [pause]

May world leaders be guided by God's plan of salvation for all . . . [pause]

May the poor, the downtrodden, and the suffering be granted the new possibilities of life God desires for them . . . [pause]

May all of us hear God's word spoken to us and respond faithfully with our yes . . . [pause]

Presider: God our Father, you sent your Son into our world to bring us the new life of salvation: hear these our prayers that we might one day enjoy everlasting life with you. We ask this through Christ our Lord. **Amen.**

Let us pray
   [as Advent draws to a close for the faith
   that opens our lives to the Spirit of God]

Pause for silent prayer

Father, all-powerful God,
your eternal Word took flesh on our earth
when the Virgin Mary placed her life
at the service of your plan.
Lift our minds in watchful hope
to hear the voice which announces his glory
and open our minds to receive the Spirit
who prepares us for his coming.

We ask this through Christ our Lord.
    Amen.

FIRST READING
2 Sam 7:1-5, 8b-12, 14a, 16

When King David was settled in his
      palace,
   and the LORD had given him rest from
      his enemies on every side,
   he said to Nathan the prophet,
   "Here I am living in a house of cedar,
    while the ark of God dwells in a tent!"
Nathan answered the king,
   "Go, do whatever you have in mind,
   for the LORD is with you."
But that night the LORD spoke to Nathan
    and said:
   "Go, tell my servant David, 'Thus says
      the LORD:
    Should you build me a house to dwell in?'

"'It was I who took you from the pasture
   and from the care of the flock
   to be commander of my people Israel.
I have been with you wherever you went,
   and I have destroyed all your enemies
      before you.
And I will make you famous like the great
    ones of the earth.
I will fix a place for my people Israel;
   I will plant them so that they may dwell
     in their place
   without further disturbance.
Neither shall the wicked continue to afflict
     them as they did of old,
   since the time I first appointed judges
     over my people Israel.
I will give you rest from all your enemies.
The LORD also reveals to you
   that he will establish a house for you.
And when your time comes and you rest
    with your ancestors,
   I will raise up your heir after you,
     sprung from your loins,
   and I will make his kingdom firm.
I will be a father to him,
   and he shall be a son to me.

Your house and your kingdom shall
    endure forever before me;
    your throne shall stand firm forever.'"

RESPONSORIAL PSALM
Ps 89:2-3, 4-5, 27, 29

R̸. (2a) Forever I will sing the goodness of
the Lord.

The promises of the LORD I will sing
    forever;
    through all generations my mouth shall
        proclaim your faithfulness.
For you have said, "My kindness is
    established forever";
    in heaven you have confirmed your
        faithfulness.

R̸. Forever I will sing the goodness of the
Lord.

"I have made a covenant with my chosen
    one,
    I have sworn to David my servant:
forever will I confirm your posterity
    and establish your throne for all
        generations."

R̸. Forever I will sing the goodness of the
Lord.

"He shall say of me, 'You are my father,
    my God, the Rock, my savior.'
Forever I will maintain my kindness
    toward him,
    and my covenant with him stands firm."

R̸. Forever I will sing the goodness of the
Lord.

SECOND READING
Rom 16:25-27

Brothers and sisters:
To him who can strengthen you,
    according to my gospel and the
        proclamation of Jesus Christ,
    according to the revelation of the
        mystery kept secret for long ages
    but now manifested through the
        prophetic writings and,
    according to the command of the
        eternal God,
    made known to all nations to bring
        about the obedience of faith,
    to the only wise God, through Jesus
        Christ
    be glory forever and ever. Amen.

About Liturgy

Reflecting on the word "mystery": "Mystery" is a favorite theme in the Pauline
corpus (see second reading); it was a favored term in the early church. So much so that
the early designation for sacraments was "the mysteries" (*mysteria*). We might detect
a use of the notion of mystery in three progressively involving ways. First, mystery
refers to the plan of salvation that God set in motion from the time of Adam and Eve's
first sin. Establishing David's throne forever is one more step in this unfolding plan
of salvation. Second, mystery refers to the birth of Jesus Christ; he himself embodies
the plan and carries it forward by his death and resurrection. Third, mystery refers to
the sacraments by which we share in God's unfolding plan of salvation. This is how
we ourselves participate in the establishment of God's everlasting reign. Liturgy is the
ritual enactment of God's mystery. Our full, conscious, and active participation in liturgy is our full, conscious, and active participation in God's mystery of salvation. Our
yes to liturgy is our "obedience of faith."

Reflecting on the word "mystery" challenges any historical approach to the Advent
and Christmas seasons. We await and prepare for Christ, but Christ is already present,
too. This Fourth Sunday of Advent specifically turns us to Christmas and tends to
blur a clear distinction between seasons. What we celebrate next week (Christ's coming) we celebrate every week—Christ is already present through God's plan of salvation, in Christ, and in us through the sacraments.

Proclamation: Greek to English: The second reading is one of those "nightmare"
proclamations in which the entire reading consists of one sentence. This works well in
Greek grammar, but it makes proclamation almost impossible in English. The kernel
of the reading is the first and last two lines: "To him who can strengthen you, . . . to
the only wise God, through Jesus Christ, be glory forever and ever. Amen." It would
be helpful especially if lectors keep these lines in mind so that their proclamation is
clearly a hymn of praise. Also, lectors need to make sure that their inflection doesn't
invite the "Amen" response from the assembly; the "Amen" belongs to the reading.

About Liturgical Music

Music suggestion: "All Who Claim the Faith of Jesus" [G, G2, GC, RS] speaks of the
fulfillment of God's promise in the incarnation of Jesus, of the blessedness of Mary
who bore him, and invites all to join Mary in her thanksgiving and gladness for what
God has done. The hymn would be appropriate for either the entrance procession or
the preparation of the gifts.

Season of Christmas

At the birth of the Son,

there was a great shouting in Bethlehem;

for the Angels came down,

and gave praise there.

Their voices were a great thunder:

at that voice of praise

the silent ones came,

and gave praise to the Son.

—St. Ephraim the Syrian
Nineteen Hymns on the Nativity of Christ in the Flesh
Hymn V

SPIRITUALITY

The Vigil Mass

GOSPEL ACCLAMATION

R̸. Alleluia, alleluia.
Tomorrow the wickedness of the earth will be
destroyed:
the Savior of the world will reign over us.
R̸. Alleluia, alleluia.

Gospel

Matt 1:1-25; L13 ABC

**The book of the genealogy of Jesus Christ,
the son of David, the son of Abraham.**

**Abraham became the father of Isaac,
Isaac the father of Jacob,
Jacob the father of Judah and his
brothers.
Judah became the father of Perez and
Zerah,
whose mother was Tamar.
Perez became the father of Hezron,
Hezron the father of Ram,
Ram the father of Amminadab.
Amminadab became the father of
Nahshon,
Nahshon the father of Salmon,
Salmon the father of Boaz,
whose mother was Rahab.
Boaz became the father of Obed,
whose mother was Ruth.
Obed became the father of Jesse,
Jesse the father of David the king.**

Continued in Appendix A, p. 262

or Matt 1:18-25 in Appendix A, p. 262.

See Appendix A, p. 263, for the other readings.

The Gospel and Living the Paschal Mystery

Key words and phrases from the gospel: name him Jesus, save his people, name him Emmanuel, God is with us

To the point: In the gospel, two names are revealed for the Infant born of Mary: Jesus, "save his people," and Emmanuel, "God is with us." The second name helps us understand the first. Our salvation is accomplished by God's very presence.

Reflection: A TV commercial a couple of years ago showed a father bringing in a large, luxurious, live-cut Christmas tree on Christmas Eve. His small son's eyes grew larger and larger and he became more and more excited. The tree was placed in the stand, then the father took a pruner and began cutting away—cutting, cutting, cutting until all the branches save a very few top ones were gone. The son's face fell and his demeanor changed to distraught sadness. Then the commercial changes scenes—it's Christmas morning. Presents are piled so high under the tree that the bare trunk of the night before is completely covered with gifts. The few branches at the top stand out majestically as the crown of the abundance. At first sight, this commercial might have caused a wrenching in us—the meaning of Christmas is not found in piled-up gifts. And yet, God's Gift to us is exactly the meaning of Christmas, and the Gift is of incalculable abundance and worth.

The Gift of the divine Son is the fulfillment of God's desire for us from the very beginning of creation. As the first reading depicts, God delights in us and desires to be in such intimate union with us that only spousal imagery can begin to capture the divine desire. God's Gift is one of presence—a whole new, unprecedented presence in which God is not only present *to* us but, by taking on human flesh, becomes present *within* us. The first reading gives us an intimate description of what happens when salvation dawns upon us in God's presence: we enjoy a whole new relationship with God. Christmas is a festival of new relationship.

In the gospel, two names are revealed for the Infant born of Mary: Jesus, "save his people," and Emmanuel, "God is with us." The second name helps us understand the first. Our salvation is accomplished by God's very presence. We are saved because we are one with the divine One who chooses to be present to us.

It is not joyful that this most wonderful time of the year—when the radio is filled with the sounds of once-a-year music, TV is abounding in images of abundance, and our neighborhoods are bristling with color and animation—is also a season of sheer contradictions. For many, the trees are piled high with presents and the tables loaded with delectable delights. For others, this is a time of acute awareness of not having the necessities of life. For some, this is a time of family togetherness and peace; for others it brings into sharp focus separations and strained relationships. The one Gift we all share is God's love, care, and presence. One challenge of Christmas is to *be* that presence for others. We must *live* the Gift and bring the joy and glory of God's presence to those who are most alienated, hurting, in need. Christmas brings demands along with the Gift. We are given the Gift so that we might share with others. This is how God desires to make salvation known.

SPIRITUALITY

Mass at Midnight

GOSPEL ACCLAMATION
Luke 2:10-11

R̸. Alleluia, alleluia.
I proclaim to you good news of great joy:
today a Savior is born for us,
Christ the Lord.
R̸. Alleluia, alleluia.

Gospel

Luke 2:1-14; L14ABC

In those days a decree
    went out from Caesar
    Augustus
that the whole world should
    be enrolled.
This was the first enrollment,
    when Quirinius was governor of
    Syria.
So all went to be enrolled, each to his
    own town.
And Joseph too went up from Galilee
    from the town of Nazareth
    to Judea, to the city of David that is
        called Bethlehem,
    because he was of the house and
        family of David,
    to be enrolled with Mary, his
        betrothed, who was with child.
While they were there,
    the time came for her to have her child,
    and she gave birth to her firstborn son.
She wrapped him in swaddling clothes
    and laid him in a manger,
    because there was no room for them
        in the inn.

Continued in Appendix A, p. 263.

See Appendix A, p. 264, for these readings:

FIRST READING
Isa 9:1-6

RESPONSORIAL PSALM
Ps 96:1-2, 2-3, 11-12, 13

SECOND READING
Titus 2:11-14

The Gospel and Living the Paschal Mystery
Key words and phrases from the gospel: her child, good news, Glory to God in the highest

To the point: "The zeal of the LORD . . . will do this!" What does God's zeal accomplish? First, the new life of Mary's Child. Second, the new life we have as we come out of darkness into Light. This new life we are given is the very life of Mary's Child. No wonder we join our voices with the angels as we sing "Glory to God in the highest"!

Reflection: During these days of Christmas celebration, we will often have occasion to sing as did the angels long ago, "Glory to God in the highest!" At this time when we celebrate the birth of "a savior [who] has been born for" us, the One who is "Wonder-Counselor, God-Hero, Father-Forever, Prince of Peace," the One who is "a great light" in the darkness of war and strife around us, we welcome an opportunity to put aside our cares and worries, bask in the joy and generosity of the season, and sing out our "Glory to God in the highest!" Yes, we celebrate the birth of our savior, Jesus Christ. The readings, however, take us beyond the birth of Jesus to the great deeds God accomplishes in us by this birth—deeds that were accomplished over two millennia ago but that God is still accomplishing in each of us, "a people as his own" (second reading). Christmas celebrates divinity and humanity in more ways than one!

Christmas is a feast of salvation (see second reading); the Son is sent to bring us from the darkness of sin into the light of glory. Through the prophets we were foretold that "a son is given us." Even in our need for cleansing and healing, God has always been faithful. Even more, God has acted with *ardor*: "The zeal of the LORD . . . will do this!" What does God's zeal accomplish? First, the new life of Mary's Child. Second, the new life we have as we come out of darkness into Light. This new life we are given is the very life of Mary's Child. No wonder we join our voices with the angels as we sing "Glory to God in the highest!" In fact, we sing a double glory: we praise God for Jesus' birth and for our own new life.

Late in the second century, St. Irenaeus wrote, "The glory of God is man [*sic*] fully alive" (*Against Heresies*, Book IV, XX, 7). Herein is the surprise of Christmas: The life of Mary's Son is *given to us*. The marriage of divinity and humanity that is the Son of Mary also is a marriage of humanity with God. *In our very selves* we give glory to God because we have been made in God's image. Mary's Son restores what was lost in the Garden of Eden and does even more than restore that lost relationship with God. Now we enjoy an even more intimate relationship, where we are given the very life of God. The Son through the Spirit dwells within each of us. By our own fidelity to this gift of new life, we are a constant chorus giving "Glory to God in the highest!"

Christmas calls us to give the most important gift of all—the very life of God—to each other. We have been given the Gift, now we share it. Christmas calls us to open our eyes and see where we ourselves can bring the joy and peace of salvation to those around us. Christmas brings demands along with the Gift. As we alleviate pain and suffering around us, we help others join in our chorus of "Glory to God in the highest!"

✚ SPIRITUALITY

Mass at Dawn

GOSPEL ACCLAMATION
Luke 2:14

℟. Alleluia, alleluia.
Glory to God in the highest,
and on earth peace to those
on whom his favor rests.
℟. Alleluia, alleluia.

Gospel

Luke 2:15-20; L15ABC

When the angels went away
   from them to heaven,
   the shepherds said to one
      another,
   "Let us go, then, to Bethlehem
   to see this thing that has taken place,
   which the Lord has made known to
      us."
So they went in haste and found Mary
   and Joseph,
   and the infant lying in the manger.
When they saw this,
   they made known the message
   that had been told them about this
      child.
All who heard it were amazed
   by what had been told them by the
      shepherds.
And Mary kept all these things,
   reflecting on them in her heart.
Then the shepherds returned,
   glorifying and praising God
   for all they had heard and seen,
   just as it had been told to them.

See Appendix A, p. 264, for these readings:

FIRST READING
Isa 62:11-12

RESPONSORIAL PSALM
Ps 97:1, 6, 11-12

SECOND READING
Titus 3:4-7

The Gospel and Living the Paschal Mystery
Key words and phrases from the gospel: angels, shepherds, the Lord has made known

To the point: We cannot know or recognize the mystery of salvation by ourselves. God alone makes this mystery known to us. God's means of communication might be heaven-sent (angels) or quite earthbound (scruffy shepherds). In any case, the message is always Good News.

Reflection: Andree was trying to draw a picture of the family's Christmas tree, which she dearly loved, to send to her grandparents. Tongue hanging out, face contorted in sheer concentration, she tried and tried but just couldn't seem to get it quite right. She could draw the tree all right, but it didn't suit her because what she drew just didn't quite catch her relationship to the tree, which made the tree what it was for her. She finally put down her green crayon and just sat quietly and stared and stared and stared. For the longest time she didn't flinch a bit. Then all of a sudden a light shone out of her face, she broke into a big smile, wriggled in excitement, chose one of the green trees she had drawn earlier, picked up a yellow crayon, drew two Christmas ornaments with smiley faces on them, and declared she had finished and could now send the picture off in the mail. When asked who the faces were, she jumped around in glee and said, "Nana and Papa—they're my Jesus." Andree had managed to draw the magic of her tree—it expressed the message she had been "reflecting on . . . in her heart." Then she "made known the message."

The message of the gospel and this whole festival is "your savior comes!" (first reading). We cannot know or recognize the mystery of salvation by ourselves. God alone makes this mystery known to us—reveals it when we take the time to reflect in our hearts and open ourselves to encounter the Mystery. Salvation is made known through the strangest means—God's means of communication might be heaven-sent (angels) or quite earthbound (scruffy shepherds). No matter how strange the means, part of the mystery of God's love is often the unexpected ways in which it is communicated. In any case, the message is always Good News.

The shepherds in the gospel model for us openness to the mystery of God's message of salvation. Sometimes we're the hearers of the Good News, and our response is simply to reflect on it in our hearts, to wait for God's message to well up within us a light that seeks to be expressed. At other times, like the shepherds, we are called to make "known the message" of salvation. Then, like Andree, we open ourselves to an encounter with the Mystery and send it along to everyone whom we meet. We ourselves, then, become bearers of the Good News.

None of us will travel to Bethlehem to behold a newborn infant lying in a manger. But all of us travel the road of daily life, when we are called to see the newborn Infant in the youngster who needs companionship, the teenager who needs a listening ear, the parent who needs a helping hand, the elder who needs someone to care. Through us the Lord makes known the message of divine love and care.

SPIRITUALITY

Mass during the Day

GOSPEL ACCLAMATION

℟. Alleluia, alleluia.
A holy day has dawned upon us.
Come, you nations, and adore the Lord.
For today a great light has come upon the earth.
℟. Alleluia, alleluia.

Gospel

John 1:1-18; L16ABC

In the beginning was the Word,
    and the Word was with God,
    and the Word was God.
He was in the beginning with God.
All things came to be through him,
    and without him nothing came to be.
What came to be through him was life,
    and this life was the light of the
        human race;
the light shines in the darkness,
    and the darkness has not
        overcome it.

A man named John was sent from God.
He came for testimony, to testify to the
    light,
    so that all might believe through him.
He was not the light,
    but came to testify to the light.

Continued in Appendix A, p. 265

or John 1:1-5, 9-14 *in Appendix A, p. 265.*

See Appendix A, p. 265–266, for the other readings.

The Gospel and Living the Paschal Mystery

Key words and phrases from the gospel: with God, was God, in the world, his fullness we have all received

To the point: The incredible joy of the Christmas message is that the One who was with God and was God from the beginning is now in the world among us (gospel), fully revealed (second reading), and directly seen (first reading). Because of Christ's birth we have received salvation—the very fullness of God.

Reflection: Our Christmas carols contain something of a seeming contradiction. Many of them are about the simplicity and joy and peace of this season such as "Silent Night" and "Joy to the World." Many sing of the sweet Babe born this night such as "Away in a Manger" or "What Child Is This?" Some tell the story of the birth of the King such as "Hark! The Herald Angels Sing" or "Angels We Have Heard on High" or "The First Noel."

But beyond the simplicity, joy, peace, newborn King, angels, stars, and *gloria*s is the stark reality of salvation. So, for example, the fourth stanza of "Hark! The Herald Angels Sing" reminds us that "Christ the Lord is born today, Christ who takes our sins away!" Both the first and third verse of "God Rest You Merry, Gentlemen" refer to Satan's power and the final, fourth verse reminds us that "This holy tide of Christmas doth bring redeeming grace." The third verse of "It Came upon the Midnight Clear" reminds us that the "world has suffered long" from "the woes of sin and strife" and we ought "hush the noise and cease [our] strife And hear the angels sing." (Check out the third and fourth verses of "O Little Town of Bethlehem" or the African-American spiritual "Go Tell It on the Mountain.")

The incredible joy of the Christmas message is that the One who was with God and was God from the beginning is now in the world among us (gospel), fully revealed (second reading), and directly seen (first reading). Because of Christ's birth we have received salvation—the very fullness of God. Yet, mixed in with all the joy and wonder and beauty of this festival is the reality of sin and salvation. The joy of this festival comes with the realization that the effects of sin are overcome; God is with us and we receive new life.

Both the first reading and gospel begin with an announcement of salvation: glad tidings, peace, good news (first reading); through the Word is life and that "life was the light of the human race" (gospel). The reason for the announcement of salvation is given in terms of what God has done on behalf of humanity: given comfort, redeemed, "bared his holy arm" for our salvation (first reading); God "gave power to become children of God" and "from his fullness we have all received" (gospel). This festival is really about the wonders God has done for us through Jesus Christ. Even more stupendous than heralding angels and adoring Magi is the invitation to each of us to accept the One who is in the world (see gospel) and become sons and daughters who have received the very fullness of God: the Word made flesh.

This season offers many opportunities for each of us to be charitable toward those less fortunate than ourselves. These readings remind us that the goodness we share with others is a continuation and symbol of the goodness God has shared with us in giving us Jesus Christ. Every good deed is a testimony to God's loving offer of salvation. This is how God makes salvation known (see responsorial psalm): through us and the works we perform. Christmas isn't a reality for us until we ourselves become lights shining in the darkness.

Model Act of Penitence

Presider: The great mystery of salvation we celebrate is that God's only-begotten Son became flesh and dwells among us. We pause to ponder this great mystery and to prepare ourselves to receive the new life Jesus offers . . . [pause]

Lord Jesus, you are the Word made flesh who dwells among us: Lord . . .

Christ Jesus, you are the true light that dispels darkness: Christ . . .

Lord Jesus, you share the glory of the Father, full of grace and truth: Lord . . .

Homily Points

• This Christmas is different from any other. This is so because each of us is different. We experience God's love in our lives in ever new ways and are continually changed.

• Salvation is none other than our experience of God's love, revealed in multiple ways, many of them unexpected and surprising. Always God acts to bring us to ever new life, from sending the Son to dwell among us to sending us to announce God's presence and love to others.

• The joy of this festival is expressed not only in our joyful songs, loving gift-giving, and gatherings with loved ones, but also in our growing awareness of God's Gift among us.

Model Prayer of the Faithful

Presider: The God who gives us the Gift of salvation will surely hear our prayers.

Response:

Lord, hear our prayer.

Cantor:

we pray to the Lord,

That the church may faithfully be a beacon of light shining in the darkness . . . [pause]

That all peoples of the world may enjoy peace and fullness of grace . . . [pause]

That the sick and suffering may be comforted by Christ who comes to them through the care of others . . . [pause]

That all of us here might share with others the fullness we ourselves have received . . . [pause]

Presider: O glorious God, you sent your Son to dwell among us: hear these our prayers that we might see your glory and one day share your everlasting life. We ask this through your Son Jesus Christ our Lord. **Amen.**

ALTERNATIVE OPENING PRAYER

(from the Mass during the Day)

Let us pray

Pause for silent prayer

God of love, Father of all,
the darkness that covered the earth
has given way to the bright dawn of your
 Word made flesh.
Make us a people of this light.
Make us faithful to your Word,
that we may bring your life to the waiting
 world.

Grant this through Christ our Lord. **Amen.**

FOR REFLECTION

· I announce God's message of salvation when . . . I receive God's message of salvation when . . .

· My manner of living reveals God's Word made flesh by . . .

· The new life from God I experience this Christmas is . . . The new life for which I long is . . .

· I express my Christmas joy throughout the year when . . .

SPIRITUALITY

℟. Alleluia, alleluia.
Let the peace of Christ control your hearts;
let the word of Christ dwell in you
    richly.
℟. Alleluia, alleluia.

Gospel

Luke 2:22-40; L17B

**When the days were completed
    for their purification
    according to the law of Moses,
    they took him up to Jerusalem
    to present him to the Lord,
    just as it is written in the law
        of the Lord,**
*Every male that opens
    the womb shall be
    consecrated to the Lord,*
and to offer the sacrifice of
*a pair of turtledoves or two young
    pigeons,*
**in accordance with the dictate in the
    law of the Lord.**

**Now there was a man in Jerusalem
    whose name was Simeon.
This man was righteous and devout,
    awaiting the consolation of Israel,
    and the Holy Spirit was upon him.
It had been revealed to him by the Holy
        Spirit
    that he should not see death
    before he had seen the Christ of the
        Lord.
He came in the Spirit into the temple;
    and when the parents brought in the
        child Jesus
    to perform the custom of the law in
        regard to him,
    he took him into his arms and blessed
        God, saying:**

Continued in Appendix A, p. 266.

or Luke 2:22, 39-40 in Appendix A, p. 266.

Reflecting on the Gospel

How many of us haven't seen someone with absolutely perfectly styled and groomed hair, and we had a wild urge to rumple it? Or we're out for a walk and come across a perfectly manicured lawn—don't we have the urge to kick off our shoes and shuffle through it? Or maybe we've heard ourselves utter this or a similar prayer: "O God, please give [so-and-so] just one fault so I can relate!" Perfection is something we humans have a hard time with. Probably this is so because we know we're not perfect—we are the children of the Fall. Yet how often don't we equate holiness with perfection? Don't we think we have to be perfectly good to be holy? No wonder this feast can be so difficult for some; after all, the Holy Family was made up of Jesus, Mary, and Joseph. How can we ever be holy like they?

Although our questions are natural, our tendency toward a narrow kind of answer that ultimately presumes we are surely not very holy shortchanges what God has begun in Christ Jesus and continues through us. God's promise of salvation (of holiness) comes to fulfillment through the enfleshment of human life: the son born to Abraham and Sarah, the Child parented by Mary and Joseph and tenderly recognized by Simeon and Anna. This promise continues to be enfleshed today as we grow in holiness. As the gospel shows, the operative word here is "grow."

"The child grew and became strong . . ." This simple affirmation about the Child says something about the whole mystery of the Incarnation, about families, about each one of us, and about holiness. Mary and Joseph, no doubt, grew into their role as parents of Jesus, beginning with their fulfilling the prescriptions of the law when they took him to the Temple to "present him to the Lord." The gospel tells us that the "child grew and became strong." Even Jesus, the Son of God, grew—physically, as he grew from baby to child to adult, but also spiritually as he grew into taking up his saving mission. We grow as individuals and as a human family as we ourselves respond to the many different ways God calls us to holiness. This is the meaning of the Incarnation: growth in God's ways. This is the meaning of holiness: not perfection, but our willingness to be open to God's promptings and grow in our relationships with God and each other. Holiness, then, is not a state of perfection to be achieved, but an openness to God's presence and promptings.

Living the Paschal Mystery

God so cared for the family of humanity that God gave us the only-begotten Son; we show our acceptance of membership in God's family by caring for each other. Of course, this begins with our own family members. This feast calls us to care for one another in practical ways. Perhaps this means phoning an elder who lives alone or is in a retirement center or nursing home. Maybe this means sharing toys more generously on the part of little ones or pitching in to help without being asked on the part of adolescents or husband and wife listening more intently to each other. These family ways of showing caring relationships are "practice" for what is even more important: responding to God's will. In fact, we respond to God's will when we care for those around us in need. Dying to self for the sake of the other is what builds up each of us and our families, and makes us holy. This is the way to having the "favor of God" upon us.

Focusing the Gospel

Key words and phrases: child grew and became strong

To the point: "The child grew and became strong . . ." This simple affirmation about the Child says something about the whole mystery of the Incarnation, about families, and about holiness. Mary and Joseph, no doubt, grew into their role as parents of Jesus, beginning with their fulfilling the prescriptions of the law. We grow as a human family as we respond to the many different ways God calls us to holiness. This is the meaning of the Incarnation: growth in God's ways.

Connecting the Gospel

to the first reading: God's promise of salvation comes to fulfillment through the enfleshment of human life: the son born to Abraham and Sarah, the Child parented by Mary and Joseph and tenderly recognized by Simeon and Anna. This promise continues to be enfleshed today as we grow in holiness.

to our lived experience: The point to this feast is not to create a tension between a notion of an ideal nuclear family and our actual experience of family. Growing in holiness is possible no matter what our family situation.

Connecting the Responsorial Psalm

to the readings: The verses of this feast's responsorial psalm are taken from Psalm 105, a lengthy song relaying the story of Israel's foundation from the days of Abraham through the event of the Exodus. The psalm is a narrative of their story of salvation probably used at festivals celebrating their identity as God's chosen people. Both the first and second readings flesh out details of this story as it pertains to Abraham and Sarah and God's covenant promise to them of numerous offspring. God was establishing a special people, holy and righteous, and granting them a homeland.

Simeon and Anna, Mary and Joseph are able to recognize God's special presence in the infant in their arms (gospel) because they have trusted in the God encountered in every retelling of this sacred story. On this feast the retelling continues, with more details in place. This time it is we who celebrate our identity as God's holy people. This time it is we who celebrate that God remembers his covenant with us (psalm refrain). This time it is we who rejoice in the holiness to which God has called us.

to cantor preparation: As you prepare this psalm you might spend some time reflecting on the God about whom you will be singing. Who is this God who wants to be in covenant with us? Who is this God who always remembers us? Who is this God who keeps acting in our favor? What might you do this week so that you can tell the community about this God with conviction?

**ASSEMBLY &
FAITH-SHARING GROUPS**
- Holiness means to me . . .
- I grow in holiness when . . . I help others grow in holiness when . . . Others help me grow in holiness when . . .
- What keeps me from growing in holiness is . . .
- What increases my desire to grow in holiness is . . .

PRESIDERS
- My own growing in holiness leads others to grow in holiness when . . .

DEACONS
- Ways I've grown in holiness because of my serving others are . . .

HOSPITALITY MINISTERS
- The manner of my greeting helps others recognize their holiness when . . .

MUSIC MINISTERS
- Lifting my voice in song is an expression of holiness because . . .

ALTAR MINISTERS
- My attentiveness to details helps the assembly grow in holiness when . . . blocks the assembly's growth in holiness when . . .

LECTORS
- I experience God's word as holy when . . . I struggle with this holiness when . . .

**EXTRAORDINARY MINISTERS
OF HOLY COMMUNION**
- I surrender to the holiness in the Body of Christ when . . .

Model Act of Penitence

Presider: This feast invites us to reflect on our relationships with each other in our own families and in the broader family of humanity. We pause and ask God to make all of us holier and better family members . . . [pause]

Lord Jesus, you grew in wisdom, age, and in grace: Lord . . .

Christ Jesus, you are the fullness of life and holiness: Christ . . .

Lord Jesus, you call us to share in the holiness of the family of God: Lord . . .

Homily Points

• All of us can name funny, tragic, uplifting, debilitating, inspiring family events. The gospels give us hints that the Holy Family had its ups and downs also. Moreover, in his adult life the family Jesus traveled with was a motley group of disciples. What is holy in all this "stuff" of family life?

• Holiness is not a state of perfection! It is, first, growth in wholesome relationships with each other (compassion, mercy, forgiveness, generosity, charity, etc.) that deepens our relationship with God. Second, holiness is the indwelling of God's grace (life).

• This feast calls us to reflect on our very human families, where even our weaknesses call us to growth. This feast enables us to be real at the same time it fills us with hope.

Model Prayer of the Faithful

Presider: Let us pray that God may bless all our families, make us holier, and draw us to stronger relationships with the family of all of humanity.

Response: Lord, hear our prayer.

Cantor: we pray to the Lord,

That the gathered church always be a welcoming and hospitable holy family . . . [pause]

That all peoples of the world grow in holiness by striving for just relationships . . . [pause]

That families suffering loss be comforted, and families in need of healing be reconciled . . . [pause]

That all of us reach out to anyone in need as our brother or sister in Christ . . . [pause]

Presider: God our Father, you created the family of humanity to share in your holiness: hear these our prayers that one day we may enjoy everlasting life with you. We ask this through Christ our brother. **Amen.**

ALTERNATIVE OPENING PRAYER

Let us pray
[as the family of God, who share in his life]

Pause for silent prayer

Father in heaven, creator of all,
you ordered the earth to bring forth life
and crowned its goodness by creating the
    family of man.
In history's moment when all was ready,
you sent your Son to dwell in time,
obedient to the laws of life in our world.

Teach us the sanctity of human love,
show us the value of family life,
and help us to live in peace with all men
that we may share in your life for ever.

We ask this through Christ our Lord.
    Amen.

FIRST READING
Gen 15:1-6; 21:1-3

The word of the LORD came to Abram in a
    vision, saying:
    "Fear not, Abram!
    I am your shield;
    I will make your reward very great."
But Abram said,
    "O Lord GOD, what good will your gifts
      be,
    if I keep on being childless
    and have as my heir the steward of my
      house, Eliezer?"
Abram continued,
    "See, you have given me no offspring,
    and so one of my servants will be my
      heir."
Then the word of the LORD came to him:
    "No, that one shall not be your heir;
    your own issue shall be your heir."
The Lord took Abram outside and said,
    "Look up at the sky and count the stars,
      if you can.
Just so," he added, "shall your descendants
      be."
Abram put his faith in the LORD,
    who credited it to him as an act of
      righteousness.

The LORD took note of Sarah as he had
    said he would;
    he did for her as he had promised.
Sarah became pregnant and bore
    Abraham a son in his old age,
    at the set time that God had stated.
Abraham gave the name Isaac to this son
    of his
    whom Sarah bore him.

RESPONSORIAL PSALM
Ps 105:1-2, 3-4, 6-7, 8-9

R̸. (7a, 8a) The Lord remembers his covenant forever.

Give thanks to the LORD, invoke his name;
 make known among the nations his
 deeds.
Sing to him, sing his praise,
 proclaim all his wondrous deeds.

R̸. The Lord remembers his covenant forever.

Glory in his holy name;
 rejoice, O hearts that seek the LORD!
Look to the LORD in his strength;
 constantly seek his face.

R̸. The Lord remembers his covenant forever.

You descendants of Abraham, his servants,
 sons of Jacob, his chosen ones!
He, the LORD, is our God;
 throughout the earth his judgments
 prevail.

R̸. The Lord remembers his covenant forever.

He remembers forever his covenant
 which he made binding for a thousand
 generations
which he entered into with Abraham
 and by his oath to Isaac.

R̸. The Lord remembers his covenant forever.

SECOND READING
Heb 11:8, 11-12, 17-19

Brothers and sisters:
By faith Abraham obeyed when he was
 called to go out to a place
 that he was to receive as an inheritance;
 he went out, not knowing where he was
 to go.
By faith he received power to generate,
 even though he was past the normal age
 —and Sarah herself was sterile—
 for he thought that the one who had
 made the promise was trustworthy.
So it was that there came forth from one
 man,
 himself as good as dead,
 descendants as numerous as the stars
 in the sky
 and as countless as the sands on the
 seashore.

Continued in Appendix A, p. 266.

See Appendix A, p. 267, for additional readings.

About Liturgy
Liturgy and holiness: All liturgy is an opportunity to grow in holiness. This means much more than simply "getting grace." It means that liturgy is one concrete way we can open ourselves to God's presence and give ourselves over to God's action so we can be transformed into ever more perfect members of the Body of Christ. Our growth in holiness begins with God's action within us. It continues with the dismissal from liturgy, when we are sent forth to live holy lives. Liturgy continues as we reach out to those who cross our paths with gentleness and kindness, justice and peace, forgiveness and reconciliation. Liturgy's fruit is God's grace borne out in the holiness of our lives.

Canticle of Simeon: Simeon's prayer in the gospel becomes the church's nightly prayer. The prayer Simeon utters when he takes the infant Jesus into his arms is now called the Canticle of Simeon or the *Nunc dimittis.* This is the proper gospel canticle for night prayer (or Compline) and has been an invariable part of Liturgy of the Hours since about the fourth century. Just as the elderly prophet Simeon could face his death with peace because he knew he had seen the Messiah so, too, when we sing this canticle every night before retiring can we sleep peacefully in the confidence that God will see us through the night since the terrors of darkness were dispelled when the Light came into the world. It is a wonderful habit to pray this prayer of confidence in God each night.

Advantage of the revised Lectionary: In order to profit from the additions to the readings in the revised Lectionary, we have chosen to go with the proper readings assigned for year B. The advantage of these extra readings is that they provide different interpretive contexts for liturgy planning and preaching. In this way the feast can stay fresh and meaningful.

About Liturgical Music
Music suggestions: Although hymns which speak of the infant Jesus and/or the Holy Family are always appropriate on this day, the readings for year B suggest using texts which sing of God's fidelity through the ages to the covenant promises and the faithful response of so many who trusted in that fidelity. "Of the Father's Love Begotten" and "Lo, How a Rose E'er Blooming," both found in most hymn resources, would be good choices on this day for the preparation of the gifts. One especially appropriate hymn which deserves wider circulation is found only in CBW3: "In the Darkness Shines the Splendor." The repeated image of Christ in "ev'ry human story" fits so well with the salvation history retold in this Sunday's readings, and with the humanness through which that story unfolds in the life events of real people. This hymn would be appropriate for either Communion or the preparation of the gifts.

DECEMBER 28, 2008
THE HOLY FAMILY OF JESUS, MARY, AND JOSEPH

✝ SPIRITUALITY

GOSPEL ACCLAMATION

R̲7̲. Alleluia, alleluia.
In the past God spoke to our ancestors through
    the prophets;
in these last days, he has spoken to us through
    the Son.
R̲7̲. Alleluia, alleluia.

Gospel

Luke 2:16-21; L18ABC

The shepherds went in
    haste to Bethlehem
    and found Mary and
    Joseph,
and the infant lying in
    the manger.
When they saw this,
    they made known the message
    that had been told them about this
    child.
All who heard it were amazed
    by what had been told them by the
    shepherds.
And Mary kept all these things,
    reflecting on them in her heart.
Then the shepherds returned,
    glorifying and praising God
    for all they had heard and seen,
    just as it had been told to them.

When eight days were completed for
    his circumcision,
he was named Jesus, the name given
    him by the angel
before he was conceived in the womb.

See Appendix A, p. 267, for these readings:

FIRST READING
Num 6:22-27

RESPONSORIAL PSALM
Ps 67:2-3, 5, 6, 8

SECOND READING
Gal 4:4-7

Reflecting on the Gospel

No one would question that a wedding day is focused on the couple being married. On the same day, nonetheless, the parents, grandparents, and (often) baptismal sponsors present also wear formal garments and receive corsages and boutonnieres, congratulations and good wishes. Honoring these people close to the bride and groom is a way of saying that they have had an important share in bringing the couple to this blessed day and are not to be forgotten. This is something of what is going on in this festival. We are in the Christmas season when we celebrate the Savior being born of human flesh and dwelling among us. The church wishes us not to forget, either, she who bore the Son of God, nursed him, and guided him in wisdom and grace to take up his mission. We honor Mary, the Mother of God, even as we rejoice in the birth of her son, our Lord and Savior.

The gospel selection opens with the shepherds seeing the "infant lying in the manger," and then leaving the manger to make known what they had seen. Others hear about this amazing event—which Mary kept in her heart, reflecting over and over on its meaning—through the witness of ordinary folk who open themselves to encountering God in the most unexpected ways. God's surprising ways of presence—as a humble infant in a manger, as the One who ransoms/saves us (see second reading)—quicken in us a resolve similar to that of the shepherds to make haste to proclaim the Good News of salvation. True encounter with God never leaves us merely reflecting—it always leads us to witness to God's presence.

Honoring Mary as the mother of God goes beyond the event of her giving birth to the Son of God. By keeping "all these things" and "reflecting on them in her heart," she exhibits a life of encountering God by hearing and seeing, and then telling of God's marvelous deeds. Like Mary, we must ponder God's entry into our own lives, making the divine presence the very "stuff" of our hearts. We, too, must see, hear, and tell others of God's marvelous deeds. And, like the shepherds, our ultimate response is to glorify and praise God.

Living the Paschal Mystery

Often New Year's resolutions are about such things as losing weight, trying to stop smoking, cleaning up our language, etc. The readings for this festival honoring Mary might challenge us and our resolution-making in another direction. Perhaps this year we might resolve to take time each day to see and hear what God is revealing to us in the ordinary things of our lives: in the grateful smile of a child, in the gift of a compliment, in the unexpected call or visit of a friend. Then we might take the time to tell of God's goodness to others.

We might also resolve to spend more time, as Mary did, pondering and reflecting in our hearts God's mystery of salvation. We might set aside a special time each day to pray and then stick to it. We might join a faith-sharing group or volunteer to read Scripture to the sight-impaired.

Living the paschal mystery means modeling our life after Christ's. From the eighth day of his life when he was named Jesus, Savior, we are reminded that our lives, too, are to be spent in saving others. This isn't necessarily something we do in big, showy ways. More often the most fruitful Christianity is that lived simply and quietly but steadily and resolutely: dying to self for the sake of a new and better life for others.

Focusing the Gospel

Key words and phrases: saw, made known, heard

To the point: Honoring Mary as the mother of God goes beyond the event of her giving birth to the Son of God. By keeping "all these things" and "reflecting on them in her heart," she exhibits a life of hearing, seeing, and telling of God's marvelous deeds.

Model Act of Penitence

Presider: At this time when we celebrate the Incarnation of the divine Son, the church gives us this festival to honor Mary, the Mother of God. With her, let us ponder the mystery of God's salvation and open our hearts to receive its grace . . . [pause]

Lord Jesus, you were conceived by the Holy Spirit in the womb of the Virgin Mary: Lord . . .

Christ Jesus, you are the Son of God and the son of Mary: Christ . . .

Lord Jesus, you are worthy of all glory and praise: Lord . . .

Model Prayer of the Faithful

Presider: On this first day of the new year let us pray for God's continued blessings on us and the world.

Response:

Lord, hear our prayer.

Cantor:

we pray to the Lord,

May all members of the church, like Mary, ponder and respond faithfully to God's marvelous deeds . . . [pause]

May all peoples of the world, like the shepherds, come to know God's salvation . . . [pause]

That the poor, sick, hungry, diseased, and discouraged may see and hear of God's blessings and peace . . . [pause]

That all of us here may resolve this year to see and hear God's blessings and tell others of God's saving power . . . [pause]

Presider: O saving God, you sent your Son, born of Mary, to dwell among us: hear these our New Year's prayers that we might receive your blessings and live in peace. We ask this through that same Son Jesus Christ our Lord. Amen.

FOR REFLECTION
· Those things I keep in my heart and reflect upon are . . .
· What helps me give time to reflect on things that trouble me or that I do not understand is . . .
· God's marvelous deeds are enacted in my life when . . .

Homily Points

• Mother's Day is the day of the year when the most long-distance phone calls are made; sometimes the landline circuits are so clogged that we must wait hours before we can get through. This solemnity honoring Mary, the Mother of God is our religious "Mother's Day."

• Mary teaches us no less than she taught Jesus: she teaches us to be open to the surprising ways God comes to us, and to reflect on God's ways in our hearts. Like Mary, our whole lives are a yes to God's presence, born to others through our faithfulness to God's ways.

SPIRITUALITY

GOSPEL ACCLAMATION
Matt 2:2

R⁊. Alleluia, alleluia.
We saw his star at its rising
and have come to do him homage.
R⁊. Alleluia, alleluia.

Gospel   Matt 2:1-12; L20ABC

When Jesus was born in Bethlehem of Judea,
  in the days of King Herod,
    behold, magi from the east arrived in
      Jerusalem, saying,
  "Where is the newborn king of the Jews?
We saw his star at its rising
  and have come to do him homage."
When King Herod heard this,
  he was greatly troubled,
  and all Jerusalem with him.
Assembling all the chief priests and the
    scribes of the people,
  he inquired of them where the Christ was
    to be born.
They said to him, "In Bethlehem of Judea,
  for thus it has been written through the
      prophet:
  And you, Bethlehem, land of Judah,
    are by no means least among the
      rulers of Judah;
  since from you shall come a ruler,
    who is to shepherd my people Israel."
Then Herod called the magi secretly
  and ascertained from them the time of
    the star's appearance.
He sent them to Bethlehem and said,
  "Go and search diligently for the child.
When you have found him, bring me word,
  that I too may go and do him homage."
After their audience with the king they set
    out.

Continued in Appendix A, p. 268.

Reflecting on the Gospel

Few of us have the luxury of time and means to begin a trip with no destination in mind, spending however much time we wish meandering about at will. For almost all of us, whenever we begin a journey either for pleasure or for business, we find security in having our route clearly laid out. We have a specific destination in mind and we use AAA or some travel website to plot out exactly how we are going to get there. The gospel for this Sunday recounts a journey, too—that of the Magi who traveled from the East (they "saw his star at its rising") to Jerusalem and then to Bethlehem to find the "newborn king."

The Magi began their journey searching for this newborn king in a most unorthodox way: they followed not a road map, but a star. They allowed themselves to be led not by human plotting of routes but by divine guidance. Nor was the Magi's route always clear, either: when they arrived at Jerusalem, the star disappeared, leaving them in darkness and uncertainty. Ignorant of the political ramifications, they sought out the most logical source for clear direction, the reigning King Herod, and inquired of him where to find the newborn king. Herod pointed them to Bethlehem, but when they resumed their journey the star once again appeared to lead them on their way. Their journey ended when the star "stopped over the place where the child was," they entered, and offered homage and gifts.

Lessons from the Magi story remind us how faithfully they followed God's lead, how diligent they were to complete their journey, how prepared they were by bringing appropriate gifts, how humbled they were to stoop to this tiny Baby and offer homage. But we also learn from this story that God leads even in darkness, even when we have lost our way, and even through the machinations of those who intend evil. *We* are the Magi today: still searching for the "newborn king," still following the light along an uncertain journey, still being surprised by what God reveals along the way and how God reveals it.

What is manifested to all of us on this feast is the *mystery* of God's presence to us in the newborn king, but also the mystery of God's presence in the loving and caring way God leads us to life eternal. We have only to do as the Magi did: surrender ourselves to God's guidance and God's surprises.

Living the Paschal Mystery

When it comes to our life journey, even though we know our destination (eternal life!), we soon discover that there is no direct or clear-cut route. The journey of faith has many detours. If we wish to arrive at our eternal destination, we must surrender our plans and expectations to a God who often takes us to unexpected places and unexpected persons.

We can hardly expect a star to guide us to our eternal destination. But this doesn't mean that God is less present to us than to the Magi, guiding us where the divine will wishes us to go. God guides us today in many and sometimes surprising ways: through the commandments, through the proclamation of Scriptures, by the model of goodness and holiness of people around us, by our consciences, during prayer, even through the actions of our enemies—in any manner or place where we look beyond ourselves to the good of others.

Recognizing God's guidance is but one part of finding our way on our life journey. Another part is dying to self; that is, we must actually follow God's guidance, even when that takes us where *we* might not want to go.

Focusing the Gospel

Key words and phrases: saw his star at its rising, Herod . . . sent them to Bethlehem, Go and search diligently, saw the child

To the point: The Magi in this gospel began a journey searching for the "newborn king of the Jews" in a most surprising way: they follow not a road map, but a star. They were guided not by their own instincts, but allowed themselves to be guided by a God whose light was often manifested in unexpected places and persons. *We* are the Magi today: still searching for the "newborn king," still following the light, still being surprised by what and how God is revealed to us along the way.

Connecting the Gospel

to the first and second readings: The Good News (the glory of God) is manifested first to Israel (see first reading) and then to all people (see second reading). Indeed, the mystery of God's presence is a "shining radiance" that enables all nations to walk by God's light.

to our experience: Whenever we begin a journey (going on vacation or a business trip), we find security in having our route clearly mapped out. When it comes, however, to the journey of our personal or spiritual growth, there is no MapQuest available. Instead, we must surrender our plans and expectations to a God who often takes us to unexpected places and is revealed through unexpected persons.

Connecting the Responsorial Psalm

to the readings: Psalm 72, from which this responsorial psalm is taken, proclaimed that all kings would pay homage to the king of Israel and all nations would serve him. The reason for such adulation had nothing to do with the personality of the king but with the belief that he was God's representative. Acting under God's directive and with God's empowerment, the king was the one above all who was to see that justice be done for the poor and the oppressed. The king was to be the personal embodiment of what God desired for the Chosen People. Much of Psalm 72 was intercessory prayer for the king that he might be able to fulfill this divinely given role.

This was a tall order and none of Israel's kings lived up to it. We sing verses of Psalm 72 this Sunday to celebrate the birth of the King who will at last fulfill God's plan. Jesus, the newborn King of the Jews, shines with the light of God (first reading) and reveals in human flesh the fullness of the mystery of God's intention (second reading). Even more, Jesus sheds the light of God's love and redemption on all nations. The Magi (gospel) represent the first of the foreign nations coming in search of this King who will bring salvation to all. They went to great lengths to find him (gospel); may we who have been given the revelation of Jesus' identity and mission go to the same lengths to lead every nation to find and adore him.

to cantor preparation: Knowing the background of this responsorial psalm will help you understand why the Lectionary chose it for the feast of the Epiphany. In Psalm 72 the Israelites prayed that their king could be faithful to his mission to care for the poorest among the people. Today you pray this psalm knowing that Jesus, the Newborn King, will fulfill God's plan of salvation, not only for Israel, but for all peoples of the world. You sing this psalm, then, not as petition but as proclamation. What is it that you proclaim? Do you believe it?

**ASSEMBLY &
FAITH-SHARING GROUPS**
· The surprises that have come to me so far in my spiritual journey are . . .
· What keeps me searching for Christ is . . .
· The unexpected people who have revealed Christ to me or have guided me on my journey are . . .
· The unexpected places where I have found Christ are . . .

PRESIDERS
· I point others to where Christ can be found when I . . .

DEACONS
· My service to those in need is a light for others when . . .

HOSPITALITY MINISTERS
· The Light shines within me and is most welcoming when . . .

MUSIC MINISTERS
· What helps my music making open a way for the assembly to find Christ is . . .

ALTAR MINISTERS
· My service at the altar manifests Christ when . . .

LECTORS
· The way I proclaim reveals the presence of Christ in the word when . . .

**EXTRAORDINARY MINISTERS
OF HOLY COMMUNION**
· What helps me be aware of the light of Christ shining in the face of each communicant is . . .

Model Act of Penitence

Presider: The Magi followed the light of the star to find the newborn King of the Jews. We follow the light of the star when we truly hear God's word and come to God's banquet table. Let us prepare ourselves well . . . [pause]

> Lord Jesus, you are the Light of the world: Lord . . .
>
> Christ Jesus, you bring salvation to all: Christ . . .
>
> Lord Jesus, you receive our homage and the gift of our hearts: Lord . . .

Homily Points

• Upon hearing this gospel, we can easily get sidetracked by focusing on the star and the "three kings." Over the years, much has been written about what the star actually was (Halley's Comet? two planets crossing paths?) and who the Magi really were (three? kings?). What Matthew is concerned with, however, is something more significant—the *universality* of salvation.

• God offers salvation to all people (Magi were Gentiles). Moreover, God offers salvation through every possible avenue (the little town of Bethlehem, the machinations of an evil king). In order for us to find the newborn King (really, a description of our journey to salvation), we must not only be diligent in our search but also be open to surprising ways in which God reveals salvation to us.

• Perhaps the biggest surprise is when God comes to us in old places and familiar faces: members of our immediate family, next-door neighbors, even our enemies. Here is where we might encounter the newborn King today. To do so we must set aside prejudices and biases which keep our eyes from seeing God's self-revelation in unexpected persons and places.

Model Prayer of the Faithful

Presider: Confident of God's promise of salvation, let us pray for our needs.

Response: Lord, hear our prayer.

Cantor: we pray to the Lord,

That the Body of Christ be a light guiding all people to salvation . . . [pause]

That all peoples share in the joy and peace of God's presence in the world . . . [pause]

That those who are poor and in need receive the revelation of God's love and care through the generosity of this community . . . [pause]

That each of us continue to search diligently for Christ along whatever pathways God leads us . . . [pause]

Presider: O God, you guide all peoples to the abundance of your salvation: hear these our prayers so that your Son Jesus Christ might be manifested for all to see clearly and follow to everlasting life. We ask this through that same Son, Jesus Christ our Lord. **Amen.**

OPENING PRAYER

Let us pray
[that we will be guided by the light of faith]

Pause for silent prayer

Father,
you revealed your Son to the nations
by the guidance of a star.
Lead us to your glory in heaven
by the light of faith.

We ask this through our Lord Jesus Christ,
   your Son,
who lives and reigns with you and the
   Holy Spirit,
one God, for ever and ever. **Amen.**

FIRST READING
Isa 60:1-6

Rise up in splendor, Jerusalem! Your light
   has come,
   the glory of the Lord shines upon you.
See, darkness covers the earth,
   and thick clouds cover the peoples;
but upon you the LORD shines,
   and over you appears his glory.
Nations shall walk by your light,
   and kings by your shining radiance.
Raise your eyes and look about;
   they all gather and come to you:
your sons come from afar,
   and your daughters in the arms of their
      nurses.

Then you shall be radiant at what you see,
   your heart shall throb and overflow,
for the riches of the sea shall be emptied
      out before you,
   the wealth of nations shall be brought
      to you.
Caravans of camels shall fill you,
   dromedaries from Midian and Ephah;
all from Sheba shall come
   bearing gold and frankincense,
   and proclaiming the praises of the LORD.

RESPONSORIAL PSALM
Ps 72:1-2, 7-8, 10-11, 12-13

℟. (cf. 11) Lord, every nation on earth will adore you.

O God, with your judgment endow the
        king,
    and with your justice, the king's son;
he shall govern your people with justice
    and your afflicted ones with judgment.

℟. Lord, every nation on earth will adore you.

Justice shall flower in his days,
    and profound peace, till the moon be no
        more.
May he rule from sea to sea,
    and from the River to the ends of the
        earth.

℟. Lord, every nation on earth will adore you.

The kings of Tarshish and the Isles shall
        offer gifts;
    the kings of Arabia and Seba shall
        bring tribute.
All kings shall pay him homage,
    all nations shall serve him.

℟. Lord, every nation on earth will adore you.

For he shall rescue the poor when he cries
        out,
    and the afflicted when he has no one to
        help him.
He shall have pity for the lowly and the
        poor;
    the lives of the poor he shall save.

℟. Lord, every nation on earth will adore you.

SECOND READING
Eph 3:2-3a, 5-6

Brothers and sisters:
You have heard of the stewardship of
        God's grace
    that was given to me for your benefit,
    namely, that the mystery was made
        known to me by revelation.
It was not made known to people in other
        generations
    as it has now been revealed
    to his holy apostles and prophets by the
        Spirit:
    that the Gentiles are coheirs, members
        of the same body,
    and copartners in the promise in Christ
        Jesus through the gospel.

About Liturgy

Liturgy and universality: Both the Christmas and Epiphany celebrations at first glance focus on this newborn King—at Christmas we celebrate his birth and at Epiphany we celebrate his manifestation to the nations. Jesus' birth marks a whole new inbreaking of God's presence among humanity and manifests God's desire for salvation for all.

One of the hallmarks of the liturgical renewal is that liturgy is not something done *for us* by the presider, but requires our full, conscious, and active participation so that liturgy truly is our communal celebration of salvation. By giving ourselves over to the ritual celebration, we make a public sign that we are concerned not only for our own salvation, but for others' as well. Liturgy is never merely a "private act," but is always the celebration of the whole church for the salvation of the world.

Liturgy has a number of places where we appropriately pray individually and personally; for example, we prepare to surrender ourselves to God's transforming action during the silent time in the act of penitence; we pray for the grace we desire at Mass during the silent time in the opening prayer; we give thanks for the gift of Eucharist in the silent time after Holy Communion. At other times during the liturgy the prayer has a clear universal character about it; for example, the prayers of the faithful are never simply focused on the needs of the local community, but always remind us to reach out to the whole church, to pray for salvation for the whole world, to be attentive to the needs of those who are poor and suffering. When we respect this universality of liturgy, we form ourselves in the unity of the Body of Christ and in solidarity with all the people of the world.

About Liturgical Music

Music suggestions: "In Deepest Night," found in CBW3 and in JS1 and 2, sings of the "morning star . . . risen plain," the light "breaking through" in God become human among us. Set to the Genevan psalter tune RENDEZ A DIEU, the hymn could be sung by the assembly during the preparation of the gifts or during Communion. Or the choir could sing Bernard Huijbers' SATB arrangement [OCP #8715] as a choral prelude. Also suitable for either the preparation of the gifts or Communion would be Bernadette Gasslein's "In the Darkness Shines the Splendour." The text builds to its climax in the final verse where the Word made flesh, "Jesus, God's epiphany," reveals not only his own glory but ours as well. Unfortunately, this fine hymn appears only in CBW3; it deserves much wider circulation. Another good hymn for the preparation of the gifts would be Herman Stuempfle's "The Silent Stars Shine Down on Us," found in the collection *Redeeming the Time* [GIA G-4699]. The text contrasts the unmindfulness of heaven's "silent stars" with the self-sacrificing love of "Christ, the bright and morning star" who "broke the silences of space" to offer all humankind hope of salvation. Dan Schutte's "Christ, the Sun of Light," found in BB and intended for use all through the Christmas season, has a verse designated for Epiphany (as well as one for the Baptism of the Lord). Set to IN DULCI JUBILO, this hymn would be excellent during Communion. A fine closing hymn would be Delores Dufner's "Infant Wrapped in God's Own Light," found in SS and in her hymn text collection *The Glimmer of Glory in Song* [GIA G-6192].

SPIRITUALITY

GOSPEL ACCLAMATION
cf. Mark 9:7

R⁄. Alleluia, alleluia.
The heavens were opened and the voice of the
   Father thundered:
This is my beloved Son, listen to him.
R⁄. Alleluia, alleluia.

Gospel

Mark 1:7-11; L21B

This is what John the Baptist
    proclaimed:
  "One mightier than I is coming after
      me.
I am not worthy to stoop and loosen the
      thongs of his sandals.
I have baptized you with water;
    he will baptize you with the Holy
      Spirit."

It happened in those days that Jesus
      came from Nazareth of Galilee
    and was baptized in the Jordan by
      John.
On coming up out of the water he saw
    the heavens being torn open
    and the Spirit, like a dove,
      descending upon him.
And a voice came from the heavens,
  "You are my beloved Son; with you I
      am well pleased."

Reflecting on the Gospel

Several times in our lives we might be asked to produce a copy of our baptismal certificates; for example, at our First Communion and confirmation or at marriage or ordination or entrance into religious life. Having a certificate and producing it when needed might lead us to believe that baptism is something that happened in the past—it is over and finished with and this certificate bears witness to that fact. It is good to recall, though, that what happened in the past that is over and completed is the *ritual ceremony* of baptism. But that is surely not all there is to baptism. An essential tenet of Christianity is that baptism plunges us into an ongoing way of living whereby our lives are patterned after Christ's. This Sunday's gospel gives us a picture of who Jesus is and that following him means taking up his saving mission—the everyday, practical way we live our baptism all our lives.

After he was "baptized in the Jordan by John," Jesus took up his saving mission as the "beloved Son." That saving mission is no less than calling each of us to such an intimate identity with Jesus that we are transformed by the new life of God that dwells within us. We are baptized by both water and the Spirit, beginning a life of turning from our thoughts and ways to God's thoughts and ways (first reading), becoming God's children (second reading), and continuing Jesus' ministry. By the indwelling of the Spirit we become adopted sons and daughters of God, God's "beloved," too. By this indwelling—God's very life— Jesus' mission is our own mission. Jesus' way of living is our own way of living. Baptism is not so much what is done to us as what we are able to do because of our new relationship through the Spirit with God and each other.

Only by opening ourselves to the action of God within us through the Spirit are we able to take up Jesus' saving mission. Indeed, baptism is more than receiving a certificate attesting that we have gone through a ceremony and are "card-carrying" members of the Body of Christ. Our baptismal commitment entails taking up Christ's saving mission.

Living the Paschal Mystery

To be initiated into Christianity means to be initiated into living the paschal mystery. Each of the readings incorporates allusions to paschal mystery dying and rising. In the gospel, "the heavens being torn open" is the same language as is used at the crucifixion (cf. Mark 15:38: "The veil of the sanctuary was torn in two from top to bottom"). The first reading from Isaiah 55 is one used at the Easter Vigil and speaks poetically and eloquently of the abundance God gives now and in everlasting life. These two readings clearly show us the dying and promised new life of the paschal mystery. Moreover, the responsorial psalm speaks of God as savior, reminding us that from all time, no matter how often we have strayed, God wishes to reach out to us in loving relationship. The second reading reminds us that Jesus "came through water and blood," yet another image reminding us of the lengths to which God will go to make us a holy people.

At his baptism Jesus took up his saving mission as the beloved Son. At our own baptism we unite ourselves with Christ as his Body (becoming God's children) and commit ourselves to take up this same saving mission. At the heart of this mission is being faithful to the relationship with God that our baptism begins, and proclaiming to others God's continued mighty deeds undertaken for our salvation.

Focusing the Gospel

Key words and phrases: he will baptize you with the Holy Spirit, Jesus . . . was baptized, my beloved Son

To the point: After Jesus was "baptized in the Jordan by John," he took up his saving mission as the "beloved Son." We are baptized by both water and the Spirit, beginning a life of turning from our thoughts and ways to God's thoughts and ways (first reading), becoming God's children (second reading), and continuing Jesus' ministry. Baptism is not so much what is done to us as what we do because of our new relationship with God and each other.

Connecting the Gospel

to the end of Christmas season and beginning of Ordinary Time: Our celebration of Christmas does not end with the infant Jesus, but with the adult Jesus being baptized and beginning his saving mission. We who have been baptized with his Spirit take up his work of salvation during Ordinary Time, continuing his mission of bringing the Good News to others.

to our Catholic culture: We tend to think of baptism only as a ritual lasting a few moments. Actually, baptism is a daily immersion in the mission of Jesus and requires lifelong commitment.

Connecting the Responsorial Psalm

to the readings: The text used for the responsorial psalm this Sunday is not taken from the Hebrew psalter, but from the book of Isaiah. The verses are part of a song celebrating God's deliverance of Israel from disaster and destruction. The psalmist proclaims God savior and calls all Israel to spread the news of God's saving intervention to "all the earth."

What is the salvation God renders? It is the gift of covenant relationship with God (first and second readings) celebrated with the fullness of the messianic banquet (first reading). It is the gift of personal relationship with God and one another marked by love (second reading). This gift is free but not without its demand that we change our manner of living (first and second readings). We can accept the gift and take on its demand, as did Jesus (gospel), because we know we have an inexhaustible source from which to draw our strength (psalm).

to cantor preparation: In this Sunday's responsorial psalm you sing about God's gift of salvation. The readings reveal that salvation means our adoption as God's children, our feasting freely at the messianic meal, and our communion with one another. How have you experienced this salvation? How have you enabled others to share in it?

ASSEMBLY & FAITH-SHARING GROUPS
- I have grown in my understanding of baptism in that . . .
- What Jesus' being called the beloved Son means for me is . . .
- For me, the greatest challenge of my baptism is . . . The greatest blessing is . . .

PRESIDERS
- I lead my people to better understand the meaning of their baptism by . . . They lead me to better understand my baptism by . . .

DEACONS
- What helps me understand my service as an expression of my baptism is . . .

HOSPITALITY MINISTERS
- My greeting helps the assembly members experience themselves as God's beloved when . . .

MUSIC MINISTERS
- One way my music ministry participates in the mission of Christ is . . .

ALTAR MINISTERS
- My service at the altar helps me better understand my baptism because . . .

LECTORS
- My proclamation of God's word challenges the assembly to deeper baptismal living when . . .

EXTRAORDINARY MINISTERS OF HOLY COMMUNION
- My manner of distributing Communion reminds the community of their unity through their baptism when . . .

Model Rite of Blessing and Sprinkling Holy Water

Presider: Dear friends, today we celebrate Jesus' baptism when the heavens were opened, the Spirit descended, and Jesus was revealed as God's beloved Son. We also celebrate the grace of our own baptism and identity as God's daughters and sons. Let us renew our commitment to take up Jesus' saving mission by the way we live.

[continue with form A or B of the blessing of water]

Homily Points

• Many of us can remember the way baptisms used to be performed: in a small baptistry; with an ornate but small font; with few people present; in a short, private ritual in Latin. Today baptism is celebrated with as many family members and friends present as possible, with everyone renewing their baptismal vows, often in the context of a parish eucharistic celebration, always with a proclamation of Scripture, by immersion in an abundance of water. The extent of this change enables us to celebrate baptism as a central event in our lives.

• Renewal of the rite, however, is only an external indication of what is meant to be a far deeper renewal: our mission as followers of Christ. Our baptismal mission is successful to the extent that we identify with Christ and continue *his* saving mission. This would seem to be an overwhelming burden, except that we are never alone in the mission, but always minister as Body of Christ, together with others.

• This is our task during Ordinary Time: to constantly *listen* to the words and actions of Jesus and seek to grow in his Spirit. This is how we truly fulfill our baptismal commitment.

Model Prayer of the Faithful

Presider: Let us pray that we be faithful to our baptismal call to continue the saving mission of Christ.

Response: Lord, hear our prayer.

Cantor: we pray to the Lord,

That all members of the church live consciously and joyfully as God's beloved daughters and sons . . . [pause]

That all peoples of the world come to salvation . . . [pause]

That the sick and suffering be strengthened by the prayer and presence of the other members of the Body of Christ . . . [pause]

That each of us be ever faithful to our baptismal call to continue the saving mission of Jesus . . . [pause]

Presider: O loving God, you name us your beloved daughters and sons: hear our prayers and fill us with the Spirit of the Lord Jesus that we may be faithful to the mission you have given us. We ask this through that same Son, Jesus Christ. **Amen.**

OPENING PRAYER

Let us pray
    [that we will be faithful to our baptism]

Pause for silent prayer

Almighty, eternal God,
when the Spirit descended upon Jesus
at his baptism in the Jordan,
you revealed him as your own beloved
    Son.
Keep us, your children born of water and
    the Spirit,
faithful to our calling.

We ask this through our Lord Jesus Christ,
    your Son,
who lives and reigns with you and the
    Holy Spirit,
one God for ever and ever. **Amen.**

FIRST READING

Isa 55:1-11

Thus says the LORD:
All you who are thirsty,
    come to the water!
You who have no money,
    come, receive grain and eat;
come, without paying and without cost,
    drink wine and milk!
Why spend your money for what is not
    bread,
    your wages for what fails to satisfy?
Heed me, and you shall eat well,
    you shall delight in rich fare.
Come to me heedfully,
    listen, that you may have life.
I will renew with you the everlasting
    covenant,
    the benefits assured to David.
As I made him a witness to the peoples,
    a leader and commander of nations,
so shall you summon a nation you knew
    not,
    and nations that knew you not shall run
        to you,
because of the LORD, your God,
    the Holy One of Israel, who has
        glorified you.

Seek the LORD while he may be found,
    call him while he is near.
Let the scoundrel forsake his way,
    and the wicked man his thoughts;
let him turn to the LORD for mercy;
    to our God, who is generous in
        forgiving.
For my thoughts are not your thoughts,
    nor are your ways my ways, says the
        LORD.
As high as the heavens are above the earth
    so high are my ways above your ways
    and my thoughts above your thoughts.

For just as from the heavens
  the rain and snow come down
and do not return there
  till they have watered the earth,
  making it fertile and fruitful,
giving seed to the one who sows
  and bread to the one who eats,
so shall my word be
  that goes forth from my mouth;
my word shall not return to me void,
  but shall do my will,
  achieving the end for which I sent it.

RESPONSORIAL PSALM
Isa 12:2-3, 4bcd, 5-6

R̘. (3) You will draw water joyfully from
the springs of salvation.

God indeed is my savior;
  I am confident and unafraid.
My strength and my courage is the LORD,
  and he has been my savior.
With joy you will draw water
  at the fountain of salvation.

R̘. You will draw water joyfully from the
springs of salvation.

Give thanks to the LORD, acclaim his name;
  among the nations make known his
    deeds,
  proclaim how exalted is his name.

R̘. You will draw water joyfully from the
springs of salvation.

Sing praise to the LORD for his glorious
    achievement;
  let this be known throughout all the
    earth.
Shout with exultation, O city of Zion,
  for great in your midst
  is the Holy One of Israel!

R̘. You will draw water joyfully from the
springs of salvation.

SECOND READING
1 John 5:1-9

Beloved:
Everyone who believes that Jesus is the
    Christ is begotten by God,
  and everyone who loves the Father
  loves also the one begotten by him.
In this way we know that we love the
    children of God
  when we love God and obey his
    commandments.

Continued in Appendix A, p. 268.

See Appendix A, p. 268, for additional readings.

✠ CATECHESIS

About Liturgy

Planning liturgy well: Notice that a number of choices for readings are possible for this feast: (1) The three readings that are assigned for L21ABC: Isa 42:1-4, 6-7; Ps 29:1-2, 3-4, 3, 9-10; Acts 10:34-38; and Matt 3:13-17; (2) using the above set of readings but substituting the year B gospel (Mark 1:7-11); or (3) using all three readings proper for year B, as the writing team has chosen for *Living Liturgy™*.

It would be entirely appropriate to use the Rite of Blessing and Sprinkling Holy Water (either blessing A or B could be used). It would also be appropriate to schedule baptisms on this Sunday at the eucharistic liturgy so that the entire parish community becomes more aware of their mutual responsibility for helping members grow in their baptismal commitment.

Environment for Ordinary Time: This feast of the Baptism of the Lord concludes the Christmas season, so Monday begins the first part of the season of Ordinary Time. It is tempting for the environment committee to leave the Christmas poinsettias in the sacred space since they tend to last a long time. However, since this flower is so closely associated with the Christmas season, it would be better to remove them. On Monday the space must clearly reflect that it is Ordinary Time.

About Liturgical Music

Music suggestions: The sprinkling rite this Sunday does not celebrate Easter, nor does it have the penitential significance of cleansing from sin, but is focused instead on discipleship. An example of a suitable text to sing during this rite would be "Send Us Flowing Water, Lord," found in VO, WC, and WS. A choir arrangement is available in WLP's *Choral Companion.* The syncopated gospel style and overlapping choir entrances of this piece communicate a sense of energy fitting for a new start into Ordinary Time.

In light of the joyfulness of the readings and the fullness of salvation that they proclaim, this would be a good Sunday to sing a more embellished setting of the responsorial psalm. Robert Batastini's "You Will Draw Water" is a lovely setting of Isaiah 12 accompanied by handbells [GIA Cantor-Congregation Series, G-2443]. The bells ring a simple ostinato arpeggio throughout the refrain and cluster chords on the verses. The final refrain can be done in canon. Furthermore, using this same setting again after the fifth reading of the Easter Vigil would reinforce the connection between Jesus' mission, its Old Testament promise, and its completion at Easter.

For other music during this liturgy, texts that call us to the Ordinary Time challenge of recommitting ourselves to the identity and mission of Jesus would be very appropriate. Alan Hommerding's "Baptized in Living Waters" speaks of our initiation into Christ and his mission and could be used during the preparation of the gifts or as a hymn of praise after Communion. "Baptized in Water" would be an excellent recessional hymn sending us back into the living of Ordinary Time.

Ordinary Time 1

✚ SPIRITUALITY

R̸. Alleluia, alleluia.
We have found the Messiah:
Jesus Christ, who brings us truth and grace.
R̸. Alleluia, alleluia.

Gospel

John 1:35-42; L65B

John was standing with two
    of his disciples,
    and as he watched Jesus
        walk by, he said,
    "Behold, the Lamb of
        God."
The two disciples heard
    what he said and
    followed Jesus.
Jesus turned and saw them
    following him and said
    to them,
    "What are you looking for?"
They said to him, "Rabbi"—which
    translated means Teacher—,
    "where are you staying?"
He said to them, "Come, and you will
    see."
So they went and saw where Jesus was
    staying,
    and they stayed with him that day.
It was about four in the afternoon.
Andrew, the brother of Simon Peter,
    was one of the two who heard John
        and followed Jesus.
He first found his own brother Simon
    and told him,
    "We have found the Messiah"—which
        is translated Christ—.
Then he brought him to Jesus.
Jesus looked at him and said,
    "You are Simon the son of John;
    you will be called Cephas"—which is
        translated Peter.

Reflecting on the Gospel

Good parents become visibly anxious if they suspect their son or daughter is becoming involved with a cult. We hear occasionally in the news of the extreme measures to which some parents go to remove their youngster from a cult and put them through "deprogramming"—often forcing them to do so. We might wonder what is the attraction of such groups, when it appears to us "uninitiated" how unhealthy they are. One attraction common to all cults is a charismatic leader—one who can mesmerize, instill ideals (be they good ones or wrong ones), coalesce individual energies into a community, motivate members to a common mission. Allegiance is never a problem; question the leader and there are dire consequences. Ideally, we who profess to follow Jesus would not have an allegiance problem, either; but, in fact, we struggle all our lives with fidelity to our call to be disciples. Clearly the problem isn't with the One whom we follow—Jesus is a charismatic leader who inspires the loftiest of ideals and the most radical of communities— we share membership in his own Body (see second reading).

John the Baptist must have been a charismatic leader as well, for the gospel mentions his "standing . . . with his disciples." Yet how easily John was able to divert the two disciples with him from himself to Jesus! Why? No doubt because his announcement, "Behold, the Lamb of God" was so believable. No doubt, too, because John's own allegiance was also to Christ. John knew that his mission was to announce the coming of the Messiah. He never wavered from his mission—he was about leading others to Christ.

Both the first reading and gospel illustrate the role of a mediator in discerning God's call: Eli mediates God's call to Samuel and in the gospel, John mediates God's call to Andrew, who then mediates the call to Simon Peter. While the role of the mediator is important, a faithful response to God's call is vastly more important—it is absolutely essential for anyone who claims to be a disciple of Jesus. Hearing and responding to God's call focuses clearly whom we follow: Samuel, the servant of Eli, becomes the servant of the Lord (see the first reading); the followers of John become disciples of Jesus. For us, too, hearing and responding to God's call sharpens our allegiance: we choose to follow Christ and to take up his mission.

Living the Paschal Mystery

We cannot truly be disciples of Christ unless we, too, hear God's call and respond by transforming our lives, evidenced in the simple willingness to be obedient to God's will and take up the saving mission of Christ. This means more than keeping commandments or even of simply going to Mass on Sunday; it means that our whole lives are directed to being faithful in our allegiance to Christ and identifying with him so completely that his life is ours, his mission is ours.

We waver in our allegiance because identity with Christ and continuing his mission make demands on us. Like Andrew in the gospel, we must boldly announce the presence of Christ in our midst and bring others to Jesus. We do this best by living as he did: caring for others, bringing a healing touch, working at developing a deeper relationship with Christ through liturgy and prayer. The demand is surely there: become so intimate with Jesus that we do not waver in our allegiance to and love for him.

Focusing the Gospel

Key words and phrases: heard, followed, stayed with him

To the point: Hearing and responding to God's call focuses clearly whom we follow: Samuel, the servant of Eli, becomes the servant of the Lord (see the first reading); the followers of John become disciples of Jesus. For us, too, hearing and responding to God's call sharpens our allegiance: we choose to follow Christ and to take up his mission.

Connecting the Gospel

to the first reading: Both the first reading and gospel are call-response narratives that invite us to reflect on our own ability to hear the voice of God and discern a faithful response.

to human experience: While our response to God must always be total, it is not always immediate. John's disciples responded at once, but Samuel was called four times. God continues to call until we respond—and respond totally.

Connecting the Responsorial Psalm

to the readings: Psalm 40 is a psalm of thanksgiving for having been rescued by God from life-threatening danger. The psalmist waited for God's help, and was not disappointed. Now she or he sings God's praises. She or he also realizes that the form of thanksgiving more desirable than the offering of a sacrifice in the Temple is obedience to God's will. The one offering is momentary, but the other is lifelong.

In the context of this Sunday's readings, these verses from Psalm 40 express our willingness to respond to God's will for the duration of our lives. With the psalmist, with Samuel (first reading), with the disciples (gospel), with Jesus himself we commit ourselves to doing God's will. Our lives, as were Samuel's and the disciples', will be changed. And this is what the journey of Ordinary Time is about.

to cantor preparation: As you prepare to sing this Sunday's responsorial psalm spend some time reflecting on why this psalm and these readings were selected for the Second Sunday in Ordinary Time. What is the liturgy calling you to? What are you as cantor calling the assembly to?

ASSEMBLY & FAITH-SHARING GROUPS

· I have heard God's call when . . . What God has called me to is . . .
· I have been helped to discern God's call by . . .
· Responding to God's call has changed my life in that . . .

PRESIDERS

· I hear God's call through the people I serve when . . . I must hear God's call through the people I serve because . . .

DEACONS

· My service to those in need is a practical response to God's call if I . . .

HOSPITALITY MINISTERS

· My hospitality encourages assembly members to respond to God when . . .

MUSIC MINISTERS

· What/who helps me experience my music ministry as a call from God is . . .

ALTAR MINISTERS

· Acts of unobtrusive service help me be faithful to God in my daily life because . . .

LECTORS

· As a lector, I mediate the call of God to the assembly when I . . .

EXTRAORDINARY MINISTERS OF HOLY COMMUNION

· My distribution of Communion deepens my allegiance to Christ because . . .

Model Act of Penitence

Presider: Just as Jesus called Andrew and Peter and the other disciples, he calls each of us to be his followers. Let us open ourselves to hear God's call in the Word today and be transformed by sharing in the table of the Lord . . . [pause]

Lord Jesus, you are the Lamb of God whom we follow: Lord . . .

Christ Jesus, you are the Messiah who is the revelation of God: Christ . . .

Lord Jesus, you are the Teacher who calls us to discipleship: Lord . . .

Homily Points

• When we begin a new challenge, we often have a great deal of energy and enthusiasm. As time goes on and the challenge becomes tedious and ordinary or, worse yet, when difficulties show up, our energy drops and enthusiasm is gone. When this happens to us—and it does, often!—what do we do? We become annoyed, get angry, certainly ask ourselves, "Is it worth it?" And sometimes we just quit.

• How true this is of our response to the call to be disciples of Jesus! When we are tempted to quit following him because of frustrations, this is the time we need to fall back on our relationship with Christ who alone can sustain us. Without a firm relationship with him, we cannot remain faithful.

• We deepen our relationship with Christ in many ways: participation in Sunday Mass, daily prayer, interaction with other followers of Christ, works of charity, etc. Our energy for discipleship is sustained by encounters with Christ in these practical ways.

Model Prayer of the Faithful

Presider: Let us pray that we be open to God's call and respond with fidelity.

Response: Lord,—— hear our prayer.

Cantor: we pray to the Lord,

That all members of the church be strengthened to respond faithfully to God's call . . . [pause]

That all peoples of the world encounter God and come to salvation . . . [pause]

That the poor, sick, and those in any need be helped by the generosity and care of Jesus' disciples . . . [pause]

That each of us here deepen our relationship with Christ through daily faithful living . . . [pause]

Presider: O God, you call us to faithful discipleship: hear these our prayers and lead us to life everlasting with you. We ask this through Christ our Lord. **Amen.**

Let us pray

Pause for silent prayer

Almighty and ever-present Father,
your watchful care reaches from end to
   end
and orders all things in such power
that even the tensions and the tragedies
   of sin
cannot frustrate your loving plans.
Help us to embrace your will,
give us the strength to follow your call,
so that your truth may live in our hearts
and reflect peace to those who believe in
   your love.

We ask this in the name of Jesus the Lord.
   Amen.

FIRST READING

1 Sam 3:3b-10, 19

Samuel was sleeping in the temple of the
   LORD
   where the ark of God was.
The LORD called to Samuel, who answered,
   "Here I am."
Samuel ran to Eli and said, "Here I am.
   You called me."
"I did not call you," Eli said. "Go back to
   sleep."
So he went back to sleep.
Again the LORD called Samuel, who rose
   and went to Eli.
"Here I am," he said. "You called me."
But Eli answered, "I did not call you, my
   son. Go back to sleep."

At that time Samuel was not familiar with
   the LORD,
   because the LORD had not revealed
      anything to him as yet.
The LORD called Samuel again, for the
   third time.
Getting up and going to Eli, he said, "Here
   I am. You called me."
Then Eli understood that the LORD was
   calling the youth.
So he said to Samuel, "Go to sleep, and if
   you are called, reply,
   Speak, LORD, for your servant is
      listening."
When Samuel went to sleep in his place,
   the LORD came and revealed his
      presence,
   calling out as before, "Samuel, Samuel!"
Samuel answered, "Speak, for your
   servant is listening."

Samuel grew up, and the LORD was with
   him,
   not permitting any word of his to be
      without effect.

RESPONSORIAL PSALM
Ps 40:2, 4, 7-8, 8-9, 10

R︎. (8a and 9a) Here am I, Lord; I come to do your will.

I have waited, waited for the LORD,
    and he stooped toward me and heard
        my cry.
And he put a new song into my mouth,
    a hymn to our God.

R︎. Here am I, Lord; I come to do your will.

Sacrifice or offering you wished not,
    but ears open to obedience you gave me.
Holocausts or sin-offerings you sought not;
    then said I, "Behold I come."

R︎. Here am I, Lord; I come to do your will.

"In the written scroll it is prescribed for
        me,
to do your will, O my God, is my delight,
    and your law is within my heart!"

R︎. Here am I, Lord; I come to do your will.

I announced your justice in the vast
        assembly;
    I did not restrain my lips, as you, O
        LORD, know.

R︎. Here am I, Lord; I come to do your will.

SECOND READING
1 Cor 6:13c-15a, 17-20

Brothers and sisters:
The body is not for immorality, but for the
        Lord,
    and the Lord is for the body;
    God raised the Lord and will also raise
        us by his power.

Do you not know that your bodies are
        members of Christ?
But whoever is joined to the Lord becomes
        one Spirit with him.
Avoid immorality.
Every other sin a person commits is
        outside the body,
    but the immoral person sins against his
        own body.
Do you not know that your body
    is a temple of the Holy Spirit within
        you,
    whom you have from God, and that you
        are not your own?
For you have been purchased at a price.
Therefore glorify God in your body.

About Liturgy
Ordinary Time: During Ordinary Time this year we proclaim the Good News according to Mark (year B), and follow the gospel narrative from the call of the disciples to confrontation with the cross. Each Sunday liturgy brings us to Mark's gospel and how salvation unfolds there. What we can unfailingly expect during Ordinary Time—if we are faithful to our paschal mystery/gospel journey—is that God will transform us in some particular way during this particular year.

During all three years of the Lectionary cycle, however, the second Sunday in Ordinary Time uses a gospel chosen from John rather than from the Synoptic Gospel assigned for the year. The reason for this is that the second Sunday "continues to center on the manifestation of the Lord, which is celebrated on the Solemnity of the Epiphany, through the traditional passage about the wedding feast at Cana [the gospel for year C] and two other passages from the Gospel of John" (ILM no. 105).

The first period of Ordinary Time (from after the Christmas season until the beginning of Lent) focuses on the early events in Jesus' public ministry, especially the call of the disciples and the beginning of Jesus' public ministry. These weeks at the beginning of the new civil year might be a good time for each of us to assess how well we hear God's relentless call to be faithful followers of Jesus. Each of us can probably recall times when we have turned deaf ears to God; if we remember that God's call is relentless (see the first reading), then we might be encouraged to listen more carefully and sooner. God won't let go!

About Liturgical Music
Music and Ordinary Time: The purpose of liturgical music is not to entertain us, but to help us surrender to the transforming action of the liturgy. During Ordinary Time the liturgy pulls us into the paschal mystery journey of ongoing Christian living. The liturgical music we sing during this period is meant to help us deepen our understanding of and participation in that journey. For this we need music that is ritually consistent rather than constantly changing. Throughout these weeks between the end of the Christmas season and the beginning of Lent, then, we need to sing the same service music—from the gospel acclamation to the Lamb of God. Selecting service music in keeping with the non-festal character of Ordinary Time and singing it consistently during these weeks will help us enter more deeply into the meaning of Ordinary Time.

One much-loved song this Sunday's readings brings immediately to mind is Dan Schutte's "Here I Am, Lord." The song is intended to be sung in responsorial fashion, with choir or cantor singing the verses (God calling us) and the assembly the refrain (our answer). Its meditative style makes it better suited for the preparation of the gifts or Communion than for the entrance or recessional.

SPIRITUALITY

GOSPEL ACCLAMATION
Mark 1:15

R̸. Alleluia, alleluia.
The kingdom of God is at hand.
Repent and believe in the Gospel.
R̸. Alleluia, alleluia.

Gospel

Mark 1:14-20; L68B

After John had been arrested,
   Jesus came to Galilee proclaiming the
      gospel of God:
   "This is the time of fulfillment.
The kingdom of God is at hand.
Repent, and believe in the gospel."

As he passed by the Sea of Galilee,
   he saw Simon and his brother
      Andrew casting their nets into
      the sea;
   they were fishermen.
Jesus said to them,
   "Come after me, and I will make you
      fishers of men."
Then they abandoned their nets and
     followed him.
He walked along a little farther
   and saw James, the son of Zebedee,
      and his brother John.
They too were in a boat mending their
     nets.
Then he called them.
So they left their father Zebedee in the
     boat
   along with the hired men and
      followed him.

Reflecting on the Gospel

Cats are creatures of habit. A mother cat gives birth where she herself was born (if that is at all possible). A cat returns to the same spot for food. Cats hunt in the same patterns. We might say that cats are not only creatures of habit, but they actually hate change. So it is with us humans. We have a number of sayings that illustrate how reluctant we are to change, for example, "Ain't broke, don't fix it"; "The devil we know is better than the devil we don't know." Change is difficult. It's easier to continue with things as they are than face something new. In terms of the Christian life, however, the ability to change is a hallmark of following Jesus. In this Sunday's gospel Jesus invited two pairs of brothers—Simon and Andrew, James and John—to change. To a huge change! They left their nets—their livelihood, their familiar life—to follow Jesus. Now rather than be fishermen, they would be followers of Jesus who fish for a far greater catch: calling others to follow Jesus as well.

Jesus' first words recorded in the Gospel of Mark call us to repentance and belief. We usually think repentance means turning from sinfulness toward God. And, indeed, this is the point of the first reading which tells how the Ninevites "turned from their evil way." The gospel, however, suggests another meaning: repentance means to change. The disciples "repented" when they left all and followed Jesus. Repentance—the willingness to change our thoughts and ways to those of God—is the foundation for daily Christian discipleship. We must cast aside whatever gets in the way of responding to Jesus' call to follow him and share in his mission to bring the "kingdom of God . . . at hand." Moreover, the repentance called for in both the first reading and gospel is not possible without belief. The people of Nineveh heard Jonah's threat and believed in God; the disciples heard Jesus' call and believed in him.

Following Jesus requires change, whether that be the radical one of leaving all to follow Jesus, or the more modest one of turning from the little everyday behaviors that cause us to focus on ourselves and our own needs rather than on Jesus and the needs of others. This means, of course, that this kind of change required for discipleship always has a cost. John preached repentance, and was arrested. Jesus preached the Gospel and suffered and died. Hearing Jesus' call to discipleship and choosing to follow him faithfully does not assure us that we will not meet adversity and suffering, as did both John and Jesus. The surprise of the gospel is not that we will face adversity. The surprise is that in preaching repentance and accepting the change in and to our lives repentance entails, the "kingdom of God is at hand." The change assures us of God's presence. Adversity from accepting the Gospel does not thwart God's presence; it hastens it.

Living the Paschal Mystery

The gospel portrays change in demanding ways: turn from evil, leave all to follow Jesus. For most of us, this is not the change that the gospel mandate of repentance requires of us—we've already done this. Rather, we must change in the little ways that are part of our every days: turn to listen to someone rather than let our minds wander; root out whatever annoys those with whom we live; think only positive thoughts, especially about others. It's these little changes that probably actually cost us the most!

Focusing the Gospel

Key words and phrases: repent, fishermen . . . fishers of men, followed him

To the point: We usually think repentance means turning from sinfulness toward God. And, indeed, this is the point of the first reading. The gospel, however, suggests another meaning: repentance means to change. The disciples "repented" when they left all and followed Jesus. Repentance—the willingness to change our thoughts and ways to those of God—is the foundation for daily Christian discipleship.

Connecting the Gospel

to the first reading: The repentance called for in both the first reading and gospel is not possible without belief. The people of Nineveh heard Jonah's threat and believed in God; the disciples heard Jesus' call and believed in him.

to culture: Change is difficult. It's easier to continue with things as they are than face something new. In terms of the Christian life, however, the ability to change is a hallmark of following Jesus.

Connecting the Responsorial Psalm

to the readings: In the refrain and verses of Psalm 25 used for this Sunday's responsorial psalm we pray that we be as responsive as the people of Nineveh (first reading) and the fishermen of Galilee (gospel) to God's call to change our lives. God initiates the call—in fact, the first reading reveals that God has continually done so throughout all of history. The call is to repentance, the promise is compassion and forgiveness (first reading and psalm), and the consequence is personal transformation (first reading and gospel). God will show us the way. Our singing of Psalm 25 is an expression of our desire to be led and our willingness to be converted.

to cantor preparation: Perhaps the greatest challenge of cantoring is the vulnerability it requires. As you sing Psalm 25 this Sunday, for example, you must become an icon for the assembly of response to God's call to conversion and discipleship. Some questions to help you prepare for this role might be, Where in your life right now is God calling you to conversion? Through whom is God calling you? What does God wish to teach you?

**ASSEMBLY &
FAITH-SHARING GROUPS**

· I hear God calling me to change . . . I find myself resisting this call because . . .

· I find it easy to repent when . . . I find it difficult to repent when . . .

· My belief in Jesus strengthens my discipleship by . . .

PRESIDERS

· I model for my people the courage to change when I . . .

DEACONS

· In order to serve more faithfully, I must change . . .

HOSPITALITY MINISTERS

· My hospitality calls a person who seems to be angry or upset to change when . . .

MUSIC MINISTERS

· Because of my participation in music ministry, I have changed . . .

ALTAR MINISTERS

· My manner of serving communicates my belief in Jesus by . . .

LECTORS

· The word of God which most clearly challenges me to repentance is . . .

**EXTRAORDINARY MINISTERS
OF HOLY COMMUNION**

· Distributing Communion has changed my attitude toward the Body of Christ from . . . to . . .

Model Act of Penitence

Presider: In today's gospel we hear Jesus call us to change our way of life and follow him. As we prepare to celebrate this liturgy well, let us be open to the change God asks of us . . . [pause]

Lord Jesus, you announce that the kingdom of God is at hand: Lord . . .

Christ Jesus, you call us to repentance and belief: Christ . . .

Lord Jesus, you send us to proclaim your Gospel to all people: Lord . . .

Homily Points

• We humans often avoid change because of how upsetting it is. We settle into the known because we are not sure how the unknown will work. We often put up with something we know isn't quite right because we fear a change could make the situation even worse. If this is our everyday experience, what must it have cost the disciples to leave their livelihood and homes to follow Jesus!

• Changing what one is doing often demands leaving the known and the familiar—the people of Nineveh put aside their comfortable but evil ways and the disciples walked away from their nets. Following Jesus is not a normal human instinct; it demands great trust, which is only possible when we truly believe in Jesus.

• We grow in our trust and belief in Jesus through our previous experience of his fidelity to us, through the witness of fellow believers, and through our own faithfulness to prayer.

Model Prayer of the Faithful

Presider: God calls us and is faithful to those who respond. And so we are encouraged to make our needs known.

Response: Lord, hear our prayer.

Cantor: we pray to the Lord,

For all members of the church to proclaim by the way they live Jesus' call to repentance and belief in the gospel . . . [pause]

For all peoples of the world to hear the Good News of salvation . . . [pause]

For the poor and the sick to be touched by the love of God through the discipleship of others . . . [pause]

For us gathered here to have the courage to change in whatever ways God calls us . . . [pause]

Presider: Gracious God, you call us to repentance and belief in the gospel: hear these our prayers that we might one day receive the fullness of life with you. We ask this through Christ our Lord. **Amen.**

Let us pray

[pleading that our vision may overcome our weakness]

Pause for silent prayer

Almighty Father,
the love you offer
always exceeds the furthest expression of our human longing,
for you are greater than the human heart.
Direct each thought, each effort of our life,
so that the limits of our faults and weaknesses
may not obscure the vision of your glory
or keep us from the peace you have promised.

We ask this through Christ our Lord.
   Amen.

FIRST READING
Jonah 3:1-5, 10

The word of the LORD came to Jonah, saying:
   "Set out for the great city of Nineveh, and announce to it the message that I will tell you."
So Jonah made ready and went to Nineveh, according to the LORD's bidding.
Now Nineveh was an enormously large city;
   it took three days to go through it.
Jonah began his journey through the city, and had gone but a single day's walk announcing,
   "Forty days more and Nineveh shall be destroyed,"
   when the people of Nineveh believed God;
   they proclaimed a fast
and all of them, great and small, put on sackcloth.

When God saw by their actions how they turned from their evil way,
   he repented of the evil that he had threatened to do to them;
   he did not carry it out.

RESPONSORIAL PSALM

Ps 25:4-5, 6-7, 8-9

℟. (4a) Teach me your ways, O Lord.

Your ways, O LORD, make known to me;
    teach me your paths,
guide me in your truth and teach me,
    for you are God my savior.

℟. Teach me your ways, O Lord.

Remember that your compassion, O LORD,
    and your love are from of old.
In your kindness remember me,
    because of your goodness, O LORD.

℟. Teach me your ways, O Lord.

Good and upright is the LORD;
    thus he shows sinners the way.
He guides the humble to justice
    and teaches the humble his way.

℟. Teach me your ways, O Lord.

SECOND READING

1 Cor 7:29-31

I tell you, brothers and sisters, the time is
    running out.
From now on, let those having wives act as
    not having them,
    those weeping as not weeping,
    those rejoicing as not rejoicing,
    those buying as not owning,
    those using the world as not using it
        fully.
For the world in its present form is
    passing away.

About Liturgy

Proclamation and believability: This Sunday's readings point out the importance of the Sunday proclamation. Through proclamation the Gospel is preached and disciples are called. For lectors, this means that their proclamation of the Scriptures must be believable. The best way for this to happen is for lectors to make a concerted effort to live the Scripture passage the week before they proclaim it in as many practical ways in their daily life as they can. In this way the believability of the proclamation comes from the conviction of their very lived experience of the Scriptures. For members of the assembly, this means that the Scriptures heard on Sunday aren't simply nice readings that one listens to and then quickly forgets, but one really, really hears the readings so that they make a difference in one's life—we hear these readings in order to be changed. The readings ought not be forgotten as soon as we're out the church doors, but they ought to be carried over into the way we live.

Fluidity in the liturgical year: At first glance the first reading and gospel might seem more appropriate for Lent than for a Sunday in Ordinary Time because they speak so strongly of repentance and fasting and penance. This challenges us to think about the liturgical year not in terms of discrete seasons with limited motifs, but as a fluidity in which the dying and rising of the paschal mystery keep showing up in different contexts. In this Sunday's readings the call to repentance comes within the context of the proclamation of the Gospel. During Lent we see a different context for repentance—preparation for or renewing our baptismal commitment and preparing to enter into the solemn Easter mysteries.

About Liturgical Music

Role of the responsorial psalm: This Sunday's responsorial psalm is an example of how the purpose of the psalm changes because of its context within the liturgical year. Psalm 25 is also sung on the First Sunday of Advent C, the First Sunday of Lent B, and the Twenty-sixth Sunday in Ordinary Time A. It is also offered as the common psalm that can be sung on all the Sundays of Advent. The refrain for each of these celebrations varies, however, to fit the particular season. There are also slight adjustments in the verses. These variations make sense when we understand that the text has been chosen not haphazardly, but specifically to fit the readings of the day. While we might be tempted to use the same refrain and verses for all of these liturgical celebrations, using the text given for the day is important because it helps us enter into this day, this season, these readings.

The refrain given for this Sunday— "Teach me your ways, O Lord"—invites us to consider the relationship between God's call and the necessity for conversion of life. In both the first reading and the gospel we see this relationship in action. Juxtaposed with the readings of the day, the psalm refrain and verses tell us what Ordinary Time is all about: listening to and learning the ways of God and opening ourselves to be forgiven and formed by the One who guides our ways.

SPIRITUALITY

GOSPEL ACCLAMATION
Matt 4:16

R⁊. Alleluia, alleluia.
The people who sit in darkness have seen a great
    light;
on those dwelling in a land overshadowed by
    death,
light has arisen.
R⁊. Alleluia, alleluia.

Gospel

Mark 1:21-28; L71B

Then they came to
    Capernaum,
    and on the sabbath Jesus
        entered the synagogue
        and taught.
The people were astonished at
    his teaching,
    for he taught them as one
        having authority and not
        as the scribes.
In their synagogue was a man with an
    unclean spirit;
    he cried out, "What have you to do
        with us, Jesus of Nazareth?
Have you come to destroy us?
I know who you are—the Holy One of
    God!"
Jesus rebuked him and said,
    "Quiet! Come out of him!"
The unclean spirit convulsed him and
    with a loud cry came out of him.
All were amazed and asked one
    another,
    "What is this?
A new teaching with authority.
He commands even the unclean spirits
    and they obey him."
His fame spread everywhere
    throughout the whole region of
    Galilee.

Reflecting on the Gospel

Three-year-old Caitlin was used to going to Sunday Mass, and her parents took time to teach her and coax her into acceptable behavior. Most Sundays she was pretty good. One Sunday, however, the music was particularly lively and it really caught her fancy. She was all ears and eyes as she riveted on the choir, joining them in all things including rhythmic moving: her little arms and hands were tapping out the beat and her little back end was going to and fro just as fast as she could make it go. Her rambunctiousness lasted pretty much the whole liturgy. At the end of Mass, she looked up at her mother and asked, "Mommy, help me behave in church." Who knows whatever prompted this little child to conclude that she had misbehaved, but her question also indicated something important about the relationship of child and parent: the child looked to her parent as one in authority—one who could teach her. In the gospel for this Sunday the people were "astonished" and "amazed" at Jesus' teaching. They exclaimed that "he taught them as one having authority." In both the case of Caitlin and of the people in the gospel, "authority" is not perceived as a negative power over, but as investing one with the wisdom and graciousness to have the people's good at heart.

Jesus' authority rests in his identity as the "Holy One of God"—indeed, his identity as the divine Son. The "new teaching with authority" about which the people are amazed is not the healing miracle in itself, but rather the display of God's face-to-face presence mediated in Jesus. The Old Testament prophets were looked to by the people to mediate God's presence and will; they were terrified to encounter God face-to-face. In Jesus, however, *God is present* and encounter with this God is not terrifying but astonishing and amazing. We, too, are privileged to encounter Jesus, and come to hear and know the Holy One's healing and compassion. God is not terrifying, but gentle and loving.

In the first reading, the people ask for a prophet to speak to them of the ways of God because to face God directly is so terrifying. In the gospel the people come in contact with Jesus, in whose person they actually do come face-to-face with God—now no longer so terrifying but, rather, astonishing and amazing. The Good News of the gospel is that God's promise is fulfilled in Jesus who comes as our own "kin" (first reading), speaking and acting with true authority and power. Jesus' authority and power was always exercised with the good of the people at heart. No wonder his "fame spread everywhere" and people sought to be near him!

Living the Paschal Mystery

Bringing forth goodness and life—the fruit of authority well exercised—is very much at the heart of the paschal mystery. Jesus' authority rested in both his word and in his power and willingness to confront evil. Paschal mystery living requires us to be so bold as Jesus in confronting whatever "demons" in us keep us from surrendering ourselves over to the growth and life to which God calls us. The call to die to self is more than idle talk—it is the ongoing demand in daily living to listen to God's word, know all that the Lord commands us, and embrace the life God offers. In the surrendering of ourselves over to God's will, in the dying to self, is the identity with the "Holy One of God" which assures us of new life. Truly, this is astonishing and amazing Good News.

Focusing the Gospel

Key words and phrases: Jesus entered, astonished, authority, amazed

To the point: In the first reading, the people ask for a prophet to speak to them of the ways of God because to face God directly is so terrifying. In the gospel the people come in contact with Jesus, in whose person they actually do come face-to-face with God—now no longer so terrifying but, rather, astonishing and amazing. The Good News of the gospel is that God's promise is fulfilled in Jesus who comes as our own "kin" (first reading), speaking and acting with true authority and power.

Connecting the Gospel

to the first reading: The stern warning and dire consequences about false prophets in the first reading are hinted at in the gospel reference to the scribes. The people already know that the scribes often speak out of self-interest, rather than fidelity to the word of God. The people experience Jesus, on the other hand, as speaking with true authority.

to our experience: We are so "expert bound," we hardly trust our own instincts about truth and authority. Moreover, we would not look for authority in a person like Jesus—one of our own "kin." Yet, that is exactly where the greatest truth and authority lie.

Connecting the Responsorial Psalm

to the readings: In the first reading Moses and the prophets speak the words of God and do so in the recognizable voice of a fellow human being, a "kinsman." In the gospel reading, Jesus also speaks the word of God in a human voice but does so with an authority far beyond anything the people have heard before. Jesus' words are a direct and victorious confrontation with the forces of evil which can possess the human heart.

The psalm, however, confronts us with a truth about ourselves we may prefer to avoid. We can refuse to surrender to the authority of Jesus' words. We can hear and harden our hearts (see refrain). The psalmist pleads with us to listen and obey, knowing full well how real is the possibility that we, like many who have gone before us, may choose otherwise. May we listen; even more, may we hear and heed!

to cantor preparation: In order for your leading of this psalm to be genuine, it needs to come from a heart that knows it sometimes struggles to hear and heed the voice of God. Spend some time this week examining when and why you struggle to heed God's voice, then use the psalm refrain as a prayer that you may overcome your resistance and open your heart to obey.

**ASSEMBLY &
FAITH-SHARING GROUPS**

· I have come face-to-face with God when . . . This astonished me because . . .

· Jesus is speaking to me with authority about . . .

· I speak with true authority and power when . . .

PRESIDERS

· What enables my presiding to speak to the people with true authority and power is . . .

DEACONS

· My service to those in need embodies true authority and power when . . .

HOSPITALITY MINISTERS

· My greeting enables assembly members to encounter God face-to-face when I . . .

MUSIC MINISTERS

· What helps me do my music ministry with fidelity to God rather than self-interest is . . .

ALTAR MINISTERS

· What enables me to encounter God face-to-face in my service ministry is . . .

LECTORS

· I proclaim the word with authority when . . .

**EXTRAORDINARY MINISTERS
OF HOLY COMMUNION**

· My distributing the Body (Blood) of Christ enables the communicants to experience a God who . . .

Model Act of Penitence

Presider: In today's gospel, Jesus speaks with authority to the people. Let us open our hearts to his word proclaimed to us in this liturgy . . . [pause]

Lord Jesus, you are the Holy One of God: Lord . . .

Christ Jesus, you are God's authority made visible among us: Christ . . .

Lord Jesus, you are the way, the truth, and the life: Lord . . .

Homily Points

• Discerning truth from fiction is difficult in a world in which we are flooded daily with so much "spin" from TV and radio commentators, print media, web blogs, etc. Often these "authorities" are concerned about selling a viewpoint, gaining ratings, or assassinating someone's character rather than with truth and the good of the people.

• The root of the word "authority" is from the Latin, *augre*, which means to increase or grow, to augment. To speak with authority, then, means to have the good of the people at heart; to lead people to grow in wisdom, understanding, and care for one another; and to speak with integrity rooted in Gospel values. In Jesus, we come face-to-face with such authority.

• We encounter the authority of Jesus not only in people with "authority," but perhaps more frequently in our own "kin"—in those most familiar to us at home and work. The gospel reminds us that in listening and responding to those nearest to us, we discern the presence of Jesus and his true authority.

Model Prayer of the Faithful

Presider: The God who authors life gives us all that we need. And so we pray.

Response: Lord,—— hear our prayer.

Cantor: we pray to the Lord,

For leaders in the church, may they always speak and act with the truth and wisdom of Jesus . . . [pause]

For leaders of nations, may their authority bring life and goodness to their people . . . [pause]

For those who are sick and suffering, may they receive healing through those who bring them the presence of Jesus . . . [pause]

For all of us here, may we continue to be formed by the teachings of Jesus . . . [pause]

Presider: Good and gracious God, you call us to life and holiness: hear our prayers that we may follow your Son Jesus more closely. We ask this through Christ our Lord. **Amen.**

Let us pray

Pause for silent prayer

Father in heaven,
from the days of Abraham and Moses
until this gathering of your Church in
    prayer,
you have formed a people in the image of
    your Son.
Bless this people with the gift of your
    kingdom.
May we serve you with our every desire
and show love for one another
even as you have loved us.

Grant this through Christ our Lord.
    Amen.

FIRST READING
Deut 18:15-20

Moses spoke to all the people, saying:
    "A prophet like me will the LORD, your
        God, raise up for you
        from among your own kin;
        to him you shall listen.
This is exactly what you requested of the
    LORD, your God, at Horeb
    on the day of the assembly, when you
        said,
    'Let us not again hear the voice of the
        LORD, our God,
    nor see this great fire any more, lest we
        die.'
And the LORD said to me, 'This was well
    said.
I will raise up for them a prophet like you
    from among their kin,
    and will put my words into his mouth;
    he shall tell them all that I command
        him.
Whoever will not listen to my words
    which he speaks in my name,
    I myself will make him answer for it.
But if a prophet presumes to speak in my
    name
    an oracle that I have not commanded
        him to speak,
    or speaks in the name of other gods, he
        shall die.'"

RESPONSORIAL PSALM

Ps 95:1-2, 6-7, 7-9

R︦. (8) If today you hear his voice, harden not your hearts.

Come, let us sing joyfully to the LORD;
    let us acclaim the rock of our salvation.
Let us come into his presence with
        thanksgiving;
    let us joyfully sing psalms to him.

R︦. If today you hear his voice, harden not your hearts.

Come, let us bow down in worship;
    let us kneel before the LORD who made
        us.
For he is our God,
    and we are the people he shepherds, the
        flock he guides.

R︦. If today you hear his voice, harden not your hearts.

Oh, that today you would hear his voice:
    "Harden not your hearts as at Meribah,
    as in the day of Massah in the desert,
    where your fathers tempted me;
        they tested me though they had seen my
            works."

R︦. If today you hear his voice, harden not your hearts.

SECOND READING

1 Cor 7:32-35

Brothers and sisters:
I should like you to be free of anxieties.
An unmarried man is anxious about the
        things of the Lord,
    how he may please the Lord.
But a married man is anxious about the
        things of the world,
    how he may please his wife, and he is
        divided.
An unmarried woman or a virgin is
        anxious about the things of the Lord,
    so that she may be holy in both body
        and spirit.
A married woman, on the other hand,
    is anxious about the things of the
        world,
    how she may please her husband.
I am telling you this for your own benefit,
    not to impose a restraint upon you,
    but for the sake of propriety
    and adherence to the Lord without
        distraction.

About Liturgy

Liturgy as prophecy: We usually think of prophecy as arising in persons called by God to announce anew the covenant with God and call the community to renewed relationship with God and commitment to the covenantal terms. And so it is. We also usually say that the last of the prophets was John the Baptist. With the coming of Jesus, a new era of divine communication and relationship was opened up. And so is this true as well. But this does not mean that prophecy has ended. Just as with the people of old, sometimes we need a way to God's presence and will to be mediated to us. Liturgy itself has a prophetic thrust; it always reminds us of our baptismal covenant with God and calls us to deeper relationship with God and a renewed commitment to live according to God's will.

Obviously, one way liturgy is prophetic is through the proclamation of Scriptures during the Liturgy of the Word. During this time we are continually reminded of God's abiding presence and love, of the divine desire to be in intimate relationship with us. We hear in the Scriptures both challenge and encouragement as we journey deeper into our relationship with God.

Another way liturgy is prophetic is through the prayers of the faithful. As we conclude our proclamation, prayer, and reflection on Scripture, we turn our hearts to the church, world, those in need, and our own local community. As we pray for all these needs, we also nudge ourselves to become involved in facing the systemic and personal harm and commit ourselves to reach out to make our church and world a better place for everyone.

Yet another way the Sunday liturgy is prophetic is by hearing the proclamation of our Christian story in the eucharistic prayer and approaching God's table of abundance to be nourished on the heavenly Food. By remembering God's great deeds for us and divine desire for salvation, we are invited to deeper commitment, remembering that our baptismal covenant has made us "kin," daughters and sons of God who are now conformed to the dying and rising of the beloved Son.

About Liturgical Music

Music suggestions: A good choice for the entrance song this Sunday would be Bryn Rees' "The Kingdom of God" [RS, W3, WC]. Its text speaks of Christ's authoritative power over sin and also of the "challenge and choice" the announcement of the kingdom lays before us. A second well-suited hymn would be "Glorious in Majesty" [G2, RS. W3]. Its text speaks of the glory of Christ victorious over the powers of darkness as well as of the invitation to come to him and live his word. This hymn could be sung for either the entrance or the recessional. A third good choice would be "God Has Spoken by His Prophets" [JS2, PMB, RS, WC]. The text is about the abiding presence and power of God's word spoken throughout the ages by the prophets, by Jesus, and by the Spirit. This hymn would work well for the entrance procession, during the preparation of the gifts, or for the recessional.

SPIRITUALITY

Gospel   Mark 1:29-39; L74B

On leaving the synagogue
    Jesus entered the house of
        Simon and Andrew with
        James and John.
Simon's mother-in-law
    lay sick with a
    fever.
They immediately
    told him about her.
He approached, grasped her hand, and
    helped her up.
Then the fever left her and she waited
    on them.

When it was evening, after sunset,
    they brought to him all who were ill
        or possessed by demons.
The whole town was gathered at the
    door.
He cured many who were sick with
    various diseases,
    and he drove out many demons,
    not permitting them to speak because
        they knew him.

Rising very early before dawn, he left
    and went off to a deserted place,
        where he prayed.
Simon and those who were with him
    pursued him
    and on finding him said, "Everyone is
        looking for you."
He told them, "Let us go on to the
    nearby villages
    that I may preach there also.
For this purpose have I come."
So he went into their synagogues,
    preaching and driving out demons
        throughout the whole of Galilee.

Reflecting on the Gospel

So many times during our life can all of us identify with Job's lament in this Sunday's first reading: "Is not [our] life on earth a drudgery?" Some of us must get up way too early in the morning to get to a job. We might sit in traffic for too many precious minutes in the morning or evening rush hours. We might work in society's or church's service sector, and feel like all we get is complaints, no matter how hard we try. We, too, like Job, might often feel like our days end "without hope." The gospel tells of the Jesus who "cured many": Peter's mother-in-law, the sick among the town, those who were possessed by demons. It is no surprise that "[e]veryone is looking" for Jesus—who wouldn't seek hope and the promise of a better life if someone were among us who could heal us of every ill? This gospel reminds us of two important and related points.

First, the significance of Jesus' healings and exorcisms goes beyond the individuals who came to him in their illness. Rather, they reveal the purpose for which Jesus came. Into a world of hopelessness described by Job and suffering depicted by the sick and possessed in the gospel, Jesus enters preaching Good News, confronting suffering, and bringing hope. Jesus is the Good News in action.

Second, we might lament that we could not have lived over two thousand years ago so that we might bring our sorrows and ailments to Jesus for healing. Yet, Jesus is present to us just as much today as to the crowds in the gospel. Like the people in the gospel, all we need do is come to him, present ourselves, ask to be healed. And Jesus gives us a clue in the gospel about how we might come to him. He rose "very early before dawn" and went out "to a deserted place" to pray, to be in communion with God. Jesus never loses sight of why he came—to preach the Good News of salvation. He does not lose sight of his mission because he never loses sight of his Father. This is how we come to Jesus today—by praying, being in communion with God. Hope is discovered in surrendering ourselves to God, coming to him in the intimacy of divine encounter, and allowing him to reach out and heal us. Yes, today, Jesus is still the Good News in action.

Living the Paschal Mystery

Like those in the gospel who come to Jesus for healing, we all come to Jesus with expectations (after all, prayers of petition are the most common prayers we pray). The challenge is to move beyond our expectations to what Jesus really wants to give us—the Good News of salvation. Jesus' presence to us today and his healing hand do not assure us that we will never suffer. Human life is full of suffering—physical, emotional, spiritual. The new life and hope Jesus brings by preaching the Good News does not give us the assurance of never suffering. The Good News does assure us, however, of having the strength to keep the suffering in perspective. Jesus assures us that suffering belongs to this life, but this is not all there is to life.

We need to allow Jesus' presence to transform us so that our every breath is a proclamation of God's saving mystery. Most of us won't go out to neighboring towns to preach. But we can smile a simple thank-you to the tired cashier in the supermarket. We can bite our tongue rather than snap at the rambunctious children. We can do something thoughtful for someone when it is not expected. Like Jesus, we can be a living Gospel, the Good News in action. Then is our normal human suffering kept in perspective.

Focusing the Gospel

Key words and phrases: Jesus entered, all who were ill or possessed, cured, Everyone is looking for you, For this purpose have I come

To the point: The significance of Jesus' healings and exorcisms goes beyond the individuals who came to him in their illness. Rather, they reveal the purpose for which Jesus came. Into a world of hopelessness described by Job (see first reading) and suffering depicted by the sick and possessed in the gospel, Jesus enters preaching Good News, confronting suffering, and bringing hope.

Connecting the Gospel

to the first reading: Job's lament in the first reading deepens our awareness of what in our human condition needs healing, and at this point in Job's miserable life he only sees "an end without hope." In the gospel Jesus is a healer whose preaching and actions instill hope.

to our experience: We tend to limit the preaching of the gospel to the spoken word. Jesus enacts the Gospel in his healings, exorcisms, and through his very life. Jesus is the Good News in action.

Connecting the Responsorial Psalm

to the readings: The reading from Job in this Sunday's Liturgy of the Word hits us with the futility, the restlessness, the "troubled nights" of the human condition. We hear these lines proclaimed with full awareness of the rest of Job's story: the destruction of his family, the loss of his property, his prolonged and painful illnesses, his degradation by friends and neighbors—all couched in the inattentiveness of a God who seems not to care. The gospel reading, however, presents us with the truth of God's response to our condition: God comes among us in the flesh of Jesus' preaching, healing, and driving out demons.

The verses of the responsorial psalm parallel the first reading and gospel by contrasting human brokenness with the cosmic power of God. What has been destroyed, God rebuilds. Those who have been scattered, God gathers. Those who are lowly, God sustains. The gospel shows us this power at its fullest in the person and mission of Jesus. In singing this psalm, we tell the world what we have come to know: that into the midst of human suffering comes a compassionate One with power to change how things are.

to cantor preparation: In the psalm refrain you call the assembly to praise God for healing the brokenhearted. In the verses you expand on the ways God does this healing. As part of your preparation, try putting names and faces on these ways. In other words, what have you seen God rebuild? Whom have you seen God regather? Whom do you watch God sustain?

**ASSEMBLY &
FAITH-SHARING GROUPS**
- What needs healing in my life is . . . I experience the healing power of Jesus when . . .
- What helps me become more aware of the suffering of others is . . .
- Jesus gives me hope by . . .

PRESIDERS
- I preach a word of hope when . . .

DEACONS
- Like Jesus, my service to those in need brings healing and hope when . . .

HOSPITALITY MINISTERS
- My greeting can be a healing word because . . .

MUSIC MINISTERS
- My music is a song of hope for the people when . . .

ALTAR MINISTERS
- My serving at the altar brings me hope by . . .

LECTORS
- Like Jesus, I put the proclaimed word into action when I . . .

**EXTRAORDINARY MINISTERS
OF HOLY COMMUNION**
- The communicants give me hope in the coming of God's kingdom by . . .

Model Act of Penitence

Presider: The purpose for which Jesus came among us was to preach the Good News, heal human suffering, and bring us hope. Let us open our hearts to encounter this compassionate Healer . . . [pause]

> Lord Jesus, you are the Healer of all those who come to you in need: Lord . . .
>
> Christ Jesus, you are the Word of hope for a weary world: Christ . . .
>
> Lord Jesus, you are the Good News of salvation: Lord . . .

Homily Points

• Suffering is part of the human condition. For Buddhists, suffering is indicative of being out of balance with self and nature, and so suffering is looked upon as an opportunity for growth. We, on the other hand, tend to understand suffering only in negative terms, and often as a punishment from God.

• In the gospel, Jesus not only heals suffering, but brings hope to those possessed by "demons." A *daimon* in Greek refers to a driving force, which is good if it helps us grow, but is bad if it leads to destruction. Our own destructive "demons" can be legion: we are driven by gluttony, hate, fear, greed, jealousy, revenge, etc.

• Jesus' driving force—the purpose for which he came—was to help people confront their destructive "demons," lead them through suffering to growth, and give them the hope of fullness of life. He continues to fulfill this purpose through and for us today.

Model Prayer of the Faithful

Presider: Let us make our needs known to our compassionate God, so that we might be healed and strengthened in the Good News.

Response:

Lord,—— hear our prayer.

Cantor:

we pray to the Lord,

For the church, entrusted with being the healing and hope-filled presence of Jesus in the world . . . [pause]

For the world, so full of suffering and hopelessness . . . [pause]

For the sick . . . for those without hope . . . for those driven by destructive demons . . . [pause]

For this community, called to continue the purpose for which Jesus came . . . [pause]

Presider: Merciful God, you hear the prayers of those who cry out to you for healing and strength: hear our prayers that we might one day enjoy everlasting life with you. We ask this through Christ our Lord. Amen.

OPENING PRAYER

Let us pray

Pause for silent prayer

Father,
watch over your family
and keep us safe in your care,
for all our hope is in you.

Grant this through our Lord Jesus Christ,
    your Son,
who lives and reigns with you and the
    Holy Spirit,
one God, for ever and ever **Amen.**

FIRST READING

Job 7:1-4, 6-7

Job spoke, saying:
    Is not man's life on earth a drudgery?
        Are not his days those of hirelings?
    He is a slave who longs for the shade,
        a hireling who waits for his wages.
    So I have been assigned months of
        misery,
        and troubled nights have been
            allotted to me.
    If in bed I say, "When shall I arise?"
        then the night drags on;
        I am filled with restlessness until the
            dawn.
    My days are swifter than a weaver's
        shuttle;
        they come to an end without hope.
    Remember that my life is like the wind;
        I shall not see happiness again.

RESPONSORIAL PSALM

Ps 147:1-2, 3-4, 5-6

℟. (cf. 3a) Praise the Lord, who heals the brokenhearted.
    or:
℟. Alleluia.

Praise the Lord, for he is good;
    sing praise to our God, for he is
        gracious;
    it is fitting to praise him.
The Lord rebuilds Jerusalem;
    the dispersed of Israel he gathers.

℟. Praise the Lord, who heals the brokenhearted.
    or:
℟. Alleluia.

He heals the brokenhearted
   and binds up their wounds.
He tells the number of the stars;
   he calls each by name.

R⁊. Praise the Lord, who heals the
brokenhearted.
   or:
R⁊. Alleluia.

Great is our Lord and mighty in power;
   to his wisdom there is no limit.
The LORD sustains the lowly;
   the wicked he casts to the ground.

R⁊. Praise the Lord, who heals the
brokenhearted.
   or:
R⁊. Alleluia.

SECOND READING
1 Cor 9:16-19, 22-23

Brothers and sisters:
If I preach the gospel, this is no reason for
      me to boast,
   for an obligation has been imposed on
      me,
   and woe to me if I do not preach it!
If I do so willingly, I have a recompense,
   but if unwillingly, then I have been
      entrusted with a stewardship.
What then is my recompense?
That, when I preach,
   I offer the gospel free of charge
   so as not to make full use of my right in
      the gospel.

Although I am free in regard to all,
   I have made myself a slave to all
   so as to win over as many as possible.
To the weak I became weak, to win over
      the weak.
I have become all things to all, to save at
      least some.
All this I do for the sake of the gospel,
   so that I too may have a share in it.

About Liturgy

The second reading during Ordinary Time: Usually during Ordinary Time the second reading does not fit with the first reading and gospel. The second reading during this season is a sequential reading of one of the New Testament letters. This is why during Ordinary Time little is said in *Living Liturgy*™ about the second reading.

   This Sunday is a happy coincidence in that the second reading reinforces the approach to the first reading and gospel taken in *Living Liturgy*™. Paul is emphasizing his (all Christians') role in preaching the Gospel, but this is no reason to boast. Paul says we must become "all things to all, to save at least some" and find our own share in the Gospel we preach by the way we live the Good News.

Who may preach: Current liturgical law limits liturgical preaching of homilies to ordained ministers (with a few exceptions, for example at Masses with children). This being said, it doesn't mean that all baptized Christians aren't called to preach the Gospel. In fact we are, by the very way we live. And sometimes the preaching by the actions of our lives is far more eloquent and fruitful than words.

About Liturgical Music

Music suggestions: Songs and hymns singing about Jesus' mission to heal abound. An excellent entrance hymn would be "Your Hands, O Lord, in Days of Old" [PWB, JS, RS, WC, W3, WS]. Fred Pratt Green's "When Jesus Came Preaching" [RS, W3] could be used for either the entrance or the recessional. "For the Healing of the Nations," found in many hymnals, ties the healing work of Jesus with our mission to continue that work. If sung to the tune ST. THOMAS or WESTMINSTER ABBEY, this text would suit either the preparation of the gifts or the recessional. If sung to the more meditative tune PICARDY, it would be better suited to the preparation of the gifts. Howard S. Olson's text "Good News" [G2, GC, GC2, LMGM, RS] uses an Ethiopian tune with refrain. The verses tell the story of Jesus' preaching, his conflict with the elders, and his death on the cross. The refrain relates the Good News to the healing of broken hearts. This song would fit the preparation of the gifts, or it could be sung by the choir alone as a prelude. Good choices for Communion include "God, Full of Mercy" [WC, choir octavo WLP #002555], "To Be Your Bread" [BB, JS, choral arrangement available in OCP's *Choral Praise Comprehensive* or as octavo #9982CC], and John Foley's "The Cry of the Poor" [BB, JS, RS, choral arrangement available in OCP's *Choral Praise Comprehensive* or as octavo #9498CC].

SPIRITUALITY

GOSPEL ACCLAMATION
Luke 7:16

R℣. Alleluia, alleluia.
A great prophet has arisen in our midst,
God has visited his people.
R℣. Alleluia, alleluia.

Gospel   Mark 1:40-45; L77B

A leper came to Jesus and kneeling
    down begged him and said,
  "If you wish, you can make me
    clean."
Moved with pity, he stretched out his
    hand,
    touched him, and said to him,
  "I do will it. Be made clean."
The leprosy left him immediately, and
    he was made clean.
Then, warning him sternly, he
    dismissed him at once.

He said to him, "See that you tell no
    one anything,
  but go, show yourself to the priest
  and offer for your cleansing what
    Moses prescribed;
  that will be proof for them."

The man went away and began to
    publicize the whole matter.
He spread the report abroad
  so that it was impossible for Jesus to
    enter a town openly.
He remained outside in deserted
    places,
  and people kept coming to him from
    everywhere.

Reflecting on the Gospel

It was a rainy summer Saturday, and Aaron, like most six-year-olds, was cooped up in the house but wanted to be outdoors playing with his friends. Feisty and boisterous, he had teased his little sister just one too many times. In exasperation, his mother turned to him and declared sternly, "You're in the doghouse." Aaron quickly retorted, "No, I'm not, that's outside; I'm in here in our house." Aaron took his mother's metaphor literally, but still understood its meaning: the doghouse put him outside and he was inside. This Sunday's gospel tells of a leper who approaches Jesus, seeking to move from being outside and excluded to being inside and included. The transformation Jesus makes in the leper goes even further.

Lepers in biblical times were required to proclaim "unclean" and live in social and religious isolation from the community (see first reading). The leper in the gospel, excluded from the community, understandably approached Jesus with doubt: "If you wish . . ." Jesus, however, has no doubt about his response, for his purpose in coming among us was to show the compassion of God for the outcast: "I do will it." Jesus' compassion gave the leper what he deeply wished—to be made clean, yes, but also to once again be included in the social and religious life of the community.

Further, the leper in the gospel, now "made clean," engages with the community by proclaiming the Good News of having been healed: he "began to publicize the whole matter." Encounter with Jesus transforms the man and the way he acts in two ways. He goes from isolation to religious ("show yourself to the priest") and social ("spread the report abroad") inclusion. He also becomes a disciple as he "spread the report abroad." Our own encounters with Jesus bring us to the same community of inclusion and discipleship. Jesus touches us in the same way today, drawing us into community and enabling us to do the same for others.

So deep was Jesus' compassion, that he even risked his own exclusion: "He remained outside in deserted places." Ultimately, Jesus' compassion brought him to the most serious isolation and exclusion of all: he was nailed to a cross between two thieves. "I do will it." Jesus wills for us nothing less than what he gave to the leper: to "[b]e made clean," that is, to share in the fruits of his cross and resurrection. This is Good News, indeed, and we, like the leper, cannot help but publicize it abroad.

Living the Paschal Mystery

The gospel begins with a leper—one who cries "Unclean!" and must remain a social outcast. The gospel ends with Jesus taking upon himself the infirmities of humanity symbolized by his "remain[ing] outside in deserted places." Living the paschal mystery means changing "If you wish" to "I do will it" and then having heaped upon ourselves the infirmities of humanity.

Jesus commands the leper to tell no one; the leper tells everyone. Jesus' commission to us is to tell everyone the Good News—do we tell no one? We must change our "wish" to "I do will it." Paschal mystery living means taking up our cross and actually doing what Jesus did—willing the good of others. In this we, too, risk isolation: being snubbed by our coworkers, being laughed at by people who think we are just religious fanatics, being ridiculed because we give of our time and possessions for the good of others. Risking this isolation in paschal mystery living, however, gains for us everything: community in the Body of Christ.

Focusing the Gospel

Key words and phrases: If you wish, Moved with pity, touched him, I do will it, began to publicize

To the point: Lepers in biblical times were required to proclaim "unclean" and live in social and religious isolation from the community (see first reading). The leper in the gospel, excluded from the community, understandably approached Jesus with doubt: "If you wish . . ." Jesus, however, has no doubt about his response, for his purpose in coming among us was to show the compassion of God for the outcast: "I do will it." Jesus touches us in the same way today, drawing us into community and enabling us to do the same for others.

Connecting the Gospel

to last Sunday: Jesus' purpose in coming was to preach Good News, confront suffering, and bring hope (last Sunday). This purpose is once again accomplished both in this healing of a leper and in the leper's "publiciz[ing] the whole matter."

to our experience: How often in life do we not struggle with who we are or where we are going. How often do we seem to be in a haze about the meaning and purpose of our lives. This was not so for Jesus. And this is Good News for us who have been baptized into his mission.

Connecting the Responsorial Psalm

to the readings: Because the readings this Sunday move so quickly from the Old Testament notion of the uncleanness of leprosy to the responsorial psalm's confession of sin and guilt, we can be misled into thinking that serious illness and serious sin are one and the same. The point of the readings and psalm, however, is quite different. What ties the first reading, gospel, and psalm together is the open admission before God and community of our condition (be it ostracizing disease or sinful behavior) and the ever-readiness of God to heal and to forgive if we but speak our need. Whatever limitations illness or sin create, God will act to counter them. And when this happens, God's loving-kindness becomes so manifest that it cannot be fenced—we must proclaim it. May we, with this psalmist and this leper, turn to God with whatever our "trouble" (psalm) is, and may we then proclaim with them the salvation we receive.

to cantor preparation: To get the full picture of what is transpiring in this Sunday's responsorial psalm between the psalmist and God—and, by implication, between yourself and God, and the assembly and God—you need to read and pray with the whole text of Psalm 32. For a long time the speaker in Psalm 32 has refused to admit her or his sinfulness and suffers because of this. When she or he finally relents and opens self to God, "groaning" is replaced by "glad cries of freedom" (vv. 3 and 7). When have you struggled to come to God with the truth about yourself and your situation, and how have you experienced release and healing when you have come to God?

**ASSEMBLY &
FAITH-SHARING GROUPS**
· The healing for which I need to ask Jesus is . . .
· What Jesus wills for me is . . . What I will for others is . . .
· One way I reach out to outcasts is . . .

PRESIDERS
· My manner of presiding makes people feel welcome and included in the community when . . .

DEACONS
· Jesus' ministry to the outcast challenges me to expand my ministry to . . .

HOSPITALITY MINISTERS
· My manner of welcoming people to the assembly expresses Jesus' compassion in that . . .

MUSIC MINISTERS
· My manner of relating to other music ministers models Jesus' embrace of others by . . .

ALTAR MINISTERS
· Serving at the altar helps others feel included when . . .

LECTORS
· My proclamation always expresses the compassion of God in that . . .

**EXTRAORDINARY MINISTERS
OF HOLY COMMUNION**
· When I take Holy Communion to the sick and homebound, I make them feel a part of our community when I . . .

Model Act of Penitence

Presider: Jesus shows his compassion in the gospel in his willingness to heal the leper. Let us prepare ourselves to encounter the compassionate Jesus during this liturgy . . . [pause]

> Lord Jesus, you are God's compassion made visible: Lord . . .
>
> Christ Jesus, you heal those who cry out to you: Christ . . .
>
> Lord Jesus, you bring salvation and healing to all: Lord . . .

Homily Points

• Most likely none of us has encountered someone with Hansen's disease. However, we have all had experience with those who are outcasts, or with feeling ourselves alienated from family or community. Today's "lepers" might well be those suffering from AIDS or substance abuse, those having a different sexual orientation, those who are homeless; or a family member guilty of crossing a line of acceptable behavior or a coworker who seems "lazy."

• "Tell me who your friends are, and I'll tell you who you are." Jesus deliberately identified himself with outcasts and the alienated: lepers, sinners, women, foreigners, tax collectors. The first thing Jesus did was accept the other; then, in some cases, he cured them and in other cases he called them to change. Always, he was compassionate.

• We, too, are called to have the compassion of Jesus and to reach out to those who seem to be or who feel alienated. Often this requires us, as it did Jesus, to run the risk of being rejected ourselves.

Model Prayer of the Faithful

Presider: Just as Jesus showed mercy and healed the leper, so surely will God show us mercy and hear our prayers.

Response:

Cantor:

May the church be a welcoming home for all who are troubled and alienated . . . [pause]

May all people of the world have the Good News of God's mercy preached to them . . . [pause]

May all those who feel isolated or alienated be touched by our compassion . . . [pause]

May each of us welcome the outcast and heal broken relationships . . . [pause]

Presider: Merciful God, you are compassionate and merciful: hear our prayers that we might be healed of all that alienates us from you and one another. We ask this through Christ our Lord. **Amen.**

OPENING PRAYER

Let us pray

Pause for silent prayer

God our Father,
you have promised to remain for ever
with those who do what is just and right.
Help us to live in your presence.

We ask this through our Lord Jesus Christ,
    your Son,
who lives and reigns with you and the
    Holy Spirit,
one God, for ever and ever. **Amen.**

FIRST READING

Lev 13:1-2, 44-46

The LORD said to Moses and Aaron,
    "If someone has on his skin a scab or
        pustule or blotch
    which appears to be the sore of leprosy,
    he shall be brought to Aaron, the priest,
    or to one of the priests among his
        descendants.
If the man is leprous and unclean,
    the priest shall declare him unclean
    by reason of the sore on his head.

"The one who bears the sore of leprosy
    shall keep his garments rent and his
        head bare,
    and shall muffle his beard;
    he shall cry out, 'Unclean, unclean!'
As long as the sore is on him he shall
        declare himself unclean,
    since he is in fact unclean.
He shall dwell apart, making his abode
        outside the camp."

RESPONSORIAL PSALM

Ps 32:1-2, 5, 11

R⁊. (7) I turn to you, Lord, in time of trouble, and you fill me with the joy of salvation.

Blessed is he whose fault is taken away,
    whose sin is covered.
Blessed the man to whom the LORD
        imputes not guilt,
    in whose spirit there is no guile.

R⁊. I turn to you, Lord, in time of trouble, and you fill me with the joy of salvation.

Then I acknowledged my sin to you,
    my guilt I covered not.
I said, "I confess my faults to the LORD,"
    and you took away the guilt of my sin.

R⁊. I turn to you, Lord, in time of trouble, and you fill me with the joy of salvation.

Be glad in the LORD and rejoice, you just;
    exult, all you upright of heart.

R⁊. I turn to you, Lord, in time of trouble, and you fill me with the joy of salvation.

SECOND READING

1 Cor 10:31–11:1

Brothers and sisters,
whether you eat or drink, or whatever you
        do,
    do everything for the glory of God.
Avoid giving offense, whether to the Jews
        or Greeks or the church of God,
    just as I try to please everyone in every
        way,
    not seeking my own benefit but that of
        the many,
    that they may be saved.
Be imitators of me, as I am of Christ.

About Liturgy

The role of hospitality ministers: Although it is every parish member's responsibility to make sure everyone feels included in both the liturgies and in the parish community, it is part of hospitality ministers' mandate as a "visible liturgical ministry" to model inclusiveness in the parish. Inadvertently, hospitality ministers (and other members of the assembly) can sometimes make others feel like religious and social "outcasts." Sometimes they are so busy catching up with friends coming into church that they miss an opportunity to say a welcome to the one they don't know. Sometimes they might miss an opportunity to help parents with young children who are restless and noisy on a particular morning feel more comfortable. Sometimes they miss an opportunity to be the first to comfort the one who might become sick during liturgy. Hospitality ministry is about inclusiveness, attending to the needs and comfort of others, and minimizing distractions and challenges so that members of the assembly can more easily surrender themselves to the transforming presence and action of God.

Another consideration for the hospitality ministers that might be a reflection derived from this Sunday's gospel is that they are not simply welcoming people to a social gathering. Their welcome helps form the members of the assembly into the one Body of Christ. Their ministry is far more than a social welcome. The heart of it concerns helping the assembly become church made visible, gathered around the visible Head, Christ. This is why there can be no outcasts—we are all members of the one Body of Christ.

About Liturgical Music

Communion processional hymns: The Communion song is meant to celebrate who we become because of our communion in the Body and Blood of Christ. The procession during Communion is a movement toward completion: we journey to the messianic banquet where we become one in the Body of Christ. Here there is food for all, love for all, healing for all. The text and style of the hymn we sing needs to express a sense of joyful completeness or fullness in the Lord which is shared with the whole Body of Christ. The song needs to focus us equally on our oneness with one another and on the One in whom this oneness is made possible.

SPIRITUALITY

GOSPEL ACCLAMATION
cf. Luke 4:18

℟. Alleluia, alleluia.
The Lord sent me to bring glad tidings to the poor,
and to proclaim liberty to captives.
℟. Alleluia, alleluia.

Gospel   Mark 2:1-12; L80B

When Jesus returned to Capernaum
    after some days,
  it became known that he was at
    home.
Many gathered together so that there
    was no longer room for them,
  not even around the door,
  and he preached the word to them.
They came bringing to him a
    paralytic carried by four men.
Unable to get near Jesus because of the
    crowd,
  they opened up the roof above him.
After they had broken through,
  they let down the mat on which the
    paralytic was lying.
When Jesus saw their faith, he said to the
    paralytic,
  "Child, your sins are forgiven."
Now some of the scribes were sitting there
    asking themselves,
  "Why does this man speak that way? He
    is blaspheming.
Who but God alone can forgive sins?"
Jesus immediately knew in his mind
what they were thinking to themselves,
  so he said, "Why are you thinking such
    things in your hearts?
Which is easier, to say to the paralytic,
  'Your sins are forgiven,'
  or to say, 'Rise, pick up your mat and
    walk'?
But that you may know
  that the Son of Man has authority to
    forgive sins on earth"
  —he said to the paralytic,
  "I say to you, rise, pick up your mat, and
    go home."
He rose, picked up his mat at once,
  and went away in the sight of everyone.
They were all astounded
  and glorified God, saying, "We have never
    seen anything like this."

Reflecting on the Gospel

We are all familiar with "iconic" brands, names so familiar there is immediate recognition. For example, Cheerios and Wheaties have almost become recognizable for cereal in general: "Have you had your Wheaties this morning?" Some brands are so recognizable that the brand name is added to our everyday vocabulary; for example, "Kodak" has become identified with camera or film. Connected with these recognizable brand names is the common sense approach not to change anything in the marketing—can one imagine Cheerios not being in a yellow box? In marketing, the attitude is "don't challenge the mother lode!" If the ploy works, leave it alone; don't change it. Yet, often change is good for us. This Sunday's first reading and gospel both speak of change in terms of something new happening—divine forgiveness.

As the gospel story unfolds, we come to see that the man carried to Jesus on a mat actually suffered from two types of paralysis: physical (he was carried to Jesus by others) and spiritual (Jesus forgives his sinfulness). Jesus looks beyond the physical paralysis of the man, and offers him the deeper healing he really needs: forgiveness. Like the actions of God toward the Israelites (see first reading), Jesus frees the paralytic (and us) from the past and opens a brand-new start in life. Forgiveness makes possible seeing something new that is happening. What is new is a whole new relationship with God—in the first reading God speaks of a "people I formed for myself." God desires such intimacy with us that forgiveness becomes an expression of divine presence, for in the first reading God announces that God wiped out Israel's offenses "for my own sake." Transgressions cause a breach in the relationship; God always acts to heal the breach, so long as we turn back toward God.

Along with the crowd in the gospel, we are astounded each time Jesus acts in the same way today to forgive us. Forgiveness is a divine act and presence that evokes a response of praise and the announcement that something new is happening. What is the "something new" that this gospel announces? That Good News is forgiveness and that God's forgiveness offers us a new start in life.

Living the Paschal Mystery

In the Our Father we pray that God forgive us as we forgive others. More important than "measuring" God's offer of forgiveness by our own, this line of the prayer reminds us that forgiving is a divine act of mercy. When we forgive others we are acting in/by God's power and, with God, bringing about something new. Through baptism we are adopted as sons and daughters of God and share in God's divine life. There is no better way for us to proclaim our own share in divinity than by forgiving others. And each time we forgive, we proclaim the Gospel.

Forgiveness is not easy. It is a kind of dying to self because we must "[r]emember not" past hurts and allow change, allow a new relationship to grow. Our acts of forgiving are a proclamation of the paschal mystery, an announcement that something new is happening—a broken relationship is restored. Together, as Body of Christ, we can once again give full-throated praise and glory to God.

Focusing the Gospel

Key words and phrases: paralytic carried by four men, your sins are forgiven, picked up his mat

To the point: As the gospel story unfolds, we come to see that the man carried to Jesus on a mat actually suffered from two types of paralysis: physical (he was carried to Jesus by others) and spiritual (Jesus forgives his sinfulness). Jesus looks beyond the physical paralysis of the man, and offers him the deeper healing he really needs. Like the actions of God toward the Israelites (see first reading), Jesus frees the paralytic (and us) from the past and opens a brand-new start in life.

Connecting the Gospel

to the first reading: How much God has to forgive Israel: their sinfulness in the desert during the Exodus, their sinfulness which precipitated the Babylonian Exile! How deep is the capacity of God to forgive and "remember no more"! This great capacity of divine forgiveness is made visible anew by Jesus in his actions toward this simple paralytic.

to our experience: Often enough we are prisoners of our own past—wallowing in past hurts and sorrows, clinging to guilt, afraid to move to a new self-understanding. This gospel calls us to be open to the many people and ways that help us move forward.

Connecting the Responsorial Psalm

to the readings: Psalm 41 is a psalm of thanksgiving for release from a grave illness which even the psalmist believed was the consequence of sin. The psalm begins with a wisdom statement that those who care for the poor will be blessed by God (vv. 2-4), then recounts a past event in which God delivered the psalmist from disease so vile that close personal friends doubted recovery would be granted (vv. 5-13). The final verse (14), used here as part of the responsorial psalm, is not really a part of Psalm 41 but the doxology concluding Book I of the Psalms (there are five books, each ending with such a doxology, Psalm 150 being the grand conclusion to the entire collection).

The Lectionary uses the wisdom introduction, collapses the saving event into three short verses, then tacks the doxology onto the final strophe. While the first strophe (the wisdom introduction) seems to have no connection with the first reading and gospel, the second and third strophes clearly relate to God's forgiveness of sins and healing of infirmities. In this responsorial psalm we acknowledge the God who raises us from sickness and sin, and we offer this God eternal praise.

to cantor preparation: As with last Sunday's psalm, this week's also speaks of the consequences of disclosing our sinfulness honestly before God: we are forgiven and healed of sin's paralyzing effects. In singing this psalm, you proclaim that you know this to be true. As part of your preparation, you might use the psalm refrain as a prayer mantra during the week. Be humble and honest about your own sinfulness. Then praise God for continued forgiveness.

**ASSEMBLY &
FAITH-SHARING GROUPS**

· What paralyzes me is . . . Who carries me to Jesus for healing is . . .

· I need to forgive myself for . . . I am able to hear Jesus' words of forgiveness when I . . .

· The new life I have received through the power of forgiveness is . . .

PRESIDERS

· While celebrating the Sacrament of Penance, I extend the compassion and healing of Jesus when I . . .

DEACONS

· Those Jesus wishes me to carry to him for healing are . . .

HOSPITALITY MINISTERS

· My greeting embodies Jesus' forgiveness and healing when . . .

MUSIC MINISTERS

· What sometimes paralyzes me in my music ministry is . . . Jesus acts to free me from this paralysis by . . .

ALTAR MINISTERS

· My ministry of service carries the burden for others because . . .

LECTORS

· My daily living announces God's word of forgiveness when . . .

**EXTRAORDINARY MINISTERS
OF HOLY COMMUNION**

· Eucharist is the sacrament of reconciliation *par excellence*. I bring forgiveness and reconciliation to others when . . .

Model Act of Penitence

Presider: In today's gospel Jesus heals the paralytic of both his physical infirmity and his sinfulness. Let us prepare ourselves to celebrate Jesus' healing and forgiveness in this Eucharist . . . [pause]

Lord Jesus, you are God's compassion made flesh among us: Lord . . .

Christ Jesus, you are the glory of God made visible: Christ . . .

Lord Jesus, you are the source of all forgiveness and healing: Lord . . .

Homily Points

• We often allow the past to control us—either we feel we are victims of the past (past hurts, failures, guilt) or we live in reaction to the past ("I'll never trust that person again"). Either way, we are paralyzed in our ability to see possibilities and choose "something new" for our life.

• Jesus never allows a person's past to cloud who that person really is or can become. His conviction of the goodness in which we are created enables his compassion to help the person grow.

• Unlike Jesus, we can't (usually) cure physical infirmities; like Jesus, we can help those trapped in their past come to forgiveness and healing. With Jesus, we can do "something new" (first reading), something "never seen . . . before" (gospel).

Model Prayer of the Faithful

Presider: Let us pray for healing and forgiveness, confident that our faithful God will grant our prayers.

Response:

Lord,—— hear our prayer.

Cantor:

we pray to the Lord,

That the church might always be a home for others, extending forgiveness and mercy . . . [pause]

That warring countries might forgive each other and seek peace . . . [pause]

That those who are paralyzed in body or spirit hear the healing word of Jesus . . . [pause]

That each of us be moved by God's mercy and forgiveness toward us to extend to others that same mercy and forgiveness. . . [pause]

Presider: Merciful God, you forgive our sins and grant us healing and mercy: hear our prayers so that one day we might enjoy the fullness of life with you. We ask this through Christ our Lord. **Amen.**

ALTERNATIVE OPENING PRAYER

Let us pray

Pause for silent prayer

Almighty God,
Father of our Lord Jesus Christ,
faith in your word is the way to wisdom,
and to ponder your divine plan is to grow
    in the truth.
Open our eyes to your deeds,
our ears to the sound of your call,
so that our every act may increase our
    sharing
in the life you have offered us.

Grant this through Christ our Lord.
    Amen.

FIRST READING

Isa 43:18-19, 21-22, 24b-25

Thus says the LORD:
Remember not the events of the past,
    the things of long ago consider not;
see, I am doing something new!
    Now it springs forth, do you not
        perceive it?
In the desert I make a way,
    in the wasteland, rivers.
The people I formed for myself,
    that they might announce my praise.
Yet you did not call upon me, O Jacob,
    for you grew weary of me, O Israel.
You burdened me with your sins,
    and wearied me with your crimes.
It is I, I, who wipe out,
    for my own sake, your offenses;
    your sins I remember no more.

RESPONSORIAL PSALM

Ps 41:2-3, 4-5, 13-14

℟. (5b) Lord, heal my soul, for I have sinned against you.

Blessed is the one who has regard for the
    lowly and the poor;
  in the day of misfortune the LORD will
    deliver him.
The LORD will keep and preserve him;
  and make him blessed on earth,
  and not give him over to the will of his
    enemies.

℟. Lord, heal my soul, for I have sinned
against you.

The LORD will help him on his sickbed,
  he will take away all his ailment when
    he is ill.
Once I said, "O LORD, have pity on me;
  heal me, though I have sinned against
    you."

℟. Lord, heal my soul, for I have sinned
against you.

But because of my integrity you sustain
    me
  and let me stand before you forever.
Blessed be the LORD, the God of Israel,
  from all eternity. Amen. Amen.

℟. Lord, heal my soul, for I have sinned
against you.

SECOND READING

2 Cor 1:18-22

Brothers and sisters:
As God is faithful,
  our word to you is not "yes" and "no."
For the Son of God, Jesus Christ,
  who was proclaimed to you by us,
    Silvanus and Timothy and me,
  was not "yes" and "no," but "yes" has
    been in him.
For however many are the promises of
    God, their Yes is in him;
  therefore, the Amen from us also goes
    through him to God for glory.
But the one who gives us security with
    you in Christ
  and who anointed us is God;
  he has also put his seal upon us
  and given the Spirit in our hearts as a
    first installment.

About Liturgy

The Sacrament of Penance: Lent begins this Wednesday, and so it is timely to reflect on the Sacrament of Penance. There is much talk in Catholic publications these days about the demise of this sacrament, how it is not being frequented enough. Many parishes offer communal penance liturgies during Lent; a good Lenten resolution might be to put aside whatever else falls on the calendar date for that evening and avail oneself of this sacrament.

Too much of the Sacrament of Penance is thought of in terms of lists of sins. Certainly our sinfulness—weakening or breaking our relationship with God—is the "matter" of this sacrament. But far more happens than mechanically reciting a list of sins. First and foremost this sacrament is an opportunity for a personal encounter with Christ and the celebration of divine mercy. It is an opportunity to praise and glorify God for always being willing to restore an intimate relationship with us humans. It gives us a chance to publicly announce that the reign of sin is vanquished and the reign of God is upon us. Our very coming to church to celebrate this sacrament is a proclamation of the Gospel—not by words, but by our deed.

Perhaps if we would cast this sacrament in the positive light of God's forgiveness, mercy, and desire for a restored relationship with each of us, more parishioners would celebrate this sacrament. Our churches ought to be packed—people spilling out the doors onto the streets, eager to celebrate God's mercy, eager to proclaim their own share in divinity. When God's forgiveness and mercy are so powerfully felt—carried over in the forgiveness and mercy we extend to each other—then it might be difficult to contain our "Alleluia!" even during Lent.

About Liturgical Music

Presentation of the gifts processional hymns: The procession with the gifts is a practical one in which we carry the bread and wine to the table to prepare them for the Liturgy of the Eucharist. The internal journey symbolized by this procession is two-pronged. One movement is internalization of the message of the gospel that has just been proclaimed; the other is final preparation of ourselves for transformation through the eucharistic prayer and Communion. A journey of this sort may be accompanied by silence, by instrumental music, by a choir piece, or by an assembly song. The most suitable text would be one based on the gospel of the day. It is important that, whatever the form, neither the style nor the text of the music entice us to drift off into private devotional prayer or become so enamored of the choir, soloist, or instrumentalist that we lose our focus on the liturgical action in which we are participating.

Season of Lent

SPIRITUALITY

GOSPEL ACCLAMATION
See Ps 95:8

If today you hear his voice,
harden not your hearts.

Gospel   Matt 6:1-6, 16-18; L219

Jesus said to his disciples:
"Take care not to perform righteous
          deeds
     in order that people may see them;
     otherwise, you will have no recompense
          from your heavenly Father.
When you give alms,
     do not blow a trumpet before you,
     as the hypocrites do in the synagogues
          and in the streets
     to win the praise of others.
Amen, I say to you,
     they have received their reward.
But when you give alms,
     do not let your left hand know what your
          right is doing,
     so that your almsgiving may be secret.
And your Father who sees in secret will
     repay you.

"When you pray,
     do not be like the hypocrites,
     who love to stand and pray in the
          synagogues and on street corners
     so that others may see them.
Amen, I say to you,
     they have received their reward.
But when you pray, go to your inner room,
     close the door, and pray to your Father in
          secret.
And your Father who sees in secret will
     repay you.

"When you fast,
     do not look gloomy like the hypocrites.
They neglect their appearance,
     so that they may appear to others to be
          fasting.
Amen, I say to you, they have received their
     reward.
But when you fast,
     anoint your head and wash your face,
     so that you may not appear to be fasting,
     except to your Father who is hidden.
And your Father who sees what is hidden
     will repay you."

See Appendix A, p. 269, for other readings.

Reflecting on the Gospel

Like Palm Sunday, Ash Wednesday seems to be one of those days that draws large numbers of people to church. Christians everywhere—even those who aren't especially fervent in the practice of their faith—have the sense that this day is important. Perhaps part of the popularity of Ash Wednesday is receiving ashes—a rather unique gesture that captures our fancy. It is seldom that we are invited to so publicly wear a badge of our Christian commitment. But

perhaps, too, part of the popularity of Ash Wednesday is that we are all aware (like the suggestion in the first reading) that we need to "return to [God] with [our] whole heart," that we know we have done wrong and hurt others, that we have a deep, inner impulse to cry out, "Spare, O Lord, your people."

Ash Wednesday begins Lent and we naturally look to ourselves and our constant need for conversion. Surprisingly, the gospel begins not with ourselves (fasting) but with others (almsgiving). Without this turning outward toward others, any inward turning to ourselves (through fasting) runs the risk of being self-centered and self-satisfied (already our reward). Reaching out to others is a means of reminding ourselves that any self-emptying is always for the sake of the other, that being in right relationship with ourselves is conditioned by our willingness to reach out to the other. Charity—centering on others—*turns us* toward right relationship with self and others.

The source and wellspring of both these practices is prayer, where we encounter the hidden God. Prayer is giving ourselves over to divine presence, the ultimate act of self-surrender. Only by losing ourselves in God are we able to reach out to God's beloved children in charity and recognize our own dignity as members of the Body of Christ. For it is in prayer that we recognize why we surrender ourselves to others—for the sake of a deeper relationship with God.

Lent is really about discipline: the self-surrender that leads to right relationships. We are marked for self-surrender. The three-pronged penance outlined in the gospel leads us to see penance as having to do with right relationships with others, God, and self; it specifies what acts help us to "return to [God] with [our] whole heart" (first reading). The ashes we receive in the form of a cross on our foreheads on this day, then, remind us that the "now" mentioned in both the first and second readings imparts a real urgency about repenting. *Now* is the time.

Living the Paschal Mystery

One of the challenges of Ash Wednesday is to see this day as a *beginning* to Lent. It is well and good that so many people come to church on this day. The ashes we receive, however, are a sign that the call to penance and conversion lasts beyond a single day. The ashes are a reminder that conversion is ongoing, lasting even beyond our forty-day Lenten observance.

Further, the ashes are a sign that penance is an essential part of paschal mystery living. This, because they remind us that dying is part of the human condition ("Remember . . . you are dust and to dust you will return") and the only way to share in risen life is to embrace dying to self. Ash Wednesday and its special rite of signing the faithful with ashes is a singular call to die to ourselves—that every day we wear ashes.

Focusing the Gospel

Key words and phrases: alms, praying, fast, Father who is hidden

To the point: Ash Wednesday begins Lent and we naturally look to ourselves and our constant need for conversion. Surprisingly, the gospel begins not with ourselves (fasting) but with others (almsgiving). The source and wellspring of both these practices is prayer, where we encounter the hidden God.

Model Prayer of the Faithful

Presider: As we begin our Lenten journey toward conversion and new life in Christ, we ask God to help us be faithful to our Lenten penance.

Response:

Lord, hear our prayer.

Cantor:

we pray to the Lord,

That all Christians everywhere embrace penance with all their hearts . . . [pause]

That all peoples everywhere rend their hearts that God's peace may enter . . . [pause]

That the poor may live with dignity and receive all they need . . . [pause]

That each of us receive our ashes as a sign of our desire for conversion . . . [pause]

Presider: Merciful God, you hear the prayers of those who cry out to you: may our Lenten penance bring us closer to you and each other. We ask this through your Son, Jesus Christ our Lord. **Amen.**

Special Features of the Rite

The blessing and distribution of ashes after the homily takes the place of the penitential rite on Ash Wednesday. This first day of Lent is the context for the meaning of the giving of ashes. Receiving ashes ritualizes our response to hearing the gospel: response in humility (remembering who we are) and response in living (turning to God).

Many parishes have introduced special Lenten soup and bread suppers and encourage families to give to the poor the money they save by fasting. These are laudable practices and help us to remember that almsgiving (charity) is one of the three prongs of traditional Christian penance. This being said, it is also good to remind ourselves that fasting has a value in itself: by emptying ourselves (of food), we are creating the space to hunger for God. Thus fasting is a way to open ourselves up to the presence of God; by being empty we are able to fill ourselves with the nourishment that lasts forever.

FOR REFLECTION

· What I will do for Lent is . . . What Lent will do for me is . . .

· What will help me remain faithful to my Lenten practices is . . . What will make it hard for me to remain faithful is . . .

· What will increase my charity is . . . What will strengthen my resolve to fast and hunger for God is . . . What will deepen my prayer life . . .

Homily Points

• Etymology suggests that the word "Lent" is a shortening of the word "lengthen," used to indicate the increasing amount of light each day—always a harbinger of spring and new life. When we think "spring," usually what pops into our heads is spring cleaning. Lent is our time of spiritual "spring cleaning." We clean up the inner clutter in order to make more room for God and neighbor.

• All three traditional practices of Christian penance—almsgiving, prayer, fasting—are intended to help us spend Lent as a time to recognize and root out the "inner clutter" that has collected over time and bring us to deeper relationships with God and each other. Spent in this way, Lent is, indeed, a preparation for the renewal of our baptismal commitment and the celebration of the new life of Easter joy.

✝ SPIRITUALITY

GOSPEL ACCLAMATION
Matt 4:4b

One does not live on bread alone,
but on every word that comes forth from the
mouth of God.

Gospel

Mark 1:12-15; L23B

**The Spirit drove Jesus out into the
desert,
and he remained in the desert for
forty days, tempted by Satan.
He was among wild beasts,
and the angels ministered to him.**

**After John had been arrested,
Jesus came to Galilee proclaiming
the gospel of God:
"This is the time of fulfillment.
The kingdom of God is at hand.
Repent, and believe in the gospel."**

Reflecting on the Gospel

There are certain times in all of our lives when we need to go off and be alone to confront the "demons" that dwell within us. A grieving person may need time alone to confront the pain of loss and perhaps even a life that must be rearranged. People serious about their spiritual life take retreat time to examine their spiritual growth. Someone contemplating a job change might spend hours alone searching out possibilities on the Internet. Although we human beings are naturally social creatures, there are times and circumstances that dictate we be alone. Jesus in this gospel went out "into the desert" alone. He is on the brink of inaugurating his public ministry. Something new and important is about to happen. He does the natural thing: going off alone to think things through and confront the demons that would dissuade him from his mission.

The structure of this Sunday's gospel highlights two distinct but interrelated movements of the Christian life: Jesus goes "into the desert" to confront Satan; then he goes into Galilee to begin his mission to "proclaim the gospel." We enter our own Lenten desert—spend more time by ourselves—to confront our temptations and turn ourselves more perfectly toward God and each other so we can emerge as an Easter people ready to proclaim the Gospel. Lent is an intensification of what our day-to-day Christian living is all about: conversion and proclamation.

Confronting temptation and the sinfulness that keeps us from righteous Christian living is a necessary first step in the ongoing process of conversion. We must turn from sinfulness before we can assume to continue Jesus' mission. Since repentance, forgiveness, and belief are so central to Christian living, proclaiming the Gospel at least means that we turn from our sinful ways, forgive others, and express our belief by saying yes to God's will for us. None of these is easy to do, which is why proclaiming the Gospel is a lifelong mission. Proclaiming the Gospel doesn't mean we all have to go out on street corners and be Bible thumpers. More eloquent proclamation than words (even sacred words!) is the life we live. Thus conversion and proclamation are vigorously related: turning from sinfulness toward God enables us to proclaim by the goodness of our lives the Gospel of repentance and forgiveness.

Living the Paschal Mystery

The first two readings this Sunday suggest that our entry into the desert and the injunction to proclaim the Gospel are part of our baptismal response. In the baptismal waters we are plunged into the death of Christ to rise to the risen life that renews the earth. Baptism is our entry into the death/resurrection mystery of Christ and our entry into Lent and Easter. We begin Lent by reminding ourselves that we are a baptized people; at the end of Lent we renew our baptismal promises at the Easter Vigil.

Our baptismal identity with Christ confers on us the same mission as Christ: to proclaim the Gospel of repentance. We know full well that we never will be rid of temptations and sinfulness. But this fact of the human condition ought not keep us from taking up our baptismal mission to proclaim the Gospel. We proclaim the Gospel not because we are sinless, but because we have aligned ourselves with Christ. Our Lenten desert affords us the opportunity to examine how well we have aligned ourselves with Christ.

Focusing the Gospel

Key words and phrases: into the desert, tempted by Satan, proclaiming the gospel

To the point: The structure of this Sunday's gospel highlights two distinct but interrelated movements of the Christian life: Jesus goes "into the desert" to confront Satan; then he goes into Galilee to "proclaim the gospel." We enter our Lenten desert to confront our temptations and turn ourselves more perfectly toward God and each other so we can emerge as an Easter people ready to proclaim the Gospel. Lent is an intensification of what our day-to-day Christian living is all about: conversion and proclamation.

Connecting the Gospel

to the first two readings: Read together, the first and second readings strengthen our understanding of God's covenant with Noah in terms of our own baptismal covenant. The gospel injunction, "Repent and believe in the gospel," is a summary of this baptismal covenant: to turn toward God and others and overcome our tendency to turn more toward self.

to our experience: There is a temptation in our busy lives to avoid self-reflection and overlook how certain negative patterns of behavior are building up. Lent calls us to take sufficient time during our busy lives to do the necessary work of reflecting on our behaviors and relationships.

Connecting the Responsorial Psalm

to the readings: The refrain to this Sunday's responsorial psalm speaks about those who keep God's covenant. The readings for this Sunday shed light on what keeping the covenant entails. First, we are to contemplate its meaning. We discover that it is God who initiates the covenant and that the relationships God establishes stretch over an ever-widening circle of inclusion from us and our descendants to all living creatures to the entire earth (see first reading). We are also reminded that this covenant is grounded in our baptism (see second reading). Second, our manner of living is to be renewed by the covenant. We are to "appeal to God for a clear conscience" (second reading) and we remind God to be faithful to the divine side of the bargain (psalm). Finally, we are to commit ourselves to proclaiming with Jesus what we have encountered through this contemplation and renewal: the Good News of repentance and belief (gospel). May our singing of this refrain express our choice to engage in the contemplation and renewal to which the season of Lent calls us.

to cantor preparation: The progression of the responsorial psalm has you do what this Sunday's readings and the season of Lent invite: move from contemplation to proclamation. In the first two strophes you talk with God. You reflect on the meaning of the covenant and ask to be led toward more faithful observance of its ways. In the third strophe you speak to the people. You proclaim the God of mercy you have come to know because of the covenant. How might you deepen the contemplation needed for truer proclamation this Lent?

ASSEMBLY & FAITH-SHARING GROUPS

· The desert to which I feel called by the Spirit is . . . What I expect to encounter there is . . .

· The conversion I need to tend to is . . .

· The Good News my day-to-day Christian living proclaims is . . .

PRESIDERS

· My role of calling the community to conversion demands of me that . . .

DEACONS

· In order to serve God's people better, the conversion I need is . . .

HOSPITALITY MINISTERS

· My greeting strengthens the covenantal relationship among the assembly members when . . .

MUSIC MINISTERS

· The "wrong notes" Lent calls me to discern in my relationship with God and with others are . . .

ALTAR MINISTERS

· My serving at the altar helps me live my baptismal covenant with God and the community because . . .

LECTORS

· My proclamation of the word encourages the self-reflection to which Lent calls me by . . .

EXTRAORDINARY MINISTERS OF HOLY COMMUNION

· The manner in which I distribute Holy Communion strengthens the community's belief in the Gospel because . . .

Model Act of Penitence

Presider: Today's gospel invites us to go off to a deserted place to confront our temptations and to believe the gospel of repentance and forgiveness. We take a moment to ask God to open us to divine action within us so that our Lenten journey may be fruitful . . . [pause]

    Confiteor: I confess . . .

Homily Points

• Isn't it strange that we live in a society that focuses so much on the external self (what we wear, what we look like, what we possess), but too often ignores the depths of who we are (our values, who and how we love, our behavior toward others). Lent offers us the opportunity to do the necessary self-reflection to come into touch with the depths of our God-given identity.

• With Jesus, we enter the Lenten desert to discern who we are called to be. We identify what tempts us to avoid growing in the gift of our God-given identity as baptized members of the Body of Christ. We emerge renewed in our ability to "believe in the gospel" and proclaim this Good News by the quality of our daily living.

• The gospels of these six Sundays of Lent invite us to deepen our identity with Christ and our baptismal call to enter into his saving life and mission. The gospels will remind us over and over that this call demands the discipline of dying to self that the world may be raised to new life.

Model Prayer of the Faithful

Presider: Let us ask God to strengthen us on our Lenten journey.

Response: Lord, hear our prayer.

Cantor: we pray to the Lord,

That the church always be faithful in her proclamation of the Gospel, bringing the Good News of repentance and forgiveness to all who would hear . . . [pause]

That all the baptized of the world renew their covenant with God, renouncing sin and believing the Gospel . . . [pause]

That those who are suffering or in need be lifted up by our Lenten almsgiving . . . [pause]

That each of us walk with those who are to be baptized this Easter, strengthening their resolve by the quality of our own Gospel living . . . [pause]

Presider: Merciful God, you are near to those who cry out to you: hear these our prayers and be with us during our Lenten journey so that we may worthily celebrate your Son's resurrection. We ask this through that same Son, our Lord Jesus Christ. **Amen.**

OPENING PRAYER
Let us pray
    [at the beginning of Lent for the spirit
    of repentance]

Pause for silent prayer

Father,
through our observance of Lent,
help us to understand the meaning
of your Son's death and resurrection,
and teach us to reflect it in our lives.

Grant this through our Lord Jesus Christ,
    your Son,
who lives and reigns with you and the
    Holy Spirit,
one God, for ever and ever. **Amen.**

FIRST READING
Gen 9:8-15

God said to Noah and to his sons with him:
"See, I am now establishing my covenant
      with you
    and your descendants after you
    and with every living creature that was
      with you:
    all the birds, and the various tame and
      wild animals
    that were with you and came out of the
      ark.
I will establish my covenant with you,
    that never again shall all bodily
      creatures be destroyed
    by the waters of a flood;
    there shall not be another flood to
      devastate the earth."
God added:
    "This is the sign that I am giving for all
      ages to come,
    of the covenant between me and you
    and every living creature with you:
I set my bow in the clouds to serve as
    a sign
    of the covenant between me and the
      earth.
When I bring clouds over the earth,
    and the bow appears in the clouds,
I will recall the covenant I have made
    between me and you and all living
      beings,
    so that the waters shall never again
      become a flood
    to destroy all mortal beings."

RESPONSORIAL PSALM
Ps 25:4-5, 6-7, 8-9

R̝. (cf. 10) Your ways, O Lord, are love and
truth to those who keep your covenant.

Your ways, O LORD, make known to me;
    teach me your paths,
guide me in your truth and teach me,
    for you are God my savior.

R̝. Your ways, O Lord, are love and truth
to those who keep your covenant.

Remember that your compassion, O LORD,
    and your love are from of old.
In your kindness remember me,
    because of your goodness, O LORD.

R̝. Your ways, O Lord, are love and truth
to those who keep your covenant.

Good and upright is the LORD,
    thus he shows sinners the way.
He guides the humble to justice,
    and he teaches the humble his way.

R̝. Your ways, O Lord, are love and truth
to those who keep your covenant.

SECOND READING
1 Pet 3:18-22

Beloved:
Christ suffered for sins once,
    the righteous for the sake of the
        unrighteous,
    that he might lead you to God.
Put to death in the flesh,
    he was brought to life in the Spirit.
In it he also went to preach to the spirits
    in prison,
    who had once been disobedient
    while God patiently waited in the days
        of Noah
    during the building of the ark,
    in which a few persons, eight in all,
    were saved through water.
This prefigured baptism, which saves you
    now.
It is not a removal of dirt from the body
    but an appeal to God for a clear
        conscience,
    through the resurrection of Jesus Christ,
    who has gone into heaven
    and is at the right hand of God,
    with angels, authorities, and powers
        subject to him.

About Liturgy

Sacramental signs: The second reading assigned for this Sunday gives us a glimpse of how sacramental signs work. Peter says the water for baptism isn't about "a removal of dirt from the body but an appeal to God for a clear conscience." In other words, water is a sign used in baptism, but while its literal meaning (washing and sustaining life) does say something about what happens in the sacrament (wash us from sin and give us new life in God), the sacramental reality goes far beyond such a literal correspondence. St. Augustine says it well: sacraments are visible signs of an invisible reality or grace.

One renewal effort in liturgy is to maximize the sacramental signs so that they can more fully speak of the grace they signify. For example, many churches now have baptismal fonts large enough for immersion in which an abundance of water can be used when baptizing. Another example: GIRM no. 321 states that the bread used at Mass ought to look like food and be large enough to be broken into pieces of which at least some are given to the faithful.

Since Lent is a period of Christian discipline, there are any number of ways we might practice maximizing the liturgical symbols we use. For example, we might pay particular attention so that our sign of the cross at the beginning of Mass be well formed and deliberate. When receiving Communion we might intentionally and carefully place one hand within another, making a fitting and reverent "throne" on which to receive the Body of Christ. Even making a concerted effort to sing the service music and hymns at Mass (even if we don't have a very good voice) can be a fuller participation in the sacramental signs.

About Liturgical Music

Music of the Lenten season: What might seem a barrenness in our music during Lent (for example, the absence of the *Gloria* and of joyful Alleluias; quieter, less elaborate service music; perhaps *a capella* singing in some places) is not barren if we recognize the power of such music to deepen our participation in the celebration of Lent. Music chosen appropriately will mold us week after week in the meaning of this season. It will not do so automatically, however. We must give the music its power by singing it with understanding.

Music suggestion: One relatively new hymn worth incorporating into the parish repertoire is Bob Hurd's "Led by the Spirit" [BB, OFUV]. The first two verses speak of the Lenten tasks to which the Spirit calls us: fasting and prayer, desert contemplation, repentance, and renewal. The final two verses speak of the Easter rebirth to which the Spirit leads us: the waters of baptism, new freedom, deepened friendship with God. The hymn would be an appropriate song for the entrance, the preparation of the gifts, or the recessional during any or all of the first several weeks of Lent.

SPIRITUALITY

GOSPEL ACCLAMATION

cf. Matt 17:5

From the shining cloud the Father's voice is
    heard:
This is my beloved Son, hear him.

Gospel

Mark 9:2-10; L26B

Jesus took Peter, James, and
    John
  and led them up a high
      mountain apart by
      themselves.
And he was transfigured
    before them,
  and his clothes became
      dazzling white,
  such as no fuller on earth
      could bleach them.
Then Elijah appeared to them along
    with Moses,
  and they were conversing with Jesus.
Then Peter said to Jesus in reply,
  "Rabbi, it is good that we are here!
Let us make three tents:
  one for you, one for Moses, and one
      for Elijah."
He hardly knew what to say, they were
    so terrified.
Then a cloud came, casting a shadow
    over them;
  from the cloud came a voice,
  "This is my beloved Son. Listen to
      him."
Suddenly, looking around, they no
    longer saw anyone
  but Jesus alone with them.

As they were coming down from the
    mountain,
  he charged them not to relate what
      they had seen to anyone,
  except when the Son of Man had
      risen from the dead.
So they kept the matter to themselves,
  questioning what rising from the
      dead meant.

Reflecting on the Gospel

Little children can be so simple, literal, and naive; often that is what brings a chuckle to us as we observe their behavior. Sometimes when children don't want to hear what their parents are telling them, they put their hands over their ears, as if pretending not to hear excuses them from obeying. Lent is a time for us to remove our hands from our ears, listen to God, and learn again how to respond in obedience.

In the first reading, Abraham stands as a model of what it means to *listen* to God and obey: "Here I am" he answered whenever God called. Even flesh and blood could not keep Abraham from turning his eyes away from God—he was totally "devoted . . . to God," totally focused on listening to God and responding in obedience to the divine will. Had Abraham not *continued* listening, he would not have heard, "Do not lay your hand on the boy." Abraham was so "devoted . . . to God" that he not only heard and obeyed God's original command to sacrifice his beloved, only son Isaac, but also continued to *listen* to God, so heard the messenger's command not to harm him.

In the gospel, when Jesus and the disciples went "apart by themselves," no doubt they were also taking time to focus themselves totally on God. Jesus' transfiguration—a glimpse of future life and glory—is the fruit of his life of *listening* obedience, a model for our own going apart to listen for God's voice. God commands us to *listen* to the "beloved Son." Like Abraham, we do not know in advance what this listening might ask of us nor how our perception of God's will might change. We do know that Jesus' listening obedience to his Father's will led him to death. Disciples go where Jesus goes. If we are faithful on the journey, we know that we will share in Jesus' death, but also in his glory. The death of Isaac means no future for Abraham—no posterity. The death of Jesus means a future for everyone—his resurrection, foreshadowed in his transfiguration. In listening to Jesus, we are hearing God's will and opening ourselves to the new life promised by his resurrection.

Living the Paschal Mystery

Although we might not put our hands over our ears like little children, we do need to quiet the many and competing voices within and outside of us so we can hear *Jesus'* voice. And perhaps the most difficult voice to quell is that which keeps us from following Jesus in his willingness to die to self for the good of others. Yet, to *listen* to Jesus is to take upon ourselves lives obedient to the divine will, a kind of living which inevitably means we put God and the good of others ahead of our own selfish desires. We must learn to die to self so we can share in transfigured glory.

When we make it a habit to key into the dying and rising of the paschal mystery, we begin to see its rhythm everywhere. In this Sunday's gospel it plays out between transfigured glory in the first part of the gospel and the allusion to Jesus' dying in the last part ("rising from the dead"). In our daily lives the paschal mystery might play out between work and leisure, between times with loved ones and times away, between success and failure, between doing something we would enjoy and doing something someone else would enjoy more. Jesus' death and resurrection assures us that our faithful dying to self assures us a share in risen life. In our own lives we must begin to look for both the dying and the rising.

Focusing the Gospel

Key words and phrases: transfigured, beloved Son, Listen to him, rising from the dead

To the point: Abraham stands as a model of what it means to *listen* to God: "Here I am" he answered whenever God called (see first reading). Had Abraham not *continued* listening, he would not have heard, "Do not lay your hand on the boy." In the gospel, God commands us to *listen* to the "beloved Son." Like Abraham, we do not know in advance what this listening might ask of us nor how our perception of God's will might change. Only this kind of listening to God leads us to the new life which Jesus' transfiguration foreshadows.

Connecting the Gospel

to the second reading: Since God "did not spare his own Son," we can truly trust that listening to and obeying whatever God asks of us will surely take us, with Christ Jesus, through death to new life.

to Lenten experience: There is always a danger that our Lenten practices and how well we have accomplished them become our focus. The purpose of our Lenten practices, however, is to discipline ourselves to listen to God and grow in obedience to whatever God is asking of us.

Connecting the Responsorial Psalm

to the readings: Even though this Sunday's psalm refrain has us walking "before the Lord," we are, in fact, walking behind. The one who leads the way—to the mountain of glory and to the mountain of the cross—is Christ. He it is who first prays that he will be God's servant, that he will offer sacrifice, that he will keep his vows to the Lord (psalm). Because of his fidelity, he knows he will walk "in the land of the living" even though he must first pass through the valley of death. In singing this psalm we indicate that we are prepared—with Jesus and Abraham (first reading)—to live the demands of our covenant relationship with God whatever the cost. What inspires such courage is our confidence—with Jesus and Abraham—that God is for us in all things (second reading). What rewards such courage is our ultimate transformation—with Jesus and Abraham—in glory (gospel and first reading).

to cantor preparation: One reason this Sunday's responsorial psalm is appropriate for the early days of Lent is because it expresses, among other things, our promise to stay with the Lenten journey. How might it help your singing if you remembered that you make this promise with Jesus who has walked the road ahead of us and who "indeed intercedes for us" (second reading)?

ASSEMBLY & FAITH-SHARING GROUPS

- What enables me to keep listening to the "beloved Son" in my everyday life is . . . What impedes my listening to him is . . .
- Where I expect to hear the "beloved Son" is . . .
- Listening to God has "transfigured" me when . . .

PRESIDERS

- I model for the assembly listening to the "beloved Son" when I . . .

DEACONS

- My service is a kind of listening in that . . .

HOSPITALITY MINISTERS

- My greeting enables assembly members to listen to God's word during liturgy when I . . .

MUSIC MINISTERS

- The kind of listening I must do in my music ministry prepares me to better listen to God by . . . My listening to God helps me do my music ministry better by . . .

ALTAR MINISTERS

- For my service at the altar to be truly efficient, I must listen to . . .

LECTORS

- My preparing to proclaim God's word requires listening in that . . .

EXTRAORDINARY MINISTERS OF HOLY COMMUNION

- I am truly able to listen to each communicant's "Amen" when . . .

Model Act of Penitence

Presider: Jesus' transfiguration gives us a glimpse of the glory that awaits us, too, when we listen to Jesus. Let us prepare ourselves to celebrate this liturgy calling to mind the times when we have not listened to Jesus and have been unfaithful to God's will . . . [pause]

    Confiteor: I confess . . .

Homily Points

• It feels to us as if thousands of voices are shouting at us all the time. Some of these "voices" are external: friends, family, TV, cell phones, job responsibilities, advertising, etc. Other "voices" are internal: fears, confusion, inordinate expectations, heartache, "gotta . . . gotta . . . gotta . . .," "shouldn't . . . shouldn't . . . shouldn't . . .," etc. In the midst of all these "voices," how do we discern the voice of God?

• In the gospel, God shows us the way to discern the divine voice: listen to Jesus. Jesus himself showed us how to listen. He regularly went apart to reflect and pray. He listened to the needs and sufferings of the people. He discerned the meaning of events as they unfolded in his life. He listened to what was going on inside himself. In all things, he gave himself over to his Father's will. This kind of listening required dying to self (ultimately, even dying on the cross)—the only way to the transfigured glory of the resurrection.

• We experience the paschal mystery in our lives when we, too, faithfully listen the way Jesus did, open ourselves to God's will, and grow into the grace of the new life God promises. We are called to not only listen *to* Jesus, but also to live and respond *as* Jesus did.

Model Prayer of the Faithful

Presider: The God who asks us to listen to the beloved Son, is also a God who will surely listen to us. And so we pray.

Response:

Lord, hear our prayer.

Cantor:
we pray to the Lord,

That all members of the church may always listen to the voice of Jesus and faithfully follow him . . . [pause]

That leaders of nations may always listen to the cries of their people for justice and peace . . . [pause]

That the sick and the suffering may find hope for healing and strength in the transfigured Jesus . . . [pause]

That our Lenten penance lead us to greater obedience to God and to transfigured glory . . . [pause]

Presider: Loving God, you clothed your Son Jesus in transfigured glory: grant these our prayers that one day we might also share in that same glory. We ask this through that same Son Jesus Christ our Lord. **Amen.**

OPENING PRAYER
Let us pray

Pause for silent prayer

God our Father,
help us to hear your Son.
Enlighten us with your word,
that we may find the way to your glory.

We ask this through our Lord Jesus Christ,
    your Son,
who lives and reigns with you and the
    Holy Spirit,
one God, for ever and ever. **Amen.**

FIRST READING
Gen 22:1-2, 9a, 10-13, 15-18

God put Abraham to the test.
He called to him, "Abraham!"
"Here I am!" he replied.
Then God said:
    "Take your son Isaac, your only one,
        whom you love,
    and go to the land of Moriah.
There you shall offer him up as a holocaust
    on a height that I will point out to you."

When they came to the place of which
        God had told him,
    Abraham built an altar there and
        arranged the wood on it.
Then he reached out and took the knife to
        slaughter his son.
But the LORD's messenger called to him
        from heaven,
    "Abraham, Abraham!"
"Here I am!" he answered.
"Do not lay your hand on the boy," said the
        messenger.
"Do not do the least thing to him.
I know now how devoted you are to God,
    since you did not withhold from me
        your own beloved son."
As Abraham looked about,
    he spied a ram caught by its horns in
        the thicket.
So he went and took the ram
    and offered it up as a holocaust in place
        of his son.

Again the LORD's messenger called to
        Abraham from heaven and said:
"I swear by myself, declares the LORD,
    that because you acted as you did
    in not withholding from me your
        beloved son,
    I will bless you abundantly
    and make your descendants as countless
    as the stars of the sky and the sands of
        the seashore;

your descendants shall take possession
of the gates of their enemies,
and in your descendants all the nations
of the earth
shall find blessing—
all this because you obeyed my
command."

RESPONSORIAL PSALM

Ps 116:10, 15, 16-17, 18-19

R̊. (116:9) I will walk before the Lord, in
the land of the living.

I believed, even when I said,
"I am greatly afflicted."
Precious in the eyes of the LORD
is the death of his faithful ones.

R̊. I will walk before the Lord, in the land
of the living.

O LORD, I am your servant;
I am your servant, the son of your
handmaid;
you have loosed my bonds.
To you will I offer sacrifice of
thanksgiving,
and I will call upon the name of the
LORD.

R̊. I will walk before the Lord, in the land
of the living.

My vows to the LORD I will pay
in the presence of all his people,
in the courts of the house of the LORD,
in your midst, O Jerusalem.

R̊. I will walk before the Lord, in the land
of the living.

SECOND READING

Rom 8:31b-34

Brothers and sisters:
If God is for us, who can be against us?
He who did not spare his own Son
but handed him over for us all,
how will he not also give us everything
else along with him?
Who will bring a charge against God's
chosen ones?
It is God who acquits us, who will
condemn?
Christ Jesus it is who died—or, rather, was
raised—
who also is at the right hand of God,
who indeed intercedes for us.

About Liturgy

Lenten Sundays: There are many reminders during the Lenten Sunday Masses that we are observing a penitential season. The readings at the Sunday Masses bring to mind Lenten motifs and spur us on to fidelity in penance. Our Lenten Masses are less celebrative than even the Masses during Ordinary Time; for example, there is no *Gloria*, no alleluia, and less exuberant instrumentation. The penitential violet purple of the vestments and other appointments keep reminding us that we are in a penitential season, as well as the simplicity of the environment and the lack of flowers.

Nevertheless, the Sundays during Lent are not Lenten days at all. At a time when the symbolism of forty was heightened, the beginning of Lent was pushed back to the Wednesday before the first Sunday of Lent so there would be forty fasting days (hence, the period of Lent is actually longer than forty days). The Sundays of Lent are still days on which we celebrate the Lord's resurrection. Especially on this second Sunday of Lent when we hear about the transfiguration of Jesus are we reminded that dying always is accompanied by rising. In our very liturgical celebrations we see the paschal mystery rhythm. Lent is a time to practice the discipline of dying to self, yet we still have one day a week on which we always celebrate the new life promised by Jesus' resurrection. What might be ways we can truly celebrate new life even on Lenten Sundays, without getting out of the spirit of Lent?

About Liturgical Music

Music suggestions: Where Christ goes we follow, both to the mountain of glory and to the mountain of death. One way to express this during the Communion procession might be to combine "Let All Mortal Flesh Keep Silence," which speaks of Christ's heavenly descent and glory, with Sylvia Dunstan's "Transform Us" [RS] which deliberately addresses our transfiguration with Christ. Since both texts are set to the same tune (PICARDY), their juxtaposition would be easy and their unity evident. The choir could sing the first hymn, using an SATB or choral setting, and the assembly follow with the Dunstan hymn, accompanied with simple handbell chords at the beginning and ending of each phrase.

✠ SPIRITUALITY

GOSPEL ACCLAMATION
John 3:16

God so loved the world that he gave his only Son,
so that everyone who believes in him might have
    eternal life.

Gospel   John 2:13-25; L29B

Since the Passover of the Jews was near,
    Jesus went up to Jerusalem.
He found in the temple area those who sold
    oxen, sheep, and doves,
    as well as the money changers seated there.
He made a whip out of cords
    and drove them all out of the temple area,
        with the sheep and oxen,
    and spilled the coins of the money
        changers
    and overturned their tables,
    and to those who sold doves he said,
"Take these out of here,
    and stop making my Father's house
        a marketplace."
His disciples recalled the words of Scripture,
Zeal for your house will consume me.
At this the Jews answered and said to him,
"What sign can you show us for doing this?"
Jesus answered and said to them,
"Destroy this temple and in three days I
    will raise it up."
The Jews said,
"This temple has been under construction
    for forty-six years,
    and you will raise it up in three days?"
But he was speaking about the temple of his
    body.
Therefore, when he was raised from the dead,
    his disciples remembered that he had
        said this,
    and they came to believe the Scripture
    and the word Jesus had spoken.

While he was in Jerusalem for the feast of
    Passover,
    many began to believe in his name
    when they saw the signs he was doing.
But Jesus would not trust himself to them
    because he knew them all,
    and did not need anyone to testify about
        human nature.
He himself understood it well.

Year A readings may be used, see Appendix A,
pp. 270–272.

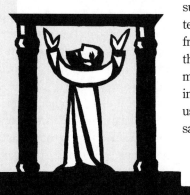

Reflecting on the Gospel

Sometimes we admire single-minded zeal and sometimes we don't. When the zeal helps others (for example, social workers who put in long hours out of compassion for the poor or for parentless children), we admire it. When the zeal hurts others (for example, when desire for promotion causes an employee to walk all over others), we disdain it. Jesus' zeal for his Father's house in this Sunday's gospel is certainly to be admired. As disciples, our driving force (zeal) must be as compelling as that of Jesus.

The zeal that drove Jesus to purify the Temple in such a dramatic way ultimately consumed him: the temple of his body was destroyed—only to be raised from the dead. His zeal was rooted in the conviction that life can come from death. Later, his disciples "remembered that he had said this" and came to believe in the resurrection. The zeal of Jesus must consume us who are his disciples today and bring us to the same belief as the disciples in the gospel—that our "deaths" can lead to new life. It is natural and good to seek life, even at all costs. The real issue becomes, however, that the life we ultimately seek can come only by embracing death. Christian commitment calls us to the same destiny as Jesus: our own bodies must be destroyed by self-giving and in this way we, too, are raised to new life.

The simple call of the gospel is to see the signs of God's presence in our midst. Unlike the signs the Jews asked to see in the gospel—signs that would justify Jesus' extraordinary action in the Temple—we are to ask and look for different signs, ones that draw us into the deepest reality of what it means to be a disciple of Jesus. Jesus showed us the signs so clearly: he was crucified (see second reading) and then raised up. Like Jesus, the zeal that ought to consume us, too, is a single-minded willingness to die to ourselves so that we, too, can live. Just as surely as God raised up Jesus from the dead, so will we be raised up. The signs are there for us to see and believe. Oh, the jealousy and fidelity of the Divine (see first reading)! Yes, God can be trusted with our very lives.

Living the Paschal Mystery

Most of us get lost in the demands of our everyday living. We get up in the morning, spend our day working, prepare and clean up after meals, shop and clean, drive the kids to soccer practice, worry about them, and do countless other things before we fall into bed at the end of the day—usually totally exhausted. In the midst of all this it is pretty difficult to be single-minded about anything except the tasks at hand. This gospel strikingly challenges us to keep doing all these everyday tasks—but for the right reason: zeal for God.

Ultimately, we are to offer up the temple of our own bodies by dying to self and only in this way can we share in the new life God offers us. This is our daily dying: not necessarily doing something different, but doing what is demanded of us out of zeal for God and the good of others. This is our daily rising: that we have kept our sight on God, have conformed ourselves more perfectly to Christ, and have believed the signs of God's presence to us.

Focusing the Gospel

Key words and phrases: Zeal . . . consume me, destroy . . . raise it up, remembered . . . believe

To the point: The zeal that drove Jesus to purify the Temple in such a dramatic way ultimately consumed him: the temple of his body was destroyed—only to be raised from the dead. His zeal was rooted in the conviction that life can come from death. Later, his disciples "remembered that he had said this" and came to believe in the resurrection. The zeal of Jesus must consume us who are his disciples today and bring us to the same belief as the disciples in the gospel—that our "deaths" can lead to new life.

Connecting the Gospel

to the second reading: Paul announces that we disciples "proclaim Christ crucified." The gospel announces that crucifixion ("Destroy this temple") always leads to resurrection ("raise it up").

to culture: Self-sacrificing zeal can lead to such singular attainments as Olympic medals, a medical or scientific breakthrough, election to public office. As personally demanding as this zeal may be, Christian zeal requires even more: that we give ourselves over, with Christ, to "death" so that we may be raised to new life.

Connecting the Responsorial Psalm

to the readings: The responsorial psalm for this Sunday is taken from Psalm 19 which unfolds in three parts. Verses 2-7 sing about the sun running its course from one end of the heavens to the other, shedding light and heat on all corners of the earth. Verses 8-11 sing about God's Law that sheds goodness over all aspects of human life. Verses 12-15 are an acknowledgment of human sin and a plea for God's help to stay faithful to the guidance the Law provides.

Just as the sun gives light to the earth, so does the Law give light to humankind. Both leave no corner in shadow. Both are gifts of God. Yet, how often humans choose to live in darkness. In the Temple, Jesus, who understands human nature well, confronts this darkness with directness and force (gospel). He is "the power . . . and the wisdom of God" (second reading) who brings the light of God's judgment to bear upon human behavior. He is the personification of the covenant and the Law whose words promise us everlasting life (psalm refrain).

to cantor preparation: The Law of God (first reading and psalm) and the wisdom of God (second reading) come together in Jesus. When you sing about the Law in the responsorial psalm, then, you sing about Jesus. As you reflect on the psalm, substitute the name of Jesus for the word "Law"; for example, "Jesus is perfect, refreshing the soul; Jesus is trustworthy, giving wisdom to the simple," etc. What insights into Jesus does this yield? How might it affect your singing of this psalm?

**ASSEMBLY &
FAITH-SHARING GROUPS**

· What really consumes me is . . .

· What strengthens my zeal to live and die as Jesus did is . . . What weakens my zeal is . . .

· I experience new life when . . .

PRESIDERS

· My zeal for God's house is evident to the assembly when . . .

DEACONS

· My zeal for those in need strengthens them and lifts them up because . . .

HOSPITALITY MINISTERS

· My greeting communicates Jesus' zeal for God's house when . . .

MUSIC MINISTERS

· The kind of zeal I need for music ministry is . . . This zeal calls me to die to myself when . . .

ALTAR MINISTERS

· My service is an expression of my zeal for dying and rising because . . .

LECTORS

· My zeal for God's word is sounded in my proclamation when . . .

**EXTRAORDINARY MINISTERS
OF HOLY COMMUNION**

· My zeal for the holy is expressed in my distribution of Holy Communion when I . . .

Model Act of Penitence

Presider: Jesus was so zealous in his love for his Father that he drove the money changers out of the Temple. As we prepare for this liturgy, may we open our hearts to God's love for us and root out anything that keeps us from zealously loving God in return . . . [pause]

Confiteor: I confess . . .

Homily Points

• We tend to shy away from anything which smacks of death or dying. For example, we spend billions on skin creams, hair dyes, and cosmetic surgeries to hide signs of inevitable aging. The increasing popularity of cryogenics indicates an attempt to avoid death altogether. We avoid dying metaphorically whenever, for example, we shy away from taking a public stand against something we know is wrong because we fear the consequences. By contrast, this Sunday's gospel calls us to confront "death" head-on and accept it.

• Jesus' zeal was such that the possibility of death did not deter him from working to bring life and new hope for all those he encountered. In fact, he knew that death was necessary for new life. In dying—giving ourselves over for the good of others—we already rise to new life.

• "Death" takes many different forms. In the gospel, Jesus stood up for what was right, even though he knew the personal price he would pay. In our own lives, for example, we might be called to die to holding onto a certain stance that prevents our growing. We might need to apologize to another, even though it "kills" us. We might have to speak out even though it is unpopular to do so. Jesus teaches us that such deaths are the necessary road to new life.

Model Prayer of the Faithful

Presider: God knows our human nature and our needs so well. We pray with confidence that we will be heard.

Response: Lord, hear our prayer.

Cantor: we pray to the Lord,

That all members of Christ's Body may be zealous in their love for God . . . [pause]

That zeal for self-giving may bring all people to salvation . . . [pause]

That zeal for those who are sick or suffering may lead us to care for their needs . . . [pause]

That those preparing for the rites of initiation at Easter may be zealous in their commitment to follow the Gospel . . . [pause]

That all of us willingly embrace dying to ourselves so that we might share in Christ's risen glory . . . [pause]

Presider: Gracious and loving God, you show infinite zeal in your care for us: hear these our prayers and increase our zeal to follow your Son through death to new life. We ask this through that same Son, Jesus Christ our Savior. **Amen.**

OPENING PRAYER

Let us pray

Pause for silent prayer

Father,
you have taught us to overcome our sins
by prayer, fasting and works of mercy.
When we are discouraged by our
     weakness,
give us confidence in your love.

We ask this through our Lord Jesus Christ,
     your Son,
who lives and reigns with you and the
     Holy Spirit,
one God, for ever and ever. **Amen.**

FIRST READING

Exod 20:1-17

In those days, God delivered all these
     commandments:
  "I, the LORD, am your God,
    who brought you out of the land of
       Egypt, that place of slavery.
You shall not have other gods besides me.
You shall not carve idols for yourselves
    in the shape of anything in the sky
       above
    or on the earth below or in the waters
       beneath the earth;
    you shall not bow down before them or
       worship them.
For I, the LORD, your God, am a jealous
     God,
    inflicting punishment for their fathers'
       wickedness
    on the children of those who hate me,
    down to the third and fourth generation;
    but bestowing mercy down to the
       thousandth generation
    on the children of those who love me
       and keep my commandments.

"You shall not take the name of the LORD,
     your God, in vain.
For the LORD will not leave unpunished
    the one who takes his name in vain.

"Remember to keep holy the sabbath day.
Six days you may labor and do all your
     work,
    but the seventh day is the sabbath of
       the LORD, your God.
No work may be done then either by you,
    or your son or daughter,
    or your male or female slave, or your
       beast,
    or by the alien who lives with you.

In six days the LORD made the heavens and
the earth,
the sea and all that is in them;
but on the seventh day he rested.
That is why the LORD has blessed the
sabbath day and made it holy.

"Honor your father and your mother,
that you may have a long life in the land
which the LORD, your God, is giving you.
You shall not kill.
You shall not commit adultery.
You shall not steal.
You shall not bear false witness against
your neighbor.
You shall not covet your neighbor's house.
You shall not covet your neighbor's wife,
nor his male or female slave, nor his ox
or ass,
nor anything else that belongs to him."

or

Exod 20:1-3, 7-8, 12-17

In those days, God delivered all these
commandments:
"I, the LORD, am your God,
who brought you out of the land of
Egypt, that place of slavery.
You shall not have other gods besides me.

"You shall not take the name of the LORD,
your God, in vain.
For the LORD will not leave unpunished
the one who takes his name in vain.

"Remember to keep holy the sabbath day.
Honor your father and your mother,
that you may have a long life in the land
which the LORD, your God, is giving you.
You shall not kill.
You shall not commit adultery.
You shall not steal.
You shall not bear false witness against
your neighbor.
You shall not covet your neighbor's house.
You shall not covet your neighbor's wife,
nor his male or female slave, nor his ox
or ass,
nor anything else that belongs to him."

RESPONSORIAL PSALM
Ps 19:8, 9, 10, 11

SECOND READING
1 Cor 1:22-25

See Appendix A, p. 269.

About Liturgy

The Lenten Lectionary: There is perhaps no other portion of the Lectionary that has such strong paschal mystery motifs as the selections for Lent. Already on the first two Sundays of Lent the gospels—the temptation in the desert and the transfiguration—speak eloquently of dying and rising. In this year B the gospels of the third to fifth Sundays of Lent (which we begin this Sunday) also focus on the dying and rising mystery which is clearly evident in the selections. Although year B draws on Mark's gospel, we notice that all three of these Lenten Sunday gospels are from John. One of the earliest ways of keeping Lent (probably dating from the third century) was to read John's gospel through, culminating in the proclamation of John's passion on Good Friday. We see this pattern clearly this year.

Unlike other Sundays of the year, the first readings don't specifically relate to the gospels (although often there are converging themes). Instead, the first readings recount major salvation history events; these remind us that the paschal mystery is already foreshadowed in God's plan of salvation unfolding from the beginning of creation.

The second readings are the least related to each other but all of them speak of Christ's dying and rising and, therefore, are commentaries on the paschal mystery. As often occurs during the festal seasons, the second readings give us insight into the meaning of the season and feast that is being celebrated. To more fully appreciate the careful construction of the Lectionary, it is always helpful to see the readings in relation to each other and the season. This hermeneutic (way of interpreting) guides all our reflections in *Living Liturgy™*.

About Liturgical Music

Music suggestions: An excellent "old standby" appropriate for this Sunday would be Lucien Deiss's "Grant to Us, O Lord" [CBW3, CH, RS, WC]. The verses speak of God's recreating us by planting the Law deep within us and forgiving our failures. Even if it is not included in the hymn book or missalette, assemblies can easily sing this refrain. The song would work well as an entrance processional with choir or cantor singing the verses and assembly repeating the refrain. The song would also be well suited for the Communion procession. David Haas' "Deep Within" expresses the same themes as "Grant to Us" and would fit either the preparation of the gifts or Communion. Bernadette Farrell's "Unless a Grain of Wheat" would be a fitting Communion song in light of the gospel reading's stark focus on the imminence of Jesus' death.

SPIRITUALITY

GOSPEL ACCLAMATION
Ps 84:5

Blessed are those who dwell in your house, O Lord,
they never cease to praise you.

Gospel   Luke 2:41-51a; L543

Each year Jesus' parents went to Jerusalem
    for the feast of Passover,
    and when he was twelve years old,
    they went up according to festival custom.
After they had completed its days, as they
        were returning,
    the boy Jesus remained behind in
        Jerusalem,
    but his parents did not know it.
Thinking that he was in the caravan,
    they journeyed for a day
    and looked for him among their
        relatives and acquaintances,
    but not finding him,
    they returned to Jerusalem to look for
        him.
After three days they found him in the
    temple,
    sitting in the midst of the teachers,
    listening to them and asking them
        questions,
    and all who heard him were astounded
    at his understanding and his answers.
When his parents saw him,
    they were astonished,
    and his mother said to him,
    "Son, why have you done this to us?
Your father and I have been looking for you
        with great anxiety."
And he said to them,
    "Why were you looking for me?
Did you not know that I must be in my
        Father's house?"
But they did not understand what he said to
    them.
He went down with them and came to
    Nazareth,
    and was obedient to them.

or Matt 1:16, 18-21, 24a in Appendix A, p. 273.

See Appendix A, p. 273, for the other readings.

Reflecting on the Gospel

The gospels rarely mention Joseph by name or even refer to him. Yet, we honor Joseph as a great saint to this very day because he was such a good and faithful father. Joseph helped form Jesus as he grew and worried about him just like any parent. The gospel mentions that Jesus "was obedient to" Mary and Joseph after they found him in the Temple and returned to Nazareth. Conversely, Joseph was also the obedient one who cooperated with God in the divine plan of salvation.

In this faithfulness and trustworthiness Joseph is a model. In all things he was guided by God, responded to God's call, and was faithful to God's plan of salvation. This simple carpenter of Nazareth models for us what remaining in "my Father's house" really means: doing God's will in all things, both the great and the simple. No doubt many times Joseph was filled with wonder, awe, and not a little bit of confusion and consternation. After all, Jesus was no ordinary child—Mary did not conceive and give birth to him like an ordinary child; no ordinary child would remain three days apart from parents and, when found, be comfortably "listening . . . and asking . . . questions" of the teachers in the Temple, seemingly unaware of the heartache he caused his parents. No, this is no ordinary child; neither is Joseph an ordinary father.

It does not surprise us that the promises of God should come to fulfillment through such great figures as David (first reading) and Abraham (second reading). But the greatest of promises (the coming of the Savior, Jesus) is entrusted to the care of a simple man and woman who were faithful to Jewish customs, looked with great anxiety for their lost Son, found him, confronted him, and took him home where he was obedient to them. This feast can teach us that God did not depend on the rich and famous to accomplish salvation; he most often chooses simple folks and only asks of them obedience and fidelity. In this we can take great comfort on this feast: God only asks of us, too, obedience and fidelity. Thus do we also cooperate in the divine plan of salvation.

Living the Paschal Mystery

Sometimes our expectations of ourselves with respect to our religious observances are great—especially during Lent. We begin with great fervor and take on demanding Lenten penance, usually only to fizzle out or continue the penance with a steadfast doggedness that borders on penance for the sake of penance and completing a task. This solemnity and St. Joseph remind us that God's promises come to fulfillment in our faithfulness to the everyday responsibilities that are ours. Holiness isn't necessarily won by great things; we grow into it by faithfulness to whatever God calls us.

Beyond the infancy narratives in which Joseph is shown as one who cooperates perfectly with God's plans for salvation, the gospels say nothing else about him. It is precisely this "hidden life" that can be both model and encouragement for us in our everyday paschal mystery living. By responding to God and being a good husband to Mary and foster father to Jesus, Joseph fulfilled his vocation. Similarly, we fulfill our own vocations in the simple, everyday tasks. Paschal mystery living is about faithfulness in the little things as much as it is about dying on the cross. Both lead to risen life. This is why we call Joseph "saint."

Focusing the Gospel

Key words and phrases: Jesus' parents, according to . . . custom, was obedient to them

To the point: It does not surprise us that the promises of God should come to fulfillment through such great figures as David (first reading) and Abraham (second reading). But the greatest of promises (the coming of the Savior, Jesus) is entrusted to the care of a simple man and woman who were faithful to Jewish customs, looked with great anxiety for their lost Son, found him, confronted him, and took him home where he was obedient to them. Although we know little else about the man Joseph, we honor him as a model of faithfulness and righteousness.

Model Act of Penitence

Presider: St. Joseph is a model for us of one who was faithful to God's plan of salvation. Hidden life though he led, he is celebrated as the patron of the universal church. Let us ask God for the grace to be faithful as Joseph . . . [pause]

> Lord Jesus, you are Son of God and foster son of Joseph: Lord . . .
>
> Christ Jesus, you now dwell in glory in your Father's house: Christ . . .
>
> Lord Jesus, you were obedient to Joseph and Mary: Lord . . .

Model Prayer of the Faithful

Presider: We make our needs known to a caring God, confident that they will be heard through the intercession of St. Joseph.

Response:

Lord, hear our prayer.

Cantor:

we pray to the Lord,

For the church, under the protection of St. Joseph . . . [pause]

For all peoples, called to salvation . . . [pause]

For laborers, whose work brings dignity . . . [pause]

For all of us here, called to be obedient to God . . . [pause]

Presider: Good and gracious God, you used the simple carpenter Joseph as an instrument for salvation: hear these our prayers that all of us might come to live with you and your Son, Jesus Christ with the Holy Spirit, one God, for ever and ever. **Amen.**

OPENING PRAYER

Let us pray

Pause for silent prayer

Father,
you entrusted our Savior to the care of
    St. Joseph.
By the help of his prayers
may your Church continue to serve its Lord,
    Jesus Christ,
who lives and reigns with you and the Holy
    Spirit,
one God, for ever and ever. **Amen.**

FOR REFLECTION

· I look for, confront, find Jesus when . . .

· What I learn from Joseph is . . .

· Like Joseph, I am faithful and righteous when . . . I am unlike Joseph when . . .

Homily Points

• Some interesting customs surround our relationship with St. Joseph. For example, someone wishing to sell a house might bury a statue of St. Joseph until the house is sold. We do such things because we depend upon such virtues as his care and protection.

• This gospel portrays the great lengths to which Mary and Joseph would go to care for and protect the child Jesus. They simply were doing what any loving parents would do. Holiness is incarnated in being faithful to the everyday demands our life situation brings us.

✠ SPIRITUALITY

GOSPEL ACCLAMATION
John 3:16

God so loved the world that he gave his only Son,
so everyone who believes in him might have
eternal life.

Gospel

John 3:14-21; L32B

Jesus said to Nicodemus:
"Just as Moses lifted up the serpent
in the desert,
so must the Son of Man be lifted up,
so that everyone who believes in him
may have eternal life."

For God so loved the world that he gave
his only Son,
so that everyone who believes in him
might not perish
but might have eternal life.
For God did not send his Son into the
world to condemn the world,
but that the world might be saved
through him.
Whoever believes in him will not be
condemned,
but whoever does not believe has
already been condemned,
because he has not believed in the
name of the only Son of God.
And this is the verdict,
that the light came into the world,
but people preferred darkness to
light,
because their works were evil.
For everyone who does wicked things
hates the light
and does not come toward the light,
so that his works might not be
exposed.
But whoever lives the truth comes to
the light,
so that his works may be clearly seen
as done in God.

Year A readings may be used, see Appendix A,
pp. 274–276.

Reflecting on the Gospel

A parish was having a Lenten mission, and for four nights precious, beautiful, freckle-faced fourth-grader Anna came to church with her mom and dad. She was especially attentive when Father explained how baptisms were celebrated in the early church. Unlike her parish, in the early church the baptismal font was large, the one to be baptized stepped down into the pool, and was pushed down and held under three times, "In the name of the Father," "and of the Son," "and of the Holy Spirit." At the end of the mission Father asked her what she learned, having come so faithfully and been so attentive. Without missing a beat, she answered, "In the fourth century they dunked people." In fact, all of us at baptism were "dunked"—if not literally, then metaphorically. The faith/belief mentioned in both the second reading and gospel allude to our self-surrender at baptism, which begins a life lived as followers of Christ. Even more: at baptism we are plunged into Christ's death so that we might rise to new life with him (see Rom 6:5). This dying and rising mystery is the paschal mystery. Through it we are joined to Christ in his work of salvation.

The gospel for this Sunday takes us to the dying and rising of the paschal mystery—Christ is "lifted up" on the cross so that those who believe "have eternal life." The mystery lies in this: "God so loved the world" that even when we are still "dead in our transgressions" (second reading) and "prefer[ ] darkness" (gospel), God sends the Light of life to us. The gospel challenges us to the kind of firm belief that leads us to "live[ ] the truth" and walk in the light. It challenges us to the kind of firm belief that even enables us to die to ourselves. This gospel, coming in the middle of Lent (this is traditionally called "*Laetare*" Sunday), is a reminder of what Lent is truly about and, indeed, what our whole Christian living is about.

The words "believe" and "light" occur five times each in this gospel and the two words are not unrelated. The light (= Christ) enables us to see; in John's gospel, seeing is believing. Our coming to the light to see and believe is expressed in "works . . . done in God." God's work is this: to die to self so that we can be raised to new life. God demonstrates great love for us by sending the Son to be lifted up on the cross and then raised to eternal life and glory. We demonstrate our great love for God by doing the work of God—dying and rising, conforming ourselves so completely to Christ that we cooperate in his very work of salvation.

Living the Paschal Mystery

The contradiction in the paschal mystery is that what we abhor—the cross—becomes the instrument of redemption. God saves the Israelites from death but in the paschal mystery we must embrace death for the only way to eternal life is by dying to ourselves, by allowing ourselves to be lifted up like Christ. Our good works (reaching out to others, doing our daily tasks with love and care, acting justly and charitably, etc.), then, are our way of being "lifted up." This is how we are crucified, so that we might live.

There are only three weeks of Lent left. Now is the time to renew our resolve to embrace dying to self so that we might truly rise in joy and life on Easter.

Focusing the Gospel

Key words and phrases: lifted up, have eternal life, God so loved, preferred darkness, lives the truth, comes to the light

To the point: This gospel takes us to the dying and rising of the paschal mystery—Christ is "lifted up" on the cross so that those who believe "have eternal life." The mystery lies in this: "God so loved the world" that even when we are still "dead in our transgressions" (second reading) and "prefer[ ] darkness" (gospel), God sends the Light of life to us. The gospel challenges us to the kind of firm belief that leads us to "live[ ] the truth" and walk in the light.

Connecting the Gospel

to the Third Sunday of Lent: The gospel for the Third Sunday of Lent also confronted us with the paschal mystery of Jesus' body being destroyed and raised up. This Sunday we see that same mystery, now demanding a choice from us—darkness or light, unbelief or belief, condemnation or salvation.

to culture: Sometimes we choose to do difficult things in our lives because the end is a good; for example, parents lose sleep for the sake of sick children or work more than one job for the sake of the family's welfare. We make these choices out of love and, moreover, they are actually a part of our own living of the paschal mystery, which leads us to new and deeper life.

Connecting the Responsorial Psalm

to the readings: Psalm 137 can only be understood in the context of Israel's exile in Babylon. The exile was devastating and the people had brought it upon themselves through their unfaithfulness to the covenant (first reading). Psalm 137 echoes the bitterness of the exile and is a reflection upon the utter barrenness of that experience. It is also a plea never again to forget what it means to be God's people.

The psalm is a direct response to this Sunday's first reading. The Israelites promise never again to forget the homeland destroyed by enemies and later restored by God. In essence they promise never to forget what God did for them in releasing them from exile. On our own lips the psalm is a promise never to forget what God has done to release us from the exile of sin and death: given the life of his own Son (gospel). May we never forget the unfathomable love God has for us. May we always walk in the light of this truth (gospel).

to cantor preparation: This Sunday's responsorial psalm will be a difficult one to sing unless you can see it as a typology of your—and everyone's—experience of sin and redemption. When have you been in exile from God and how has God drawn you back?

ASSEMBLY & FAITH-SHARING GROUPS

· I have experienced God's great love for me when . . .

· I am prone to "prefer[ ] darkness" when . . . Who and what lead me back to the Light are . . .

· I help others come to believe in Jesus by . . .

PRESIDERS

· My ministry helps others believe in God's love for them when I . . .

DEACONS

· My service lifts up Jesus for all to see when . . .

HOSPITALITY MINISTERS

· My greeting incarnates God's love for the members of the assembly when I . . .

MUSIC MINISTERS

· My music ministry is a "work . . . done in God" when . . .

ALTAR MINISTERS

· My service at the altar calls me to die to self in these ways . . .

LECTORS

· My prayerful reading of Scripture and preparation for proclamation leads me to the Light by . . .

EXTRAORDINARY MINISTERS OF HOLY COMMUNION

· Bringing Holy Communion to the sick and homebound shows God's great love for them when . . .

✝ CELEBRATION

Model Act of Penitence

Presider: On this fourth Sunday of Lent we are reminded once again that Jesus was lifted up on the cross to give us eternal life. Let us take a moment to reflect on God's gift to us in Jesus and ask God's pardon for our failures . . . [pause]

    Confiteor: I confess . . .

Homily Points

• Throughout our lives we undergo many passages. As we grow up, we experience many kinds of "growing pains" (physical, emotional, spiritual), and our parents are often the ones who explain, encourage, and allay our fears. We also experience many kinds of transitions: from parents providing a home to independent living; from high school to college; from single life to married life. All of these passages bring challenge, excitement, fear. This is no less true of our growing in being followers of Jesus. Looking to Jesus, we find the One who, having gone before us, can help us pass over to new life.

• The most important and continuing "passing over" we face is begun in baptism where we are plunged into Christ's death so to rise to new life. This *is* the paschal mystery. The dying and rising rhythm of the paschal mystery is the *very pattern* of our Christian living and discipleship.

• Daily living calls us to die to self for the good of others. In the very dying, we pattern ourselves after the life and ministry of Jesus who, although exhausted spoke to the little ones, always cured those who came to him, fully accepted people who were sinners. In this dying is our life.

Model Prayer of the Faithful

Presider: The God who loved the world so much to give the only Son for us will surely hear and answer our prayers.

Response: Lord, hear our prayer.

Cantor: we pray to the Lord,

For all members of the church, that by dying to themselves for the sake of others they might have eternal life . . . [pause]

For all people of the world, that by believing in God's mercy and love they might have eternal life . . . [pause]

For all those in need, that they might receive from the bounty of others . . . [pause]

For all those preparing for the Easter sacraments, that they might come to greater belief and commitment . . . [pause]

For all of us here, that our belief might be firm and our love might be full . . . [pause]

Presider: God of mercy and love, you call us out of darkness to eternal light: hear these our prayers that we might one day live forever with you and your Son Jesus Christ, together with the Holy Spirit, one God, for ever and ever. **Amen.**

ALTERNATIVE OPENING PRAYER

Let us pray

Pause for silent prayer

God our Father,
your Word, Jesus Christ, spoke peace to a
    sinful world
and brought mankind the gift of
    reconciliation
by the suffering and death he endured.
Teach us, the people who bear his name,
to follow the example he gave us:
may our faith, hope, and charity
turn hatred to love, conflict to peace, death
    to eternal life.

We ask this through Christ our Lord.
    Amen.

FIRST READING

2 Chr 36:14-16, 19-23

In those days, all the princes of Judah, the
    priests, and the people
    added infidelity to infidelity,
    practicing all the abominations of the
        nations
    and polluting the LORD's temple
    which he had consecrated in Jerusalem.

Early and often did the LORD, the God of
    their fathers,
    send his messengers to them,
    for he had compassion on his people
        and his dwelling place.
But they mocked the messengers of God,
    despised his warnings, and scoffed at
        his prophets,
    until the anger of the LORD against his
        people was so inflamed
    that there was no remedy.
Their enemies burnt the house of God,
    tore down the walls of Jerusalem,
    set all its palaces afire,
    and destroyed all its precious objects.
Those who escaped the sword were
    carried captive to Babylon,
    where they became servants of the king
        of the Chaldeans and his sons
    until the kingdom of the Persians came
        to power.
All this was to fulfill the word of the LORD
    spoken by Jeremiah:
    "Until the land has retrieved its lost
        sabbaths,
    during all the time it lies waste it shall
        have rest
    while seventy years are fulfilled."

In the first year of Cyrus, king of Persia,
   in order to fulfill the word of the LORD
      spoken by Jeremiah,
   the LORD inspired King Cyrus of Persia
   to issue this proclamation throughout
      his kingdom,
   both by word of mouth and in writing:
"Thus says Cyrus, king of Persia:
All the kingdoms of the earth
   the LORD, the God of heaven, has given
      to me,
   and he has also charged me to build him
      a house
   in Jerusalem, which is in Judah.
Whoever, therefore, among you belongs to
      any part of his people,
   let him go up, and may his God be with
      him!"

RESPONSORIAL PSALM
Ps 137:1-2, 3, 4-5, 6

R̸. (6ab) Let my tongue be silenced, if I
ever forget you!

By the streams of Babylon
   we sat and wept
   when we remembered Zion.
On the aspens of that land
   we hung up our harps.

R̸. Let my tongue be silenced, if I ever
forget you!

For there our captors asked of us
   the lyrics of our songs,
and our despoilers urged us to be joyous:
   "Sing for us the songs of Zion!"

R̸. Let my tongue be silenced, if I ever
forget you!

How could we sing a song of the LORD
   in a foreign land?
If I forget you, Jerusalem,
   may my right hand be forgotten!

R̸. Let my tongue be silenced, if I ever
forget you!

May my tongue cleave to my palate
   if I remember you not,
if I place not Jerusalem
   ahead of my joy.

R̸. Let my tongue be silenced, if I ever
forget you!

SECOND READING
Eph 2:4-10

See Appendix A, p. 274.

About Liturgy

Best way to prepare for the liturgy: Because Scripture and the Lectionary are open to many interpretations, it is especially important that we reflect on the Scriptures before we come to Sunday Mass so we can be ready to hear God's word with all its depth and richness. The best preparation for the Liturgy of the Word is by reading the Sunday Scriptures—especially the gospel—over early in the week before and then see how God's word begins to play itself out in our daily living. Let that word challenge us to live differently. Let that word invite us to new understanding. Let that word encourage us to die to ourselves every day so that we might more perfectly live the truth that only comes from God's light.

There is no substitution for good preparation of liturgy and the best preparation is by the way we live. A wonderful celebration of liturgy will be greatly aided by preparing well to hear the word on Sunday and by the kind of Christian living that evidences we are consciously trying to live God's word in our everyday lives. This is when liturgy comes alive and is, indeed, a true celebration.

About Liturgical Music

Music suggestions: "By the Babylonian Rivers" [RS, W3] is a paraphrase of Psalm 137 set to a Latvian folk tune. The final verse connects cross and resurrection, "Let the Cross be benediction For those bound in tyranny; by the power of resurrection Loose them from captivity." The hymn would be suitable for the entrance song or for the preparation of the gifts.

Psalm 137 occurs as the responsorial psalm only this once in the three-year Lectionary cycle. Its intensely plaintive text calls for an equally plaintive setting. RS and W3 use a Gelineau tone effectively set for either organ or woodwinds. The refrain by Frank Schoen is chromatically intense, and may be difficult for the assembly to get on first hearing, but is worth the effort. WC has a through-composed setting by Mike Hay that requires a competent cantor who can handle a high tessitura and a melodic line independent from the accompaniment. Both of these settings are immensely expressive of the psalm text.

On another note, the early church used the image of a harp hanging on a tree as a typology of the crucifixion. Knowing the typology sheds new light on our use of this psalm this Sunday. In Old Testament times it was common practice to hang Aeolian-type harps on trees so that the wind could play them. Because prophetic trances were sometimes induced by playing on "lyres, tambourines, flutes and harps" (1 Sam 10:5) to "hang up the harp" was a metaphor for the cessation of prophecy. Harps and prophecy were also associated with David whom Scripture celebrates as a harpist and later Jewish tradition considers a prophet. In Christian typology, which pairs Jesus with all kinds of Old Testament symbols, Jesus is not only the star of David and from the House of David, he is also referred to as the harp of David. Thus, to hang the harp (Jesus) on the tree (cross) became a typology for the crucifixion.

SPIRITUALITY

GOSPEL ACCLAMATION
John 1:14ab
The Word became flesh and made his dwelling
    among us
and we saw his glory.

Gospel   Luke 1:26-38; L545

The angel Gabriel was sent from God
    to a town of Galilee called Nazareth,
    to a virgin betrothed to a man named
        Joseph,
    of the house of David,
    and the virgin's name was Mary.
And coming to her, he said,
    "Hail, full of grace! The Lord is with you."
But she was greatly troubled at what was said
    and pondered what sort of greeting this
        might be.
Then the angel said to her,
    "Do not be afraid, Mary,
    for you have found favor with God.
Behold, you will conceive in your womb and
        bear a son,
    and you shall name him Jesus.
He will be great and will be called Son of
        the Most High,
    and the Lord God will give him the throne
        of David his father,
    and he will rule over the house of Jacob
        forever,
    and of his Kingdom there will be no end."
But Mary said to the angel,
    "How can this be,
    since I have no relations with a man?"
And the angel said to her in reply,
    "The Holy Spirit will come upon you,
    and the power of the Most High will over-
        shadow you.
Therefore the child to be born
    will be called holy, the Son of God.
And behold, Elizabeth, your relative,
    has also conceived a son in her old age,
    and this is the sixth month for her who
        was called barren;
    for nothing will be impossible for God."
Mary said, "Behold, I am the handmaid of
        the Lord.
May it be done to me according to your
        word."
Then the angel departed from her.

See Appendix A, p. 276, for the other readings.

Reflecting on the Gospel

Lent invites us to consider this annunciation gospel in light of the paschal mystery. Jesus' name (=savior) reminds us that his body becomes an "offering . . . once for all" (second reading) and is also destined for glory (gospel: "of his kingdom there will be no end"). Moreover, we ourselves "have been consecrated" and so, like Mary, offer our own bodies to ceaselessly incarnate Christ in our world through our dying to self for the salvation of the world. From the very moment of his conception, Jesus was announced as "savior" (Jesus = "savior"), a foreshadowing of the challenges the paschal mystery always announces. Neither Mary nor Jesus was exempt from these challenges.

Instead of experiencing security, Mary was "greatly troubled at what was said" and asked, "How can this be . . . ?" Instead of being wrapped securely in a protecting diaper, this Man wore a loin cloth as he offered up his body for our sake. Instead of a throne, this Man was lifted up on a cross to the jeer, "He saved others; he cannot save himself. Let the Messiah, the King of Israel, come down now from the cross that we may see and believe" (Mark 15:31b-32a). Here there is no security for either the Baby or mother. Instead of adoration and honor this Baby is met with derision and asked to bear the weight of the sins of the world.

Lent and Triduum and paschal mystery all call for dying. Mary's "May it be done to me according to your word" is the model for our own oblation of our very selves (see second reading), a self-emptying for the sake of the other that is one essential facet of the saving import of the annunciation of this Baby. But this is only one facet of the mystery. The other facet of the mystery was also announced by Gabriel: This Son "will be great . . . will be called Son of the Most High . . . he will rule . . . and of his kingdom there will be no end" (gospel). The oblation of Body is the elevation of the whole world to a share in divine life.

Both Jesus and Mary said yes to the Father's will (see second reading and gospel). Such readiness to place self at the service of God's plan of salvation is the paschal mystery in action. Our Lenten practices of prayer, fasting, and charity are meant to lead us to this same gift of self. Lent is far more than a season of mere discipline. It is a time of conversion during which we enter more deeply into the paschal mystery announced at our baptism, modeled in our saying yes every day to God's call, and embraced for the sake of everlasting life. Gabriel's annunciation of Jesus' conception and taking on human flesh is also the annunciation of our own initiation into the paschal mystery and a share in God's plan of salvation.

Living the Paschal Mystery

Since "nothing [is] impossible for God," we ought not fear spending our lives as oblation by dying to ourselves for the sake of the other. Gabriel not only announces Jesus' conception in Mary's womb; in the course of salvation history Jesus' annunciation is the pledge of a new life we all receive. All we must do is die to ourselves. Just as Jesus was destined for glory, so are we. Lent, Triduum, and Easter remind us that dying and rising are two facets of an incredible mystery: that God loves us so much as to offer us a share in divine life.

Focusing the Gospel

Key words and phrases: conceive . . . and bear a son, Jesus, of his kingdom there will be no end, May it be done to me

To the point: Both Jesus and Mary said yes to the Father's will (see second reading and gospel). Such readiness to place self at the service of God's plan of salvation is the paschal mystery in action. Our Lenten practices of prayer, fasting, and charity are meant to lead us to this same gift of self.

Model Act of Penitence

Presider: In today's gospel for the solemnity of the Annunciation of the Lord Mary says yes to God's request that she become the mother of the Savior. Let us reflect on our own yes to God in our everyday living . . . [pause]

Lord Jesus, you are the Son of the Most High: Lord . . .

Christ Jesus, your reign is forever: Christ . . .

Lord Jesus, you offered your body for our salvation: Lord . . .

Model Prayer of the Faithful

Presider: God graciously sent the Son to redeem us from our sins and bring us new life. Let us pray that God's life may increase in us.

Response: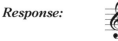

Lord, hear our prayer.

Cantor:

we pray to the Lord,

That all members of the church, like Mary, always say yes to God's call to co-operate in the divine plan of salvation . . . [pause]

That all people of the world might be open to the graciousness of God's presence . . . [pause]

That the sick and suffering find in Mary a source of consolation and strength . . . [pause]

That each of us here die to self for the good of others . . . [pause]

Presider: Gracious God, the power of your Spirit overshadowed Mary who conceived your Son: hear these our prayers that we might share everlasting life with you, through the offering of your Son and in the power of that same Holy Spirit, one God, for ever and ever. **Amen.**

OPENING PRAYER

Let us pray

Pause for silent prayer

God our Father,
your Word became man and was born of
    the Virgin Mary.
May we become more like Jesus Christ
whom we acknowledge as our Redeemer,
    God and man.

We ask this through our Lord Jesus Christ,
    your Son,
who lives and reigns with you and the Holy
    Spirit,
one God, for ever and ever. **Amen.**

FOR REFLECTION

· Like Mary, I have said yes to God and incarnated Jesus for others when . . . I have said no when . . .

· My gift of self for others through prayer is . . . through fasting is . . . through charity is . . .

· This solemnity leads me to embrace more deeply the dying and rising of the paschal mystery in that . . .

Homily Points

• Such total gift of self exemplified by Jesus and Mary seems so beyond our reach. Yet, the only *dying* God asks of us is to meet our everyday demands with fidelity and graciousness. Our yes in little things is very much a part of God's plan of salvation.

• The angel Gabriel addresses Mary as "full of grace." By our baptism, we also are graced by God, already sharing in the *risen life* of Jesus. Thus, cooperation in God's plan of salvation is not totally dependent on us and our yes, but is always made possible by God's help—"for nothing will be impossible for God."

✠ SPIRITUALITY

GOSPEL ACCLAMATION
John 12:26

Whoever serves me must follow me, says the
  Lord;
and where I am, there also will my servant be.

Gospel

John 12:20-33; L35B

Some Greeks who had come to
    worship at the Passover
    Feast
  came to Philip, who was from
    Bethsaida in Galilee,
  and asked him, "Sir, we would
    like to see Jesus."
Philip went and told Andrew;
  then Andrew and Philip went
    and told Jesus.
Jesus answered them,
  "The hour has come for the Son
    of Man to be glorified.
Amen, amen, I say to you,
  unless a grain of wheat falls to the
    ground and dies,
  it remains just a grain of wheat;
  but if it dies, it produces much fruit.
Whoever loves his life loses it,
  and whoever hates his life in this
    world
  will preserve it for eternal life.
Whoever serves me must follow me,
  and where I am, there also will my
    servant be.
The Father will honor whoever serves
  me.

"I am troubled now. Yet what should I
    say?
'Father, save me from this hour'?
But it was for this purpose that I came
    to this hour.
Father, glorify your name."
Then a voice came from heaven,
  "I have glorified it and will glorify it
    again."

Continued in Appendix A, p. 277.
Year A readings may be used, see Appendix A,
pp. 277–279.

Reflecting on the Gospel

The parents had spent a good bit of time during Lent talking with their three children about Jesus, his death and resurrection, and that what we do with our Lenten penance is unite ourselves with Jesus and his self-giving sacrifice. Although the children were still rather young (preschool and primary), the parents talked with the children about dying to self for the good of others. They explained that when the eldest, Aaron, is upset with his little brother, rather than hit him he should "die to self." One day after school on a rainy day the three were particularly feisty and no matter what Mom said, they were at each other. After repeated warnings to behave, the little ones still kept up the bickering. Finally, patience having been lost, Mom grabbed Aaron to put him in the time-out corner, at which point Aaron looked up and said, "Mommy, what happened to the paschal mystery?"

Good question! In the gospel for this Sunday, Jesus gives three different descriptions of the paschal mystery: the grain of wheat must die to produce good fruit; to lose our life we must hate it; we must follow Jesus as servants. All three images lead us to the basic truth of the paschal mystery: by dying to self for the good of others we come to new life.

The goal of Lent and of all Christian living is voiced by the Greeks in the gospel: "We would like to see Jesus." We truly "see" Jesus when we are faithful to *his* law written on our hearts (see first reading). The "new covenant" that God writes "upon [our] hearts" (first reading) is spelled out in the gospel in an unexpected way. The law is not precepts merely to be obeyed, but is a way of life. And this is his "law": become the seed that dies, the life that loses itself, and the servant who follows. Our lives glorify God (as did Jesus' life) when we willingly give our lives for the sake of others.

Giving ourselves for the sake of others is never easy. Sometimes it even makes demands on us that seem impossible. Both the gospel and second reading make clear that Jesus did not want to suffer. Gospel: "I am troubled now . . . save me"; second reading: "he offered prayers and supplications with loud cries and tears" to his Father. We hear a similar plaintive cry when Jesus prays to his Father in the Garden of Gethsemane, asking his Father to save him from the cup of suffering he must drink. Jesus, however, taught us the most important lesson about the paschal mystery: suffering (self-denial) and death (dying to self) is the way—the only way—to life. The dying itself is a gift and grace because it is a harbinger of new life.

Our continual response of dying to self strengthens our ability to die. As the second reading reminds us, Jesus "learned obedience from what he suffered." As Jesus was obedient to his Father, we are to be obedient to Jesus: die to self. Thus we learn obedience and receive new life as we take up the habit of dying to self for the good of others.

Living the Paschal Mystery

When we struggle with dying to self, we are in good company: Jesus himself was "troubled" (gospel) by this and cried out to be delivered from it (see second reading). We don't enter the paschal mystery as the dying and rising rhythm of our Christian living apart from Jesus. When we do take up the cross and die—not in the physical sense but by laying down our lives in service—we are able to see that the cross is the means of glory—for the Father, for Jesus, and for us.

Focusing the Gospel

Key words and phrases: see Jesus, grain . . . dies, follow me, glorify your name

To the point: The goal of Lent and of all Christian living is voiced by the Greeks: "We would like to see Jesus." We truly "see" Jesus when we are faithful to *his* law written on our hearts (see first reading). And this is his "law": become the seed that dies, the life that loses itself, and the servant who follows. Our lives glorify God (as did Jesus' life) when we willingly give our lives for the sake of others.

Connecting the Gospel

to the first reading: The "new covenant" that God writes "upon [our] hearts" (first reading) is spelled out in the gospel in an unexpected way. The law is not precepts merely to be obeyed, but is a way of life: die to self.

to our experience: When we struggle with dying to self, we are in good company: Jesus himself was "troubled" (gospel) by this and cried out to be delivered from it (see second reading).

Connecting the Responsorial Psalm

to the readings: The connection between this Sunday's responsorial psalm and the first reading is readily apparent. In the reading God establishes a new covenant with Israel, forgiving the sins that had destroyed the first covenant. In Psalm 51 the psalmist admits sinfulness, asks God's forgiveness, and begs for a new start ("a clean heart"). Fully confident of God's compassion and mercy, the psalmist promises to call other sinners back home.

For us the mediator of forgiveness and renewed covenant relationship with God is Jesus who lays down his life for us (gospel, second reading). When he "falls to the ground and dies," he is paradoxically "lifted up." In his glory all see the mercy and plan of God. Perhaps the clean heart we pray for in the psalm is the clear-sightedness to see who we are—sinners in need of forgiveness—and who Jesus is—the one who draws us through his death back to God.

to cantor preparation: Like most psalm verses, these verses from Psalm 5 are first-person address to God. The one admitting sin, asking for mercy, begging to be cleansed and restored is yourself. Singing such a text publicly requires great vulnerability, but it is your very vulnerability that invites the assembly to enter this same level of conversation with God. In your vulnerability you show them the "ways" of God. You also show them Jesus (see gospel) who is the way to our salvation.

ASSEMBLY & FAITH-SHARING GROUPS

· What draws me to want to "see" Jesus is . . .

· I see Jesus in the way others live when . . . Others see Jesus in my manner of living when . . .

· I resist dying to self when . . . I am willing to die to self when . . .

PRESIDERS

· My presiding calls me to die to self because . . . This dying opens the door to new life for me and the assembly in that . . .

DEACONS

· My service is truly a dying to self when . . .

HOSPITALITY MINISTERS

· The manner of my greeting helps others "see" Jesus when . . .

MUSIC MINISTERS

· The assembly can "see" Jesus in my manner of doing music ministry when . . .

ALTAR MINISTERS

· My service at church leads others to be drawn to Jesus when I . . .

LECTORS

· The steps I take in preparation for my ministry to ensure that God's words will be written on people's hearts are . . .

EXTRAORDINARY MINISTERS OF HOLY COMMUNION

· Some ways that I might manifest the Eucharist as both the suffering of the cross and the glory of the resurrection are . . .

Model Act of Penitence

Presider: The gospel today calls us to be grains of wheat that die to bear fruit, to lose life to find new life, and to follow Jesus faithfully. Let us empty ourselves of anything that keeps us from dying to self and beg God's forgiveness and mercy for the times when we have failed . . . [pause]

> *Confiteor:* I confess . . .

Homily Points

• We have many expressions that use "dying" but we don't really mean that we "die." For example, we might exclaim, "I'm dying for some chocolate" or "I just died when she said that" or "It just kills me when I have to . . ." When Jesus speaks of dying, however, he really means it.

• We tend to think of Jesus' dying in terms of his death on the cross. In fact, the cross is a summary of his whole life of dying to self for the good of others. Jesus always practiced what he preached in this Sunday's gospel. He continually died to himself when he reached out to sinners and outcasts, when he stood up to those who were threatening him, when he was frustrated with his close friends but didn't terminate the relationship.

• Dying to self defines followers of Jesus, and this must characterize our daily living. What renders us capable of such dying to self is, first, the realization that Jesus himself embraced this dying even though it was difficult; and, second, that Jesus showed us that new life only comes through this dying to self. The more we align ourselves with Jesus as his followers, the more are we aware that his "law" of dying to self is written deeply in our hearts.

Model Prayer of the Faithful

Presider: The God who calls us to life through death will give us the grace we need to be faithful.

Response: Lord, hear our prayer.

Cantor: we pray to the Lord,

That all members of the church may willingly die to self to bear fruit for the good of others . . . [pause]

That leaders of the world faithfully model self-giving for the good of others . . . [pause]

That those who are suffering or dying may see in Jesus the promise of new life . . . [pause]

That those preparing for the Easter sacraments enter into Jesus' death and resurrection with confidence and joy . . . [pause]

That each of us continue our Lenten journey of dying to self, confident in Jesus' promise of new life . . . [pause]

Presider: Merciful and loving God, you are glorified by those who follow your Son Jesus Christ into death and resurrection: hear these our prayers that we might share eternal life with you. We ask this through that same Jesus Christ. **Amen.**

OPENING PRAYER

Let us pray
  [for the courage to follow Christ]

Pause for silent prayer

Father,
help us to be like Christ your Son,
who loved the world and died for our
    salvation.
Inspire us by his love,
guide us by his example,
who lives and reigns with you and the
    Holy Spirit,
one God, for ever and ever. **Amen.**

FIRST READING

Jer 31:31-34

The days are coming, says the LORD,
    when I will make a new covenant with
      the house of Israel
    and the house of Judah.
It will not be like the covenant I made with
    their fathers
    the day I took them by the hand
    to lead them forth from the land of
      Egypt;
    for they broke my covenant,
    and I had to show myself their master,
      says the LORD.
But this is the covenant that I will make
    with the house of Israel after those
      days, says the LORD.
I will place my law within them and write
    it upon their hearts;
    I will be their God, and they shall be my
      people.
No longer will they have need to teach
    their friends and relatives
    how to know the LORD.
All, from least to greatest, shall know me,
    says the LORD,
    for I will forgive their evildoing and
      remember their sin no more.

RESPONSORIAL PSALM
Ps 51:3-4, 12-13, 14-15

R̶. (12a) Create a clean heart in me, O God.

Have mercy on me, O God, in your
    goodness;
    in the greatness of your compassion
      wipe out my offense.
Thoroughly wash me from my guilt
    and of my sin cleanse me.

R̶. Create a clean heart in me, O God.

A clean heart create for me, O God,
    and a steadfast spirit renew within me.
Cast me not out from your presence,
    and your Holy Spirit take not from me.

R̶. Create a clean heart in me, O God.

Give me back the joy of your salvation,
    and a willing spirit sustain in me.
I will teach transgressors your ways,
    and sinners shall return to you.

R̶. Create a clean heart in me, O God.

SECOND READING
Heb 5:7-9

In the days when Christ Jesus was in the
    flesh,
    he offered prayers and supplications
      with loud cries and tears
    to the one who was able to save him
      from death,
    and he was heard because of his
      reverence.
Son though he was, he learned obedience
    from what he suffered;
    and when he was made perfect,
    he became the source of eternal
      salvation for all who obey him.

About Liturgy

Lent, baptism, and covenant: The first reading from the prophet Jeremiah speaks of the covenant God made with the Israelites: "I will be their God, and they shall be my people." Lent is a time of the year when we especially join with those preparing for the Easter sacraments. Lent is a time for preparing for or renewing our baptismal covenant, which makes us the new people of God—the Body of Christ.

We misunderstand covenant if we liken it to our notion of contract. When we enter into a contractual agreement with another the desire is to agree on as even terms as possible—maybe even one "putting it over" on the other and making a very good deal. God's covenants with us are never on even terms—God always gives more than we give. God made Israel God's chosen people and gave them a land of plenty and in return all Israel had to do was obey the laws of God. In our baptismal covenant God makes of us members of the Body of Christ by instilling in us the divine life of the Spirit, and in return all we need do is become a servant follower of Jesus.

Yet we know that we fail in keeping our covenant about as many times as Israel failed! If we constantly keep the terms of the baptismal covenant before us (which is why we renew our baptismal commitments each Easter), then perhaps we will allow the good terms of our covenant with God to entice us to give ourselves over to Gospel living. Lenten penance is to help us gain the discipline of dying to ourselves. Easter glory is a glimpse of what God ultimately has in store for those who keep the covenant by living the paschal mystery.

Liturgy committee: Next Sunday begins the long liturgies connected with the annual celebration of Christ's death and resurrection. It is usually a very busy time for the liturgy committee and environment ministers. One principle to remember is that the liturgy always takes precedence; sometimes committee members get so caught up in elaborate preparations that they forget what these liturgies are really all about: Christ's dying and rising. Elaborate isn't always better.

About Liturgical Music

Music suggestions: The songs recommended for the third Sunday of Lent—Lucien Deiss's "Grant to Us, O Lord"; David Haas' "Deep Within"; and Bernadette Farrell's "Unless a Grain of Wheat"—would be excellent choices again this week. Repeating appropriate pieces such as these is a good way to communicate the unity of a season. With each repetition we allow the power of the music to collaborate with and support the transformative power of the season. And to the extent that we are allowing the season to shape our daily living, we will sing the pieces each week with deeper understanding. Thus life, liturgy, and our liturgical singing become one.

SPIRITUALITY

GOSPEL ACCLAMATION
Phil 2:8-9

Christ became obedient to the point of death,
even death on a cross.
Because of this, God greatly exalted him
and bestowed on him the name which is above
  every name.

Gospel at the procession with palms

John 12:12-16; L37B (Mark 11:1-10 may also
be read.)

**When the great crowd that had come to
    the feast heard
    that Jesus was coming to Jerusalem,
    they took palm branches and went
        out to meet him, and cried out:
    "Hosanna!
    Blessed is he who comes in the
        name of the Lord,
        the king of Israel."
Jesus found an ass and sat upon it, as
    is written:
    *Fear no more, O daughter Zion;
    see, your king comes, seated upon
        an ass's colt.*
His disciples did not understand this at
    first,
    but when Jesus had been glorified
    they remembered that these things
        were written about him
    and that they had done this for him.**

Gospel at Mass   Mark 14:1–15:47; L38B
or Mark 15:1–39; L38B *in Appendix A,
pp. 280–283.*

Reflecting on the Gospel

Anna was to make her First Holy Communion, and when it came time for family catechesis, four-year-old Christian was brought to the session, too. Much to the parents' surprise, Christian was good as gold throughout the entire time. More than good—Christian seemed to be rapt in attention during the whole hour. After they got into the car to go home, Dad complimented Christian on his stellar behavior and asked him, "What did you pay such close attention to?" Christian answered his dad with another question, "Daddy, why did the teacher keep saying my name so often?" Perhaps this was the first time Christian was confronted with the fact that he shared his name with so many others. We all, in fact, call ourselves Christian because we have the common identity of Body of Christ. Growing into this identity and acting consistent with its demands is a lifelong task. This was no less true for Jesus and the disciples, too.

On this, Palm Sunday, we proclaim two contrasting gospels, both declaring something quite different about Jesus' identity and both indicating to us just how utterly consistent Jesus was with who he truly was. Yet Jesus' "disciples did not understand" (gospel at the procession) that Jesus' entrance into Jerusalem was not about immediate acclamation and glory ("Hosanna . . . king of Israel") but about a glory realized only through the cross: "Truly this man was the Son of God!" Jesus humbled himself to become human, "even [to] death on a cross" (second reading). In the passion account, Jesus shows us how humbly and completely he embraced humanity: he submitted to denial, betrayal, abandonment, torture, mockery, crucifixion. As disciples of Jesus, we, too, are called to humble ourselves. We are to bend our knees before Jesus (see second reading). Even more: like him, we are to bend our knees in humility before one another.

Mark paints a vivid picture of the sufferings of Jesus. At the same time his passion account—and even his whole gospel—rises to a crescendo in the centurion's amazing proclamation of faith: "Truly this man was the Son of God!" The one both hailed and derided as king of the Jews, the one crucified, is finally revealed in his deepest identity as Son of God. His mission is accomplished— in the shedding of his blood he gives his blood as the new Fruit of the vine in which we all share each time we commemorate him. We might "roll a stone against the entrance of the tomb" where he lay dead; but we cannot contain his true identity and mission.

Living the Paschal Mystery

The essence of discipleship is that we don't simply receive the fruit of Jesus' suffering and death; the essence of discipleship is that we align our own identity with that of Jesus, accept self-denial and self-giving, and in this way walk with him to the cross. Disciples go wherever the Master goes.

Coming to understand who Jesus is, his mission, and how that relates to us his disciples is no easy task; it takes a lifetime. Like Jesus, to be faithful followers by taking up our cross means we will feel this to the depths of our humanity: we will suffer, we will lose heart, we will cry out to God to take life's miserable lot away from us. But also like Jesus, we have divine life that gives us the strength to carry our cross. It is divine life pulsing within us—which we first receive at our baptism—that raises up our humanity, enabling us to be faithful disciples carrying our crosses, faithful disciples consistent with our identity as Christians, as Body of Christ.

Focusing the Passion Gospel

Key words and phrases: deny me, betrayer, left him and fled, scourged, mocked, crucified, forsaken me

To the point: Jesus humbled himself to become human, "even [to] death on a cross" (second reading). In the passion account, Jesus shows us how fully and humbly he embraced humanity: he submitted to denial, betrayal, abandonment, torture, mockery, crucifixion. As disciples of Jesus, we, too, are called to humble ourselves. We are to bend our knees before Jesus (see second reading). Even more: like him, we are to bend our knees in humility before one another.

Connecting the Gospel

to the procession with palms: Jesus' "disciples did not understand" (gospel at the procession) that Jesus' entrance into Jerusalem was not about immediate acclamation and glory ("Hosanna . . . king of Israel") but about a glory realized only through the cross: "Truly this man was the Son of God!"

to our experience: We often think of humility in terms of self-effacement. At its deepest level, humility is about embracing the truth of who we really are and who we are called to become.

Connecting the Responsorial Psalm

to the readings: The verses chosen from Psalm 22 for Palm Sunday progress in the opposite direction from the movement set up between the gospel read at the opening of this liturgy and the passion proclaimed during the Liturgy of the Word. With these readings we begin with the crowd shouting praise and end with the story of Christ's degradation and death. In the responsorial psalm, however, we begin with the psalmist's cries of agony and abandonment and end with a song of praise.

Thus from opposite directions this responsorial psalm and these readings pull us into the true meaning of glory. A crowd's adulation in itself means nothing; in God's eyes it is suffering and death undertaken for the sake of redemption that means all. When we willingly enter this mystery with Christ—this Holy Week and every day of our lives—we find our tongues praising God (psalm). And we find God's tongue praising us (second reading).

to cantor preparation: The few verses used from Psalm 22 this Sunday do not do justice to the psalm's depth and its connection with the meaning of what we celebrate this Sunday and throughout Holy Week. Set aside some time this week to read the psalm in its entirety and to reflect on the relationship between suffering and praise of God. Then pray for the grace to enter Christ's suffering so that with him you may sing God's praise.

**ASSEMBLY &
FAITH-SHARING GROUPS**

· Jesus' true mission was not about receiving accolades of hosanna, but in shedding his blood for the many. I shed my blood for others when . . .

· I bend my knee before Jesus by . . . I bend my knee before others by . . .

· Jesus embraced my humanity; I embrace my humanity by . . .

PRESIDERS

· I model the humanity of Jesus when . . .

DEACONS

· My service is a way of bending my knee before others when . . .

HOSPITALITY MINISTERS

· Hospitality demands self-emptying, "taking the form of a slave"; I embrace this same posture when . . .

MUSIC MINISTERS

· I am tempted to exalt myself through my music ministry when . . . What leads me instead to humble myself is . . .

ALTAR MINISTERS

· My serving at the altar is truly a humble service when . . .

LECTORS

· Good proclamation demands humility of me in that . . .

**EXTRAORDINARY MINISTERS
OF HOLY COMMUNION**

· Jesus' dying and rising is proclaimed in my ministry when . . .

Model Act of Penitence [only used at Masses with the simple entrance]

Presider: Today we begin the most solemn of weeks in the whole Christian year. Today reminds us of two contradictory events: the crowd triumphantly hailing Jesus as king of the Jews and the soldiers mocking and deriding Jesus for the same title. We pause and consider how we have been willing to follow Jesus in times of glory but perhaps have abandoned him when it comes to carrying his cross . . . [pause]

    Confiteor: I confess . . .

Homily Points

• The word "humility" comes from the Latin, *humus*, meaning "earth" or "soil." To be humble, then, is to be grounded in who we really are. Moreover, God so cherishes who we really are in our humanity—clay made into the divine image—that God chose in Jesus to become one of us.

• Jesus is the Son of God who, in humility, deemed to become human. We are called to embrace, in humility, both the earthiness of our humanity and the divine life we have been given in Christ.

• Embracing both our earthiness and the divine life given us in Christ means being willing to undergo with Christ his passage through death to new life. Every year on this day—Palm Sunday of the Lord's Passion—we enter into this passage in heightened ritual form. May we continue this journey with Christ through Holy Week and enter with him into glory on Easter Sunday.

Model Prayer of the Faithful

Presider: The God who calls us to new life through death gives us what we need. And so we pray.

Response: Lord, hear our prayer.

Cantor: we pray to the Lord,

That all members of the church walk with Jesus in his passion and so share abundantly in the new life he offers . . . [pause]

That all peoples of the world come to salvation . . . [pause]

That those suffering pain and loss might find hope and consolation in the suffering Christ . . . [pause]

That each of us humble ourselves before God and come to full humanity . . . [pause]

Presider: Redeeming God, you sent your Son to lead us to salvation: hear these our prayers that one day we might share eternal glory with him. We ask this through Christ our Lord. **Amen.**

OPENING PRAYER

Let us pray

Pause for silent prayer

Almighty, ever-living God,
you have given the human race Jesus
    Christ our Savior
as a model of humility.
He fulfilled your will by becoming man
and giving his life on the cross.
Help us to bear witness to you
by following his example of suffering
and make us worthy to share in his
    resurrection.

We ask this through our Lord Jesus Christ,
    your Son,
who lives and reigns with you and the
    Holy Spirit,
one God, for ever and ever. **Amen.**

FIRST READING

Isa 50:4-7

The Lord God has given me
  a well-trained tongue,
that I might know how to speak to the
    weary
  a word that will rouse them.
Morning after morning
  he opens my ear that I may hear;
and I have not rebelled,
  have not turned back.
I gave my back to those who beat me,
  my cheeks to those who plucked my
    beard;
my face I did not shield
  from buffets and spitting.

The Lord God is my help,
  therefore I am not disgraced;
I have set my face like flint,
  knowing that I shall not be put to
    shame.

RESPONSORIAL PSALM

Ps 22:8-9, 17-18, 19-20, 23-24

℟. (2a) My God, my God, why have you abandoned me?

All who see me scoff at me;
  they mock me with parted lips, they
    wag their heads:
"He relied on the Lord; let him deliver him,
  let him rescue him, if he loves him."

℟. My God, my God, why have you abandoned me?

Indeed, many dogs surround me,
    a pack of evildoers closes in upon me;
they have pierced my hands and my feet;
    I can count all my bones.

R℣. My God, my God, why have you
abandoned me?

They divide my garments among them,
    and for my vesture they cast lots.
But you, O LORD, be not far from me;
    O my help, hasten to aid me.

R℣. My God, my God, why have you
abandoned me?

I will proclaim your name to my brethren;
    in the midst of the assembly I will
        praise you:
"You who fear the LORD, praise him;
    all you descendants of Jacob, give glory
        to him;
    revere him, all you descendants of
        Israel!"

R℣. My God, my God, why have you
abandoned me?

SECOND READING
Phil 2:6-11

Christ Jesus, though he was in the form
    of God,
    did not regard equality with God
    something to be grasped.
Rather, he emptied himself,
    taking the form of a slave,
    coming in human likeness;
    and found human in appearance,
    he humbled himself,
    becoming obedient to the point of
        death,
    even death on a cross.
Because of this, God greatly exalted him
    and bestowed on him the name
    which is above every name,
    that at the name of Jesus
    every knee should bend,
    of those in heaven and on earth and
        under the earth,
    and every tongue confess that
    Jesus Christ is Lord,
    to the glory of God the Father.

About Liturgy

Why choose John 12:12-16 as the gospel at the procession with palms?
Two choices are given for year B for the gospel proclaimed before the procession with palms; it would be natural that the selection from Mark be used since this is the year we proclaim Mark. Yet we suggest that the Johannine selection be proclaimed because it clearly sets out the tension about Jesus' entry into Jerusalem: the crowd greets Jesus with the joyful accolades due to the one whose arrival they perceive to be the messiah-king, but this entry into the City of David is not the moment of Jesus' glory. The "disciples did not understand" that Jesus' glory could only be achieved by suffering and death; death on the cross leads to the glory of risen life.

This tension marks the vicissitudes of our own Christian living. We are willing to follow Jesus—but we would like it to be an easy road to glory. Contrary, Christian living is the hard work of proclaiming the gospel by the way we live, a proclamation such that people can see us and, seeing how we live, proclaim, "Truly this person reveals the Son of God!" We cannot stress enough in our reflection and our preaching that this tension is a critical one, one that reminds us of the reality of the cross.

About Liturgical Music

Music and the paschal mystery: Perhaps more than any other week in the liturgical year, Holy Week makes evident the importance and power of the music we sing during the liturgy. The choir and music ministers will have put a great deal of extra time and effort into the music for these liturgies. Their intent, however, is not to entertain, but to enable us to enter more deeply into the mystery we celebrate in ritual form: our participation with Christ in his death and resurrection. When we sing, we actualize this very mystery as we die to ourselves to become one in heart and song with each other. May we sing this Holy Week with full and conscious awareness of what we are doing and who we are becoming.

Easter Triduum

. . . Seeing the blood,
I will pass over you . . .
Jesus knew that his hour had come
to pass from this world
to the Father.

—Exod 12:13b; John 13:1

Reflecting on the Triduum

Transitions are a fact of human living. The first one, of course, is the transition from the warmth and security of the mother's womb to the "outside" world where the newborn must breathe and eat. Then there is the transition from home to school, from school to work. Transitions occur during job changes and moving a household. Life-changing transitions occur when going from single to married, from nonordained to ordained, from healthy to unhealthy, from life to death. It ought be no surprise, then, that transitions occur in our spiritual and worship lives. These transitions, too, are life changing.

During the Triduum we celebrate the core mystery of our Christian faith: we ritualize Jesus' transition from life to death to risen life, and our own participation in that timeless mystery. Rather than "transition," however, we tend to use another word that more distinctly images for us what happens during these days; that word is "passover." We hear the expression during the first reading and gospel on Holy Thursday evening. This establishes the context for what we celebrate throughout the Triduum. "It is the Passover of the LORD."

When the Hebrews were about to leave Egypt they celebrated the first "Passover" meal. At this time the blood of the sacrificial lamb was to be smeared on their doorposts and lintels so the angel of death would "pass over" them, sparing the Hebrew's firstborn children. Their posture and garb as people about to make a journey connects this meal clearly with the exodus event. The Exodus is a founding event for God's people. They became God's chosen ones. They were cared for and protected by God. They passed over from slavery to freedom, and from being strangers in a foreign land to being at home in the land God gave them, one flowing with milk and honey. "It is the Passover of the LORD."

Numerous passages in the New Testament refer to Jesus as the Lamb of God or the Passover lamb. His sacrificial offering brought the mercy, care, and redemption God had offered Israel to a new and more consummate realization. Not merely symbolized by the blood of a lamb, this new Passover is accomplished by the blood of the divine Son. Not merely establishing a chosen people, this new Passover accomplishes God's adopting us as beloved daughters and sons and ones who share in divine life. As Jesus passed over from life to death to life, we pass over from human limits to divine indwelling. "It is the Passover of the LORD."

Living the Paschal Mystery

It is so easy this time of year to celebrate these days as a historical commemoration. After all, Jesus really did celebrate a Last Supper with his disciples, really did undergo a trial, really did suffer, really was crucified, really did die, really did rise from the dead. Nevertheless, we are doing far more than recalling these historical facts. What Jesus did for us has consequence for all people at all times. His life, death, and resurrection happened to him, but they also happen to all of us who claim to be his followers. These days, then, are a reminder and celebration of who we ourselves are and what our own lives are about.

As we celebrate the mystery of Jesus' passing from life to death to life, we actually celebrate the same passing over in our own lives. Jesus' self-sacrifice opened the way for us to share in new life. But this does require our own cooperation in God's divine plan of salvation. We must pass over our lives into God's hands and imitate the self-giving of God's Son. This is the way to Life. "It is the Passover of the LORD."

TRIDUUM

"Triduum" comes from two Latin words (*tres* and *dies*) that mean "a space of three days." But since we have four days with special names—Holy Thursday, Good Friday, Holy Saturday, and Easter Sunday—the "three" may be confusing to some.

The confusion is cleared up when we understand how the days are reckoned. On all high festival days the Church counts a day in the same way as Jews count days and festivals; that is, from sundown to sundown. Thus, the Triduum consists of *three* twenty-four-hour periods that stretch over four calendar days.

Therefore, the Easter Triduum begins at sundown on Holy Thursday with the Mass of the Lord's Supper and concludes with Easter evening prayer at sundown on Easter Sunday; its high point is the celebration of the Easter Vigil (GNLYC no. 19).

SOLEMN PASCHAL FAST

According to the above calculation, Lent ends at sundown on Holy Thursday; thus, Holy Thursday itself is the last day of Lent. This doesn't mean that our fasting concludes on Holy Thursday, however; the church has traditionally kept a solemn forty-hour fast from the beginning of the Triduum until the fast is broken at Communion during the Easter Vigil.

✝ SPIRITUALITY

I give you a new commandment, says the Lord:
love one another as I have loved you.

Gospel   John 13:1-15; L39ABC

Before the feast of Passover, Jesus knew
    that his hour had come
    to pass from this world to the Father.
He loved his own in the world and he loved
    them to the end.
The devil had already induced Judas, son of
    Simon the Iscariot, to hand him over.
So, during supper,
    fully aware that the Father had put
        everything into his power
    and that he had come from God and
        was returning to God,
    he rose from supper and took off his
        outer garments.
He took a towel and tied it around his
    waist.
Then he poured water into a basin
    and began to wash the disciples' feet
    and dry them with the towel around his
        waist.
He came to Simon Peter, who said to him,
    "Master, are you going to wash my feet?"
Jesus answered and said to him,
    "What I am doing, you do not understand
        now,
    but you will understand later."
Peter said to him, "You will never wash my
    feet."
Jesus answered him,
    "Unless I wash you, you will have no
        inheritance with me."
Simon Peter said to him,
    "Master, then not only my feet, but my
        hands and head as well."
Jesus said to him,
    "Whoever has bathed has no need except
        to have his feet washed,
        for he is clean all over;
    so you are clean, but not all."
For he knew who would betray him;
    for this reason, he said, "Not all of you
        are clean."

Continued in Appendix A, p. 284.
See Appendix A, p. 284, for the other readings.

Reflecting on the Gospel and Living the Paschal Mystery

Key words and phrases from the gospel: Passover, never wash . . . Unless I wash, betray, master . . . washed your feet, model to follow

To the point: Jesus is the Passover Lamb. On this night his passing over strikingly presents saving events: he passed over from being free to being an arrested criminal; he also passed over from being master to slave, thus modeling for us how we are to follow him. Peter, however, is reluctant—he doesn't want his feet washed, jeopardizing his being inaugurated into this saving mystery and its glory of eternal inheritance. With Peter, we must submit to the Lord so that we can "wash [the] feet" of others. This must also be our own passover night.

Reflection: How easy are misunderstandings! We might misunderstand someone's intentions, motives, actions, words. The potential for misunderstanding really is there any time interaction between persons occurs. When the persons don't know each other very well, the potential to take something amiss is much greater than when people have known each other a long time and have established patterns of behaviors and expectations. Peter has known Jesus for a while; he has traveled with him, heard him preach, witnessed his miracles. Yet when Jesus stoops to wash his feet, he misunderstands Jesus' intention as well as his action. Jesus' intention was not to do what a slave does and wash feet; it was to model self-giving. His action was more than about washing; it would reveal those who betray him and challenge faithful ones to follow him by living lives spent for the sake of others.

Jesus' action at the Supper is a culmination of everything the disciples had witnessed while being with him. All Jesus' life and being is summed up in "as I have done for you, you should also do." Jesus is the Passover Lamb. On this night his passing over strikingly presents saving events: he passed over from being free to being an arrested criminal; he also passed over from being master to slave, thus modeling for us how we are to follow him. Peter, however, is reluctant—he is embarrassed to have his feet washed, jeopardizing his being inaugurated into this saving mystery and its glory of eternal inheritance. With Peter, we must submit to the Lord so that we can "wash [the] feet" of others. This must also be our own passover night.

Unlike Peter, we have the benefit of centuries of interpretation of the Scriptures so we don't misunderstand Jesus' intention and action. We have the benefit of holy people who have gone before us modeling lives of faithful response to Jesus' invitation to follow him. We have the benefit of this night to ponder and reflect on our own lives and our response to Jesus' invitation. We have been given every possible thing so that we don't misunderstand what Jesus modeled for us and asked of his followers.

Living every day as a passover is never easy. It demands of us constant sensitivity to the needs of others. It asks of us generous self-giving. It begs of us humility, faithfulness, and the kind of love that God has shown us. Our motivation for taking up such a way of life is spelled out by Jesus in the gospel: to have inheritance with him. Passover is just the beginning. Ultimately, our following Jesus and undertaking actions for the good of others is our own passing over from death to life.

Model Act of Penitence

Presider: Tonight we begin the most solemn three days of our Christian year—the Easter Triduum. Tonight we remember God's mighty deeds in passing over and saving from death the firstborn of the Israelites and bringing them safely from slavery to freedom. Tonight we remember Jesus' gift of life in giving us his Body and Blood for nourishment and his passing over from master to slave as he modeled for us how we are to give our lives in service. Let us prepare well to celebrate these great mysteries . . . [pause]

> Lord Jesus, you are our Passover Lamb: Lord . . .
>
> Christ Jesus, you give us your Body and Blood as heavenly Food: Christ . . .
>
> Lord Jesus, you model for us a life spent for the good of others: Lord . . .

Homily Points

• We have the expression, "It is better to give than to receive." There are those of us who find it difficult to allow others to give to us, to help us, to be present to us. But to receive from another is also to give oneself. Like Peter, we must "pass over" to a new understanding of what it means to receive from Jesus.

• When Jesus stooped to wash the feet of his disciples, he modeled for them what we also must do. Jesus was inviting them to receive this gesture as a sign of his gift of himself on their behalf. He was also inviting them to imitate such self-giving in their own lives. Only by imitating Jesus' own self-giving can we grow into the fullness of life we desire.

• Jesus' self-giving is continued in each celebration of the Eucharist. At this Supper we receive from Jesus and once again witness his self-giving to us as a call for our own lives to grow in self-giving. Every Eucharist is an invitation to both receiving and giving—to receive the Eucharist includes the responsibility to give self for others.

Model Prayer of the Faithful

Presider: With confidence let us pray to the God who lavishes on us all good things and promises us eternal inheritance.

Response:

Cantor:

That all members of the church generously pour out their lives in service of others . . . [pause]

That all people know the redeeming love of God who desires for them fruitful life . . . [pause]

That those enslaved by poverty or sickness pass over to a better life and health . . . [pause]

That all of us here gathered grow in our appreciation for the great gift of Self Jesus gives us in the Eucharist and its demands to live selflessly for others . . . [pause]

Presider: Redeeming God, you bring your people from slavery to freedom: hear these prayers that we might one day enjoy an everlasting inheritance with you. We ask this through Christ our Lord. **Amen.**

OPENING PRAYER

Let us pray

Pause for silent prayer

God our Father,
we are gathered here to share in the supper
which your only Son left to his Church to
reveal his love.
He gave it to us when he was about to die
and commanded us to celebrate it as the
new and eternal sacrifice.
We pray that in this eucharist
we may find the fullness of love and life.

Grant this through our Lord Jesus Christ,
your Son,
who lives and reigns with you and the Holy
Spirit,
one God, for ever and ever. **Amen.**

FOR REFLECTION

· Like Peter, I misunderstand what Jesus is asking of me whenever I . . . I find it easiest to be clear about what Jesus asks of me whenever I . . .

· The people whose feet I find it easiest to wash are . . . Those whose feet are most difficult for me to wash are . . .

· Jesus has stooped to wash my feet when . . . This has brought me to pass over from . . . to . . .

✚ SPIRITUALITY

GOSPEL ACCLAMATION
Phil 2:8-9

Christ became obedient to the point of death,
even death on a cross.
Because of this, God greatly exalted him
and bestowed on him the name which is above
    every other name.

Gospel   John 18:1–19:42; L40ABC

Jesus went out with his disciples across
    the Kidron valley
    to where there was a garden,
    into which he and his disciples entered.
Judas his betrayer also knew the place,
    because Jesus had often met there with
        his disciples.
So Judas got a band of soldiers and guards
    from the chief priests and the Pharisees
    and went there with lanterns, torches,
        and weapons.
Jesus, knowing everything that was going to
        happen to him,
    went out and said to them, "Whom are
        you looking for?"
They answered him, "Jesus the Nazorean."
He said to them, "I AM."
Judas his betrayer was also with them.
When he said to them, "I AM,"
    they turned away and fell to the ground.
So he again asked them,
    "Whom are you looking for?"
They said, "Jesus the Nazorean."
Jesus answered,
    "I told you that I AM.
So if you are looking for me, let these men
        go."
This was to fulfill what he had said,
    "I have not lost any of those you gave
        me."
Then Simon Peter, who had a sword, drew
        it,
    struck the high priest's slave, and cut off
        his right ear.
The slave's name was Malchus.
Jesus said to Peter,
    "Put your sword into its scabbard.
Shall I not drink the cup that the Father
        gave me?"

Continued in Appendix A, pp. 285–286.
See Appendix A, p. 287, for the other readings.

Reflecting on the Gospel and Living the Paschal Mystery
Key words and phrases from the gospel: I find no guilt in him, handed him over, It is finished, he handed over the spirit

To the point: Our jurisprudence system rests on the assumption that one is innocent until proven guilty. In John's passion account, Pilate explicitly states that "I find no guilt in him." Yet Jesus was handed over, crucified, and died. A man known to be innocent had his life taken. He passed over from life to death: "It is finished." Is it?

Reflection: Popes and bishops alike have condemned capital punishment. Among many reasons given for this position, one is that sometimes innocent people's lives are taken for crimes they didn't commit. While every effort is made to determine truthfully whether one is guilty, sometimes mistakes are made. We never punish—especially by the death penalty—someone we know is innocent. Our jurisprudence system rests on the assumption that one is innocent until proven guilty. In John's passion account, Pilate explicitly states that "I find no guilt in him." Yet Jesus was handed over, crucified, and died. A man known to be innocent had his life taken. He passed over from life to death: "It is finished." Is it?

This gospel is filled with passovers: Judas passes over from being a disciple to betrayer; Peter passes over from acknowledging Jesus is the Messiah to denying him; Barabbas passes over from being a prisoner to being freed; Mary and the beloved disciple pass over into each other's care; Jesus passed over from life to death; the soldiers passed over Jesus' body without breaking a bone; Joseph and Nicodemus passed over from being secretive about their relationship with Jesus to openly caring for his dead body. Sometimes the "passing over" is a step toward renewed relationship and life. In the case of Joseph and Nicodemus, for example, Jesus' death moved them to act toward him in a way they couldn't have when he was alive. Jesus' death gave them courage to act boldly. At other times "passing over" is from life-giving relationship with Jesus to isolation and despair. In the case of Judas, for example, his betrayal severed the master-disciple relationship.

Jesus' passing over from life to death has consequences for all of us. His passing over never leaves us unaffected; we, too, must embrace our own passover. The challenge of Good Friday is that we cannot celebrate this mystery of our salvation fruitfully without deciding once again to pass over into a deeper relationship with this innocent One who was crucified. Our passing over, then, ultimately means that we, too, must be willing to be innocent victims sacrificed for the good of others. We must willingly die to ourselves if we are to follow Jesus through death to new life. Jesus can say "It is finished" with respect to his mortal body; but the mystery itself is not finished. The mystery of life and death is broken open and manifested in Jesus' "carrying the cross himself"—he willingly died so that we might live. The mystery of life and death is not finished: *we* must take up Jesus' cross, carry it ourselves, and continue his self-giving sacrifice.

This is why Good Friday is a quiet day: we are silenced, awed by the depth and power of this mystery of death bringing life. This is why Good Friday is not a sad day: Jesus' death means resurrection for him and a share in that eternal life for us.

Homily Points

- Death scares most of us. It is an utter unknown. It happens once for each of us. The death we soberly and quietly celebrate this day is like no other. This death does not scare us, but draws us into the deepest mystery of our faith: through death comes life.

- This liturgy begins in silence and with a profound gesture that we only see (with rare exceptions) on this one day of the year. The ministers enter and prostrate themselves on the ground. This gesture models what we celebrate this day: an act of total self-surrender, total self-giving. Jesus' death on the cross is an unprecedented event, the magnitude of self-giving hardly able to be grasped by us. The Son of God surrenders his mortal body, passing from life to death, so that we might pass from death to eternal life.

- The kind of dying to self Jesus models for us by being sacrificed on the cross calls forth from us a daily response of self-giving. We do this by the little acts that strengthen our relationships with others—family, coworkers, neighbors, strangers. No act of kindness, love, generosity, forgiveness, peacemaking is so small that it does not have awesome implications. These acts are our "practice" in passing over from death to life.

Suggestions for Music

Singing the solemn prayers: Just as the Easter Vigil is the mother of all vigils, so the Good Friday solemn prayers are the mother and model of all general intercessions. Because of their solemnity they are meant to be sung using the simple chant given in the Sacramentary, and to include short periods of silent prayer after each statement of intention. If it is not possible that these intercessions be sung, they should be spoken with solemnity with time allowed for the appropriate silent pauses.

Music during the Veneration of the Cross: As the title of this part of this day's liturgy—"Veneration of the Cross"—indicates, what we honor in this procession is not the One crucified but the Cross, which embodies the mystery of his (and our) redemptive triumph over sin and death. Because we are not *historicizing* or reenacting a past event, but *ritualizing* the meaning of this event for our lives here and now, this procession is not one of sorrow or expiation but of gratitude, of triumph, and of quiet and confident acceptance (the very sentiments expressed in the responsorial psalm). The music during this procession needs, then, to sing about the mystery and triumph of the cross rather than about the details of Jesus' suffering and death. Examples of appropriate hymns include: "We Acclaim the Cross of Jesus"; "O Cross of Christ, Immortal Tree"; "Behold, Before Our Wond'ring Eyes." Examples of appropriate choir-assembly pieces include Ricky Manalo's "We Should Glory in the Cross" [OCP 11355CC] and Francis Patrick O'Brien's "Tree of Life and Glory" [GIA G-5452]. Gerard Chiusano's choral setting of the entrance antiphon for Holy Thursday, "We Should Glory in the Cross" [OCP 10884,] would be an excellent piece for the choir to sing. If already sung as part of the Holy Thursday liturgy, repeating it would emphasize the unity of these celebrations.

Music during the Communion procession: Examples of songs appropriate for Communion include texts such as "Only This I Want," "What Wondrous Love Is This," and Marty Haugen's "In the Cross of Christ."

OPENING PRAYER

Let us pray

Pause for silent prayer

Lord,
by shedding his blood for us,
your Son, Jesus Christ,
established the paschal mystery.
In your goodness, make us holy
and watch over us always.

We ask this through Christ our Lord.
Amen.

FOR REFLECTION

- Celebrating Jesus' death brings about these "passing overs" in me . . .
- Jesus' death renews my relationship to him in that . . .
- Jesus' death spurs me on to greater self-giving when . . .

SPIRITUALITY

Gospel

Mark 16:1-7; L41B

When the sabbath was over,
  Mary Magdalene, Mary, the
    mother of James, and Salome
  bought spices so that they might
    go and anoint him.
Very early when the sun had risen,
  on the first day of the week, they
    came to the tomb.
They were saying to one another,
  "Who will roll back the stone for
    us
  from the entrance to the tomb?"
When they looked up,
  they saw that the stone had been
    rolled back;
  it was very large.
On entering the tomb they saw a
    young man
  sitting on the right side, clothed in a
    white robe,
  and they were utterly amazed.
He said to them, "Do not be amazed!
You seek Jesus of Nazareth, the
    crucified.
He has been raised; he is not here.
Behold the place where they laid him.
But go and tell his disciples and Peter,
  'He is going before you to Galilee;
    there you will see him, as he told
      you.'"

Readings continued in Appendix A, pp. 288–293.

Reflecting on the Gospel and Living the Paschal Mystery

Key words and phrases from the gospel: when the sun had risen, You seek Jesus, he has been raised, there you will see him

To the point: Mary and the other women come to Jesus' gravesite to anoint him. Hardly were they prepared for what they encountered: not a dead body, but a live "young man" who declared to them, "He has been raised." They are told to go to Galilee and "there you will see him." We know what they found in Galilee: Jesus the risen One. We know what we also find in our midst: Jesus the risen One.

Reflection: Darkness has always been a time of fear for little children, a time of mischief at Halloween for older youngsters, a time of crime for many adults. We tend to associate much of life's unpleasantries with darkness. When it gets dark outside, we want to be inside, safe and comfortable. Yet on this night, we Christians venture out. No, we go out purposefully and gladly. For after the sun dies, we begin our celebration of life. In the darkness we are not afraid. This night darkness passes over into the light of risen life. This is what we celebrate this night: passing over from darkness to light, from death to life, from sober quietness to exuberant joy. This night our alleluias that have been silent for forty days ring out in a crescendo of hope and glory.

If we hear carefully the proclamations during this Easter Vigil in the Holy Night of Easter, we hear over and over again that "This is the Passover of the Lord" (from the instruction at the beginning of the Service of Light). Yes, surely this night we begin our fifty-day celebration of the Lord's resurrection. After we are invited to rejoice at the beginning of the *Exsultet*, it is declared that "This is our Passover feast." *Our* passover feast. We rejoice because it is not only the Lord's passover from death to life this night, but it is also our own passover. This is why this night is a preeminent time for celebrating baptism, and why all of us renew our baptismal promises. We celebrate the new life we have been given in Christ.

No matter what we humans do that is unfaithful, our generous and merciful God is always faithful and invites us to salvation. All along God only desired for us life. "When the sun had risen," the Son rises. What an image! Concern for the weight of the stone at the entrance is allayed by seeing that it is already rolled back. What a sight! The women are greeted with the words, "Do not be amazed!" What words! How can we not be amazed? All the Scriptures had prepared us, but we could not quite imagine this zenith of God's plan of salvation: the One who was crucified is now raised to new life.

Mary and the other women come to Jesus' gravesite to anoint him. Hardly were they prepared for what they encountered: not a dead body, but a live "young man" who declared to them, "He has been raised." They are told to go to Galilee and "there you will see him." We know what they found in Galilee: Jesus the risen One. We know what we also find in our midst: Jesus the risen One. Not in Galilee, but right here among us. This is why Easter also celebrates our own passing over into new life—we still encounter the risen One among us and in the good we do for each other. This is also our passover night. Alleluia!

Homily Points

• It seems that for some, life has become quite disposable in our society: rampant crime takes life all too often; unhealthy lifestyles and eating habits leave all too many with diminished energy and shortened life spans. For others, life is quite precious and grasped with all one's might: the terminally ill desperately search for healing; we spend monumental amounts of money on products that will keep us young. Between these two extremes is the reality we celebrate this night: life as we know it comes to an end. But this end is just the beginning.

• Jesus' resurrection is more than a celebration of his new life. Easter is a time for each of us to come to greater awareness of the share in Jesus' risen life that we have been given. Just as the women were commanded to "go and tell" and seek Jesus, so does this define our own discipleship in new life. We are to share the joyous message of salvation and seek Jesus with all our hearts.

• Easter joy is not something we can sustain for 365 days a year. Quickly we get back to the everyday demands of our busy lives. What can be sustained each and every day is gratitude for the life we have been given, a willingness to bring that life to others by goodness and care, and the deep inner peace that comes from seeking the risen One in all we do. When this characterizes our daily living, then our whole life is a living alleluia.

Model Prayer of the Faithful

Presider: On this glorious night when the newly baptized join us for the first time in our priestly prayer, let us confidently present our needs to God.

Response: Lord, hear our prayer.

Cantor: we pray to the Lord,

For the newly baptized and all members of the church, that we may be faithful to our baptismal dignity as sons and daughters of God . . . [pause]

For all peoples of the world, that they may find salvation, hope, and peace in the God who gives new life . . . [pause]

For those in need, that they might live a fulfilled life through the presence of the risen Christ in us . . . [pause]

For all of us gathered here on this holy night, that we might be renewed in life by the joy we share . . . [pause]

Presider: God of life and salvation, you raised your divine Son up to new life: help us to celebrate with renewed life and joy, so that one day we might share everlasting life with you. We ask this through your risen Son, Jesus Christ our Lord. **Amen.**

OPENING PRAYER

Let us pray

Pause for silent prayer

Lord God,
you have brightened this night
with the radiance of the risen Christ.
Quicken the spirit of sonship in your Church;
renew us in mind and body
to give you whole-hearted service.

Grant this through our Lord Jesus Christ,
    your Son,
who lives and reigns with you and the Holy
    Spirit,
one God, for ever and ever. **Amen.**

FOR REFLECTION

· I encounter the risen One in my daily life whenever I . . .

· My Easter joy spills over into care for others when . . .

· I am the risen presence of Christ for others when . . .

Special Features of the Rite

Liturgy of Baptism: Every time the Christian community celebrates baptisms it is a special occasion, but from earliest times the Easter Vigil was the privileged time for celebrating the initiation sacraments. On this night when we celebrate risen life, the newly baptized share in that new life of Christ for the first time and are invited to profess their faith, pray the priestly prayers of the faithful, and come to the Table for their Passover feast. The Liturgy of Baptism includes symbols (water, light, white garment, chrism) that remind us of new life, particularly noted in the language of rebirth. The blessing of the water is filled with imagery that is drawn from Scriptural references to water: the Spirit breathed on the chaotic waters at creation, the flood, the Red Sea that saved Israel and destroyed the Egyptians, the Jordan in which Jesus was baptized, the water that flowed from Jesus' side on the cross, Jesus' command after the resurrection to baptize in the name of the Trinity.

✚ SPIRITUALITY

GOSPEL ACCLAMATION
cf. 1 Cor 5:7b-8a

Ry. Alleluia, alleluia.
Christ, our paschal lamb, has been
    sacrificed;
let us then feast with joy in the Lord.
Ry. Alleluia, alleluia.

Gospel

John 20:1-9; L42ABC

On the first day of the week,
    Mary of Magdala came to the
        tomb early in the morning,
    while it was still dark,
    and saw the stone removed
        from the tomb.
So she ran and went to Simon Peter
    and to the other disciple whom Jesus
        loved, and told them,
    "They have taken the Lord from the
        tomb,
    and we don't know where they put him."
So Peter and the other disciple went out
    and came to the tomb.
They both ran, but the other disciple ran
    faster than Peter
    and arrived at the tomb first;
    he bent down and saw the burial cloths
        there, but did not go in.
When Simon Peter arrived after him,
    he went into the tomb and saw the
        burial cloths there,
    and the cloth that had covered his head,
    not with the burial cloths but rolled up
        in a separate place.
Then the other disciple also went in,
    the one who had arrived at the tomb
        first,
    and he saw and believed.
For they did not yet understand the
    Scripture
    that he had to rise from the dead.

or

Mark 16:1-7; L41B *in Appendix A, p. 294*

or, at an afternoon or evening Mass

Luke 24:13-35; L46 *in Appendix A, p. 294.*

See Appendix A, p. 295 for the other readings.

Reflecting on the Gospel and Living the Paschal Mystery
Key words and phrases from the gospel: tomb [six times], did not yet understand, he had to rise from the dead

To the point: Death leads all of us to the unbelieving and misunderstanding stance of those early disciples. After all, our only experience of death as humans is that it is final. The suffering and death of Good Friday we can grasp; that is within our human experience. The joy and glory of Easter Sunday we can hardly grasp; it is outside of our human experience. No, the disciples didn't understand. Neither do we. But they came to believe. So can we.

Reflection: The paschal mystery is not complete until death gives way to life, "the glory of Jesus' resurrection" (sequence). It is no surprise that the Easter sequence—an embellishment of the gospel alleluia—is more poetic than prose in composition. The open-ended language of poetry perhaps tries to capture best the mystery of Jesus risen from the dead. And yet we know that any language at all falls short of expressing the mystery. Maybe this is why our alleluias ring out: this musical, single word captures and expresses the uncontainable joy in our hearts because Jesus "had to rise from the dead." Alleluia is our way of saying we believe in the resurrection. No wonder we sing alleluia over and over all year long and it is so difficult to bury it during Lent. Taking away our alleluias is like taking away our life. We are lost without it.

Death leads all of us to the unbelieving and misunderstanding stance of those early disciples. After all, our only experience of death as humans is that it is final. The suffering and death of Good Friday we can grasp; that is within our human experience. The joy and glory of Easter Sunday we can hardly grasp; it is outside of our human experience. No, the disciples didn't understand. Neither do we. But they came to believe. So can we.

The disciples saw the empty tomb and believed Mary's report that the body of Jesus was not there. When they encountered the risen Lord, they remembered Jesus' promise that he would be raised up after three days. Thus they came to believe. To help us come to believe, we have the preaching of eyewitnesses (witness is used three times and testify once in the first reading). Our "seeing" comes through hearing an unbroken chain of witnesses who have encountered the risen Lord and preached Christ raised from the dead. Jesus commissioned his disciples to preach; they preach not only the good news of forgiveness of sins and the coming of God's reign, but disciples also preach by their witness to new life in Christ.

Easter Sunday, then, is more than a celebration of the resurrection *of Christ*. It is also an invitation to each of us to preach the gospel and take our place in the long line of witnesses to Jesus' risen life. Perhaps this is why we are so awed at the mystery: not just that Jesus was raised from the dead, but that God entrusts us with Jesus' mission and with being witnesses to God's mighty deed of resurrection. It appears as though God trusts us a great deal. The issue and challenge of this Easter Sunday isn't so much to pass over from misunderstanding to belief; it is to pass over from receiving a share in Jesus' risen life to, like Mary and the early disciples, proclaiming the good news to all we meet. No wonder we continually sing out alleluia!—it means so many things: Christ's risen life and our share in it; seeing and believing; witnessing to these great events. And so we sing again, alleluia!

Model Act of Penitence

Presider: Today our Lenten penance gives way to the exuberant joy of celebrating Christ's resurrection. Let us resolve to witness by our lives to this new life and ready ourselves to give heartfelt thanks and praise . . . [pause]

Lord Jesus, you were raised up to new life by your Father: Lord . . .

Risen Christ, you are victor over death, reigning over everlasting life: Christ . . .

Lord Jesus, you send us to witness to your risen life: Lord . . .

Homily Points

• There is an interesting contrast between the gifts of Christmas and the gifts of Easter. At Christmas, the gifts are openly displayed under the tree, easy to find. At Easter, the eggs are hidden and it takes effort to find them even when they are concealed in familiar places. Like the early disciples, the empty tomb nudges us to keep searching—not merely for a dead body, but for the risen Lord.

• Part of the good news is that we don't search for the risen Lord alone. We have many witnesses who testify to the presence of resurrection in the midst of "death." And as we grow in our belief, we ourselves also become part of the company of these witnesses.

• Jesus is risen and here among us and we must grow in our ability to recognize when we are encountering him. How many of us haven't had an experience we were convinced was "deadly" (e.g., betrayal, suffering, failure). Often it is the witness of another person whose experience was similar to ours who helps us to see and believe the new life that can come from death. Easter challenges us to encounter and witness to the fact that God is true to the divine promise to bring forth life from death.

Model Prayer of the Faithful

Presider: In the joy and hope of the resurrection let us pray to our wondrous God for our needs.

Response:

Lord, hear our prayer.

Cantor:

we pray to the Lord,

That all members of the church witness to Christ's resurrection by the goodness of their lives . . . [pause]

That all peoples of the world come to see and believe in God's gift of salvation . . . [pause]

That those who are disheartened may find joy, those who are sick may find healing, those who are downtrodden may be lifted up . . . [pause]

That all of us here receive new faith and hope through our celebration of Christ's resurrection . . . [pause]

Presider: O saving God, you planned from the beginning of creation to shower us with life and light: hear these our prayers that one day we might enjoy everlasting life with you and the risen Son, with the Holy Spirit, one God, for ever and ever. **Amen.**

FOR REFLECTION
· I have "told" others about Jesus' risen life in which I share by . . .
· What brings me the greatest joy and helps me come to greater belief in the new life God offers me is . . .
· This Easter I wish that . . .

Special Features of the Rite

Sequence: This short, poetic text for Easter Sunday is a perfect example of how a sequence is a meditation on the verse for the gospel acclamation: "Christ, our paschal lamb, has been sacrificed; let us then feast with joy in the Lord." Attributed to one Burgundian Wipo (who lived in the eleventh century), the text is a dialogue between Mary of Magdala (see the gospel in which she runs to Peter and the Beloved Disciple to witness to them about the empty tomb) and the church—Mary even today remains a witness to the resurrection.

One historical use of the sequence was as an embellishment of the gospel acclamation. On the two Sundays when we have an obligatory sequence (Easter and Pentecost), it would be well to combine the sequence with the alleluia and have an extended gospel procession among all the assembly. For those near the aisles perhaps they might touch or kiss the book out of reverence for the proclamation to which we are all called to give witness.

Season of Easter

✚ SPIRITUALITY

R̸. Alleluia, alleluia.
You believe in me, Thomas, because you have
    seen me, says the Lord;
blessed are those who have not seen me, but still
    believe!
R̸. Alleluia, alleluia.

Gospel   John 20:19-31; L44B

On the evening of that first day of the
    week,
    when the doors were locked, where the
        disciples were,
    for fear of the Jews,
    Jesus came and stood in their midst
    and said to them, "Peace be with you."
When he had said this, he showed them
    his hands and his side.
The disciples rejoiced when they saw the
    Lord.
Jesus said to them again, "Peace be with
    you.
As the Father has sent me, so I send you."
And when he had said this, he breathed
    on them and said to them,
    "Receive the Holy Spirit.
Whose sins you forgive are forgiven them,
    and whose sins you retain are retained."

Thomas, called Didymus, one of the
    Twelve,
    was not with them when Jesus came.
So the other disciples said to him, "We
    have seen the Lord."
But he said to them,
    "Unless I see the mark of the nails in
        his hands
    and put my finger into the nailmarks
    and put my hand into his side, I will not
        believe."

Now a week later his disciples were again
    inside
    and Thomas was with them.
Jesus came, although the doors were
    locked,
    and stood in their midst and said,
        "Peace be with you."

Continued in Appendix A, p. 296.

Reflecting on the Gospel

"Oh, I see!" someone may say to us. Little children play peek-a-boo and say "I see you!" "Go and see who's at the door," a parent might say to one of their youngsters. The word "see" has many meanings, although in one way or another they are all related. When we "see" in the literal sense of using our eyes, we mean to regard or notice something. Metaphorically, to see means to comprehend, understand, have something dawn on us; it always implies an awakening.

As Thomas says to the other disciples in this Sunday's gospel, he must *see* the risen Lord for himself, or he "will not believe." Thomas is actually bridging the literal and metaphoric meanings. He wants to "see" in the sense of real—he wants to put his "finger into the nailmarks and put [his] hand into his side." He also wants to go from disbelief to belief.

With the appearance of the risen Lord on Easter evening, the disciples (less Thomas) pass over from fear to rejoicing, from disbelief to belief. This transformation, however, is incomplete—a week later, the disciples are still hiding behind locked doors. Yet the risen Lord does not abandon them, but continues to make his presence known not only to the disciples who saw him the week before, but now also to Thomas who is present, sees, and comes to belief. This is good news for us. No matter how halting our belief in the resurrection, the risen Lord is relentless in leading us to belief and to the new life this belief brings.

Thomas is a convenient stand-in for all of us as we strive to deepen our belief in the risen Lord. Unlike Thomas, however, we do not literally "see" the risen Lord. We do encounter Christ in the ministry of the believing community: being of "one heart and mind," bearing "witness," sharing our goods so that there is "no needy person among" us (first reading). This is also how the risen Lord comes among us: in those in need, in those who reach out in self-giving to help those in need. Going from disbelief to belief is not a mental exercise. It is encountering the risen Lord in the people and circumstances around us.

Living the Paschal Mystery

Belief always goes beyond what we can prove, and often means we must go out on a limb. Belief can make us vulnerable; for example, we can be taken advantage of or we might gain a reputation for being gullible. Belief in the risen Lord means that we die to self so that we can encounter the risen Lord around us. This means, at times, that we ourselves might have "nail marks" or we might be wounded. Dying to self always runs a risk of being vulnerable. So it was with Jesus. Out of his vulnerability, love, and self-giving came risen life!

The challenge of this gospel is that we put aside our own fears and embrace belief, with all its consequences. Just as the risen Lord was relentless in bringing the disciples from disbelief to belief, so is he with us. He is also just as relentless with us as he was with the disciples in bringing them to the cross. Even after his resurrection, Jesus always challenges us to both dying and rising.

Having passed over from our Lenten discipline to Easter rejoicing doesn't mean that we can forget about the dying required for living the paschal mystery. Now, however, our "seeing" is heightened: we have experienced once again Easter joy, a glimpse and promise of the fullness to come.

Focusing the Gospel

Key words and phrases: doors were locked, fear, Jesus . . . in their midst, rejoiced, seen the Lord, come to believe

To the point: With the appearance of the risen Lord on Easter evening, the disciples pass over from fear to rejoicing, from disbelief to belief. This transformation, however, is incomplete—a week later, the disciples are still hiding behind locked doors. Yet the risen Lord does not abandon them, but continues to make his presence known not only to the disciples who saw him the week before, but now also to Thomas who is present, sees, and comes to belief. This is good news for us. No matter how halting our belief in the resurrection, the risen Lord is relentless in leading us to belief and to the new life this belief brings.

Connecting the Gospel

to the first two readings: This Sunday's gospel focuses on the gradual growth in belief of the disciples in the upper room. The first two readings present us with a picture of the ongoing demands of mature belief: sharing of goods, care for the needy, loving one another, and keeping God's commandments.

to culture: Saying, "I believe you" (I believe the facts of what you are saying) is different from saying, "I believe *in* you" (I trust you as a person). Believing in the resurrection is more than believing in a *fact*; it is trusting in Jesus.

Connecting the Responsorial Psalm

to the readings: For the Israelites, the rejected stone become cornerstone of Psalm 118 may have represented the stone of the Temple, the symbol of God the immovable rock of their salvation. Or it may have represented themselves, a puny nation thought easy to conquer but proven surprisingly staunch because of the supportive power of God. In either case the stone was something people could "see" and in doing so they could come to believe in God's wonderful works and everlasting love.

Following Christian tradition, the Lectionary interprets the rejected stone as Christ risen from death to become the foundation of the church. Because of Christ's resurrection, we sing thanks to God for love and mercy, victory and salvation. This is "wonderful in our eyes" (psalm) and we want the world to know it. But we tell them through more than just our singing. It is our loving one another, caring for the needy, and keeping the commandments (first and second readings) that proclaim most loudly the wonderful work of God wrought in Christ. Our behavior becomes the cornerstone of faith for others, and this is "wonderful in [all] eyes."

to cantor preparation: In singing these verses from Psalm 118, you invite the assembly to give God thanks for the wonderful gift of the resurrection. In the context of the readings, you also invite them to give thanks for the gift of faith and the gift of loving, righteous living borne out of that faith. You might spend some time this week identifying where you encounter the resurrecting work of God in the lives of believers. Where also have you seen a rejected (or impeding) stone become a cornerstone of faith?

ASSEMBLY & FAITH-SHARING GROUPS

· I have grown in my belief in the risen Lord in that . . . I know my belief needs to be deeper in that . . .

· I have experienced Jesus calling me to greater belief when . . .

· My faith community leads me from fear to rejoicing when . . . from doubt to faith when . . .

PRESIDERS

· My moments of doubt have, like Thomas, led me to deeper faith by . . .

DEACONS

· My service leads others to believe in the risen Lord when . . .

HOSPITALITY MINISTERS

· My welcome, care, and concern helps those gathering for liturgy to experience community as being "of one heart and mind" when . . .

MUSIC MINISTERS

· In my music ministry, I have encountered the presence of the risen Lord when . . . I have helped my fellow music ministers encounter this presence by . . .

ALTAR MINISTERS

· My belief in the risen Lord helps me serve better because . . .

LECTORS

· "[T]hese [words] are written that you may come to believe." My prayerful preparation with the word leads me to a deeper belief when . . .

EXTRAORDINARY MINISTERS OF HOLY COMMUNION

· The way I express my belief in the risen Lord in my daily living is carried over in how I distribute Holy Communion by . . .

Model Rite of Blessing and Sprinkling Holy Water

Presider: Dear friends, this water we bless reminds us of our baptism and our identity as the Body of Christ. Thomas doubted and came to belief through his encounter with the risen Lord. Let us open ourselves to encounter this same risen Lord . . . [pause]

[continue with form C of the blessing of water]

Homily Points

• How often isn't it true that our strengths are affirmed by another, and that we are helped to overcome weaknesses by knowing that another has faced and mastered the same weaknesses? The testimony of others can have a powerful effect on us, encouraging and assuring us in our hesitations and doubts. Not so with Thomas; even the rejoicing of the disciples in seeing the Lord wasn't able to bring Thomas to belief in the resurrection.

• Thomas asks for physical proof that Jesus is alive. He could have seen the proof in the disciples themselves who had been transformed from fear to rejoicing because of their encounter with the risen Lord. Yet, he was unbelieving—blind, unseeing—to the possibility of life coming from death.

• The challenge in the gospel is for Thomas to go from unbelief to belief in the risen Lord. The challenge for us is to go from paying lip service to belief in the resurrection to its being a dynamic believing, which makes an actual difference in the way we live our daily lives and how we ultimately approach each other in relationships. We ourselves are called to be the presence of the risen Lord in today's world, bringing life out of death.

Model Prayer of the Faithful

Presider: Christ is risen and present among us. Let us ask for what we need to live as his faithful disciples.

Response: Lord, hear our prayer.

Cantor: we pray to the Lord,

That all members of the church come to a deeper faith by encountering the risen Lord in each other . . . [pause]

That all nations of the world grow in lasting peace . . . [pause]

That those who are poor and in need be supported by the care and concern of the community of the church . . . [pause]

That all of us here gathered may rejoice in the risen Lord and receive new life from him . . . [pause]

Presider: Gracious God, you raised your Son Jesus to risen life and brought us to belief: hear these our prayers that we might one day live with you and your Son Jesus Christ for ever and ever. **Amen.**

ALTERNATIVE OPENING PRAYER

Let us pray
 [as Christians thirsting for the risen life]

Pause for silent prayer

Heavenly Father and God of mercy,
we no longer look for Jesus among the
 dead,
for he is alive and has become the Lord
 of life.
From the waters of death you raise us
 with him
and renew your gift of life within us.
Increase in our minds and hearts
the risen life we share with Christ
and help us to grow as your people
toward the fullness of eternal life with
 you.

We ask this through Christ our Lord.
 Amen.

FIRST READING

Acts 4:32-35

The community of believers was of one
 heart and mind,
 and no one claimed that any of his
 possessions was his own,
 but they had everything in common.
With great power the apostles bore
 witness
 to the resurrection of the Lord Jesus,
 and great favor was accorded them all.
There was no needy person among them,
 for those who owned property or houses
 would sell them,
 bring the proceeds of the sale,
 and put them at the feet of the apostles,
 and they were distributed to each
 according to need.

RESPONSORIAL PSALM

Ps 118:2-4, 13-15, 22-24

℟. (1) Give thanks to the Lord for he is good, his love is everlasting.
 or:
℟. Alleluia.

Let the house of Israel say,
 "His mercy endures forever."
Let the house of Aaron say,
 "His mercy endures forever."
Let those who fear the LORD say,
 "His mercy endures forever."

℟. Give thanks to the Lord for he is good, his love is everlasting.
 or:
℟. Alleluia.

I was hard pressed and was falling,
    but the LORD helped me.
My strength and my courage is the LORD,
    and he has been my savior.
The joyful shout of victory
    in the tents of the just.

R̸. Give thanks to the Lord for he is good,
his love is everlasting.
    or:
R̸. Alleluia.

The stone which the builders rejected
    has become the cornerstone.
By the LORD has this been done;
    it is wonderful in our eyes.
This is the day the LORD has made;
    let us be glad and rejoice in it.

R̸. Give thanks to the Lord for he is good,
his love is everlasting.
    or:
R̸. Alleluia.

SECOND READING
1 John 5:1-6

Beloved:
Everyone who believes that Jesus is the
    Christ is begotten by God,
    and everyone who loves the Father
    loves also the one begotten by him.
In this way we know that we love the
    children of God
    when we love God and obey his
        commandments.
For the love of God is this,
    that we keep his commandments.
And his commandments are not
    burdensome,
    for whoever is begotten by God
        conquers the world.
And the victory that conquers the world is
    our faith.
Who indeed is the victor over the world
    but the one who believes that Jesus is
        the Son of God?

This is the one who came through water
    and blood, Jesus Christ,
    not by water alone, but by water and
        blood.
The Spirit is the one that testifies,
    and the Spirit is truth.

About Liturgy

Easter octave: Two great festivals still retain an octave on the 1969 Revised General Roman Calendar: Christmas and Easter. For eight days we celebrate with great solemnity the joy of the festival; for example, we may sing the sequence every day during the octave of Easter and no other celebration may take the place of these eight days.

Eight is an important symbolic number and its meaning for an octave is something of the same meaning as when the early Christians called Sunday the "eighth day." Our week has seven days and so to speak of an eighth day is to speak of a day beyond our human reckoning of time—beyond time, belonging to the end times. Theologically, this refers to "eschatological" time when Jesus Christ will return in all his glory to gather everything back to God at the end and fullness of time. Thus, the Easter octave means more than simply going from one Sunday to the next; it heightens our expectation that the risen life we celebrate is the same life that we will one day share with the Trinity in everlasting glory.

Significance of the proclaimed word and the ministry of lector: The gospel for this Sunday makes clear that one way we come to belief is through the proclamation of the word. As caretakers of the word, lectors' ministry is intimately connected with the assembly's encountering Christ and coming to belief. Before lectors can proclaim the word effectively so that Christ is encountered, they themselves must have encountered Christ in the word. Their proclamation must ring with their own belief so that the assembly is moved to respond, "My Lord and my God!" The way to come to this kind of proclamation is twofold: lectors must pray and reflect deeply and long on the word they will proclaim; lectors must live the word in their life so they know from their own experience of the word's challenges and blessings.

About Liturgical Music

Seasons and style of acclamations: The interplay between festal seasons and Ordinary Time is an expression of the dying-rising dynamic that defines the paschal mystery. Throughout the course of the year, the liturgy draws us into this dynamic. The style of acclamations we sing during each season helps us understand this dynamic and participate in it. The acclamations we sing, then, need to fit the purpose and mood of each season. Singing the wrong style of acclamations for a given season actually impedes our participation in the broader scheme of the whole liturgical year.

Easter is the season to use the most festive, energetic, musically embellished acclamations in the parish repertoire. Select such a set, then reserve its use for this season only. Over time the assembly will recognize it as their "Easter setting." To emphasize the relationship between Easter and the solemnities celebrated during the year—for example, All Saints, Christ the King—use this set on those days also.

✠ SPIRITUALITY

GOSPEL ACCLAMATION
cf. Luke 24:32

R̸. Alleluia, alleluia.
Lord Jesus, open the Scriptures to us;
make our hearts burn while you speak to us.
R̸. Alleluia, alleluia.

Gospel Luke 24:35-48; L47B

The two disciples recounted what had
    taken place on the way,
    and how Jesus was made known to them
    in the breaking of bread.

While they were still speaking about this,
    he stood in their midst and said to them,
    "Peace be with you."
But they were startled and terrified
    and thought that they were seeing a ghost.
Then he said to them, "Why are you troubled?
And why do questions arise in your hearts?
Look at my hands and my feet, that it is I
    myself.
Touch me and see, because a ghost does not
    have flesh and bones
    as you can see I have."
And as he said this,
    he showed them his hands and his feet.
While they were still incredulous for joy
    and were amazed,
    he asked them, "Have you anything here
    to eat?"
They gave him a piece of baked fish;
    he took it and ate it in front of them.

He said to them,
    "These are my words that I spoke to you
        while I was still with you,
    that everything written about me in the
        law of Moses
    and in the prophets and psalms must be
        fulfilled."
Then he opened their minds to understand
    the Scriptures.
And he said to them,
    "Thus it is written that the Christ would
        suffer
    and rise from the dead on the third day
    and that repentance, for the forgiveness
        of sins,
    would be preached in his name
    to all the nations, beginning from
        Jerusalem.
You are witnesses of these things."

Reflecting on the Gospel

Despite the reports of the two Emmaus disciples (opening lines of the gospel) and other eyewitnesses as well, when Jesus appeared to the gathered disciples they "were startled and terrified and thought that they were seeing a ghost" (gospel). Similar to last Sunday with Thomas, Jesus invites the disciples to "Look at my hands and my feet, that it is I myself." "Look . . . touch . . . see." How concretely Jesus relates to the disciples. How understanding! How quickly their

terror was changed to incredulous joy! How amazed they were as this risen One ate before them the "piece of baked fish." It is as though Jesus is doing everything possible to help the disciples understand how real this new life of resurrection is. Then Jesus brings it home to the disciples in specific terms to which human beings can readily relate. His death and resurrection were not isolated events only in the life of Jesus; they have meaning for all Jesus' disciples.

The reality of his passing over from death to life is carried forward by those who witness to these things: repentance and forgiveness of sins.

It is perhaps surprising that repentance and forgiveness (acts we much more readily associate with Lent) figure so prominently in all three readings assigned to this third Sunday of Easter. The readings suggest to us that we, unlike the disciples to whom Jesus appeared after the resurrection, cannot "Look . . . touch . . . see." But Jesus gives us another and just as concrete a means to come to belief in the new life of resurrection. For repentance and forgiveness are themselves encounters with the risen Lord, an invitation to greater belief, and an experience of our own resurrection.

In this Sunday's gospel, Jesus invites all the disciples to do what (in John's gospel last Sunday) he had invited Thomas to do, "Touch me," so that they might come to believe in his resurrection. This belief, however, is not passive. Our belief in the risen Lord is made visible when we "preach in his name" the kind of repentance leading to the new life of forgiveness. We "touch" Jesus today when we repent of our sins and forgive others—an encounter with this same risen Lord that makes him present in our world today. Jesus "was made known" in the breaking of the bread and in repentance and forgiveness. This is risen life: "You are forgiven." This is our witness to the resurrection: "I forgive you."

Living the Paschal Mystery

Our belief in the risen One is not some elite intellectual exercise, but an embodied faith expressed in actions. Our faith is seen both in us by our assent to God's will and in our actions by our witness to repentance and forgiveness of sins. Forgiveness is part of the reality of risen life; it is the effect of death and resurrection. We should walk and act like a forgiven people.

Repentance and forgiveness do not belong simply to Lent—there, that's over for another year. Instead, they are very much a part of the Easter mystery. Forgiveness is the virtue that enables us not to allow past hurts to determine our decisions and actions in the here and now. Forgiveness opens up the space for creating together with the one forgiven a new future where we can "fall peacefully asleep" (responsorial psalm). Giving and receiving forgiveness is a resurrection activity. This is how Jesus is known.

Focusing the Gospel

Key words and phrases: Touch me, repentance, forgiveness of sins, preached in his name

To the point: In this Sunday's gospel, Jesus invites all the disciples to do what (in John's gospel last Sunday) he had invited Thomas to do, "Touch me," so that they might come to believe in his resurrection. This belief leads to preaching a gospel of repentance and forgiveness, which invites all peoples to "touch" Jesus and be raised to new life.

Connecting the Gospel

to the first two readings: Peter (first reading) and the first Letter of St. John (second reading) witness ways that the early communities obeyed Jesus' command in the gospel to preach repentance and forgiveness.

to experience: We usually think of repentance of wrongdoing and forgiveness as difficult and negative experiences. All three readings remind us that these are life-giving actions leading to an encounter with the risen Lord.

Connecting the Responsorial Psalm

to the readings: All three readings this Sunday reveal how we as human beings prefer darkness to light, death to life, sin to righteousness. Darkness may be the realm of death, but it is the familiar. Christ risen from the dead, offering forgiveness for sin, is the unexpected. Can we believe? Are we forgiven? "Yes," answer the readings. We need only repent (first reading), return to righteous living (second reading), believe in the risen, forgiving Christ whom we encounter in the breaking of the bread, in Scripture, and in the witnessing of others (gospel).

Between our ongoing human struggle and God's redemptive answer stands the responsorial psalm. Honest about ourselves, we beg God to shine the face of the risen Christ upon the darkness of our unbelief and our sinfulness. We know already from personal experience (psalm) and the witness of others (all three readings) that God will respond. We have only to ask for the light (psalm refrain).

to cantor preparation: Spend some time this week looking honestly at your own struggles with unbelief and sin. Look with the eyes of God who, never surprised by human behavior, continually comes with evidence of resurrection and offers of forgiveness (all three readings). As you sing this responsorial psalm, then, you will be able to call to God out of real need and speak to the assembly out of real confidence.

**ASSEMBLY &
FAITH-SHARING GROUPS**

· Jesus has "touched" me when . . . I have "touched" others with the presence of the risen Lord when . . .

· Examples of how I have experienced the risen Lord through repentance and forgiveness are . . .

· The new life I have experienced this Easter season is . . .

PRESIDERS

· I have helped another to repent and be forgiven when . . .

DEACONS

· My service of others makes Jesus known to them by . . .

HOSPITALITY MINISTERS

· My greeting helps those gathering to experience the risen Lord when . . .

MUSIC MINISTERS

· As a music minister I need to seek forgiveness for . . . Seeking this forgiveness witnesses to the presence of the risen Lord by . . .

ALTAR MINISTERS

· My serving at the altar is a fruitful expression of my repentance and forgiveness when . . .

LECTORS

· My proclamation opens the minds of the assembly to understand the Scriptures when . . .

**EXTRAORDINARY MINISTERS
OF HOLY COMMUNION**

· The Eucharist has inspired and nourished me to be repentant and forgiving by . . .

Model Rite of Blessing and Sprinkling Holy Water

Presider: Dear friends, our baptismal commitment urges us to preach repentance and forgiveness. We ask God to bless this water and we sprinkle it as a sign and renewal of our baptism and of our desire to be faithful to that commitment . . . [pause]

  [continue with form C of the blessing of water]

Homily Points

• Too often we think of people who apologize and ask for forgiveness as weak and insecure. But actually such behavior reveals great inner strength and often generates genuine admiration and respect. The ability to apologize and seek forgiveness is a worthy human trait; it is also necessary if we are to grow in our relationships.

• The readings this Sunday are less concerned with hammering at us for our human faults and sins than they are with God's offer of new life through repentance and forgiveness. It is not God's judgment Peter preaches about, for example, but God's mercy and our conversion of heart to which this mercy calls us.

• In the gospel Jesus reveals that he died and rose to bring us to repentance and forgiveness, and he missions us to continue this life-giving preaching. We are to do this not only in words, but we are to make repentance and forgiveness of others the identifiable characteristic of those of us who follow the risen Lord.

Model Prayer of the Faithful

Presider: The God who raised Jesus from the dead calls us to repentance and offers us new life. And so we pray.

Response: Lord, hear our prayer.

Cantor: we pray to the Lord,

That the church always be a font of mercy and forgiveness . . . [pause]

That all people hear God's call to repentance and celebrate the new life of forgiveness . . . [pause]

That those burdened by guilt be freed by Jesus' promise of forgiveness . . . [pause]

That each of us gathered here be sincere in our repentance and quick to forgive . . . [pause]

Presider: Merciful God, you are forgiving and offer new life beyond compare: hear these our prayers that we might enjoy new life now and always. We ask this through the risen One, Jesus Christ our Lord. **Amen.**

ALTERNATIVE OPENING PRAYER
Let us pray

Pause for silent prayer

Father in heaven, author of all truth,
a people once in darkness has listened to
   your Word
and followed your Son as he rose from the
   tomb.
Hear the prayer of this newborn people
and strengthen your Church to answer
   your call.
May we rise and come forth into the light
   of day
to stand in your presence until eternity
   dawns.
We ask this through Christ our Lord.
   Amen.

FIRST READING
Acts 3:13-15, 17-19

Peter said to the people:
"The God of Abraham,
   the God of Isaac, and the God of Jacob,
   the God of our fathers, has glorified his
      servant Jesus,
   whom you handed over and denied in
      Pilate's presence
   when he had decided to release him.
You denied the Holy and Righteous One
   and asked that a murderer be released
      to you.
The author of life you put to death,
   but God raised him from the dead; of
      this we are witnesses.
Now I know, brothers,
   that you acted out of ignorance, just as
      your leaders did;
   but God has thus brought to fulfillment
   what he had announced beforehand
   through the mouth of all the prophets,
   that his Christ would suffer.
Repent, therefore, and be converted, that
   your sins may be wiped away."

RESPONSORIAL PSALM

Ps 4:2, 4, 7-8, 9

℟. (7a) Lord, let your face shine on us.
or:
℟. Alleluia.

When I call, answer me, O my just God,
   you who relieve me when I am in
      distress;
   have pity on me, and hear my prayer!

℟. Lord, let your face shine on us.
or:
℟. Alleluia.

Know that the LORD does wonders for his
   faithful one;
   the LORD will hear me when I call upon
      him.

℟. Lord, let your face shine on us.
or:
℟. Alleluia.

O LORD, let the light of your countenance
   shine upon us!
   You put gladness into my heart.

℟. Lord, let your face shine on us.
or:
℟. Alleluia.

As soon as I lie down, I fall peacefully
   asleep,
   for you alone, O LORD,
   bring security to my dwelling.

℟. Lord, let your face shine on us.
or:
℟. Alleluia.

SECOND READING

1 John 2:1-5a

My children, I am writing this to you
   so that you may not commit sin.
But if anyone does sin, we have an
      Advocate with the Father,
   Jesus Christ the righteous one.
He is expiation for our sins,
   and not for our sins only but for those
      of the whole world.
The way we may be sure that we know
   him is to keep
   his commandments.
Those who say, "I know him," but do not
   keep his commandments
   are liars, and the truth is not in them.
But whoever keeps his word,
   the love of God is truly perfected in
      him.

About Liturgy

Sacrament of Penance: Much is being written in the Catholic press these days about the demise of the Sacrament of Penance—too few are making use of this sacrament of healing, especially as private confession between the typical twice-a-year (Advent and Lent) communal penance liturgies in our parishes. Perhaps part of the problem lies in a rather narrow understanding of this sacrament—that it is about acknowledging sins. This is true, but it is only one dimension of the sacrament. Far more important is that our seeking and receiving forgiveness, our firm resolve of repentance, and our doing some penance as an expression of our desire for conversion are all opportunities for encounters with the risen Christ.

Like all liturgy, the Sacrament of Penance makes present the paschal mystery. Perhaps we focus too much on the dying aspect of this mystery (confession of sins) and not enough on the rising (encounter with Christ and the restoration of our relationship with God). Like all sacraments, the Rite of Reconciliation includes a proclamation of the word, even when it is celebrated as private confession. Perhaps a good practice would be to reflect on some New Testament passage on forgiveness for a significant time before confession; perhaps this Sunday's gospel would be a good choice since it reminds us so well of the connection of forgiveness and risen life.

Since this is the third and last Sunday of Easter for which the gospel selection proclaims a resurrection appearance, this would be a good Sunday to mark our calendars for times for us to receive the Sacrament of Penance. This is one way to prolong the Easter celebration into Ordinary Time.

About Liturgical Music

Music suggestions: An excellent hymn for either the entrance or the Communion procession this Sunday would be "That Easter Day with Joy Was Bright" [CBW3, CG, CH, RS, W3]. This fifth-century text speaks of Christ standing before his disciples, his "risen flesh with radiance glowed; His wounded hands and feet he showed." The triple meter of the tune usually coupled with it, PUER NOBIS, dances with the joy of encounter with the risen Christ (CBW3 uses LASST UNS ERFREUEN which gives the text a broader feel). "Christ the Lord Is Risen Today," James Leeson's translation of the Easter sequence *Victimae paschali laudes*, speaks of "God and sinners reconciled," a significant theme in all of this Sunday's readings. RS uses a long setting with alleluia refrain which would fit the Communion procession. BB, JS2, SS, and WC use a shorter tune which would work well for the entrance procession.

SPIRITUALITY

GOSPEL ACCLAMATION
John 10:14

R̸. Alleluia, alleluia.
I am the good shepherd, says the Lord;
I know my sheep, and mine know me.
R̸. Alleluia, alleluia.

Gospel

John 10:11-18; L50B

Jesus said:
    "I am the good shepherd.
A good shepherd lays down his
        life for the sheep.
A hired man, who is not a
        shepherd
    and whose sheep are not his
        own,
    sees a wolf coming and leaves
        the sheep and runs away,
    and the wolf catches and
        scatters them.
This is because he works for pay
        and has no concern for the sheep.
I am the good shepherd,
    and I know mine and mine know me,
    just as the Father knows me and I
        know the Father;
    and I will lay down my life for the
        sheep.
I have other sheep that do not belong to
        this fold.
These also I must lead, and they will
        hear my voice,
    and there will be one flock, one
        shepherd.
This is why the Father loves me,
    because I lay down my life in order to
        take it up again.
No one takes it from me, but I lay it
        down on my own.
I have power to lay it down, and power
        to take it up again.
This command I have received from my
    Father."

Reflecting on the Gospel

"Selective hearing" is a phrase we sometimes hear. It means that we hear what we want, and "tune out" what we don't want to hear. Children have selective hearing when they can't hear a parent telling them to quit the computer game and do their homework, but they hear the parent calling them to supper. Adults hear many "voices" in the course of a day, and choose which ones to pay attention to and which ones to tune out. In the gospel this Sunday Jesus declares himself to be the "good shepherd" whose flock must hear his voice. Moreover, we who hear his voice must follow it. Following Jesus, as the gospel says, means that we must "lay down [our] life" for the sake of others. We can do this, because the Good Shepherd has already done this for us.

In this gospel parable the hired man doesn't have a sufficiently deep or committed relationship to the sheep and so he runs away when danger comes. The good shepherd, however, is the one who owns the sheep and has much more at stake than the hired hand. The good shepherd is concerned about, cares for, and protects the sheep even to the point of laying down the shepherd's life. Jesus requires of us disciples the same mission—to lay down our lives (this phrase occurs five times in the gospel), too.

Shepherding, then, is serious business. It means that we cannot run away from danger like the hired man, but we must meet danger head-on for the sake of God's beloved. Because of the resurrection, we share in the new life of Christ; our entry into this new life is dying to ourselves—laying down our own lives. Jesus proclaims that he is the "good shepherd," that his flock hear his voice, and that he lays down his life for them. In the context of the second reading, however, we are more than Jesus' flock: we are "children of God" who are to "be like him." This means that we are not only sheep who hear our Good Shepherd's voice, but we also are to become shepherds ourselves. Transformed from sheep to shepherd, we take up the life he has laid down and take up his saving mission to shepherd others to new life.

Taking up Jesus' mission means that we actually adopt selective hearing as a way of life. Now, however, the selective hearing isn't a matter of following our own will or completing a task of our own liking. The selective hearing of Jesus' disciples is a sharpening of our hearing so that Jesus' voice is the guiding element in our daily living. By sorting through all the diverse voices we hear each day, and hearing in some of them the voice of Jesus, we know the fold to which we belong—"we are God's children now" (second reading). Hearing Jesus' voice, we know that "[t]here is no salvation through anyone else" (first reading). And we willingly lay down our own lives so that others can come to the same awesome truth: a share in Easter life, the "love the Father has bestowed on us" (second reading).

Living the Paschal Mystery

Laying down our lives for the sake of others doesn't mean that we will be nailed to a cross. It does mean that we commit ourselves to "good deeds" (first reading) such as caring for the sick, forgiving those who wrong us (last Sunday's gospel), giving thanks and praise to God (responsorial psalm), loving others as God has loved us (second reading). These good deeds are the very "stuff" of our everyday living. We don't have to go out of our way to be good shepherds. We need only relate as one filled with new life in Christ to those who come our way.

Focusing the Gospel

Key words and phrases: good shepherd, lays down his life, sheep, hear my voice, take it up again

To the point: In the gospel for this Sunday, Jesus proclaims that he is the "good shepherd," that his flock hear his voice, and that he lays down his life for them. In the context of the second reading, however, we are more than Jesus' flock: we are "children of God" who are to "be like him." This means that we are not only sheep who hear our Good Shepherd's voice, but we also are to become shepherds ourselves. Transformed from sheep to shepherd, we take up the life he has laid down.

Connecting the Gospel

to the first reading and Pentecost: This Sunday's first reading already exemplifies the mission conferred on the disciples at Pentecost, and hinted at in the gospel. "Peter, filled with the Holy Spirit," carries out Jesus' commission to heal the sick and proclaim the Good News.

to Catholic culture: The image of the Good Shepherd (pictures on our walls or statues on our mantels) is not only a promise of divine care and protection; it is also a call to Christian mission.

Connecting the Responsorial Psalm

to the readings: The readings and responsorial psalm for this Sunday present us with two very different images of Christ: cornerstone and good shepherd. One is an image of rock, the other of flesh and blood and their juxta-position deepens our understanding of who Jesus is for us. As cornerstone he stands as our foundation, the one upon whom we can build our lives. As shepherd he knows us intimately and loves us so profoundly that he lays down his life for us. Both images tell us we can count on Christ because he is rock-solid. There is no salvation through anyone else (first reading). He lays down his life for us on his own power (gospel). Rejection by other powers-that-be poses no ultimate threat to his mission of salvation (first reading, psalm). Christ—the one who never crumbles, the one who never flinches from the demands of saving us; the one who supports, the one who loves; the one on whom we stand and the one whom we follow—Christ, the savior for whom in singing this psalm we give thanks.

to cantor preparation: As you prepare to sing this Sunday's responsorial psalm, you might reflect on questions such as these: How is Christ the foundation of your life? How does Christ lead and support you? How is Christ faithful to you at all costs? How do you give Christ thanks?

ASSEMBLY & FAITH-SHARING GROUPS
· I experience Jesus as Good Shepherd when . . . I am a good shepherd for others when . . .
· I hear Jesus' voice calling me to . . .
· Like Jesus, I lay down my life for others when I . . . Others lay down their life for me when . . .

PRESIDERS
· As shepherd, I lay down my life for the assembly when . . .

DEACONS
· In my ministry, I take up the life Jesus laid down by . . .

HOSPITALITY MINISTERS
· My greeting prepares people to hear the voice of the Good Shepherd in the liturgy when . . .

MUSIC MINISTERS
· My music ministry helps the assembly become one flock led by Jesus when I . . .

ALTAR MINISTERS
· Often the voice of Jesus calls me through my service of the altar and I . . .

LECTORS
· The assembly hears the voice of Jesus in my proclamation when . . .

EXTRAORDINARY MINISTERS OF HOLY COMMUNION
· Distributing Holy Communion is an act of taking up new life for me when . . . for the communicants when . . .

Model Rite of Blessing and Sprinkling Holy Water

Presider: Dear friends, we ask God to bless this water as a reminder of our baptism through which we are empowered to hear the voice of Jesus the Good Shepherd. Let us pray that we may also be good shepherds, helping each other come to the fullness of life . . . [pause]

[continue with form C of the blessing of water]

Homily Points

• We have a romanticized notion of shepherds; in reality, they were the dregs of society doing a work no one wanted to do. Shepherding was a dirty, lonely, thankless job with animals who are notoriously stupid and stinky. Often outcasts and criminals were given this job of shepherding, and it was no surprise that they would abandon the sheep when trouble or danger threatened.

• Jesus proclaims himself to be the *good* shepherd because he is more concerned about the welfare of the sheep than about his own welfare. He lays down his life for the sheep. Moreover, he takes his life up again, first, in his resurrection, but not only that. He also takes up his life *through us* his flock who hear his voice and follow him. Now, as disciples, we become like him (see second reading), good shepherds, who similarly lay down our own lives.

• Like "dumb sheep," we often wander around and get ourselves into all kinds of trouble; for example, we blindly follow the crowd even when they are going in a wrong direction or we get ourselves tangled up in knotty situations—both examples descriptive of the human condition. The voice of Jesus calls us back to the right track. His voice also calls us to make the transformation from being sheep to being shepherd. The transformation is never total; we remain always both sheep and shepherd, listening to the voice of Jesus calling us to deeper discipleship.

Model Prayer of the Faithful

Presider: Confident that our Good Shepherd never abandons us, we now lift our needs to God.

Response: Lord, hear our prayer.

Cantor: we pray to the Lord,

That all members of the church faithfully listen to the voice of the Good Shepherd calling them to discipleship and mission . . . [pause]

That all leaders of nations be good shepherds, concerned for the welfare of their people . . . [pause]

That those who are suffering or downtrodden be lifted up by the embrace of the Good Shepherd . . . [pause]

That we always have the courage to lay down our lives so that new life can burst forth in others . . . [pause]

Presider: Loving God, your Son is the Good Shepherd who laid down his life for us: hear these our prayers that we might be faithful in laying down our own lives and come to the new life promised us. We ask this through Christ our Lord. **Amen.**

Let us pray

Pause for silent prayer

Almighty and ever-living God,
give us new strength
from the courage of Christ our shepherd,
and lead us to join the saints in heaven,
where he lives and reigns with you and the
  Holy Spirit,
one God, for ever and ever. **Amen.**

FIRST READING

Acts 4:8-12

Peter, filled with the Holy Spirit, said:
  "Leaders of the people and elders:
  If we are being examined today
  about a good deed done to a cripple,
  namely, by what means he was saved,
  then all of you and all the people of
    Israel should know
  that it was in the name of Jesus Christ
    the Nazarene
  whom you crucified, whom God raised
    from the dead;
  in his name this man stands before you
    healed.
He is *the stone rejected by you, the builders,*
  which has become the cornerstone.
There is no salvation through anyone else,
  nor is there any other name under
    heaven
  given to the human race by which we
    are to be saved."

RESPONSORIAL PSALM

Ps 118:1, 8-9, 21-23, 26, 28, 29

℟. (22) The stone rejected by the builders
has become the cornerstone.
  or:
℟. Alleluia.

Give thanks to the LORD, for he is good,
  for his mercy endures forever.
It is better to take refuge in the LORD
  than to trust in man.
It is better to take refuge in the LORD
  than to trust in princes.

℟. The stone rejected by the builders has
become the cornerstone.
  or:
℟. Alleluia.

I will give thanks to you, for you have
    answered me
  and have been my savior.
The stone which the builders rejected
  has become the cornerstone.
By the LORD has this been done;
  it is wonderful in our eyes.

R⁊. The stone rejected by the builders has
become the cornerstone.
  or:
R⁊. Alleluia.

Blessed is he who comes in the name of
    the LORD;
  we bless you from the house of the
    LORD.
I will give thanks to you, for you have
    answered me
  and have been my savior.
Give thanks to the LORD, for he is good;
  for his kindness endures forever.

R⁊. The stone rejected by the builders has
become the cornerstone.
  or:
R⁊. Alleluia.

SECOND READING
1 John 3:1-2

Beloved:
See what love the Father has bestowed
    on us
  that we may be called the children of
    God.
Yet so we are.
The reason the world does not know us
  is that it did not know him.
Beloved, we are God's children now;
  what we shall be has not yet been
    revealed.
We do know that when it is revealed we
    shall be like him,
  for we shall see him as he is.

About Liturgy

The fifty-day Easter Lectionary: The gospels for the eight Sundays from Easter to Pentecost form a wonderfully cohesive progression from Jesus' resurrection to our taking up Jesus' mission to preach the gospel. There is movement from Jesus, the risen One, to ourselves as disciples who, set afire by the Spirit, continue his saving mission in our world today.

The gospels for the first three Sundays of Easter always feature appearance accounts of the risen Lord to the disciples. During this time we focus on Jesus who has passed through death to risen life. We become convinced in our believing hearts that this Jesus is still present to us. Now, on this fourth Sunday of Easter, we are invited to reflect on Jesus' great love and care for us and be assured that he will not abandon us. On Good Shepherd Sunday during this year B, there is also a strong suggestion that we must take up Jesus' mission through our discipleship (especially pronounced in the other two readings). This notion of our taking up and continuing Jesus' mission moves us into the second half of the Easter season when the gospels explicitly focus on us as disciples. These Sunday gospels prepare us for the celebration of the descent of the Spirit at Pentecost, a Spirit who now dwells within us, conforms us to Christ, and strengthens us to take up his saving mission.

About Liturgical Music

The collective "I" of the psalms and of liturgical singing: As with many psalms, the speaker in parts of this Sunday's responsorial psalm is first person singular. The psalms are a good example of texts where the use of the first person singular is not introspective, but is directed outward toward the relationship of the whole community with God. When sung liturgically, the "I" of the psalms is collective: all of Israel, all of the church. Such a collective use calls us to participation in our common identity as God's people beloved, forgiven, redeemed, and called to proclaim God's goodness and mercy to all the world. How apropos this understanding is to Jesus' words in this Sunday's gospel! And how apropos that we keep this understanding in mind in all our liturgical singing. Some songs which use "I" language are not suitable for liturgy; others, like the psalms, draw us to a collective understanding of that "I." The issue is not the use of "I," but whether its use focuses our attention inward to private prayer or outward to shared identity and mission.

Music suggestions: Songs about the Good Shepherd abound. One which connects Jesus' shepherding with our mission to be shepherds ("May we with a shepherd's heart Love the people round us . . .") is Fred Kaan's "Jesus, Shepherd of Our Souls" [GC, W3]. Its gentle tune would make it fitting for the preparation of the gifts.

Russell Woollen's "One Fold, One Shepherd" [WLP octavo 000660] is a choral setting of this Sunday's gospel text. This lovely piece would make an excellent choir prelude. In light of the texts of the first reading and psalm, another good choice for a choral prelude would be Karen Schneider-Kirner and Steven Warner's "Come to the Living Stone" [VO2; WLP octavo 7243], an energetic choir piece with conga or djembe drum accompaniment. In fact, this piece would make an appropriate choral prelude on any Sunday of the Easter season. The choral parts are not difficult to learn and the rhythms—choral and drum—communicate Easter joy.

✠ SPIRITUALITY

GOSPEL ACCLAMATION
John 15:4a, 5b

℟. Alleluia, alleluia.
Remain in me as I remain in you, says the Lord.
Whoever remains in me will bear much fruit.
℟. Alleluia, alleluia.

Gospel

John 15:1-8; L53B

Jesus said to his
    disciples:
    "I am the true vine,
        and my Father is
        the vine grower.
He takes away every
        branch in me that
        does not bear fruit,
    and every one that does he prunes so
        that it bears more fruit.
You are already pruned because of the
        word that I spoke to you.
Remain in me, as I remain in you.
Just as a branch cannot bear fruit on
        its own
    unless it remains on the vine,
    so neither can you unless you remain
        in me.
I am the vine, you are the branches.
Whoever remains in me and I in him
        will bear much fruit,
    because without me you can do
        nothing.
Anyone who does not remain in me
    will be thrown out like a branch and
        wither;
    people will gather them and throw
        them into a fire
    and they will be burned.
If you remain in me and my words
        remain in you,
    ask for whatever you want and it will
        be done for you.
By this is my Father glorified,
    that you bear much fruit and become
        my disciples."

Reflecting on the Gospel

For many elementary students, long division is their mathematical downfall. As long as the division is simple, it is generally manageable. But when it gets to larger numbers, it gets difficult. And no small part of this difficulty is the "remainder"—what in the world do we do with what is left over? So, for example, thirty-two divided by eight is four—that's simple. But what do we do with something like 2009 ÷ 5? What do we do with the remainder, what's left over? This is a stumbling block for many youngsters. This Sunday's gospel talks about "remaining" in Jesus. In a sense, we are "remainders," we are "left over" to do his work of bearing fruit. And just like long division, the willingness to remain with Jesus, be pruned, and bear fruit can be a stumbling block for us, too.

We must "remain" in Jesus because this is the only way to be in relationship with the Father. Our attachment to Jesus—our relationship with the divine—is a choice of heart that is affirmed and confirmed not only "in word or speech but in deed and truth" (second reading). Further, to "remain" in Jesus, we must be willing to be pruned. Even so, pruning is both the problem and the solution. Pruning is a problem because it is painful and we humans avoid what causes us pain. Yet, however painful this pruning may be, it is being done by a God whom we call Father. We bear fruit as disciples because, like with Jesus, the Father ("the vine grower") lovingly tends to us. All the Father's work in Jesus continues as we remain in Jesus. Only by this personal attachment to the Son can we be in personal relationship with the Father and receive all we need to bear fruit.

Just as God planted and tended the true vine Jesus, so does God tend us who remain in Jesus so that we, too, might "bear much fruit." God prunes from us whatever does not give life, and nourishes within us whatever does. Our remaining in Jesus, our bearing fruit as disciples, our believing in the Son and keeping the commandments (see second reading) are all the work of the Father who lovingly tends the life we share with Jesus ("I am the vine, you are the branches").

Living the Paschal Mystery

In the first reading the disciples were afraid to relate to Saul because of his past reputation for persecuting Christians. Barnabas, a member of the community, took Paul under his wings and witnessed to the community on his behalf. In this way was Paul accepted so he could preach the word. Barnabas witnessed to how Paul was "pruned" by his encounter with the risen Jesus, an encounter so intense that he was "pruned" from his old zealous hatred of this new Jewish sect and became a disciple himself, one who "remained" in Jesus.

Part of our living the paschal mystery—its dying and rising—requires that we be willing to be pruned. We must allow God to tend us, so that we might rid ourselves of whatever gets in the way of our being a faithful disciple who not only proclaims the Gospel, but also lives it in "deed and truth." First of all, this means that we must witness to an intimate relationship with God. We do this through prayer and worship—both private and public acts of glorifying God. We also witness in "deed and truth" through how we relate to others. Taking someone troubled under our wing to help them is but one example of how we remain in Jesus through our caring for others.

Focusing the Gospel

Key words and phrases: I am the true vine, my Father is the vine grower, Remain in me, bear much fruit

To the point: Just as God planted and tended the true vine Jesus, so does God tend us who remain in Jesus so that we, too, might "bear much fruit." God prunes from us whatever does not give life, and nourishes within us whatever does. Our remaining in Jesus, our bearing fruit as disciples, our believing in the Son and keeping the commandments (see second reading) are all the work of the Father who lovingly tends the life we share with Jesus ("I am the vine, you are the branches").

Connecting the Gospel

to the first two readings: The Spirit is the "sap" that brings the fruit of discipleship to life. The early church bore fruit in its rapid expansion and its righteous living (see first reading). We bear fruit by keeping the commandments and loving one another (see second reading).

to experience: We tend to think that the word "remaining" implies being stagnant, staying put, not moving forward. Paradoxically, "remaining" in Jesus means growing, changing, and bearing fruit.

Connecting the Responsorial Psalm

to the readings: For what in this Sunday's psalm refrain do we praise God? We praise God for the growth of the church (first reading). We praise God for the presence of the Spirit who enables us to remain connected to Christ and to one another in love (second reading). Finally, we praise God for the pruning which enables us to bear fruit because of our relationship with Christ (gospel). This pruning is not easy or without struggle, as the experience of Paul shows us (first reading). But Paul's experience led him to praise God before others, both those who would listen and those who would not, and his efforts bore fruit—the company of believers grew by leaps and bounds (first reading). May we, like Paul, speak everywhere of God. And may our praise of God, like Paul's, bear fruit.

to cantor preparation: It is one thing to praise God for the resurrection, and another to praise God for pruning those parts of us which impede risen life. In this Sunday's responsorial psalm, you give thanks to God for both. You thank God for both the rising and the dying. What might you do this week to help yourself grow in understanding that when what is not of Christ in you dies, God is doing the work of resurrection?

ASSEMBLY & FAITH-SHARING GROUPS

- God has tended my growth when . . . I have experienced God's pruning when . . .
- What "remain in" Jesus means to me is . . .
- The fruit my life has already borne is . . . New fruit I sense is budding in me is . . .

PRESIDERS

- I call the community to "remain in" Jesus by . . . The community helps me to "remain in" Jesus by . . .

DEACONS

- As the Father tends me, I tend others by . . .

HOSPITALITY MINISTERS

- The manner of my welcome helps the assembly "remain in" Jesus because . . .

MUSIC MINISTERS

- My music ministry lovingly tends to the faith of the assembly when . . .

ALTAR MINISTERS

- The abundant fruit my service at the altar bears is . . .

LECTORS

- My proclamation of the word bears fruit "in deed and truth" (second reading) when . . .

EXTRAORDINARY MINISTERS OF HOLY COMMUNION

- My ministry makes visible the unity of the Vine and the branches as I . . .

127

Model Rite of Blessing and Sprinkling Holy Water

Presider: Dear friends, through baptism we became branches grafted onto the vine Christ. Let us open ourselves to whatever pruning is necessary in our lives so that we can be fruitful and glorify God . . . [pause]

[continue with form C of the blessing of water]

Homily Points

• In nature, the process of "pruning" produces new life. For example, when forest fires occur naturally (such as by lightning), the old trees and ground cover are destroyed, but newer, fresher, healthier, more abundant growth follows. Our human "pruning" also produces new life, but we often react against this experience of being pruned because it is painful. We know, however, that pain can be a sign of growth and that something right is happening.

• The Father-Vine Grower in the gospel is the Creator-God whose pruning shapes us into more perfect icons of the divine image intended at creation. Jesus, aware of how God works, invites us to be open to the pruning necessary for this to happen. We become once again icons of the divine image as we "remain in" Jesus; that is, put on his mind and face.

• It is natural for us to react against the pain of the pruning process. Yet, we embrace the pain (dying to self) because the gain is so great: remaining in Jesus, becoming like him, and bearing much fruit.

Model Prayer of the Faithful

Presider: God is the faithful Vine-Grower who tends us lovingly. We are confident that this God hears our prayers.

Response:

Lord, hear our prayer.

Cantor:

we pray to the Lord,

That all members of the church grow in the Spirit of Jesus and bear much fruit . . . [pause]

That all world leaders tend tirelessly to those in their care . . . [pause]

That the sick and suffering be sustained by the compassionate love of this community . . . [pause]

That those initiated at Easter always remain in Christ, growing in love and truth . . . [pause]

That each of us remain in Jesus and obey his commands . . . [pause]

Presider: Gracious God, you carefully watch over us and help us to bear fruit: hear these our prayers that we might always remain in your risen Son Jesus Christ our Lord. **Amen.**

OPENING PRAYER

Let us pray

Pause for silent prayer

God our Father,
look upon us with love.
You redeem us and make us your children
    in Christ.
Give us true freedom
and bring us to the inheritance you
    promised.

We ask this through our Lord Jesus Christ,
    your Son,
who lives and reigns with you and the
    Holy Spirit,
one God, for ever and ever. **Amen.**

FIRST READING   Acts 9:26-31

When Saul arrived in Jerusalem he tried to
    join the disciples,
    but they were all afraid of him,
    not believing that he was a disciple.
Then Barnabas took charge of him and
    brought him to the apostles,
    and he reported to them how he had
      seen the Lord,
    and that he had spoken to him,
    and how in Damascus he had spoken
      out boldly in the name of Jesus.
He moved about freely with them in
    Jerusalem,
    and spoke out boldly in the name of the
      Lord.
He also spoke and debated with the
    Hellenists,
    but they tried to kill him.
And when the brothers learned of this,
    they took him down to Caesarea
    and sent him on his way to Tarsus.
The church throughout all Judea, Galilee,
    and Samaria was at peace.
It was being built up and walked in the
    fear of the Lord,
    and with the consolation of the Holy
      Spirit it grew in numbers.

RESPONSORIAL PSALM

Ps 22:26-27, 28, 30, 31-32

℟. (26a) I will praise you, Lord, in the assembly of your people.
   or:
℟. Alleluia.

I will fulfill my vows before those who fear
    the LORD.
    The lowly shall eat their fill;
they who seek the LORD shall praise him:
    "May your hearts live forever!"

℟. I will praise you, Lord, in the assembly of your people.
   or:
℟. Alleluia.

All the ends of the earth
    shall remember and turn to the LORD;
all the families of the nations
    shall bow down before him.

R̸. I will praise you, Lord, in the assembly
of your people.
    or:
R̸. Alleluia.

To him alone shall bow down
    all who sleep in the earth;
before him shall bend
    all who go down into the dust.

R̸. I will praise you, Lord, in the assembly
of your people.
    or:
R̸. Alleluia.

And to him my soul shall live;
    my descendants shall serve him.
Let the coming generation be told of the
    LORD
    that they may proclaim to a people yet
        to be born
    the justice he has shown.

R̸. I will praise you, Lord, in the assembly
of your people.
    or:
R̸. Alleluia.

SECOND READING
1 John 3:18-24

Children, let us love not in word or speech
    but in deed and truth.
Now this is how we shall know that we
        belong to the truth
    and reassure our hearts before him
    in whatever our hearts condemn,
    for God is greater than our hearts and
        knows everything.
Beloved, if our hearts do not condemn us,
    we have confidence in God
    and receive from him whatever we ask,
    because we keep his commandments
        and do what pleases him.
And his commandment is this:
    we should believe in the name of his
        Son, Jesus Christ,
    and love one another just as he
        commanded us.
Those who keep his commandments
        remain in him, and he in them,
    and the way we know that he remains
        in us
    is from the Spirit he gave us.

About Liturgy

Mother's Day: This Sunday is Mother's Day, and although we never focus our weekly celebration of the resurrection on this civil holiday, nevertheless it is always fitting to remind ourselves of how one responsibility of mothers is to "prune" their children so that they are formed into being faithful disciples of Jesus. There may be a fifth intention added to the prayer of the faithful; for example, "That all mothers nurture the fruit of their womb to remain in Jesus as faithful and fruitful disciples . . . [pause]." The Book of Blessings gives an "Order for the Blessing of Mothers on Mother's Day" (chapter 55).

Liturgy of the Word: One way to remain in the risen Christ is to allow God's words to remain in us, shape us, and help us bear fruit. This suggests that the Liturgy of the Word during Mass is more than just moral exhortation or a structural element of the liturgy that brings us to the Liturgy of the Eucharist. In the proclamation of the word we are being "pruned" so that we can remain in Christ.

Clearly, good proclamation is essential if the Liturgy of the Word is to be fruitful. Proclamation is more than good reading—it implies that the lector has lived the word in his or her life (in "deed and truth"), is committed to its message, and allows the word to remain in him or her. Without this the word cannot be a living word nor can it be as fruitful.

About Liturgical Music

Music suggestions: The bilingual song "Pues Si Vivimos/If We Are Living" [in many hymnals] speaks of living and dying in Christ, of bearing fruit, and of belonging to God—all aspects of the vine imagery in this Sunday's gospel. The tempo and style of this song would make it appropriate for the Communion procession. Another good choice for Communion would be Delores Dufner's "Make Your Home in Me" [PMB, WC]. The text speaks of Jesus as the vine and us as the branches. The final verse offers this prayer: "Jesus, living vine, keep your branches Flourishing with life in your love. Prune away whatever is useless, That we may bear fruit in your name."

A third appropriate hymn (and one which deserves wider publication) would be Jaroslav Vajda's "Amid the World's Bleak Wilderness" [CH]. Despite its title (simply a repeat of the first phrase of v. 1), this hymn is not about Lent but our relationship with Christ the vine. Verses 1-2 tell of the vineyard planted by the Lord with "promise green." Verse 3 speaks of us the branches who "feel the dresser's knife" and verse 4 of our life-giving connection to Christ from whom we "draw the juice of life" and for whom we "supply his winery." Verse 5 is our prayer addressed to Christ: "Vine, keep what I was meant to be: Your branch, with your rich life in me." The hymn could be sung during the preparation of the gifts, or it could be sung during the Communion procession with verse 5 interpolated as a refrain.

✚ SPIRITUALITY

GOSPEL ACCLAMATION
John 14:23

℟. Alleluia, alleluia.
Whoever loves me will keep my word, says the Lord,
and my Father will love him and we will come to him.
℟. Alleluia, alleluia.

Gospel

John 15:9-17; L56B

Jesus said to his disciples:
"As the Father loves me, so I also love you.
Remain in my love.
If you keep my commandments, you will remain in my love,
just as I have kept my Father's commandments
and remain in his love.

"I have told you this so that my joy may be in you
and your joy might be complete.
This is my commandment: love one another as I love you.
No one has greater love than this,
to lay down one's life for one's friends.
You are my friends if you do what I command you.
I no longer call you slaves,
because a slave does not know what his master is doing.
I have called you friends,
because I have told you everything I have heard from my Father.
It was not you who chose me, but I who chose you
and appointed you to go and bear fruit that will remain,
so that whatever you ask the Father in my name he may give you.
This I command you: love one another."

Reflecting on the Gospel

Society's frequent projection of what love is—feelings, affection, eroticism, Valentine's hearts, liking someone, etc.—is hardly a context for understanding this Sunday's Scriptures. The word *love* is repeated so often in the second reading and gospel (nine times in each) that we might think we have tuned into one of the daytime soaps or MTV. Love is almost exclusively presented as an everlasting honeymoon, where the relationship is perfect, there are no problems, and life is completely satisfying to the love partners. No problems, everlasting bliss, complete happiness—is this really what love is? This kind of love seems to imply that love is without cost, just happens, and is easy to maintain. Or when cracks begin to occur in the love relationship, the partners are free to just walk away, with supposedly no consequences. From the purview of this Sunday's readings, we almost need to completely clear our minds of all the media's projections and notions about love and begin from scratch. The gospel and first reading each give us a context for understanding what Christian love really is and demands. The second reading establishes how this is borne out in deeds.

The gospel begins with God, not us. It describes in extensive detail the unparalleled, intimate relationship to which the Father and Jesus invite us: chosen by them, given a share in their joy, called friends by them, told everything by them, appointed by them to bear fruit, and given whatever we ask in Jesus' name. In response, we are to incarnate this divine-human relationship in our relationships with each other: "love one another as I love you." God's love is so freely and lavishly given. In turn, we are to empty ourselves and give that love to those we meet.

What may sound like a convoluted gospel text using the word *love* way too many times boils down to something really quite simple: remain in Jesus' love, keep the commandments, love one another. The second reading and gospel help us understand how we are to bring this down to something measurable in our everyday living. God expressed divine love by sending the Son "as expiation for our sins" (second reading). Likewise, we express our love by "laying down" our lives (gospel). Love is no "pie-in-the-sky" feeling; it is concrete deeds—laying down our lives, keeping God's commandments, loving one another. God's love for us is the model: Jesus sacrificed his life, so must we. This is the cost of discipleship; this is why we need the gift of the Spirit; this is why we prepare for Pentecost.

Living the Paschal Mystery

The gospel command to "love one another" demands a different kind of love than is projected by the media and society in general. Our love for one another is to emulate God's love—a love that is total, demanding, self-emptying, self-giving. Jesus doesn't ask us to do anything that he hasn't done first.

Yes, the command is simple: "love one another." The demand is imposing: lay down our lives. Keeping God's commandments is laying down our lives—we surrender our will to doing God's will and in this is the dying. Caring for and reaching out to others is laying down our lives—also a dying. Doing the little things every day, not because we have to but because we see the other as the beloved of God, is dying. We choose all these and other ways of dying because we know this is love and love is risen Life rising to kiss us with a share in divinity.

Focusing the Gospel

Key words and phrases: Jesus said, As the Father loves me, I also love you, love one another

To the point: The gospel describes in extensive detail the unparalleled, intimate relationship we have with the Father and Jesus: chosen by them, given a share in their joy, called friends by them, told everything by them, appointed by them to bear fruit, and given whatever we ask in Jesus' name. In response, we are to incarnate this divine-human relationship in our relationships with each other: "love one another as I love you."

Connecting the Gospel

to the first and second readings: The Good News is that "God shows no partiality" in extending love and friendship to disciples (gospel) and Gentiles (first reading) alike. Just so are we to "love one another" (second reading).

to experience: We are very aware of the obligations that accompany any commitment. Growth in authentic spiritual living, however, flows not from mere obligation, but primarily from the knowledge and experience of being loved by God.

Connecting the Responsorial Psalm

to the readings: The verses of Psalm 98 used for this Sunday's responsorial psalm express Israel's gradual discovery that God's plan of salvation extended beyond the "house of Israel" to "all nations." Similarly, Peter and the other Jewish believers with him were astounded to see the Holy Spirit "fall upon" Gentiles listening to the word (first reading). The ritual of baptism, Peter declared, cannot be refused those who have already received the Spirit.

In singing this responsorial psalm, we acknowledge that the God who first loves us (second reading, gospel) calls us to open our hearts as wide as the divine embrace. Like Peter and the early church community, we are to recognize God's saving presence and activity among all peoples. Like the psalmist, we are to sing of God's love and faithfulness before all the world.

to cantor preparation: As the Israelites experienced God's love more deeply, they saw more clearly that this love was not limited to them. The same is true for us. Each of us is able to live our baptismal call to love others as Jesus loves because we know first of all how much we are loved by God. As you prepare to sing this Sunday's responsorial psalm, you might spend some time reflecting on God's love for you. Then let your gratitude spill out as you sing the psalm.

ASSEMBLY & FAITH-SHARING GROUPS

· I am most aware of being loved by God when . . . I struggle with feeling loved by God because . . .
· I experience joy in the Lord when . . .
· What helps me love others as God loves me is . . .

PRESIDERS

· I incarnate God's love for the assembly when I . . .

DEACONS

· My service brings God's joy to those in need when I . . .

HOSPITALITY MINISTERS

· My greeting expresses God's love for the people of God when . . .

MUSIC MINISTERS

· As a music minister, the command to love others as God loves me is most challenging when . . . It is easiest when . . .

ALTAR MINISTERS

· My joy is more evident when serving at the altar when . . .

LECTORS

· My proclamation of the word challenges the assembly to "love one another as I love you" when . . .

EXTRAORDINARY MINISTERS OF HOLY COMMUNION

· The manner in which I distribute Holy Communion helps communicants move from Jesus' love for them to their love for others when I . . .

Model Rite of Blessing and Sprinkling Holy Water

Presider: Dear friends, we ask God to bless this water as a reminder of our baptismal initiation into the Christian community. Let us celebrate Jesus' love for us and renew our commitment to love one another . . . [pause]

> *[continue with form C of the blessing of water]*

Homily Points

• The adage that "love is blind" is incorrect; infatuation is blind. All relationships have a "honeymoon" period during which we tend to overlook behaviors that later become annoying. By contrast, genuine love sees others as they truly are. We look beneath strengths and weaknesses to see the innate goodness we know is there. This is the kind of love that forms the foundation of lasting care and commitment.

• With God there is no honeymoon period; there is genuine love from the very beginning to the end of time. Jesus understood perfectly the human heart and knew full well human weaknesses. He himself experienced betrayal and disappointment, denial and obtuseness from his "friends." Yet, he loved to the end.

• We are called to love each other as Jesus loves us. This is not easy for us because of past hurts and resentments, others' idiosyncrasies, anger, stubbornness, others' refusal to do what we want, etc. We look to Jesus and his response to people to see how we are to respond to those around us, and love as he loved.

Model Prayer of the Faithful

Presider: Having recalled God's unparalleled love for us, we are emboldened to ask in Jesus' name for all that we need.

Response: Lord, hear our prayer.

Cantor: we pray to the Lord,

That all members of the church might express their joy in the risen Christ's love by loving others in word and deed . . . [pause]

That all persons in positions of power and authority model for those they serve Jesus' self-sacrificing love . . . [pause]

That those in need be lifted up by the generous deeds of Christ's disciples . . . [pause]

That each of us here bear fruit by loving others as Jesus loves us . . . [pause]

Presider: Loving God, you sent your Son to live among us and love us to the end: hear these our prayers that we might love others as he has taught us. We ask this through that same risen Christ our Lord. **Amen.**

OPENING PRAYER

Let us pray

Pause for silent prayer

Ever-living God,
help us to celebrate our joy
in the resurrection of the Lord
and to express in our lives
the love we celebrate.

Grant this through our Lord Jesus Christ, your Son,
who lives and reigns with you and the Holy Spirit,
one God, for ever and ever. **Amen.**

FIRST READING
Acts 10:25-26, 34-35, 44-48

When Peter entered, Cornelius met him
    and, falling at his feet, paid him
        homage.
Peter, however, raised him up, saying,
    "Get up. I myself am also a human
        being."

Then Peter proceeded to speak and said,
    "In truth, I see that God shows no
        partiality.
Rather, in every nation whoever fears him
        and acts uprightly
    is acceptable to him."

While Peter was still speaking these
        things,
    the Holy Spirit fell upon all who were
        listening to the word.
The circumcised believers who had
        accompanied Peter
    were astounded that the gift of the Holy
        Spirit
    should have been poured out on the
        Gentiles also,
    for they could hear them speaking in
        tongues and glorifying God.
Then Peter responded,
    "Can anyone withhold the water for
        baptizing these people,
    who have received the Holy Spirit even
        as we have?"
He ordered them to be baptized in the
        name of Jesus Christ.

RESPONSORIAL PSALM

Ps 98:1, 2-3, 3-4

℞. (cf. 2b) The Lord has revealed to the
nations his saving power.
or:
℞. Alleluia.

Sing to the LORD a new song,
    for he has done wondrous deeds;
his right hand has won victory for him,
    his holy arm.

℞. The Lord has revealed to the nations
his saving power.
or:
℞. Alleluia.

The LORD has made his salvation known:
    in the sight of the nations he has
        revealed his justice.
He has remembered his kindness and his
    faithfulness
    toward the house of Israel.

℞. The Lord has revealed to the nations
his saving power.
or:
℞. Alleluia.

All the ends of the earth have seen
    the salvation by our God.
Sing joyfully to the LORD, all you lands;
    break into song; sing praise.

℞. The Lord has revealed to the nations
his saving power.
or:
℞. Alleluia.

SECOND READING

1 John 4:7-10

Beloved, let us love one another,
    because love is of God;
        everyone who loves is begotten by God
            and knows God.
Whoever is without love does not know
    God, for God is love.
In this way the love of God was revealed
    to us:
    God sent his only Son into the world
    so that we might have life through him.
In this is love:
    not that we have loved God, but that he
        loved us
    and sent his Son as expiation for our
        sins.

About Liturgy

Eucharist as love feast: The *Didache* (the "Teachings"), a church document probably originating from early in the second century, is divided into two parts. The first describes "two ways" of conducting oneself: do good and live, or do evil and die. The second part of this important document reports on early church services. Chapters nine and ten describe what today we call the Mass. Scholars are divided whether this really refers to a celebration of the Lord's Supper, or an *agape* (love) banquet. What is clear in both parts is that love and care for one another are essential for how Christians are to conduct themselves and how Christians are to worship.

Eucharist is a celebration of a love feast from two directions. First, in the Eucharist God expresses divine love and care for us in giving us the Body and Blood of our Lord Jesus Christ for our nourishment and strength. Each celebration makes present Jesus' supreme act of self-giving to us. From our direction, Eucharist is not a private act. It is always the act of the whole church for the whole church, an expression of the community's unity in the Body of Christ which is always made concrete in acts of charity and goodness, especially toward the less fortunate. At any number of places in the Eucharist are we reminded of our bond of love and charity toward one another: in the times we ask for forgiveness for wrongdoing; in praying for the needs of the church, world, those in need, and for the local community during the prayer of the faithful; in presenting our gifts of bread and wine, of goods for the poor, of ourselves to be transformed; in the sign of peace where we embrace each other as members of Christ's Body, beloved of God and each other; in Holy Communion where we are fed at God's lavish messianic banquet table.

Eucharist is always a love feast, reminding us that our first responsibility as baptized members of the Body of Christ is to do as Jesus taught us: love one another as he has loved us.

About Liturgical Music

Music suggestions: : On these latter Sundays of Easter season when the readings focus on our call to participate in Jesus' mission of redeeming death-resurrection, the Easter hymns we sing need to share this same focus. For instance, the strong imagery of "We Know That Christ Is Raised" identifies us as the risen Body of Christ. Note how the thought of one verse is continued and completed by succeeding verses; for example, "The Spirit's power stirs [in some hymnals this reads: "fission shakes"] the Church of God . . . As Christ's new body takes on flesh and blood. The universe restored and whole will sing" (v. 3-4). Combined with the equally powerful tune ENGELBERG, this hymn would be excellent for either the entrance procession or a hymn of praise after Communion.

A choral piece well suited to this Sunday's readings is Robert Kreutz' "Love Song" [WLP octavo 7934]. Verse 1 reminds us that we are loved first by God whose love for us is unquenchable. Verse 2 calls us to love one another "in deed and truth, Not merely make the word resound." Verse 3 states that love gave us life and love awaits us when we die. The piece could be sung by the choir as a prelude or during the preparation of the gifts.

✠ SPIRITUALITY

GOSPEL ACCLAMATION
Matt 28:19a, 20b

Ry. Alleluia, alleluia.
Go and teach all nations, says the Lord;
I am with you always, until the end of the world.
Ry. Alleluia, alleluia.

Gospel

Mark 16:15-20; L58B

Jesus said to his
    disciples:
"Go into the whole
    world
and proclaim the
    gospel to every
    creature.
Whoever believes and is
    baptized will be saved;
whoever does not believe
    will be condemned.
These signs will accompany those who
    believe:
in my name they will drive out
    demons,
they will speak new languages.
They will pick up serpents with their
    hands,
and if they drink any deadly thing, it
    will not harm them.
They will lay hands on the sick, and
    they will recover."

So then the Lord Jesus, after he spoke
    to them,
was taken up into heaven
and took his seat at the right hand of
    God.
But they went forth and preached
    everywhere,
while the Lord worked with them
and confirmed the word through
    accompanying signs.

Reflecting on the Gospel

Most parents hope their children will walk in their footsteps. When it comes to the family and religious values that parents try to instill in their children, we see this as a good and worthy desire. Sometimes one or both of the parents push their children to fulfill their personal expectations, often with respect to career. A youngster might be forced into a family business, for example, and be very loyal to the parents, but the individual's heart just isn't there. Something is missing: the commitment, the love, the desire to excel out of personal devotion.

Jesus expects his disciples to walk in his footsteps. The difference between Jesus and parents pushing youngsters into the wrong profession is that Jesus always *invites* us (gospel: "whoever believes"; second reading: "call you have received") to share in his ministry, never forces us. Jesus invites us through our belief—nothing less than our own expression of our commitment, love, and personal devotion to Jesus.

The ascension marks the completion of Jesus' historical ministry and the beginning of our own commission to proclaim the Gospel. We are not forced to proclaim the Gospel, nor do we do this on our own authority. We undertake our mission "through the Holy Spirit" (first reading) and manifest the Holy Spirit through our mission. But always the mission is Christ's. At first this might seem an impossible commission: how can we expect to fill Jesus' footsteps?

On our own authority we cannot preach the Gospel nor bear fruit by this preaching. We can fill Jesus' footsteps when we hear the "instructions [given] through the Spirit" (first reading). Jesus invites us to be disciples and commissions us to preach the Gospel, and then gives us all we need to fulfill our mission. Jesus also makes clear, however, that gifts are given us not for our own sake but for "building up the body of Christ" (second reading). The mission is always Christ's.

What an awesome honor it is to be disciples of Christ—we fill his footsteps! What meaning this accords the ascension—by returning to his rightful place at the hand of God, Jesus entrusts his mission to us. Our mission is to proclaim the Good News of salvation. In this work the Lord is present in us and in the mission we undertake.

Living the Paschal Mystery

Before we even celebrate Pentecost we are already hearing about our taking up the mission of Christ. This mission describes our Christian living—preaching the Gospel. Ascension is a call to all the baptized, reminding us that baptism is far more than having original sin taken away; it is a receiving of the Spirit by which we are grafted onto the Body of Christ. Baptism is our Pentecost and it includes a mission.

The gospel reminds us that the bearers of the Good News—those who continue Jesus' saving mission today—are *ordinary people*. This would seem to be an overwhelming and impossible task. How can we represent God and continue the divine saving work? We can't, on our own. But Jesus assured us that he would work with us. Always, the mission is Christ's and we accomplish it by the strength and life of the Spirit who dwells in the baptized. It is the Spirit who works in us. This is why ordinary people can with enthusiasm, commitment, and love take up Jesus' mission.

Focusing the Gospel

Key words and phrases: go, proclaim the gospel, the Lord worked with them

To the point: The ascension marks the completion of Jesus' historical ministry and the beginning of our own commission to proclaim the Gospel. We do not do this on our own authority. We undertake our mission "through the Holy Spirit" (first reading) and manifest the Holy Spirit through our mission. But always the mission is Christ's.

Connecting the Gospel

to Easter and Pentecost: Our own taking up the mission to proclaim the Gospel (Ascension) is always in light of the risen Christ (Easter) and empowered by the Spirit (Pentecost). Easter, Ascension, Pentecost are all one mystery and we participate in this mystery by proclaiming the Gospel.

to our religious experience: It is easy to be distracted by the spectacular signs mentioned in this gospel (snake handling, drinking deadly poison) and lose sight of the hard work of living the real message of the gospel (humility, gentleness, bearing with one another; see second reading).

Connecting the Responsorial Psalm

to the readings: The verses we sing from Psalm 47 for the solemnity of the Ascension are about more than the historical event of Jesus' being lifted up into the heavens. They are also a promise about our ultimate victory over sin and death. Jesus' victory will be our victory, for the one who has commissioned us to proclaim the Gospel (gospel) has also promised us the power to do so (first reading). Paul reminds us that each of us has been given the grace of Christ to carry out our particular part of the mission, and this is the "hope of our calling" (second reading). On dark days, then, when we do not know when the kingdom is to come (first reading), when we must wait with patient fidelity to the daily virtues of Christian living (second reading), we can still shout, "God mounts his throne" (psalm refrain), and so do we!

to cantor preparation: Your task in singing this responsorial psalm is to move the assembly beyond only remembering a past historical event in Jesus' life to celebrating a present reality in their own lives. As with the resurrection, the ascension is not just about Jesus—it is about us, the disciples of Christ called to be his Body. This responsorial psalm is a song of hope, a sure promise that in Christ we will complete the mission given us in baptism. As part of your preparation, you might spend some time identifying where—in your own life, in the church, in the world—you see this hope already being fulfilled.

**ASSEMBLY &
FAITH-SHARING GROUPS**

· My life proclaims the Gospel when . . . One way I need to grow in living the Gospel is . . .

· One sign that the risen Lord is working in and through me is . . .

· I pray to the Holy Spirit for . . .

PRESIDERS

· What helps me realize that I act not on my own authority, but on the authority of Christ is . . .

DEACONS

· My proclamation of the Gospel takes place in both word and action when . . .

HOSPITALITY MINISTERS

· My hospitality manifests the Spirit by building up the Body of Christ when I . . .

MUSIC MINISTERS

· I am aware of Christ working through me in my music ministry when . . .

ALTAR MINISTERS

· My service at the altar truly proclaims the Gospel because . . .

LECTORS

· My proclamation of the word leads the assembly to better hear the proclamation of the Gospel when . . .

**EXTRAORDINARY MINISTERS
OF HOLY COMMUNION**

· My distribution of Holy Communion continues Jesus' mission in that . . .

135

Model Rite of Blessing and Sprinkling Holy Water

Presider: Dear friends, today we commemorate the risen Lord's ascension into heaven and his commissioning of the disciples to preach the Gospel. We sprinkle this water as a sign of our own baptism, when we, too, became Jesus' disciples and were commissioned to preach his Good News . . . [pause]

  [continue with form C of the blessing of water]

Homily Points

• We live in a culture that expects people to be well prepared for their profession: teachers, doctors, lawyers must have certificates/licenses. Even more than that, they must have extensive on-the-job training: student teachers, interns, junior lawyers. The confidence the public tends to place in a professional is directly proportional to the individual's level of training and length of experience.

• Despite their having been with Jesus during his public ministry, despite their having experienced his death and resurrection, the individuals Jesus sends out on mission still don't grasp who he is and what he is about (see second reading). Nevertheless, this is the lot Jesus commissions. And, through the power of the Spirit, they manage to proclaim the Gospel, thus continuing Jesus' mission into today.

• By our standards, Jesus didn't wait for his disciples to be fully prepared in order to take on his mission. In fact, part of the Good News is a basic trust in the Spirit of Jesus, who guides us. Gospel living itself and the ongoing demands of discipleship provide "on-the-job training" for continuing Jesus' mission.

Model Prayer of the Faithful

Presider: Let us pray that God will strengthen us to preach the Gospel well by how we live our everyday lives.

Response: Lord, hear our prayer.

Cantor: we pray to the Lord,

May the church always and everywhere proclaim the Good News . . . [pause]

May all leaders of nations govern with humility and gentleness, with patience and love . . . [pause]

May those who are sick and suffering be healed by the gentle touch of this community . . . [pause]

May each of us here faithfully manifest the Spirit in both word and deed . . . [pause]

Presider: God of life, your risen Son now sits at your right hand in glory: hear these our prayers that we might continue faithfully his mission and make his Gospel known. We ask this through that same Son Jesus Christ. **Amen.**

ALTERNATIVE OPENING PRAYER

Let us pray

Pause for silent prayer

Father in heaven,
our minds were prepared for the coming
 of your kingdom
when you took Christ beyond our sight
so that we might seek him in his glory.

May we follow where he has led
and find our hope in his glory,
for he is Lord for ever. **Amen.**

FIRST READING

Acts 1:1-11

In the first book, Theophilus,
  I dealt with all that Jesus did and taught
  until the day he was taken up,
  after giving instructions through the
   Holy Spirit
  to the apostles whom he had chosen.
He presented himself alive to them
  by many proofs after he had suffered,
  appearing to them during forty days
  and speaking about the kingdom of
   God.
While meeting with them,
  he enjoined them not to depart from
   Jerusalem,
  but to wait for "the promise of the
   Father
  about which you have heard me speak;
  for John baptized with water,
  but in a few days you will be baptized
   with the Holy Spirit."

When they had gathered together they
  asked him,
  "Lord, are you at this time going to
   restore the kingdom to Israel?"
He answered them, "It is not for you to
   know the times or seasons
  that the Father has established by his
   own authority.
But you will receive power when the Holy
   Spirit comes upon you,
  and you will be my witnesses in
   Jerusalem,
  throughout Judea and Samaria,
  and to the ends of the earth."
When he had said this, as they were
   looking on,
  he was lifted up, and a cloud took him
   from their sight.

While they were looking intently at the
    sky as he was going,
      suddenly two men dressed in white
        garments stood beside them.
They said, "Men of Galilee,
    why are you standing there looking at
      the sky?
This Jesus who has been taken up from
    you into heaven
    will return in the same way as you have
      seen him going into heaven."

RESPONSORIAL PSALM

Ps 47:2-3, 6-7, 8-9

℟. (6) God mounts his throne to shouts of
joy: a blare of trumpets for the Lord.
    or:
℟. Alleluia.

All you peoples, clap your hands,
    shout to God with cries of gladness,
for the LORD, the Most High, the awesome,
    is the great king over all the earth.

℟. God mounts his throne to shouts of joy:
a blare of trumpets for the Lord.
    or:
℟. Alleluia.

God mounts his throne amid shouts of joy;
    the LORD, amid trumpet blasts.
Sing praise to God, sing praise;
    sing praise to our king, sing praise.

℟. God mounts his throne to shouts of joy:
a blare of trumpets for the Lord.
    or:
℟. Alleluia.

For king of all the earth is God;
    sing hymns of praise.
God reigns over the nations,
    God sits upon his holy throne.

℟. God mounts his throne to shouts of joy:
a blare of trumpets for the Lord.
    or:
℟. Alleluia.

SECOND READING

Eph 1:17-23

or

Eph 4:1-13

or

Eph 4:1-7, 11-13

See Appendix A, p. 296.

About Liturgy

Celebrating Ascension on Sunday: Most dioceses have transferred the celebration of the Ascension to the seventh Sunday of Easter. In addition to the obvious pastoral reasons for this decision—more people will actually celebrate this important mystery if it takes place on Sunday when people are used to coming to Mass—there are also good theological reasons for this transfer of the festival from Thursday to Sunday.

The synoptic gospels present a different time frame for the Easter-Ascension-Pentecost events than does John's gospel. Matthew, Mark, and Luke take a more historical approach: Ascension happened on the fortieth day after the resurrection (John's gospel has Jesus ascending on Easter evening), with Pentecost being celebrated on the fiftieth day. With the transference of ascension to Sunday, Easter, Ascension, and Pentecost are all celebrated on the same day of the week—Sunday. The advantage of this is that it gets us out of a historical mentality and helps us integrate these events into a single mystery of salvation. Our annual celebration of the paschal mystery is not a historical reenactment of those events of long ago, but a here-and-now celebration of the reality of what it means to be baptized into Jesus' death and resurrection, what it means for us to receive the Holy Spirit, and how we are to continue today Jesus' saving mission.

If the celebration of Ascension is transferred from Thursday to Sunday, then the liturgy of the Seventh Sunday of Easter is omitted. The Lectionary does make a rubrical note on the Sixth Sunday of Easter that when Ascension is transferred, the second reading and gospel from the Seventh Sunday may be proclaimed on the Sixth Sunday. If some kind of a rotation between Sixth and Seventh Sunday readings were observed, then the Seventh Sunday readings would be proclaimed, say, every other year and not be lost.

About Liturgical Music

Music suggestions: This solemnity would be a particularly appropriate day on which to sing a post-Communion hymn of praise. Examples of songs which speak of the commission given us by the ascended Christ include the South African "Halleluya! We Sing Your Praises" [G2, GC, GC2, RS], Ruth Duck's "As a Fire Is Meant for Burning" [G2, GC, GC2, RS], and her "You Are Called to Tell the Story" [G2, GC, RS]. The tune given in G2, GC, and RS for this last hymn (GHENT) makes the text more suitable for the Communion procession itself, but the more strongly metered 4/4 tune (REGENT SQUARE) used in the Ruth Duck collection *Dancing in the Universe* [GIA G-3833] and the GC2 setting (ROSEMARY) are just right for post-Communion.

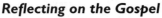

SPIRITUALITY

GOSPEL ACCLAMATION
cf. John 14:18

℟. Alleluia, alleluia.
I will not leave you orphans, says the Lord.
I will come back to you, and your
   hearts will rejoice.
℟. Alleluia, alleluia.

Gospel

John 17:11b-19; L60B

**Lifting up his eyes to heaven,
   Jesus prayed, saying:
"Holy Father, keep them in
   your name that you have
   given me,
so that they may be one just
   as we are one.
When I was with them I protected them
   in your name that you gave me,
and I guarded them, and none of
   them was lost
except the son of destruction,
in order that the Scripture might be
   fulfilled.
But now I am coming to you.
I speak this in the world
   so that they may share my joy
   completely.
I gave them your word, and the world
   hated them,
   because they do not belong to the
   world
   any more than I belong to the world.
I do not ask that you take them out of
   the world
   but that you keep them from the evil
   one.
They do not belong to the world
   any more than I belong to the world.
Consecrate them in the truth. Your
   word is truth.
As you sent me into the world,
   so I sent them into the world.
And I consecrate myself for them,
   so that they also may be consecrated
   in truth."**

Reflecting on the Gospel

We say prayers together all the time; for example, at Mass with the community, at home with family at meals, or in the parish before a meeting begins. Most of us are quite comfortable with this because the words have been given to us in the many prayers we have learned as small children (for example, the Our Father and Hail Mary, meal prayers, Glory be to the Father). When our prayer, however, is intensely personal, when we are pouring our hearts out to God in our own words, we are much slower to say these out loud so that others might hear. If we are called upon to pray in some situation where a memorized prayer won't fit, we tend to fumble for words and keep our prayer very short. This kind of intensely personal prayer is very self-revealing.

The gospels often indicate that Jesus went off alone to pray. Of course, we expect this of Jesus. The gospel for this Sunday is unusual because it doesn't simply show us Jesus at prayer, but it includes one of the rare instances where we actually hear the words of Jesus' prayer. We are eavesdropping on Jesus' very intensely personal prayer. What do we hear? That Jesus wants for us what he has with his Father—unity.

Just like our own intensely personal prayer, Jesus' prayer is very self-revealing. In Jesus' prayer for his disciples we can feel his anguish, love, and concern. He knows that if we speak the same words of truth that he spoke the world will hate us, too. Jesus trusts that his disciples will take up his mission, and knows full well that we will face the same fate as he is facing—death. No wonder his prayer is so intense and personal!

Jesus is not naive about sending out disciples. His lengthy prayer for them (and us) recognizes that there will be resistance ("the world hated them") to the word of truth. Nevertheless, Jesus' prayer assures us that we are never alone. Such confidence Jesus spawns in us by his prayer! This is our joy: to be so intimately loved, cared for, protected, guarded, and guided by Jesus—all for the sake of the world.

Living the Paschal Mystery

All of the confidence and protection Jesus promises in his prayer rests on our surrendering to Jesus' discipleship—we must speak words of truth to a world that may or may not receive our words. The evangelist John's "world" is everything that is opposed to Jesus—yet God clearly loves the world because the Son was sent to redeem the world. We may die because of the hatred the world has for the truth; but what life we find in God's love!

It doesn't take too many nights of watching the evening news to figure out that much of our world, too, is opposed to Jesus and what he taught. Violence, crime of all kinds, selfishness, disrespect for life and property—the list goes on and on of all the "wrongs" of our world. We may grow discouraged in our discipleship if we think that our deeds must make the nightly news and obviously turn our world around. Yet, this is not what Jesus asks of us.

Jesus asks that we do not "belong to the world" but to him. This means that in our ordinary daily living we act with the same protection and guardianship as Jesus extends to us. We do this by respecting life and property, by paying attention to the needs of those around us, by caring for ourselves. Doing the simple, everyday tasks well and relating to others with genuine love and joy is already an answer to Jesus' gospel prayer for us.

Focusing the Gospel

Key words and phrases: Jesus prayed, keep them, protected, guarded, world

To the point: Jesus is not naive about sending out disciples. His lengthy prayer for them (and us) recognizes that there will be resistance ("the world hated them") to the word of truth. Nevertheless, Jesus' prayer assures us that we are never alone. Jesus prays that even in this world we might be kept, protected, guarded—and all for the sake of the world.

Connecting the Gospel

to the second reading and Pentecost: The assurance that we have the ability to carry out our mission as disciples rests in the fact "that he has given us of his Spirit" (second reading). Pentecost celebrates what we have already received.

to our experience of prayer: During times of crisis and personal need, we readily ask others to pray for us and we invoke the intercession of the saints. As powerful and comforting as this is for us, we have an even more powerful intercessor—Jesus himself is praying for us.

Connecting the Responsorial Psalm

to the readings: In this Sunday's responsorial psalm we bless God for "kindness" shown us and "benefits" given. What is this kindness, these benefits? They are numerous: understanding of our situation both in terms of our own weaknesses (the "transgressions" forgiven in the psalm) and the world's antagonism (gospel); guidance as we, the community of disciples, make decisions for the carrying out of the mission (first reading); protection from "the evil one" (gospel); and above all intimate, loving personal presence (second reading). The psalm reveals that Christ who prays with such intimate self-revelation in our midst (gospel) also sits with power and glory above us. Could we have a more powerful benefactor or a more effective prayer-partner?

to cantor preparation: As we wait for the coming of the Spirit, as we engage in the daily decisions and works of discipleship, as we strive to love as we are called to love, we have among us (gospel, second reading) and above us (responsorial psalm) a steady Presence and sure Protector. How might you deepen your trust in this Presence-Protector that you might lead the assembly to greater trust in the One whose "throne [is] in heaven"?

ASSEMBLY & FAITH-SHARING GROUPS

- Knowing that Jesus prays for me, I . . .
- Some of the resistance I've met in being faithful to Jesus' mission is . . . Who/what has helped me overcome this resistance is . . .
- My prayer for others helps them by . . .

PRESIDERS

- I assure the assembly of Jesus' presence and protection when I . . .

DEACONS

- My ministry to others is the "answer" to Jesus' prayer when . . .

HOSPITALITY MINISTERS

- My hospitality helps others come to know and believe in the love Jesus has for us when . . .

MUSIC MINISTERS

- A tension with the "world" I experience in my music ministry is . . . I sense God's love helping me deal with this tension by . . .

ALTAR MINISTERS

- My service at the altar is worthy and true when . . .

LECTORS

- My proclamation is strength and protection for the assembly when . . .

EXTRAORDINARY MINISTERS OF HOLY COMMUNION

- My distribution of Holy Communion is itself a prayer for unity when . . .

Model Rite of Blessing and Sprinkling Holy Water

Presider: Dear friends, this water blessed and sprinkled is a reminder of our baptism, which strengthens us to speak Christ's word of truth to the world. Let us pray that we are faithful to this mission . . . [pause]

[continue with form C of the blessing of water]

Homily Points

• Sometimes the biggest block in our being faithful to a vision is ourselves because we are afraid of resistance or failure. Sometimes the block is other people who oppose our vision. Sometimes the block is the enormity of the vision itself. At times like these, what gives us courage to be faithful to the vision can come in the most unexpected ways.

• No vision is more challenging nor meets more opposition than the vision of living and preaching God's word of truth to the world. This is exactly what we disciples are to do. No vision has a more surprising source of support: Jesus' own prayer for us.

• If we believe in the love and protection of Jesus, then we will be open to watch for the unexpected ways that Jesus' prayer in the gospel is manifested to us today. Also, we will believe that we can come into touch with this love of Jesus through others who are filled with his Spirit.

Model Prayer of the Faithful

Presider: Let us pray that we may be faithful disciples even when God's word of truth is rejected and hated.

Response: Lord, hear our prayer.

Cantor: we pray to the Lord,

That all members of the church have the vision and the courage to bring God's word of truth to the world . . . [pause]

That all peoples be protected and guarded from harm . . . [pause]

That those persecuted or imprisoned for the sake of the Gospel find courage and strength . . . [pause]

That each of us be the prayer and strength of Jesus to each other . . . [pause]

Presider: Loving God, you guard and protect those who are one with your risen Son Jesus Christ: hear these our prayers that we might be consecrated in truth and one day have everlasting joy with you. We ask this through Christ our Lord. **Amen.**

OPENING PRAYER

Let us pray

Pause for silent prayer

Father,
help us keep in mind that Christ our
    Savior
lives with you in glory
and promised to remain with us until the
    end of time.

We ask this through our Lord Jesus Christ,
    your Son,
who lives and reigns with you and the
    Holy Spirit,
one God, for ever and ever. **Amen.**

FIRST READING

Acts 1:15-17, 20a, 20c-26

Peter stood up in the midst of the brothers
    —there was a group of about one
        hundred and twenty persons
    in the one place—.
He said, "My brothers,
    the Scripture had to be fulfilled
    which the Holy Spirit spoke beforehand
    through the mouth of David, concerning
        Judas,
    who was the guide for those who
        arrested Jesus.
He was numbered among us
    and was allotted a share in this ministry.

"For it is written in the book of Psalms:
    May another take his office.

"Therefore, it is necessary that one of the
        men
    who accompanied us the whole time
    the Lord Jesus came and went among us,
    beginning from the baptism of John
    until the day on which he was taken up
        from us,
    become with us a witness to his
        resurrection."
So they proposed two, Judas called
        Barsabbas,
    who was also known as Justus, and
        Matthias.
Then they prayed,
    "You, Lord, who know the hearts of all,
    show which one of these two you have
        chosen
    to take the place in this apostolic
        ministry
    from which Judas turned away to go to
        his own place."
Then they gave lots to them, and the lot
        fell upon Matthias,
    and he was counted with the eleven
        apostles.

RESPONSORIAL PSALM
Ps 103:1-2, 11-12, 19-20

R̲Ɉ. (19a) The Lord has set his throne in heaven.
or:
R̲Ɉ. Alleluia.

Bless the LORD, O my soul;
  and all my being, bless his holy name.
Bless the LORD, O my soul,
  and forget not all his benefits.

R̲Ɉ. The Lord has set his throne in heaven.
or:
R̲Ɉ. Alleluia.

For as the heavens are high above the earth,
  so surpassing is his kindness toward those who fear him.
As far as the east is from the west,
  so far has he put our transgressions from us.

R̲Ɉ. The Lord has set his throne in heaven.
or:
R̲Ɉ. Alleluia.

The LORD has established his throne in heaven,
  and his kingdom rules over all.
Bless the LORD, all you his angels,
  you mighty in strength, who do his bidding.

R̲Ɉ. The Lord has set his throne in heaven.
or:
R̲Ɉ. Alleluia.

SECOND READING
1 John 4:11-16

Beloved, if God so loved us,
  we also must love one another.
No one has ever seen God.
Yet, if we love one another, God remains in us,
  and his love is brought to perfection in us.

This is how we know that we remain in him and he in us,
  that he has given us of his Spirit.
Moreover, we have seen and testify
  that the Father sent his Son as savior of the world.
Whoever acknowledges that Jesus is the Son of God,
  God remains in him and he in God.
We have come to know and to believe in the love God has for us.

God is love, and whoever remains in love
  remains in God and God in him.

About Liturgy

Memorial Day: Monday is Memorial Day and many parishioners will be celebrating liturgy or attending other memorial services. It would not be appropriate to use patriotic songs either Sunday or Monday at the liturgies because the music at liturgy has its own requirements that are dictated by the liturgy and liturgical year. An intention could be added at the prayer of the faithful for either Sunday or Monday that might read: That those who have given their lives in defense of the values of our country may enjoy the peace of eternal life . . . [pause].

Historicizing salvation events: We tend to think linearly through the liturgical year, beginning with anticipation of Jesus' birth; his birth and epiphany; beginnings of his public ministry; suffering, death, and resurrection; ascension and Pentecost. The Lectionary often seems to encourage a historicizing interpretation and this Sunday is a good example. Last Thursday was ascension and so the gospel makes temporal sense when it has Jesus saying, "I am coming to you"; the first reading records an event that also occurs after the ascension.

The point is that liturgy isn't a celebration of historical events (even though they are sometimes put to us in that way) but the celebration of saving events. This isn't to deny the fact of those historical events, but it is to underscore that liturgy breaks us out of a temporal time frame and helps us focus on God's saving events happening at all times for all peoples.

About Liturgical Music

Music suggestions: If you celebrate the ascension on this Sunday, then you might sing one of the hymns suggested for that day as a post-Communion hymn of praise. If you celebrated ascension last Thursday, you might repeat either "As a Fire Is Meant for Burning" or "You Are Called to Tell the Story" during the preparation of the gifts (here either tune for "You Are Called to Tell the Story" would be appropriate). A good choice for the Communion procession for the Seventh Sunday of Easter would be "We Who Once Were Dead" [CBW3] which speaks of Jesus our head leading us forward through hardship, pain, and death to resurrection.

MAY 24, 2009
SEVENTH SUNDAY OF EASTER
or CELEBRATION OF ASCENSION

✦ SPIRITUALITY

GOSPEL ACCLAMATION

R̸. Alleluia, alleluia.
Come, Holy Spirit, fill the hearts of your faithful
and kindle in them the fire of your love.
R̸. Alleluia, alleluia.

Gospel   John 20:19-23; L63B

On the evening of that first day of the week,
    when the doors were locked, where the
        disciples were,
    for fear of the Jews,
    Jesus came and stood in their midst
    and said to them, "Peace be with you."
When he had said this, he showed them his
    hands and his side.
The disciples rejoiced when they saw the
    Lord.
Jesus said to them again, "Peace be with
    you.
As the Father has sent me, so I send you."
And when he had said this, he breathed on
    them and said to them,
    "Receive the Holy Spirit.
Whose sins you forgive are forgiven them,
    and whose sins you retain are retained."

or John 15:26-27; 16:12-15

Jesus said to his disciples:
    "When the Advocate comes whom I will
        send you from the Father,
    the Spirit of truth that proceeds from the
        Father,
    he will testify to me.
And you also testify,
    because you have been with me from the
        beginning.

"I have much more to tell you, but you
    cannot bear it now.
But when he comes, the Spirit of truth,
    he will guide you to all truth.
He will not speak on his own,
    but he will speak what he hears,
    and will declare to you the things that are
        coming.
He will glorify me,
    because he will take from what is mine
        and declare it to you.
Everything that the Father has is mine;
    for this reason I told you that he will take
        from what is mine
    and declare it to you."

Reflecting on the Gospel

Often school spirit manifests itself most strongly when a sport team has advanced toward tournament play. If the team makes the state (high school) or national (college) finals, school spirit can reach a frenzied, feverish pitch. We even speak of "March madness" when the NCAA basketball tournament takes place. At times like these, even those who are not ordinarily interested in sports become staunch fans. An entire school seems to be caught up in the "spirit" with a common mission: win! The spirit takes over and knits students who were strangers on campus into a shouting body of one voice. This Sunday we celebrate our "Christian Spirit." This Spirit wells up within us, too, and we can't contain the Goodness within us. This Spirit knits us together into a proclaiming, testifying Body.

We celebrate this Sunday a wondrous and unprecedented gift of God—"the Spirit of truth." This truth God gives is relational. Similar but far more powerful than school spirit, the Spirit of truth changes us—through the Spirit we share a common identity as the Body of Christ and take up a common mission to proclaim the Gospel by the sheer goodness of our lives. The Spirit enables us to live with one another in a new way: with "love, joy, peace, patience, kindness, generosity," etc. (second reading). The Spirit propels us to engage with the world in a new way: we "testify" (gospel) to the "mighty acts of God" (first reading) through the very way that we live. The truth God gives transforms us and, through us, transforms the world.

This Pentecost commemoration does not simply recall a past event, but celebrates what God is doing within us now. In baptism each of us received the Spirit; that is our Pentecost. The Spirit is not something we have, is not a possession. The Spirit dwells within us as divine life, enabling us to be faithful and true disciples. The Spirit is given for the sake of mission: to proclaim the gospel ("you also testify"), to be molded as disciples ("the Spirit . . . will guide you to all truth"), and, ultimately, to worship ("glorify me"). The indwelling of the Spirit is a continual Pentecost so that everyone can hear of the "mighty acts of God" (first reading) and thus bring glory to God.

Living the Paschal Mystery

Our daily living is to "testify" to the Spirit of truth who dwells within us. We often think of "truth" in terms of "truths"—dogmas to believe. The gospel leads us to something far more dynamic, relational. The Spirit who dwells in each of us enfleshes within us the "mighty acts of God." Truth is being faithful to the identity and mission offered us.

If we are to be living icons of the Spirit of truth dwelling within us, then the good choices we make daily testify to this divine indwelling. Simply put, Pentecost invites us to act like God! If, then, we are to exude the fruits of the Spirit (see second reading), we must be willing to die to ourselves. We cannot love another if we do not give of ourselves to others. We cannot have joy if we are turned in on ourselves. We cannot have peace if we are distracted by getting and doing only what we want. We cannot have patience if we do not respect the dignity of others. We cannot have gentleness if we do not see the need in others. We cannot have self-control if we don't put the good of others first.

Come, Holy Spirit!

Focusing the Gospel

Key words and phrases: I will send, the Spirit of truth, guide you, testify

To the point: We celebrate this Sunday a wondrous and unprecedented gift of God—"the Spirit of truth." This truth God gives is relational. The Spirit enables us to live with one another in a new way: with "love, joy, peace, patience, kindness, generosity," etc. (second reading). The Spirit propels us to engage with the world in a new way: we "testify" (gospel) to the "mighty acts of God" (first reading) through the very way that we live. The truth God gives transforms us and, through us, transforms the world.

Connecting the Gospel

to the second reading from Galatians 5:16-25: Having received the Spirit, we are confronted with a choice: to "live by the Spirit" or to live by what is opposed to the Spirit.

to experience: Mission statements try to capture the spirit of an organization. Everyone belonging to the organization is expected to buy into that "spirit" and embody it in their specific tasks. How much more are we to embody Jesus' Spirit to carry on his mission!

Connecting the Responsorial Psalm

to the readings: In the responsorial psalm for Pentecost, we beg God to send the Spirit of renewal. The gospel reading reveals that what the Spirit renews is our capacity to receive truth and to give testimony. The second reading suggests that part of the truth received is discernment of virtue from vice and part of the testimony given is lived out of this discernment. The Spirit-truth, then, sends us on our mission by transforming our way of living. When we allow this to happen, the "theme" of our lives (psalm)—what we say and what we do—is truly "pleasing" to God. Furthermore, we are enabled by the Spirit to communicate the Good News of this salvation in whatever tongue is necessary for people to hear and understand (first reading). What we pray for in this responsorial psalm, then, is neither extraneous to our personal lives nor minuscule in scope. The Spirit recreates the face of the earth (psalm refrain) by first recreating us.

to cantor preparation: As you sing the responsorial psalm for Pentecost, you celebrate the Spirit's wonderful deeds and renewing energies. But you also pray for your own transformation. You pray that your words and deeds become "pleasing" to God. The renewal of the earth for which you pray is not outside yourself, but actually begins within you. How might your preparation of this psalm during the week include a renewal of your willingness to allow the Spirit to continue transforming you?

**ASSEMBLY &
FAITH-SHARING GROUPS**

· I am aware of the gift of the Spirit transforming me when . . . This transformation is challenging for me when . . .

· I see the Spirit transforming my family . . . parish . . . city . . . world . . .

· The way I live testifies to the Spirit of truth when . . .

PRESIDERS

· I open the assembly to being transformed by the Spirit when I . . .

DEACONS

· My service builds up the community in the Spirit when I . . .

HOSPITALITY MINISTERS

· My greeting makes visible the fruits of the Spirit when . . .

MUSIC MINISTERS

· The tasks and relationships of music ministry challenge me to become transformed in the Spirit by . . .

ALTAR MINISTERS

· My service builds up the gift of the Spirit for the community because . . .

LECTORS

· I know my preparation for and proclamation of the word are both Spirit-filled when . . .

**EXTRAORDINARY MINISTERS
OF HOLY COMMUNION**

· The manner in which I encounter each communicant embodies the fruits of the Spirit in that . . .

Model Rite of Blessing and Sprinkling Holy Water

Presider: Dear friends, we ask God to bless this water as a reminder of the gift of the Spirit given us at baptism. Let us celebrate with great joy and pray to live faithfully the life to which the Spirit calls us . . . [pause]

[continue with form C of the blessing of water]

Homily Points

• We all have had experiences of being exhausted, worn down, discouraged— "dispirited." Often something unexpected and surprising lifts our spirits—for example, someone calls us on the phone, sends an e-mail, or stops to talk with us and says just the "right thing."

• God's gift of the Spirit is not an incidental presence, but an abiding one. At all times the Spirit is present within us and in the community, nudging us to see the giftedness still latent within us, within one another, and in our ordinary lives. Our challenge is to get in touch with manifestations of the Spirit's abiding presence, and to act upon this new awareness.

• Recognizing the presence of the Spirit happens, for example, by being open to others (even those who seemingly don't live by the Spirit), by being faithful to reflection and prayer, by noticing the fruits our good deeds have already borne. Acting upon the presence of the Spirit sometimes means taking risks, speaking up, seizing new possibilities; at other times it means simply remaining faithful, continuing to do ordinary things with love, doing routine or tedious tasks patiently.

Model Prayer of the Faithful

Presider: Let us pray to be faithful to the Spirit of truth who dwells within each of us.

Response:
Lord, hear our prayer.

Cantor:
we pray to the Lord,

That all members of the church respond faithfully to the enlivening presence of the Spirit . . . [pause]

That all peoples share in the fullness of life offered by the Spirit . . . [pause]

That those in need be lifted up by the love and care of the community in whom the Spirit dwells . . . [pause]

That the Spirit guide each of us to proclaim the gospel with sincerity and truth . . . [pause]

Presider: Gracious God, you send your Spirit to be with us and to guide us in all things: hear these our prayers that we might manifest the gift of the Spirit in our daily lives. We ask this through Christ our Lord. **Amen.**

OPENING PRAYER
Let us pray

Pause for silent prayer

God our Father,
let the Spirit you sent on your Church
to begin the teaching of the gospel
continue to work in the world
through the hearts of all who believe.

We ask this through our Lord Jesus Christ,
    your Son,
who lives and reigns with you and the
    Holy Spirit,
one God, for ever and ever. **Amen.**

FIRST READING
Acts 2:1-11

When the time for Pentecost was fulfilled,
    they were all in one place together.
And suddenly there came from the sky
    a noise like a strong driving wind,
    and it filled the entire house in which
        they were.
Then there appeared to them tongues as
    of fire,
    which parted and came to rest on each
        one of them.
And they were all filled with the Holy Spirit
    and began to speak in different tongues,
    as the Spirit enabled them to proclaim.

Now there were devout Jews from every
    nation under heaven
        staying in Jerusalem.
At this sound, they gathered in a large
    crowd,
    but they were confused
    because each one heard them speaking
        in his own language.
They were astounded, and in amazement
    they asked,
    "Are not all these people who are
        speaking Galileans?
Then how does each of us hear them in
    his native language?
We are Parthians, Medes, and Elamites,
    inhabitants of Mesopotamia, Judea and
        Cappadocia,
    Pontus and Asia, Phrygia and Pamphylia,
    Egypt and the districts of Libya near
        Cyrene,
    as well as travelers from Rome,
    both Jews and converts to Judaism,
        Cretans and Arabs,
    yet we hear them speaking in our own
        tongues
    of the mighty acts of God."

RESPONSORIAL PSALM
Ps 104:1, 24, 29-30, 31, 34

℟. (cf. 30) Lord, send out your Spirit, and renew the face of the earth.
or: ℟. Alleluia.

Bless the Lord, O my soul!
  O Lord, my God, you are great indeed!
How manifold are your works, O Lord!
  The earth is full of your creatures.

℟. Lord, send out your Spirit, and renew the face of the earth.
or: ℟. Alleluia.

If you take away their breath, they perish
  and return to their dust.
When you send forth your spirit, they are created,
  and you renew the face of the earth.

℟. Lord, send out your Spirit, and renew the face of the earth.
or: ℟. Alleluia.

May the glory of the Lord endure forever;
  may the Lord be glad in his works!
Pleasing to him be my theme;
  I will be glad in the Lord.

℟. Lord, send out your Spirit, and renew the face of the earth.
or: ℟. Alleluia.

SECOND READING
1 Cor 12:3b-7, 12-13

or

Gal 5:16-25

SEQUENCE

See Appendix A, p. 297.

About Liturgy

Pentecost sequence: The Pentecost sequence is a remarkably beautiful composition attributed to the late-twelfth, early thirteenth-century Archbishop of Canterbury Stephen Langton. This composition beautifully captures a wide range of activities of the Spirit, among them bringer of light, source of goods for the poor and all of us, comforter, sweet refreshment, solace, healer, strength, guide, source of joy. It would be well to spend some time meditating on all these activities of the Spirit. Moreover, if these activities are attributed to the Spirit, then because of the gift of the Spirit's indwelling we, too, are to live in this way.

Optional readings: In addition to the year A readings (permitted to be used any year), the revised Lectionary has given us an optional set of readings for each of the three years of the Lectionary cycle for Pentecost, and this year we have opted to reflect on those proper for year B in *Living Liturgy*™. These new choices of readings not only provide us with exposure to more Scripture texts, but they also offer fresh avenues for exploring the insights and meaning of this solemnity.

About Liturgical Music

Music suggestions: Pentecost celebrates our full insertion into the life, death, and mission of Jesus. Hymns which convey the urgency and import of this mission are especially relevant to this celebration. "We Know That Christ Is Raised" combines a strong text with a strong tune. Verses such as "A new creation comes to life and grows As Christ's new body takes on flesh and blood. The universe restored and whole will sing: Alleluia!" capture well the meaning of Pentecost. This hymn would be excellent for the entrance procession. Another hymn with equally strong text and tune is "The Church of Christ in Every Age," which could be used for either the entrance or the preparation of the gifts.

The Pentecost sequence is a required element in this day's liturgy. GIRM indicates that the sequence is sung before the Alleluia (no. 64), but the Introduction of the Order of Mass issued by the U.S. Bishops' Committee on the Liturgy states that it is sung after the Alleluia (no. 90). Perhaps the best—and most pastorally effective—way to sing the sequence is to honor its historical roots as an extended gospel acclamation and combine it with a solemn and prolonged gospel procession. WC and WS set the text to the familiar O FILII ET FILIAE with an Alleluia refrain (they have done the same with the Easter sequence). The assembly could easily sing the refrain while cantor or choir sings the verses. BB and JS2 set the text to HYMN TO JOY, using an internal refrain of "Come, O Holy Spirit, come!" Cantor or choir can sing the verses with the assembly chiming in on the refrain, with the whole framed at beginning and end by the Mode VI Easter Alleluia. While the sequence is sung, have the deacon or presider process throughout the entire assembly space holding the Book of the Gospels high for all to see.

Ordinary Time II

✝ SPIRITUALITY

GOSPEL ACCLAMATION
Rev 1:8

R̸. Alleluia, alleluia.
Glory to the Father, the Son, and the Holy Spirit;
to God who is, who was, and who is to come.
R̸. Alleluia, alleluia.

Gospel

Matt 28:16-20; L165B

The eleven disciples went to Galilee,
    to the mountain to which Jesus had
        ordered them.
When they all saw him, they
    worshiped, but they doubted.
Then Jesus approached and said to
    them,
    "All power in heaven and on earth
        has been given to me.
Go, therefore, and make disciples of all
    nations,
    baptizing them in the name of the
        Father,
    and of the Son, and of the Holy
        Spirit,
    teaching them to observe all that I
        have commanded you.
And behold, I am with you always, until
    the end of the age."

Reflecting on the Gospel

As a human like us, Jesus experienced the same challenges and frustrations with relationships as we do. The eleven disciples who met Jesus in Galilee had been with him from the beginning; they had seen his miracles, heard his teaching, witnessed his healing, saw him die, and now see him alive, the risen One. Yet, "they doubted." Beyond doubt, the disciples had denied him, betrayed him, resisted him. It would seem that this would put a strain on any relationship! Instead of giving up on the disciples, Jesus commands them to carry forth his mission. These disciples who strain relationships are trusted to carry forth Jesus' very ministry! Jesus' faithfulness to and trust in his followers lets us glimpse something of the mystery and wonder of who God is, which cannot be separated from God as the One who desires to be in relationship with God's people at all costs. The readings show us a God who always acts on our behalf, strengthening the intimate bond of love and relationship between God and us.

On this Sunday honoring the Trinity, the first reading describes what our Creator-God did for the Israelites: made them heirs of the land and of a long life. This reading says something about who God is, but does so in terms of God as the doer of mighty deeds: God creates, elects a nation to be God's own people, enjoins the people to keep the "statutes and commandments" which God gives, desires life and prosperity for the chosen people. This passage from Deuteronomy suggests all that God does is really an extension of who God is (strong and beneficent).

The second reading describes what God does for us in Christ. The depth and intimacy of God's relationship with us goes to our own identity—"we are children of God" and "heirs of God and joint heirs with Christ." As children and heirs, we share in the identity of Christ and, therefore, of God (compare 2 Peter 1:4: "share in the divine nature"). Moreover, we participate in God's saving work because we share in the power and mission of Christ (gospel) through the Spirit (see second reading). Sharing in divine identity is to share in divine doing—we, too, are to do mighty deeds. To be formed into the identity of Christ (and of God), therefore, is to be formed into his mission.

The gospel rather succinctly and clearly lays out the mission with which Jesus charged the disciples (and us) before he ascended into heaven: make disciples, baptize in the name of the Trinity, teach, and observe "all that [Jesus] has commanded." Jesus can entrust this mission to us because we share in his identity through the power of the Spirit. Has anything more wondrous or greater happened before?

Living the Paschal Mystery

Liturgy does for us what the Deuteronomy texts did for Israel of old: helps us remember God's mighty deeds and enter into a covenantal relationship with the Divine. Liturgy calls us together to ask, "Who is this God?"

Knowing God isn't something we can find out in the abstract; knowing God is sought and expressed in our own doing—in taking up Christ's mission and living our own privileged identity as daughters and sons of God "until the end of the age." Without doing as Jesus did, we cannot answer "Who is God?" This doing is nothing less than to "suffer with" Christ (second reading), which means a constant dying to self. By our own self-emptying are we filled with the divine identity.

Focusing the Gospel

Key words and phrases: Jesus . . . said, power, go . . . make disciples

To the point: On this Sunday honoring the Trinity, the first reading describes what our Creator-God did for the Israelites: made them heirs of the land and of a long life. The second reading and gospel describe what God does for us in Christ: makes us God's own sons and daughters and heirs of divine life. Moreover, we participate in God's saving work because we share in the power and mission of Christ (gospel) through the Spirit (see second reading).

Connecting the Gospel

to the second reading: We participate in the power and mission of Jesus "if only we suffer with him" (second reading). As with Jesus, dying to ourselves brings new life to others and, ultimately, leads us to be "glorified with him."

to Catholic experience: The Trinity is much more than a theological concept. How our Triune God has acted toward us is the pattern for our taking up the mission of Jesus and living the paschal mystery.

Connecting the Responsorial Psalm

to the readings: The verses of Psalm 33 chosen for this Sunday's responsorial psalm convey the utmost trust we can have in God whose word is true, whose works are reliable, whose kindness is granted to all who hope. The readings reveal even more: God chooses us to participate in the intimate personal relationship which is the very essence of the divine nature. At the core of both the mystery of the Trinity and the mystery of redemption stands a person-to-person relationship. God creates humankind, then takes Israel as "a nation to himself" (first reading). God adopts us as children (second reading). Jesus promises us his personal presence "until the end" (gospel). Truly, we are blessed who have been chosen for such love (psalm refrain).

But the love doesn't stop with us. Jesus' command in the gospel indicates that God desires "all nations" to be brought into the divine embrace. Today we celebrate how blessed we are for having been chosen as God's own, and we take on the mission of letting all peoples know they, too, are called to the same blessedness.

to cantor preparation: In this Sunday's first reading Moses invites the community of Israel to renew their covenant relationship with the God who has created, chosen, and redeemed them. In the responsorial psalm you invite the Christian community to do the same. How might you this week celebrate your covenant relationship with the triune God? How might you let others know they are called to this same relationship (see gospel)?

ASSEMBLY & FAITH-SHARING GROUPS

· For me, the Trinity touches my life when . . .
· The Trinity influences how I relate to others by . . .
· The Spirit urges me with renewed courage to continue the mission of Jesus when . . .

PRESIDERS

· My presiding helps the assembly to see themselves as God's sons and daughters when . . .

DEACONS

· My care of those in need incarnates the loving community life of the Trinity by . . .

HOSPITALITY MINISTERS

· My greeting helps the gathering assembly see themselves as a trinitarian community when . . .

MUSIC MINISTERS

· What helps me do my music ministry "in the name of" the Trinity is . . .

ALTAR MINISTERS

· The unobtrusiveness of my ministry reflects the hidden life of the Trinity because . . .

LECTORS

· Careful preparation for proclaiming the word is a continuation of Jesus' mission in that . . .

EXTRAORDINARY MINISTERS OF HOLY COMMUNION

· Jesus promises, "I am with you always" (gospel). This promise is fulfilled in me when . . .

Model Act of Penitence

Presider: We honor today the Blessed Trinity in whose name we have been baptized and sent on mission. Let us call upon the Lord Jesus to enable us to be faithful . . . [pause]

Lord Jesus, all power is yours: Lord . . .

Christ Jesus, you are with us always: Christ . . .

Lord Jesus, you call disciples to continue your saving work: Lord . . .

Homily Points

• Perhaps the most life-giving aspect of human experience is found in the relationships we have with one another. Perhaps our most painful experience is the cessation or absence of relationships. Much of our time and energy is directed toward establishing and maintaining healthy and deep family ties, meaningful friendships, and good working relationships with our colleagues.

• It is virtually impossible to maintain healthy human relationships without constant self-giving. This is hard work for us humans, and we are often tempted to give up. This yearly celebration of the Trinity reminds us how willingly and to what extent God reaches out to us in love, calling us into ever deeper relationships. Jesus incarnated this love of the Trinity for us; he also incarnated how we are to love one another.

• Jesus commissions us to be disciples who continue to incarnate the Trinity's love in our world. While we are sometimes tempted to give up on our relationships, our baptism calls us to embrace another option: to love each other the way God loves us. Such love is only possible when we give of ourselves. We practice this in the little things: forgiving hurts, expressing gratitude, offering compliments, listening patiently—dying to self daily.

Model Prayer of the Faithful

Presider: God continually cares for us and so we are encouraged to make our needs known.

Response:

Lord, hear our prayer.

Cantor:

we pray to the Lord,

That all members of the church be strengthened for their mission to carry on the saving work of Jesus . . . [pause]

That all peoples of the world may come to salvation . . . [pause]

That those in need may receive generously from the community of the baptized . . . [pause]

That all of us remain faithful as disciples of Jesus, strengthening one another in community by our love and care . . . [pause]

Presider: Triune God, you are present to your people in your mighty deeds and dwell within us by your grace: hear these our prayers that we might one day enjoy everlasting life in your presence. We ask this in Christ and through the Holy Spirit, one God, for ever and ever. **Amen.**

Let us pray
[to our God who is Father, Son, and Holy Spirit]

Pause for silent prayer

God, we praise you:
Father all-powerful, Christ Lord and
      Savior, Spirit of love.
You reveal yourself in the depths of our
      being,
drawing us to share in your life and your
      love.
One God, three Persons,
be near to the people formed in your
      image,
close to the world your love brings to life.
We ask this, Father, Son, and Holy Spirit,
one God, true and living, for ever and ever.
      Amen.

FIRST READING
Deut 4:32-34, 39-40

Moses said to the people:
      "Ask now of the days of old, before
            your time,
      ever since God created man upon the
            earth;
      ask from one end of the sky to the
            other:
      Did anything so great ever happen
            before?
Was it ever heard of?
Did a people ever hear the voice of God
      speaking from the midst of fire, as you
            did, and live?
Or did any god venture to go and take a
      nation for himself
      from the midst of another nation,
      by testings, by signs and wonders, by
            war,
      with strong hand and outstretched arm,
            and by great terrors,
      all of which the LORD, your God,
      did for you in Egypt before your very
            eyes?
This is why you must now know,
      and fix in your heart, that the LORD is
            God
      in the heavens above and on earth
            below,
      and that there is no other.
You must keep his statutes and
      commandments that I enjoin on you
            today,
      that you and your children after you
            may prosper,
      and that you may have long life on the
            land
      which the LORD, your God, is giving you
            forever."

RESPONSORIAL PSALM
Ps 33:4-5, 6, 9, 18-19, 20, 22

R̸. (12b) Blessed the people the Lord has chosen to be his own.

Upright is the word of the LORD,
  and all his works are trustworthy.
He loves justice and right;
  of the kindness of the LORD the earth
    is full.

R̸. Blessed the people the Lord has chosen to be his own.

By the word of the LORD the heavens were
    made;
  by the breath of his mouth all their
    host.
For he spoke, and it was made;
  he commanded, and it stood forth.

R̸. Blessed the people the Lord has chosen to be his own.

See, the eyes of the LORD are upon those
    who fear him,
  upon those who hope for his kindness,
to deliver them from death
  and preserve them in spite of famine.

R̸. Blessed the people the Lord has chosen to be his own.

Our soul waits for the LORD,
  who is our help and our shield.
May your kindness, O LORD, be upon us
  who have put our hope in you.

R̸. Blessed the people the Lord has chosen to be his own.

SECOND READING
Rom 8:14-17

Brothers and sisters:
Those who are led by the Spirit of God are
    sons of God.
For you did not receive a spirit of slavery
    to fall back into fear,
  but you received a Spirit of adoption,
  through whom we cry, "Abba, Father!"
The Spirit himself bears witness with our
    spirit
  that we are children of God,
  and if children, then heirs,
  heirs of God and joint heirs with Christ,
  if only we suffer with him
so that we may also be glorified with
    him.

About Liturgy

Return to Ordinary Time: It might be tempting to think of this Sunday as a continuation of the festive Easter season, since this solemnity comes immediately after Pentecost. After all, this is just one more high festival in a whole string of them. It seems like we have been celebrating resurrection and new life for a long time, and we have—for a full fifty days. It is good to remind ourselves at this point in the liturgical year that we resumed Ordinary Time on the Monday after Pentecost, so Trinity Sunday is a solemnity during Ordinary Time. It is now that we consciously take up Jesus' paschal mission and live what we have been celebrating. All good things come to an end and we must get on with our life. So it is with Easter. The constant celebration has come to an end. Now we must live what the celebration means.

About Liturgical Music

Music suggestions: There are a number of contemporary trinitarian hymns worth considering for this Sunday's liturgy. John Bell's "Today I Awake" [G2, GC] combines a freshly poetic text with a melody that sweeps an octave and more. Because the tune may be a stretch for many assemblies, this hymn might work best as a choir prelude with a soloist on verse 1, another soloist on verse 2, duo on verse 3, and the entire choir on verse 4. Brian Wren's "How Wonderful the Three-in-One" [in many hymnals] also offers fresh imagery for reflecting on the Trinity. Set to an early American Southern Harmony tune, this hymn is easy for most assemblies to sing even on first hearing (having a cantor sing the first verse solo would, however, give them added encouragement). This hymn would work well for either the preparation of the gifts or as an assembly song of praise after Communion. Sylvia Dunstan's "This Holy Covenant Was Made" [RS] describes the unique role of each Person of the Trinity in the covenant God maintains with us. The song would suit the preparation of the gifts or the Communion procession.

✠ SPIRITUALITY

GOSPEL ACCLAMATION
John 6:51

R̸. Alleluia, alleluia.
I am the living bread that came down from heaven,
says the Lord; whoever eats this bread will live
forever.
R̸. Alleluia, alleluia.

Gospel   Mark 14:12-16, 22-26; L168B

On the first day of the Feast of
    Unleavened Bread,
    when they sacrificed the Passover lamb,
    Jesus' disciples said to him,
    "Where do you want us to go
    and prepare for you to eat the
        Passover?"
He sent two of his disciples and said to
    them,
    "Go into the city and a man will meet
        you,
    carrying a jar of water.
Follow him.
Wherever he enters, say to the master of
    the house,
    'The Teacher says, "Where is my guest
        room
    where I may eat the Passover with my
        disciples?"'
Then he will show you a large upper room
    furnished and ready.
Make the preparations for us there."
The disciples then went off, entered the city,
    and found it just as he had told them;
    and they prepared the Passover.

While they were eating,
    he took bread, said the blessing,
    broke it, gave it to them, and said,
    "Take it; this is my body."
Then he took a cup, gave thanks, and gave
    it to them,
    and they all drank from it.
He said to them,
    "This is my blood of the covenant,
    which will be shed for many.
Amen, I say to you,
    I shall not drink again the fruit of the vine
    until the day when I drink it new in the
        kingdom of God."
Then, after singing a hymn,
    they went out to the Mount of Olives.

Reflecting on the Gospel

We undertake nothing significant in our lives without preparation. We spend years in school before we take on a profession. We spends months preparing for a wedding or years preparing for ordination or profession of vows in a religious congregation. We pore over blueprints and go over specs with an architect for months before building a house. Yes, big events in our lives take careful preparation. We notice that the entire first half of the gospel for this solemnity is about preparation. Jesus sends two of his disciples ahead to procure a room and make preparations for the supper. We would suspect that such careful preparation means something significant is about to happen. And so it does. Jesus does something entirely new and unimaginably significant: he gives himself—his very body and blood—to us as our heavenly Food. This is the mystery we celebrate this Sunday.

The story of our redemption unfolds as a progressive deepening of God's personal presence and self-gift to us. The blood of bulls was sprinkled on the Israelites as a sign of their acceptance of the Mosaic covenant (see first reading). Now, the blood of Jesus is the sign of a new covenant (see gospel). By our drinking of the blood of Jesus and our eating of his body, we accept this new covenant of divine self-gift and personal presence. Even more: we *are* that presence for the world, called to the same self-giving. The Eucharist is the source and summit of our own self-giving in ministry and life.

Jesus' identity as the suffering servant who obtained redemption for us "with his own blood" (second reading) is, truly, the same as his mission—to give of himself without counting the cost, even if its cost is his very body and blood. In Eucharist we are given the sacrificed Body to eat and the sacrificed Blood to drink (the Israelites, by contrast, were merely sprinkled with the blood). Our yes to this eucharistic food seals our new covenant with God and nourishes us to spend ourselves in the same sacrificial self-giving as Jesus modeled for us.

This solemnity is an opportunity to celebrate the action of God's delivering us and to accept the divine invitation to participate in this deliverance—both to receive the deliverance as the Bread of life and the Blood of covenantal relationship and to extend God's deliverance to others by our own self-giving. O wondrous mystery: the Body of self-giving is the Son of God; the Blood of the new covenant brings us to the "kingdom of God" and "the promised eternal inheritance." We drink of divine Life, and this becomes our pledge of self-giving for the sake of others.

Living the Paschal Mystery

The covenant God made with Israel and sealed through the sprinkling of the sacrificial animal blood was a relationship with God in which they were to hear God's word and keep his commandments. Now, rather than being sprinkled "with the blood of goats and calves" (second reading), we drink the blood of the risen Lord and by that action seal our new covenant with God. We are still to hear God's word and keep his commandments, like of old, but now something else is added: we ourselves are to take up God's redemptive work as we conform ourselves more perfectly to Christ and continue his self-giving ministry.

Our everyday living is preparation for sharing in the Eucharist and receiving eternal life. We sprinkle among the people with whom we live and work little acts of self-giving, sealing our relationship with them and with God. This is how we "worship the living God" (second reading): by self-giving.

Focusing the Gospel

Key words and phrases: body, Take it, drank from it, blood of the covenant, shed for many

To the point: The story of our redemption unfolds as a progressive deepening of God's personal presence and self-gift to us. The blood of bulls was sprinkled on the Israelites as a sign of their acceptance of the Mosaic covenant (see first reading). Now, the blood of Jesus is the sign of a new covenant (see gospel). By our drinking of the blood of Jesus and our eating of his body, we accept this new covenant of divine self-gift and personal presence. Even more: we *are* that presence for the world, called to the same self-giving.

Connecting the Gospel

to the second reading: The second reading seems not to be about the gift of the Eucharist that we celebrate on this Sunday. Jesus' self-offering on the cross, however, is inseparable from his gift of self in the Eucharist.

to Catholic experience: Truly the bread and wine become the Body and Blood of Christ. Just as truly do we who consume this Bread and Wine become more perfectly the Body of Christ.

Connecting the Responsorial Psalm

to the readings: What does it mean for us to "take the cup of salvation" (psalm refrain)? For a Hebrew this phrase meant taking a cup of wine and pouring it out as a libation in thanksgiving for some saving deed on God's part. In the introductory sections of Psalm 116, the psalmist tells about an imminent threat of death, about the fear and desperation with which she or he cried out for God's intervention, and about how graciously and mercifully God responded. In the closing verses the supplicant vows to make public thanksgiving so that all the people may know what God has done.

In the context of this Sunday's solemnity, we sing this refrain with added layers of meaning. The cup of salvation that is poured out is Christ's Blood, his very life given for our salvation (second reading). We take up this cup in thanksgiving, not, however, to pour it out but to drink it (gospel) so that our blood, transformed into Christ's, may be poured out for others. The libation we make in thanksgiving for God's saving deeds in Christ is to tip over the cup of our own hearts in self-sacrificing love. How precious is such death in God's eyes and how challenging such a commitment on our part (psalm)! May we sing this refrain with full awareness of what we are saying.

to cantor preparation: The context into which this Sunday's solemnity puts these verses from Psalm 116 challenges you to the core of your identity as Body of Christ. You sing not only in thanksgiving for what God has done in redeeming you, but also in promise that you will act as God's faithful servant. And this means laying down your life as Christ has done. You "take [up] the cup of salvation" in the same way that Christ does in the gospel reading: as your own blood to be poured out for others. Where in your life at this moment are you being called to pour out your blood? In what way(s) can you call upon God to help you?

ASSEMBLY & FAITH-SHARING GROUPS
- I accept my covenantal relationship with God when . . . This covenant is a particular challenge to me when . . .
- I am strengthened by the Body and Blood of Christ to . . .
- I find it easiest to give myself for the sake of others when . . . I find it most difficult when . . .

PRESIDERS
- I keep the self-giving of Jesus alive in me when presiding by . . . in my daily ministry when . . .

DEACONS
- My ministry of service encourages others to be self-giving when . . .

HOSPITALITY MINISTERS
- The manner in which I greet others is a presence of Christ for them when . . .

MUSIC MINISTERS
- When I am truly present to others, my music ministry is . . . The Eucharist helps me grow in being really present to others by . . .

ALTAR MINISTERS
- My service helps people grasp the deepest meaning of the eucharistic celebration because . . .

LECTORS
- The word has deepened my participation in the Eucharist by . . . The Eucharist has deepened my awareness of Christ's presence in the word by . . .

EXTRAORDINARY MINISTERS OF HOLY COMMUNION
- The manner of my distributing Holy Communion calls others to a deeper appreciation for the presence of Christ in that . . .

Model Act of Penitence

Presider: Today we honor the Most Holy Body and Blood of Christ. Let us prepare ourselves for this celebration by opening our hearts to give thanks for all God has given us . . . [pause]

Lord Jesus, you are the Body given for our salvation: Lord . . .

Christ Jesus, you are the Blood poured out for us: Christ . . .

Lord Jesus, you are the Nourishment we need as we journey to eternal life: Lord . . .

Homily Points

• We've all experienced times when being present to another is demanding: we must listen even if we are distracted or tired; we must put aside our own agendas to attend to another's; to understand another, we must put ourselves into their shoes. Likewise, we've all had experiences when another was so genuinely present to us that we felt attended to, cherished, significant.

• The gospels abound with stories showing how amazingly present to people Jesus was (for example, touching lepers, embracing children, attending to weeping women). These incidents of personal presence, however, were time-bound and limited. In the self-gift of the Eucharist, Jesus makes himself present to us for all time: "Do this in memory of me" (Luke 22:19).

• Eucharist is more than a gift for us; it is a gift through us for others. The celebration of Eucharist always sends us forth to a life of self-giving, so totally modeled by Jesus. We are to bring the presence of the risen Christ to others.

Model Prayer of the Faithful

Presider: With hearts grateful for this gift of Christ's Body and Blood, we pray for strength to give ourselves for the sake of others.

Response: Lord, hear our prayer.

Cantor: we pray to the Lord,

That all members of the church truly live as Christ's presence in the world . . . [pause]

That all people of the world come to unity and peace through self-giving for the sake of others . . . [pause]

That those without food and drink receive sufficient nourishment to live healthy and strong lives . . . [pause]

That each of us proclaim by just deeds and worthy lives the mystery of Christ's self-giving . . . [pause]

Presider: Gracious God, you have given us your Son's Body and Blood as nourishment: hear these our prayers that we might come to everlasting life. We ask this through Jesus Christ our Lord. **Amen.**

ALTERNATIVE OPENING PRAYER

Let us pray
   [for the willingness to make present in
   our world the love of Christ shown to us
   in the eucharist]

Pause for silent prayer

Lord Jesus Christ,
we worship you living among us
in the sacrament of your body and blood.
May we offer to our Father in heaven
a solemn pledge of undivided love.
May we offer our brothers and sisters
a life poured out in loving service of that
      kingdom
where you live with the Father and the
      Holy Spirit,
one God, for ever and ever. **Amen.**

FIRST READING
Exod 24:3-8

When Moses came to the people
   and related all the words and ordinances
      of the LORD,
   they all answered with one voice,
   "We will do everything that the LORD
      has told us."
Moses then wrote down all the words of
   the LORD and,
   rising early the next day,
   he erected at the foot of the mountain
      an altar
   and twelve pillars for the twelve tribes
      of Israel.
Then, having sent certain young men of
   the Israelites
   to offer holocausts and sacrifice young
      bulls
   as peace offerings to the LORD,
Moses took half of the blood and put it
   in large bowls;
   the other half he splashed on the altar.
Taking the book of the covenant, he read
   it aloud to the people,
   who answered, "All that the LORD has
      said, we will heed and do."
Then he took the blood and sprinkled it on
   the people, saying,
   "This is the blood of the covenant
   that the LORD has made with you
   in accordance with all these words of
      his."

RESPONSORIAL PSALM
Ps 116:12-13, 15-16, 17-18

R̹. (13) I will take the cup of salvation, and call on the name of the Lord.
or:
R̹. Alleluia.

How shall I make a return to the LORD
   for all the good he has done for me?
The cup of salvation I will take up,
   and I will call upon the name of the
     LORD.

R̹. I will take the cup of salvation, and call on the name of the Lord.
or:
R̹. Alleluia.

Precious in the eyes of the LORD
   is the death of his faithful ones.
I am your servant, the son of your
     handmaid;
   you have loosed my bonds.

R̹. I will take the cup of salvation, and call on the name of the Lord.
or:
R̹. Alleluia.

To you will I offer sacrifice of
     thanksgiving,
   and I will call upon the name of the
     LORD.
My vows to the LORD I will pay
   in the presence of all his people.

R̹. I will take the cup of salvation, and call on the name of the Lord.
or:
R̹. Alleluia.

SECOND READING
Heb 9:11-15

OPTIONAL SEQUENCE

See Appendix A, p. 298.

About Liturgy

Preparing for and appreciating the mystery: The General Instruction of the Roman Missal provides that there be a brief period of silence or hymn of praise after Communion (see GIRM nos. 88 and 164). Thus the ritual action itself encourages us to spend some time reflecting on and praising God for the gracious and wondrous gift of the Body and Blood of Christ. Even if we faithfully do this every Mass, we know that we cannot begin to have sufficient time to reflect on the depths of the mystery or to give sufficient thanks for it. For this reason it is always appropriate to spend some other devotional time before the Blessed Sacrament. Our time of adoration and thanksgiving, however, must always flow from the action of the Eucharist itself and lead us to witness more clearly in our lives the self-giving of Jesus. This great Gift always—during Mass and at times of adoration—leads us to identify our lives more closely with Christ. We are reminded, then, that this Gift has its cost: we, too, are to give ourselves for others. Anything less than this is to rob the mystery of its greatest depth—the fact that we eat and drink Christ's true Body and Blood and become what we eat so that we can be the self-giving Christ for others.

Since we naturally take sufficient preparation time for significant events in our lives, it would seem that this would also be part of our weekly celebration of Eucharist. Perhaps because it is a weekly event, far too many of us take little or no time to prepare for this most important event of our week. The church gives us ways to prepare: every Friday is a day of penance, on which we fast, pray, and do acts of charity to prepare ourselves spiritually for the Gift we receive on Sunday. Every act of self-giving for the good of others is also preparation for celebrating Eucharist. Reading the Scriptures ahead of time so we can better hear God's word proclaimed is another way to prepare. Dressing in something other than everyday or work clothes is another way we prepare ourselves and also witness to others the importance of Eucharist in our lives.

About Liturgical Music

Music suggestions: It is tempting especially at Communion this Sunday to sing hymns which are devotional in nature. It is very important, however, that we distinguish between hymns meant for adoration of the Blessed Sacrament and hymns meant for the eucharistic liturgy. Traditional hymns such as "Jesus, My Lord, My God, My All" and "O Jesus, We Adore Thee" are devotional because their texts move persons to private adoration. For this reason they are not appropriate for the eucharistic celebration. Examples of songs appropriate for the Communion procession at Mass, and particularly fitting for this solemnity, include John Foley's "One Bread, One Body"; Alexander Peloquin's "In Memory of You" [RS], which combines the traditional "Ave Verum" with a refrain that speaks of the assembly's active participation in the doing of Eucharist; Delores Dufner's "Let the Hungry Come to Me," an alternative text for "Adoro Te Devote" [CH]; and Laurence Rosania's "the Supper of the Lord" [BB], which sings of the "Precious body, precious blood, here in bread and wine . . ."

JUNE 14, 2009
THE SOLEMNITY OF THE MOST HOLY BODY AND BLOOD OF CHRIST

✦ SPIRITUALITY

GOSPEL ACCLAMATION
Matt 11:29ab

R⁊. Alleluia, alleluia.
Take my yoke upon you, says the Lord;
and learn from me, for I am meek and humble
    of heart.
R⁊. Alleluia, alleluia.

or

1 John 4:10b

R⁊. Alleluia, alleluia.
God first loved us
and sent his Son as expiation for our sins.
R⁊. Alleluia, alleluia.

Gospel   John 19:31-37; L171B

Since it was preparation day,
   in order that the bodies might not
      remain on the cross on the
      sabbath,
   for the sabbath day of that week was a
      solemn one,
   the Jews asked Pilate that their legs be
      broken
   and they be taken down.
So the soldiers came and broke the legs
   of the first
   and then of the other one who was
      crucified with Jesus.
But when they came to Jesus and saw
   that he was already dead,
   they did not break his legs,
   but one soldier thrust his lance into his
      side,
   and immediately blood and water
      flowed out.
An eyewitness has testified, and his
      testimony is true;
   he knows that he is speaking the truth,
   so that you also may come to believe.
For this happened so that the Scripture
      passage might be fulfilled:
   Not a bone of it will be broken.
And again another passage says:
   They will look upon him whom they
      have pierced.

See Appendix A, p. 299, for the other readings.

Reflecting on the Gospel

How much is one's all? Parents often give to their sick child, losing sleep until they think they will drop, and then reach down to find some reserve of strength to keep on. Sometimes the ones who most generously respond to the needs of others are those who have little or nothing themselves. Martyrs continue to give their lives for the sake of the Gospel and others' salvation and even after their death continue to influence people to follow Christ. Like the mystery of God itself, giving one's all seems to have no end. Always more can be given. We never run out. Surely, neither does God!

The first reading from the prophet Hosea tells eloquently and tenderly of God's great love for the people Israel in spite of their constant infidelity—God loved, called, taught, enveloped Israel with divine "bands of love," fed, and healed. The second reading from the letter to the Ephesians concludes that the "breadth and length and height and depth" of the love of Christ still surpasses everything we can know and fills us "with all the fullness of God." These poetic texts stretch our giving our all beyond a love we think we can endure. Then the gospel makes this concrete.

The lance thrust into the heart of Jesus, an apparently pointless act ("he was already dead"), opens up a sign of the totality of Jesus' self-giving ("immediately blood and water flowed out") and a pledge of future life. This sign and pledge are the "love of Christ which surpasses knowledge" referred to in the second reading and the divine tender love overwhelmingly poured out in the first reading. Just when Jesus had given his all, even to the point of death, he opens himself and pours out more life for us. His crucified body bears the red mark of the lance's thrust so that we can "look upon him whom they have pierced" and come to believe. Without this further testimony to Jesus' great love perhaps we could miss the real import of his death—not for political reasons or out of misguided goals, but so we can "come to believe" in God's tender care for us. God's tender love. This is no passive love, no intellectual love, no cheap love. This is a love borne from creation through Israel's infidelity and through our own infidelity to the end of time so that "the plan of the mystery hidden from ages past . . . might now be made known through the church" and "accomplished in Christ Jesus our Lord" (second reading)—God's remarkable plan for our salvation. God has taken the greatest of care to ensure that we have life, even to the point of sacrificing the divine Son whose heart was pierced.

Living the Paschal Mystery

The Sacred Heart of Jesus has been a popular devotion; the traditional Litany of the Sacred Heart contains language that reminds us of the real demand of discipleship: "Heart of Jesus, abode of justice and love . . . of Whose fullness we have all received . . . patient and most merciful . . . obedient unto death . . . our life and resurrection." We have received fullness of life from God through the death and resurrection of Jesus; now we must be abodes of justice and love, patient and more merciful, obedient even unto death. Although this solemnity speaks of God's great tenderness in loving us, even this has its demand. It is God's tenderness that encourages us to have our own hearts pierced so that others might receive the fullness of life through us. We can do this because God loved us first.

Focusing the Gospel

Key words and phrases: already dead, thrust his lance, blood and water flowed out

To the point: The lance thrust into the heart of Jesus, an apparently pointless act ("he was already dead"), opens up a sign of the totality of Jesus' self-giving ("immediately blood and water flowed out") and a pledge of future life. This sign and pledge are the "love of Christ which surpasses knowledge" referred to in the second reading and the divine tender love overwhelmingly poured out in the first reading.

Model Act of Penitence

Presider: On this solemnity of the Sacred Heart we celebrate God's great love for us and the gift of life we receive through the sacrifice of the divine Son. Let us open our hearts to receive new life from the Table of the Word and the Table of the Eucharist . . . [pause]

Lord Jesus, you died on the cross for our salvation: Lord . . .

Christ Jesus, the blood and water of life flowed from your side: Christ . . .

Lord Jesus, your love for us draws us to believe in you: Lord . . .

Model Prayer of the Faithful

Presider: Assured of God's great and tender love, we do not hesitate to ask for what we need.

Response: Lord, hear our prayer.

Cantor: we pray to the Lord,

That Christ's self-sacrificing love be manifested through the community of the church . . . [pause]

That Christ's pouring out of his life come to fulfillment in the salvation of all people . . . [pause]

That Christ's generous self-giving be a beacon of hope for the needy . . . [pause]

That Christ's pierced heart motivate us to love our brothers and sisters by our own self-giving . . . [pause]

Presider: Loving God, you have cared for us from the moment we first breathed life: hear these our prayers that each of us may one day join you in everlasting life. We ask this through the Sacred Heart of your divine Son Jesus Christ. **Amen.**

FOR REFLECTION

· The image of the heart of Jesus emphasizes for me . . .

· When I look upon "him whom they have pierced," I . . . I am willing to let my heart be pierced for the sake of others when . . .

· The self-giving of Jesus which touches me the most is . . .

· I have encountered the love of Jesus in . . . through . . . by . . .

Homily Points

• Parents readily identify with the imagery the prophet Hosea uses in the first reading to try and capture the deep, intimate love God has for us: calls us children; teaches us to walk; hugs, feeds, heals us. While no human can express the "breadth and length and height and depth" of God's love for us, this divine love remains the call to us to love each other.

• Divine love is incarnated and fully expressed in Jesus' self-giving—perfectly summed up in the "sacred heart." This love now manifested through us is spilled out from our hearts aflame with the love of God.

SPIRITUALITY

GOSPEL ACCLAMATION

Luke 7:16

R⁊. Alleluia, alleluia.
A great prophet has risen in our midst,
God has visited his people.
R⁊. Alleluia, alleluia.

Gospel

Mark 4:35-41; L95B

**On that day, as evening drew on, Jesus
said to his disciples:
"Let us cross to the other side."
Leaving the crowd, they took Jesus
with them in the boat just as he
was.
And other boats were with him.
A violent squall came up and waves
were breaking over the boat,
so that it was already filling up.
Jesus was in the stern, asleep on a
cushion.
They woke him and said to him,
"Teacher, do you not care that we are
perishing?"
He woke up,
rebuked the wind, and said to the
sea, "Quiet! Be still!"
The wind ceased and there was great
calm.
Then he asked them, "Why are you
terrified?
Do you not yet have faith?"
They were filled with great awe and
said to one another,
"Who then is this whom even wind
and sea obey?"**

Reflecting on the Gospel

Even when we think we are safe, violent storms scare us and we do all we can to protect ourselves from their potential destruction. We buy expensive surge protectors to safeguard our electronic equipment from lightning strikes. We put plywood over windows and batten down our property as best we can in face of a predicted hurricane or tornado. We store nonperishable food and bottled water in case deep snow keeps us from getting out. Almost all of us can identify with the disciples' fright when they are out at sea and a "violent squall" comes up. After all, Jesus is with experienced fishermen who know well the peril of a storm at sea.

What they do not "yet" know fully is the extent of Jesus' power and of his "care" for them. The fishermen are frightened, and Jesus is comfortably "asleep on a cushion." Either Jesus was especially tired—it was evening—or Jesus displayed a trust in his Father that the disciples did not share with him. So, we might ask, from what disaster does Jesus really save the disciples? From a storm? Yes, but much more: he saves them from their own lack of faith and trust in him—an even bigger disaster than a storm at sea. Storms can destroy property or hurt us physically or even take our lives. The surprise of the gospel is that this isn't the biggest concern of Jesus. His biggest concern is that the disciples do not have sufficient faith and trust in him.

As the first reading demonstrates, God has power over the might of creation. God assures Job "out of the storm" that it was divine power that contained the seas and set its limits: "here shall your proud waves be stilled!" The disciples were experiencing a similar might of nature: "waves were breaking over the boat." When Jesus commanded the sea to be "Quiet! Be still!" it obeyed him. The response that welled up in the disciples was one of "great awe" which led them to ask about Jesus' identity. And here is the crunch of the gospel: only God has power over nature. When Jesus asked faith of the disciples, he was asking them to grow in their relationship to him as more than a "Teacher." He was revealing further that he was the long-expected Messiah, the Son of God (which is revealed later in Mark's Gospel). When Jesus asked faith of the disciples, then, he was not asking faith in him as their Teacher and leader. He was asking them to have faith and trust in him as the divine One with power to save.

After Jesus commanded the sea to be quiet, "there was great calm." We might surmise that a similar calm washed over the disciples—that their "great awe" brought them to humble silence before this Teacher who had such extraordinary power. Calm comes out of trust. And thus is diverted the real "storm" at sea. The disciples' faith was tested, and this became an occasion for them to grow in faith. So it is with us. The "storms" of our own lives become occasions for us to grow in faith and trust that God is ever present to us, calming whatever threatens us, bringing us to a deeper relationship with the God who cares for us.

Living the Paschal Mystery

In our daily living we tend to ward off as much disaster as we can. We spend a great deal of time planning ahead—having gas in the car, food on our pantry shelves, well-organized calendars so we can keep our appointments straight. This gospel challenges us to meet whatever challenges come our way—and no matter how much planning and preparing we do, the challenges will come—as opportunities to grow in faith and trust in God as well as in those who live and work with us.

Focusing the Gospel

Key words and phrases: violent squall, do you not care, Do you not yet have faith, filled with great awe

To the point: Jesus is with experienced fishermen who know well the peril of a storm at sea. What they do not "yet" know fully is the extent of Jesus' power and of his "care" for them. So from what disaster does Jesus really save the disciples? From a storm? Yes, but much more: he saves them from their own lack of faith and trust in him—an even bigger disaster than a storm at sea. So does Jesus do for us.

Connecting the Gospel

to the first reading: The first reading describes a theophany: God speaks to Job in the midst of a storm and assures him of divine power over creation. The gospel, too, describes a theophany in the midst of a "violent squall" which reveals Jesus' divine identity.

to human experience: We human beings prefer to have sufficient proof that something will work before we venture forth into an unknown. For example, after the Discovery shuttle disaster, NASA spent years amassing proof that shuttle travel would be safe. Nevertheless, it took great trust for the next team of astronauts to venture forth into space. Proof is easier than trust.

Connecting the Responsorial Psalm

to the readings: Psalm 107 as a whole relates the story of God's continual intervention to save Israel from distress and terror. The psalm conveys these terrors through vivid images of thirst experienced in the desert, fear felt in face of primordial darkness, agony suffered because of fatal illness, and perils undergone at sea. In every situation the persons in danger called upon God and were saved, and Israel called them to thank God for steadfast love and wonderful deeds on behalf of humankind.

In line with this Sunday's gospel, the verses chosen from the psalm are those depicting a devastating storm at sea. The verses invite us to place the same trust in God as did Israel. When dangers and disasters mark our journey of discipleship, we needn't be either surprised or terrified. Such traumas are inevitable, but so is the intervention of the One who has power over the sea (first reading and gospel). The psalm reminds us that our all-powerful God will calm not only these "storms" but also our own overwhelmed hearts. No matter the weakness of our faith, God's activity on our behalf will remain constant. And for this we give thanks (psalm refrain).

to cantor preparation: It is important that you not let the concrete imagery of this responsorial psalm sidetrack you from its real meaning. The storm is but a metaphor: you are not singing about dangers at sea, but about the ongoing reality of faithful discipleship. How does this metaphor shed light on your own experience of discipleship? How does it strengthen your trust in the God who saves?

ASSEMBLY & FAITH-SHARING GROUPS

· The "violent squall" in life of which I am most fearful is . . .

· A "violent squall" which tested my faith and trust in Jesus was . . . It also strengthened by faith and trust in that . . .

· I experience Jesus' great care for me when . . . This has brought me to greater faith and trust in that . . .

PRESIDERS

· My ministry enables me to help others calm the storms in their lives when . . .

DEACONS

· My service is a theophany of Jesus' care in the midst of stress whenever . . .

HOSPITALITY MINISTERS

· My hospitality has a calming effect when . . . for . . .

MUSIC MINISTERS

· One of the "squalls" that keeps coming up in my music ministry is . . . I experience Jesus calming this squall by . . .

ALTAR MINISTERS

· My unobtrusive service has a calming effect to the extent that . . .

LECTORS

· My ongoing reflection on God's word has deepened my faith and trust in Jesus by . . .

EXTRAORDINARY MINISTERS OF HOLY COMMUNION

· My ministry has increased my trust in Jesus' abiding presence within the community by . . .

Model Act of Penitence

Presider: In the gospel today Jesus calms the storm at sea and leads the disciples to greater faith and trust in him. As we prepare to celebrate this liturgy, let us open ourselves to Jesus' abiding presence and deep care for us . . . [pause]

Lord Jesus, you care for those entrusted to you: Lord . . .

Christ Jesus, you are the divine One who has power over creation: Christ . . .

Lord Jesus, you are the One in whom we believe and trust: Lord . . .

Homily Points

• Parents understand well the responsibility and privilege of calling their children beyond where they are at any stage in their lives. For example, encouraging a toddler to walk, a youngster to ride a bike, a teenager to make right decisions, etc. Basic to this process is parents teaching their children to trust their own innate abilities and grow into capable and independent adults. Our faith journey is a similar process.

• Even though the disciples had already experienced some of Jesus' miracles, this new situation at sea was different: the violence of the storm threatened *their* lives and was beyond their power to control. Jesus' care for them and his power over creation led them to greater faith and trust.

• Jesus is the "parent" who calls us, his disciples today, to go beyond our own previous experiences and our limited understanding of his presence in our lives. In the "storms" of our own lives, Jesus is always present—through other people, within ourselves, in the very challenge of the situation. Each challenge in life offers us more and more reasons to trust in Jesus—concrete evidence of our continual growth in faith.

Model Prayer of the Faithful

Presider: The God who has power over all creation and cares for us will surely hear our prayers and give us all we need to grow in faith and trust. And so we pray.

Response:

Lord, hear our prayer.

Cantor:

we pray to the Lord,

That each member of the church witness to Jesus' abiding presence and care by their concern for others . . . [pause]

That all people grow into a greater trust in God's power over evil . . . [pause]

That those overwhelmed by danger or disaster find courage in Jesus' abiding presence and power . . . [pause]

That members of this faith community lead one another to greater faith and trust in Jesus . . . [pause]

Presider: Almighty God, you still the storms of our lives and care for your people: hear these our prayers that one day we might enjoy everlasting peace with you. We ask this through Christ our Lord. **Amen.**

OPENING PRAYER

Let us pray
   [to God whose fatherly love keeps us safe]

Pause for silent prayer

Father,
guide and protector of your people,
grant us an unfailing respect for your
    name,
and keep us always in your love.

Grant this through our Lord Jesus Christ,
    your Son,
who lives and reigns with you and the
    Holy Spirit,
one God, for ever and ever. **Amen.**

FIRST READING

Job 38:1, 8-11

The Lord addressed Job out of the storm
    and said:
  Who shut within doors the sea,
    when it burst forth from the womb;
  when I made the clouds its garment
    and thick darkness its swaddling
      bands?
  When I set limits for it
    and fastened the bar of its door,
  and said: Thus far shall you come but
      no farther,
    and here shall your proud waves be
      stilled!

RESPONSORIAL PSALM

Ps 107:23-24, 25-26, 28-29, 30-31

℞. (1b) Give thanks to the Lord, his love is everlasting.
  or:
℞. Alleluia.

They who sailed the sea in ships,
    trading on the deep waters,
these saw the works of the Lord
    and his wonders in the abyss.

℞. Give thanks to the Lord, his love is everlasting.
  or:
℞. Alleluia.

His command raised up a storm wind
    which tossed its waves on high.
They mounted up to heaven; they sank to
    the depths;
    their hearts melted away in their plight.

℞. Give thanks to the Lord, his love is everlasting.
  or:
℞. Alleluia.

They cried to the LORD in their distress;
  from their straits he rescued them,
he hushed the storm to a gentle breeze,
  and the billows of the sea were stilled.

R̸. Give thanks to the Lord, his love is
everlasting.
  or:
R̸. Alleluia.

They rejoiced that they were calmed,
  and he brought them to their desired
    haven.
Let them give thanks to the LORD for his
  kindness
  and his wondrous deeds to the children
    of men.

R̸. Give thanks to the Lord, his love is
everlasting.
  or:
R̸. Alleluia.

SECOND READING
2 Cor 5:14-17

Brothers and sisters:
The love of Christ impels us,
  once we have come to the conviction
    that one died for all;
  therefore, all have died.
He indeed died for all,
  so that those who live might no longer
    live for themselves
  but for him who for their sake died and
    was raised.

Consequently, from now on we regard no
    one according to the flesh;
  even if we once knew Christ according
    to the flesh,
  yet now we know him so no longer.
So whoever is in Christ is a new creation:
  the old things have passed away;
  behold, new things have come.

About Liturgy

Why not celebrate Father's Day? Many important days occur throughout the year and we may be struck by the fact that most of these are not included on the liturgical calendar. It isn't that the church wants to ignore important days such as this Sunday, Father's Day, or birthdays, or most national holidays. These are important times for us and to say they are not part of our religious lives is to split ourselves in two—spiritual selves and everyday get-on-with-our-business selves. To help us understand why we seem to ignore so much, we must keep in mind what liturgy is really all about. The church keeps the liturgy for celebrating what is absolutely central to us Christians—the paschal mystery, events that mark it, and saints who have lived it and now share in everlasting glory.

Nevertheless, although these kinds of holidays do not have a place on our liturgical calendar, we don't have to ignore them altogether. Liturgy always encompasses the whole person, which means that there are ways to incorporate these days into our liturgical celebrations. It is always good to pray when marking these other celebrations, and so it would be appropriate to add a fifth intercession this Sunday for fathers; for example, "For all fathers to teach their children the goodness and care of our triune God and to live the gospel faithfully . . ." The Book of Blessings in chapter 56 provides other sample intercessions and a prayer over the people that may be used before the blessing of the people during the concluding rite.

About Liturgical Music

Service music for Ordinary Time: As we return to Sundays in Ordinary Time, it is once again important to begin singing a set of service music which fits this season. It might be well to have two sets in place, one to use from now through the Twenty-third Sunday in Ordinary Time, the other to begin singing on the Twenty-fourth Sunday when the gospel readings begin to take on a different flavor, moving us toward Jerusalem and the cross.

Music suggestions: Maintaining our faith in the person and power of Jesus even when we cannot see, hear, or touch him is well-expressed in the familiar hymn "We Walk by Faith." The hymn is suitable for the preparation of the gifts, or it could be used as a recessional. A second hymn suited for this Sunday is Ralph Wright's "Sing of One Who Walks Beside Us" [CBW3; also found in GIA's *Hymnal for the Hours*]. The hymn speaks of Christ's continuing presence with us as we journey forward in discipleship, dining with us, sharing his wisdom, and freeing us from every fear. Finally, the well-known Quaker hymn "How Can I Keep from Singing" with its refrain "No storm can shake my inmost calm, While to that rock I'm clinging. Since Love is Lord of heaven and earth, how can I keep from singing?" is perfect for this Sunday. This hymn would work well during the preparation of the gifts or Communion.

SPIRITUALITY

GOSPEL ACCLAMATION
cf. Luke 1:76

R∕. Alleluia, alleluia.
You, child, will be called prophet of the Most High,
for you will go before the Lord to prepare his way.
R∕. Alleluia, alleluia.

Gospel   Luke 1:57-66, 80; L587

When the time arrived for Elizabeth to
       have her child
    she gave birth to a son.
Her neighbors and relatives heard
    that the Lord had shown his great
           mercy toward her,
    and they rejoiced with her.
When they came on the eighth day to cir-
       cumcise the child,
    they were going to call him Zechariah
           after his father,
    but his mother said in reply,
    "No. He will be called John."
But they answered her,
    "There is no one among your relatives
           who has this name."
So they made signs, asking his father what
       he wished him to be called.
He asked for a tablet and wrote, "John is his
       name,"
    and all were amazed.
Immediately his mouth was opened, his
       tongue freed,
    and he spoke blessing God.
Then fear came upon all their neighbors,
    and all these matters were discussed
       throughout the hill country of Judea.
All who heard these things took them to
       heart, saying,
    "What, then, will this child be?"
For surely the hand of the Lord was with him.

The child grew and became strong in spirit,
    and he was in the desert until the day
    of his manifestation to Israel.

See Appendix A, p. 300, for the other readings.

FIRST READING
Isa 49:1-6

RESPONSORIAL PSALM
Ps 139:1b-3, 13-14ab, 14c-15

SECOND READING
Acts 13:22-26

162

Reflecting on the Gospel

We have all heard of or seen child prodigies and admire their stupendous ability demonstrated at such an early age. If there is so much talent so young, what giftedness might this child showcase at a mature age? We, too, might ask the question in the gospel, "What, then, will this child be?"

What is interesting about this particular gospel story is that the neighbors were amazed at this babe who had as yet done nothing. The source of their amazement was the unusual circumstances surrounding the conception and birth of this child: elderly parents beyond childbearing years, father unable to speak for no apparent reason, choice of a name outside the family and expectations, father once again able to speak and bless God. But the real amazement the gospel prompts comes from the utter fidelity to God's plan that the gospel portrays. Elizabeth and Zechariah's obedience to the angel's choice of a name for this child is more than a decision about a name. The neighbors and relatives expected that "they were going to call him Zechariah after his father." By naming him according to the instruction of Gabriel when he appeared to Zechariah in the Temple, John's parents already announced that this child was not theirs (not "after his father"), but the gift of a gracious God ("John" = "Yahweh is gracious"). Thus the naming already equates John's identity as God's gracious gift with his mission to herald the coming of the Messiah: "formed . . . as [God's] servant from the womb" (first reading), John announced the "one . . . coming after" (second reading) him who was the "word of salvation" that was sent. Like his parents, John was obedient to the mission for which he was born; he was utterly faithful to God's plan of salvation.

John evoked amazement from others as a baby and as an adult carrying on the mission given him. "What, then, will this child be?" John "grew and became strong in spirit," he prepared himself for his public ministry by dwelling in the desert alone, he was humble in face of his Savior cousin, he spoke boldly the truth, and he was beheaded.

John's birth came about because "the Lord had shown his great mercy." Faithful to his death, John the Baptist is celebrated today as the prophet who announced the new reign of God. John, the gracious gift, fulfilled his mission to herald the coming of the Messiah who was God's most gracious gift of all. "What, then, will this child be?" John is remembered as one who said, "I am not worthy to unfasten the sandals of [the Savior's] feet," and yet through him God showed his glory (see first reading). His mission was accomplished; the Word of salvation was heralded. John as God's gracious gift now lives forever in God's eternal glory.

Living the Paschal Mystery

None of us had such striking incidents surround our conception and birth as did John; we didn't grow up in a desert wearing strange clothes and eating weird food. We are just simple, ordinary folks who, nevertheless, are also called to herald the Word of salvation in our midst. We do this by a truthful word, a courageous word, a humble word. Like John, we are called to die to self so that Christ might be announced to the world. We celebrate this day John's identity and mission—which is ours, too: we are God's gracious gift to the world, called to be faithful to God and to announce the reign of salvation.

Focusing the Gospel

Key words and phrases: the Lord had shown his great mercy; "John is his name"; "What, then, will this child be?"

To the point: In Hebrew the name "John" means "Yahweh is gracious." The birth of John signals God acting graciously to raise up a herald for the coming of the savior (second reading). In this way John's very identity (embodying God's graciousness) discloses his mission (to herald the savior, the most astounding embodiment of God's graciousness).

Model Act of Penitence

Presider: Today we celebrate the birth of John the Baptist, the prophet sent to herald the coming of Jesus our savior. Let us prepare ourselves to hear God's word and celebrate these mysteries . . . [pause]

Lord Jesus, you are a Light to all nations: Lord . . .

Christ Jesus, you are the Savior of the world: Christ . . .

Lord Jesus, you are the Messiah announced by John the Baptist: Lord . . .

Model Prayer of the Faithful

Presider: The God who acted so graciously in giving John to the elderly Elizabeth and Zechariah will show mercy to us and hear our prayers.

Response:

Lord, hear our prayer.

Cantor:

we pray to the Lord,

That the church may graciously herald the presence of the Savior in the world . . . [pause]

That world leaders may graciously guide their people to peace and prosperity . . . [pause]

That all newborn infants may grow in grace and become strong in spirit . . . [pause]

That all of us gathered here may recognize the many gracious gifts God bestows on each of us . . . [pause]

Presider: Gracious God, you give us all things to bring us to salvation: hear these our prayers, help us to rejoice on this festival of the birth of John the Baptist, and one day be with you in eternal glory. We ask this through Jesus Christ our Lord. **Amen.**

FOR REFLECTION

· Those who have been John the Baptist for me are . . . I have been John the Baptist for others when . . .

· God has been gracious to me in these ways . . . I have helped others see God's graciousness in their lives when . . .

· Like Elizabeth and Zechariah, I am faithful to God's plan for me when . . .

Homily Points

• The birth of an infant almost always is cause for real joy and a deep sense in the parents that this newborn is a precious gift. This is no less true for the birth of John to Elizabeth and Zechariah. John is God's gracious gift to them in their senior, childless years. But John is also gracious in his being gift to others—he never drew others to himself, but kept his life and mission focused on the coming of the Messiah, whose sandals he felt he was not worthy to unfasten.

• Just as John was God's gracious gift and graciously gave of himself for the sake of salvation, so are we God's gracious gift to our families, friends, the church, the world. We, too, must graciously give of ourselves so that others might come to know Jesus and receive God's offer of new life.

✠ SPIRITUALITY

GOSPEL ACCLAMATION
cf. 2 Tim 1:10

R̸. Alleluia, alleluia.
Our Savior Jesus Christ destroyed death
and brought life to light through the Gospel.
R̸. Alleluia, alleluia.

Gospel   Mark 5:21-43; L98B

When Jesus had crossed again in the
    boat
    to the other side,
    a large crowd gathered around him,
        and he stayed close to the sea.
One of the synagogue officials,
    named Jairus, came forward.
Seeing him he fell at his feet and
    pleaded earnestly with him, saying,
"My daughter is at the point of death.
Please, come lay your hands on her
    that she may get well and live."
He went off with him,
    and a large crowd followed him and
        pressed upon him.

There was a woman afflicted with
    hemorrhages for twelve years.
She had suffered greatly at the hands of
    many doctors
    and had spent all that she had.
Yet she was not helped but only grew
    worse.
She had heard about Jesus and came up
    behind him in the crowd
    and touched his cloak.
She said, "If I but touch his clothes, I
    shall be cured."
Immediately her flow of blood dried up.
She felt in her body that she was healed
    of her affliction.
Jesus, aware at once that power had gone
    out from him,
    turned around in the crowd and asked,
        "Who has touched my clothes?"
But his disciples said to Jesus,
    "You see how the crowd is pressing
        upon you,
    and yet you ask, 'Who touched me?'"

Continued in Appendix A, p. 301.

Reflecting on the Gospel

We have a tendency to label people and situations, probably for several reasons. Our experience might have taught us how to react to certain people or in particular situations, which saves us from thinking things through anew each time. Labeling might serve as a protecting mechanism, preparing us to act appropriately. Labeling might be a way we avoid the heartache and disappointment of unfulfilled expectations. Labeling might be an expression of hardheaded realism

in which we coldly look at the facts, just the facts. It would seem that the people in the two situations depicted in this Sunday's gospel are good at labeling. The disciples are aghast at Jesus' seemingly stupid question, "Who touched me?" when the crowds were pressing around him. The crowd at Jairus's house are telling him not to bother Jesus because the daughter was already dead. These would seem to be typical, normal responses of people who used their experience and labeled the people and situations. After all, the woman was "afflicted with hemorrhages for twelve years"—surely long enough to figure out that she wouldn't probably be getting better. The child is dead—what can be done in face of that? The disciples and crowd use their heads to assess the situation. What they were not prepared for is that Jesus takes familiar, old, labeled situations and treats them as whole new opportunities to call forth faith.

Both healing events in the long form of this Sunday's gospel disclose great faith and trust in Jesus on behalf of the petitioners. On the other hand, the disciples were critical of Jesus, and the crowd gathered in Jairus's house ridiculed him until the raising of the child to life left them "utterly astounded." The faith of Jairus and the woman stand in opposition to the hardheaded realism of the disciples and the crowd. Encounter with Jesus always changes experience, situations, expectations. It is precisely Jairus's and the woman's faith that a new situation with different outcome would be ushered in by the presence of Jesus that opened the door to the new life Jesus offered. These humble petitioners incarnate the faith to which the disciples, the crowd, and we are called.

The crowd is "utterly astounded" after Jesus raises Jairus's daughter back to life. The miracle cued them into the new situation. The challenge of this gospel is that we must see a new situation in all of life's circumstances, precisely because Jesus is present and absolutely nothing is the same. The challenge is to see the little "miracles" that happen every day in our lives simply because God has as much care for us as Jesus had care for Jairus's daughter and the woman. Labels don't work in faith life, because God always can bring something new out of the ordinary, out of pain, out of even death. The Good News of Jesus' life and mission is that suffering and death are not hopeless situations, but out of them come life. All we need is faith and trust in Jesus.

Living the Paschal Mystery

It is hard to shake off labels and labeling and develop a spirituality that is open to the constant in-breaking of God's life. Our own faith must grow in a way that enables us to see God at work in all circumstances of our lives. Even something so ordinary and simple as getting over a cold and feeling good again is a sign of God's presence which brings us a healing touch. By recognizing these signs of God's presence are we able to see new possibilities in old situations and hear Jesus' command, "Go in peace."

Focusing the Gospel

Key words and phrases: come lay your hands on her, If I but touch his clothes, yet you ask, your faith has saved you, why trouble the teacher, just have faith, utterly astounded

To the point: Both healing events in the long form of this Sunday's gospel disclose great faith and trust in Jesus on behalf of the petitioners. On the other hand, the disciples were critical of Jesus, and the crowd gathered in Jairus's house ridiculed him until the raising of the child to life left them "utterly astounded." The faith of Jairus and the woman stand in opposition to the hard-headed realism of the disciples and the crowd. But it is precisely their faith that opened the door to the new life Jesus offered. These humble petitioners incarnate the faith to which the disciples, the crowd, and we are called.

Connecting the Gospel

to the first reading: God's desire that all things have life (see first reading) is assured in the presence and ministry of Jesus.

to human experience: Instinctively we cling to things that confirm our experience. Jesus, on the other hand, is not so quick to rule out the possibility of life where disease and death seem to prevail.

Connecting the Responsorial Psalm

to the readings: The Sunday Lectionary uses Psalm 30 four times (Easter Vigil 4, Third Sunday of Easter C, Tenth Sunday in Ordinary Time C, and this Sunday) and each time the readings deal with our need to be delivered from death. The "pit" from which the psalmist is rescued is Sheol, the land of the dead (not the same as the Christian concept of hell). Notice how much of the text is in past tense. The psalmist rests confident in deliverance yet to come because of deliverance already given by God.

The first reading tells us God has made all things for life. Nonetheless, we experience death coming toward us over and over, in many guises. We find ourselves caught in the middle of a cosmic struggle between the force of life and the force of death. The good news, as the gospel so concretely dramatizes, is that Christ holds the ultimate power in this struggle. By singing these verses from Psalm 30, we acknowledge what oftentimes only our faith can see: that death with its contingent weeping and mourning is not the end of the story—life is. No wonder we sing with such confidence!

to cantor preparation: When you sing this psalm, you embody the confidence of the entire Body of Christ that God saves from death, even when the whole world groans under its threat. Pray this week for those who are facing death in any form—physical, mental, emotional. Pray that you may be a voice of hope for them.

**ASSEMBLY &
FAITH-SHARING GROUPS**

· Those who incarnate faith and call me to growth in faith are . . .

· I struggle with faith when . . .

· My faith has opened a door to new life when . . .

PRESIDERS

· My ministry to the sick increases my faith in that . . .

DEACONS

· My service brings new life to others when . . .

HOSPITALITY MINISTERS

· My hospitality ministry opens a door for others to encounter Jesus and receive new life when . . .

MUSIC MINISTERS

· Whenever the task of music ministry becomes draining or lifeless for me, Jesus comes and . . .

ALTAR MINISTERS

· My serving at the altar increases my faith and helps me encounter Jesus when . . .

LECTORS

· God's word brings new life and hope to me and others when . . .

**EXTRAORDINARY MINISTERS
OF HOLY COMMUNION**

· When I see the communicants as those who want healing and new life from Jesus, my ministry becomes . . .

Model Act of Penitence

Presider: In this Sunday's gospel Jesus heals a woman and raises a young girl from the dead. Let us prepare ourselves for Jesus to heal us and give us new life during this liturgy . . . [pause]

Lord Jesus, you are the Source of healing and Lord of life: Lord . . .

Christ Jesus, you are Victor over death: Christ . . .

Lord Jesus, you are the Hope of those who trust in you: Lord . . .

Homily Points

• Most of us have encountered what seem to be hopeless situations. For example, no one thought Helen Keller could ever read, write, or speak, but Annie Sullivan thought differently. Parents with physically or mentally challenged children persist beyond what seems to be human strength to help the children achieve to the best of their ability. While these are dramatic examples, all of us tend to place limits on ourselves and others because of past experiences or misconceived expectations.

• Jesus, on the other hand, did not allow expectations of people or situations to be limited by the past or the predictable. He could see the spark of faith in persons who came to him, and responded to them in miraculous ways. He is the Source of healing and the Lord of life.

• For us the issue is to continue to hope and believe beyond our limitations and normal expectations, and ask for what we need as did Jairus and the woman. Sometimes this may bring ridicule or rebuke from others, especially in face of what seems to be a hopeless request. Sometimes even our request is not met to our expectation. Nevertheless, Jesus invites us to the kind of faith and trust that does work miracles.

Model Prayer of the Faithful

Presider: Let us bring our needs to the God who calls us to faith and new life.

Response:

Lord, hear our prayer.

Cantor:

we pray to the Lord,

That all members of the church may continue to grow in faith . . . [pause]

That all people may receive the fullness of life God desires for them . . . [pause]

That the sick and suffering be strengthened and healed . . . [pause]

That this community inspire others to believe in the life-giving goodness of God . . . [pause]

Presider: God of all life, you formed us in your own image: hear these our prayers that one day we may share everlasting life with you. We ask this through Christ our Lord. **Amen.**

OPENING PRAYER

Let us pray

Pause for silent prayer

Father,
you call your children
to walk in the light of Christ.
Free us from darkness
and keep us in the radiance of your truth.

We ask this through our Lord Jesus Christ,
    your Son,
who lives and reigns with you and the
    Holy Spirit,
one God, for ever and ever. **Amen.**

FIRST READING
Wis 1:13-15; 2:23-24

God did not make death,
    nor does he rejoice in the destruction of
        the living.
For he fashioned all things that they might
        have being;
    and the creatures of the world are
        wholesome,
and there is not a destructive drug among
        them
    nor any domain of the netherworld on
        earth,
    for justice is undying.
For God formed man to be imperishable;
    the image of his own nature he made
        him.
But by the envy of the devil, death entered
        the world,
    and they who belong to his company
        experience it.

RESPONSORIAL PSALM

Ps 30:2, 4, 5-6, 11, 12, 13

℟. (2a) I will praise you, Lord, for you have rescued me.

I will extol you, O LORD, for you drew me clear
    and did not let my enemies rejoice over me.
O LORD, you brought me up from the netherworld;
    you preserved me from among those going down into the pit.

℟. I will praise you, Lord, for you have rescued me.

Sing praise to the LORD, you his faithful ones,
    and give thanks to his holy name.
For his anger lasts but a moment;
    a lifetime, his good will.
At nightfall, weeping enters in,
    but with the dawn, rejoicing.

℟. I will praise you, Lord, for you have rescued me.

Hear, O LORD, and have pity on me;
    O LORD, be my helper.
You changed my mourning into dancing;
    O LORD, my God, forever will I give you thanks.

℟. I will praise you, Lord, for you have rescued me.

SECOND READING

2 Cor 8:7, 9, 13-15

Brothers and sisters:
As you excel in every respect, in faith, discourse,
    knowledge, all earnestness, and in the love we have for you,
    may you excel in this gracious act also.

For you know the gracious act of our Lord Jesus Christ,
    that though he was rich, for your sake he became poor,
    so that by his poverty you might become rich.
Not that others should have relief while you are burdened,
    but that as a matter of equality
    your abundance at the present time should supply their needs,
    so that their abundance may also supply your needs,
    that there may be equality.
As it is written:
    Whoever had much did not have more,
    and whoever had little did not have
    less.

About Liturgy

Liturgical labeling, people, and situations: Liturgy always challenges us to examine our labels and expectations. If we come looking for what liturgy is not supposed to do, we tend to go away disappointed, often labeling and lashing out at the people who work hard to help liturgy unfold gracefully and prayerfully.

Primarily liturgy is about enacting in our present situation and lives the dying and rising mystery of Christ. In the here and now we celebrate the mystery into which we were plunged at baptism and that defines our daily living. As members of the Body of Christ, we are to live with the self-giving, care, compassion, and openness to new life that Jesus demonstrated in his life. This is not always easy, especially when we want to make liturgy something very personal, satisfying our own prayer, aesthetic, and relational needs. Liturgy, then, calls us to come to each celebration as if for the first time. It calls us to drop our preconceived notions and expectations—derived from countless liturgical experiences—and be open to each celebration as a new encounter with God and each other. The satisfaction of liturgy must come much less from our own personal needs and taste and much more from our surrendering ourselves to God's action within each of us and within the community as a whole.

If we form ourselves in an attitude that each liturgy is new, then we have prepared ourselves for whatever surprises God may have in store for us. Liturgy is rarely an emotional climax, nor should it be. But it is always an opportunity to encounter God and each other in faith, celebrating what is defining for us: the life, death, and resurrection of Jesus Christ and our participation in it.

About Liturgical Music

Music suggestions: "God's Word throughout the Ages" [HG] tells the story of Jesus raising Jairus's daughter from death. The final verse applies the story to us, the community of the church: "The church is like a daughter Who oversleeps in death; Lord, touch her with your Spirit and bring her back to life." This song would be appropriate for the preparation of the gifts. In the refrain of Randall DeBruyn's "Jesus, Lord" [BB, JS2], we call on Jesus to strengthen our faith in him and fill us with trust in his love. This song would be a fitting choice for Communion with cantor or choir singing the verses and assembly the refrain.

JUNE 28, 2009
THIRTEENTH SUNDAY IN ORDINARY TIME

SPIRITUALITY

GOSPEL ACCLAMATION
Matt 16:18

R⁊. Alleluia, alleluia.
You are Peter and upon this rock I will build my
    church,
and the gates of the netherworld shall not
    prevail against it.
R⁊. Alleluia, alleluia.

Gospel   Matt 16:13-19; L591

When Jesus went into the region of
    Caesarea Philippi
  he asked his disciples,
    "Who do people say that the Son
      of Man is?"
They replied, "Some say John the
      Baptist, others Elijah,
  still others Jeremiah or one of the
      prophets."
He said to them, "But who do you say that
  I am?"
Simon Peter said in reply,
    "You are the Christ, the Son of the liv-
      ing God."
Jesus said to him in reply, "Blessed are
    you, Simon son of Jonah.
For flesh and blood has not revealed this
    to you, but my heavenly Father.
And so I say to you, you are Peter,
  and upon this rock I will build my
      Church,
  and the gates of the netherworld shall
      not prevail against it.
I will give you the keys to the Kingdom of
    heaven.
Whatever you bind on earth shall be
    bound in heaven;
  and whatever you loose on earth shall
      be loosed in heaven."

See Appendix A, p. 302, for the other readings.

FIRST READING
Acts 12:1-11

RESPONSORIAL PSALM
Ps 34:2-3, 4-5, 6-7, 8-9

SECOND READING
2 Tim 4:6-8, 17-18

Reflecting on the Gospel

One of Aesop's fables tells the story of a cat who fell hopelessly in love with a young man. The cat showered affection on the man, but the man did not return the love. Disheartened, the cat went for help to Venus, the goddess of love and beauty. Venus willingly changed the cat into a fair damsel, the man fell in love with her, and they married and were enormously happy. Venus, however, was curious whether the change in the cat's form also changed the cat's nature. So she sent a mouse into the room where the couple were sitting. The damsel saw the mouse, jumped up, and pounced on the mouse as if she would devour it, much to the dismay of the husband. Since the cat had revealed her unchanged, true nature by these actions, Venus turned the damsel back into a cat.

Like the cat, both Peter and Paul underwent great changes in their lives. Neither began as a rock, a pillar of the church. Simon, a simple fisherman and one who doubted and denied Jesus, becomes Peter, the outspoken leader of the apostles and the one who announces clearly Jesus' identity as the Christ. Paul, a devout Pharisee who persecuted Christians (Acts 9 and 22), becomes the evangelizer of the Gentiles (see second reading). With both of these great apostles the change was not merely in form, but (unlike the cat in the fable) the changes were truly of their very being.

This gospel and these two great apostles call us to willingness to change. This is how we come to know Jesus: in the very willingness to change, to identify with him more, to grow in our own identity as his disciples who continue his mission. Our answer to the identity question Jesus asks cannot be based only on what we have heard about him or on the witness or authority of others, as was the first answer of some of the disciples in the gospel. Jesus' question is a *personal* one that each of us must, like Peter, answer from the depths of who we have come to know Jesus to be *for us*. Then we, too, are rocks upon which the church is built and the missionaries through whom "the proclamation [of Christ] might be completed" (second reading).

To recognize and proclaim Jesus' identity requires a response: total conformity to "Christ, the Son of the living God." We can speak of the church being built upon these two great apostles because of their total conformity to Christ. Both the identity and mission of the church are the same: to be Christ. This is the rock upon which the church is built: utter conformity and fidelity to being the Body of Christ.

Living the Paschal Mystery

We ourselves are called to change in the same way as Peter and Paul—not simply a change in form that is external but a change in being that conforms us completely to Christ. This is the challenge of this solemnity honoring the two great apostles Peter and Paul: totally conform to Christ. The netherworld cannot prevail against those who carry the identity of the Body of Christ. Like Peter and Paul, this conformity promises us that "the crown of righteousness awaits" us, too. Unlike Peter and Paul, most of us won't suffer and die a martyr's death. But like Peter and Paul, we are all called to put Christ first in our lives. This means that sometimes we may have to make choices that make us unpopular at home or in the workplace. This is the cost of faithful conformity to Christ.

Focusing the Gospel

Key words and phrases: But who do you say that I am, You are the Christ, rock . . . church

To the point: Our answer to the identity question Jesus asks cannot be based only on what we have heard about him or on the witness or authority of others, as was the first answer of some of the disciples in the gospel. His question is a *personal* one that each of us must, like Peter, answer from the depths of who we have come to know Jesus to be *for us*. Then we, too, are rocks upon which the church is built and the missionaries through whom "the proclamation [of Christ] might be completed" (second reading).

Model Act of Penitence

Presider: God raised up two great apostles, Peter and Paul, to be pillars of his church and models of faithful discipleship. As we begin our celebration, let us pray for the strength to walk in the footsteps of Peter and Paul . . . [pause]

> Lord Jesus, you are the Christ, the Son of the living God: Lord . . .
>
> Christ Jesus, you named Peter, the rock upon which you built your church: Christ . . .
>
> Lord Jesus, you called Paul, the apostle to the nations: Lord . . .

Model Prayer of the Faithful

Presider: We pray for the strength to conform our lives totally to Christ and to be faithful witnesses of the Gospel.

Response:

Lord, hear our prayer.

Cantor:

we pray to the Lord,

That all members of the church be faithful to their identity as the Body of Christ . . . [pause]

That world leaders seek to dispel hatred among nations, races, and peoples . . . [pause]

That those imprisoned or persecuted for spreading the faith be restored to their communities . . . [pause]

That all of us faithfully bring the message of the Gospel to all we meet by the way we live our lives in conformity to Christ . . . [pause]

Presider: O living God, you raised up for us Peter and Paul to teach us to live your ways: hear these our prayers that one day we might join them in sharing your everlasting glory. We ask this through Christ our Lord. **Amen.**

OPENING PRAYER
Let us pray
Pause for silent prayer

God our Father,
today you give us the joy
of celebrating the feast of the apostles
    Peter and Paul.
Through them your Church first received
    the faith.
Keep us true to their teaching.

Grant this through our Lord Jesus Christ,
    your Son,
who lives and reigns with you and the Holy
    Spirit,
one God, for ever and ever. **Amen.**

FOR REFLECTION

· Jesus puts the question of his identity to me when . . . My answer is . . .

· Others have revealed to me who Jesus is by . . .

· I fruitfully proclaim the Gospel by . . .

Homily Points

• We know that if we are to grow emotionally, psychologically, and spiritually, we need to be changed in ways that move us beyond where we are. This was surely true of both Peter and Paul as they struggled to come to know Jesus and understand his mission of salvation for the whole world—they both changed dramatically. This change was because of Christ working with and within them.

• We ourselves are initially changed by our baptism into being the Body of Christ. But it is over time that we come to know Jesus intimately and to participate in his saving mission by boldly proclaiming the Gospel. Only by being faithful disciples can we be rocks upon which the church continues to be built.

✠ SPIRITUALITY

GOSPEL ACCLAMATION
cf. Luke 4:18

R⁄. Alleluia, alleluia.
The Spirit of the Lord is upon me,
for he sent me to bring glad tidings to the poor.
R⁄. Alleluia, alleluia.

Gospel

Mark 6:1-6; L101B

Jesus departed from
    there and came to
    his native place,
    accompanied by his
    disciples.
When the sabbath
    came he began
    to teach in the
    synagogue,
    and many who heard him were
        astonished.
They said, "Where did this man get all
    this?
What kind of wisdom has been given
    him?
What mighty deeds are wrought by his
    hands!
Is he not the carpenter, the son of
    Mary,
    and the brother of James and Joses
        and Judas and Simon?
And are not his sisters here with us?"
And they took offense at him.
Jesus said to them,
    "A prophet is not without honor
        except in his native place
    and among his own kin and in his
        own house."
So he was not able to perform any
    mighty deed there,
    apart from curing a few sick people
        by laying his hands on them.
He was amazed at their lack of faith.

Reflecting on the Gospel

Many of us face misunderstandings and rejection in our daily living. We might make a comment to someone which is taken the wrong way. Our values and lifestyle might turn people away from us. No matter who is involved in this misunderstanding and rejection, it always hurts. It hurts even more so when the hurt comes from those close to us—family and friends. Shockingly, in this Sunday's gospel Jesus encounters resistance and rejection "among his own kin and in his own house." This, because Jesus' words and deeds went beyond his neighbors' understanding of who he was ("the carpenter"). Similarly, who we think Jesus is determines our response to him: resistance or faith. Jesus' hometown neighbors were "astonished" at his teaching, wisdom, and mighty deeds: "Where did this man get all this?" We are amazed along with Jesus: Can they not hear his teaching, recognize his wisdom, and see his mighty deeds? Jesus is amazed at the townspeople's lack of faith because they are rejecting the very thing that brings them life.

Jesus came to his "native place" offering gifts of wisdom and healing. Amazingly, the townspeople "took offense at him." God continually offers us what we need for life, but we often resist it. *Our receptivity* to how and through whom God speaks to us, however, is *decisive*. Our receptivity is key for hearing God's word and receiving the gifts of healing which God offers. The rejected prophet has no power to influence the behavior of the people (see first reading); Jesus is unable to work miracles for those who do not believe in him. God always offers new life; it is for us to recognize and receive it. Our very receptivity to God's presence and gifts is an act of faith, and this is decisive for whether we receive God's ultimate gift of eternal life. On the other hand, our rebellion, obstinacy, lack of faith (all really the same thing) keep us from recognizing God's presence and works in our midst, keep us from recognizing Jesus.

The shock of the gospel is the weight that our faith or lack of faith has. God never pushes salvation on us; it is a faithful gift, but one freely given and only asking of us a free response. Jesus "was not able" to perform miracles in his hometown because of the townspeople's lack of faith. Yet, as the first reading reminds us, God will carry on in spite of our rebellion or lack of faith ("they shall know that a prophet has been among them"). God never quits on us or abandons us; it is we who choose to resist or have faith. It is we who choose . . . is Jesus able to perform any mighty deed or not?

Living the Paschal Mystery

Our "mighty deeds" which bring forth faith in others lie in our doing our daily tasks the best we can, accepting others for who they are, being patient with others' responses to us. We may not do the "mighty deed" of healing the sick, but we can surely visit them and bring a word of hope. We might not all be theologians, but we can speak from our hearts the conviction of God's word in Scripture which we've heard over and over again at Mass and in private prayer.

We are anointed prophets in baptism. We receive the wisdom of the Holy Spirit. We are empowered to do the mightiest of mighty deeds: be the Body of Christ, bringing Christ's risen presence to our broken world. What will people say of us? We will shock them into taking a second look at who we are only when we live as Jesus did—giving ourselves for others.

Focusing the Gospel

Key words and phrases: What . . . wisdom, What . . . deeds, took offense at him, amazed at their lack of faith

To the point: Jesus came to his "native place" offering gifts of wisdom and healing. Amazingly, the townspeople "took offense at him." God continually offers us what we need for life, but we often resist it. *Our receptivity* to how and through whom God speaks to us, however, is *decisive*. The rejected prophet has no power to influence the behavior of the people (see first reading); Jesus is unable to work miracles for those who do not believe in him. God always offers new life; it is for us to recognize and receive it. Our very receptivity to God's presence and gifts is an act of faith.

Connecting the Gospel

to the first reading: In spite of rejection, rebellion, non-receptivity, God is always faithful, assuring us that there will be "a prophet . . . among [us]" (first reading) to teach us and bring us new life (gospel).

to experience: We find it easier to confine encounters with God to amazing places or events (for example, apparitions). But God's normative manner of coming to us is in the ordinary circumstances of our daily lives ("native place") and in the human beings closest to us ("among his own kin and in his own house").

Connecting the Responsorial Psalm

to the readings: How clearly this Sunday's gospel shows us that fidelity to the mission of proclaiming the Good News inevitably stirs up opposition and foments rejection! The first reading shows us that this story is not a new one. Yet God continues to send prophets to the people and, finally, sends Jesus, a man like themselves—"carpenter . . . son . . . and brother" (gospel)—whose very familiarity makes him unacceptable.

With its simple imagery of eyes turned toward master/mistress, the responsorial psalm expresses the sense of self before God as willing and ready servant, then speaks pointedly of the pain of being mocked and held in contempt by those who despise God. The essence of the psalm is the willingness to stay focused on God whether standing ready to serve or suffering rejection because of that service. How poignantly, and perhaps how often, Jesus himself must have prayed these words! May we the baptized join him in remaining ever ready for the mission, steadfastly attuned to God and confident of the mercy that sustains us.

to cantor preparation: In this responsorial psalm you pray that God see and care about the personal opposition you experience because of your fidelity to the Gospel. You need to know that God is as attentive to you (refrain and third strophe) as you are to God (first two strophes). How human a need! And how confident you can be of the divine response! How can you let both your need and your confidence be evident to the assembly as you sing?

ASSEMBLY & FAITH-SHARING GROUPS

· Someone who opens to me the wisdom of God is . . . Someone who brings me the healing of God is . . .

· I am a source of God's wisdom and healing for others when . . . I sometimes block God's wisdom or healing when . . .

· My receptivity to God and others is an act of faith for me when . . .

PRESIDERS

· My priestly ministry helps others be receptive of God's gifts when . . .

DEACONS

· My self-giving service is truly an act of faith-filled receptivity when . . .

HOSPITALITY MINISTERS

· My ministry increases in those gathering for liturgy the capacity for receptivity by . . .

MUSIC MINISTERS

· I encounter God in the humanness of my fellow music ministers when I . . .

ALTAR MINISTERS

· I have been astonished and surprised to experience the mighty prophet of God in the mundane, lowly business of service when . . .

LECTORS

· My manner of proclaiming the Scripture makes it easier for people to receive God's word and live it when . . .

EXTRAORDINARY MINISTERS OF HOLY COMMUNION

· My distributing Holy Communion primes me to recognize Jesus among my "own kin" and "in [my] own house" because . . .

Model Act of Penitence

Presider: The gospel today describes the rejection of Jesus by those most familiar with him—his kin and neighbors. Let us prepare ourselves to encounter Jesus in this liturgy and receive him in faith . . . [pause]

  Lord Jesus, you were a carpenter from Nazareth and the prophet from God: Lord . . .

  Christ Jesus, you are the One in whom we have faith: Christ . . .

  Lord Jesus, you are the Source of all wisdom and healing: Lord . . .

Homily Points

• Why do we accept something being said from one person, but not accept the same thing from another? Some people say things to us that we hear and accept; others say things to us that we take with a grain of salt. The credibility of persons rests to a large extent on the relationship we have with them, the reputation or credentials that precede them, or their actions which speak louder than their words. Yet our growing in knowledge of and appreciation for others depends on a level of receptivity much deeper than simply hearing and accepting.

• The townspeople in the gospel had every reason to believe what Jesus was saying—they knew him well, he had a reputation for teaching and healing, and his actions had already revealed his power. But they did not receive him. Why? They lacked faith—that leap into letting go of preconceived expectations to receive the Person who could bring them new gifts and life.

• The gospel invites us to reflect on how open we are and to whom. Jesus is present to us now with his gifts of wisdom and healing through those whom *we* might least suspect—those nearest to us. Here is our leap of faith: that others can be the presence and power of God for us, bringing us untold gifts.

Model Prayer of the Faithful

Presider: God sends Jesus with wisdom and healing. Let us ask to receive these gifts with open hearts.

Response:

Lord, hear our prayer.

Cantor:

we pray to the Lord,

For all members of the church, may they deepen their faith through encounters with the risen Christ in others . . . [pause]

For all world leaders, may they govern with wisdom and justice . . . [pause]

For the sick and suffering, may they be strengthened and healed by the presence of Christ through the care and concern of this community . . . [pause]

For each of us here, may we always see in others the revelation of the presence and gifts of God . . . [pause]

Presider: God of faith and mighty deeds: you are present to us and give us all good gifts: hear these our prayers that we might always recognize Christ among us. We pray through that same Jesus Christ our Lord. **Amen.**

ALTERNATIVE OPENING PRAYER
Let us pray

Pause for silent prayer

Father,
in the rising of your Son
death gives birth to new life.
The sufferings he endured restored hope to
    a fallen world.
Let sin never ensnare us
with empty promises of passing joy.
Make us one with you always,
so that our joy may be holy,
and our love may give life.

We ask this through Christ our Lord.
  Amen.

FIRST READING
Ezek 2:2-5

As the LORD spoke to me, the spirit entered
    into me
  and set me on my feet,
  and I heard the one who was speaking
    say to me:
  Son of man, I am sending you to the
    Israelites,
  rebels who have rebelled against me;
  they and their ancestors have revolted
    against me to this very day.
Hard of face and obstinate of heart
  are they to whom I am sending you.
But you shall say to them: Thus says the
    LORD God!
And whether they heed or resist—for they
    are a rebellious house—
  they shall know that a prophet has been
    among them.

RESPONSORIAL PSALM
Ps 123:1-2, 2, 3-4

R̞. (2cd) Our eyes are fixed on the Lord,
pleading for his mercy.

To you I lift up my eyes
    who are enthroned in heaven—
as the eyes of servants
    are on the hands of their masters.

R̞. Our eyes are fixed on the Lord,
pleading for his mercy.

As the eyes of a maid
    are on the hands of her mistress,
so are our eyes on the LORD, our God,
    till he have pity on us.

R̞. Our eyes are fixed on the Lord,
pleading for his mercy.

Have pity on us, O LORD, have pity on us,
    for we are more than sated with
        contempt;
our souls are more than sated
    with the mockery of the arrogant,
    with the contempt of the proud.

R̞. Our eyes are fixed on the Lord,
pleading for his mercy.

SECOND READING
2 Cor 12:7-10

Brothers and sisters:
That I, Paul, might not become too elated,
    because of the abundance of the
        revelations,
    a thorn in the flesh was given to me, an
        angel of Satan,
    to beat me, to keep me from being too
        elated.
Three times I begged the Lord about this,
    that it might leave me,
    but he said to me, "My grace is
        sufficient for you,
    for power is made perfect in weakness."
I will rather boast most gladly of my
        weaknesses,
    in order that the power of Christ may
        dwell with me.
Therefore, I am content with weaknesses,
        insults,
    hardships, persecutions, and
        constraints,
    for the sake of Christ;
    for when I am weak, then I am strong.

About Liturgy
Gospel and Creed: Each Sunday at Mass we hear the gospel proclaimed and profess our faith. Perhaps there is a challenge this Sunday in the readings to connect these two—gospel and creedal statement. In the proclamation of the gospel we hear of Jesus' mighty deeds; as we proclaim what Jesus does we learn more about who he was. Jesus' deeds are a window into who Jesus is. More than a carpenter, he was a prophet speaking the word of God on our behalf and showing us how we must live in order for God's reign to come. It is as response to this gospel proclamation of Christ in our midst that we profess our faith.

The challenge is always to make the Creed more than a superficial recitation of some tenets of our faith. The assent of our belief is expressed in how we live. As we recite the Creed, we might think back to what has just been proclaimed in the gospel on a particular Sunday. Then "We believe" means that we commit ourselves to doing in our everyday lives what Jesus was doing in the gospel. This is why the Creed is included every Sunday: so that we might publicly profess that we are the Body of Christ and will act this week as Jesus shows us in the gospel.

About Liturgical Music
Music suggestions: "Word of God, Come Down on Earth" begs Christ the Word to "touch our hearts and bring to birth faith and hope and love unending" (v. 1) and to make our blind eyes see and our deaf ears hear (v. 3). The hymn would work well either for the entrance procession or during the preparation of the gifts on this Sunday when Christ meets so much opposition to the wonders of healing and faith he has come to bring (gospel). "We Walk by Faith," with its cry that Christ help our unbelief and make our faith abound (v. 3), would be appropriate for the preparation of the gifts. Both CH and W3 use tunes different from the familiar one by Marty Haugen; all three are lovely and easily accessible for any assembly. Finally, Bernadette Farrell's "Praise to You, O Christ, Our Savior" is a general song about Christ as the Word which would fit this Sunday or any Sunday in Ordinary Time. This hymn is a strong processional piece which can be sung responsorially between cantor/choir and assembly or sung directly by everyone.

✚ SPIRITUALITY

GOSPEL ACCLAMATION
cf. Eph 1:17-18

℟. Alleluia, alleluia.
May the Father of our Lord Jesus Christ
enlighten the eyes of our hearts,
that we may know what is the hope that
belongs to our call.
℟. Alleluia, alleluia.

Gospel

Mark 6:7-13; L104B

Jesus summoned the Twelve and
   began to send them out two
   by two
   and gave them authority over
      unclean spirits.
He instructed them to take nothing
   for the journey
   but a walking stick—
   no food, no sack, no money in their
      belts.
They were, however, to wear sandals
   but not a second tunic.
He said to them,
   "Wherever you enter a house, stay
      there until you leave.
Whatever place does not welcome you
   or listen to you,
   leave there and shake the dust off
      your feet
   in testimony against them."
So they went off and preached
   repentance.
The Twelve drove out many demons,
   and they anointed with oil many who
      were sick and cured them.

Reflecting on the Gospel

Ask a little child what she or he wants to do when they grow up, and the answer usually comes rather quickly. They want to be the latest action figure in the cartoons, or an astronaut, or president. Usually the child's answer leans toward larger-than-life persons or careers. The ordinary or mundane are not part of the child's vision. Yet, for the most part, we grow up to be ordinary people doing ordinary things. This is what makes the world go around—ordinary people living well. From the gospel perspective, however, we are ordinary people called to do extraordinary things. The extraordinary, however, does not lie in what we do as such—the simple, everyday things—but in the fact that God is continuing salvation through us.

In this Sunday's gospel Jesus sends his disciples on mission and counsels them to take nothing extra on the way. All they need for success is the commission of Jesus and the authority he gives them. We who are Jesus' disciples today are sent in the same way: though we travel light, we carry with us the weight of Jesus' own authority. This "authority" is not power or control. It is the ability to author life—to bring to people the fullness of what they need and seek most. This is why it must be Jesus' mission: on our own we cannot bring the life that is only God's to give. By acting faithfully on Jesus' authority, we are an ordinary instrument of God doing the extraordinary divine activity of bringing life and healing to others.

It is an awesome thought that Jesus entrusts his mission to us. The mission of Jesus is so important that he must use others to reach out to all people at all times to bring them salvation. But the only way we can be successful is to make sure that our mission is, indeed, that of Jesus. Who Jesus is, disciples are—prophets sent on a mission (see the first reading). With our own power and talent we can do little; with the authority with which Jesus invests his disciples we can do much. And this truly is extraordinary!

Living the Paschal Mystery

In our own lives and times we carry much baggage on our journey as disciples of Jesus. We have closets full of clothes, pantries and refrigerators full of food; many of us are armed with college degrees. The practical instructions of Jesus to his Twelve would not serve us well today; it would be irresponsible to divest ourselves of all our possessions. At the same time this gospel does invite us to examine what it is that hinders us from fulfilling the mission on which Jesus sends all of us, beginning with our baptism. Each of us is a disciple who is sent. What distracts us from our mission?

For most of us the greatest distractions probably don't come from our possessions, but from our interior emotions and attitudes. We don't like rejection—so it is difficult to preach an unpopular gospel with its demands for righteousness and love. We don't like the risk of being unsuccessful—so it is easier to live our religion by saying prayers rather than by ceaseless self-giving. We don't like pushing our own faith to its limits—so it is easier to be more concerned with right doctrine than with right living. In spite of our excuses and human weakness, Jesus is clear: "Go . . . to my people" (first reading). We must keep moving forward with his mission. We must do the extraordinary in the ordinariness of our daily lives.

Focusing the Gospel

Key words and phrases: send them, gave them authority, take nothing, went

To the point: In this Sunday's gospel Jesus sends his disciples on mission and counsels them to take nothing extra on the way. All they need for success is the commission of Jesus and the authority he gives them. We who are Jesus' disciples today are sent in the same way: though we travel light, we carry with us the weight of Jesus' own authority.

Connecting the Gospel

to the first reading: As with the sending of the disciples in the gospel, Amos was sent and preached by the authority of God. God's call and authority are this shepherd's justification for being prophet.

to experience: Even in Jesus' time going on a journey with no provisions was foolhardy. This gospel reminds us of our need for radical dependence on God to carry on the mission.

Connecting the Responsorial Psalm

to the readings: Both the first reading and the gospel for this Sunday indicate that the mission to preach God's message is not self-appointed. Amos declares that it was God who sent him as prophet to Israel (first reading). The apostles journey forth to preach and heal because Jesus sends them (gospel). The responsorial psalm also reminds us that the work of salvation is God's initiative. It is God's kindness we shall see, God's salvation we shall be granted (refrain), God's word which is proclaimed (first strophe). The call to be prophet, the mission to preach, and the power to confront evil and cure disease come not from ourselves but from God. The Good News is that, despite opposition (first reading and gospel), God moves forward relentlessly with the work of salvation. "Kindness and truth shall meet; justice and peace shall kiss." We can count on it. We need only pray for its coming and respond, as did Amos and the apostles, when enlisted in its service.

to cantor preparation: Do you hear the proclamation God is making in the world? Do you see God's kindness? Do you see justice and peace coming together? In what ways is God calling you to proclaim what you hear and see? How in singing this responsorial psalm are you prophet of God's saving work?

ASSEMBLY & FAITH-SHARING GROUPS
- I know myself to be a disciple sent on mission by Jesus because . . . when . . .
- The authority of Jesus that I have is . . . I live out of this authority when . . .
- Traveling light because of discipleship gives me freedom to . . . is difficult for me when . . .

PRESIDERS
- To preside with Jesus' authority, I must shed . . .

DEACONS
- To serve with Jesus' authority feels like . . . looks like . . .

HOSPITALITY MINISTERS
- The manner of my greeting helps those who gather for liturgy to shed their extra baggage when . . .

MUSIC MINISTERS
- As a music minister, Jesus has given me authority to . . .

ALTAR MINISTERS
- As an altar minister, I have authority to . . . Exercising this authority is truly discipleship when . . .

LECTORS
- I proclaim the word with Jesus' authority when . . .

EXTRAORDINARY MINISTERS OF HOLY COMMUNION
- I am commissioned to . . .

Model Act of Penitence

Presider: Jesus gave his apostles the authority to go out and preach and heal in his name. Let us open ourselves to hear God's word and be nourished at this Table so that we might take up the mission of Jesus . . . [pause]

> Lord Jesus, you have all authority in heaven and on earth: Lord . . .
>
> Christ Jesus, you emptied yourself to enrich others: Christ . . .
>
> Lord Jesus, you give us authority to take up your mission: Lord . . .

Homily Points

• People today are perceived to have "authority" because they have power, wealth, weapons, position, fame. Sometimes this authority is self-serving and coercing; it does not always bring forth greater life in people nor is it always focused on the well-being of others. Yet we also know people who are greatly admired because they use their "authority" for the good of others (for example, Nelson Mandela, Bill Gates, Paul Newman, Bono).

• Jesus' exercise of authority originated with his love and concern for the people and carried forth his mission to call people to new life and growth. It is this same mission to which he calls us and for which he gives us authority.

• The Christian perception of mission and authority is very different from that of our popular culture. When we see and respond to the needs of others, we are carrying forth Jesus' mission and acting on the authority he is giving us. Being sent by Jesus with authority to continue his mission is as simple as doing our everyday tasks with his love, care, and purpose.

Model Prayer of the Faithful

Presider: We ask God to give us what we need to continue Jesus' mission faithfully.

Response:

Lord, hear our prayer.

Cantor:

we pray to the Lord,

That the church may faithfully continue the mission of Jesus . . . [pause]

That all peoples of the world may come to salvation through the faithful ministry of others . . . [pause]

That the sick and suffering may be lifted up by the care and concern of this community of disciples . . . [pause]

That all of us gathered here may be bold in living the Gospel so that our very lives continue Jesus' mission . . . [pause]

Presider: Loving God, you send us forth with your authority to do good in our world: hear these our prayers that we might be strengthened for the task at hand. We ask this through Christ our Lord. **Amen.**

OPENING PRAYER

Let us pray

Pause for silent prayer

God our Father,
your light of truth
guides us to the way of Christ.
May all who follow him
reject what is contrary to the gospel.

We ask this through our Lord Jesus Christ,
    your Son,
who lives and reigns with you and the
    Holy Spirit,
one God, for ever and ever. **Amen.**

FIRST READING

Amos 7:12-15

Amaziah, priest of Bethel, said to Amos,
    "Off with you, visionary, flee to the land
        of Judah!
There earn your bread by prophesying,
    but never again prophesy in Bethel;
        for it is the king's sanctuary and a royal
            temple."
Amos answered Amaziah, "I was no
    prophet,
        nor have I belonged to a company of
            prophets;
    I was a shepherd and a dresser of
        sycamores.
The LORD took me from following the
    flock, and said to me,
    Go, prophesy to my people Israel."

RESPONSORIAL PSALM

Ps 85:9-10, 11-12, 13-14

R꙳. (8) Lord, let us see your kindness, and
grant us your salvation.

I will hear what God proclaims;
    the LORD—for he proclaims peace.
Near indeed is his salvation to those who
        fear him,
    glory dwelling in our land.

R꙳. Lord, let us see your kindness, and
grant us your salvation.

Kindness and truth shall meet;
    justice and peace shall kiss.
Truth shall spring out of the earth,
    and justice shall look down from
        heaven.

R꙳. Lord, let us see your kindness, and
grant us your salvation.

The LORD himself will give his benefits;
    our land shall yield its increase.
Justice shall walk before him,
    and prepare the way of his steps.

R꙳. Lord, let us see your kindness, and
grant us your salvation.

SECOND READING

Eph 1:3-14

Blessed be the God and Father of our Lord
　　Jesus Christ,
　　who has blessed us in Christ
　　with every spiritual blessing in the
　　　　heavens,
　　as he chose us in him, before the
　　　　foundation of the world,
　　to be holy and without blemish before
　　　　him.
In love he destined us for adoption to
　　　　himself through Jesus Christ,
　　in accord with the favor of his will,
　　for the praise of the glory of his grace
　　that he granted us in the beloved.
In him we have redemption by his blood,
　　the forgiveness of transgressions,
　　in accord with the riches of his grace
　　　　that he lavished upon us.
In all wisdom and insight, he has made
　　　　known to us
　　the mystery of his will in accord with
　　　　his favor
　　that he set forth in him as a plan for the
　　　　fullness of times,
　　to sum up all things in Christ, in heaven
　　　　and on earth.

In him we were also chosen,
　　destined in accord with the purpose of
　　　　the One
　　who accomplishes all things according
　　　　to the intention of his will,
　　so that we might exist for the praise of
　　　　his glory,
　　we who first hoped in Christ.
In him you also, who have heard the word
　　　　of truth,
　　the gospel of your salvation, and have
　　　　believed in him,
　　were sealed with the promised Holy
　　　　Spirit,
　　which is the first installment of our
　　　　inheritance
　　toward redemption as God's possession,
　　　　to the praise of his glory.

or Eph 1:3-10

See Appendix A, p. 302.

About Liturgy

Second reading during Ordinary Time: Since the second reading during Ordinary Time is not chosen to accord with the gospel and first reading but is a semi-continuous reading from one of the letters of the New Testament, we suggest that the short form (when given as a choice, such as on this Sunday) always be proclaimed. This is not to say that all of Sacred Scripture isn't important, for surely it is. It does remind us that the centerpiece of the Liturgy of the Word is the gospel and that the first reading and responsorial psalm are specifically chosen to relate to it. During the festal seasons even the second reading accords with the rest of the Liturgy of the Word, often being a theological commentary on the feast or season.

This Sunday we begin reading from the letter to the Ephesians and will complete it on the Twenty-first Sunday in Ordinary Time. This letter stresses the unity of the church and the Body of Christ (see chapters 1 and 2) as well as the church's mission to the world and the gifts given to fulfill this mission (see chapters 3 and 4). It is a good letter to begin reading on this Sunday when the gospel relates Jesus' sending the apostles on their mission. The letter to the Ephesians is not without its admonitions to right living, either (see chapters 5 and 6). This letter is a good blueprint for Ordinary Time: the church sent on mission living rightly. This characterizes our journey with Christ.

About Liturgical Music

Music suggestions: John Bell's "The Summons" captures the sense of being called by Christ for a mission, which promises risk and demands personal transformation. Verses 1-4 are the voice of Christ asking the assembly if they are willing to take on this mission. Verse 5 is their response. Letting a cantor or two cantors in alternation sing verses 1-4 and the assembly respond with verse 5 would emphasize the dialogic structure of this song. The song would be appropriate for the preparation of the gifts as a further reflection on the gospel.

A second fitting hymn for this Sunday is Michael Perry's "How Shall They Hear the Word of God" [W3]. The verses are set up in question-and-answer form. How shall people hear the gospel? How shall people come to know God's saving action in their lives? Each question is answered with a petition that God bless those engaged in the mission of Christ. The final petition, "So send us, Lord," is the clincher: in singing it the assembly asks to be the ones sent on mission. Because each phrase begins with a pick-up beat, the hymn exudes a forward impulse which fits the sense of mission about which it speaks. The hymn would work well during the preparation of the gifts as a reflection on the gospel. Or it would make an appropriate assembly hymn after Communion where the "So send us, Lord" prepares for the dismissal to follow.

SPIRITUALITY

GOSPEL ACCLAMATION
John 10:27

R⁊. Alleluia, alleluia.
My sheep hear my voice, says the Lord;
I know them, and they follow me.
R⁊. Alleluia, alleluia.

Gospel

Mark 6:30-34; L107B

The apostles gathered together with Jesus
and reported all they had done and taught.
He said to them,
"Come away by yourselves to a deserted place and rest a while."
People were coming and going in great numbers,
and they had no opportunity even to eat.
So they went off in the boat by themselves to a deserted place.
People saw them leaving and many came to know about it.
They hastened there on foot from all the towns
and arrived at the place before them.

When he disembarked and saw the vast crowd,
his heart was moved with pity for them,
for they were like sheep without a shepherd;
and he began to teach them many things.

Reflecting on the Gospel

It's the nature of most children to take their parents for granted. They expect mom and dad to take care of them and meet their every need at the drop of a hat. After these youngsters have grown up, marry, and have their own children, they might remark, "I just don't know how my mom and dad did it." They learn what an exhausting job parenting can be, and this on top of keeping up a home and holding down a job to pay the bills. We get the hint in this Sunday's gospel that the apostles have now learned firsthand for themselves how demanding is the ministry of bringing the Good News of salvation to others, and how many exhausting demands have been placed on Jesus by the crowds. Last Sunday Jesus sent the apostles off on mission; this Sunday they face the harsh reality that the mission wears them out.

Jesus, the true shepherd of God, always responds to the needs of others: with a listening ear, food, and rest for the weary apostles; with teaching for the "vast crowd." Jesus is ever the caring shepherd. Jeremiah is reproving the shepherds who mislead God's people and scatter them (see the first reading); Jesus is the divine shepherd who both knows the needs of others and responds to them. By his own good example, Jesus teaches the disciples that caring relationships are at the heart of bringing his mission to completion. By paying attention to the needs of people can we serve them, giving them all they need to encounter the God who brings all good things to those who are open to divine presence.

As disciples of Jesus, we are both shepherds and sheep: like Jesus, we respond to those in need, as well as receive care when we are the ones in need. By this exchange of giving and receiving, we are no longer a scattered crowd, but a community of God's people. Giving and receiving help form a bond of community because these mutual exchanges are essentially *relational*. In mutual relationship—characterized by giving and receiving—do we take up Jesus' own example of self-giving for others as well as create the condition for receiving all that God offers us. In the mutual giving and receiving we share in common both our abundance (we give what we have) and our need (we are empty, willing to be filled from the goodness of others).

Living the Paschal Mystery

We all need to go off to a "deserted place" occasionally to "rest a while." Whether this means taking some time alone each day to pray and rest in God, making Sunday truly a day of rest, or setting aside a few days a year to make a retreat, all of us need time to regain our strength so we can take up our own shepherding tasks. If the mission overwhelms us, we are unable to persevere.

Achieving a balance between the work of discipleship and the need to rest from weariness can be no easy task in itself. Like Jesus, we are called to shepherd—to care, teach, heal, listen, etc. At the same time, we must know when it is time for us to be on the receiving end, to balance our work of sharing the Gospel with rest, with time to replenish our spirit and energy. Self-giving and rest are two parallel poles to the dying and rising dynamic of the paschal mystery. Too much dying can crush us. Too much rest can lull us into being uncaring shepherds.

Focusing the Gospel

Key words and phrases: rest a while, vast crowd, moved with pity, sheep without a shepherd, began to teach them

To the point: Jesus, the true shepherd of God, responds to the needs of others: with a listening ear, food, and rest for the weary apostles; with teaching for the "vast crowd." As disciples of Jesus, we are both shepherds and sheep: we respond to those in need, as well as receive care when we are the ones in need. By this exchange of giving and receiving, we are no longer a scattered crowd, but a community of God's people.

Connecting the Gospel

to the first reading: Jeremiah foresees God entrusting the shepherding role to a king of the house of David. Jesus is that royal shepherd.

to experience: We tend to see ourselves as being either leaders or followers, haves or have-nots, those who give or those who receive, etc. The fullness of human growth comes when we accept that sometimes we are one, sometimes the other.

Connecting the Responsorial Psalm

to the readings: Psalm 23 is perhaps the best known and most loved of all the psalms. Its verses use two images—shepherd and host—to communicate how unstintingly God cares for, feeds, nurtures, and protects us. It is easy to see the appropriateness of singing verses of this psalm on this Sunday when the readings reveal that God never abandons the people. In Jeremiah when the appointed leaders fail to care, God intervenes and promises to call forth new shepherds (first reading). In the gospel when the disciples are exhausted and the crowd lost and leaderless, Jesus responds to both with tender attention.

We might ask as we sing this psalm whether we are the crowd in need of care and direction or the disciples in need of rest. If we look deeply enough, we will see that the answer is "both" and that to every need Jesus pays heed. May we rest in him from both the labors of discipleship and the pain of every need.

to cantor preparation: As a baptized member of the Body of Christ, you are called to shepherd others. But you are also shepherded by the One who calls. You might spend some time this week reflecting on the ways Christ pays heed to you. When are you most vulnerable? When are you in need? How have you experienced Christ's attentiveness and care at these times? Do you tell Christ of your struggles? Do you let yourself hear his answer?

ASSEMBLY & FAITH-SHARING GROUPS

· I experience God's care for me when . . .
· I need to shepherd when . . . I need to be shepherded when . . .
· The communities in which I find growth and care are . . . The "vast crowd[s]" in which I find myself lost are . . .

PRESIDERS

· As pastor, I am able to shepherd my people better when . . .

DEACONS

· My service eases others' suffering and needs best when . . .

HOSPITALITY MINISTERS

· My greeting helps those who gather be welcomed into a caring community when . . .

MUSIC MINISTERS

· My music ministry helps those who have gathered become a community with one Shepherd when . . .

ALTAR MINISTERS

· My service at the altar is primarily about giving. I also receive when . . .

LECTORS

· God's word shepherds me by . . . From this I receive . . .

EXTRAORDINARY MINISTERS OF HOLY COMMUNION

· I experience my ministry of distributing Holy Communion as both giving and receiving when . . .

Model Act of Penitence

Presider: Jesus is the caring shepherd who listens to us and gives us rest. Let us open ourselves in this liturgy to Jesus' caring presence . . . [pause]

Lord Jesus, you are the One in whom we find our rest: Lord . . .

Christ Jesus, you are the Shepherd who cares for your people: Christ . . .

Lord Jesus, you are the One who teaches the ways of goodness to those who come to you: Lord . . .

Homily Points

• Americans are known to be a nation of rugged individualists, but isn't it interesting that this coveted value is also the source of our being a lonely crowd? On the one hand, we fear depending on others ("I owe you"); but, on the other hand, we long to be connected with others in deep, lasting relationships of giving and receiving.

• Jesus' life is a perfect example of how both giving and receiving strengthen the bonds of community. He receives the apostles when they return from their tiring missionary activities and report what they have experienced as they "gathered together" with him. Jesus also gives of himself as he cares for his exhausted apostles and teaches the "vast crowd" who have searched him out.

• Giving and receiving fashion the bonds of interrelatedness which is the basis for any caring community. Together giving and receiving establish a sense of fundamental equality, joy or satisfaction in mutual sharing, completion in receiving from another, and comfort with dependence on another. None of this diminishes who we are, but expands who we are into being the Body of Christ.

Model Prayer of the Faithful

Presider: We pray now to our caring God who through Jesus hears our prayers and grants our needs.

Response:

Lord, hear our prayer.

Cantor:

we pray to the Lord,

That the church always be a haven of rest for those weary in body and spirit . . . [pause]

That nations find creative ways to feed their hungry and care for their downtrodden . . . [pause]

That those worn out by the demands of discipleship find rest in Christ . . . [pause]

That this community excel in giving and receiving, thus deepening their bond as Body of Christ . . . [pause]

Presider: Shepherd God, you grant rest to the weary and fill the needs of those who come to you: hear these our prayers that one day we may enjoy eternal rest with you. We ask this through Christ our Lord. **Amen.**

Let us pray

Pause for silent prayer

Father,
let the gift of your life
continue to grow in us,
drawing us from death to faith, hope, and
    love.
Keep us alive in Christ Jesus.
Keep us watchful in prayer
and true to his teaching
till your glory is revealed in us.

Grant this through Christ our Lord.
    Amen.

FIRST READING

Jer 23:1-6

Woe to the shepherds
    who mislead and scatter the flock of my
        pasture,
    says the LORD.
Therefore, thus says the LORD, the God of
    Israel,
    against the shepherds who shepherd my
        people:
    You have scattered my sheep and driven
        them away.
You have not cared for them,
    but I will take care to punish your evil
        deeds.
I myself will gather the remnant of my
    flock
    from all the lands to which I have driven
        them
    and bring them back to their meadow;
        there they shall increase and multiply.
I will appoint shepherds for them who will
    shepherd them
    so that they need no longer fear and
        tremble;
    and none shall be missing, says the
        LORD.

Behold, the days are coming, says the
    LORD,
    when I will raise up a righteous shoot
        to David;
as king he shall reign and govern wisely,
    he shall do what is just and right in the
        land.
In his days Judah shall be saved,
    Israel shall dwell in security.
This is the name they give him:
    "The LORD our justice."

RESPONSORIAL PSALM

Ps 23:1-3, 3-4, 5, 6

℞. (1) The Lord is my shepherd; there is nothing I shall want.

The LORD is my shepherd; I shall not want.
In verdant pastures he gives me repose;
beside restful waters he leads me;
he refreshes my soul.

℞. The Lord is my shepherd; there is nothing I shall want.

He guides me in right paths
for his name's sake.
Even though I walk in the dark valley
I fear no evil; for you are at my side
with your rod and your staff
that give me courage.

℞. The Lord is my shepherd; there is nothing I shall want.

You spread the table before me
in the sight of my foes;
you anoint my head with oil;
my cup overflows.

℞. The Lord is my shepherd; there is nothing I shall want.

Only goodness and kindness follow me
all the days of my life;
and I shall dwell in the house of the LORD
for years to come.

℞. The Lord is my shepherd; there is nothing I shall want.

SECOND READING

Eph 2:13-18

Brothers and sisters:
In Christ Jesus you who once were far off
have become near by the blood of
Christ.

For he is our peace, he who made both one
and broke down the dividing wall of
enmity, through his flesh,
abolishing the law with its
commandments and legal claims,
that he might create in himself one new
person in place of the two,
thus establishing peace,
and might reconcile both with God,
in one body, through the cross,
putting that enmity to death by it.
He came and preached peace to you who
were far off
and peace to those who were near,
for through him we both have access in
one Spirit to the Father.

About Liturgy

Sunday—a day of rest: The emperor Constantine in the fourth century made Sunday a day of rest for all the people of the realm. It was a day when fasting and kneeling were forbidden, but also a day given over to acts of mercy and kindness. Sunday as a day of celebration and rest has given Christians time for enjoyment of and appreciation for God's gifts and for redeemed life in all its human dimensions. Sunday rest is more than merely abstaining from productive work; the rest encourages the realization of the work of God's redeeming power which frees us. Sunday rest reminds us that all we have is really a gift from a provident and generous God; that the fruitful work of our hands is sharing in God's creative power.

Unfortunately, for all too many Christians, Sunday is as busy a day as any other. Stores are all open so the numbers of people who must work have increased dramatically. It takes constant effort and a great deal of planning and commitment to make Sunday a special day. But, like the message of this Sunday's gospel, there must be a balance in our lives between productive work and rest, between weekdays and Sunday. Changing the rhythm of our week so that Sunday is truly a day of rest—marked by quality time for God and family—has its built-in rewards. We find not only a better balance in our lives, but find our God as well.

About Liturgical Music

Music suggestions: Settings of Psalm 23 abound. One of the finest is Gelineau's classic in which the accompaniment mimics a shepherd's flute moving in counterpoint to the melody of the psalm tone. Another classic setting is the well-known one by Vermulst/Westendorf [WC, WS]. Settings such as these are good choices because they allow the text to shine as the dominant element rather than the music.

John Bell's "The Summons" merits repeating this Sunday because it expresses the intimate personal relationship with the shepherding Christ which disciples on mission need. As was suggested last Sunday, letting cantors sing the words of Christ (vv. 1-4) and the assembly sing their response (v. 5) would make the dialogic structure of the text evident. Hymns which speak of Jesus reaching out to us when we are in need of either rest or leadership include "Come to Me, O Weary Traveler" [G2, GC, GC2, RS]; "I Heard the Voice of Jesus Say" [in most hymnals]; "Jesus, Lead the Way" [GC, GC2, RS, W3]; "With a Shepherd's Care" [G2, GC, GC2, RS, SS]; and Delores Dufner's "Come to Me" [JS2, PMB, WC].

SPIRITUALITY

GOSPEL ACCLAMATION
Luke 7:16

℞. Alleluia, alleluia.
A great prophet has risen in our midst.
God has visited his people.
℞. Alleluia, alleluia.

Gospel

John 6:1-15; L110B

Jesus went across the
        Sea of Galilee.
A large crowd followed
        him,
    because they saw
        the signs he was
        performing on
        the sick.
Jesus went up on the mountain,
    and there he sat down with his disciples.
The Jewish feast of Passover was near.
When Jesus raised his eyes
    and saw that a large crowd was coming
        to him,
    he said to Philip,
    "Where can we buy enough food for
        them to eat?"
He said this to test him,
    because he himself knew what he was
        going to do.
Philip answered him,
    "Two hundred days' wages worth of
        food would not be enough
    for each of them to have a little."
One of his disciples,
    Andrew, the brother of Simon Peter,
        said to him,
    "There is a boy here who has five barley
        loaves and two fish;
    but what good are these for so many?"
Jesus said, "Have the people recline."
Now there was a great deal of grass in that
        place.
So the men reclined, about five thousand in
        number.

Continued in Appendix A, p. 303.

Reflecting on the Gospel

"Big" seems to be in. Some of the burger fast-food chains use "super size" as a marketing ploy—the fries and drinks are larger, appealing to a hungrier appetite as well as a good deal. Fishermen love to tell fish stories; but notice that the fish never get smaller but always larger in the retelling. We might interpret Jesus' multiplication of the loaves (gospel) as a kind of "one-upmanship" over Elisha (first reading: crowd is larger, more left over) or one great fish story that has gotten larger in the telling. And, actually, supersizing the story is exactly the point, for the multiplication account has more to do with what Jesus was saying about the future than about feeding a hungry crowd. The abundance in the account is an eschatological sign of risen life. The multiplication of the loaves points to a time of fulfillment when God's plan for redemption is finally realized.

The context of this gospel is Passover—Israel's annual celebration of God's mighty deeds on their behalf. The wondrous and impressive sign that Jesus works on this occasion—feeding 5000 with five loaves—points beyond taking care of the hunger of the "large crowd." Rather, Jesus' sign points to a time when God's mighty deeds come to fulfillment—a time when all people are abundantly filled and every need is met. The question about having food to feed the crowd is put to two particular apostles (Philip and Andrew) who traditionally are considered to be ministers to the Gentiles ("Jesus went across the Sea of Galilee" = to Gentile territory); in the messianic reign even the Gentiles will share in the abundance and be saved. The bread is specified as barley, the grain used by the poor; in the messianic reign the poor will also share in God's abundance. Twelve baskets of bread fragments were gathered up after all had their fill; the leftovers and the number twelve points to the new Israel in its eschatological perfection.

Jesus' unprecedented miracle of abundance doesn't warrant his being made an earthly king, in spite of the crowd's understandable enthusiasm; rather, "he withdrew . . . alone" so that the miracle of abundance points to the establishment of a new kingdom, a new Israel. Jesus supersedes both the apostles' and the crowd's expectations of God's reign: with little he feeds many and thus reveals that he is not an earthly king but, ironically, Jesus is a king. Jesus himself is an eschatological sign of abundance—of God's lavish presence.

Living the Paschal Mystery

This gospel account is far more than an interesting "super size" story; it primes us to ponder the great mystery of Jesus himself as the Bread of Life (which we will hear about on subsequent Sundays) and his self-giving that enables us to share in it. The challenge for us is far more than believing in Jesus' power to multiply loaves and fishes; the challenge is recognizing Jesus' self-giving as a sign of fulfillment and promise of eschatological glory that we share even now. We Christians are to see our lives through the lens of God's lavish abundance. Do we?

It is too easy to think of God's lavish abundance primarily (maybe exclusively?) in terms of the Eucharist we share each Sunday. Indeed, this is a mighty act of God on our behalf, and Eucharist always is an eschatological sign of God's abundance and a time of future fulfillment. However, we ought not let this lull us into missing other signs of God's abundance: the abundance of family and friends, steady job, support and care of others. God's abundance is "super size" and it is all around us.

Focusing the Gospel

Key words and phrases: five barley loaves, five thousand, had their fill, more than they could eat, saw the sign

To the point: The context of this gospel is Passover—Israel's annual celebration of God's mighty deeds on their behalf. The wondrous and impressive sign that Jesus works on this occasion—feeding 5000 with five loaves—points beyond taking care of the hunger of the "large crowd." Rather, Jesus' sign points to a time when God's mighty deeds come to fulfillment—a time when all people are abundantly filled and every need is met.

Connecting the Gospel

to the first reading: In the first reading Elisha miraculously uses twenty loaves to feed 100 people with "some left over." In the gospel Jesus uses only five loaves to feed 5000 with "twelve wicker baskets" left over. No one could be prepared for the superabundance of God's gifts that Jesus brings.

to our culture: In our society abundance is usually a sign of inheritance, hard work, or lucky investments. In the first reading and gospel this Sunday, abundance is a sign of God's free gift.

Connecting the Responsorial Psalm

to the readings: Psalm 145 is an acrostic poem, meaning that each verse begins with the next letter of the Hebrew alphabet. The psalm is a hymn of praise for the continuity of God's goodness from the beginning of things to their end.

Looked at in the context of the past two Sundays the theme of Psalm 145 becomes even more evident. The first reading and gospel of the 15th Sunday show God acting relentlessly to bring about salvation; Psalm 85 describes the future promised us by such a God. The first reading and gospel of the 16th Sunday reveal God shepherding the people to this future; Psalm 23 celebrates how timely, tender, and intimate this shepherding is. This Sunday brings the message full circle. The future promise of Psalm 85 and the present tenderness of Psalm 23 are completed in Jesus' multiplication of the loaves (gospel), sign of himself as the eschatological banquet where all will have more than their fill. Truly in the Eucharist the Lord "feeds us [and] answers all our needs" (psalm refrain). How readily we can look to the future with hope (psalm) for we know from present experience what is being promised us.

to cantor preparation: This Sunday's responsorial psalm promises that God will feed all who hunger. The gospel shows us that this nourishment will be from the hand of Christ. As you prepare to sing the psalm you might reflect on questions such as these: For what do you hunger? For what do you look hopefully? How in the Eucharist do you experience Jesus' longing to nourish you?

ASSEMBLY & FAITH-SHARING GROUPS
- Some of God's superabundance given to me over the years is . . .
- God's mighty deeds on my behalf are . . .
- I hunger to be fed when . . .

PRESIDERS
- I help people experience God's superabundant gifts by . . .

DEACONS
- What frustrates me about not being able to meet every need is . . . Jesus helps me with this frustration by . . .

HOSPITALITY MINISTERS
- My hospitality is a sign of God's lavishness for the people when . . .

MUSIC MINISTERS
- Jesus helps me feed the assembly through my music ministry by . . . He feeds me by . . .

ALTAR MINISTERS
- In light of Jesus' example of abundance, the true spirit of Christian service for me is . . .

LECTORS
- God's word is superabundant nourishment for me in that . . .

EXTRAORDINARY MINISTERS OF HOLY COMMUNION
- I experience the superabundance of God's gifts in distributing Holy Communion when . . .

Model Act of Penitence

Presider: Jesus embodies for us the abundance of God freely given to us, symbolized by the gospel account of the feeding of the 5000. We pause now to remember God's abundant gifts to us and especially the gift of Eucharist in which we now share . . . [pause]

Lord Jesus, you are the fullness of God's love: Lord . . .

Christ Jesus, you are the fullness of divine life given to us: Christ . . .

Lord Jesus, you are the fullness of all that we seek: Lord . . .

Homily Points

• Many people who find themselves in impossible situations are saved through human intervention. A single parent might be juggling two jobs and rearing children. Someone might have lost a job and is faced with paying rent, food, utilities. Or someone may be in emotional or spiritual distress. Relief and help often come from the awareness, generosity, and sensitivity of others.

• Elisha's servant (in the first reading) thinks it an impossible situation for Elisha to feed so many with so little. In the gospel, the disciples felt that five loaves was an impossible amount to satisfy 5000 people. Divine intervention meets these impossible situations in most amazing ways; in both cases people are filled to satisfaction, with some left over. God's abundance is incalculable; we need never doubt the extent of God's gifts and care for us.

• One sign of God's abundance and care for us now is the goodness and generosity of those around us. Our participation in this self-giving hastens the coming of the fullness of life that God is offering us.

Model Prayer of the Faithful

Presider: God abundantly provides for all people. We confidently raise our prayers to such a generous God.

Response:

Lord, hear our prayer.

Cantor:

we pray to the Lord,

That the church willingly open her stores of abundance to those in need . . . [pause]

That all people be able to share in the fullness and goodness of life . . . [pause]

That the hungry always have their fill . . . [pause]

That we always take time to gather the leftovers so that nothing of God's abundance be wasted . . . [pause]

Presider: God of abundance, you lavish on us all good gifts: hear these our prayers that one day we might be with you in the fullness of everlasting life. We ask this through Christ our Lord. **Amen.**

OPENING PRAYER

Let us pray

Pause for silent prayer

God our Father and protector,
without you nothing is holy,
nothing has value.
Guide us to everlasting life
by helping us to use wisely
the blessings you have given to the world.

We ask this through our Lord Jesus Christ,
your Son,
who lives and reigns with you and the
Holy Spirit,
one God, for ever and ever. **Amen.**

FIRST READING

2 Kgs 4:42-44

A man came from Baal-shalishah bringing
to Elisha, the man of God,
twenty barley loaves made from the
firstfruits,
and fresh grain in the ear.
Elisha said, "Give it to the people to eat."
But his servant objected,
"How can I set this before a hundred
people?"
Elisha insisted, "Give it to the people to
eat.
For thus says the LORD,
'They shall eat and there shall be some
left over.'"
And when they had eaten, there was some
left over,
as the LORD had said.

RESPONSORIAL PSALM
Ps 145:10-11, 15-16, 17-18

R℣. (cf. 16) The hand of the Lord feeds us;
he answers all our needs.

Let all your works give you thanks, O
  Lord,
  and let your faithful ones bless you.
Let them discourse of the glory of your
  kingdom
  and speak of your might.

R℣. The hand of the Lord feeds us; he
answers all our needs.

The eyes of all look hopefully to you,
  and you give them their food in due
  season;
you open your hand
  and satisfy the desire of every living
  thing.

R℣. The hand of the Lord feeds us; he
answers all our needs.

The Lord is just in all his ways
  and holy in all his works.
The Lord is near to all who call upon him,
  to all who call upon him in truth.

R℣. The hand of the Lord feeds us; he
answers all our needs.

SECOND READING
Eph 4:1-6

Brothers and sisters:
I, a prisoner for the Lord,
  urge you to live in a manner worthy of
    the call you have received,
  with all humility and gentleness, with
    patience,
  bearing with one another through love,
  striving to preserve the unity of the
    spirit through the bond of peace:
  one body and one Spirit,
  as you were also called to the one hope
    of your call;
  one Lord, one faith, one baptism;
  one God and Father of all,
  who is over all and through all and in
    all.

About Liturgy

John 6—the Bread of Life discourse: John's gospel is read extensively during the festal seasons, but there is no block of Sundays during these high celebration times when the beautiful Bread of Life discourse from John's sixth chapter could be included without breaking it up. Those who compiled the Lectionary made the decision to include extensive portions of this sixth chapter from John's gospel on five consecutive Sundays during year B as a theological commentary on the multiplication of the loaves and, by extension, on the Eucharist. It is inserted in Mark's gospel just at the point of Mark's multiplication account.

This decision reminds us that the Lectionary is not a Bible, but is a liturgical book with its own purpose. Since, further, the Lectionary is a liturgical book used primarily during the celebration of Eucharist, it should come as no surprise to us that the intent is precisely to draw our attention to the mystery of the Eucharist.

In Reflecting on the Gospel we mentioned a number of indicators in the text that the passage is eschatological, that is, refers to the final fulfillment at the end times. The gospel for this Sunday also includes indicators that the passage is eucharistic. For example, Jesus gives thanks; the Greek term used here is *eucharistēsas*, the word, of course, from which we derive our term Eucharist. Further, unlike the account in Mark, in the Johannine account Jesus *himself* distributes the bread to the hungry crowd, pointing to himself as the bread of life. Finally, the Passover and eschatological contexts remind us that Eucharist is a sacrament related to the end times and our share in Christ's risen life.

About Liturgical Music

Music suggestions: An excellent choice for the entrance procession or for an assembly hymn of thanksgiving after Communion would be Sylvia Dunstan's "All Who Hunger, Gather Gladly"/"All Who Hunger." Her images of "com[ing] from wilderness and wand'ring . . . from restlessness and roaming . . . from loneliness and longing" identify the hungry crowd facing Jesus that day on the mountain (gospel) as well as those who gather for Eucharist today. G2, GC, GC2, and RS set the text to a Bob Moore melody; SS and RS also set it to the American folk tune HOLY MANNA. A further tune possibility would be NETTLETON.

The well-known classic "Gift of Finest Wheat"/"You Satisfy the Hungry Heart" would be excellent for the Communion procession. OCP publishes the original SATB arrangement by Robert Kreutz [octavo 8005CC] and includes choral versions in *Choral Praise* and *Choral Praise Comprehensive*. GIA publishes a lovely arrangement by John Ferguson [G-3089]. Verses 1, 3, and 5 are SATB. Verses 2 and 4 are unison with organ doubling the melody in the pedal and manuals playing open chords in counterpoint on flute or string stops. These verses can also be played without pedal, keeping strings on both manuals and letting a flutist double the melody.

✠ SPIRITUALITY

GOSPEL ACCLAMATION
Matt 4:4b

R/. Alleluia, alleluia.
One does not live on bread alone, but by every
word that comes forth from the mouth of God.
R/. Alleluia, alleluia.

Gospel

John 6:24-35; L113B

When the crowd saw that
  neither Jesus nor his
  disciples were there,
they themselves got into
  boats
and came to Capernaum
  looking for Jesus.
And when they found him
  across the sea they said to him,
"Rabbi, when did you get here?"
Jesus answered them and said,
  "Amen, amen, I say to you,
  you are looking for me not because
    you saw signs
  but because you ate the loaves and
    were filled.
Do not work for food that perishes
  but for the food that endures for
    eternal life,
  which the Son of Man will give you.
For on him the Father, God, has set his
  seal."
So they said to him,
  "What can we do to accomplish the
    works of God?"
Jesus answered and said to them,
  "This is the work of God, that you
    believe in the one he sent."
So they said to him,
  "What sign can you do, that we may
    see and believe in you?
What can you do?
Our ancestors ate manna in the desert,
  as it is written:
  *He gave them bread from heaven to
    eat.*"

Continued in Appendix A, p. 303.

Reflecting on the Gospel

After being fed the bread and fish abundantly provided by Jesus (last Sunday's gospel about the multiplication of the loaves), it is natural that the crowd would look for Jesus. What they were not prepared for was that the bread Jesus offers is so much more than food that satisfies their immediate hunger; the food that Jesus offers satisfies the hunger for eternal life. Jesus is trying to help the crowd who has followed him to Capernaum make a shift in their understanding of him. He is trying to help them move from human expectations and satisfaction to believing in and embracing what "endures for eternal life." This was no easy shift for the crowd to make, nor is it an easy shift for us.

Seeing the manna on the ground, the Israelite community asks, "*What* is this?" (first reading). Moses answers that this is the bread God has given them to eat. At the heart of their questioning of Jesus in the gospel, the crowd is really asking, "*Who* is this?" Jesus answers, "I am the bread of life" sent by God. The nourishment God sends us now is not a perishable substance but the very person of Jesus. Moreover, *this* Bread "endures for eternal life," and so long as we encounter Jesus among us, we will "never hunger," "never thirst." This bread promises more than all the perishable bread in the world. The bread Jesus offers is "bread from heaven," a share in the fullness of life that only our encounters with Jesus can bring.

God's abundance is a sign of messianic times, of God's reign being established, of eternal life. Our sharing in this abundance is already a sharing in the fullness of life to come. The "bread of God . . . which comes down from heaven . . . gives life to the world." Our way to share in this life is to "believe in the one [God] sent." We need look nowhere else for signs—only to Jesus who is the Bread of Life. Believing leads to life; Jesus is the Bread of Life, the gift of Life itself, the gift of himself. We consume the bread from heaven so that the mystery of Life may consume us, drawing us to eternal life.

Living the Paschal Mystery

What we need to receive Eucharist fruitfully is a personal relationship with Jesus. This "bread from heaven" is ultimately a person, Jesus Christ. If Jesus is the bread from heaven given for us and we are the Body of Christ, then we must conclude that we ourselves are to be bread from heaven that fosters eternal life for others. As God has "set his seal" on Jesus, so through baptism and confirmation has God "set his seal" on us. Jesus gives himself as bread from heaven; we give ourselves to others as bread from heaven when we live our baptismal commitment by doing the ordinary things of every day as Jesus would—with care, compassion, love, generosity, patience.

The very person of Jesus is *everything* for which we long. Jesus is the deep well of what's beyond our immediate satisfaction, the deep well that brings us face to face with our longing and dissatisfaction. Just as the crowd followed Jesus across the lake, looking for him to satisfy them, so must we follow Jesus as faithful disciples. We both look for him in our everyday lives—in the people and circumstances around us—as well as faithfully bring that divine presence to others. The bread God offers us is the abiding presence of Jesus among us, always reaching out to satisfy us with what is imperishable, what endures forever: eternal life.

Focusing the Gospel

Key words and phrases: food that perishes, food that endures, see and believe in you, true bread, I am the bread of life

To the point: Seeing the manna on the ground, the Israelite community asks, "*What* is this?" (first reading). Moses answers that this is the bread God has given them to eat. At the heart of their questioning of Jesus in the gospel, the crowd is really asking, "*Who* is this?" Jesus answers, "I am the bread of life" sent by God. The nourishment God sends us now is not a perishable substance but the very person of Jesus. Moreover, *this* Bread "endures for eternal life."

Connecting the Gospel

to the first reading: In the first reading, the Israelites grumble about being hungry and look to their past experience in Egypt where they had their "fill of bread." In the gospel Jesus is calling the crowd to look beyond their having been filled with bread to what is unimaginable—being filled with Jesus who is the "bread of life."

to our culture: As human beings, we are always dissatisfied, always longing for more. In Jesus, God gives us all that we long for; we have only to see and believe.

Connecting the Responsorial Psalm

to the readings: Psalm 78 retells the history of God's continual interventions to save the Israelites, their constant failure to remember what God has done for them, and God's efforts to bring Israel to faithfulness. The psalmist is reminding the Israelites of his day that this is their story and is calling them to the fidelity their ancestors ignored. The verses from Psalm 78 used for this Sunday's responsorial psalm connect directly with the first reading, relating God's saving deed of providing the Israelites with manna in the desert. The first strophe sings about remembering and passing on the story of God's "glorious deeds" from one generation to the next. The third strophe remembers how their desert journey ended: God led them into the holy land they had been promised.

By using these verses from Psalm 78, the Lectionary reminds us that this story is also ours. God acts to save us; like the Israelites we can see and believe or we can grumble (first reading). God calls us to relationship, above all by sending Jesus, the Bread of Life who nourishes us on our journey to eternal life (gospel). Will we eat and be faithful, or eat and forget? The responsorial psalm invites us to remember the nourishment and the new life we are continually given in Christ, the "bread from heaven."

to cantor preparation: The psalmist of Psalm 78 is a storyteller relaying the history of God's relationship with Israel and calling the people to remember that story and be faithful to the God who generates it. You need to recognize that this Sunday you are the storyteller for your eucharistic assembly. The bread from heaven you sing about is the person of Jesus given to the community yesterday, today, and forever. In your singing you call the community to celebrate this gift and remain faithful to the relationship it establishes. As a way of helping yourself connect past and present in your "storytelling" you might pray the psalm refrain each day this week in the present tense, "The Lord gives us bread from heaven." You might also pray it in first person singular, "The Lord gives me bread from heaven."

ASSEMBLY & FAITH-SHARING GROUPS
- The "what" God feeds me with is . . . The "who" God feeds me with is . . .
- Jesus satisfies my hungers by . . .
- I encounter Jesus as the "bread of life" when . . .

PRESIDERS
- My ministry calls me to be the "bread of life" for others in that . . .

DEACONS
- My ministry of service satisfies these hungers in others . . .

HOSPITALITY MINISTERS
- My greeting of those who gather for Eucharist invites them to encounter the Bread of Life when . . .

MUSIC MINISTERS
- My music making is bread that nourishes the faith of the assembly when . . .

ALTAR MINISTERS
- Preparing the table from which the community receives the Bread of Life humbles me in that . . . nourishes me in that . . .

LECTORS
- The Word of Life I proclaim is the Bread of Life when . . .

EXTRAORDINARY MINISTERS OF HOLY COMMUNION
- Distributing the Bread of Life to the community nourishes my own daily living by . . .

Model Act of Penitence

Presider: Jesus is the Bread of Life, given to us that we might come to believe in him. We pray during this Eucharist to come to a deeper relationship with Jesus by hearing his word and sharing in the sacrament of life . . . [pause]

> Lord Jesus, you are the true Bread from heaven: Lord . . .
>
> Christ Jesus, you are the Food that brings life: Christ . . .
>
> Lord Jesus, you are Nourishment for all who hunger: Lord . . .

Homily Points

- Our daily living conditions us to immediacy. We tend to seek instant gratification, evidenced by our "consumer" mentality. We purchase the highest speed of telecommunications and the fastest computer chips. We are impatient with long lines or with delays. While we live in immediacy, we also hunger, however, for what endures—love, security, satisfaction.

- Jesus both satisfied the crowd's immediate need (he fed the 5000) as well as helped them look beyond the immediate to deeper and more lasting needs. His signs were never simply for the sake of satisfying immediate physical needs (hunger, healing, etc.); they always pointed beyond to what is enduring and what, ultimately, our seeing and believing in him is about—growing into eternal life.

- Our hungers are not only for food and shelter—they also include the need for acceptance, recognition, insight, support, security, etc. Jesus satisfied physical needs and also recognized and addressed the far deeper needs. He came to give us life in all its fullness and he would do so by offering his very self as what nourishes us. Encountering Jesus is our deepest satisfaction and greatest nourishment because the very person of Jesus *is the life* for which we long.

Model Prayer of the Faithful

Presider: God sends Jesus to be the Bread that nourishes and sustains us. And so we pray.

Response: Lord, hear our prayer.

Cantor: we pray to the Lord,

That the church, nourished by Jesus, be bread for the world . . . [pause]

That all peoples of the world might believe in God and receive the goodness and compassion of God . . . [pause]

That those who suffer from any hunger be nourished by this community which has been fed at the table of the Lord . . . [pause]

That each of us here grow deeper in our relationship with Jesus, the Bread of Life . . . [pause]

Presider: God of blessings, you send bread from heaven so that we might have eternal life: give us this bread always. We ask this through the Bread of Life, Jesus Christ our Lord. **Amen.**

Let us pray

Pause for silent prayer

God our Father,
gifts without measure flow from your
    goodness
to bring us your peace.
Our life is your gift.
Guide our life's journey,
for only your love makes us whole.
Keep us strong in your love.

We ask this through Christ our Lord.
    Amen.

FIRST READING

Exod 16:2-4, 12-15

The whole Israelite community grumbled
    against Moses and Aaron.
The Israelites said to them,
    "Would that we had died at the LORD's
        hand in the land of Egypt,
    as we sat by our fleshpots and ate our
        fill of bread!
But you had to lead us into this desert
    to make the whole community die of
        famine!"

Then the LORD said to Moses,
    "I will now rain down bread from
        heaven for you.
Each day the people are to go out and
        gather their daily portion;
    thus will I test them,
    to see whether they follow my
        instructions or not.

"I have heard the grumbling of the
        Israelites.
Tell them: In the evening twilight you shall
        eat flesh,
    and in the morning you shall have your
        fill of bread,
    so that you may know that I, the LORD,
        am your God."

In the evening quail came up and covered
        the camp.
In the morning a dew lay all about the
        camp,
    and when the dew evaporated, there on
        the surface of the desert
    were fine flakes like hoarfrost on the
        ground.
On seeing it, the Israelites asked one
        another, "What is this?"
    for they did not know what it was.
But Moses told them,
    "This is the bread that the LORD has
        given you to eat."

RESPONSORIAL PSALM
Ps 78:3-4, 23-24, 25, 54

R̸. (24b) The Lord gave them bread from heaven.

What we have heard and know,
  and what our fathers have declared to us,
we will declare to the generation to come
  the glorious deeds of the Lord and his strength
  and the wonders that he wrought.

R̸. The Lord gave them bread from heaven.

He commanded the skies above
  and opened the doors of heaven;
he rained manna upon them for food
  and gave them heavenly bread.

R̸. The Lord gave them bread from heaven.

Man ate the bread of angels,
  food he sent them in abundance.
And he brought them to his holy land,
  to the mountains his right hand had won.

R̸. The Lord gave them bread from heaven.

SECOND READING
Eph 4:17, 20-24

Brothers and sisters:
I declare and testify in the Lord
  that you must no longer live as the
    Gentiles do,
  in the futility of their minds;
  that is not how you learned Christ,
  assuming that you have heard of him
    and were taught in him,
  as truth is in Jesus,
  that you should put away the old self of
    your former way of life,
  corrupted through deceitful desires,
  and be renewed in the spirit of your
    minds,
  and put on the new self,
  created in God's way in righteousness
    and holiness of truth.

About Liturgy

Eucharist, believing, and action: Believing in the Eucharist is more than believing in the Real Presence. Or, to put it another way, believing in the Real Presence—the Eucharist is truly the Body and Blood of Christ—demands something of us. Eucharist nourishes us, transforms us into being more perfectly the Body of Christ, so that we might live this holy mystery more effectively in our daily lives. As St. Augustine said in his famous Sermon 272, "If you are the Body of Christ and members of it, then it is that mystery which is placed on the Lord's table: you receive the mystery, which is to say the Body of Christ, your very self. You answer Amen to who you are and in the answer embrace yourself. You hear Body of Christ and answer Amen. Be a member of Christ's Body, that your Amen will be true."

Believing itself is an action—a commitment to a relationship. To say we believe in Jesus as the Bread of Life and to say Amen to the Body and Blood we receive at Communion is to make a commitment: that we live who we are, the Body of Christ. The only way our Amen to the Body and Blood of Christ can be true is for each of us to be Christ in our everyday actions. This is a tall order! On our own we could not do it. But Jesus himself is our strength and helps us say our Amen.

About Liturgical Music

Music suggestions: "All Who Hunger, Gather Gladly"/ "All Who Hunger," suggested for last Sunday could well be repeated this Sunday for either the entrance or the Communion song. Using the tune HOLY MANNA would be a good choice because of the references to manna in the first reading and gospel. If the text is too short for the Communion procession, supplement it with instrumental or choral interludes. As with many pentatonic folk melodies, this tune can be sung in canon at the distance of one measure. For one interlude the melody might be played in canon using solo instruments or contrasting organ stops, and for another the choir might repeat a verse in canon *a cappella*. A third option would be to have the tenors and basses sing an ostinato open fifth (the tonic and dominant of whatever key you are in) beneath the treble voices singing a verse. Have the men sing the words "taste and see" throughout in the rhythm of dotted quarter-eighth note–half note.

AUGUST 2, 2009
EIGHTEENTH SUNDAY IN ORDINARY TIME

SPIRITUALITY

GOSPEL ACCLAMATION
John 6:51

R⁊. Alleluia, alleluia.
I am the living bread that came down
     from heaven, says the Lord;
whoever eats this bread will live
     forever.
R⁊. Alleluia, alleluia.

Gospel

John 6:41-51; L116B

The Jews murmured about Jesus
     because he said,
  "I am the bread that came down from
     heaven,"
  and they said,
  "Is this not Jesus, the son of Joseph?
Do we not know his father and mother?
Then how can he say,
  'I have come down from heaven'?"
Jesus answered and said to them,
  "Stop murmuring among yourselves.
No one can come to me unless the
     Father who sent me draw him,
  and I will raise him on the last day.
It is written in the prophets:
     They shall all be taught by God.
Everyone who listens to my Father and
     learns from him comes to me.
Not that anyone has seen the Father
     except the one who is from God;
  he has seen the Father.
Amen, amen, I say to you,
  whoever believes has eternal life.
I am the bread of life.
Your ancestors ate the manna in the
     desert, but they died;
  this is the bread that comes down
     from heaven
  so that one may eat it and not die.
I am the living bread that came down
     from heaven;
  whoever eats this bread will live
     forever;
  and the bread that I will give is my
     flesh for the life of the world."

Reflecting on the Gospel

Last Sunday the Israelites were grumbling about food; this Sunday the crowd is murmuring about who Jesus says he is. At least we notice a progression in the discontent—now we are murmuring about what is really important— the identity of Jesus and how we gain eternal life. In reality, murmuring shows shortsightedness more than obstinacy. The Jews were murmuring because of their limited understanding of who Jesus is; after all, "Is this not . . . the son of Joseph?" They were struggling with coming to understand Jesus as more than they immediately perceived. Jesus is trying to teach the crowd that he is the way to eternal life. Furthermore, we can never gain eternal life on our own. Always, it is God's gift. The surprise of the readings this Sunday is how persistent God is in bringing us to new and eternal life.

In the first reading, Elijah is worn out to the point of death. Twice God sends an angel to feed him and set him back on his feet to continue his journey to Horeb, "the mountain of God." In the gospel, despite the murmuring of the crowd, Jesus persists in revealing himself as the bread sent by God to nourish them (and us) for the journey to eternal life. Jesus gives his life so that we might have new life: "the bread that I will give is my flesh for the life of the world." The surprise of the gospel is that Jesus himself, as the "bread . . . from heaven," is both the promise and fulfillment of the eternal life for which we long. Jesus declares himself to be "the living bread" and when we share in this Bread we "will live forever."

The ultimate act of God's persistence in bringing us to new and eternal life is to send the Son who gives his life for us. And herein is another new revelation in the text: the bread of heaven isn't without its cost. For Jesus, the cost is the cross ("the bread that I will give is my flesh for the life of the world"). The bread of life is the bread of self-sacrifice. Here is the real source of the murmuring and here is the giant step forward in this gospel passage: to eat the bread of life is to eat the bread of suffering. To encounter Jesus by eating the bread of life is to take upon ourselves Jesus' life of self-giving. This is why the gospel is so difficult, why the Jews are really murmuring: we, too, must die in order to live forever.

Living the Paschal Mystery

We always like the language about receiving eternal life; language about death and self-sacrifice is much more difficult for us to take in. However, in the mystery of Christ we are reminded that the two always go together. If we wish to live, we must be willing to die to ourselves. Lest we get too discouraged, we must always remember that the paschal mystery is a rhythm of dying and rising. We are able to embrace dying to self because, through Jesus, we know that in the very dying is new life. Jesus has gone before us and taught us that death brings life. The rhythm of the paschal mystery enables us to identify with Jesus in this great mystery of dying and eternity. Cross leads to resurrection. Dying leads to eternal life.

God's persistence in bringing us life is a gift, indeed. But the gift invites more than our own openness to receive it. To receive God's gift of life—Jesus as living bread—is to pledge ourselves also to bring that life of God to others. We are not "come down from heaven"; we have our feet planted firmly on this good earth, giving our own "flesh for the life of the world" through the good we do every day for others.

Focusing the Gospel

Key words and phrases: murmured, bread . . . come down from heaven, I am the bread of life, my flesh for the life of the world

To the point: God is persistent in bringing us to new life. In the first reading, Elijah is worn out to the point of death. Twice God sends an angel to feed him and set him back on his feet to continue his journey to Horeb. In the gospel, despite the murmuring of the crowd, Jesus persists in revealing himself as the bread sent by God to nourish them (and us) for the journey to eternal life. Jesus gives his life so that we might have new life: "the bread that I will give is my flesh for the life of the world."

Connecting the Gospel

to the first reading: In the first reading, the bread Elijah was given strengthened him to reach his goal—the mountain of God. In the gospel, the bread Jesus gives us—his very self—*is* the goal.

to our experience: When someone sets himself or herself up before as "God's gift to humankind," we automatically bristle, so we can understand well the murmuring of the crowd against Jesus in the gospel. In Jesus' case, he speaks out of accurate self-knowledge and a deep desire to give us the life God offers through him.

Connecting the Responsorial Psalm

to the readings: In the beginning of this Sunday's first reading, Elijah is resistant to God. He is tired of life and wants to die. Even after his first feeding by an angel, he wants only to continue sleeping. But God will not leave him to either his despair or his exhaustion. God sends more food and Elijah is strengthened to complete his walk to the mountain.

The food God sent was not just physical bread, however. More importantly, what God sent was the grace to believe and respond. In the gospel reading, Jesus points out to his challengers that anyone who has "learned from" the Father will know whom they encounter when they meet Jesus. In the words of the responsorial psalm, those who have "tasted and seen the goodness of the Lord" will recognize Jesus and come to him. They will hunger for what they have already acquired a taste. As we sing this responsorial psalm, may we who have already been fed by God hunger for more and come gladly to receive the More that is offered.

to cantor preparation: In every verse of this Sunday's responsorial psalm you address the assembly. You sing about your experience of God's goodness and invite them to respond to God with the same confidence and joy. You might spend some time this week reflecting on who and what in your life has led you to "taste and see" God's goodness. Offer God thanksgiving and ask for the grace to hunger for more.

**ASSEMBLY &
FAITH-SHARING GROUPS**

· I am worn out to the point of death when . . . by . . .
· God persistently offers me new life when . . . by . . .
· I have experienced Jesus as the Bread of Life when . . .

PRESIDERS

· I call the people to recognize Jesus as the Bread of Life by . . .

DEACONS

· People experience Jesus as the Bread of Life through my ministry when . . .

HOSPITALITY MINISTERS

· My greeting opens people to receive God's offer of new life when . . .

MUSIC MINISTERS

· When, like Elijah, I am exhausted by the demands of music ministry, Jesus feeds me by . . .

ALTAR MINISTERS

· My ministry enables me to see how Jesus offers me new life when . . .

LECTORS

· My proclamation of the word calls the assembly to new life when . . .

**EXTRAORDINARY MINISTERS
OF HOLY COMMUNION**

· Like the angel ministering to Elijah, I nourish people for their journey to new life in these ways . . .

Model Act of Penitence

Presider: God desires eternal life for us and sent the Son as Bread from heaven to nourish us and strengthen us. Let us prepare ourselves to hear God's word and share in this heavenly Bread . . . [pause]

Lord Jesus, you are the Bread of Life: Lord . . .

Christ Jesus, you are the Promise of eternal life: Christ . . .

Lord Jesus, you give your flesh for the life of the world: Lord . . .

Homily Points

• Children are often picky eaters! Parents respond by saying things like "Eat it, it's good for you" or "Try it, you'll like it," neither of which do the children believe. Yet parents persistently coax their children to try what they know leads to new delights and healthy life. The well-being of their children is why parents persist against the children's balking. Even more is at stake in God's persistence in bringing us to new life.

• Jesus, ever the patient one, is persistent in offering us the bread of life despite any resistance. And he persists even to the point of giving his own life. His sacrifice on the cross is, indeed, bread for our journey and his resurrection is the ultimate promise of new life. This is what we make present in every celebration of Eucharist and in the ordinary circumstances of our lives.

• The bread God offers us in Jesus doesn't always "taste good" because it's the bread of self-sacrifice. Nonetheless, it is necessary to eat this bread in order to have life. We can't be "picky eaters" when it comes to Eucharist and its implications for daily living.

Model Prayer of the Faithful

Presider: The God who offers us new life in Jesus hears our prayers and grants our needs. And so we pray.

Response: Lord, hear our prayer.

Cantor: we pray to the Lord,

For all members of the church, may they persist in bringing new life to others through self-giving lives . . . [pause]

For all peoples of the world, may they persist in seeking God with all their hearts . . . [pause]

For those who are sick and suffering, may they persist in hope and receive what they need for well-being . . . [pause]

For each of us here, may we persist in growing in our understanding of and living the Eucharist . . . [pause]

Presider: God in heaven, you give us your Son as the Bread of Life: hear our prayers and bring us to eternal life. We ask this through Jesus Christ our Lord. **Amen.**

ALTERNATIVE OPENING PRAYER

Let us pray
[that through us others may find the way to life in Christ]

Pause for silent prayer

Father,
we come, reborn in the Spirit,
to celebrate our sonship in the Lord Jesus Christ.
Touch our hearts,
help them grow toward the life you have promised.
Touch our lives,
make them signs of your love for all men.

Grant this through Christ our Lord.
Amen.

FIRST READING
1 Kgs 19:4-8

Elijah went a day's journey into the desert,
until he came to a broom tree and sat beneath it.
He prayed for death, saying:
"This is enough, O LORD!
Take my life, for I am no better than my fathers."
He lay down and fell asleep under the broom tree,
but then an angel touched him and ordered him to get up and eat.
Elijah looked and there at his head was a hearth cake
and a jug of water.
After he ate and drank, he lay down again,
but the angel of the LORD came back a second time,
touched him, and ordered,
"Get up and eat, else the journey will be too long for you!"
He got up, ate, and drank;
then strengthened by that food,
he walked forty days and forty nights
to the mountain of God, Horeb.

RESPONSORIAL PSALM
Ps 34:2-3, 4-5, 6-7, 8-9

R̸. (9a) Taste and see the goodness of the Lord.

I will bless the LORD at all times;
   his praise shall be ever in my mouth.
Let my soul glory in the LORD;
   the lowly will hear me and be glad.

R̸. Taste and see the goodness of the Lord.

Glorify the LORD with me,
   let us together extol his name.
I sought the LORD, and he answered me
   and delivered me from all my fears.

R̸. Taste and see the goodness of the Lord.

Look to him that you may be radiant with
     joy,
   and your faces may not blush with
     shame.
When the afflicted man called out, the
     LORD heard,
   and from all his distress he saved him.

R̸. Taste and see the goodness of the Lord.

The angel of the LORD encamps
   around those who fear him and delivers
     them.
Taste and see how good the LORD is;
   blessed the man who takes refuge in
     him.

R̸. Taste and see the goodness of the Lord.

SECOND READING
Eph 4:30–5:2

Brothers and sisters:
Do not grieve the Holy Spirit of God,
   with which you were sealed for the day
     of redemption.
All bitterness, fury, anger, shouting, and
     reviling
   must be removed from you, along with
     all malice.
And be kind to one another,
     compassionate,
   forgiving one another as God has
     forgiven you in Christ.

So be imitators of God, as beloved
     children, and live in love,
   as Christ loved us and handed himself
     over for us
   as a sacrificial offering to God for a
     fragrant aroma.

About Liturgy

Eucharist, cross, and sacrifice: Eucharist and cross go together because, in the Christian mystery, dying and rising go together. There has been a long-standing tradition in the church to use the image of sacrifice in relation to Eucharist. One aspect of sacrifice surely refers to Jesus' physical death on the cross. Another aspect is that Jesus' death embodies his total giving of himself, holding back nothing. The shedding of his blood is the pouring out of his life for us. Eucharist, as well, is a total giving of himself to us for our strength and nourishment. When we celebrate Eucharist, then, we are doing more than reenacting Calvary and the Last Supper. We are enacting in the present moment the continual gift of Jesus' self-giving. The cross and the Last Supper are once-and-for-all unrepeatable historical events. Jesus' acts of self-giving are an ongoing outpouring of his love for us. But there is more.

Our sharing in Eucharist is the concrete manifestation of our encounter with Christ and our participation in his mystery. Eating and drinking Christ's Body and Blood transforms us more perfectly into being the Body of Christ. This means that we ourselves are better equipped to embrace the dying to self that is an essential prerequisite for rising to eternal life. We must embrace the cross of self-giving each time we share in the Bread of eternal life. This is the power of the mystery: to transform us into believers committed to self-surrender.

About Liturgical Music

The Communion hymn, part 1: The ongoing proclamation of Jesus' Bread of Life discourse is a fitting time to reflect on the purpose of the Communion song. According to GIRM no. 86, the Communion song has three purposes: (1) to express the communicants' unity by means of the unity of their voices, (2) to give evidence of a joyful heart, and (3) to highlight more the common action of the Communion procession.

The first purpose indicates the Communion song is an outward expression of our inward unity in Christ. This means the song is itself sacramental. It both celebrates our communion and assists it to happen. It is never to be lightly omitted, either by the liturgy planners or by an individual member of the assembly who chooses not to sing. For the planners this means keeping in mind, when choosing Communion songs, the assembly's ability to sing them well and easily. For the individual assembly member this means choosing to enter into the communal singing even when the hymn is somewhat unfamiliar, or not to one's liking, or a distraction from private prayer. It means entering in with full heart and letting the community's common voice carry one's singular struggling voice. It means entering in with full heart and letting the text of the hymn transform one's private prayer into the shared prayer of the Body of Christ.

THE ASSUMPTION OF THE BLESSED VIRGIN MARY

SPIRITUALITY

GOSPEL ACCLAMATION

R⁊. Alleluia, alleluia.
Mary is taken up to heaven;
a chorus of angels exults.
R⁊. Alleluia, alleluia.

Gospel   Luke 1:39-56; L622

Mary set out
   and traveled to the hill country in haste
   to a town of Judah,
   where she entered the house of
      Zechariah
   and greeted Elizabeth.
When Elizabeth heard Mary's greeting,
   the infant leaped in her womb,
   and Elizabeth, filled with the Holy Spirit,
   cried out in a loud voice and said,
   "Blessed are you among women,
   and blessed is the fruit of your womb.
And how does this happen to me,
   that the mother of my Lord should
      come to me?
For at the moment the sound of your
      greeting reached my ears,
   the infant in my womb leaped for joy.
Blessed are you who believed
   that what was spoken to you by the
      Lord
   would be fulfilled."

And Mary said:
   "My soul proclaims the greatness of
      the Lord;
   my spirit rejoices in God my Savior
      for he has looked with favor on his
         lowly servant.
   From this day all generations will call
      me blessed:
      the Almighty has done great things
         for me,
      and holy is his Name.
   He has mercy on those who fear him
      in every generation.
   He has shown the strength of his arm,
      and has scattered the proud in their
         conceit.

Continued in Appendix A, p. 303.
See Appendix A, pp. 303–304, for the other readings.

194

Reflecting on the Gospel

The context for Mary speaking her *Magnificat*—the visit to her elderly, pregnant cousin Elizabeth—explains why her heart overflowed with praise of God as well as why the church honors her with this festival. She is "the mother of [our] Lord," to be sure. But more: in saying yes to being the mother of the Redeemer and in going to Elizabeth in her need, Mary demonstrates the heart of discipleship—giving self to bring the Lord's presence to others. For this has God raised her on high.

After the annunciation by Gabriel that she would conceive a Son and name him Jesus, Mary "sets out" to visit her elderly, pregnant cousin Elizabeth. Mary's immediate response to the announcement that she would be the mother of God is one of self-giving and thinking of another in need. Further, Elizabeth's greeting to Mary reveals that Elizabeth perceives that Mary is blessed not only in her pregnancy, but also because she "believed . . . what was spoken to [her] by the Lord." Mary's yes to God and her self-giving in going to Elizabeth expressed God's action through her and the divine desire that the "Lord should come to" us.

Mary's yes unleashed a unique relationship with Jesus and in this she models for us the basis for faithful discipleship—an intimate, enduring relationship with Jesus. For nine months she would nurture in her womb the Life that would bring life to all. For nine months she would give her body so that the Son incarnate might be born. For three months she would stay with Elizabeth, helping the older pregnant cousin come to full term with he who would announce the identity of the fruit of her own womb. Mary is blessed because she said yes to God's invitation to place herself at the disposal of the divine will. Mary is blessed because her body gave life to the Word incarnate. This is why we believe that her body is assumed into heaven: hers was a uniquely blessed body. Mary had the singular privilege of nourishing with her body the Lord. Body and soul, she was assumed into heaven to enjoy eternal life with the divine Word, her Son. Because she said yes. Not just once to Gabriel. Not just to Elizabeth's need. But she said yes that rings out through the centuries into our own hearts, reminding us that life is a gift both received and given.

Living the Paschal Mystery

Mary's yes is a model for our own self-giving and shows us the possibilities of our own intimate relationship with Jesus. When we say yes to God and express it through a life of self-giving, like Mary, we also bear the Lord within us. Our yes to God makes the space within ourselves to be the Body of Christ that nourishes others.

Elizabeth's meeting with Mary caused John in her womb to "leap for joy." Our own yes to the Body of Christ must be so strong that we bring others we meet to leap for joy. Sometimes self-giving can be seen in only a negative, death-dealing sense. And self-giving does involve a dying to self. The gospel for this festival reminds us that there is joy in self-giving as well. The joy that comes from seeing the suffering of another lightened, or a smile brought to the face of someone who is lonely, or the peace of little ones tucked safely into bed for the night is an incarnation in our midst of the Savior. Our self-giving won't lead to any of us being pregnant with the Son of God, nor even to our being led to die on a cross. Our self-giving unfolds in the simple events of our days that embody our own yes to God, which in turn overflows into our own *Magnificat*.

Focusing the Gospel

Key words and phrases: Mary set out, greeted Elizabeth, mother of my Lord, My soul proclaims the greatness of the Lord

To the point: The context for Mary's speaking her *Magnificat*—the visit to her elderly, pregnant cousin Elizabeth—explains why her heart overflowed with praise of God as well as why the church honors her with this festival. She is "the mother of [our] Lord," to be sure. But more: in agreeing to be the mother of the Redeemer and in going to Elizabeth in her need, Mary demonstrates the heart of discipleship—giving self to bring the Lord's presence to others. For this has God raised her on high.

Model Act of Penitence

Presider: We celebrate today the mystery that Mary was taken into heaven body and soul to enjoy eternal life with her divine Son. We prepare to celebrate these sacred mysteries by opening ourselves to God's Word and saying yes to God's invitations . . . [pause]

Lord Jesus, you were the Fruit of Mary's womb: Lord . . .

Christ Jesus, you live in eternal glory, united with Mary your mother: Christ . . .

Lord Jesus, you lift up the lowly and fill the hungry with good things: Lord . . .

Model Prayer of the Faithful

Presider: The God who raises the lowly and fills the hungry will hear our every need. And so we pray.

Response:

Lord, hear our prayer.

Cantor:

we pray to the Lord,

That all members of the church faithfully imitate the openness and self-giving of Mary . . . [pause]

That all people of the world have their fill of God's good things . . . [pause]

That pregnant women bring forth healthy life and nurture their children with love and care . . . [pause]

That we gathered here, like Mary, find holiness in the ordinary circumstances of our daily lives . . . [pause]

Presider: God of our Savior, you entrusted Mary to be the mother of your Son and brought her to share in your eternal glory: hear these our prayers that one day we might share that same glory. We ask this through Christ our Lord. **Amen.**

ALTERNATIVE OPENING PRAYER

Let us pray

Pause for silent prayer

Father in heaven,
all creation rightly gives you praise,
for all life and holiness come from you.
In the plan of your wisdom
she who bore the Christ in her womb
was raised body and soul in glory to be
    with him in heaven.
May we follow her example in reflecting
    your holiness
and join in her hymn of endless life and
    praise.
We ask this through Christ our Lord.
    Amen.

FOR REFLECTION

· Those I must set out to help are . . .
· Like Mary, my self-giving overflows in praise of God when . . .
· Like Mary, God uplifts me when . . .

Homily Points

• Mary was wonderfully open to God and to others. She listened to the many different ways that God spoke to her and, consequently, she was able to perceive and respond to the needs of others. As Jesus' mother, she was the primary role model of these same virtues for him.

• This day we celebrate the heights to which God has raised Mary, yet the gospel reminds us how immersed Mary was in the ordinary circumstances of human life. It is here, in everyday life, that she found holiness. She is not beyond our experience or our imitation.

SPIRITUALITY

GOSPEL ACCLAMATION
John 6:56

R⁊. Alleluia, alleluia.
Whoever eats my flesh and drinks my blood
remains in me and I in him, says the Lord.
R⁊. Alleluia, alleluia.

Gospel   John 6:51-58; L119B

Jesus said to the crowds:
  "I am the living bread
      that came down
      from heaven;
  whoever eats this
      bread will live
      forever;
  and the bread that I
      will give
  is my flesh for the life
      of the world."

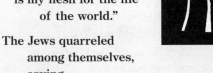

The Jews quarreled
      among themselves,
      saying,
  "How can this man give us his flesh to
      eat?"
Jesus said to them,
  "Amen, amen, I say to you,
  unless you eat the flesh of the Son of
      Man and drink his blood,
  you do not have life within you.
  Whoever eats my flesh and drinks my
      blood
  has eternal life,
  and I will raise him on the last day.
  For my flesh is true food,
  and my blood is true drink.
  Whoever eats my flesh and drinks my
      blood
  remains in me and I in him.
  Just as the living Father sent me
  and I have life because of the Father,
  so also the one who feeds on me
  will have life because of me.
  This is the bread that came down from
      heaven.
  Unlike your ancestors who ate and still
      died,
  whoever eats this bread will live
      forever."

Reflecting on the Gospel

The couple were "empty nesters" as far as their children were concerned, but for the past twelve years the wife's mother had been living with them. At first, she was a great help—especially by having a hot dinner ready for them each night as they came home from work. But as the years rolled by age wasn't so kind to her and she began to diminish in energy and enthusiasm. Then she was diagnosed with terminal cancer. She had only a short time to live. She wanted to die in her familiar surroundings; the couple agreed, knowing full well the round-the-clock care she would need, but not knowing whether she would be with them for weeks or for months. Time passed. The couple continued their loving care. Their heartaches were many: the pain of the wife's mother; her constant demands on their time and patience; the unknowns of the dying process; the struggle to juggle other family obligations, work, full-time care. But the biggest heartache was plaintively expressed by the wife, when she shared with a friend, "I've not been to Mass for so long. I just can't leave Mom nor do I have the energy to get there." Little did this overburdened daughter know that eucharistic acts are as common as bread and wine, as common as the self-sacrificing love we freely give to others.

For four weeks now we've been proclaiming the evangelist John's lofty eucharistic theology. At this point in John's Bread of Life discourse, our table is finally set. Not, however, with meat and wine (see first reading), but with the very Body and Blood of Jesus. Jesus' self-giving, fulfilled on the cross, is now made present in the Eucharist. Our eating his flesh and drinking his blood draws us into this same mystery of self-giving.

The language Jesus uses to describe this food—his very own flesh and blood—is reminiscent of sacrificial language with which the crowds in the gospel would have been familiar. In the Temple the flesh of the sacrificial animals was roasted and eaten and the blood was poured out. To share in the sacrificial meal by eating the roasted flesh was to become a participant in the sacrifice. The victim's life was given to God and, in turn, became food returned from God to the giver. This sacrificial food was no ordinary food; those who gave up the life of the victim received life from the very victim that had been sacrificed.

The mystery of life and death is at the heart of sacrifice. It is at the heart of what Jesus was teaching about his being the "living bread" given for us. The mystery of life and death is at the heart of Eucharist, present to us on the altars of sacrifice during Mass and on the altars of sacrifice of our daily living as we give ourselves over for the good of others.

Living the Paschal Mystery

The development of the Bread of Life discourse leads us to a broader understanding of Eucharist. Jesus' invitation in giving us his flesh and blood to eat and drink is an invitation to enter into his own self-giving. Eucharist is self-giving. We can be self-giving like Jesus because by eating his flesh and drinking his blood we become Jesus, the Body of Christ. This is why we can "remain" in Jesus—we are transformed by what we eat. Our relationship to Jesus, then, becomes a relationship of indwelling, of divine life. This is why Eucharist is a promise of eternal life: because we already have divine life within us.

Eucharist is both gift given and an invitation to self-giving. The mystery of Eucharist strengthens us for our daily dying and rising, our daily giving of ourselves for the sake of others so that we all might share more abundantly in divine life. How can we afford not to say Amen?

Focusing the Gospel

Key words and phrases: bread . . . I will give, flesh for the life of the world, eats my flesh, drinks my blood

To the point: At this point in John's Bread of Life discourse, our table is finally set. Not, however, with meat and wine (see first reading), but with the very Body and Blood of Jesus. Jesus' self-giving, fulfilled on the cross, is now made present in the Eucharist. Our eating his flesh and drinking his blood draws us into this same mystery of self-giving.

Connecting the Gospel

to the first reading: The challenge to "advance in the way of understanding" (first reading) aptly applies to the mystery of the Eucharist. The mystery requires not only that we live it, but that we contemplate its depths and grow in its demands.

to Catholic culture: A venerable Catholic tradition is eucharistic adoration. This adoration flows from our full and active participation in the eucharistic liturgy and leads to a life of self-giving.

Connecting the Responsorial Psalm

to the readings: In the first reading, Wisdom calls both the simple and the foolish to eat of her table so that they may gain true understanding. In the gospel reading, Jesus asks the same of his hearers. What is the food wisdom provides (first reading) and Jesus offers (gospel), if not the goodness of God (psalm)? And what is the goodness of God, if not the person of Jesus come to lay down his life for the world (gospel)?

None of us completely understands the mystery of Christ or of the Eucharist. Rather, we come to the table of the Lord acknowledging our need for deeper understanding. Here we eat of the goodness of God (psalm) and discover, over and over again, that this gift is no mere physical food and drink, but the person of Jesus himself. Feeding on him, we gain understanding and eternal life (gospel). Our faces become radiant and our hearts burn with the desire to tell all those who can hear where true wisdom and life can be found. In singing this responsorial psalm, we proclaim that we have tasted of Jesus and want to call others to the table.

to cantor preparation: As you prepare to call others in this Sunday's responsorial psalm to feast on the goodness of God, you might take some time to reflect on who first called you to the table of the Lord. Who calls you now to keep coming? Who witnesses for you that feasting again and again on the Body and Blood of Christ transforms their life?

ASSEMBLY & FAITH-SHARING GROUPS

· The table God sets for me is . . . The table I set for others is . . .

· What and who have helped me grow in my understanding of the Eucharist are . . . I help others grow in their understanding of Eucharist by . . .

· My daily self-giving is an expression of Eucharist when . . .

PRESIDERS

· My presiding over the Eucharist helps me live the Eucharist in daily life by . . . My daily living Eucharist helps me be a better presider when . . .

DEACONS

· My self-giving ministry brings Eucharist to others in that . . .

HOSPITALITY MINISTERS

· My greeting those who gather for Eucharist is an act of self-giving in that . . .

MUSIC MINISTERS

· Music making is an essential part of "setting the table" for the Eucharist in that . . .

ALTAR MINISTERS

· My setting the altar table helps others enter into the spirit of the Eucharist by . . .

LECTORS

· My proclamation helps the assembly connect the table of the word with the table of the Eucharist when . . .

EXTRAORDINARY MINISTERS OF HOLY COMMUNION

· My ministry calls me to self-giving beyond the act of distributing Holy Communion . . .

Model Act of Penitence

Presider: Jesus invites us in the gospel today to eat his Body and drink his Blood. Let us prepare ourselves to participate in this great mystery . . . [pause]

Lord Jesus, your Body and Blood nourish us for our journey to eternal life: Lord . . .

Christ Jesus, you are the Bread of Life: Christ . . .

Lord Jesus, you are the resurrection and the life: Lord . . .

Homily Points

• If we were asked what are the "eucharistic things" we do in our ordinary daily lives, would the question even make sense to us and what might we answer?

• Sometimes the language Jesus uses in the Bread of Life discourse we hear proclaimed these weeks is so extraordinary as to be beyond our ken and we tune out. This is high theology, indeed! Yet, Jesus also tells us that the mystery of the Eucharist is as ordinary as bread and wine and as common as a meal shared in love.

• Eucharistic living is both lofty and ordinary. Jesus modeled for us how to live this challenge. Daily he spent himself for others: he healed, preached, fed, listened, taught, forgave, prayed, etc. Eucharist is lofty for us in that weekly (for some, even daily) we are privileged to come to the Lord's table and be fed. It is ordinary in that daily we are privileged to spend our lives in sometimes very simple ways for others. The challenge of the gospel is to see in both the lofty and ordinary the mystery of Eucharist.

Model Prayer of the Faithful

Presider: We place our needs before God, mindful that God nourishes us and strengthens us.

Response:

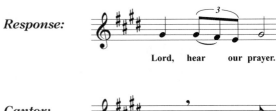

Lord, hear our prayer.

Cantor:

we pray to the Lord,

That members of the church always raise grateful hearts in praise for the gift of Eucharist . . . [pause]

That all nations enjoy the peace that anticipates everlasting life . . . [pause]

That those who are hungry be fed through our kindness . . . [pause]

That all of us nourished by the Eucharist give ourselves in self-sacrifice for the sake of others . . . [pause]

Presider: O wondrous God, you give us the gift of your Son's Body and Blood: hear these our prayers that we might one day live forever with you. We ask this through that same Jesus Christ our Lord. **Amen.**

Let us pray

Pause for silent prayer

God our Father,
may we love you in all things and above
	all things
and reach the joy you have prepared for us
beyond all our imagining.

We ask this through our Lord Jesus Christ,
	your Son,
who lives and reigns with you and the
	Holy Spirit,
one God, for ever and ever. **Amen.**

FIRST READING
Prov 9:1-6

Wisdom has built her house,
	she has set up her seven columns;
she has dressed her meat, mixed her wine,
	yes, she has spread her table.
She has sent out her maidens; she calls
	from the heights out over the city:
"Let whoever is simple turn in here;"
	To the one who lacks understanding,
		she says,
"Come, eat of my food,
	and drink of the wine I have mixed!
Forsake foolishness that you may live;
	advance in the way of understanding."

RESPONSORIAL PSALM
Ps 34:2-3, 4-5, 6-7

R̅. (9a) Taste and see the goodness of the Lord.

I will bless the Lord at all times;
    his praise shall be ever in my mouth.
Let my soul glory in the Lord;
    the lowly will hear me and be glad.

R̅. Taste and see the goodness of the Lord.

Glorify the Lord with me,
    let us together extol his name.
I sought the Lord, and he answered me
    and delivered me from all my fears.

R̅. Taste and see the goodness of the Lord.

Look to him that you may be radiant with
    joy,
    and your faces may not blush with
        shame.
When the poor one called out, the Lord
        heard,
    and from all his distress he saved him.

R̅. Taste and see the goodness of the Lord.

SECOND READING
Eph 5:15-20

Brothers and sisters:
Watch carefully how you live,
    not as foolish persons but as wise,
    making the most of the opportunity,
    because the days are evil.
Therefore, do not continue in ignorance,
    but try to understand what is the will of
        the Lord.
And do not get drunk on wine, in which
        lies debauchery,
    but be filled with the Spirit,
    addressing one another in psalms and
        hymns and spiritual songs,
    singing and playing to the Lord in your
        hearts,
    giving thanks always and for
        everything
    in the name of our Lord Jesus Christ to
        God the Father.

About Liturgy

Mass, Communion, Eucharist: We know that one of our seven sacraments is Eucharist. We also know that it is the third and final of our initiation sacraments (baptism makes us members of the Body of Christ, confirmation seals us through the Holy Spirit in our new identity, Eucharist nourishes us on our life's journey). But if we would survey members of the liturgical assembly about what "Eucharist" means, we would probably get various answers, chief among them being Mass, Communion, or Christ's real Body and Blood. All of these are correct, of course, but a few remarks might clarify these terms.

Mass (the name is derived from the Latin dismissal, *Ite, missa est*) is the ritual action we gather to celebrate at least every Sunday and for some people, almost every day. We call it a "ritual action" because its structure is something that has come down to us through the Tradition of the church and, for the most part, is a sequence of repeated actions; we are familiar with how it unfolds. Mass is broader than Communion, which is one ritual element of Mass, the time during which we process to the altar (the symbol in the sacred space of Christ and his messianic banquet) to receive the Body and Blood of Christ. The term "Eucharist" includes both Mass and Communion, but it also has an even broader meaning. As we have been reflecting on these gospels from John chapter 6, Eucharist includes our giving thanks to God for these wondrous gifts, a thanksgiving that is concretized by our emulating Christ's life of self-giving. Eucharist, then, goes beyond the walls of the church building and characterizes our lives as Christians. The greatest thanks we can give God for this marvelous Gift is to give of ourselves to others to build up the Body of Christ.

About Liturgical Music

The Communion hymn, part 2: GIRM no. 86 indicates the second purpose of the Communion song is to give evidence of a joyful heart. The Communion song is meant to express the joy we experience in being called to the messianic table to feast on the Body and Blood of Christ and become together the one Body of Christ. Appropriate Communion hymns express praise, thanksgiving, joy in being fed and filled, gratitude for being healed and forgiven, gladness in being one in Christ, etc.

This purpose is especially important to keep in mind during the festal seasons when we often sing a seasonal song during Communion. Songs of expectation during Advent, nativity carols during Christmas season, hymns filled with alleluias during Easter season easily accord with expressing our joy of heart at approaching the banquet of eternal life. But songs expressing sorrow or penitence, even when it is Lent, would seem to contradict the spirit of the Communion procession. Even during Lent we need to sing Communion songs that carry an undercurrent of joy. The most appropriate Lenten Communion songs are those that invite us to the greater self-giving, the deeper transformation, and the new ways of living that are the foundations of our eucharistic joy.

✠ SPIRITUALITY

GOSPEL ACCLAMATION
John 6:63c, 68c

R⁷. Alleluia, alleluia.
Your words, Lord, are Spirit and life;
you have the words of everlasting life.
R⁷. Alleluia, alleluia.

Gospel

John 6:60-69; L122B

Many of Jesus' disciples who
    were listening said,
  "This saying is hard; who can
    accept it?"
Since Jesus knew that his
    disciples were murmuring
    about this,
  he said to them, "Does this shock
    you?
What if you were to see the Son of
    Man ascending
  to where he was before?
It is the spirit that gives life,
  while the flesh is of no avail.
The words I have spoken to you are
    Spirit and life.
But there are some of you who do not
    believe."
Jesus knew from the beginning the
    ones who would not believe
  and the one who would betray him.
And he said,
  "For this reason I have told you that
    no one can come to me
  unless it is granted him by my
    Father."

As a result of this,
  many of his disciples returned to
    their former way of life
  and no longer accompanied him.
Jesus then said to the Twelve, "Do you
    also want to leave?"
Simon Peter answered him, "Master, to
    whom shall we go?
You have the words of eternal life.
We have come to believe
  and are convinced that you are the
    Holy One of God."

Reflecting on the Gospel

We have spent the last four Sundays listening to Jesus' teaching about the Bread of Life—and now this Sunday we hear the conclusion to the discourse. Jesus has taught many wondrous things, summarized in the statement that he is the bread of life who brings us eternal life. This is gift beyond imagining. We might think that everyone would be open to this gift. But this Sunday's gospel says otherwise: "many of his disciples returned to their former way of life and no longer accompanied him." So, although the gift is freely given and promises so much, there remains a choice to accept the gift or not. Why would anyone not choose this wondrous gift? Why would many leave? The answers aren't so easy as they appear. We might mistakenly think some of these disciples are just plain stubborn. After all, they've witnessed Jesus' signs; they've seen his wondrous miracles. Why not accept the gift? The answer is really quite simple: the gift has its demands.

Just as Joshua sets before the Israelites a choice ("decide today whom you will serve") so, too, does Jesus set before us a choice ("Do you also want to leave?"). Jesus' teaching about the Eucharist is the fulcrum upon which the choice rests, for it is the Eucharist that draws together our relationship with Jesus as well as with one another in lives of self-giving. And this is what makes choosing the Gift so difficult: the demand of the Gift is that we be like the Giver and give ourselves over for the good of others. On our own, we could not even make such a demanding and all-encompassing choice. But Jesus also reminds us that we are not alone; the Spirit is given us as well and enables us to make the choice to which Jesus calls us.

Choosing Jesus and his teaching requires letting go of what we know of God and allowing God to act in a whole new way toward us. Israel's expectations of God and who the Messiah would be blocked the way for some to see God acting in a new way and offering a whole new way of relating to us. Never before had Israel heard of a God who becomes incarnate and dwells among the people. Never before had God demanded so much of the people—to give one's life for others. To share in Jesus' Body and Blood demands of us this same kind of self-giving. The gift transforms us and in this it makes harsh demands on us, for we become like the Master and can expect to have done to us what the Master had done to him. Choosing to follow Jesus and accept his gift of Self to us is a challenge to see beyond the sacrifice of self-giving and continual dying for the sake of others to the life that comes from this self-sacrifice. It is always good to remember that Jesus is the Bread of Life. Self-giving always leads to new life and this is why we are able to make the choice to stay with the Master—he has "the words of eternal life."

Living the Paschal Mystery

"It is the spirit that gives life." The Holy Spirit dwells within us and is the source of our life in Christ and of our commitment to follow Jesus wholeheartedly. Without the Spirit we would not be able to shoulder the demands of the Gift, and we would return to our "former way of life." The Spirit enables us to enter into the rhythm of paschal mystery living—of dying and rising, of self-giving and celebrating the indwelling of God. Constant vigilance and openness to the Spirit within nudges any halfhearted response to a wholehearted one to choose Jesus and the Gift he offers us.

Focusing the Gospel

Key words and phrases: who can accept, Spirit and life, Do you also want to leave?

To the point: Just as Joshua sets before the Israelites a choice ("decide today whom you will serve") so, too, does Jesus set before us a choice ("Do you also want to leave?"). Jesus' teaching about the Eucharist is the fulcrum upon which the choice rests, for it is the Eucharist that draws together our relationship with Jesus as well as with one another in lives of self-giving. It is the Spirit who enables us to make the choice to which Jesus calls us.

Connecting the Gospel

to the first reading: The Israelites chose to serve the Lord. Our choice to receive Eucharist is also a choice to serve the Lord in one another.

to human experience: It is easier to live out of habit and routine than to see our participation in the Eucharist as a continual choice that carries consequences.

Connecting the Responsorial Psalm

to the readings: The verses from Psalm 34 used this Sunday are different from those used the previous weeks; they move from one voice to many and from past to ongoing tense. These changes subtly capture a progressive development in our understanding of Jesus' gift of himself to us. The gift of God's goodness in Christ is not given for private consumption but for the sake of others, especially the distressed, the brokenhearted, the crushed (psalm). And the gift is not a once-in-a-lifetime bequest of some thing, but a lifelong engagement in a personal relationship. Accepting the gift means making a commitment to this relationship. Peter and the disciples who stood with him did so (gospel) just as did Joshua and the people who stood with him (first reading).

The psalm this Sunday calls us to decide: will we "taste and see the goodness of the Lord"? Will we take on the relationship we have tasted, knowing from the life of Christ the price we will pay?

to cantor preparation: Last week part of your preparation to sing the responsorial psalm included reflection about who first called you to the table of the Lord and who calls you today. This week you might spend time with these reflection questions: Whom do you call to the table? For whom do you witness that your eating and drinking of Christ transforms who you are and how you live?

ASSEMBLY & FAITH-SHARING GROUPS

· The daily choices I continually make are . . .

· I am conscious of the Spirit's help in choosing to be a faithful disciple of Jesus when . . .

· Eucharist deepens my relationship with both God and others by . . .

PRESIDERS

· My presiding helps the assembly choose faithful discipleship when . . . The assembly's participation helps me choose faithful discipleship when . . .

DEACONS

· My self-giving ministry strengthens others' belief in the Eucharist in that . . .

HOSPITALITY MINISTERS

· My manner of greeting reveals my choice to remain faithful to Jesus in that . . .

MUSIC MINISTERS

· My music ministry deepens my participation in the Eucharist by . . .

ALTAR MINISTERS

· My choice to be an altar minister strengthens my discipleship when . . .

LECTORS

· My proclamation of the word reveals whom I have chosen to serve when . . .

EXTRAORDINARY MINISTERS OF HOLY COMMUNION

· My ministry is to serve Holy Communion, but it is also . . .

Model Act of Penitence

Presider: Today's gospel challenges us to choose Jesus as the center of our lives. Let us prepare ourselves to celebrate well this Eucharist in which we encounter Jesus and his call to discipleship . . . [pause]

Lord Jesus, you are the Holy One of God: Lord . . .

Christ Jesus, you are both truth and life: Christ . . .

Lord Jesus, you are the Word of eternal life: Lord . . .

Homily Points

• Every day we make oodles of choices, most of which are unreflective. For example, we buy certain brands out of habit, we follow the same route to work or school, we maintain unchanged attitudes and expectations about others, etc. But when it comes to the more consequential choices of our lives such as marriage, profession, or even vacation, we are much more reflective. With Eucharist, we really cannot afford to be unreflective creatures of habit; more is at stake with this choice than with any other we make.

• The choice for Eucharist is the choice for discipleship. Both Eucharist and discipleship demand the choice to take on the self-giving attitudes and actions of Jesus, to enter into ever deeper relationships with Jesus and others, and to be open to and guided by the Spirit.

• The simple act of gathering for the eucharistic celebration is, therefore, a concrete expression of our choice for discipleship, as well as a call to be accepting, forgiving, supportive, etc. Conversely, our response to the eucharistic celebration is to live out our choice for discipleship.

Model Prayer of the Faithful

Presider: Let us pray that we might make the choice always to be faithful followers of Jesus who is the Bread of Life.

Response:

Lord, hear our prayer.

Cantor:

we pray to the Lord,

That all members of the church choose faithful discipleship without counting the cost . . . [pause]

That the people of the world choose to live in a way open to the Spirit's guidance . . . [pause]

That those who are struggling with serious choices be guided by the Spirit and come to peace . . . [pause]

That we here gathered choose to live Eucharist as a concrete expression of our choice for discipleship . . . [pause]

Presider: Gracious God, your Son Jesus gives us the words of eternal life: hear these our prayers that we might share in your glory. We ask this through that same Jesus Christ our Lord. **Amen.**

Let us pray

Pause for silent prayer

Father,
help us to seek the values
that will bring us lasting joy in this
    changing world.
In our desire for what you promise
make us one in mind and heart.

Grant this through our Lord Jesus Christ,
    your Son,
who lives and reigns with you and the
    Holy Spirit,
one God, for ever and ever. **Amen.**

FIRST READING
Josh 24:1-2a, 15-17, 18b

Joshua gathered together all the tribes of
    Israel at Shechem,
    summoning their elders, their leaders,
    their judges, and their officers.
When they stood in ranks before God,
    Joshua addressed all the people:
    "If it does not please you to serve the
    LORD,
    decide today whom you will serve,
    the gods your fathers served beyond the
    River
    or the gods of the Amorites in whose
    country you are now dwelling.
As for me and my household, we will
    serve the LORD."

But the people answered,
    "Far be it from us to forsake the LORD
    for the service of other gods.
For it was the LORD, our God,
    who brought us and our fathers up out
    of the land of Egypt,
    out of a state of slavery.
He performed those great miracles before
    our very eyes
    and protected us along our entire journey
    and among the peoples through whom
    we passed.
Therefore we also will serve the LORD, for
    he is our God."

RESPONSORIAL PSALM
Ps 34:2-3, 16-17, 18-19, 20-21

℟. (9a) Taste and see the goodness of the
Lord.

I will bless the LORD at all times;
    his praise shall be ever in my mouth.
Let my soul glory in the LORD;
    the lowly will hear me and be glad.

℟. Taste and see the goodness of the Lord.

The LORD has eyes for the just,
    and ears for their cry.
The LORD confronts the evildoers,
    to destroy remembrance of them from
        the earth.

R̸. Taste and see the goodness of the Lord.

When the just cry out, the LORD hears them,
    and from all their distress he rescues
        them.
The LORD is close to the brokenhearted;
    and those who are crushed in spirit he
        saves.

R̸. Taste and see the goodness of the Lord.

Many are the troubles of the just one,
    but out of them all the LORD delivers him;
he watches over all his bones;
    not one of them shall be broken.

R̸. Taste and see the goodness of the Lord.

SECOND READING
Eph 5:21-32

Brothers and sisters:
Be subordinate to one another out of
    reverence for Christ.
Wives should be subordinate to their
    husbands as to the Lord.
For the husband is head of his wife
    just as Christ is head of the church,
    he himself the savior of the body.
As the church is subordinate to Christ,
    so wives should be subordinate to their
        husbands in everything.
Husbands, love your wives,
    even as Christ loved the church
    and handed himself over for her to
        sanctify her,
    cleansing her by the bath of water with
        the word,
    that he might present to himself the
        church in splendor,
    without spot or wrinkle or any such thing,
    that she might be holy and without
        blemish.
So also husbands should love their wives
    as their own bodies.
He who loves his wife loves himself.
For no one hates his own flesh
    but rather nourishes and cherishes it,
    even as Christ does the church,
    because we are members of his body.
For this reason a man shall leave his father
    and his mother
    and be joined to his wife,
    and the two shall become one flesh.
This is a great mystery,
    but I speak in reference to Christ and
        the church.

or Eph 5:2a, 25-32 in Appendix A, p. 304.

About Liturgy

Eucharist—doctrine and response: For all too many Christians Eucharist is a matter primarily of believing in the right teachings. Right doctrine is important—we believe that the substance of the bread and wine truly are changed into the substance of the Body and Blood of Christ. (This is what "transubstantiation" means: substance is changed). We aren't just saying Jesus' Body and Blood are given to us for our nourishment; the change in substance is real. At the same time that we struggle with right doctrine, we are also faced with a choice every time we go to Communion: to become more perfectly the Body of Christ and to live as Jesus did. Eucharist always demands a self-giving response.

Whether our believing in Jesus' Body and Blood stops at the level of doctrine or is carried over into our living is measured by how much over time we (and others) can actually see a difference in our lives. Are we becoming more charitable, more just, more holy? Is this measurable in our everyday actions—for example, do we say fewer unkind words, are we more aware of others' needs, are we happier individuals? Eucharist must make a difference in our lives.

We often hear that we are a eucharistic church, that Eucharist defines who we are. What this means in a nutshell is that we are a self-giving people, concerned always for the good of others. The Eucharist is a great gift; the gift is received not only when we eat and drink Jesus' Body and Blood, but also when we live the self-giving this Gift demands. Eucharist changes us, changes our church, and changes our world. But only when we truly live who we become in Jesus—"the Holy One of God."

About Liturgical Music

The Communion hymn, part 3: The third purpose of the Communion hymn is to highlight the communal action of the Communion procession (see GIRM no. 86). This purpose is two-pronged. First, the song is meant to direct our attention outward toward communal celebration rather than inward toward private prayer. This means that hymns which speak of adoration of the Blessed Sacrament (hymns proper to Benediction and to times of eucharistic adoration) are not appropriate during the Communion procession at Mass. Suitable hymns have texts which speak of our being brought together as the one Body of Christ, as the community of the church, and/or of our mission to be this Body, this church in the world.

Second, the song is meant to support our processional movement to and from the eucharistic table. The procession is symbolic of what is taking place: all of us—the able and the lame, the ready and the not-so-ready, the healed and those in need of healing—march together to the messianic table to celebrate the fullness of our union in Christ as one redeemed body. Our singing is a way that we engage our hearts with our bodies in this important processional movement. And it is a way that we keep ourselves engaged with the whole Body of Christ even after we have concluded our individual movement to and from the table. More than any other activity at this moment in the Mass, our singing together is perhaps the one which most effectively draws us out of our separate worlds into the shared world of the Body of Christ.

AUGUST 23, 2009
TWENTY-FIRST SUNDAY
IN ORDINARY TIME

✠ SPIRITUALITY

GOSPEL ACCLAMATION
James 1:18

R⁄. Alleluia, alleluia.
The Father willed to give us birth by the word
of truth
that we may be a kind of firstfruits of his
creatures.
R⁄. Alleluia, alleluia.

Gospel

Mark 7:1-8, 14-15, 21-23; L125B

When the Pharisees with some
scribes who had come from
Jerusalem
gathered around Jesus,
they observed that some of his
disciples ate their meals
with unclean, that is, unwashed,
hands.
—For the Pharisees and, in fact, all Jews,
do not eat without carefully washing
their hands,
keeping the tradition of the elders.
And on coming from the marketplace
they do not eat without purifying
themselves.
And there are many other things that
they have traditionally observed,
the purification of cups and jugs and
kettles and beds.—
So the Pharisees and scribes
questioned him,
"Why do your disciples not follow the
tradition of the elders
but instead eat a meal with unclean
hands?"
He responded,
"Well did Isaiah prophesy about you
hypocrites, as it is written:
*This people honors me with their
lips,*
but their hearts are far from me;
in vain do they worship me,
*teaching as doctrines human
precepts.*

Continued in Appendix A, p. 304.

Reflecting on the Gospel

The Coca-Cola company put a new product on the shelves—Coke Plus—which was fortified with vitamins. If folks' drink of choice is soda, then the idea is to fortify it with what's good for us. One way or another, we'll get our vitamins! This is an example of the attitude, "Can't lick them, join them": if we are going to drink Coke, then let's put the vitamins we need to stay healthy in that drink. More than we like to think, we tend to do what others do. Most of advertising is based on a "herd mentality" premise. In the gospel today, the Pharisees and scribes have a herd mentality. They questioned Jesus about observing traditions and raise issues of clean and unclean. Jesus' response helps us sort out what enables us to be truly clean, that is, acceptable before God. In their goal to be acceptable before God, some Pharisees and scribes became caught up in mere human traditions. Jesus insists on the priorities of God's Law—that which keeps our hearts focused on God.

The Jewish leaders in this gospel specify religious purity in largely external ritual terms—washing hands, purifying pots, etc. Jesus reconnects law and tradition to the historical context from which they grew and the goal toward which they are oriented: hearts focused on God. Jesus calls us to look at what is deep within us: honoring God or "evils come from within." It is not external behaviors that define religious fidelity, but the internal dispositions of heart from which behavior flows.

What constitutes cleanliness and defilement? Jesus makes clear that cleanliness and defilement are not solely connected to something "outside" like keeping laws. One can keep the letter of the law and miss entirely the point of the law—moral living is a sign of covenantal relationship with God. Israel's taking possession of the land (see first reading) is a realization of salvation—God delivered them from their enemies as a sign that God is faithful to the covenant that God made with Israel. Israel, in turn, is to observe God's commands. But a "wise and intelligent people" doesn't merely keep the commandments; this people knows that the commandments are a sign of their faithful covenantal relationship with God.

Paying mere lip service to God's commands is evidenced by "hearts . . . far from" God; purity before God flows from a heart turned to God. We can't afford only to pay lip service to God. When our hearts are turned to God, we have life. This is what is at stake.

Living the Paschal Mystery

It's easier to clean the pots and pans than to clean one's heart! It's also easy to dismiss this gospel because our tradition has never emphasized this kind of ritual impurity. Yet, the gospel hits home closer than we may think. What traditions do we blindly cling to? Perhaps it is enough for us just to go to Mass on Sunday; after all, this is what most of us grew up doing; this is the "herd mentality" that gives evidence we are Catholics. Or perhaps we cling to rote prayers that we learned as a child rather than stretch our relationship with God to find new prayer expressions. Perhaps we relegate God in our lives to only an hour on Sunday.

We need to look at the way we live, and this will tell us whether we have hearts truly turned toward God—all the time. Purity of heart is expressed in righteous living—self-giving for the sake of others. This is how we have life.

Focusing the Gospel

Key words and phrases: tradition of the elders, honors me, hearts are far from me, from outside, from within

To the point: The Jewish leaders in this gospel specify religious purity in largely external ritual terms—washing hands, purifying pots, etc. Jesus reconnects law and tradition to the historical context from which they grew and the goal toward which they are oriented: hearts focused on God. Jesus calls us to look at what is deep within us: honoring God or "evils come from within." It is not external behaviors that define religious fidelity, but the internal dispositions of heart from which behavior flows.

Connecting the Gospel

to the first reading: God gives us commandments so we "may live." The purpose of keeping the Law is not a matter of blind obedience, but rather about growing closer to the Lord God who has first come "so close" to us.

to human experience: It is easier to do "outside" actions such as cleaning "jugs and kettles" than it is to do the harder work of cleaning one's heart. But it is as we do the "inside" work of the heart that our "outside" actions become pure.

Connecting the Responsorial Psalm

to the readings: Psalm 15 was a liturgical psalm used by the Israelites in a ritual renewal of their covenant with God. The psalm begins with the question, "Lord, who may abide in your tent?" and proceeds to answer the question by describing a person who treats others with justice. The mark of fidelity to the covenant, then, is acting justly toward one's neighbor.

In the first reading Moses commands the people to be faithful to all the statutes and decrees given them by God because the Law was a sign of God's closeness to them and was a guide to justice. When the Pharisees and scribes confront Jesus about the failure of his disciples to keep the ritual laws of washing before eating, they are not concerned with either closeness to God or justice, but with their desire to undermine the authority of Jesus (gospel). Jesus responds by calling the people, literally, back to the heart. Fidelity to the Law comes from living a deep interiorization of its precepts.

This psalm invites us to an interiorized way of living God's Law that will be evident in our acting with justice. In singing it, we proclaim our desire to be persons of "wisdom and intelligence" who are very near to God (first reading).

to cantor preparation: This Sunday's responsorial psalm is different from most because its text is didactic. Rather than offering prayer to God, the psalm offers teachings about right living. This will make the text more difficult to sing unless you turn your preparation time into prayer. Ask God to show you where you need to grow in just living. Ask God for the grace to interiorize this teaching so that it flows out of your being into your daily living.

ASSEMBLY & FAITH-SHARING GROUPS

· The "pots and kettles" which command my attention are . . . I must turn my heart toward . . .

· I would describe my internal dispositions of heart right now as . . .

· When I experience the pull between good and evil within me, Jesus . . .

PRESIDERS

· As a presider, I tend to get caught up in only the externals when . . . What helps me refocus is . . .

DEACONS

· The manner in which I serve others helps them grow in having hearts focused on God when . . .

HOSPITALITY MINISTERS

· My hospitality goes beyond external niceties when . . .

MUSIC MINISTERS

· I find mere human observance shaping my music ministry when . . . What helps me refocus on God is . . .

ALTAR MINISTERS

· My ministry calls me to focus on the "pots and kettles." What helps me put this in perspective is . . .

LECTORS

· What keeps my proclamation from being mere lip service is . . . It originates from a heart near the Lord when . . .

EXTRAORDINARY MINISTERS OF HOLY COMMUNION

· While my distribution of Holy Communion is an external act, it arises from my heart when . . .

Model Act of Penitence

Presider: In the gospel today, Jesus invites us to reflect on whether our behaviors arise from hearts turned to God. Let us open our hearts to hear his life-giving word . . . [pause]

Lord Jesus, you lead us to new life: Lord . . .

Christ Jesus, you summon our hearts to turn toward you: Christ . . .

Lord Jesus, you teach by word and deed: Lord . . .

Homily Points

• "Wash your hands!" "Eat your vegetables!" "Make your bed!" "Stop picking on your little sister!" These are common orders parents give children. From where do these rules come and to what are they directed? They are rules to protect the well-being and health of the children and the relationships within the family.

• Religious commands, too, are rooted in common behaviors that promote well-being and healthy relationships. By the time of Jesus, this connection to the deeper meaning of law and covenant had become glossed over by mere human traditions. Jesus called the Jewish leaders (and the whole community) back to right attitudes and behaviors toward each other rooted in hearts turned to God.

• The gospel today is challenging us to take a serious look at where our hearts lie and why we do what we do. Do we obey laws merely out of habit, or because we've been told to do so, or because of peer pressure? On the other hand, do we obey laws because we have internalized the love of God and neighbor toward which law directs us? The gospel reminds us that the ultimate measure of how we regard law is the growth of our relationships with each other and with our God. Ultimately, this is what Jesus gave his very life for, and there was no law about that.

Model Prayer of the Faithful

Presider: Keeping God's commandments and living rightly is demanding. Let us pray for the strength to have hearts turned to God.

Response: Lord, hear our prayer.

Cantor: we pray to the Lord,

That the actions of all members of the church may always come from hearts turned to God . . . [pause]

That nations not allow cultural traditions and differences to lead to hatred and war . . . [pause]

That the sick and suffering be strengthened by the generosity of this community's tender heart . . . [pause]

That each of us grow in our understanding of God's Law and come to new life . . . [pause]

Presider: All-powerful God, you gave your people commandments to guide them to right relationship with you and each other: hear these our prayers that our hearts may always be turned to you so that one day we might enjoy everlasting life. We ask this through Christ our Lord. **Amen.**

ALTERNATIVE OPENING PRAYER

Let us pray

Pause for silent prayer

Lord God of power and might,
nothing is good which is against your will,
and all is of value which comes from your hand.
Place in our hearts a desire to please you
and fill our minds with insight into love,
so that every thought may grow in wisdom
and all our efforts may be filled with your peace.

We ask this through Christ our Lord.
Amen.

FIRST READING
Deut 4:1-2, 6-8

Moses said to the people:
"Now, Israel, hear the statutes and decrees
which I am teaching you to observe,
that you may live, and may enter in and take possession of the land
which the LORD, the God of your fathers, is giving you.
In your observance of the commandments of the LORD, your God,
which I enjoin upon you,
you shall not add to what I command you nor subtract from it.
Observe them carefully,
for thus will you give evidence
of your wisdom and intelligence to the nations,
who will hear of all these statutes and say,
'This great nation is truly a wise and intelligent people.'
For what great nation is there
that has gods so close to it as the LORD, our God, is to us
whenever we call upon him?
Or what great nation has statutes and decrees
that are as just as this whole law
which I am setting before you today?"

RESPONSORIAL PSALM

Ps 15:2-3, 3-4, 4-5

℟. (1a) The one who does justice will live in the presence of the Lord.

Whoever walks blamelessly and does
     justice;
  who thinks the truth in his heart
  and slanders not with his tongue.

℟. The one who does justice will live in the presence of the Lord.

Who harms not his fellow man,
  nor takes up a reproach against his
       neighbor;
by whom the reprobate is despised,
  while he honors those who fear the
     LORD.

℟. The one who does justice will live in the presence of the Lord.

Who lends not his money at usury
  and accepts no bribe against the
       innocent.
Whoever does these things
  shall never be disturbed.

℟. The one who does justice will live in the presence of the Lord.

SECOND READING

Jas 1:17-18, 21b-22, 27

Dearest brothers and sisters:
All good giving and every perfect gift is
     from above,
  coming down from the Father of lights,
  with whom there is no alteration or
       shadow caused by change.
He willed to give us birth by the word of
     truth
  that we may be a kind of firstfruits of
       his creatures.

Humbly welcome the word that has been
     planted in you
  and is able to save your souls.

Be doers of the word and not hearers only,
     deluding yourselves.

Religion that is pure and undefiled before
     God and the Father is this:
  to care for orphans and widows in their
       affliction
  and to keep oneself unstained by the
       world.

About Liturgy

Second reading fits this Sunday: By happy coincidence the second reading corresponds nicely with the gospel—it gives the counterpart behaviors for the list of sins with which the gospel selection concludes. This would be a good Sunday to spend some time reflecting on the second reading.

Liturgy and life: The gospel's inclusion of the quotation from Isaiah (29:13) is a strong reminder for us of the necessity of an inherent relationship between liturgy and life. The prophets often sounded the warning that worship without right living is not acceptable to God (for example, Micah 6:6-8 and Amos 5:21-24). Our Christian liturgy, however, demands more of us than simply doing just deeds. Our liturgy forms us into a just people so that our good deeds come from within us. Both liturgy and life are rooted in the paschal mystery with its demand to die to self so that we can rise to new life. This isn't something we can do occasionally—it is a way of life.

What is at stake in this way of life is a relationship with God evidenced in keeping God's Law. Obedience goes way beyond blind obedience—it is really about coming closer to the Lord God. Paying attention to the presence of God dwelling within us and then living out of this intimate relationship with the divine is what brings us to the good way of living described in the second reading.

About Liturgical Music

Post-Communion hymn: No. 88 of GIRM repeats the directive of the 1985 Instruction that after Communion the community may spend some time in silent prayer or may sing a psalm or hymn. The singing of a post-Communion hymn is meant to enhance the assembly's sense of eucharistic celebration as a communal act. Having completed the Communion procession, the assembly stands together to sing its communal thanksgiving to the One who has called them to his table, blessed them with nourishment, and transformed them more fully into being the Body of Christ. The text sung should not be one that draws the assembly into private prayer, but one that leads them to communal thanksgiving and praise of God, to celebration of their oneness in Christ, and to the acknowledgment that they have been nourished for mission to the world. The melody should be metrically strong and energetic rather than meditative.

When a post-Communion song is sung, the Communion hymn which precedes it should be ended in ample time to allow for an appropriate transition (GIRM no. 86). A good way to handle this would be to finish the Communion procession with instrumental music only. Furthermore, when singing a post-Communion hymn of praise, it would make sense to omit a recessional hymn.

AUGUST 30, 2009
TWENTY-SECOND SUNDAY IN ORDINARY TIME

✝ SPIRITUALITY

GOSPEL ACCLAMATION
cf. Matt 4:23

R℣. Alleluia, alleluia.
Jesus proclaimed the Gospel of the
    kingdom
and cured every disease among the
    people.
R℣. Alleluia, alleluia.

Gospel

Mark 7:31-37; L128B

**Again Jesus left the district
    of Tyre
    and went by way of Sidon
        to the Sea of Galilee,
    into the district of the
        Decapolis.
And people brought to him a deaf man
    who had a speech impediment
    and begged him to lay his hand on
        him.
He took him off by himself away from
    the crowd.
He put his finger into the man's ears
    and, spitting, touched his tongue;
    then he looked up to heaven and
        groaned, and said to him,
    "Ephphatha!"—that is, "Be
        opened!"—
And immediately the man's ears were
    opened,
    his speech impediment was removed,
    and he spoke plainly.
He ordered them not to tell anyone.
But the more he ordered them not to,
    the more they proclaimed it.
They were exceedingly astonished and
    they said,
    "He has done all things well.
He makes the deaf hear and the mute
    speak."**

Reflecting on the Gospel

We often use "see" metaphorically, going well beyond physical seeing to imply-ing understanding and insight; for example, we use expressions such as "Oh, I see your point," or "I see that you are happy." What enables us to go beyond what is physically evident is a history or relationship with the other person. The better we know someone, the better we can get "inside" of them and "see" what is really going on. When we consider our relationship to God, all our "seeing" is metaphoric. We cannot *see* God, but we can surely come to a deep understanding of God's pres-ence and deeds among us. Signs of God's salvation among us (see first reading) are visible for those who have eyes to see. The people in the gospel are "exceedingly astonished" when they see the deaf and mute man hear and speak; they are fascinated by and proclaim the *miracle*. This is what they first see. Understood only as an external sign, however, the miracle falls short of the reality. What must be proclaimed is not the sign itself, but that to which it points: God's presence bringing salvation (see first reading).

Jesus touches the tongue of the deaf man who could not speak before he commands, "Be opened!" The touch and com-mand unleash a progression of events: a miracle takes place (the man can hear and speak plainly) and the healed man and people proclaim what has taken place. We surmise that something very profound must have happened between Jesus and the deaf man even before the miracle that brought the deaf and mute man to a profound insight about Jesus. Jesus must have communicated some-thing to him that resonated deep within the man's very being and changed him. This is why he could not help but proclaim the miracle—his encounter with Jesus changed him. The deaf man was able to see beyond the miracle to the wholeness (salvation) that Jesus had brought him.

The crowd recognized that Jesus is the fulfillment of Isaiah's prophecy (see first reading) when they say, "He has done all things well. He makes the deaf hear and the mute speak." Jesus' miracle points beyond himself as a miracle worker to himself as the one who has come to save us. The miracles are a sign of salvation—God's new life is breaking in on humanity and changing who we are and giving us a whole new insight into our relationship with God. We now see God's mighty deeds, know Jesus is our savior, and proclaim God's salvation. This Good News cannot be contained.

Living the Paschal Mystery

In terms of Christian discipleship, we must come to know Jesus before we can proclaim who he is. Looking to mighty deeds that we think may be unfolding around us today—reports of miracles, etc.—is not where this gospel leads us. Rather, the gospel leads us to see Christ in the little things around us—the caring touch, the encouraging smile, the unexpected friendly phone call—and interpret these as the real miracles which evidence God's presence and salva-tion. We ought to be "astonished" today by the many manifestations of God's presence in and through the people around us. We ought to be astonished at how God uses us as instruments to proclaim the Good News of salvation. We ought to be so keyed into Jesus' presence that we, too, cannot contain ourselves, but must proclaim God's mighty deeds on our behalf.

Focusing the Gospel

Key words and phrases: man's ears were opened, speech impediment was removed, proclaimed it, exceedingly astonished

To the point: The people in the gospel are "exceedingly astonished" when they see the deaf and mute man hear and speak; they are fascinated by and proclaim the *miracle*. Understood only as an external sign, however, the miracle falls short of the reality. What must be proclaimed is not the sign itself, but that to which it points: God's presence bringing salvation (see first reading).

Connecting the Gospel

to the first reading: There's more to this gospel than the healing miracle because there's more to Jesus than being a miracle worker—he is the fulfillment of Isaiah's prophecy ("the ears of the deaf be cleared . . . the tongue of the mute will sing"). This event discloses Jesus as savior: "Here is your God . . . he comes to save you." This is the deepest reality to which the gospel miracle points.

to experience: When we are astonished at something—swept off our feet—we tend to be caught up in what is at hand, what is immediate. Some experiences of astonishment need go no further. Others, however, lead us to the kind of reflection that brings new insight.

Connecting the Responsorial Psalm

to the readings: Psalm 146 is the first of five psalms that together form the conclusion to the whole collection of psalms. These five are a shout of praise to the God who throughout all of human history continually saves the people, transforming impairment to wholeness, injustice to right, and suffering to joy. Isaiah proclaims the promise of God to do these very things (first reading). The gospel story of the healing of the deaf-mute shows us this promise become fully incarnate—touching and touchable—in Jesus.

Yet unlike the psalmist who over and over again commands us to shout praise for God's saving deeds (psalm refrain), Jesus commands the crowd to keep quiet about the miracle they have witnessed. In these contradictory commands, both the psalmist and Jesus want the same thing—that we see beneath the physical miracles to the deeper reality of God at work for our salvation. We are called to do more than merely shout about wonder-working. We are called to shape our lives around God. May this be the praise we offer.

to cantor preparation: In this Sunday's responsorial psalm you tell the story of God's saving deeds and invite the assembly to sing God's praise. In order to sing this story with authenticity, you must yourself believe it. Do you? Do you shape your life according to it? Does the way you live proclaim God's praise?

ASSEMBLY & FAITH-SHARING GROUPS

· I have been "exceedingly astonished" when . . .

· An astonishing incident that led me to deeper insight has been . . .

· An astonishing experience that has led me to reflection on God's nearness was . . . on God's saving power was . . .

PRESIDERS

· The assembly has astonished me and brought me to a deeper understanding of God when . . .

DEACONS

· My service to those in need is a sign of . . .

HOSPITALITY MINISTERS

· My greeting in itself is not important; what is important is . . . and this proclaims to those gathering that . . .

MUSIC MINISTERS

· My music making leads the assembly to a greater sense of God's loving presence when . . .

ALTAR MINISTERS

· The nature of my service is neither extraordinary nor astonishing, but it is a sign of God's saving presence when . . .

LECTORS

· What I proclaim is . . .

EXTRAORDINARY MINISTERS OF HOLY COMMUNION

· I am astonished by the presence of God in those who come forward to receive Holy Communion when . . .

Model Act of Penitence

Presider: Jesus works mighty deeds; in today's gospel he heals the deaf man with the speech impediment. The gospel calls us to look beyond the miracle to see who Jesus is—the One who comes to save us. Let us prepare ourselves to meet this saving God . . . [pause]

Lord Jesus, you come to us with healing touch: Lord . . .

Christ Jesus, you are the Savior of the world: Christ . . .

Lord Jesus, you astonish us with your mighty deeds: Lord . . .

Homily Points

• We have the saying, "missing the forest for the trees," meaning we have a tendency to zero in on details and miss the depth and breadth of the whole picture. For example, parents can be so caught up in the busy-ness of getting children to the next practice or game, the next dance lesson, the next social event, that they can miss being astonished at the real miracle taking place: the children's gradual growth into being independent, wholesome beings.

• In the miracles of Jesus, God's love and concern for us become dramatically evident and present, but these miracles are not ends in themselves—they are not the "trees." They are meant to reveal the deeper reality of all God's saving actions on our behalf. Discipleship—proclaiming what we have seen—entails both seeking deeper insight ourselves into the meaning of Jesus and his ministry as well as leading others to that deeper insight.

• Jesus is still present among us, his disciples, working "miracles" that challenge us to deeper insight into God's presence and saving deeds. For example, when we see someone deaf to words of praise and we help them come to feel better about themselves, our sensitivity to them can be God's saving presence. Or when we stand by someone mute in face of injustice and encourage them to speak out, our support can be God's care and concern.

Model Prayer of the Faithful

Presider: Our God touches us and we are saved. Let us pray that we might be open to such mighty deeds.

Response: Lord, hear our prayer.

Cantor: we pray to the Lord,

That always and everywhere the church proclaim God's mighty deeds . . . [pause]

That leaders of nations be instruments of God's healing touch that brings peace to all . . . [pause]

That the physically, mentally, or spiritually challenged be healed in body or spirit . . . [pause]

That all of us here proclaim the presence of our saving Christ by the way we live . . . [pause]

Presider: Lord our God, you work mighty deeds on our behalf and draw us to yourself by your tender care: in your justice and mercy hear these our prayers. We ask this through Christ our Lord and Savior. **Amen.**

ALTERNATIVE OPENING PRAYER

Let us pray

Pause for silent prayer

Lord our God,
in you justice and mercy meet.
With unparalleled love you have saved us
    from death
and drawn us into the circle of your life.
Open our eyes to the wonders this life sets
    before us,
that we may serve you free from fear
and address you as God our Father.

We ask this in the name of Jesus the Lord.
    Amen.

FIRST READING
Isa 35:4-7a

Thus says the LORD:
    Say to those whose hearts are
        frightened:
        Be strong, fear not!
    Here is your God,
        he comes with vindication;
    with divine recompense
        he comes to save you.
    Then will the eyes of the blind be
        opened,
        the ears of the deaf be cleared;
    then will the lame leap like a stag,
        then the tongue of the mute will sing.
    Streams will burst forth in the desert,
        and rivers in the steppe.
    The burning sands will become pools,
        and the thirsty ground, springs of
            water.

RESPONSORIAL PSALM
Ps 146:7, 8-9, 9-10

℞. (1b) Praise the Lord, my soul!
or:
℞. Alleluia.

The God of Jacob keeps faith forever,
    secures justice for the oppressed,
    gives food to the hungry.
The LORD sets captives free.

℞. Praise the Lord, my soul!
or:
℞. Alleluia.

The LORD gives sight to the blind;
    the LORD raises up those who were
        bowed down.
The LORD loves the just;
    the LORD protects strangers.

℞. Praise the Lord, my soul!
or:
℞. Alleluia.

The fatherless and the widow the LORD
    sustains,
    but the way of the wicked he thwarts.
The LORD shall reign forever;
    your God, O Zion, through all
        generations.
Alleluia.

℞. Praise the Lord, my soul!
or:
℞. Alleluia.

SECOND READING
Jas 2:1-5

My brothers and sisters, show no
    partiality
    as you adhere to the faith in our
        glorious Lord Jesus Christ.
For if a man with gold rings and fine
    clothes
    comes into your assembly,
    and a poor person in shabby clothes
        also comes in,
    and you pay attention to the one
        wearing the fine clothes
    and say, "Sit here, please,"
    while you say to the poor one, "Stand
        there," or "Sit at my feet,"
    have you not made distinctions among
        yourselves
    and become judges with evil designs?

Listen, my beloved brothers and sisters.
Did not God choose those who are poor in
    the world
    to be rich in faith and heirs of the
        kingdom
    that he promised to those who love him?

About Liturgy

Labor Day: This is Labor Day weekend, and it would be appropriate to add a fifth intention at the prayer of the faithful. For example, "That all laborers, by the quality of their work, give witness to God's care and love for all people."

Lectors, assembly, and proclamation of the word: Proclamation involves more than just speaking and hearing. True proclamation demands a commitment of self on the part of both lector and assembly that is evident in the way one lives. This is why being a lector is much more than being a good reader. One might read flawlessly, but the word would not necessarily be proclamation. True proclamation comes from the lived experience of the lector (the individual has already lived God's word during the week before proclamation) and rings so true that it moves the assembly to live the word as well. In other words, proclamation demands something of the proclaimer and something of the hearer. If either is lacking, then the proclamation is lacking.

    Good proclamation requires living what we might call a "spirituality of the word." This means that one isn't a lector just on the Sunday when one proclaims, but is a lector every moment of every day. It also means that the assembly is called to live the word proclaimed as well. Proclamation of God's word becomes a way of life that is evident in the way one speaks in ordinary daily living (kind, uplifting words; no profanity; encouragement and challenge; etc.). A spirituality of the word would also be characterized by one who spends extra time with God's word—the Bible or Lectionary—perhaps reading a few verses every day and keeping them in mind while one goes about the day. In this way God's word becomes so familiar as to become the very words of the individual.

About Liturgical Music

Music suggestions: The text of "When the King Shall Come Again" [found in many hymn books] is strongly related to this Sunday's readings. The tune's rhythmic switching from duple to triple meter plus the surprise of the hemiola (a time pattern in a 3:2 ratio) in the third phrase forces us to pause over what we are singing. Both text and tune would make a strong entrance processional song. "Your Hands, O Lord, in Days of Old" [found in many hymn books] sings of the healing miracles Jesus worked long ago and begs him to continue using his saving power today "In ev'ry street, in ev'ry home. In ev'ry troubled friend" (v. 2). The energetic tune would work well for the entrance procession. In "O Christ, You Speak the Names of God" [BB, JS2] Genevieve Glen looks at the mystery of Christ from multiple angles, inviting us to see in each a different aspect of God's self-revelation and saving presence. The song would be suitable for either the preparation of the gifts or Communion. Finally, Delores Dufner's "Jesus Christ, by Faith Revealed" [PMB, WC, WS] speaks of Christ revealed in the signs of the gathered church, the Word proclaimed, water, oil, Bread and Wine, and in our deeds of justice and charity. The song would make an excellent entrance hymn.

SEPTEMBER 6, 2009
TWENTY-THIRD SUNDAY IN ORDINARY TIME

SPIRITUALITY

GOSPEL ACCLAMATION
Gal 6:14

℟. Alleluia, alleluia.
May I never boast except in the cross of our Lord
through which the world has been crucified to
    me and I to the world.
℟. Alleluia, alleluia.

Gospel

Mark 8:27-35; L131B

Jesus and his disciples set out
    for the villages of Caesarea Philippi.
Along the way he asked his disciples,
    "Who do people say that I am?"
They said in reply,
    "John the Baptist, others Elijah,
    still others one of the prophets."
And he asked them,
    "But who do you say that I am?"
Peter said to him in reply,
    "You are the Christ."
Then he warned them not to tell anyone
    about him.

He began to teach them
    that the Son of Man must suffer greatly
    and be rejected by the elders, the chief
        priests, and the scribes,
    and be killed, and rise after three days.
He spoke this openly.
Then Peter took him aside and began to
    rebuke him.
At this he turned around and, looking at
    his disciples,
    rebuked Peter and said, "Get behind
    me, Satan.
You are thinking not as God does, but as
    human beings do."

He summoned the crowd with his
    disciples and said to them,
    "Whoever wishes to come after me
        must deny himself,
    take up his cross, and follow me.
For whoever wishes to save his life will
    lose it,
    but whoever loses his life for my sake
    and that of the gospel will save it."

Reflecting on the Gospel

We know what it means to reach a point of no return. Sometimes the point of no return is fairly inconsequential, and we just keep doggedly going. For example, we may begin a hike along a trail in a park, and the going is more demanding than we thought. But once we've gone halfway, we know it doesn't make sense to turn back. At other times, the point of no return has far more serious consequences. For example, the strains on a relationship might reach a point of no return and the relationship is terminated. This Sunday's gospel captures a turning point—something of a point of no return—for the disciples.

Jesus asks his disciples a seemingly simple but puzzling question. After all, how long had the disciples been with Jesus? Peter acknowledges that Jesus is the Messiah, but misses the deeper point. He has a preconceived notion of who Jesus is and also of who the Messiah would be. For this reason does Peter take Jesus aside and rebuke him after Jesus makes explicit what will happen to him. But Jesus also makes something else explicit—disciples must also "take up [their] cross" if they are to follow Jesus. The disciples are hardly prepared for the relationship of Jesus' identity as the Christ—the Messiah—to the demands of following him.

The process of growing into discipleship is always a surprise and always a struggle. Jesus is not the Messiah of the disciples' expectations, but One who "must suffer greatly and be rejected"—a surprise because this doesn't make sense; a struggle because this requires that the disciples also must "take up his cross" to follow him. The first reading describes what our commitment to discipleship must look like: we must "set [our] face like flint." It also reveals what enables us to be faithful to the commitment to discipleship: God, our help, upholds us. Alone, the demands of discipleship would be impossible, the struggle beyond us. But with God as our help, we can begin to think as God does, not as humans. And how does God think? Not in terms of beatings, buffets, pain, ridicule, or death as being too great a sacrifice to endure so that all can be brought to new life. God only wills for us what is good for us and what brings us to new life. What we might endure on the road to new life, well, all that is just human setbacks to divine glory. Disciples embrace the surprise and struggle of discipleship because that alone is the road to new life.

Living the Paschal Mystery

This gospel makes explicit the parameters of discipleship: self-denial, bearing hardship. It makes equally explicit why in the world anyone would follow Jesus: because this is the way to have life. Herein is a clear gospel presentation of the paschal mystery: it means death and new life, it means making a choice, it means that we, too, must embrace this way of living if we are to receive the gift of salvation Jesus offers.

It is no small coincidence that this gospel begins with the question of Jesus' identity and then ends with the cost of discipleship. Identity and discipleship are inextricably related because who we are actually is the same as how we follow. Our identity through baptism is that of Body of Christ; by being united with him in identity, we are also united with him in his life, death, *and* resurrection. Unlike him, we will not die on a cross. Like him, we are called to be followers who give themselves for the good of others.

Focusing the Gospel

Key words and phrases: You are the Christ, suffer greatly, Peter . . . began to rebuke him, take up . . . cross, follow me, life

To the point: This Sunday's gospel captures a turning point for the disciples. Peter acknowledges that Jesus is the Messiah, but misses the deeper point. The process of growing into discipleship is always a surprise and always a struggle. Jesus is not the Messiah of their expectations, but One who "must suffer greatly and be rejected"—a surprise because this doesn't make sense; a struggle because this requires that the disciples also must "take up his cross" to follow him. Disciples embrace the surprise and struggle because that alone is the road to new life.

Connecting the Gospel

to the first reading: The first reading describes what our commitment to discipleship must look like: we must "set [our] face like flint." It also reveals what enables us to be faithful to the commitment to discipleship: God, our help, upholds us.

to experience: We naturally shun or put off what is distasteful, difficult, or painful. Yet, we often endure these very things because they are the only road to something we want, for example, completing physical therapy to regain physical well-being.

Connecting the Responsorial Psalm

to the readings: Psalm 116 was a song of thanksgiving prayed by an individual while offering a sacrifice to God in gratitude for having been delivered from grave danger. On this Sunday when both the first reading and gospel place the necessity of death before us, this psalm is our statement of profound confidence in God's ultimate presence and protection. The suffering servant of Isaiah faces persecution without "turn[ing] back" (first reading). Jesus begins to teach that the cost of following him is the cross (gospel). If we remain faithful to discipleship, then, we are indeed in grave danger. But we can face the danger because we know, like the psalmist, that no danger—even death—is greater than God's desire to give us life. With Jesus, then, we can walk resolutely toward our death, knowing that we walk "before the Lord, in[to] the land of the living" (psalm refrain).

to cantor preparation: To sing this psalm well, you must combine confidence in God's protection with willingness to take up the cross. How in your life does the one feed the other?

**ASSEMBLY &
FAITH-SHARING GROUPS**

· Turning points in my life have been . . . Spiritual turning points for me have been . . .

· Times when I have embraced painful or difficult challenges to experience new life have been . . .

· When I hear Jesus' call to carry his cross, I . . .

PRESIDERS

· Ordained ministry has surprised me in that . . . I struggle with it when . . .

DEACONS

· I suffer in my ministry to those in need when . . .

HOSPITALITY MINISTERS

· My manner of greeting supports those gathering for liturgy in carrying their daily cross in that . . .

MUSIC MINISTERS

· The struggles I have met in being faithful to music ministry have brought me new life by . . .

ALTAR MINISTERS

· When I carry the cross in processions, I feel . . .

LECTORS

· My proclamation brings hope and strength to those who struggle with carrying their cross when . . .

**EXTRAORDINARY MINISTERS
OF HOLY COMMUNION**

· My participation in the suffering of Jesus has made me a better eucharistic minister because . . .

Model Act of Penitence

Presider: In today's gospel Jesus makes known that he is the Messiah who will suffer, die, and rise. Let us prepare ourselves to hear his words and his call to follow him through death to new life . . . [pause]

Lord Jesus, you are the Christ who died and rose for our sake: Lord . . .

Christ Jesus, you are Victor over death: Christ . . .

Lord Jesus, you call us to take up your cross and follow you: Lord . . .

Homily Points

• We often create expectations about the way things should be that destroy our ability to appreciate how things actually are. For example, is the Grand Canyon the most breathtaking natural wonder, or just a big hole? Does this restaurant really serve the best meals one will ever eat? It's natural to have expectations, but they must be realistic. Often there is nothing wrong with a reality, but with our expectations of it.

• Because of their expectations, the disciples were not prepared for what Jesus tells them in this Sunday's gospel. Jesus speaks openly of the reality of what it means for him to be the Messiah and what it means to be his disciples. Here we have the reversal of our usual experience, however. Whereas unrealistic expectations often ruin actual experience, Jesus' "reality check" about discipleship opens up possibilities for new and richer life.

• Jesus offers us, his disciples today, the same reality check through our reflection on his words in Scripture, through our sharing in his paschal meal at the eucharistic table, and through the support we offer one another as we share stories of our own experiences of dying and rising.

Model Prayer of the Faithful

Presider: God is our help who upholds us. We are encouraged to ask for all we need.

Response:

Lord,   hear   our   prayer.

Cantor:

we   pray   to   the   Lord,

That all members of the church faithfully follow Jesus even when their difficulties and suffering seem overwhelming . . . [pause]

That the expectations of world leaders be rooted in the real needs of their people . . . [pause]

That those whose cross of suffering seems unbearable be strengthened by the support and care of this Christian community . . . [pause]

That all of us here grow in our conviction that accepting the cross of discipleship is the road to new life . . . [pause]

Presider: Loving God, you sent your Son to be our Messiah and Savior: be with us always as we follow him faithfully and come to eternal life. We ask this through Christ our Lord. **Amen.**

OPENING PRAYER

Let us pray
[that God will keep us faithful in his service]

Pause for silent prayer

Almighty God,
our creator and guide,
may we serve you with all our heart
and know your forgiveness in our lives.

We ask this through our Lord Jesus Christ,
your Son,
who lives and reigns with you and the
Holy Spirit,
one God, for ever and ever. **Amen.**

FIRST READING
Isa 50:4c-9a

The Lord GOD opens my ear that I may
hear;
and I have not rebelled,
have not turned back.
I gave my back to those who beat me,
my cheeks to those who plucked my
beard;
my face I did not shield
from buffets and spitting.

The Lord GOD is my help,
therefore I am not disgraced;
I have set my face like flint,
knowing that I shall not be put to
shame.
He is near who upholds my right;
if anyone wishes to oppose me,
let us appear together.
Who disputes my right?
Let that man confront me.
See, the Lord GOD is my help;
who will prove me wrong?

RESPONSORIAL PSALM
Ps 116:1-2, 3-4, 5-6, 8-9

R̸. (9) I will walk before the Lord, in the
land of the living.
or:
R̸. Alleluia.

I love the LORD because he has heard
my voice in supplication,
because he has inclined his ear to me
the day I called.

R̸. I will walk before the Lord, in the land
of the living.
or:
R̸. Alleluia.

The cords of death encompassed me;
    the snares of the netherworld seized
        upon me;
    I fell into distress and sorrow,
and I called upon the name of the LORD,
    "O LORD, save my life!"

R̸. I will walk before the Lord, in the land
of the living.
    or:
R̸. Alleluia.

Gracious is the LORD and just;
    yes, our God is merciful.
The LORD keeps the little ones;
    I was brought low, and he saved me.

R̸. I will walk before the Lord, in the land
of the living.
    or:
R̸. Alleluia.

For he has freed my soul from death,
    my eyes from tears, my feet from
        stumbling.
I shall walk before the LORD
    in the land of the living.

R̸. I will walk before the Lord, in the land
of the living.
    or:
R̸. Alleluia.

SECOND READING
Jas 2:14-18

What good is it, my brothers and sisters,
    if someone says he has faith but does
        not have works?
Can that faith save him?
If a brother or sister has nothing to wear
    and has no food for the day,
    and one of you says to them,
        "Go in peace, keep warm, and eat well,"
    but you do not give them the necessities
        of the body,
    what good is it?
So also faith of itself,
    if it does not have works, is dead.

Indeed someone might say,
    "You have faith and I have works."
Demonstrate your faith to me without
        works,
    and I will demonstrate my faith to you
        from my works.

About Liturgy

Turning point: This gospel selection from Mark 8 is one of this gospel's two structural climaxes. The other occurs in chapter 15, when the centurion at the foot of the cross exclaims, "Truly this man was the Son of God!" (v. 39). In both instances Jesus' identity is revealed in the context of his suffering and death. These climaxes highlight the overall thrust of Mark's Gospel with its focus on Jesus' identity and the demands of discipleship.

This Sunday might also mark something of a turning point in our own journey through the liturgical year (notice the change in music for the prayer of the faithful). We are into mid-September, a time when the new school year has begun, vacations are over, the feel of fall is beginning to creep in (in the northern states), and we have a sense of "hunkering down." However well we have paid attention or however much we have learned through our journey through Mark's Gospel during Ordinary Time of this year B, it is never too late to ask ourselves two questions: Have we encountered Jesus and learned more of who he is for us? Have we learned better how to shoulder the cost of discipleship, discovered new ways to be faithful, and recognized that in the very dying—in conforming ourselves to Jesus in our own style of self-giving—we are already rising to new life?

About Liturgical Music

Music suggestions: This Sunday marks a turning point in the tenor of the first reading and gospel from now until the close of the liturgical year. Setting his "face like flint" (first reading), Jesus begins his resolute journey to Jerusalem where he will face his passion and death and then be raised to new life (gospel). He makes explicit to his disciples that they, too, must lose their lives if they wish to save them. One way to mark this change is to switch to a different musical setting of the service music for Mass (and why *Living Liturgy*™ changes the musical setting for the prayer of the faithful [see facing page]). The purpose for switching to a different setting is not simply to add variety to the music, but to help us notice the shift in mood occurring with this Sunday.

Hymns that invite us to take up the cross would be appropriate for this Sunday; for example, "Take Up Your Cross," "Only This I Want," "Before the Fruit Is Ripened by the Sun." Because the readings also speak of God's promise to bring life out of death, this might be a good Sunday to sing a post-Communion hymn celebrating resurrection, such as "Sing with All the Saints in Glory."

SPIRITUALITY

GOSPEL ACCLAMATION
cf. 2 Thess 2:14

R⁊. Alleluia, alleluia.
God has called us through the Gospel
to possess the glory of our Lord Jesus Christ.
R⁊. Alleluia, alleluia.

Gospel

Mark 9:30-37; L134B

Jesus and his disciples left
    from there and began a
    journey through Galilee,
but he did not wish anyone
    to know about it.
He was teaching his
    disciples and telling them,
"The Son of Man is to be handed
    over to men
and they will kill him,
and three days after his death the
    Son of Man will rise."
But they did not understand the saying,
    and they were afraid to question him.

They came to Capernaum and, once
    inside the house,
he began to ask them,
"What were you arguing about on the
    way?"
But they remained silent.
They had been discussing among
    themselves on the way
who was the greatest.
Then he sat down, called the Twelve,
    and said to them,
"If anyone wishes to be first,
he shall be the last of all and the
    servant of all."
Taking a child, he placed it in their
    midst,
and putting his arms around it, he
    said to them,
"Whoever receives one child such as
    this in my name, receives me;
and whoever receives me,
    receives not me but the One who sent
    me."

Reflecting on the Gospel

The disciples in this gospel selection are a little bit like the child caught with his or her hand in the cookie jar—sheepish at getting caught, they are reduced to silence. What contrasts this gospel presents! Jesus is speaking of dying; the disciples are speaking of greatness! The disciples "did not understand" yet "were afraid to question" Jesus. The disciples (and all of us humans) are prone to illusions of grandeur; Jesus calls us to "be the last of all." In face of such contrasts, perhaps the only response really is silence. But not a silence of sheepish embarrassment; rather the silence necessary in face of the challenge of the cross.

The context for this gospel selection is significant—"Jesus and his disciples left from there and began a journey . . ." This was a significant journey for two reasons. First, the journey would be to Jerusalem and the cross. Jesus was ready to embrace his mission; the disciples preferred not to understand. Second, Jesus "began a journey" he "did not wish anyone to know about." It is as though Jesus needed uninterrupted time to teach his disciples what he is really about—giving his life for others. In sharp contrast, what is on the disciples' mind is status—"who was the greatest" among them. Undaunted, Jesus doesn't give up, but tries another tack: he says that a disciple must be "the servant of all" and then he does just that by embracing a child. Ultimately, to be the greatest is to be servant, and to be servant is to give one's life. Here is what being "greatest" entails: dying.

The first reading surprises us with exactly how God brings about dying and coming to new life in us. We humans test God and each other all the time; our transgressions are all too evident in the world around us. It is as though we are like those wicked folks in the first reading—we push and push to see how far we can go. Undaunted, God does "take care of" us, but not in the way we think. God did not spare the Son from "revilement and torture"; God delivered him by raising him from death. The same is true for Jesus' disciples. We will be tested and God will care for us, too. But along the way we can expect others to revile us, too. Being a disciple means that we will be obnoxious to some people (those for whom transgression is a way of life). This is the risk of discipleship.

Jesus uses the model of a little child to illustrate his point. Children are innocent and without pretensions. They naturally embody what "least of all" means. This also illustrates to what extent the disciple is to become the "servant of all" by receiving even the "least of all." The total self-emptying that enables one to receive the "least of all" describes the disciple. This is how we receive Jesus—by receiving the least. No one is insignificant. Everyone is worth dying for.

Living the Paschal Mystery

No wonder Jesus focused his time on the journey to Jerusalem on his disciples—this teaching is so hard to hear! No wonder the disciples do not understand—this teaching is so hard to accept! We are no different from the disciples. How often do we fail to come to Jesus to question him so that we can understand the cost of discipleship? We are afraid to question Jesus about discipleship when we choose the easy way that is not discipleship: when we ignore the plea of others for help; when we only spend time with people in our own inner circle; when we harbor racial, sexual, or religious prejudices; when we . . .

Focusing the Gospel

Key words and phrases: The Son of Man is to be handed over, they did not understand, who was the greatest, be . . . servant of all

To the point: In the gospel, Jesus "began a journey" he "did not wish anyone to know about." It is as though Jesus needed uninterrupted time to teach his disciples what he is really about—giving his life for others. In sharp contrast, what is on the disciples' mind is status—"who was the greatest" among them. Undaunted, Jesus doesn't give up, but tries another tack: he says that a disciple must be "the servant of all" and then he does just that by embracing a child. Ultimately, to be the greatest is to be servant, and to be servant is to give one's life.

Connecting the Gospel

to the first reading: ". . . if the just one be the son of God, God will . . . deliver him." God did, indeed, deliver the Son—not by sparing him from "revilement and torture" but by raising him from death.

to biblical culture: The Greek word for "child" [*paidíon*] also means "servant," implying the insignificance of children in Greco-Roman culture where they had no social or legal status. In Isaiah 53:2 "*paidíon*" is used to describe the "suffering servant." Receiving a child/servant is, indeed, receiving Christ who is the suffering servant.

Connecting the Responsorial Psalm

to the readings: The first reading and responsorial psalm for this Sunday present us with markedly different conversations. In the reading, the wicked discuss how to kill a just person who has confronted them for their doings. With cynicism they suggest that God will defend their victim. In the psalm, the just one talks with God about the evil plot being planned. With absolute confidence the just one knows that God will uphold and save him or her.

In the context of the gospel, the first reading and psalm show us that there is no getting out of death, which comes with discipleship. Jesus knows this and tells his disciples. But they fail to understand and fall into a conversation of their own which misses the point: who among them is the greatest? Jesus offers them an alternative view: the greatest is the one who serves. The psalm invites us to enter Jesus' way of thinking, to "freely . . . offer" ourselves in praise of God's goodness. Such offering will lead to justice and service and will cost us our lives. We can make the choice because, like Jesus and the psalmist, we know Who will uphold us.

to cantor preparation: It is one thing to praise God for saving deeds that heal illness, cure disease, end hunger, and protect from destitution (see, for example, the responsorial psalm for the 23rd Sunday). It is another to praise God for upholding you while you undergo death for the sake of discipleship. Discipleship—paschal mystery living—will not protect you from death, but will lead you into death. Can you sing this responsorial psalm with the psalmist's confidence? Can you follow the path laid out by Jesus (gospel)? Do you truly trust that God will uphold you?

ASSEMBLY & FAITH-SHARING GROUPS

· I need uninterrupted time to hear Jesus say to me . . .

· I find myself worrying about status when . . . At these times Jesus gently calls me to be servant by . . .

· I am the least when . . . I am the greatest when . . .

PRESIDERS

· My ordained ministry constantly calls me to die to self. This is a joy to me when . . . This is a burden to me when . . .

DEACONS

· I embrace the least in Jesus' name when . . . I am the one Jesus embraces when . . .

HOSPITALITY MINISTERS

· My greeting incarnates Jesus' words, "Whoever receives one . . . in my name, receives me," when . . .

MUSIC MINISTERS

· Whenever I find myself vying with other music ministers over status, what helps me die to self and choose to be least and servant is . . .

ALTAR MINISTERS

· My ministry naturally draws me to be the "servant of all." This means to me . . .

LECTORS

· What helps me remain undaunted in my efforts to lead people to understand God's word is . . .

EXTRAORDINARY MINISTERS OF HOLY COMMUNION

· When I give the Body of Christ, I also am receiving the Body of Christ. This requires dying to self in that . . .

Model Act of Penitence

Presider: Jesus teaches the disciples in today's gospel about who they ought to be: servants of all. Let us pray during this Mass that we can follow the Master where he went—giving our all, even when it means coming to the cross . . . [pause]

Lord Jesus, you were handed over to die on the cross: Lord . . .

Christ Jesus, you were raised on the third day: Christ . . .

Lord Jesus, you became the Savior of all by being the servant of all: Lord . . .

Homily Points

• How disconcerting we find it when we need to tell another something of great importance and that person is clearly not listening! Their lack of response is hurtful and we experience personal rejection. Oftentimes we decide never again to confide anything of great importance to that person.

• Not so with Jesus. The most important concern of his ministry was to help others grow in new life, and to accomplish this he realized that he must suffer and die. The disciples don't want to hear about it. Jesus doesn't give up on them, but persists in teaching them what he is really about. In this very persistence did Jesus choose to die to self, become servant of all, and continue to lead others to new understanding and life.

• Jesus persists in teaching us today with the same intensity. We hear his word proclaimed, we see his goodness in others, we take up his cross to follow him. In all of this, we too are called to be persistent in doing as Jesus did: die to self and so help each other find new life.

Model Prayer of the Faithful

Presider: Jesus instructs us to become servants of all. Let us pray that we can die to ourselves so we can bring life to others.

Response:

Lord, hear our prayer.

Cantor:

we pray to the Lord,

That all members of the church always make the Sign of the Cross as a pledge of dying to self for the good of others . . . [pause]

That all people come to salvation through a willingness to die to self for the sake of others . . . [pause]

That the least among us be lifted up by the selfless service of others . . . [pause]

That we become servants of all, thus truly being faithful disciples of Jesus . . . [pause]

Presider: O God, you sent your Son to teach us how to serve and care for others: hear these our prayers that we might one day take our place with you in glory. We ask this through Christ our Lord. **Amen.**

OPENING PRAYER

Let us pray
[that we may grow in the love of God
and of one another]

Pause for silent prayer

Father,
guide us, as you guide creation
according to your law of love.
May we love one another
and come to perfection
in the eternal life prepared for us.

Grant this through our Lord Jesus Christ,
your Son,
who lives and reigns with you and the
Holy Spirit,
one God, for ever and ever. **Amen.**

FIRST READING

Wis 2:12, 17-20

The wicked say:
Let us beset the just one, because he is
obnoxious to us;
he sets himself against our doings,
reproaches us for transgressions of the
law
and charges us with violations of our
training.
Let us see whether his words be true;
let us find out what will happen to
him.
For if the just one be the son of God,
God will defend him
and deliver him from the hand of his
foes.
With revilement and torture let us put
the just one to the test
that we may have proof of his
gentleness
and try his patience.
Let us condemn him to a shameful
death;
for according to his own words, God
will take care of him.

RESPONSORIAL PSALM

Ps 54:3-4, 5, 6-8

℞. (6b) The Lord upholds my life.

O God, by your name save me,
   and by your might defend my cause.
O God, hear my prayer;
   hearken to the words of my mouth.

℞. The Lord upholds my life.

For the haughty have risen up against me,
   the ruthless seek my life;
   they set not God before their eyes.

℞. The Lord upholds my life.

Behold, God is my helper;
   the Lord sustains my life.
Freely will I offer you sacrifice;
   I will praise your name, O LORD, for its
     goodness.

℞. The Lord upholds my life.

SECOND READING

Jas 3:16–4:3

Beloved:
Where jealousy and selfish ambition exist,
   there is disorder and every foul practice.
But the wisdom from above is first of all
     pure,
   then peaceable, gentle, compliant,
   full of mercy and good fruits,
   without inconstancy or insincerity.
And the fruit of righteousness is sown in
     peace
   for those who cultivate peace.

Where do the wars
   and where do the conflicts among you
     come from?
Is it not from your passions
   that make war within your members?
You covet but do not possess.
You kill and envy but you cannot obtain;
   you fight and wage war.
You do not possess because you do not
     ask.
You ask but do not receive,
   because you ask wrongly, to spend it on
     your passions.

About Liturgy

Communion and greatness: In this Sunday's gospel the disciples are arguing about "who was the greatest" and Jesus teaches them that true discipleship consists in becoming "the last of all." The dynamic is from greatest to least. It is interesting that in the Communion rite exactly the opposite dynamic happens; we go from least to greatest.

At the invitation of the presider to begin the Communion procession ("This is the Lamb of God . . . Happy are those who are called to his supper") we respond with "Lord, I am not worthy . . ." Before coming to the messianic Table to participate in the Lord's feast we declare that we are the least among God's people. Then we come to the Table and share in the feast and, indeed, become the greatest because we eat the Body and Blood and become what we eat—the Body of Christ.

The biblical source for this familiar liturgical text is Matthew 8:8, where the Capernaum centurion approaches Jesus and asks him to heal his servant. When Jesus answers that he will come, the servant replies, "Lord, I am not worthy to have you enter under my roof . . . only say the word." The centurion's word is a substitution for the visit—Lord, don't come; you only have to give the word. At Communion these words are an invitation to Jesus to visit us, now in the most wondrous gift of his Body and Blood. In addition to a confession of humility, these words we utter just before Communion are also an expression of confidence that our Lord will come to us—to nourish us, heal us, strengthen us, save us.

About Liturgical Music

Music suggestions: "Lord, Whose Love in Humble Service" [found in many hymn books] speaks of Christ as the model of service and calls the church to compassionate service with him. All three of the tunes to which it is set (HOLY MANNA, IN BABILONE, BEACH SPRING) would function well for the entrance procession.

Hymns about carrying the cross, normally reserved for Lent, would also be a good choice for this Sunday. For example, "Before the Fruit Is Ripened by the Sun" [CH, W3] would make an excellent hymn during the preparation of the gifts. Also appropriate for the preparation of the gifts would be Dan Schutte's "Only This I Want" [BB, CBW3, G2, GC]. Depending on which tune chosen, "Take Up Your Cross" [BB, CBW3, CH, GC, RS, WC] would be suitable for either the entrance procession or the preparation of the gifts.

SPIRITUALITY

GOSPEL ACCLAMATION
cf. John 17:17b, 17a

℟. Alleluia, alleluia.
Your word, O Lord, is truth;
consecrate us in the truth.
℟. Alleluia, alleluia.

Gospel Mark 9:38-43, 45, 47-48; L137B

At that time, John said to Jesus,
  "Teacher, we saw someone driving out
      demons in your name,
  and we tried to prevent him because he
      does not follow us."
Jesus replied, "Do not prevent him.
There is no one who performs a mighty deed
      in my name
  who can at the same time speak ill of me.
For whoever is not against us is for us.
Anyone who gives you a cup of water to drink
  because you belong to Christ,
    amen, I say to you, will surely not lose his
      reward.

"Whoever causes one of these little ones who
      believe in me to sin,
  it would be better for him if a great
      millstone
  were put around his neck
  and he were thrown into the sea.
If your hand causes you to sin, cut it off.
It is better for you to enter into life maimed
  than with two hands to go into Gehenna,
  into the unquenchable fire.
And if your foot causes you to sin, cut if off.
It is better for you to enter into life crippled
  than with two feet to be thrown into Gehenna.
And if your eye causes you to sin, pluck it out.
Better for you to enter into the kingdom of
      God with one eye
  than with two eyes to be thrown into
      Gehenna,
  where 'their worm does not die, and the fire
      is not quenched.'"

Reflecting on the Gospel

Anyone who has adolescents or has worked with them knows how important belonging to a group is to them. It's perhaps the most important aspect of their young lives; the need to belong is at the basis of peer group pressure—they will do anything at all in order to belong. Being part of and accepted by a circle of close friends is how these young people begin to sort out their self-identity. It's how they learn who they are. Although as we grow older this intense need for belonging lessens somewhat and it isn't the most important driving force in our lives, adults still have need for membership in groups. Some primary groups are a given—family, for example. Some groups are essential—our work associates, for example. Some groups have membership by choice—social groups and clubs, for example. Whatever the group, we belong because there are advantages. Membership has its privileges. In the gospel this Sunday we hear that mere membership in a group is certainly not the last word. Membership also has its responsibilities. When it comes to membership in the community of disciples, we must take on the vision and goals of Jesus and work diligently to implement them in daily life. This is true discipleship—this ultimately is true membership.

The disciples ask Jesus a question about group membership; Jesus answers with the deeper meaning of what following him really means. Following Jesus is not about being a card-carrying Christian; it's not about having a baptismal certificate framed and hanging on a wall. Even if one is counted a disciple—is part of the group—but causes harm to another, that one is not a follower of Jesus. Following Jesus means that the hard work of discipleship is being true to Jesus, not only in our words but especially in our actions and behaviors. The disciples were worried about other people's behavior who were not part of their group, and Jesus admonishes them to look to their own behavior. We are to root out the cause of sin in us at all costs—root out whatever is not consistent with who Jesus calls us to be. What is at stake is "enter[ing] into the kingdom of God," entering into fullness of life.

Discipleship is decided by our *behavior* rather than by our being in the inner circle. What is crucial to discipleship is how we act. Jesus uses extreme terms to tell us that we must turn from whatever is inconsistent with acting in his name. Any behavior that causes us to sin or to lead others into sin must be cut off. Any attitude that limits the presence and power of the Spirit must also be cut off (see first reading). Being a disciple demands radical choices about how we live and relate to others.

Living the Paschal Mystery

Through our baptismal anointing we truly are prophets (see first reading); all of us are commissioned to speak and do deeds in the Lord's name. Thus baptism is more than initiation into a group—it is the transformation of ourselves into disciples of Christ who follow the Teacher by faithful service "in [his] name." Faithful service is not expressed in occasional good deeds but in ongoing patterns of unselfish, life-giving behaviors.

As a follower of Christ, discipleship means doing something so great as volunteering for one of the liturgical ministries or so simple as taking the garbage out without being asked. It means that our words and actions are consistent with Gospel values. It means that we are ruthless about choosing to cut out behaviors inconsistent with Jesus' values and gentle about choosing to do the works of the Teacher.

Focusing the Gospel

Key words and phrases: belong to Christ, sin, cut it off, It is better, enter into life

To the point: Discipleship is decided by our *behavior* rather than by our being in the inner circle. What is crucial to discipleship is how we act. Jesus uses extreme terms to tell us that we must turn from whatever is inconsistent with acting in his name. Any behavior that causes us to sin or to lead others into sin must be cut off. Any attitude that limits the presence and power of the Spirit must also be cut off (see first reading). Being a disciple demands radical choices about how we live and relate to others.

Connecting the Gospel

to the first reading and baptism: "Would that the LORD might bestow his spirit on them all!" At baptism God does exactly this: gives us the Spirit through whom we are commissioned to speak and do good works in the Lord's name.

to experience: We tend to make decisions based solely on our immediate needs and wants rather than on their effect on us as well as on others. The gospel challenges us that "[i]t is better" to sacrifice the immediate so that we might gain the ultimate—"to enter into life."

Connecting the Responsorial Psalm

to the readings: This Sunday's responsorial psalm reminds us that the stumbling blocks to faithful discipleship arise not only from enemies who oppose us but also from unsuspected regions within our own hearts. The readings this Sunday and last Sunday give us concrete examples. On our journey of discipleship we may find ourselves vying with one another (last Sunday's gospel), being jealous of the good others do (gospel, first reading), or, more seriously, even leading the innocent astray (gospel). Jesus lays down a harsh line of defense against such behaviors: we are to cut off whatever leads us or others to sin (gospel).

The responsorial psalm offers us a softer line of defense: the surest safeguard against infidelity is fidelity to the Law of God. The truth and justice of this Law will lead us to wisdom. Even unconscious movements against God and neighbor will have no "rule over [us]." We can sustain the harsh demands of discipleship when we adhere to a Law that has been lovingly given for our salvation. In singing this responsorial psalm we express our understanding of the life-giving nature of the Law and our willingness to make it our rule of life.

to cantor preparation: As you prepare to sing this Sunday's responsorial psalm, you might reflect on questions such as these: What does the Law of God ask of you? What wisdom have you gained because of your obedience to it? What sacrifices has such obedience required? What joys have resulted?

ASSEMBLY & FAITH-SHARING GROUPS

· My discipleship looks like . . . It calls me to . . .

· What I need to "cut . . . off" in order to be a more faithful disciple is . . .

· An attitude I have which limits the working of the Spirit is . . . I am aware of the Spirit's presence helping me be a better disciple when . . .

PRESIDERS

· The decisive choices I must continually make in order to be a good presider are . . .

DEACONS

· The decisive choices I must continually make in order to serve "these little ones" are . . .

HOSPITALITY MINISTERS

· The decisive choices I must continually make in order to be inclusive in my welcoming those gathering are . . .

MUSIC MINISTERS

· The decisive choices I must continually make in order to do my music making in Jesus' name are . . .

ALTAR MINISTERS

· The decisive choices I must continually make in order that my unobtrusive service lead others to "belong to Christ" are . . .

LECTORS

· The decisive choices I must continually make in order to proclaim God's word effectively are . . .

EXTRAORDINARY MINISTERS OF HOLY COMMUNION

· The decisive choices I must continually make in order to receive all communicants as members of the Body of Christ are . . .

221

Model Act of Penitence

Presider: Discipleship calls us to make radical choices about how we live as followers of Jesus. We ask God's pardon for times we have failed and ask for the strength to be faithful disciples . . . [pause]

Lord Jesus, you are the Word who calls us to discipleship: Lord . . .

Christ Jesus, you are the Way to eternal life: Christ . . .

Lord Jesus, you are the Prophet who teaches all truth: Lord . . .

Homily Points

• We often make difficult choices to gain what we want. For example, we choose what and how we eat in order to have a svelte body; we choose to curtail expenses in order to have money for a new car; we choose certain relationships in order to find support and understanding as well as challenge when we need it. The gospel calls us to make even more radical choices that go beyond our immediate desires.

• Jesus calls us to choose life, even when this involves something extremely radical: cut off whatever behaviors lead ourselves or others away from him and truly acting in his name. Choosing discipleship means aligning our way of thinking and acting to be that of Jesus. Discipleship must shape our daily choices, both in terms of what we curtail (destructive behaviors) and what we expand (our understanding of where and in whom we see the Spirit working). Choose life!

• Membership is by action, not by card. Simply having a card (baptismal certificate) doesn't mean we belong in the deepest sense of what "belonging" truly means. Belonging to the community of the church means taking on the vision and goals of Jesus and working diligently to implement them in daily life. This is true discipleship.

Model Prayer of the Faithful

Presider: We pray now that we may be faithful followers of Jesus the Teacher.

Response:

Cantor:

Lord, hear our prayer.

we pray to the Lord,

That all members of the church be faithful disciples leading others to new life in Christ . . . [pause]

That all peoples be freed from sin and come to eternal life . . . [pause]

That the poor and lowly have their fill of the good things of God . . . [pause]

That all of us here support one another in making the radical choices faithful discipleship demands . . . [pause]

Presider: Good and gracious God, you are merciful to the sinner and kind to those who follow your Son: hear these our prayers that we might one day enjoy with you eternal life. We ask this through that same Son, Jesus Christ our Lord. **Amen.**

OPENING PRAYER

Let us pray

Pause for silent prayer

Father,
you show your almighty power
in your mercy and forgiveness.
Continue to fill us with your gifts of love.
Help us to hurry toward the eternal life
    you promise
and come to share in the joys of your
    kingdom.

Grant this through our Lord Jesus Christ,
    your Son,
who lives and reigns with you and the
    Holy Spirit,
one God, for ever and ever. **Amen.**

FIRST READING

Num 11:25-29

The Lord came down in the cloud and
    spoke to Moses.
Taking some of the spirit that was on
    Moses,
    the Lord bestowed it on the seventy
      elders;
    and as the spirit came to rest on them,
      they prophesied.

Now two men, one named Eldad and the
    other Medad,
    were not in the gathering but had been
      left in the camp.
They too had been on the list, but had not
    gone out to the tent;
    yet the spirit came to rest on them also,
    and they prophesied in the camp.
So, when a young man quickly told Moses,
    "Eldad and Medad are prophesying in
      the camp,"
    Joshua, son of Nun, who from his youth
      had been Moses' aide, said,
    "Moses, my lord, stop them."
But Moses answered him,
    "Are you jealous for my sake?
Would that all the people of the Lord were
    prophets!
Would that the Lord might bestow his
    spirit on them all!"

RESPONSORIAL PSALM

Ps 19:8, 10, 12-13, 14

℟. (9a) The precepts of the Lord give joy to the heart.

The law of the Lord is perfect,
    refreshing the soul;
the decree of the Lord is trustworthy,
    giving wisdom to the simple.

℟. The precepts of the Lord give joy to the heart.

The fear of the LORD is pure,
  enduring forever;
the ordinances of the LORD are true,
  all of them just.

R⁊. The precepts of the Lord give joy to the heart.

Though your servant is careful of them,
  very diligent in keeping them,
yet who can detect failings?
  Cleanse me from my unknown faults!

R⁊. The precepts of the Lord give joy to the heart.

From wanton sin especially, restrain your
    servant;
  let it not rule over me.
Then shall I be blameless and innocent
  of serious sin.

R⁊. The precepts of the Lord give joy to the heart.

SECOND READING
Jas 5:1-6

Come now, you rich, weep and wail over
      your impending miseries.
Your wealth has rotted away, your clothes
      have become moth-eaten,
  your gold and silver have corroded,
  and that corrosion will be a testimony
      against you;
  it will devour your flesh like a fire.
You have stored up treasure for the last
      days.
Behold, the wages you withheld from the
      workers
  who harvested your fields are crying
      aloud;
  and the cries of the harvesters
  have reached the ears of the Lord of
      hosts.
You have lived on earth in luxury and
      pleasure;
  you have fattened your hearts for the
      day of slaughter.
You have condemned;
  you have murdered the righteous one;
  he offers you no resistance.

✝ CATECHESIS

About Liturgy

Penitential rite: If we could go back in time and be present at a Mass celebrated during the first few centuries of the church (say, up until Charlemagne during the ninth century), one of the things that would strike us is that the Mass had much more lengthy petitionary prayer than it has today. In these earlier periods the beginning of the Mass included lengthy petitions which culminated in the opening prayer. The opening prayer used to be called the "collect" because it "collected together" in a general formula all the prayers that had just been prayed. (When the third edition of the Sacramentary is approved and implemented in the U.S. church, the opening prayer will once again be called a "collect.")

In those earlier centuries the *Kyrie* (Lord, have mercy) belonged to the genre of petitionary prayer. It was used at the hours of the Divine Office as well as at Mass. At this time the "Lord, have mercy" was a response to petitions (called "tropes") that were most often presented in the form of a litany; the list of petitions would vary, of course, but usually included prayers for the whole church, clergy, rulers, the people, the sick, benefactors, the poor, and for peace. Eventually in some churches the *Kyrie* stood alone and was simply repeated a number of times—anywhere from three to forty! Another development is that the tropes became an embellishment of the invocation (Lord or Christ). It is this latter form that is used in the models in the Sacramentary for the third form of the penitential rite and the one that we use in *Living Liturgy*™. The *Kyrie* litany "is a chant by which the faithful praise the Lord and implore his mercy" (GIRM no. 52).

The important point to remember is that the beginning of Mass is a time for prayer. This is the time when we dispose ourselves toward God so that God's actions can take root in us and change us, so that our behaviors are more consistent with the vision and values of Jesus.

About Liturgical Music

Music suggestions: Singing an entrance hymn that connects explicitly with the text of the gospel reading unifies the liturgy, but it is not always possible, nor even necessary, to do so. During the season of Ordinary Time any song that speaks of the gathering of the church for worship or of the offering praise to God is a good choice. Some examples of songs which do this well are Delores Dufner's "Sing a New Church" [BB]; Carl Daw's "As We Gather at Your Table" [CBW3, GC2, JS, RS, SS]; Pamela Stotter and Margaret Daly's "Church of God" [CBW3, G2, GC, PMB, RS, WC]; Herman Stuempfle's "We Are Your People" [PMB, RS, SS, WC, WS]; Bob Hurd's "Gather Your People" [BB, GC2, JS]; Fred Pratt Green's "God Is Here! As We His People" [GC, GC2, JS, PMB, RS, SS, W3, WC]; Bob Moore's "Gather We Now" [BB].

This having been said, one hymn which does coincide well with this Sunday's gospel is Bryn Rees' "The Kingdom of God" with its reminder that the kingdom "is challenge and choice." The hymn would make a strong entrance song or recessional.

SEPTEMBER 27, 2009
TWENTY-SIXTH SUNDAY
IN ORDINARY TIME

SPIRITUALITY

GOSPEL ACCLAMATION
1 John 4:12

R̶̅. Alleluia, alleluia.
If we love one another, God remains in us
and his love is brought to perfection in us.
R̶̅. Alleluia, alleluia.

Gospel

Mark 10:2-16; L140B

The Pharisees approached
   Jesus and asked,
"Is it lawful for a
   husband to divorce
   his wife?"
They were testing him.
He said to them in reply,
"What did Moses com-
   mand you?"
They replied,
"Moses permitted a husband to write
   a bill of divorce
and dismiss her."
But Jesus told them,
"Because of the hardness of your
   hearts
he wrote you this commandment.
But from the beginning of creation,
   God made them male and female.
For this reason a man shall leave his
   father and mother
   and be joined to his wife,
   and the two shall become one flesh.
So they are no longer two but one flesh.
Therefore what God has joined together,
   no human being must separate."
In the house the disciples again questioned Jesus about this.
He said to them,
"Whoever divorces his wife and marries another
commits adultery against her;
and if she divorces her husband and
   marries another,
she commits adultery."

Continued in Appendix A, p. 305.

or Mark 10:2-12, in Appendix A, p. 305.

Reflecting on the Gospel

Something of one's interior attitudes and dispositions is often revealed in the face. We might speak of someone with a gentle face: the muscles are relaxed, a smile comes easily, there is openness and welcome written in the softness. We might also speak of someone as having a hard face: the muscles are tight, a smile is seldom seen, the face is stormy and uninviting. We are naturally attracted to gentle persons, naturally avoid those whom we perceive as hard and unyielding. In the gospel for this Sunday Jesus exposes the hardness of the Pharisees' hearts. It challenges us to look deep within our own hearts.

The context for this gospel is confrontation ("They were testing him," "the disciples rebuked them") and the content is about divorce ("Is it lawful for a husband to divorce his wife?"). But digging deeper into the text, we find that the reverberating message of the gospel is about hardness of hearts: "Because of the hardness of your hearts [Moses] wrote you this commandment." The Pharisees show "hardness of . . . hearts" by putting the law of Moses (which allows divorce) ahead of the plan of God ("what God has joined together, no human being must separate"). Even the disciples show "hardness of . . . hearts" in rebuking the children. The plan of God, as revealed in creation (see first reading), is the blueprint for creation's completion. "[H]ardness of . . . hearts" cuts us off from the blueprint. Jesus always challenges human traditions when they diverge from action hindering our entering fully the life and blessing God offers us.

The world in which the Creator blessed marriage is the world before sin. The world in which Jesus and the Pharisees debate divorce is a world in which sin abounds, and so one must be directed by laws. One purpose of law is to delineate clear parameters for making right choices. This is necessary in a world where sin and hard hearts cloud people's judgment and sometimes lead them to make selfish choices rather than self-giving choices. The Pharisees ask about a point of the law and Jesus answers by pointing to God's intention. This gospel presents the tension between God's plan and sin, between the divine ideal and concessions to human weakness. Jesus champions the ideals of unity and goodness embedded in creation and of blessing and compassion offered to little ones.

In the deepest recesses of our hearts, we all desire to live in union with one another as God intends. The gospel intimates that the kingdom of God belongs to those who yield "hardness of . . . hearts" to the open embrace Jesus models. Just as the gospel moves from shortsighted confrontation over Mosaic laws of divorce to Jesus' tender embrace of little children, so must our lives move from our own shortsightedness to the wide embrace of God's ultimate plan—the blessing of union with one another.

Living the Paschal Mystery

God's design for all of creation is that it be harmonious and whole. Paradoxically, it's the rhythm of the paschal mystery—between dying and rising—that keeps us harmonious and whole. Dying to self means that our own selfish interests are not put ahead of the good of another—which promotes harmony. The new life that always comes from self-giving is a sign of wholeness. Always what stands in the way of harmony and wholeness is hardness of heart—our own or another's. The challenge is in the example of Jesus: embrace and bless even the little ones.

Focusing the Gospel

Key words and phrases: testing him, hardness of . . . hearts, Let the children come to me, embraced them, blessed them

To the point: In the deepest recesses of our hearts, we all desire to live in union with one another as God intends. The gospel intimates that the kingdom of God belongs to those who yield "hardness of . . . hearts" to the open embrace Jesus models. Just as the gospel moves from shortsighted confrontation over Mosaic laws of divorce to Jesus' tender embrace of little children, so must our lives move from our own shortsightedness to the wide embrace of God's ultimate plan—the blessing of union with one another.

Connecting the Gospel

to the first reading: God's plan from the very beginning of creation is a suitable partnership between husband and wife. The greatest deterrent to our living in union with one another is "hardness of . . . hearts."

to experience: In human history, divorce has always been problematic. The Pharisees tested Jesus, which is to say they used a thorny issue to nail him. Jesus moves them from a specific theological debate to the larger perspective of the ways of God's kingdom.

Connecting the Responsorial Psalm

to the readings: This Sunday's responsorial psalm is one of a sequential set (Pss 120–134) some scholars suggest were sung by the Israelites as they traveled to Jerusalem for the major feasts every year. Psalm 128 might have been a song of blessing over the people as they began their journey back home. The psalm sings about the blessings which fidelity to "walking in [God's] ways" brings. The Israelites considered the blessings of a happy and fruitful marriage among the greatest signs of God's care and salvation. But the image of the happy family was also the symbol par excellence of Israel's covenant relationship with God. The blessings described—fruitfulness, fulfillment, prosperity, and peace—extended to all Jerusalem. Thus Psalm 128 is not only about the blessings of marriage, but also about the blessings of a way of life faithful to the "ways" of God.

The gospel reading suggests what it means for us to live such a way. We are to surrender any "hardness of heart" we bear toward one another, we are to live in union, we are to become humble and receptive as little children. May our singing of this psalm be a prayer of blessing over one another and over the whole church, that we truly walk in this way.

to cantor preparation: Because on the surface level the text of this Sunday's responsorial psalm addresses only the blessings of marriage and parenthood, it is important that you understand these images as a paradigm of the fruitfulness God pours upon all those who are faithful to the covenant. How has your own fidelity born fruit? How has it done so for others as well as for yourself?

ASSEMBLY & FAITH-SHARING GROUPS

· What helps me live in union with others is . . . I struggle to live in union with others when . . .

· The hardness of heart I experience is . . .

· I experience the tender embrace of Jesus when . . .

PRESIDERS

· My presiding embraces all members of the assembly when I . . .

DEACONS

· My serving others is Jesus' tender embrace of them when . . .

HOSPITALITY MINISTERS

· My greeting enables those gathering for liturgy to be united as the Body of Christ when . . .

MUSIC MINISTERS

· My singing expresses unity in the Body of Christ when . . . My singing disrupts this unity when . . .

ALTAR MINISTERS

· My unobtrusive service witnesses to God's wide embrace of blessing because . . .

LECTORS

· God's word is challenging and demanding. My manner of proclamation helps others embrace it in that . . .

EXTRAORDINARY MINISTERS OF HOLY COMMUNION

· Distributing and receiving Holy Communion is both an embrace by and blessing of God in that . . .

Model Act of Penitence

Presider: The Pharisees in today's gospel show hardness of hearts toward Jesus. Let us begin this liturgy by examining our own hearts and ask for the healing embrace of Jesus . . . [pause]

Lord Jesus, you embrace us and bless us: Lord . . .

Christ Jesus, from the beginning you are the Word of our Creator-God: Christ . . .

Lord Jesus, you bring us unity and peace: Lord . . .

Homily Points

• Sometimes little children are less than ideal in their behavior. For example, they can be picky about what they eat; they get cranky when tired or hungry; they vie to be the center of attention. Yet little children also have admirable traits. For example, they are trusting, open, guileless, unpretentious, without hardness of heart. As we grow older, we learn to be cautious, suspicious, duplicitous. We begin to harden our hearts.

• Throughout his life, Jesus modeled how to approach people and situations with a wide embrace of love and care rather than with hardness of heart. He did not shy away from anyone or any contentiousness because he saw in every person and every situation an opportunity to lead people to union with God and one another.

• We begin life trusting and innocent, but let's face it: life experiences bring all of us to the hardness of heart which breeds discord and disunity. Those open to Jesus' embrace learn to embrace others with his trust and goodness, and thus grow in peace and unity with one another.

Model Prayer of the Faithful

Presider: From the very beginning of creation, we are called to union with God and each other. Let us pray that this union be strong.

Response:

Lord, hear our prayer.

Cantor:

we pray to the Lord,

That all members of the church grow in openness to Jesus' presence and embrace . . . [pause]

That all levels of government enact only laws that promote God's plan for creation . . . [pause]

That the lowly, downtrodden, and the disadvantaged be embraced and given a new hope in life . . . [pause]

That all of us here gathered live in harmony and peace, with our hearts turned only to God . . . [pause]

Presider: Compassionate God, you embrace us and draw us together in peace: hear these our prayers that one day we might enjoy everlasting union with you and your Son, Jesus Christ our Lord. **Amen.**

OPENING PRAYER

Let us pray

Pause for silent prayer

Father,
your love for us
surpasses all our hopes and desires.
Forgive our failings,
keep us in your peace
and lead us in the way of salvation.

We ask this through our Lord Jesus Christ,
    your Son,
who lives and reigns with you and the
    Holy Spirit,
one God, for ever and ever. **Amen.**

FIRST READING
Gen 2:18-24

The LORD God said: "It is not good for the
    man to be alone.
I will make a suitable partner for him."
So the LORD God formed out of the ground
    various wild animals and various birds
        of the air,
    and he brought them to the man to see
        what he would call them;
    whatever the man called each of them
        would be its name.
The man gave names to all the cattle,
    all the birds of the air, and all wild
        animals;
    but none proved to be the suitable
        partner for the man.

So the LORD God cast a deep sleep on the
    man,
    and while he was asleep,
    he took out one of his ribs and closed
        up its place with flesh.
The LORD God then built up into a woman
    the rib
    that he had taken from the man.
When he brought her to the man, the man
    said:
    "This one, at last, is bone of my bones
        and flesh of my flesh;
    this one shall be called 'woman,' for
        out of 'her man' this one has been
            taken."
That is why a man leaves his father and
    mother
    and clings to his wife,
    and the two of them become one flesh.

RESPONSORIAL PSALM
Ps 128:1-2, 3, 4-5, 6

℟. (cf. 5) May the Lord bless us all the days of our lives.

Blessed are you who fear the LORD,
  who walk in his ways!
For you shall eat the fruit of your
    handiwork;
  blessed shall you be, and favored.

℟. May the Lord bless us all the days of our lives.

Your wife shall be like a fruitful vine
  in the recesses of your home;
your children like olive plants
  around your table.

℟. May the Lord bless us all the days of our lives.

Behold, thus is the man blessed
  who fears the LORD.
The LORD bless you from Zion:
  may you see the prosperity of Jerusalem
  all the days of your life.

℟. May the Lord bless us all the days of our lives.

May you see your children's children.
  Peace be upon Israel!

℟. May the Lord bless us all the days of our lives.

SECOND READING
Heb 2:9-11

Brothers and sisters:
He "for a little while" was made "lower
    than the angels,"
  that by the grace of God he might taste
    death for everyone.

For it was fitting that he,
  for whom and through whom all things
    exist,
  in bringing many children to glory,
  should make the leader to their
    salvation perfect through suffering.
He who consecrates and those who are
    being consecrated
  all have one origin.
Therefore, he is not ashamed to call them
  "brothers."

About Liturgy

Lectionary hermeneutic: "Hermeneutic" is a word that means "interpretation." The phrase "Lectionary hermeneutic" means that when the compilers of the Lectionary chose the particular passages for a given day, they had a particular interpretation in mind. The various choices are themselves a kind of interpretation of Sacred Scripture. Thus, the Lectionary isn't just a shortened Bible; it has a built-in interpretive stance that has to do with the unfolding of the liturgical year. Sometimes a particular combination of readings might even lead us to interpret a passage of Scripture in a slightly different way from its context in the Bible. Liturgy is the context for the Lectionary and that celebration provides the interpretive clue. This Sunday's selection of readings is a good case in point.

The second creation account in Genesis that describes the relationship between husband and wife ("and the two of them become one flesh"), the responsorial psalm that speaks of family blessings, and the question the Pharisees in the gospel put to Jesus about divorce would all tend to lead us to focus this Sunday on the relationship of husband and wife, on marriage and divorce, and this is certainly one interpretive direction to take. When we take into account the last verses of the gospel (which is why choosing the longer form of the gospel changes how one might approach the Scriptures for this Sunday) and where we are in Mark's gospel, other interpretive stances emerge, such as delving into the ramifications of "hardness of . . . hearts."

About Liturgical Music

Music suggestions: This Sunday is the third in a row on which Christ uses children or "little ones" (26th Sunday) to teach the meaning of discipleship. An excellent Communion hymn for all three weeks might be Herbert Brokering's "Take the Bread, Children" [RS], set to music by Carl Schalk (also available in a simple choir setting with verses 1-2 split between women and men, verse 3 *a cappella* SATB, and verses 4-5 melody with descant [GIA #G-3368]). In sequence the verses lay out the traditional four-fold action of the Eucharist: take the bread, bless the bread, break the bread, give/eat the bread. Even with the choir version the hymn is somewhat short for the Communion procession and will need to be lengthened with instrumental interludes.

OCTOBER 4, 2009
TWENTY-SEVENTH SUNDAY
IN ORDINARY TIME

SPIRITUALITY

GOSPEL ACCLAMATION
Matt 5:3

R̸. Alleluia, alleluia.
Blessed are the poor in spirit,
for theirs is the kingdom of heaven.
R̸. Alleluia, alleluia.

Gospel   Mark 10:17-30; L143B

As Jesus was setting out on a
      journey, a man ran up,
   knelt down before him, and asked him,
   "Good teacher, what must I do to inherit
      eternal life?"
Jesus answered him, "Why do you call me
      good?
No one is good but God alone.
You know the commandments: *You shall not
      kill;*
   you shall not commit adultery;
   you shall not steal;
   you shall not bear false witness;
   you shall not defraud;
   honor your father and your mother."
He replied and said to him,
   "Teacher, all of these I have observed
      from my youth."
Jesus, looking at him, loved him and said to
      him,
   "You are lacking in one thing.
Go, sell what you have, and give to the poor
   and you will have treasure in heaven; then
      come, follow me."
At that statement his face fell,
   and he went away sad, for he had many
      possessions.

Jesus looked around and said to his
      disciples,
   "How hard it is for those who have wealth
   to enter the kingdom of God!"
The disciples were amazed at his words.
So Jesus again said to them in reply,
   "Children, how hard it is to enter the
      kingdom of God!
It is easier for a camel to pass through the
      eye of a needle
   than for one who is rich to enter the
      kingdom of God."

Continued in Appendix A, p. 305.

Reflecting on the Gospel

Judging from the explosion in the number of game shows on TV and the large viewing audiences they attract, there is really nothing that compares to riches (compare the first reading: "I . . . deemed riches nothing in comparison to [wisdom]"); a whole TV game show network has developed out of our get-rich-with-little-effort craze. When someone wins a fair amount of money, the host usually asks the contestant what he or she plans to do with it. Answers vary, but often include taking a long vacation, buying a house or car, paying off debts. There seems to be a "more is better" attitude that drives us. Once in a great while, though, someone might even mention that they would give some to their favorite charity. But has anyone ever said he or she will give it all away, sell everything else they have and give even that to the poor, and then follow Jesus?

How openly and eagerly the young man in the gospel comes to Jesus! How dejectedly he leaves, for "he went away sad." If we find it hard to follow Jesus, we should not be surprised—it is *very* hard! The man in the gospel, having faithfully kept the commandments, learns that even this is not enough. To follow Jesus we, too, must give all, even—and perhaps especially—what we prize most. The Good News is that by giving all (even our very lives), we are given all—the fullness of life.

Giving our all to follow Jesus doesn't mean that we literally sell everything; we all have family and social obligations that make having things a necessity. Jesus is saying that we can't let possessions (or anything else, for that matter) divide our hearts. Too often possessions possess us; we must let go so only God possesses us. Riches are a stumbling block to following Jesus when they command our attention so that we are not turned toward doing right—which is what following Jesus means.

The man in the gospel turned away from Jesus because he couldn't let go. It's not impossible to enter the kingdom of God because "all things are possible for God." But it is hard to enter the kingdom of God because too often our hearts are divided—we want to let go and follow Jesus at the same time we want to hang onto our possessions and, indeed, even to their commanding our attention and focus of life. Divided hearts just won't do. We can't have and give all to follow Jesus at the same time. The very hard demands of following Jesus include not swerving from what is central to us—allowing ourselves to be possessed by Jesus fully and completely so that we receive the hundredfold promised those who are faithful: "eternal life."

Living the Paschal Mystery

The "rich man" who couldn't "give up" his wealth was not ready to follow Jesus. After all, following Jesus leads to the cross—where everything is given up! Following Jesus goes beyond keeping the commandments to paschal living. This means that "giving up" is more than dispossessing ourselves of what we have. It means that we make our very lives available—this is what following Jesus truly entails. Jesus' teaching about giving up everything is very hard and demanding, but this is the only way to receive a hundredfold now and in eternal life. This is another description of discipleship, of paschal living: "giving up" is dying, receiving a hundredfold now is experienced in terms of already sharing in the glory of eternal life.

Focusing the Gospel

Key words and phrases: ran up, went away sad, How hard, given up everything, followed you, receive a hundred times more, life

To the point: How openly and eagerly the young man in the gospel comes to Jesus! How dejectedly he leaves, for "he went away sad." If we find it hard to follow Jesus, we should not be surprised—it is *very* hard! The man in the gospel, having faithfully kept the commandments, learns that even this is not enough. To follow Jesus we, too, must give all, even—and perhaps especially—what we prize most. The Good News is that by giving all (even our very lives), we are given all—the fullness of life.

Connecting the Gospel

to the first reading: Jesus is the wisdom of God—no riches compare to him and through him all good things come to us.

to experience: It is a human tendency to do the minimum—just enough to get by. According to Jesus, keeping the commandments is the minimum; much more is required.

Connecting the Responsorial Psalm

to the readings: Although in different words, both the young man and the disciples in this Sunday's gospel ask the same question: "How can we be saved?" Jesus answers that salvation comes only through dispossessing self of all that stands in the way of making God the complete focus of one's life. The teaching is hard—the young man walks away from it and the disciples question their ability to do it.

To all who ask, God offers the wisdom to see the reward offered (first reading, psalm, gospel) and the price required (first reading, gospel). The price is nothing less than our willingness to give whatever discipleship costs; the reward is nothing less than all and more than we need to live, now and forever. God alone can give us the wisdom we need to see the reward and the strength we need to pay the price. The narrator in the first reading asks for and joyfully receives these gifts of grace from God. The young man in the gospel asks for what he needs, but turns sadly away when he hears the answer. Today it is we who in the psalm ask for what we need for fullness of life, and it is we who must choose our response.

to cantor preparation: In singing this Sunday's responsorial psalm, you make a dangerous request: you ask God for the "wisdom of heart," which will lead to deeper demands in discipleship. You are, in a sense, the young man in the gospel reading. You are also the disciples who struggle with Jesus' answer. Are you willing to make the request?

ASSEMBLY & FAITH-SHARING GROUPS
- I find it hardest to follow Jesus when . . .
- What I have given up to follow Jesus is . . . What I have yet to give up is . . .
- I have experienced the hundredfold promised to those who follow Jesus in that . . .

PRESIDERS
- What I must give up in order to be a better presider is . . . What I receive is . . .

DEACONS
- What I must give up in order to better serve those in need is . . . What I receive from them is . . .

HOSPITALITY MINISTERS
- What I must give up in order to be more hospitable is . . . What I receive from those gathering for liturgy is . . .

MUSIC MINISTERS
- What I must give up in order to better lead the assembly in song is . . . What I receive in return is . . .

ALTAR MINISTERS
- What I must give up in order to serve the liturgy more effectively is . . . What I receive from serving the liturgy is . . .

LECTORS
- What I must give up in order to proclaim the word of God with authenticity is . . . What I receive when I proclaim is . . .

EXTRAORDINARY MINISTERS OF HOLY COMMUNION
- What I must give up in order to openly and eagerly receive each communicant as the Body of Christ is . . . What I receive from them is . . .

Model Act of Penitence

Presider: Jesus promises a hundredfold abundance to those who give all in order to be his followers. Let us open our hearts to hear his call and to surrender ourselves to being his disciples . . . [pause]

Lord Jesus, you are the good Teacher who shows us the way to eternal life: Lord . . .

Christ Jesus, you are the Savior who gave even your very life for us: Christ . . .

Lord Jesus, you are the Hundredfold who blesses us with all good things: Lord . . .

Homily Points

• What we think gives us a feeling of satisfaction might be, for example, physical possessions, reputation, or power over others. What is curious is that once we have what we thought would make us happy, we find ourselves restless and wanting more. In the gospel, Jesus offers us a completely different and surprising avenue to satisfaction—in order to have all, we must give up all and follow him.

• Jesus' awareness that we must give all we have and are in order to have fullness of life came from his own personal experience. No matter how tired he was, no matter how frustrated he was with people's lack of understanding, no matter how daunted he was by those who opposed him, Jesus reached out to others with an offer of new life. And in giving them life, he himself received risen life and offers that same life to us.

• No matter what our cost of discipleship, what keeps us from not walking away like the man in the gospel is our commitment to Jesus alone as the way to eternal life. Furthermore, as we grow stronger in our commitment, we grow stronger in the realization that our self-giving discipleship not only brings others to deeper love and relationships, but it also strengthens our own love and relationships. This is already the hundredfold.

Model Prayer of the Faithful

Presider: The God who promises a hundredfold to those who follow Jesus will surely hear our prayers and answer our needs.

Response:

Lord, hear our prayer.

Cantor:

we pray to the Lord,

For all baptized followers of Jesus, may they value faithful discipleship more than any earthly possessions . . . [pause]

For all peoples of the world, may they come to peace and justice by keeping God's commandments . . . [pause]

For all those who are poor, may they have a more equitable share in God's abundance through the self-giving of this faith community . . . [pause]

For each of us here, may we have hearts grateful for the hundredfold God has already given us . . . [pause]

Presider: Good God, you provide us with all things and keep us in your loving care: hear these our prayers that one day we might enjoy fullness of life with you in the age to come. We ask this through Christ our Lord. **Amen.**

OPENING PRAYER

Let us pray

Pause for silent prayer

Lord,
our help and guide,
make your love the foundation of our
    lives.
May our love for you express itself
in our eagerness to do good for others.

Grant this through our Lord Jesus Christ,
    your Son,
who lives and reigns with you and the
    Holy Spirit,
one God, for ever and ever. **Amen.**

FIRST READING

Wis 7:7-11

I prayed, and prudence was given me;
    I pleaded, and the spirit of wisdom
        came to me.
I preferred her to scepter and throne,
and deemed riches nothing in comparison
    with her,
    nor did I liken any priceless gem to her;
because all gold, in view of her, is a little
    sand,
    and before her, silver is to be accounted
        mire.
Beyond health and comeliness I loved her,
and I chose to have her rather than the
    light,
    because the splendor of her never yields
        to sleep.
Yet all good things together came to me in
    her company,
    and countless riches at her hands.

RESPONSORIAL PSALM
Ps 90:12-13, 14-15, 16-17

R̊. (14) Fill us with your love, O Lord, and we will sing for joy!

Teach us to number our days aright,
   that we may gain wisdom of heart.
Return, O LORD! How long?
   Have pity on your servants!

R̊. Fill us with your love, O Lord, and we will sing for joy!

Fill us at daybreak with your kindness,
   that we may shout for joy and gladness
      all our days.
Make us glad, for the days when you
      afflicted us,
   for the years when we saw evil.

R̊. Fill us with your love, O Lord, and we will sing for joy!

Let your work be seen by your servants
   and your glory by their children;
and may the gracious care of the LORD our
      God be ours;
   prosper the work of our hands for us!
   Prosper the work of our hands!

R̊. Fill us with your love, O Lord, and we will sing for joy!

SECOND READING
Heb 4:12-13

Brothers and sisters:
Indeed the word of God is living and
      effective,
   sharper than any two-edged sword,
   penetrating even between soul and
      spirit, joints and marrow,
   and able to discern reflections and
      thoughts of the heart.
No creature is concealed from him,
   but everything is naked and exposed to
      the eyes of him
   to whom we must render an account.

About Liturgy

Presentation of the gifts: The entire eucharistic liturgy is an invitation to empty ourselves, to dispossess ourselves of anything that stands in the way of our being transformed more perfectly into the Body of Christ. One concrete symbol of this dispossession takes place at the presentation of the gifts. This procession is more than a practical way to get the bread and wine on the altar; if this were the case, they could simply be placed there by an altar minister after the prayer of the faithful (which, for simplicity, is often what happens during a weekday Mass).

The procession with the bread and wine is symbolic of our own journey from this life to eternal life when we will stand at the messianic banquet "in the age to come." The bread and wine are also symbolic of ourselves; just as the bread and wine are substantially changed into the real Body and Blood of Christ, so are we transformed into more perfect members of that Body. Finally, when the gifts of the community include food, necessities, and money for the poor, this is wonderfully symbolic of our willingness to "give to the poor" and putting Jesus' invitation to follow him into visible practice. It is a concrete way for us to show our willingness not to be possessed by our riches, but to give of ourselves, emptying ourselves to better follow Jesus with an undivided heart. Therefore, the presentation of the gifts is symbolic of our own desire for dispossession—to have an undivided heart when following Jesus.

About Liturgical Music

Music suggestions: "Seek Ye First" fits this Sunday's readings very well and would be a good choice for the preparation of the gifts. Michael Joncas' "The Love of the Lord" relates to both the readings and the responsorial psalm refrain. The verses speak of riches, wealth, honors, all that one cherishes as worthless "in the light of the love of the Lord." The refrain connects this abandonment of all things with the satisfaction that comes from a "share in [Christ's] suffering and death." Because of its meditative mood, this song would work well either as a choir prelude or as an assembly hymn at the preparation of the gifts. Cantor or choir only might sing the verses with the assembly joining in on the refrain.

Another good choice for the preparation of the gifts would be the Shaker song "Simple Gifts." Some hymn books give only the original single verse and refrain, others include additional verses written by Joyce Merman. If the hymn resource used contains only the one verse, the assembly could sing that verse, cantor or choir could sing the additional verses with assembly joining in on the refrain, and everyone could repeat the first verse and refrain at the end. Access to the additional verses can be obtained from Shawnee Press, Inc.

Also suitable this Sunday would be songs about God's Wisdom given to us that we may have fuller life. Ruth Duck's "Holy Wisdom, Lamp of Learning" would fit the preparation of the gifts. Omer Westendorf's "Wisdom's Feast" would be an excellent song for Communion.

✠ SPIRITUALITY

℟. Alleluia, alleluia.
The Son of Man came to serve
and to give his life as a ransom for many.
℟. Alleluia, alleluia.

Gospel   Mark 10:35-45; L146B

James and John, the sons of Zebedee,
    came to Jesus and said to him,
  "Teacher, we want you to do for us
      whatever we ask of you."
He replied, "What do you wish me to do
    for you?"
They answered him, "Grant that in your
    glory
  we may sit one at your right and the
      other at your left."
Jesus said to them, "You do not know
    what you are asking.
Can you drink the cup that I drink
  or be baptized with the baptism with
      which I am baptized?"
They said to him, "We can."
Jesus said to them, "The cup that I drink,
    you will drink,
  and with the baptism with which I am
      baptized, you will be baptized;
  but to sit at my right or at my left is not
      mine to give
  but is for those for whom it has been
      prepared."
When the ten heard this, they became
    indignant at James and John.
Jesus summoned them and said to them,
  "You know that those who are recognized
      as rulers over the Gentiles
  lord it over them,
  and their great ones make their authority
      over them felt.
But it shall not be so among you.
Rather, whoever wishes to be great among
    you will be your servant;
  whoever wishes to be first among you will
      be the slave of all.
For the Son of Man did not come to be served
  but to serve and to give his life as a
      ransom for many."

or Mark 10:42-45

See Appendix A, p. 306.

Reflecting on the Gospel

How often hasn't each of us eagerly agreed to do something, but then we want to back off when we get details and begin to realize the demands. Youngsters eagerly join ball teams seeking the glory of winning, but then parents hassle with them about the responsibility of being faithful to practices despite their demands and pains. We might load up our calendar with social engagements seeking the glory of popularity, but then end up wishing that we had some time alone in quiet. Or elderly grandparents might ask to have the grandchildren visit for a whole week seeking the glory of being needed, but then end up too exhausted to enjoy them. This Sunday's gospel begins with apostles seeking glory, learning that there is more demand to being disciples than would appear, and finally facing that true glory is not found where we usually seek it. We receive true glory when we finally give up pursuing it and instead pursue Jesus and the demanding life he offers.

Like all of us ordinary human beings, James and John seek glory for themselves when they ask Jesus for places at his right and left. Jesus surprises them—and us—by responding that true glory comes only from a life lived and given for others. Sharing in Jesus' glory demands drinking his cup of suffering, being baptized into his death, and becoming the slave of all. Who would think that glory comes out of self-giving, suffering, and dying? What a contradiction!

This gospel does more than predict Jesus' passion and the consequences of being Jesus' disciples. It points to and challenges the basic human tendency to seek fleeting glory and makes clear that the only behavior that brings lasting glory—an eternal share in the glory of Jesus himself—is to embrace who a servant-disciple of Jesus truly is: one who "gives his life" (first reading) for the sake of the other, just as Jesus gave his life.

There is nothing in this life that can bring us lasting glory—the eternal life that has been prepared for us and in which we already share—except self-giving for the sake of others, a self-giving that conforms us more closely to Jesus' own self-identity as the suffering servant. Thus a share in Jesus' glory ultimately means that we faithfully live our baptism into Jesus' death and thus identify with Jesus and his saving work.

Jesus responds to the apostles' request for a share in his glory by saying that discipleship isn't about raw power ("lord it over them," "make their authority felt"). Discipleship is about servanthood, even when it entails suffering and giving one's life (see first reading). The only way to glory is by self-emptying, serving, giving one's life. The apostles weren't ready for this—they abandoned Jesus at his passion and death. Are we ready to follow?

Living the Paschal Mystery

Much of our doing for others is simply part of our everyday circumstances, for example, parents taking care of their children or a worker cooperating with others on a team job. Being the servant of all isn't always something extra or big; most of the time it is simply doing our everyday tasks generously and with integrity while keeping in mind that others are the Body of Christ. If we can do these everyday tasks with loving care, then when something big comes along we won't deny Jesus like the apostles, but will say "we can." And mean it, knowing full well the demands that identity with Christ entails.

Focusing the Gospel

Key words and phrases: glory, cup, baptism, slave

To the point: Like all of us ordinary human beings, James and John seek glory for themselves. Jesus surprises them—and us—by responding that true glory comes only from a life lived and given for others. Sharing in Jesus' glory demands drinking his cup of suffering, being baptized into his death, and becoming the slave of all. Who would think that glory comes out of self-giving, suffering, and dying?

Connecting the Gospel

to the first reading: This selection is read as part of the first reading on Good Friday, drawing us clearly and immediately into Jesus' passion and death. James and John desire glory. Jesus reveals the stark requirement for sharing in his glory: drink his cup of suffering, be baptized into his death.

to our experience: Like James and John, how readily we say "we can" to a commitment which promises glory and appears easy. Jesus, however, hides none of the fine print—our "we can" takes us to the cross.

Connecting the Responsorial Psalm

to the readings: At first glance this Sunday's responsorial psalm seems to have no connection with the readings of the day. But further reflection on the first reading and gospel shows how aptly it has been chosen. In the psalm refrain we pray over and over again for God's mercy. We need God's mercy because of our frequent wanderings from the path of true discipleship. How often like James and John do we want our association with Jesus to be an avenue for our own glory (gospel)? How often do we avoid the death-to-self demands of true identification with him?

We also need God's mercy every time we choose to remain faithful to discipleship. Unlike James and John we know what is in store for those who beg to sit next to Jesus in glory: we must give our life for the sake of others (first reading, gospel). We need the mercy of the One who will lead us through this death to new life and true glory. Our singing of this psalm is a cry for this mercy and a pledge of trust that it will be granted us.

to cantor preparation: As you read this Sunday's responsorial psalm in the context of the first reading and gospel, pay attention to its internal structure. This psalm captures the entire journey of discipleship in three short strophes. In the first strophe you tell the assembly about the trustworthiness of God. In the second you invite them to place their hope in God who will deliver them from death. In the third strophe you speak not to them but for them as you voice surrender to God in hope and trust. As you prepare to sing about this journey, spend some time reflecting on how you walk it and how God supports you along its way.

ASSEMBLY & FAITH-SHARING GROUPS

· The glory I often discover myself seeking is . . . The glory Jesus invites me to seek is . . .

· What helps me drink Jesus' cup of suffering more willingly is . . .

· One person who shows me the glory that comes from self-giving is . . .

PRESIDERS

· The glory I seek from my presiding is . . . The glory I receive from my presiding is . . .

DEACONS

· My ordination calls me to be "slave of all" by . . .

HOSPITALITY MINISTERS

· My hospitality ministry brings me closer to Jesus, the One who "did not come to be served but to serve" when . . .

MUSIC MINISTERS

· I find myself using my music ministry as an avenue to personal glory when . . . Who/what calls me back to a ministry of service is . . .

ALTAR MINISTERS

· I experience "greatness" through my service when . . .

LECTORS

· My preparation of the word leads me to serve others in my daily living when . . .

EXTRAORDINARY MINISTERS OF HOLY COMMUNION

· The cup of Blood that I drink and minister is not only a precious gift of Jesus, but also the demand to live as "slave of all" when . . .

Model Act of Penitence

Presider: In today's gospel Jesus reminds us that we receive glory by becoming the servant of all. Let us prepare to celebrate this liturgy by calling upon the Lord Jesus to help us respond to others the way he did . . . [pause]

Lord Jesus, you gave your life as a ransom for many: Lord . . .

Christ Jesus, through your passion and death you came into everlasting glory: Christ . . .

Lord Jesus, you call us to be servant of all: Lord . . .

Homily Points

• Much of what we recognize in life as "glory" is measured by external accolades such as parades, awards, TV appearances, financial bonuses, etc. Sometimes such accolades are merited; sometimes not; always they are fleeting. Nonetheless, they remain appealing and motivate our behaviors.

• The apostles want a ticker-tape parade; Jesus promises suffering and death as the road to true glory. How different Jesus' glory is! Despite the paradox that it demands dying to self—"be the slave of all"—the glory of which Jesus speaks in the gospel is stronger and more full of life than human "glory."

• What does this fullness of life look like for us and when have we experienced it? Daily we are called to die to ourselves, for example, we forgive when we have been hurt, reach out to those in need, bite our tongue and hold back a cutting remark, speak the truth even when we know it will not be welcome, etc. In these simple acts we experience new life: the strengthening of our relationships with Jesus and each other, the peace we feel when not giving in to hurting another, the sense of integrity that comes from speaking the truth. Ultimately, what must motivate our behavior is Jesus himself, the way he lived, and our being baptized into his very life.

Model Prayer of the Faithful

Presider: Let us confidently approach God's throne of glory and present our needs.

Response:

Lord, hear our prayer.

Cantor:

we pray to the Lord,

For the church, the Body of Christ called to be servant of all . . . [pause]

For world leaders, called to serve the common good of all . . . [pause]

For those suffering and dying, called to be united with Christ in glory . . . [pause]

For all of us here, called to embrace Jesus' life of self-giving . . . [pause]

Presider: Almighty and ever-living God, you always hear the prayers of your humble servants: grant our needs that one day we might share in your eternal glory. We ask this through Christ our Lord. **Amen.**

OPENING PRAYER

Let us pray
[for the gift of simplicity and joy in our service of God and man]

Pause for silent prayer

Almighty and ever-living God,
our source of power and inspiration,
give us strength and joy
in serving you as followers of Christ,
who lives and reigns with you and the
      Holy Spirit,
one God, for ever and ever. **Amen.**

FIRST READING
Isa 53:10-11

The LORD was pleased
   to crush him in infirmity.

If he gives his life as an offering for sin,
   he shall see his descendants in a long
      life,
   and the will of the LORD shall be
      accomplished through him.

Because of his affliction
   he shall see the light in fullness of days;
through his suffering, my servant shall
      justify many,
   and their guilt he shall bear.

RESPONSORIAL PSALM
Ps 33:4-5, 18-19, 20, 22

R̸. (22) Lord, let your mercy be on us, as we place our trust in you.

Upright is the word of the LORD,
  and all his works are trustworthy.
He loves justice and right;
  of the kindness of the LORD the earth
    is full.

R̸. Lord, let your mercy be on us, as we place our trust in you.

See, the eyes of the LORD are upon those
    who fear him,
  upon those who hope for his kindness,
to deliver them from death
  and preserve them in spite of famine.

R̸. Lord, let your mercy be on us, as we place our trust in you.

Our soul waits for the LORD,
  who is our help and our shield.
May your kindness, O LORD, be upon us
  who have put our hope in you.

R̸. Lord, let your mercy be on us, as we place our trust in you.

SECOND READING
Heb 4:14-16

Brothers and sisters:
Since we have a great high priest who has
    passed through the heavens,
  Jesus, the Son of God,
  let us hold fast to our confession.
For we do not have a high priest
  who is unable to sympathize with our
    weaknesses,
  but one who has similarly been tested in
    every way,
  yet without sin.
So let us confidently approach the throne
    of grace
  to receive mercy and to find grace for
    timely help.

About Liturgy

Parish ministry and servanthood: Every Sunday at Mass we see any number of men, women, and children selflessly give of themselves by means of the various liturgical ministries—presiders, deacons, hospitality ministers, music ministers, altar ministers (including servers, sacristans, janitors, environment committee members), lectors, extraordinary ministers of Holy Communion. These are quite visible to all those who come to Sunday Mass. Additionally, there are many other parish ministers (e.g., members of the pastoral council, education board, etc.) who, generally, work behind the scenes. Yet when we add all these numbers together, sad to say, the persons actively ministering in a parish remain a rather small percentage of the whole parish census. Two points might be worth our reflection time.

First, the parish ministries express real servanthood. Many people sacrifice much of themselves in order to minister in their parishes and this is truly part of what Jesus asks when we are to be the servant of all. If we truly believe that the parish is really the people, then being serious about our commitment to follow Christ means that our service begins with our own parish community.

Second, we ought to encourage and thank one another for this faithful commitment of service. One time someone mentioned that she had given selflessly for twenty-three years to her parish and no one had ever come up to her and said "thank you." This is a sad commentary on how much we take for granted! Perhaps our greatest expression of servanthood is to recognize and thank those who selflessly model for us what serving all really means.

This being said, we must always remember that the primary locus for our self-emptying is in serving the world, marketplace, home. The primary role of the church is to serve the world and be a sign of God's reign in our midst.

About Liturgical Music

Singing the Lamb of God: The plea for God's mercy in this Sunday's responsorial psalm refrain makes a great deal of sense in light of the reminder in the first reading and gospel that discipleship means dying with Christ that others might live. Our singing of the Lamb of God at the fraction rite makes the same kind of sense. The Lamb of God is not filler music used to cover the time it takes for the eucharistic ministers to gather in the sanctuary. Rather it is a litany we sing to accompany the presider's action of breaking the bread and preparing it for distribution. It is a litany we sing as a final act of preparation for what we are about to do: eat this Bread and drink this Cup. This Bread is Christ's Body; this Wine, his Blood given for the world. We who consume this Bread become Christ's Body meant to be broken that the world may eat; and we who drink this Wine become his Blood meant to be poured out that others may live. The Lamb of God is a litany of petition that Christ have mercy on us for what we are about to undertake. Do we realize why we are singing these particular words at this particular moment? Do our presiders break the bread with deliberation? Do we watch with attention and awareness? Finally, does the style and tempo of the Lamb of God we sing fit the awesomeness of what we are doing at this moment in the liturgy?

SPIRITUALITY

Gospel

Mark 10:46-52; L149B

As Jesus was leaving Jericho with his
    disciples and a sizable crowd,
  Bartimaeus, a blind man, the son of
      Timaeus,
  sat by the roadside begging.
On hearing that it was Jesus of
    Nazareth,
  he began to cry out and say,
  "Jesus, son of David, have pity on
      me."
And many rebuked him, telling him to
    be silent.
But he kept calling out all the more,
  "Son of David, have pity on me."
Jesus stopped and said, "Call him."
So they called the blind man, saying to
    him,
  "Take courage; get up, Jesus is
      calling you."
He threw aside his cloak, sprang up,
    and came to Jesus.
Jesus said to him in reply, "What do
    you want me to do for you?"
The blind man replied to him, "Master,
    I want to see."
Jesus told him, "Go your way; your
    faith has saved you."
Immediately he received his sight
  and followed him on the way.

Reflecting on the Gospel

Billboards and print ads, media commercials and junk mail are all about entic-
ing us to leap before we think. There is a whole psychology about advertising
that is rooted in making us think we need or want something whether we do or
not. Advertising is about a leap to buy. This Sunday's gospel is about leaps, too.
But these leaps are of a very different kind: they too involve needs and wants,
but also they bring us to leap to action that has everlasting consequences: increase in faith and in steadfastly following Jesus.

In the gospel the blind beggar Bartimaeus makes two leaps. First, he makes
a leap of trust when he cries out to Jesus to "have pity on" him. Then, when
Jesus stops and calls him, he "sprang up"—a leap of anticipation and hope.
Bartimaeus persists in prayer, relies on Jesus' pity, and comes when called. He
receives his sight and is ultimately saved by his faith. We are saved by our own
faith when we pursue Jesus, speak boldly to him of our needs, and say to him
"I want to see" knowing full well that what we are really asking is to follow him
unreservedly as disciples. Faith is the insight of action. It is a leap that brings
salvation.

This gospel gives us a blueprint for faith and salvation—both what they
are and what they demand. The dynamic between Bartimaeus and Jesus is a
perfect description of what faith is: Bartimaeus heard Jesus, cried out to him,
persisted in his prayer, came to Jesus when he called, and then spoke boldly of
his need. All these actions—hearing, crying out, coming, speaking—describe a
relationship between Bartimaeus and Jesus that is borne out in concrete action.
This blind man was able to take in what Jesus had tried so desperately on the
road to Jerusalem to get through to his disciples—that faith has its costs, that
one must leave all ("threw aside his cloak") and follow. Once he was cured of
his blindness and able to see (seeing here is a metaphor for faith), Bartimaeus
accepted the demand of faith and followed Jesus.

Bartimaeus is a model of Christian discipleship; he lets his faith lead him to
Jesus and then follows him. The link between faith and following is an encounter with Jesus: "Jesus, Son of David, have pity on me." We can speak of faith as
the insight of action because faith brings us more eagerly and surely to make
leaps of trust and hope concerning what is ultimately most important to us
when our ordinary human tendency would counsel caution. Bartimaeus' cry to
Jesus was for sight; he received that, but also a deeper faith and a lifelong journey of following Jesus. Jesus tells Bartimaeus that his "faith has saved" him.
Saved him from begging? Saved him from . . . ?

Living the Paschal Mystery

Without persistence in prayer it will be impossible for us to follow Jesus faithfully. Encounters with Jesus in prayer keep our relationship to him healthy and
strong. The prayer of petition reminds us that disciples can do nothing on their
own without Jesus' help. Only with Jesus will we disciples not stumble (see first
reading).

The paschal mystery rhythm of dying and rising plays itself out in many
ways—this Sunday in a rhythm of faith and action. In practical, everyday
terms this means that at times we are doing our faith—reaching out to those
around us in need; at other times we are being our faith—taking time to call out
to God to have pity on us.

Focusing the Gospel

Key words and phrases: cry out . . . have pity . . . call him, came to Jesus, I want to see, faith, followed him

To the point: In the gospel Bartimaeus persists in prayer, relies on Jesus' pity, and comes when called. He receives his sight and is ultimately saved by his faith. We are saved by our own faith when we pursue Jesus, speak boldly to him of our needs, and say to him "I want to see" knowing full well that what we are really asking is to follow him unreservedly as disciples. Faith is the insight of action.

Connecting the Gospel

to the first reading: Using many images of healing, the first reading describes the salvation ultimately given to Bartimaeus and to us: deliverance, homecoming, consolation, guidance, life-giving water, and level roads where no one stumbles.

to our experience: Usually when we ask for something, we know clearly what it is we want. When we ask Jesus for sight we also know clearly what it is we want: to follow him. However, what we don't always know clearly or want is all that discipleship entails.

Connecting the Responsorial Psalm

to the readings: Psalm 126 was probably composed at the time when Israel was freed from its captivity in Babylon. The first two strophes speak of Israel's rejoicing at God's saving intervention and of the amazement of other nations. The last two express Israel's confidence that the God who has saved them in the past will save them again in the future.

The connection of the psalm to the first reading and gospel is immediately apparent: God brings Israel out of captivity; Jesus delivers Bartimaeus from blindness. The context of where we are at this point in the journey of Ordinary Time, however, generates an even deeper connection. Bartimaeus' cure and immediate pursuit of Jesus down the road become a metaphor for our own healing from whatever blocks us from seeing our mission clearly and whatever immobility prevents us from moving forward in discipleship. The response of Jesus reveals that we can be healed simply by asking him for help. This is an ironic healing, however, for its outcome leaves us walking with open eyes toward the cross. And though it may not appear to be so, this is indeed a "great thing" God is doing for us (psalm refrain).

to cantor preparation: This Sunday's responsorial psalm needs to be prepared not only in relation to the first reading and gospel, but also in relation to where we are on this year's journey through Ordinary Time. As Jesus nears Jerusalem, conflict with his enemies intensifies and the cross looms more and more prominently on the horizon. So does the struggle of the disciples to accept the cross as necessary to discipleship. In this light one of the "great things" God does (see psalm) is grant you the grace to follow Jesus to the cross. Are you prepared to accept this kind of "great thing"? Do you believe that the weeping the cross brings will be turned into joy?

**ASSEMBLY &
FAITH-SHARING GROUPS**

· I am like Bartimaeus when . . . I am like the crowds around Bartimaeus when . . .

· When I pray, I ask for . . .

· My faith leads me to . . .

PRESIDERS

· As presider I lead the assembly to call out to Jesus and follow him more faithfully by . . .

DEACONS

· My service helps those in need to encounter the pity of Jesus by . . .

HOSPITALITY MINISTERS

· I open the door to God's saving action when . . .

MUSIC MINISTERS

· My music making helps the assembly see Jesus more clearly and follow him more faithfully when I . . .

ALTAR MINISTERS

· My service of the altar is a way of asking Jesus for sight when . . .

LECTORS

· My faith-filled insight into God's word deepens the assembly's faith when . . .

**EXTRAORDINARY MINISTERS
OF HOLY COMMUNION**

· I am the compassion of Jesus to the crowd approaching me to receive Holy Communion because . . .

Model Act of Penitence

Presider: In the gospel today Bartimaeus the blind beggar asks Jesus to see and Jesus grants him his sight. Seeing is a gospel way of speaking about faith—about encountering Jesus and then following him. As we prepare for this liturgy we open our hearts to Jesus and ask that we, too, might see and follow . . . [pause]

Lord Jesus, you are the compassion of God: Lord . . .

Christ Jesus, you are the Light of faith: Christ . . .

Lord Jesus, you answer our every prayer: Lord . . .

Homily Points

• Often in life we are called to make leaps of faith that we resist. For example, we might be asked to do a job for which we feel inadequate and are afraid of failure. Yet despite our fear and uncertainty, we take the step because life has taught us that growth and good come from leaps of faith.

• In the gospel Bartimaeus takes a great leap of faith. He may not have been able to see, but he had trust in Jesus because he knew who Jesus was ("son of David"). When Jesus called, Bartimaeus came without hesitation to where Jesus stood. His faith in Jesus not only gained him his physical sight, but his leap of faith brought him even more than he asked for: Bartimaeus' faith was confirmed, he was "saved," and he "followed [Jesus] on the way."

• Faith is the insight of action when we pursue who Jesus is for us, allow him to heal us, and faithfully follow him. Although we sometimes hold back and are afraid to run the risk of taking a leap of faith, Jesus is always present to us and calling us to ever deeper life. In the midst of need, fear, and uncertainty, we learn to call out to Jesus to help us take new risks and continue to follow Jesus "on the way."

Model Prayer of the Faithful

Presider: God is compassionate toward those with needs. Let us pray with confidence.

Response: Lord, hear our prayer.

Cantor: we pray to the Lord,

For all members of the church to have the faith to come confidently to Jesus when in need . . . [pause]

For the people of all nations to have the faith to seek salvation . . . [pause]

For the sick and the suffering to have the faith to trust in Jesus' healing presence . . . [pause]

For each of us to have the faith to persist in prayer and come to a deeper relationship with Jesus . . . [pause]

Presider: Gracious God, you give us all we need to follow your Son Jesus to eternal glory: hear these our prayers that our faith might be deepened and our discipleship strengthened. We ask this through that same Son, Jesus Christ our Lord. **Amen.**

OPENING PRAYER

Let us pray

Pause for silent prayer

Almighty and ever-living God,
strengthen our faith, hope, and love.
May we do with loving hearts
what you ask of us
and come to share the life you promise.

We ask this through our Lord Jesus Christ,
　　your Son,
who lives and reigns with you and the
　　Holy Spirit,
one God, for ever and ever. **Amen.**

FIRST READING

Jer 31:7-9

Thus says the LORD:
Shout with joy for Jacob,
　　exult at the head of the nations;
　　proclaim your praise and say:
The LORD has delivered his people,
　　the remnant of Israel.
Behold, I will bring them back
　　from the land of the north;
I will gather them from the ends of the
　　world,
　　with the blind and the lame in their
　　　midst,
the mothers and those with child;
　　they shall return as an immense throng.
They departed in tears,
　　but I will console them and guide them;
I will lead them to brooks of water,
　　on a level road, so that none shall
　　　stumble.
For I am a father to Israel,
　　Ephraim is my firstborn.

RESPONSORIAL PSALM

Ps 126:1-2, 2-3, 4-5, 6

Ry. (3) The Lord has done great things for us; we are filled with joy.

When the LORD brought back the captives of Zion,
　　we were like men dreaming.
Then our mouth was filled with laughter,
　　and our tongue with rejoicing.

Ry. The Lord has done great things for us; we are filled with joy.

Then they said among the nations,
  "The Lord has done great things for
    them."
The Lord has done great things for us;
  we are glad indeed.

R̶ʒ. The Lord has done great things for us;
we are filled with joy.

Restore our fortunes, O Lord,
  like the torrents in the southern desert.
Those that sow in tears
  shall reap rejoicing.

R̶ʒ. The Lord has done great things for us;
we are filled with joy.

Although they go forth weeping,
  carrying the seed to be sown,
they shall come back rejoicing,
  carrying their sheaves.

R̶ʒ. The Lord has done great things for us;
we are filled with joy.

SECOND READING
Heb 5:1-6

Brothers and sisters:
Every high priest is taken from among
    men
  and made their representative before
    God,
  to offer gifts and sacrifices for sins.
He is able to deal patiently with the
    ignorant and erring,
  for he himself is beset by weakness
  and so, for this reason, must make sin
    offerings for himself
  as well as for the people.
No one takes this honor upon himself
  but only when called by God,
  just as Aaron was.
In the same way,
  it was not Christ who glorified himself
    in becoming high priest,
  but rather the one who said to him:
    *You are my son: this day I have
      begotten you;*
  just as he says in another place:
    *You are a priest forever according to
      the order of Melchizedek.*

About Liturgy

Petitions during liturgy: By now all of us are familiar with having petitions at Mass, especially in the form of the prayer of the faithful. This is an ancient custom, and in the early history of the church petitions abounded in several places during the liturgy, sometimes becoming quite lengthy (even running to several pages of text). We remarked on the Twenty-sixth Sunday in Ordinary Time in the catechesis on the penitential rite that originally one form of the *Kyrie* included a litany of petitions to which the "Lord, have mercy" was a common response. We still have petitions in our eucharistic prayers for both the living and the dead. One interesting form of petitions is called "diptychs" which are lists of individuals mentioned right in the liturgy—surely martyrs, but we think some were even living benefactors. An example of this still remains in our contemporary liturgy in the list of men and women martyrs that are part of Eucharistic Prayer I.

Some people have grumbled about the constant petitions during Mass, especially that there seems to be so much repetition—we are praying for the same things all the time. One response to this attitude is to consider the blind man in this Sunday's gospel. Having cried out to Jesus for pity and been rebuked, rather than giving up Bartimaeus "kept calling out all the more." He gives us an example of persistence in our petitionary prayer—not that we are frustrated that God does not seem to hear all our prayers, but that persistence reminds us of how utterly dependent upon God we are.

A good practice during the prayer of the faithful is to have a pause of reasonable length after the announcement of each intention (the model suggested in *Living Liturgy*™). This pause allows time for personal prayer, for making the general intentions very much our own prayer. In this way even general intercessions which seem similar or repetitious can take on individuality.

About Liturgical Music

Music suggestion: One perfect hymn for this Sunday is "Amazing Grace" with its reference to blindness and healing. This hymn would fit best either at the preparation of the gifts or as a choral prelude. The hymn may need to be given a lift out of the overfamiliarity that often plagues it, however. One way to inject new life into this song would be to sing a verse or two in canon, beginning the second voice at the end of the second full measure. Another way would be to sing it in 4/4 rather than the usual 3/4. *Songs of Zion* (Nashville: Abingdon Press, 1981) contains an excellent 4/4 arrangement by J. Jefferson Cleveland. The stretch of that extra beat adds great intensity and breadth to the text. Try it, you'll like it!

OCTOBER 25, 2009
THIRTIETH SUNDAY
IN ORDINARY TIME

SPIRITUALITY

GOSPEL ACCLAMATION
Matt 11:28

R̸. Alleluia, alleluia.
Come to me, all you who labor and are burdened
and I will give you rest, says the Lord.
R̸. Alleluia, alleluia.

Gospel Matt 5:1-12a; L667

When Jesus saw the crowds, he went up
    the mountain,
    and after he had sat down, his disciples
        came to him.
He began to teach them, saying:
    "Blessed are the poor in spirit,
        for theirs is the Kingdom of heaven.
    Blessed are they who mourn,
        for they will be comforted.
    Blessed are the meek,
        for they will inherit the land.
    Blessed are they who hunger and thirst
        for righteousness,
        for they will be satisfied.
    Blessed are the merciful,
        for they will be shown mercy.
    Blessed are the clean of heart,
        for they will see God.
    Blessed are the peacemakers,
        for they will be called children of God.
    Blessed are they who are persecuted
        for the sake of righteousness,
        for theirs is the Kingdom of heaven.
    Blessed are you when they insult you
        and persecute you
    and utter every kind of evil against
        you falsely because of me.
Rejoice and be glad,
    for your reward will be great in
        heaven."

Reflecting on the Gospel

Sometimes the phrase "that blessed event" is used to refer to the birth of a child, especially a firstborn or one who has been conceived with difficulty. We have a sense that birth—bringing forth new life—is a wondrous, mysterious event. It establishes a special relationship usually with tangible results: assurance of care when vulnerable and promised inheritance when older. In the Beatitudes Jesus speaks of a similar care and promise and spells out the great assurance of our faith—that there is glory awaiting us: "Rejoice and be glad, for your reward will be great in heaven." This solemnity celebrates more than those who have gone before us and already share fully in that glory. It also celebrates those of us who "are God's children now" (second reading) who already enjoy the inheritance of new life. This unique relationship of being God's blessed children is really a share in the new life Jesus promised as well as a pledge of eternal life.

Inheritance is normally a consequence of *identity*—we inherit because of a biological or relational connection. As children of our parents, we may inherit a house or money. As children of the promise, Israel inherited a land flowing with milk and honey. Jesus, however, startlingly reveals an unimaginable inheritance now offered to us in him: being the very "children of God" with the promised inheritance of a share in God's life now and eternally in the "kingdom of heaven."

The *promise* of the Beatitudes is that certain ways of living (poor, meek, merciful, etc.) surely lead to inheriting a place in the heavenly kingdom. The *challenge* of the Beatitudes is to embrace these ways of living and thus make present in the here and now God's reign. The "land" of inheritance is both heavenly and earthly, both future and now—always God's gift to "God's children now" (second reading) who are the blessed ones, the saints.

There are many ways to be blessed. One of the attractions of honoring saints is that they offer a great deal of variety and richness of life for us to emulate. No matter what situation in life we find ourselves or what difficulty we face, some saint offers us a model for perseverance in our blessedness and the assurance of care. This solemnity reminds us that our life of blessedness rests on an intimate relationship with God and each other expressed through enduring bonds of mutual care, mercy, humility, and self-giving.

Living the Paschal Mystery

We often think of the saints as out-of-this-world holy people who are far beyond our own experience or sense of our own goodness. When we pray the Litany of All Saints (for example, before the baptisms during the Easter Vigil) we ask the intercession of very many saints who lived centuries ago in a very different time and culture. They seem far away. This solemnity reminds us that at one time they were ordinary people just like us.

This festival is one of encouragement—God doesn't judge us only on our weaknesses but on persevering in our willingness to live as God's blessed children. The simple, everyday things we do well wash us in the blood of the Lamb (see first reading). Our smile is a saintly one. Our gesture of kindness is an expression of blessedness. Others' holy gestures toward us are reminders that there is glory awaiting us. To each of us who embraces our blessedness: ours "is the kingdom of heaven."

Focusing the Gospel

Key words and phrases: theirs is the kingdom of heaven [2 x], children of God, Rejoice and be glad

To the point: The *promise* of the Beatitudes is that certain ways of living (poor, meek, merciful, etc.) surely lead to inheriting a place in the heavenly kingdom. The *challenge* of the Beatitudes is to embrace these ways of living and thus make present in the here and now God's reign. The "land" of inheritance is both heavenly and earthly, both future and now—always God's gift to "God's children now" (second reading) who are the blessed ones, the saints.

Connecting the Gospel

to the first reading: The rejoicing and gladness and great reward in heaven mentioned at the end of the Beatitudes is expressed most sublimely in heavenly worship where there is an unending chorus of blessing and giving glory to God.

to our experience: While the Beatitudes are a challenging blueprint for Christian living, they are not an impossible goal. We all know people who have fruitfully taken up the challenge of the Beatitudes and thus inspire us to saintly living.

Connecting the Responsorial Psalm

to the readings: Psalm 24 was used by the Israelites as part of a ritual for gaining entrance into the Temple on high holy days. As worshipers approached the entryway a designated person would ask, "Who can ascend the mountain of the Lord?" and the people would respond, "One whose hands are sinless, whose heart is clean, who desires not what is vain." Having expressed their fidelity to the covenant, they would be granted entrance into the presence of God.

On this solemnity we honor those who stand in the presence of God because they have been faithful both to the covenant of old and to the new covenant laid out by Jesus in the Beatitudes. These holy ones now see fully the face for which they longed and they have discovered fully their own face: they look like God (see second reading). These are the blessed ones who have crossed the threshold into the fullness of light. We stand at the door and sing their praises.

to cantor preparation: Your role in singing this psalm is like that of the official who granted faithful Israelites entrance into the Temple. You remind the people that they must be faithful to the covenant, and you remind God that these are God's people. What a position in which to stand! How might you prepare yourself to fulfill this role with grace and humility?

**ASSEMBLY &
FAITH-SHARING GROUPS**

- The most challenging Beatitude for me is . . . The most encouraging Beatitude for me is . . .
- I experience the reign of God present on earth when . . .
- Persons who inspire me to saintly living are . . .

PRESIDERS

- My ministry encourages the assembly to live the Beatitudes more fully when . . .

DEACONS

- My service ministry embodies the deepest challenge of the Beatitudes in that . . .

HOSPITALITY MINISTERS

- My ministry helps the gathering assembly know where their true home is when . . .

MUSIC MINISTERS

- My ministry joins the singing of this assembly with the singing of the heavenly choir when . . .

ALTAR MINISTERS

- My servant ministry reflects the presence of God's reign when . . .

LECTORS

- My proclamation of the word is both promise and challenge when . . .

**EXTRAORDINARY MINISTERS
OF HOLY COMMUNION**

- What helps me recognize the saintliness of those who come for Holy Communion is . . .

Model Act of Penitence

Presider: We are reminded by this solemnity that each of us already shares in the blessedness of the saints who have gone before us whenever we are faithful to our baptismal life of self-giving. We prepare for this liturgy by looking into our hearts and recognizing there the blessedness of being God's beloved children . . . [pause]

Lord Jesus, you are the Teacher who calls us to a life of blessedness: Lord . . .

Christ Jesus, you are the Lamb who receives blessing and glory, wisdom and thanksgiving, honor, power, and might: Christ . . .

Lord Jesus, you give eternal life to those who follow you: Lord . . .

Homily Points

• We tend to equate holiness more with pious acts rather than with right living. While spending lots of time at prayer, being at church more than required, and wearing medals are laudable in themselves, they are not sufficient in themselves for being holy. Saintliness always requires the kind of daily living that is characterized by concern for others, generosity, justice, simplicity, etc.

• In the Beatitudes Jesus gives a blueprint both for pious acts as well as for right living. While the specific tenets of the Beatitudes might seem idealistic—poor in spirit, meek, etc.—they actually are quite ordinary and accessible to anyone serious about faithful discipleship. Moreover, they are the very attitudes that lead to what Jesus promises—a share in the "kingdom of heaven."

• Today's solemnity places before us the canonized saints in heaven, those whom we've known in our lives who are also in heaven, as well as those living among us now who model for us right living. Surely this is a great company of saints who call us to live saintly lives ourselves! While we look to those in heaven to support us by their prayers, we look to those on earth to support us by their example.

Model Prayer of the Faithful

Presider: We are confident to lift our prayers to God through the intercession of all the saints.

Response:

Lord, hear our prayer.

Cantor:

we pray to the Lord,

That the church, washed in the blood of the Lamb at baptism, always be a sign of God's blessings . . . [pause]

That all peoples of the world share in the blessings of creation . . . [pause]

That those who are poor, oppressed, in mourning, or persecuted receive God's blessedness through our ministry . . . [pause]

That all of us, washed in the blood of the Lamb at baptism, give ourselves selflessly for others . . . [pause]

Presider: Loving God, you raise up holy men and women in every age to offer hope and encouragement: hear these our prayers that one day we might join with them in eternal joy with you. We ask this through our Lord Jesus Christ. **Amen.**

Let us pray

Pause for silent prayer

God our Father,
source of all holiness,
the work of your hands is manifest in your saints,
the beauty of your truth is reflected in their faith.
May we who aspire to have part in their joy
be filled with the Spirit that blessed their lives,
so that having shared their faith on earth
we may also know their peace in your kingdom.

Grant this through Christ our Lord. **Amen.**

FIRST READING
Rev 7:2-4, 9-14

I, John, saw another angel come up from the East,
    holding the seal of the living God.
He cried out in a loud voice to the four angels
    who were given power to damage the land and the sea,
    "Do not damage the land or the sea or the trees
    until we put the seal on the foreheads of the servants of our God."
I heard the number of those who had been marked with the seal,
    one hundred and forty-four thousand marked
    from every tribe of the children of Israel.

After this I had a vision of a great multitude,
    which no one could count,
    from every nation, race, people, and tongue.
They stood before the throne and before the Lamb,
    wearing white robes and holding palm branches in their hands.
They cried out in a loud voice:
    "Salvation comes from our God,
    who is seated on the throne,
    and from the Lamb."
All the angels stood around the throne
    and around the elders and the four living creatures.
They prostrated themselves before the throne,
    worshiped God, and exclaimed:
    "Amen. Blessing and glory, wisdom and thanksgiving,
    honor, power, and might
    be to our God forever and ever. Amen."

Then one of the elders spoke up and said
    to me,
    "Who are these wearing white robes,
        and where did they come from?"
I said to him, "My lord, you are the one
        who knows."
He said to me,
    "These are the ones who have survived
        the time of great distress;
    they have washed their robes
    and made them white in the Blood of
        the Lamb."

RESPONSORIAL PSALM
Ps 24:1bc-2, 3-4ab, 5-6

℟. (cf. 6) Lord, this is the people that longs
to see your face.

The LORD's are the earth and its fullness;
    the world and those who dwell in it.
For he founded it upon the seas
    and established it upon the rivers.

℟. Lord, this is the people that longs to see
your face.

Who can ascend the mountain of the
    LORD?
    or who may stand in his holy place?
One whose hands are sinless, whose heart
    is clean,
    who desires not what is vain.

℟. Lord, this is the people that longs to see
your face.

He shall receive a blessing from the LORD,
    a reward from God his savior.
Such is the race that seeks him,
    that seeks the face of the God of Jacob.

℟. Lord, this is the people that longs to see
your face.

SECOND READING
1 John 3:1-3

Beloved:
See what love the Father has bestowed
        on us
    that we may be called the children of
        God.
Yet so we are.
The reason the world does not know us
    is that it did not know him.
Beloved, we are God's children now;
    what we shall be has not yet been
        revealed.
We do know that when it is revealed we
    shall be like him,
    for we shall see him as he is.
Everyone who has this hope based on him
    makes himself pure,
    as he is pure.

About Liturgy

Origin of the festival of All Saints: We humans have always honored our departed loved ones. Ancestors' pictures often adorn our walls. Buildings are named after long-deceased benefactors. Accomplishments are marked with obelisks or monuments. It is not surprising, then, that from earliest times the church has also desired to honor the faithful departed.

The earliest cult of the saints focused on the martyrs, those who courageously gave their life out of commitment to Christ. From at least the fourth century the Eastern church had a festival honoring all the saints who have departed; in Rome in the fifth century the pagan Pantheon was consecrated as a church honoring Mary and the martyrs. By the eighth century the cult of the saints is extended beyond the martyrs to honor others who lived selfless, faithful Christian lives. At this time there is the first indication that the festival was fixed on November 1 in the West.

This festival is not primarily about remembering the faithful departed (we do that on November 2). It is about honoring those who have been faithful disciples of Jesus, those who model for us gospel living, those who inspire us to be likewise faithful.

About Liturgical Music

Music suggestions: On this solemnity a setting of the Beatitudes would be excellent for the Communion procession. In addition to David Haas' well-known "Blest Are They," there is Darryl Ducote's "Beatitudes" with its syncopated rhythms and uplifting refrain [found in BB and JS2], and Harry Hagan's "Rejoice with All the Saints" [in JS2 and in the hymn collection *Awake, My Soul*, OCP #11641]. In Alan Hommerding's lovely "We Sing of the Saints [PMB, WC] we sing about those we know to be saints, those sainted but unnamed, and ourselves called to be "living saints here below." This hymn would fit well for the preparation of the gifts.

Douglas E. Wagner's "Canticle for All the Saints" [H.W.Gray Publications] is a combination prelude-entrance hymn. The choir sings first about the famous who are remembered because of the mark they have made on history, then about those for whom there is "no memorial." The concluding phrase "but their names liveth forevermore" blossoms dramatically into full congregational singing of "For All the Saints."

NOVEMBER 1, 2009
ALL SAINTS

SPIRITUALITY

GOSPEL ACCLAMATION
cf. John 6:40

This is the will of my Father, says the Lord,
that everyone who sees the Son and believes in
    him
may have eternal life.

Gospel

John 6:37-40; L668

Jesus said to the crowds:
"Everything that the Father gives
        me will come to me,
    and I will not reject anyone who
        comes to me,
    because I came down from
        heaven not to do my own
        will
    but the will of the one who sent
        me.
And this is the will of the one who sent
        me,
    that I should not lose anything of
        what he gave me,
    but that I should raise it on the last
        day.
For this is the will of my Father,
    that everyone who sees the Son and
        believes in him
    may have eternal life,
    and I shall raise him up on the last
        day."

See Appendix A, p. 306, for the other readings.

FIRST READING
Dan 12:1-3; L1011.7

RESPONSORIAL PSALM
Ps 27:1, 4, 7, 8b, 9a, 13-14

SECOND READING
Rom 6:3-9

*or any other readings from L668 or any readings
from the Masses for the Dead (L1011–1015)*

Reflecting on the Gospel

Sometimes when little children want something very much, they close their eyes tightly, purse their lips in concentration, hold their breath, and make a wish with all their hearts. Often they receive what it is they wish—no small thanks to the generosity and love of their parents. The amazing assurance of this gospel is that God *wills* that we all be saved ("this is the will of my father . . . everyone . . . may have eternal life") and this has already been accomplished in Christ (see second reading). God our Father extends divine generosity and love toward us in Christ for the wildest wish possible: that we "have eternal life" and are raised up with Christ "on the last day." Christ assures us that this is the will of the Father for us.

Yes, indeed, here is the good news: God *wills* that we all be saved (gospel). Here is more good news: our salvation has already been accomplished in Christ through whom we are dead to sin and alive with new life (see second reading). Our share in new and eternal life rests wholly on our identity with Christ and our firm belief in him. Because of Christ those who have been faithful will not disappear into darkness but will shine brightly forever (see first reading).

This feast day reminds us that God is faithful to God's promise to save and that the victory of salvation is possible for all. We begin our lives by belonging to the Father who wills that not one of us be lost. God's will that we gain everlasting life is so strong that God sent the only-begotten Son to unite with us in our weak humanity so that we can be raised to a share in divine life. But temptations abound; we make choices selfishly to serve ourselves rather than gracefully serve others and God. Truly, there is a choice to be made in face of God's will for our salvation.

This festival honoring all the faithful departed also reminds us that victory is possible. On November 1 we celebrated the solemnity of All Saints. This November 2 commemoration of all the faithful departed is not a totally different feast. The souls in purgatory are like all of us weak human creatures; they have sinned. But they also have already won the victory; they have believed in the Son and are not lost. All that remains is the satisfaction for their weak moments and righting their relationships with God and others in the Body of Christ. The souls in purgatory are not lost; they have won their victory. We pray for them as brothers and sisters in Christ.

Living the Paschal Mystery

In the immediacy of our everyday lives we don't see how our specific choices to be faithful disciples are related to how we spend eternity. This festival in general and the gospel in particular remind us that we must believe in Christ. Belief, however, is not something passive. It is the right living that evidences our commitment to live our baptismal plunge into Christ's death and resurrection. This is the only way to new and eternal life.

Each choice we make to believe in Christ and live as faithful disciples—no matter how small and seemingly insignificant—truly does take us either closer to God and each other or farther away. The gospel invites us to think of our everyday choices as having consequences—eternal life.

Focusing the Gospel

Key words and phrases: will of my father, everyone who . . . believes, have eternal life

To the point: Here is the good news: God wills that we all be saved (gospel). Here is more good news: our salvation has already been accomplished in Christ through whom we are dead to sin and alive with new life (see second reading). Our share in new and eternal life rests wholly on our identity with Christ. Because of him those who have been faithful will not disappear into darkness but will shine brightly forever (see first reading).

Model Act of Penitence

Presider: Today we commemorate the faithfulness of the souls in purgatory and pray that they might come to the fullness of risen life. We pause to open ourselves to the great mystery of God's mercy . . . [pause]

Lord Jesus, you came that not one of God's beloved be lost: Lord . . .

Christ Jesus, you were crucified on the cross and were raised to life on the third day: Christ . . .

Lord Jesus, you call both the sinner and the righteous to new life: Lord . . .

Model Prayer of the Faithful

Presider: We make our needs known to the God of mercy who desires that all be saved.

Response: Lord, hear our prayer.

Cantor: we pray to the Lord,

That the faithfulness of all members of the church be a beacon of hope for eternal life to others . . . [pause]

That all the faithful departed come to rest forever in God's love and mercy . . . [pause]

That those mourning the loss of a loved one find hope and consolation in God's promise of eternal life . . . [pause]

That each of us here may remain faithful to our baptismal promises and one day enjoy eternal life . . . [pause]

Presider: Merciful God, you will that all people gain eternal life: hear these our prayers that one day we might live with you forever through your Son, Jesus Christ. **Amen.**

OPENING PRAYER (FROM THE FIRST MASS)

Let us pray

Pause for silent prayer

Merciful Father,
hear our prayers and console us.
As we renew our faith in your Son,
whom you raised from the dead,
strengthen our hope that all our departed
    brothers and sisters
will share in his resurrection,
who lives and reigns with you and the Holy
    Spirit,
one God, for ever and ever. **Amen.**

FOR REFLECTION

· What I do to grow in my identity with Christ as the center of my life is . . .

· My will to do good is in conformity with God's will for all to have eternal life when . . .

· This feast day gives me hope for all those who have died in that . . .

Homily Points

• The long-standing Catholic practice of praying for the souls in purgatory is laudable, but is not to be misconstrued. The souls in purgatory are already saved and have already received of God's mercy. Purgatory is seen as a time of purification for rebuilding the relationship with God diminished through sin.

• This celebration is not about sorrow, but about hope. The source of our hope is Christ crucified in whom we have been baptized, and his resurrection through which we have the promise of eternal life. What better promise can we have than this sureness of being raised with Christ?

245

✚ SPIRITUALITY

GOSPEL ACCLAMATION
Matt 5:3

℟. Alleluia, alleluia.
Blessed are the poor in spirit,
for theirs is the kingdom of heaven.
℟. Alleluia, alleluia.

Gospel

Mark 12:38-44; L155B

In the course of his teaching Jesus
    said to the crowds,
  "Beware of the scribes, who
      like to go around in long robes
  and accept greetings in the
      marketplaces,
  seats of honor in synagogues,
  and places of honor at banquets.
They devour the houses of widows and,
    as a pretext
  recite lengthy prayers.
They will receive a very severe
    condemnation."

He sat down opposite the treasury
  and observed how the crowd put
      money into the treasury.
Many rich people put in large sums.
A poor widow also came and put in two
    small coins worth a few cents.
Calling his disciples to himself, he said
    to them,
  "Amen, I say to you, this poor widow
      put in more
  than all the other contributors to the
      treasury.
For they have all contributed from their
    surplus wealth,
  but she, from her poverty, has
      contributed all she had,
  her whole livelihood."

or Mark 12:41-44

See Appendix A, p. 307.

Reflecting on the Gospel

Many parishes regularly schedule a social time of coffee, juice, and donuts after the Sunday Masses. Most parishes have a basket out on one of the tables for donations to help defray the cost of the refreshments. One Sunday a family with three little children in tow approached the table for juice and donuts, and Dad put a couple of bills into the basket. Not to be outdone, Cory reached into pants pocket and put something in the basket, too. Later when the hospitality minister collected the bills in the basket, she found a nickel and penny there as well. That must have been Cory's donation—no doubt all that he had. Her smile suggested that the two small coins were of not much monetary value for paying bills, but they were priceless in other ways: Cory was learning to share, to carry his weight of the cost of the social time, that few things in life come without cost. Further, he learned to give because he saw his father giving. So much to learn from giving so little!

The gospel this Sunday is about Jesus observing how people of his time were making donations. But another layer of interpretation might be opened up. This gospel is really a metaphor for true discipleship, a central theme in the Gospel of Mark. What does it mean to be a disciple of Jesus? Jesus tells us when he contrasts the behavior of the self-important scribes and the rich with the action of a poor and seemingly insignificant widow. Without calculating the cost to herself, the widow gave "all she had." Disciples, too, give all they have without counting the cost, calculating self-gain, or seeking attention. The "whole livelihood" disciples give is their very selves. Simply contributing isn't the issue; it matters not whether what we give is large or small. What ultimately matters is the gift of self which marks a true disciple of Jesus.

Similar to the surplus of meaning in the gospel, the first reading is really about more than a widow who risks the last bit of her flour and oil to respond to Elijah's need. Elijah rewards her obedience and generous hospitality—out of her need—with an abundance of flour and oil, enough to feed herself and her son for a whole year. The story depicts the hundredfold God returns to those who are so exceptionally generous. Paradoxically, by being generous to others we open ourselves to God's unbounded generosity toward us. Such is the hundredfold of those who are faithful disciples. Disciples give their all, and in turn receive what our generous God offers: "salvation to those who eagerly await him" (second reading).

Living the Paschal Mystery

Just as Cory learned to contribute for the refreshments from his father, so do we learn how to be good disciples from others who follow Jesus faithfully. The gospel holds up the poor widow as a model for the total self-giving of the true disciple. We need but look around us to find strong models for faithful discipleship. Nor is it always a matter of these disciple-models giving large sums of money. Giving a bit of time each week for the good of another, participating in at least some parish activities beyond going to Mass and contributing to the collection basket, signing up when volunteers are needed are all ways of contributing a little which makes a huge difference in overall parish life. Even "something" can be our "all."

Focusing the Gospel

Key words and phrases: Beware of the scribes, poor widow, put in more, contributed all she had, her whole livelihood

To the point: What does it mean to be a disciple of Jesus? Jesus tells us when he contrasts the behavior of the self-important scribes and the rich with the action of a poor and seemingly insignificant widow. Without calculating the cost to herself, the widow gave "all she had." Disciples, too, give all they have without counting the cost, calculating self-gain, or seeking attention. The "whole livelihood" disciples give is their very selves.

Connecting the Gospel

to the first reading: The first reading is really about more than a widow who risks the last bit of her flour and oil to respond to Elijah's need. The story depicts the hundredfold God returns to those who are so exceptionally generous.

to culture: The law of survival tells us to watch out for ourselves first. Jesus condemns those who live by this law ("receive a very severe condemnation") and praises those who choose to give even out of their little.

Connecting the Responsorial Psalm

to the readings: Psalm 146 tells of how God cares without fail for those in need—the hungry, the disabled, the bowed down, the widowed. We sang these verses from Psalm 146 on the Twenty-third Sunday in Ordinary Time when Jesus cured a deaf-mute brought to him by the crowd. This Sunday we catch a glimpse of two widows who have lost almost everything yet willingly give to God the little they have left. God rewards the first with abundant sustenance; Jesus identifies the second as the model for all discipleship. If we are to be fully committed disciples we must give all we have for the sake of the kingdom. Nothing can be held back. When we find ourselves left with nothing because of the kingdom, we needn't fear, for we will have staked our security on a God who holds nothing back in return (psalm).

to cantor preparation: This responsorial psalm needs to be sung with confidence in God's providence and protection. But unless you give all that you have—your whole heart—you will never discover what God is giving in return. What do you hold back? What would give you the courage to give it?

ASSEMBLY & FAITH-SHARING GROUPS
- I am like the scribes when I . . . I am like the poor widow when I . . .
- For me, the cost of discipleship is . . . I find myself counting this cost when . . . I find myself risking when . . .
- I have experienced God's hundredfold generosity to me when . . .

PRESIDERS
- As presider I model for the assembly what it means to give all despite sometimes feeling I have little when . . .

DEACONS
- I find it easy to serve those in need when I have extra time and energy. When I don't have that extra time and energy . . .

HOSPITALITY MINISTERS
- Like Jesus, my role as a hospitality minister is to recognize those who seem insignificant. I find this difficult when . . . I find this easy when . . .

MUSIC MINISTERS
- I find myself "holding back" in my music ministry when . . . What helps me give my all is . . .

ALTAR MINISTERS
- The "all" I give each time I minister at the altar is . . .

LECTORS
- I give my all to my ministry of proclamation when . . .

EXTRAORDINARY MINISTERS OF HOLY COMMUNION
- I experience God's gift of a hundredfold during my distribution of Holy Communion when . . .

Model Act of Penitence

Presider: The gospel today tells about the poor widow who gave two small coins to the Temple treasury. As we prepare to celebrate this liturgy, let us look into our hearts and see what we are prepared to give to the Lord Jesus . . . [pause]

Lord Jesus, you are the Source of all we have and are: Lord . . .

Christ Jesus, you are the Gift of God's presence among us: Christ . . .

Lord Jesus, you call us to become self-giving disciples: Lord . . .

Homily Points

• In circumstances where we find our resources limited, we often hold back on what we give. For example, if we lose our job, Christmas gift-giving might be less extravagant. When not feeling well, we tend to engage in less interaction with others. When we feel under pressure from work, we are far less willing to take on additional commitments. This Sunday's readings, especially the gospel, challenge us to give all we have and are even when we feel we have little or nothing to give.

• When Jesus chose his disciples, they were not yet willing to take the risk of giving all, no matter what the cost. The disciples try to dissuade Jesus from his passion and death and in the end abandon him in his hour of need. In this Sunday's gospel Jesus holds up the widow as a model of the total giving necessary for true discipleship. Ultimately his disciples grew into being model disciples in their total self-giving.

• What are the "coins" that the widow gave and we are invited to give? Giving a little bit of time listening to someone in spite of being very busy; a sick mother still takes care of family; a friendly hello to someone who seems alone or down are all examples of small "coins" that bring life and hope into people's lives. It matters not whether what we give is large or small. What matters is the gift of self which, for the disciple, is really the greatest gift of all: the presence of Jesus.

Model Prayer of the Faithful

Presider: Knowing that we need God's help to be faithful disciples, let us make our needs known.

Response:

Lord, hear our prayer.

Cantor:

we pray to the Lord,

That all members of the church be generous in self-giving and kind to those in need . . . [pause]

That leaders of nations may lift up the poor and needy entrusted to their care . . . [pause]

That those who have lost family or support may be comforted by this Christian community . . . [pause]

That this Christian community continue to grow in true discipleship . . . [pause]

Presider: Gracious God, you sent your Son to show us your love: hear these our prayers that one day we might enjoy everlasting life. We ask this through that same Son, Jesus Christ our Lord. *Amen.*

Let us pray

Pause for silent prayer

Almighty Father,
strong is your justice and great is your mercy.
Protect us in the burdens and challenges of life.
Shield our minds from the distortion of pride
and enfold our desire with the beauty of truth.
Help us to become more aware of your loving design
so that we may more willingly give our lives in service to all.
We ask this through Christ our Lord.
Amen.

FIRST READING

1 Kgs 17:10-16

In those days, Elijah the prophet went to Zarephath.
As he arrived at the entrance of the city,
a widow was gathering sticks there; he called out to her,
"Please bring me a small cupful of water to drink."
She left to get it, and he called out after her,
"Please bring along a bit of bread."
She answered, "As the LORD, your God, lives,
I have nothing baked; there is only a handful of flour in my jar
and a little oil in my jug.
Just now I was collecting a couple of sticks,
to go in and prepare something for myself and my son;
when we have eaten it, we shall die."
Elijah said to her, "Do not be afraid.
Go and do as you propose.
But first make me a little cake and bring it to me.
Then you can prepare something for yourself and your son.
For the LORD, the God of Israel, says,
'The jar of flour shall not go empty,
nor the jug of oil run dry,
until the day when the LORD sends rain upon the earth.'"
She left and did as Elijah had said.
She was able to eat for a year, and he and her son as well;
the jar of flour did not go empty,
nor the jug of oil run dry,
as the LORD had foretold through Elijah.

RESPONSORIAL PSALM
Ps 146:7, 8-9, 9-10

R̞. (1b) Praise the Lord, my soul!
or:
R̞. Alleluia.

The LORD keeps faith forever,
    secures justice for the oppressed,
    gives food to the hungry.
The LORD sets captives free.

R̞. Praise the Lord, my soul!
or:
R̞. Alleluia.

The LORD gives sight to the blind;
    the LORD raises up those who were
        bowed down.
The LORD loves the just;
    the LORD protects strangers.

R̞. Praise the Lord, my soul!
or:
R̞. Alleluia.

The fatherless and the widow he sustains,
    but the way of the wicked he thwarts.
The LORD shall reign forever;
    your God, O Zion, through all
        generations. Alleluia.

R̞. Praise the Lord, my soul!
or:
R̞. Alleluia.

SECOND READING
Heb 9:24-28

Christ did not enter into a sanctuary made
        by hands,
    a copy of the true one, but heaven itself,
    that he might now appear before God
        on our behalf.
Not that he might offer himself repeatedly,
    as the high priest enters each year into
        the sanctuary
    with blood that is not his own;
    if that were so, he would have had to
        suffer repeatedly
    from the foundation of the world.
But now once for all he has appeared at
        the end of the ages
    to take away sin by his sacrifice.
Just as it is appointed that human beings
        die once,
    and after this the judgment, so also
        Christ,
    offered once to take away the sins of
        many,
    will appear a second time, not to take
        away sin
    but to bring salvation to those who
        eagerly await him.

About Liturgy

Discipleship and intercession for the dead: We have recently celebrated All Souls Day, and we customarily keep all of November as a month when we remember the dead. Rather than remembering the dead just being a rote or mechanical practice, we might consciously place our prayers for the dead in the larger context of discipleship. Prayers for the dead beyond our own loved ones is an act of discipleship because it evidences our connection to each other as members of the Body of Christ and our continued care and concern for one another.

Traditionally the church prays for the faithful departed each night at the intercessions during evening prayer and this is structurally where this intention belongs. Since most of our parishioners do not regularly celebrate Liturgy of the Hours, this presents a pastoral problem—when do we as a community pray for the dead? Many parishes include an intention for those who have died as part of the prayer of the faithful at Sunday Mass. Although there is nothing "wrong" with this, it might be kept in mind that this practice is by way of exception and pastoral sensitivity rather than tradition. The principle here is that as a Christian community we do pray together for the faithful departed. Perhaps a good pastoral compromise might be to include at Sunday Mass an intention for the deceased only when someone in the parish has died during that week. A model might be "That N. and all the faithful departed enjoy everlasting life, joining with Jesus at the messianic banquet . . . [pause]."

About Liturgical Music

Music suggestions: An excellent choice for the preparation of the gifts would be Herman Stuempfle's "The Temple Rang with Golden Coins" [found in HG, W3]. The hymn is based on this Sunday's gospel story and connects the widow's offering of all she had with Christ's self-offering on the cross. Another good choice for either the preparation of the gifts or Communion would be Michael Joncas' "The Love of the Lord," which names sharing in the suffering and death of Christ as the ultimate wealth worth more than all other wealth and possessions. Other appropriate suggestions for the preparation of the gifts or Communion are "I Surrender All" and "Is Your All on the Altar" [both found in LMGM]. The first sings peacefully about the self-gift already given; the second asks repeatedly if the gift has been made.

NOVEMBER 8, 2009
THIRTY-SECOND SUNDAY
IN ORDINARY TIME

SPIRITUALITY

GOSPEL ACCLAMATION
Luke 21:36

℟. Alleluia, alleluia.
Be vigilant at all times
and pray that you have the strength to stand
    before the Son of Man.
℟. Alleluia, alleluia.

Gospel

Mark 13:24-32; L158B

Jesus said to his disciples:
"In those days after that
        tribulation
    the sun will be darkened,
    and the moon will not give its
        light,
    and the stars will be falling from
        the sky,
    and the powers in the heavens
        will be shaken.

"And then they will see 'the Son of
        Man coming in the clouds'
    with great power and glory,
    and then he will send out the angels
    and gather his elect from the four
        winds,
    from the end of the earth to the end
        of the sky.

"Learn a lesson from the fig tree.
When its branch becomes tender and
        sprouts leaves,
    you know that summer is near.
In the same way, when you see these
        things happening,
    know that he is near, at the gates.
Amen, I say to you,
    this generation will not pass away
    until all these things have taken
        place.
Heaven and earth will pass away,
    but my words will not pass away.

"But of that day or hour, no one knows,
    neither the angels in heaven, nor the
        Son, but only the Father."

Reflecting on the Gospel

We humans live in the future more than we think. We are always hoping and living to buy some new gadget, receive a promotion, have better health, awaken new friendships, achieve some accomplishment, and on and on. This "future living" has the positive benefit of giving us goals to strive for that carry us beyond ourselves, challenging us to grow. At the same time, too much "future living" can cause us to miss all the goodness that is already at hand, right before our eyes.

At this time when we near the end of another liturgical year, we always hear gospels about the end times that call for us to look far into the future. These gospels inevitably paint a dark and dismal picture of calamity and doom, and so we often dismiss them. The apocalyptic imagery of this Sunday's gospel ("sun will be darkened," "moon will not give its light," "stars will be falling from the sky," and "powers in the heavens will be shaken") is no exception. We are tempted to ask, "When, Lord?" Jesus' answer, "no one knows," ought to bring us to pay more attention to the present. Now is an opportune time for the in-breaking of Christ. Now is what counts.

Apocalyptic language is always uttered by people undergoing difficult times (at the time of the writing of Mark's gospel, the Temple in Jerusalem had been destroyed and the Jewish people saw themselves once again challenged as a nation). The word "apocalyptic" comes from the Greek, meaning to "uncover" or "reveal." What is revealed in the apocalyptic passages of the gospels is the hope and promise of Christ's abiding presence *now* and not just in terms of a future promise. The words of Jesus in this gospel communicate hope: when our world is falling apart, he is breaking in and will "gather his elect" to share in his "great power and glory."

We think of Jesus' second coming as a future event. In fact, the darkening of the sun and moon and stars is already happening in the trials and tribulations that not only beset the first disciples, but also are part of our own lives. Jesus promises that all these things will happen. He further promises that he is "near, at the gates." This gospel is about the ultimate victory over darkness that belongs to those who are faithful. That victory is now.

What ought to startle us into sober reality is that we know the end will come. Like the gospel, Daniel's vision describes in the first reading "a time unsurpassed in distress." Also like the gospel, his vision reveals the victory of those "written in the book": they "shall shine brightly . . . forever" and thereby give hope to people of their own time. We have all the means at hand to face darkness and evil with confidence, sure that one day we "shall live forever." The future holds no fear for us; rather than fear, we anticipate our future with joyful expectation, because the one we await is within and among us now.

Living the Paschal Mystery

Just as big calamities are not what the future is really about, neither are big deeds what our present is about. Our present is about doing the little things well, and we know how we "lead the many to justice" (first reading): by listening to Jesus' words. Jesus has already given us all we need to have our names "written in the book." We just need to live like he did, with compassion and understanding, wisdom and care, love and hope.

Focusing the Gospel
Key words and phrases: darkened; near, at the gates

To the point: We think of Jesus' second coming as a future event. In fact, the darkening of the sun and moon and stars is already happening in the trials and tribulations that not only beset the first disciples, but also are part of our own lives. Jesus promises that all these things will happen. He further promises that he is "near, at the gates." This gospel is about the ultimate victory over darkness that belongs to those who are faithful. That victory is now.

Connecting the Gospel
to the first reading: Like the gospel, Daniel's vision describes "a time unsurpassed in distress." Also like the gospel, his vision reveals the victory of those "written in the book": they "shall shine brightly . . . forever" and thereby give hope to people of their own time.

to religious experience: The words of Jesus in this gospel communicate hope: when our world is falling apart, he is breaking in.

Connecting the Responsorial Psalm
to the readings: The first reading and gospel tell us there will come a time of great tribulation and suffering when the world as we know it will end and certainties will be shattered. But Christ reminds us that this collapse of things will be no more than the announcement of his coming when he will send his angels to gather the elect (gospel)—those who have lived by wisdom and justice (first reading)—into life everlasting. No one knows the moment of his coming (gospel), but the readings and psalm promise life-giving judgment for those who have been faithful.

Whether we envision these catastrophes and tribulations as events in the far-off future or as experiences we encounter in the present, the readings and psalm invite us to see them as revelations of hope rather than harbingers of destruction. Catastrophes, tragedies, sufferings open new ways for Christ to enter our world and our consciousness (gospel) and offer us new ways to trust in God's abiding promise to give us life even in the midst of death (psalm). We stand already and always in the presence of Christ and we possess already and always an eternal inheritance—God's very Self—that nothing can destroy (psalm refrain).

to cantor preparation: The joy and confidence you sing about in this Sunday's responsorial psalm is not naive. You are not a "happy-go-lucky" beginner, but an experienced disciple on a road that you know will lead to suffering and death. Your choice to make God your "inheritance" is made with full confidence of its reward as well as full awareness of its cost. In what ways have you already encountered its cost? In what ways have you already experienced its reward? How might these reflections help you sing this psalm with more conviction?

ASSEMBLY & FAITH-SHARING GROUPS
· The darkness I experience today in the world is . . . in my life is . . .
· I experience Jesus "near, at the gates" when I . . . His presence dispels darkness by . . .
· I experience hope for the world because . . . I experience hope for the church because . . .

PRESIDERS
· I am the promise of hope for my people when . . .

DEACONS
· My service lifts others out of darkness into hope when . .

HOSPITALITY MINISTERS
· My open-hearted hospitality gathers people "from the end of the earth to the end of the sky" to the nearness of Jesus in that . . .

MUSIC MINISTERS
· My music ministry enables the presence of Christ to break forth within the assembly when . . .

ALTAR MINISTERS
· My lighting the candles is symbolic of Jesus' dispelling darkness when . . .

LECTORS
· The manner of my proclamation reveals Jesus' presence when . . .

EXTRAORDINARY MINISTERS OF HOLY COMMUNION
· When I bring Holy Communion to the sick and homebound, I bring the light of Christ in that . . .

Model Act of Penitence

Presider: Today's gospel speaks of the tribulations accompanying Jesus' second coming; it also assures us of his abiding presence now. As we prepare to celebrate this liturgy, let us open ourselves to his presence among us . . . [pause]

> Lord Jesus, your words will not pass away: Lord . . .
>
> Christ Jesus, you will come in glory at the end of time: Christ . . .
>
> Lord Jesus, you are our hope and salvation: Lord . . .

Homily Points

• Today we have our own apocalyptic visionaries—environmentalists warn of global destruction and activists warn of nuclear annihilation. We ourselves are apocalyptic visionaries when we, for example, warn our children to stop destructive behavior, chide ourselves to healthy diet and exercise, or moan one more time, "Where's this all going to end?" Such apocalyptic outcries call us to see likely futures so that we might change present ways.

• Jesus teaches us to respond to life's inevitable darkness by finding in this very darkness his in-breaking presence. Jesus uses apocalyptic language not primarily to talk about the future, but to call us to the hope that is in the present situation. The source of this hope is his abiding presence.

• We can come to hope in Jesus' abiding presence through very human ways. Often, for example, when we face difficulties it is others who come to us with a word of comfort or insight, help us see more clearly the whole situation, give us strength to make changes in our lives through their presence and compassion. Or our own past experience of growth through the challenge of difficulties brings us to deeper wisdom. We don't find Jesus "in the clouds," but here on earth; we don't await victory over darkness only at the end of time, but find it here and now.

Model Prayer of the Faithful

Presider: God sends the Son as our hope and strength. And so we pray with confidence for our needs.

Response:

Lord, hear our prayer.

Cantor:

we pray to the Lord,

For all members of the church to be beacons of hope where there is darkness . . . [pause]

For the salvation of the world . . . [pause]

For the poor and sick, the lonely and desperate . . . [pause]

For all of us to be open to the many faces of Jesus' presence . . . [pause]

Presider: God of heaven and earth, you gather all people into your loving care: hear these our prayers that we might be found written in the book and invited to enjoy everlasting life with you. We ask this through your Son, Jesus Christ, who is to come in glory. **Amen.**

ALTERNATIVE OPENING PRAYER

Let us pray

Pause for silent prayer

Father in heaven,
  ever-living source of all that is good,
  from the beginning of time you promised
    man salvation
through the future coming of your Son,
    our Lord Jesus Christ.
Help us to drink of his truth
and expand our hearts with the joy of his
    promises,
so that we may serve you in faith and in
    love
and know for ever the joy of your
    presence.

We ask this through Christ our Lord.
  Amen.

FIRST READING
Dan 12:1-3

In those days, I, Daniel,
  heard this word of the Lord:
"At that time there shall arise
    Michael, the great prince,
    guardian of your people;
it shall be a time unsurpassed in distress
    since nations began until that time.
At that time your people shall escape,
    everyone who is found written in the
    book.

"Many of those who sleep in the dust of
    the earth shall awake;
    some shall live forever,
    others shall be an everlasting horror
      and disgrace.

"But the wise shall shine brightly
    like the splendor of the firmament,
and those who lead the many to justice
    shall be like the stars forever."

RESPONSORIAL PSALM
Ps 16:5, 8, 9-10, 11

R̸. (1) You are my inheritance, O Lord!

O LORD, my allotted portion and my cup,
 you it is who hold fast my lot.
I set the LORD ever before me;
 with him at my right hand I shall not be
 disturbed.

R̸. You are my inheritance, O Lord!

Therefore my heart is glad and my soul
 rejoices,
 my body, too, abides in confidence;
because you will not abandon my soul to
 the netherworld,
 nor will you suffer your faithful one to
 undergo corruption.

R̸. You are my inheritance, O Lord!

You will show me the path to life,
 fullness of joys in your presence,
 the delights at your right hand forever.

R̸. You are my inheritance, O Lord!

SECOND READING
Heb 10:11-14, 18

Brothers and sisters:
Every priest stands daily at his ministry,
 offering frequently those same sacrifices
 that can never take away sins.
But this one offered one sacrifice for sins,
 and took his seat forever at the right
 hand of God;
 now he waits until his enemies are made
 his footstool.
For by one offering
 he has made perfect forever those who
 are being consecrated.

Where there is forgiveness of these,
 there is no longer offering for sin.

About Liturgy
Parousia and eschatology: "Parousia" is a technical theological term that refers to Jesus' Second Coming. This Sunday's gospel only mentions the great cosmic events that will accompany his return. Additionally, when Christ comes at the end of time there will be the general judgment (see Matt 25) and general resurrection. If this Second Coming would be all there is at the end times, then perhaps there could be reason for fear. However, the parousia isn't all there is—it ushers in the final age of fulfillment. This time of fulfillment is theologically referred to as the "eschatological times." This strange term comes from two Greek words meaning the study of finality or end times. Eschatology, then, marks the point (not to be understood chronologically) in time when God's reign will be finally established.

It is easy to put these future events out of our heads; most of us (when we think of them at all, usually on these last Sundays of the liturgical year) think of the end times as way off in the future. Contrary, in the very early church they thought that Christ would return immediately and so they lived their lives in a most radical way—sharing all things in common, devoting themselves to prayer, etc. (see, for example, Acts 2:42-47 and Acts 4:32-35). One of the challenges of these future events is that we, too, learn to live in the present and to be faithful disciples, making Christ's saving presence known in our world. We are to live in expectation, not in fear.

About Liturgical Music
Music suggestions: Issac Watts' quiet but powerful "O God, Our Help in Ages Past" would make an appropriate opening or closing song for this Sunday's liturgy. Timothy Dudley-Smith's text "When the Lord in Glory Comes" identifies the voice and face of Christ as what will be most important at the Second Coming; Bob Moore's setting would make an effective song during the preparation of the gifts. Grayson Warren Brown's "When He Comes" exudes the joy God and all creation will feel when Christ returns in glory and "the children of ages will die nevermore." It could be used as an assembly song during the preparation of the gifts or as a choir prelude [WLP #007002]. David Haas' energetic "My Lord Will Come Again" also sings of the joy Christ's return will engender and would make an excellent choral prelude [GIA G-3654]. David Music's setting of Timothy Dudley-Smith's "Name of All Majesty" [GIA G-4791] would provide a choral prelude of a very different style. The setting moves from modal to major and from chant to homophony, effectively coloring the text with both ethereal majesty and earthy presence. Finally, the well known Quaker hymn "How Can I Keep from Singing" sings of our hope in the midst of tumult and tribulation because we know "love is Lord of heaven and earth." This hymn would work well as an assembly song during the Communion procession, or could be used as a choral prelude [see Paul Gibson's arrangement for assembly, choir, organ, and brass quintet, OCP #9202].

SPIRITUALITY

Gospel

John 18:33b-37; L161B

Pilate said to Jesus,
    "Are you the King
        of the Jews?"
Jesus answered, "Do
    you say this on
        your own
    or have others told
        you about me?"
Pilate answered, "I
    am not a Jew,
    am I?
Your own nation and the chief priests
    handed you over to me.
What have you done?"
Jesus answered, "My kingdom does not
    belong to this world.
If my kingdom did belong to this world,
    my attendants would be fighting
    to keep me from being handed over
        to the Jews.
But as it is, my kingdom is not here."
So Pilate said to him, "Then you are a
    king?"
Jesus answered, "You say I am a king.
For this I was born and for this I came
    into the world,
    to testify to the truth.
Everyone who belongs to the truth
    listens to my voice."

Reflecting on the Gospel

Since most of us have never lived in a kingdom and have no experience of relating to a king, our notion of kings and kingdoms tends to be along the lines of Camelot filled with handsome men, fair damsels, great wealth, easy comfort, eye-popping love, pristine peace. It's a grand dream for a kingdom of this world. This festival and the readings, however, hardly take us to this kind of kingdom. The gospel is part of the dialogue between Jesus and Pilate at Jesus' trial. This is not exactly Camelot!

On this last Sunday of the liturgical year we clearly see that Jesus' kingdom is not of this world. Christ's kingdom is not a spacial place ("does not belong to this world"), but an interior identity defined by our relationship to Christ the King. And here is where we can have a little bit of Camelot. This Sunday we celebrate a King whose presence and power we have already experienced: Christ, whose kingdom is not territory but virtue, not power but service, not wealth but grace. This King has loved us with his very life. He has shown us Camelot.

"My kingdom does not belong to this world." Where is Jesus' kingdom? It exists wherever people embody Jesus' manner of acting and relating ("belongs to the truth"), wherever the Spirit of Jesus is the rule of life. We enter into Jesus' kingdom whenever we listen to his voice and proclaim him "the Alpha and the Omega" (second reading) of all that is. This kingdom does not belong to this world, but is meant to transform this world. The liturgical year culminates with a summary statement of the identity of Jesus—"Christ the King." As Christ, he is worthy of our worship. As King he is deserving of our service. As we celebrate this enthronement of Christ in glory (compare first reading), we also look forward to his victory in us when we are "freed . . . from our sins" and "made . . . into a kingdom" (second reading).

Thus this solemnity invites us to renew our commitment to serve him with all our hearts. It invites us to renew our self-giving stance as disciples who follow the King. In our self-giving are we transformed and as we are transformed so is the world because he has made us into a kingdom (second reading). The surprise of this festival is that we are God's kingdom already. We already share in his victory for we are "freed from our sins."

At the end of this liturgical year we are invited by the liturgy once again to fall in love with our King who has won for us eternal life. "To him be glory and power forever and ever. Amen."

Living the Paschal Mystery

Self-giving service is a small price to pay for our share in this eternal glory. Living the paschal mystery means that we don't count the cost, but always find strength, hope, encouragement in the glimpse of final victory that we are repeatedly given throughout the liturgical year. Living the paschal mystery means that we see the victorious Christ even in the everyday trials and difficulties that we face. Living the paschal mystery means that we are ever faithful to the rhythm of dying and rising as it unfolds in our every day prayer, work, leisure. Living the paschal mystery means that we are "priests" (that is, mediators) for those whom we meet—that we are the Body of Christ leading others to holier lives and happier commitment. If someone should then ask us, "What have you done?" (see gospel) our answer would come quickly and surely—we have served our King. We have loved our King. In doing so, we have shared in the greatest wealth possible—his kingdom where is all glory.

Focusing the Gospel

Key words and phrases: My kingdom does not belong to this world, belongs to the truth, listens to my voice

To the point: "My kingdom does not belong to this world." Where is Jesus' kingdom? It exists wherever people embody Jesus' manner of acting and relating ("belongs to the truth"), wherever the Spirit of Jesus is the rule of life. We enter into Jesus' kingdom whenever we listen to his voice and proclaim him "the Alpha and the Omega" (second reading) of all that is. This kingdom does not belong to this world, but is meant to transform this world.

Connecting the Gospel

to the first and second readings: The liturgical year culminates with a summary statement of the identity of Jesus—"Christ the King." As Christ, he is worthy of our worship. As King he is deserving of our service. As we celebrate this enthronement of Christ in glory (compare first reading), we also look forward to his victory in us when we are "freed . . . from our sins" and "made . . . into a kingdom" (second reading).

to our experience: We have a limited understanding of kings today, and when we think about them, it tends to be from history and/or memory rather than from our immediate experience. This Sunday we celebrate a King whose presence and power we have experienced: Christ, whose kingdom is not territory but virtue, not power but service, not wealth but grace.

Connecting the Responsorial Psalm

to the readings: The ancient Hebrew community conceived of the earth as a platform balanced on the chaotic waters of a raging sea. The surging waters constantly threatened to overwhelm the earth and would have done so were it not for the constant intervention of a more stabilizing force: the hand of God. Psalm 93, from which this responsorial psalm is taken, uses this imagery to express the cosmic conflict going on between God and the forces of evil and assures us that God has the upper hand: "[God] has made the world firm, not to be moved" (psalm).

On this day we celebrate the full and final victory of God over evil through the person of Christ. We also celebrate our faithful discipleship. Throughout another year of Ordinary Time we have listened to Jesus' words and obeyed his call to discipleship. We have walked with him to Jerusalem and the cross. Today we celebrate the glory which awaits us beyond the cross. Christ is King and he has made us his kingdom (see second reading).

to cantor preparation: In this Sunday's responsorial psalm you shout what you have believed in and remained faithful to even when factors of everyday life made it appear otherwise: Christ is King, the Alpha and Omega (see second reading), the meaning and endpoint of all existence. The joy with which you sing this psalm will be directly related to the faithfulness with which you have walked this year's journey through Ordinary Time. Take time this week to thank Christ for showing you the way and for strengthening you when you felt weak and weary. Take time also to thank Christ for the many other faithful disciples who have walked with you.

ASSEMBLY & FAITH-SHARING GROUPS
- Jesus' kingdom is evident to others through my manner of acting and relating when . . .
- Who/what helps me listen to Jesus' voice is . . .
- I experience the transforming power of Jesus' kingdom in . . .

PRESIDERS
- My way of relating to the assembly invites them to encounter Christ the King when . . .

DEACONS
- My proclamation of any gospel reading is always the proclamation of Christ as "the Alpha and the Omega" because . . .

HOSPITALITY MINISTERS
- My manner of welcoming members of the assembly creates a sense of coming into Christ's kingdom by . . .

MUSIC MINISTERS
- My manner of doing music ministry makes the kingdom of Christ present by . . .

ALTAR MINISTERS
- My ministry of service exemplifies the spirit of Christ's kingdom by . . .

LECTORS
- My awareness of belonging "to the truth" helps me proclaim better the word of God because . . .

EXTRAORDINARY MINISTERS OF HOLY COMMUNION
- My manner of distributing Holy Communion helps people experience more fully their coming to the Banquet of the King when . . .

Model Act of Penitence

Presider: Today we acclaim Christ as our King. Let us look into our hearts and see how Christ is enthroned there . . . [pause]

Lord Jesus, you are King forever: Lord . . .

Christ Jesus, you love us and have freed us from our sins: Christ . . .

Lord Jesus, you deserve all dominion and glory and service: Lord . . .

Homily Points

• We are a nation founded upon independence; our national holiday is called "Independence Day." We made a choice as a people not to be ruled by a king. But we did not give up the rule of law or the centrality of acquiescing to the common good. At the same time, how hard it is for us to put the common good first, when our tendency is to watch out for our own interests. This tension subtly contrasts the "kingdoms" of this world with Jesus' kingdom which is not of this world.

• Jesus as King and the kingdom he promises us does not erase this tension but rather heightens it because of the radical manner of acting and relating to which Jesus calls us. Our lives are totally about the good of the other. And this is the radical life Christ the King modeled for us: he "loves us" and "has freed us from our sins by his blood" (second reading).

• Jesus' kingdom exists wherever people act and relate as he did. Consequently, our lives are to be just as radical in giving ourselves over to the common good as was his. We are called to be his priests (see second reading), the mediators of God's love among us.

Model Prayer of the Faithful

Presider: Let us pray for the grace to continue to build Christ's kingdom here on earth.

Response: Lord, hear our prayer.

Cantor: we pray to the Lord,

That Christ's reign be visible through the loving service of all members of the church . . . [pause]

That Christ's reign be visible through all peoples' faithful witness to God's presence . . . [pause]

That Christ's reign be visible through our active concern for the suffering of the poor, imprisoned, persecuted . . . [pause]

That Christ's reign be visible through each of us in our daily efforts to serve the common good . . . [pause]

Presider: Father all-powerful, God of love, you raised your Son to new life and seated him at your right hand in glory where he could reign as King for ever: hear these our prayers and help us to be faithful in our service of others. We ask this in the name of Jesus Christ the King now and for ever. **Amen.**

Let us pray
[that the kingdom of Christ may live in our hearts and come to our world]

Pause for silent prayer

Father all-powerful, God of love,
you have raised our Lord Jesus Christ from death to life,
resplendent in glory as King of creation.
Open our hearts,
free all the world to rejoice in his peace,
to glory in his justice, to live in his love.
Bring all mankind together in Jesus Christ your Son,
whose kingdom is with you and the Holy Spirit,
one God, for ever and ever. **Amen.**

FIRST READING
Dan 7:13-14

As the visions during the night continued,
    I saw
    one like a Son of man coming,
        on the clouds of heaven;
    when he reached the Ancient One
        and was presented before him,
    the one like a Son of man received
        dominion, glory, and kingship;
    all peoples, nations, and languages
        serve him.
    His dominion is an everlasting dominion
        that shall not be taken away,
        his kingship shall not be destroyed.

RESPONSORIAL PSALM
Ps 93:1, 1-2, 5

R︎. (1a) The Lord is king; he is robed in majesty.

The LORD is king, in splendor robed;
    robed is the LORD and girt about with
      strength.

R︎. The Lord is king; he is robed in majesty.

And he has made the world firm,
    not to be moved.
Your throne stands firm from of old;
    from everlasting you are, O LORD.

R︎. The Lord is king; he is robed in majesty.

Your decrees are worthy of trust indeed;
    holiness befits your house,
    O LORD, for length of days.

R︎. The Lord is king; he is robed in majesty.

SECOND READING
Rev 1:5-8

Jesus Christ is the faithful witness,
    the firstborn of the dead and ruler of
      the kings of the earth.
To him who loves us and has freed us from
    our sins by his blood,
    who has made us into a kingdom,
      priests for his God and Father,
    to him be glory and power forever and
      ever. Amen.
Behold, he is coming amid the clouds,
    and every eye will see him,
    even those who pierced him.
All the peoples of the earth will lament
    him.
    Yes. Amen.

"I am the Alpha and the Omega," says the
    Lord God,
    "the one who is and who was and who
      is to come, the almighty."

About Liturgy

Celebration: Just as Lent opens onto Easter, if we have patiently worked our way through Ordinary Time—and, indeed, through the whole of this past liturgical year—when we come to this solemnity we are ready for a jubilant celebration. The fruits of our labors will be consistent with the extent of our labors. If our liturgical year has been rather lackadaisical, then these high festivals probably won't move us. We will depend on the environment and the music to carry us rather than on the inner strength that comes from watching ourselves be transformed ever more perfectly into the Body of Christ during this past year.

Liturgical celebration has little to do with "whoop-dee-do" and much to do with self-emptying. Our greatest joy and celebration come not from what we do but from the deep experience of what God has done in us. We need to be careful that we don't cloud the real meaning of these high festivals with externals that actually keep us from the deepest and most satisfying feasting. Celebration is really the play between surrender and encounter in which we are transformed. Anything less than this gets in the way of our being God's presence, God's reign in this redeemed world.

About Liturgical Music

Music suggestions: Closing the journey of Ordinary Time, this solemnity is like a second Easter. We need to make this liturgy a celebration not only of Christ's kingship but also of the church's fidelity through another year of Ordinary Time. Sing your most festive service music (your Easter season set). Use an SATB setting of the responsorial psalm. Do a full gospel procession with an extended Alleluia. Use "Lift High the Cross" for the entrance procession (most appropriate this year when the gospel reading is taken from the passion of John) and add full brass. Use Suzanne Toolan's adaptable "Jesus Christ, Yesterday, Today and for Ever" with its prayerful, Taizé-like refrain for the Communion procession.

NOVEMBER 22, 2009
THE SOLEMNITY OF OUR LORD JESUS CHRIST THE KING

✠ SPIRITUALITY

GOSPEL ACCLAMATION
℟. Alleluia, alleluia.
In all circumstances, give thanks,
for this is the will of God for you in Christ Jesus.
℟. Alleluia, alleluia.

Gospel   Luke 17:11-19;
L947.6

As Jesus continued
    his journey to
        Jerusalem,
    he traveled through
        Samaria and
        Galilee.
As he was entering a vil-
    lage, ten lepers met him.
They stood at a distance from him and
    raised their voices, saying,
    "Jesus, Master! Have pity on us!"
And when he saw them, he said,
    "Go show yourselves to the priests."
As they were going they were cleansed.
And one of them, realizing he had been
    healed,
    returned, glorifying God in a loud voice;
    and he fell at the feet of Jesus and
        thanked him.
He was a Samaritan.
Jesus said in reply,
    "Ten were cleansed, were they not?
Where are the other nine?
Has none but this foreigner returned to
    give thanks to God?"
Then he said to him, "Stand up and go;
    your faith has saved you."

See Appendix A, p. 307, for the other readings.

FIRST READING
Sir 50:22-24; L943.2

RESPONSORIAL PSALM
Ps 67:2-3, 5, 6, 8; L919.1

SECOND READING
1 Cor 1:3-9; L944.1

*Additional reading choices may be found in the
Lectionary for Mass, vol. IV, "In Thanksgiving to
God," nos. 943–947.*

Reflecting on the Gospel

The origin of this civil holiday goes back to the Pilgrims when their governor called them to prayer and then a meal that they shared among themselves and with friendly Native Americans. Yet these people had a collective memory of a death-filled, difficult voyage to a land that was also harsh to them. There was not a family who had not lost at least one member and still they stopped to give God thanks. It takes a magnanimous heart, indeed, to recognize that even in the midst of difficulties and sometimes death, we are dependent upon a God who loves us and gives us all good things.

As the first reading from Sirach reminds us, we bless God because God "has done wondrous things on earth." The second reading picks up on the same theme: we "continually thank" God "because of the favor he has bestowed on [us] in Christ Jesus." It is essential for us to have grateful hearts, even in face of hardship and death. Gratitude reminds us that we are never bereft of gifts, even when it seems like we are as low as we can get. The pilgrims and thanksgiving remind us that if we forget all we receive as gift—especially the little things in life—we lose our giftedness—our hearts turned toward others.

How much God does for us, how attentive to every detail of our lives: creation, life itself, joy and peace (first reading); grace, knowledge, spiritual gifts (second reading); cleansing, healing, salvation (gospel). How much Jesus did for the ten lepers by healing them! One of them chose not to take this divine goodness for granted, and in returning to say thanks, he received even more: salvation.

When the Samaritan leper realized he had been healed, he returned to the Source of his healing. Herein is salvation: not only the wholeness that God continually offers us, but also the grace to seek out the God who is good to us beyond our estimation. In seeking God, in giving thanks, in acknowledging God's goodness to us, we recognize that God's faithfulness brings us to grace and peace (see second reading). God's generosity is boundless; our thanksgiving ought be as boundless.

Living the Paschal Mystery

What is the difference between the one who returned to thank Jesus and the nine who didn't? All ten were cured. All ten received the gift of healing from Jesus. Only one, though, went beyond the joy all ten must have felt in being healed; only one transcended self and returned to thank the Giver of the gift. Self-awareness was not simply self-centered; the leper's self-awareness of healing prompted him to forget self and give thanks for the gift of healing that came from outside of himself.

Thanksgiving Day is a national time for giving thanks for all the abundance with which our nation has been blessed. Like the leper, though, we must transcend ourselves and express our gratitude in concrete acts of generous thanksgiving. More than going to church (as important as that is), we also express our gratitude by reaching out to those less fortunate than ourselves, to those who don't seem to share in the abundance of our nation in the same way. Genuine gratitude calls us to die to ourselves by giving of our own abundance so that others may share in God's gracious gifts, receiving life more abundantly themselves. Thankfulness is more than words—it is actions expressed in loving service of others, giving to them as God has given to us.

Focusing the Gospel

Key words and phrases: ten persons with leprosy; cleansed; realizing he had been healed, returned . . . and thanked him; saved you

To the point: How much God does for us, how attentive to every detail of our lives: creation, life itself, joy and peace (first reading); grace, knowledge, spiritual gifts (second reading); cleansing, healing, salvation (gospel). How much Jesus did for the ten lepers by healing them! One of them chose not to take this divine goodness for granted, and in returning to say thanks, he received even more: salvation. God's generosity is boundless; our thanksgiving ought be as boundless.

Model Act of Penitence

Presider: We gather today as a nation to give thanks to God for the many blessings bestowed upon us. Let us pause and prepare to celebrate well this Eucharist, through which we give thanks to God for salvation, our most precious gift . . . [pause]

Lord Jesus, you are God's gracious Gift to us: Lord . . .

Christ Jesus, you are our salvation: Christ . . .

Lord Jesus, you give us your Body and Blood which we receive in thanksgiving: Lord . . .

Model Prayer of the Faithful

Presider: The God who has blessed us with all good things, will continue to give us what we need. And so we pray.

Response:

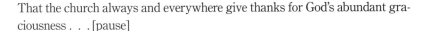

Lord, hear our prayer.

Cantor:

we pray to the Lord,

That the church always and everywhere give thanks for God's abundant graciousness . . . [pause]

That nations share their abundance so that all peoples have what they need . . . [pause]

That the poor be lifted out of poverty and the sick be healed . . . [pause]

That each of us express daily our thankfulness to God for our blessings by reaching out in service to those in need . . . [pause]

Presider: Gracious God, you have given us all good things: hear these our prayers, that in sharing our prosperity with others all may know your goodness and blessings. We ask this through the intercession of your most gracious Gift to us of all, Jesus Christ our Lord. **Amen.**

FOR REFLECTION

· What helps me stop and realize God's goodness to me is . . .

· God's generosity to me looks like . . . I am most grateful to God for . . .

· When I give God thanks, the "more" I receive is . . .

Homily Points

• The origin of this civil holiday is rooted in the Pilgrims who came together to thank God for the good things they had, even in the midst of death and hardship. This models for us that giving God thanks is evoked by more than good things; it is our expression of our need for and intimate relationship with God.

• The ten lepers were all healed, whether they gave thanks or not. But when the Samaritan leper returned to give thanks, he was given even more: salvation. Recognition of God's good gifts to us and gratitude for all we receive opens us to even more gifts.

Readings *(continued)*

The Immaculate Conception of the Blessed Virgin Mary, *December 8, 2008*

Gospel (cont.)
Luke 1:26-38; L689

But Mary said to the angel,
  "How can this be,
  since I have no relations with a man?"
And the angel said to her in reply,
  "The Holy Spirit will come upon you,
  and the power of the Most High will overshadow you.
Therefore the child to be born
  will be called holy, the Son of God.
And behold, Elizabeth, your relative,
  has also conceived a son in her old age,
  and this is the sixth month for her who was called barren;
  for nothing will be impossible for God."
Mary said, "Behold, I am the handmaid of the Lord.
May it be done to me according to your word."
Then the angel departed from her.

FIRST READING
Gen 3:9-15, 20

After the man, Adam, had eaten of the tree,
  the LORD God called to the man and asked
    him, "Where are you?"
He answered, "I heard you in the garden;
  but I was afraid, because I was naked,
  so I hid myself."
Then he asked, "Who told you that you were
  naked?
You have eaten, then,
  from the tree of which I had forbidden you
    to eat!"
The man replied, "The woman whom you put
  here with me—
  she gave me fruit from the tree, and so I
    ate it."
The LORD God then asked the woman,
  "Why did you do such a thing?"
The woman answered, "The serpent tricked
  me into it, so I ate it."

Then the LORD God said to the serpent:
  "Because you have done this, you shall be
    banned
    from all the animals
    and from all the wild creatures;
  on your belly shall you crawl,
    and dirt shall you eat
    all the days of your life.
  I will put enmity between you and the
    woman,
    and between your offspring and hers;
  he will strike at your head,
    while you strike at his heel."

The man called his wife Eve,
  because she became the mother of all the
    living.

RESPONSORIAL PSALM
Ps 98:1, 2-3, 3-4

R̂. (1a) Sing to the Lord a new song, for he has done marvelous deeds.

Sing to the LORD a new song,
  for he has done wondrous deeds;
his right hand has won victory for him,
  his holy arm.

R̂. Sing to the Lord a new song, for he has done marvelous deeds.

The LORD has made his salvation known:
  in the sight of the nations he has revealed
    his justice.
He has remembered his kindness and his
    faithfulness
  toward the house of Israel.

R̂. Sing to the Lord a new song, for he has done marvelous deeds.

All the ends of the earth have seen
  the salvation by our God.
Sing joyfully to the LORD, all you lands;
  break into song; sing praise.

R̂. Sing to the Lord a new song, for he has done marvelous deeds.

SECOND READING
Eph 1:3-6, 11-12

Brothers and sisters:
Blessed be the God and Father of our Lord
    Jesus Christ,
  who has blessed us in Christ
  with every spiritual blessing in the
    heavens,
  as he chose us in him, before the foundation
    of the world,
  to be holy and without blemish before him.
In love he destined us for adoption to himself
    through Jesus Christ,
  in accord with the favor of his will,
  for the praise of the glory of his grace
  that he granted us in the beloved.

In him we were also chosen,
  destined in accord with the purpose of the
    One
  who accomplishes all things according to the
    intention of his will,
  so that we might exist for the praise of his
    glory,
  we who first hoped in Christ.

Gospel (cont.)
Matt 1:1-25; L13ABC

David became the father of Solomon,
 whose mother had been the wife of Uriah.
Solomon became the father of Rehoboam,
 Rehoboam the father of Abijah,
 Abijah the father of Asaph.
Asaph became the father of Jehoshaphat,
 Jehoshaphat the father of Joram,
 Joram the father of Uzziah.
Uzziah became the father of Jotham,
 Jotham the father of Ahaz,
 Ahaz the father of Hezekiah.
Hezekiah became the father of Manasseh,
 Manasseh the father of Amos,
 Amos the father of Josiah.
Josiah became the father of Jechoniah and his brothers
 at the time of the Babylonian exile.

After the Babylonian exile,
 Jechoniah became the father of Shealtiel,
 Shealtiel the father of Zerubbabel,
 Zerubbabel the father of Abiud.
Abiud became the father of Eliakim,
 Eliakim the father of Azor,
 Azor the father of Zadok.
Zadok became the father of Achim,
 Achim the father of Eliud,
 Eliud the father of Eleazar.
Eleazar became the father of Matthan,
 Matthan the father of Jacob,
 Jacob the father of Joseph, the husband of Mary.
Of her was born Jesus who is called the Christ.

Thus the total number of generations
 from Abraham to David
 is fourteen generations;
 from David to the Babylonian exile,
 fourteen generations;
 from the Babylonian exile to the Christ,
 fourteen generations.

Now this is how the birth of Jesus Christ came about.
When his mother Mary was betrothed to Joseph,
 but before they lived together,
 she was found with child through the Holy Spirit.
Joseph her husband, since he was a righteous man,
 yet unwilling to expose her to shame,
 decided to divorce her quietly.

Such was his intention when, behold,
 the angel of the Lord appeared to him in a dream and said,
 "Joseph, son of David,
 do not be afraid to take Mary your wife into your home.
For it is through the Holy Spirit
 that this child has been conceived in her.
She will bear a son and you are to name him Jesus,
 because he will save his people from their sins."
All this took place to fulfill
 what the Lord had said through the prophet:
  Behold, the virgin shall conceive and bear a son,
   and they shall name him Emmanuel,
  which means "God is with us."
When Joseph awoke,
 he did as the angel of the Lord had commanded him
 and took his wife into his home.
He had no relations with her until she bore a son,
 and he named him Jesus.

or Matt 1:18-25

This is how the birth of Jesus Christ came about.
When his mother Mary was betrothed to Joseph,
 but before they lived together,
 she was found with child through the Holy Spirit.
Joseph her husband, since he was a righteous man,
 yet unwilling to expose her to shame,
 decided to divorce her quietly.
Such was his intention when, behold,
 the angel of the Lord appeared to him in a dream and said,
 "Joseph, son of David,
 do not be afraid to take Mary your wife into your home.
For it is through the Holy Spirit
 that this child has been conceived in her.
She will bear a son and you are to name him Jesus,
 because he will save his people from their sins."
All this took place to fulfill
 what the Lord had said through the prophet:
  Behold, the virgin shall conceive and bear a son,
   and they shall name him Emmanuel,
  which means "God is with us."
When Joseph awoke,
 he did as the angel of the Lord had commanded him
 and took his wife into his home.
He had no relations with her until she bore a son,
 and he named him Jesus.

The Nativity of the Lord, *December 25, 2008 (Vigil Mass)*

FIRST READING
Isa 62:1-5

For Zion's sake I will not be silent,
    for Jerusalem's sake I will not be quiet,
until her vindication shines forth like the dawn
    and her victory like a burning torch.

Nations shall behold your vindication,
    and all the kings your glory;
you shall be called by a new name
    pronounced by the mouth of the LORD.
You shall be a glorious crown in the hand of
    the LORD,
    a royal diadem held by your God.
No more shall people call you "Forsaken,"
    or your land "Desolate,"
but you shall be called "My Delight,"
    and your land "Espoused."
For the LORD delights in you
    and makes your land his spouse.
As a young man marries a virgin,
    your Builder shall marry you;
and as a bridegroom rejoices in his bride
    so shall your God rejoice in you.

RESPONSORIAL PSALM
Ps 89:4-5, 16-17, 27, 29

R. (2a) Forever I will sing the goodness of the Lord.

I have made a covenant with my chosen one,
    I have sworn to David my servant:
forever will I confirm your posterity
    and establish your throne for all
        generations.

R. Forever I will sing the goodness of the Lord.

Blessed the people who know the joyful shout;
    in the light of your countenance, O LORD,
        they walk.
At your name they rejoice all the day,
    and through your justice they are exalted.

R. Forever I will sing the goodness of the Lord.

He shall say of me, "You are my father,
    my God, the rock, my savior."
Forever I will maintain my kindness toward
    him,
    and my covenant with him stands firm.

R. Forever I will sing the goodness of the Lord.

SECOND READING
Acts 13:16-17, 22-25

When Paul reached Antioch in Pisidia and
        entered the synagogue,
    he stood up, motioned with his hand, and
        said,
    "Fellow Israelites and you others who are
        God-fearing, listen.
The God of this people Israel chose our
    ancestors
    and exalted the people during their sojourn
        in the land of Egypt.
With uplifted arm he led them out of it.
Then he removed Saul and raised up David
        as king;
    of him he testified,
    'I have found David, son of Jesse, a man
        after my own heart;
    he will carry out my every wish.'
From this man's descendants God, according
        to his promise,
    has brought to Israel a savior, Jesus.
John heralded his coming by proclaiming a
        baptism of repentance
    to all the people of Israel;
    and as John was completing his course, he
        would say,
    'What do you suppose that I am? I am not he.
Behold, one is coming after me;
    I am not worthy to unfasten the sandals of
        his feet.'"

The Nativity of the Lord, *December 25, 2008 (Mass at Midnight)*

Gospel (cont.)
Luke 2:1-14; L14ABC

Now there were shepherds in that region living in the fields
    and keeping the night watch over their flock.
The angel of the Lord appeared to them
    and the glory of the Lord shone around them,
    and they were struck with great fear.
The angel said to them,
    "Do not be afraid;
    for behold, I proclaim to you good news of great joy
    that will be for all the people.
For today in the city of David
    a savior has been born for you who is Christ and Lord.
And this will be a sign for you:
    you will find an infant wrapped in swaddling clothes
    and lying in a manger."
And suddenly there was a multitude of the heavenly host with the
        angel,
    praising God and saying:
        "Glory to God in the highest
            and on earth peace to those on whom his favor rests."

The Nativity of the Lord, *December 25, 2008 (Mass at Midnight)*

FIRST READING
Isa 9:1-6

The people who walked in darkness
    have seen a great light;
upon those who dwelt in the land of gloom
    a light has shone.
You have brought them abundant joy
    and great rejoicing,
as they rejoice before you as at the harvest,
    as people make merry when dividing
        spoils.
For the yoke that burdened them,
    the pole on their shoulder,
and the rod of their taskmaster
    you have smashed, as on the day of Midian.
For every boot that tramped in battle,
    every cloak rolled in blood,
    will be burned as fuel for flames.
For a child is born to us, a son is given us;
    upon his shoulder dominion rests.
They name him Wonder-Counselor, God-Hero,
    Father-Forever, Prince of Peace.
His dominion is vast
    and forever peaceful,
from David's throne, and over his kingdom,
    which he confirms and sustains
by judgment and justice,
    both now and forever.
The zeal of the LORD of hosts will do this!

RESPONSORIAL PSALM
Ps 96:1-2, 2-3, 11-12, 13

R̰. (Luke 2:11) Today is born our Savior,
Christ the Lord.

Sing to the LORD a new song;
    sing to the LORD, all you lands.
Sing to the LORD; bless his name.

R̰. Today is born our Savior, Christ the Lord.

Announce his salvation, day after day.
    Tell his glory among the nations;
    among all peoples, his wondrous deeds.

R̰. Today is born our Savior, Christ the Lord.

Let the heavens be glad and the earth rejoice;
    let the sea and what fills it resound;
    let the plains be joyful and all that is in
        them!
Then shall all the trees of the forest exult.

R̰. Today is born our Savior, Christ the Lord.

They shall exult before the LORD, for he
    comes;
    for he comes to rule the earth.
He shall rule the world with justice
    and the peoples with his constancy.

R̰. Today is born our Savior, Christ the Lord.

SECOND READING
Titus 2:11-14

Beloved:
The grace of God has appeared, saving all
    and training us to reject godless ways and
        worldly desires
    and to live temperately, justly, and devoutly
        in this age,
as we await the blessed hope,
    the appearance of the glory of our great
        God
    and savior Jesus Christ,
who gave himself for us to deliver us from
    all lawlessness
and to cleanse for himself a people as his
    own,
eager to do what is good.

The Nativity of the Lord, *December 25, 2008 (Mass at Dawn)*

FIRST READING
Isa 62:11-12

See, the LORD proclaims
    to the ends of the earth:
say to daughter Zion,
    your savior comes!
Here is his reward with him,
    his recompense before him.
They shall be called the holy people,
    the redeemed of the LORD,
and you shall be called "Frequented,"
    a city that is not forsaken.

RESPONSORIAL PSALM
Ps 97:1, 6, 11-12

R̰. A light will shine on us this day: the Lord
is born for us.

The LORD is king; let the earth rejoice;
    let the many islands be glad.
The heavens proclaim his justice,
    and all peoples see his glory.

R̰. A light will shine on us this day: the Lord
is born for us.

Light dawns for the just;
    and gladness, for the upright of heart.
Be glad in the LORD, you just,
    and give thanks to his holy name.

R̰. A light will shine on us this day: the Lord
is born for us.

SECOND READING
Titus 3:4-7

Beloved:
When the kindness and generous love
    of God our savior appeared,
not because of any righteous deeds we had
    done
    but because of his mercy,
he saved us through the bath of rebirth
    and renewal by the Holy Spirit,
whom he richly poured out on us
    through Jesus Christ our savior,
so that we might be justified by his grace
    and become heirs in hope of eternal life.

Gospel (cont.)
John 1:1-18; L16ABC

The true light, which enlightens everyone,
was coming into the world.

He was in the world,
and the world came to be through him,
but the world did not know him.
He came to what was his own,
but his own people did not accept him.

But to those who did accept him
he gave power to become children of God,
to those who believe in his name,
who were born not by natural generation
nor by human choice nor by a man's decision
but of God.

And the Word became flesh
and made his dwelling among us,
and we saw his glory,
the glory as of the Father's only Son,
full of grace and truth.

John testified to him and cried out, saying,
"This was he of whom I said,
'The one who is coming after me ranks ahead of me
because he existed before me.'"
From his fullness we have all received,
grace in place of grace,
because while the law was given through Moses,
grace and truth came through Jesus Christ.
No one has ever seen God.
The only Son, God, who is at the Father's side,
has revealed him.

or John 1:1-5, 9-14

In the beginning was the Word,
and the Word was with God,
and the Word was God.
He was in the beginning with God.
All things came to be through him,
and without him nothing came to be.
What came to be through him was life,
and this life was the light of the human race;
the light shines in the darkness,
and the darkness has not overcome it.

The true light, which enlightens everyone,
was coming into the world.

He was in the world,
and the world came to be through him,
but the world did not know him.
He came to what was his own,
but his own people did not accept him.

But to those who did accept him
he gave power to become children of God,
to those who believe in his name,
who were born not by natural generation
nor by human choice nor by a man's decision
but of God.

And the Word became flesh
and made his dwelling among us,
and we saw his glory,
the glory as of the Father's only Son,
full of grace and truth.

FIRST READING
Isa 52:7-10

How beautiful upon the mountains
are the feet of him who brings glad tidings,
announcing peace, bearing good news,
announcing salvation, and saying to Zion,
"Your God is King!"

Hark! Your sentinels raise a cry,
together they shout for joy,
for they see directly, before their eyes,
the LORD restoring Zion.
Break out together in song,
O ruins of Jerusalem!
For the LORD comforts his people,
he redeems Jerusalem.
The LORD has bared his holy arm
in the sight of all the nations;
all the ends of the earth will behold
the salvation of our God.

RESPONSORIAL PSALM
Ps 98:1, 2-3, 3-4, 5-6

R℣. (3c) All the ends of the earth have seen the
saving power of God.

Sing to the LORD a new song,
for he has done wondrous deeds;
his right hand has won victory for him,
his holy arm.

R℣. All the ends of the earth have seen the
saving power of God.

The LORD has made his salvation known:
in the sight of the nations he has revealed
his justice.
He has remembered his kindness and his
faithfulness
toward the house of Israel.

R℣. All the ends of the earth have seen the
saving power of God.

All the ends of the earth have seen
the salvation by our God.
Sing joyfully to the LORD, all you lands;
break into song; sing praise.

R℣. All the ends of the earth have seen the
saving power of God.

Sing praise to the LORD with the harp,
with the harp and melodious song.
With trumpets and the sound of the horn
sing joyfully before the King, the LORD.

R℣. All the ends of the earth have seen the
saving power of God.

The Nativity of the Lord, December 25, 2008 (Mass During the Day)

SECOND READING
Heb 1:1-6

Brothers and sisters:
In times past, God spoke in partial and
     various ways
   to our ancestors through the prophets;
in these last days, he has spoken to us
     through the Son,
   whom he made heir of all things
   and through whom he created the universe,
   who is the refulgence of his glory, the very
        imprint of his being,
     and who sustains all things by his
        mighty word.
   When he had accomplished purification
        from sins,

he took his seat at the right hand of the
     Majesty on high,
   as far superior to the angels
     as the name he has inherited is more
        excellent than theirs.

For to which of the angels did God ever say:
   *You are my son; this day I have begotten
        you?*
Or again:
   *I will be a father to him, and he shall be a
        son to me?*
And again, when he leads the firstborn into
     the world, he says:
   Let all the angels of God worship him.

The Holy Family of Jesus, Mary, and Joseph, December 28, 2008

Gospel (cont.)
Luke 2:22-40; L17B

"Now, Master, you may let your servant go
   in peace, according to your word,
for my eyes have seen your salvation,
   which you prepared in sight of all the peoples,
a light for revelation to the Gentiles,
   and glory for your people Israel."
The child's father and mother were amazed at what was said about
   him;
and Simeon blessed them and said to Mary his mother,
   "Behold, this child is destined
for the fall and rise of many in Israel,
and to be a sign that will be contradicted
—and you yourself a sword will pierce—
so that the thoughts of many hearts may be revealed."
There was also a prophetess, Anna,
   the daughter of Phanuel, of the tribe of Asher.
She was advanced in years,
   having lived seven years with her husband after her marriage,
   and then as a widow until she was eighty-four.
She never left the temple,
   but worshiped night and day with fasting and prayer.
And coming forward at that very time,
   she gave thanks to God and spoke about the child
   to all who were awaiting the redemption of Jerusalem.

When they had fulfilled all the prescriptions
   of the law of the Lord,
   they returned to Galilee,
   to their own town of Nazareth.
The child grew and became strong, filled with wisdom;
   and the favor of God was upon him.

or

Luke 2:22, 39-30

When the days were completed for their purification
   according to the law of Moses,
   they took him up to Jerusalem
   to present him to the Lord.

When they had fulfilled all the prescriptions
   of the law of the Lord,
   they returned to Galilee,
   to their own town of Nazareth.
The child grew and became strong, filled with wisdom;
   and the favor of God was upon him.

SECOND READING (cont.)
Heb 11:8, 11-12, 17-19

By faith Abraham, when put to the test, offered up Isaac,
   and he who had received the promises was ready to offer
      his only son,
   of whom it was said,
   "Through Isaac descendants shall bear your name."
He reasoned that God was able to raise even from the dead,
   and he received Isaac back as a symbol.

The Holy Family of Jesus, Mary, and Joseph, *December 28, 2008*

FIRST READING
Sir 3:2-6, 12-14

God sets a father in honor over his children;
  a mother's authority he confirms over her
    sons.
Whoever honors his father atones for sins,
  and preserves himself from them.
When he prays, he is heard;
  he stores up riches who reveres his mother.
Whoever honors his father is gladdened by
    children,
  and, when he prays, is heard.
Whoever reveres his father will live a long life;
  he who obeys his father brings comfort to
    his mother.

My son, take care of your father when he is
    old;
  grieve him not as long as he lives.
Even if his mind fail, be considerate of him;
  revile him not all the days of his life;
kindness to a father will not be forgotten,
  firmly planted against the debt of your sins
  —a house raised in justice to you.

RESPONSORIAL PSALM
Ps 128:1-2, 3, 4-5

R̥. (cf. 1) Blessed are those who fear the Lord
and walk in his ways.

Blessed is everyone who fears the LORD,
  who walks in his ways!
For you shall eat the fruit of your handiwork;
  blessed shall you be, and favored.

R̥. Blessed are those who fear the Lord and
walk in his ways.

Your wife shall be like a fruitful vine
  in the recesses of your home;
your children like olive plants
  around your table.

R̥. Blessed are those who fear the Lord and
walk in his ways.

Behold, thus is the man blessed
  who fears the LORD.
The LORD bless you from Zion:
  may you see the prosperity of Jerusalem
  all the days of your life.

R̥. Blessed are those who fear the Lord and
walk in his ways.

SECOND READING
Col 3:12-21

Brothers and sisters:
Put on, as God's chosen ones, holy and
    beloved,
  heartfelt compassion, kindness, humility,
    gentleness, and patience,
  bearing with one another and forgiving one
    another,
  if one has a grievance against another;
  as the Lord has forgiven you, so must you
    also do.
And over all these put on love,
  that is, the bond of perfection.
And let the peace of Christ control your
    hearts,
  the peace into which you were also called in
    one body.
And be thankful.

Let the word of Christ dwell in you richly,
  as in all wisdom you teach and admonish
    one another,
  singing psalms, hymns, and spiritual songs
  with gratitude in your hearts to God.
And whatever you do, in word or in deed,
  do everything in the name of the Lord
    Jesus,
  giving thanks to God the Father through
    him.

Wives, be subordinate to your husbands,
  as is proper in the Lord.
Husbands, love your wives,
  and avoid any bitterness toward them.
Children, obey your parents in everything,
  for this is pleasing to the Lord.
Fathers, do not provoke your children,
  so they may not become discouraged.

Solemnity of the Blessed Virgin Mary, Mother of God, *January 1, 2009*

FIRST READING
Num 6:22-27

The LORD said to Moses:
  "Speak to Aaron and his sons and tell them:
  This is how you shall bless the Israelites.
Say to them:
  The LORD bless you and keep you!
  The LORD let his face shine upon
    you, and be gracious to you!
  The LORD look upon you kindly and
    give you peace!
So shall they invoke my name upon the
    Israelites,
  and I will bless them."

RESPONSORIAL PSALM
Ps 67:2-3, 5, 6, 8

R̥. (2a) May God bless us in his mercy.

May God have pity on us and bless us;
  may he let his face shine upon us.
So may your way be known upon earth;
  among all nations, your salvation.

R̥. May God bless us in his mercy.

May the nations be glad and exult
  because you rule the peoples in equity;
  the nations on the earth you guide.

R̥. May God bless us in his mercy.

May the peoples praise you, O God;
  may all the peoples praise you!
May God bless us,
  and may all the ends of the earth fear him!

R̥. May God bless us in his mercy.

SECOND READING
Gal 4:4-7

Brothers and sisters:
When the fullness of time had come, God sent
    his Son,
  born of a woman, born under the law,
  to ransom those under the law,
  so that we might receive adoption as sons.
As proof that you are sons,
  God sent the Spirit of his Son into our
    hearts,
  crying out, "Abba, Father!"
So you are no longer a slave but a son,
  and if a son then also an heir, through God.

The Epiphany of the Lord, *January 4, 2009*

Gospel (cont.)
Matt 2:1-12; L20ABC

And behold, the star that they had seen at its rising preceded them,
  until it came and stopped over the place where the child was.
They were overjoyed at seeing the star,
  and on entering the house
  they saw the child with Mary his mother.
They prostrated themselves and did him homage.
Then they opened their treasures
  and offered him gifts of gold, frankincense, and myrrh.
And having been warned in a dream not to return to Herod,
  they departed for their country by another way.

The Baptism of the Lord, *January 11, 2009*

SECOND READING (cont.)
1 John 5:1-9

For the love of God is this,
  that we keep his commandments.
And his commandments are not burdensome,
  for whoever is begotten by God conquers
    the world.
And the victory that conquers the world is
  our faith.
Who indeed is the victor over the world
  but the one who believes that Jesus is the
    Son of God?
This is the one who came through water and
    blood, Jesus Christ,
  not by water alone, but by water and blood.
The Spirit is the one who testifies,
  and the Spirit is truth.
So there are three that testify,
  the Spirit, the water, and the blood,
  and the three are of one accord.
If we accept human testimony,
  the testimony of God is surely greater.
Now the testimony of God is this,
  that he has testified on behalf of his Son.

FIRST READING
Isa 42:1-4, 6-7

Thus says the LORD:
Here is my servant whom I uphold,
  my chosen one with whom I am pleased,
upon whom I have put my spirit;
  he shall bring forth justice to the nations,
not crying out, not shouting,
  not making his voice heard in the street.

A bruised reed he shall not break,
  and a smoldering wick he shall not quench,
until he establishes justice on the earth;
  the coastlands will wait for his teaching.

I, the LORD, have called you for the victory of
    justice,
  I have grasped you by the hand;
I formed you, and set you
  as a covenant of the people,
  a light for the nations,
to open the eyes of the blind,
  to bring out prisoners from confinement,
  and from the dungeon, those who live in
    darkness.

RESPONSORIAL PSALM
Ps 29:1-2, 3-4, 3, 9-10

℞. (11b) The Lord will bless his people with
peace.

Give to the LORD, you sons of God,
  give to the LORD glory and praise,
give to the LORD the glory due his name;
  adore the LORD in holy attire.

℞. The Lord will bless his people with peace.

The voice of the LORD is over the waters,
  the LORD, over vast waters.
The voice of the LORD is mighty;
  the voice of the LORD is majestic.

℞. The Lord will bless his people with peace.

The God of glory thunders,
  and in his temple all say, "Glory!"
The LORD is enthroned above the flood;
  the LORD is enthroned as king forever.

℞. The Lord will bless his people with peace.

SECOND READING
Acts 10:34-38

Peter proceeded to speak to those gathered
  in the house of Cornelius, saying:
  "In truth, I see that God shows no
    partiality.
Rather, in every nation whoever fears him
  and acts uprightly
  is acceptable to him.
You know the word that he sent to the
    Israelites
  as he proclaimed peace through Jesus
    Christ, who is Lord of all,
  what has happened all over Judea,
  beginning in Galilee after the baptism
  that John preached,
  how God anointed Jesus of Nazareth
  with the Holy Spirit and power.
He went about doing good
  and healing all those oppressed by the
    devil,
  for God was with him."

Ash Wednesday, *February 25, 2009*

FIRST READING
Joel 2:12-18

Even now, says the LORD,
    return to me with your whole heart,
    with fasting, and weeping, and mourning;
Rend your hearts, not your garments,
    and return to the LORD, your God.
For gracious and merciful is he,
    slow to anger, rich in kindness,
    and relenting in punishment.
Perhaps he will again relent
    and leave behind him a blessing,
Offerings and libations
    for the LORD, your God.

Blow the trumpet in Zion!
    proclaim a fast,
    call an assembly;
Gather the people,
    notify the congregation;
Assemble the elders,
    gather the children
    and the infants at the breast;
Let the bridegroom quit his room
    and the bride her chamber.
Between the porch and the altar
    let the priests, the ministers of the LORD,
        weep,
And say, "Spare, O LORD, your people,
    and make not your heritage a reproach,
    with the nations ruling over them!
Why should they say among the peoples,
    'Where is their God?'"

Then the LORD was stirred to concern for his
    land
    and took pity on his people.

RESPONSORIAL PSALM
Ps 51:3-4, 5-6ab, 12-13, 14, and 17

R℣. (see 3a) Be merciful, O Lord, for we have
sinned.

Have mercy on me, O God, in your goodness;
    in the greatness of your compassion wipe
        out my offense.
Thoroughly wash me from my guilt
    and of my sin cleanse me.

R℣. Be merciful, O Lord, for we have sinned.

For I acknowledge my offense,
    and my sin is before me always:
"Against you only have I sinned,
    and done what is evil in your sight."

R℣. Be merciful, O Lord, for we have sinned.

A clean heart create for me, O God,
    and a steadfast spirit renew within me.
Cast me not out from your presence,
    and your Holy Spirit take not from me.

R℣. Be merciful, O Lord, for we have sinned.

Give me back the joy of your salvation,
    and a willing spirit sustain in me.
O Lord, open my lips,
    and my mouth shall proclaim your praise.

R℣. Be merciful, O Lord, for we have sinned.

SECOND READING
2 Cor 5:20—6:2

Brothers and sisters:
We are ambassadors for Christ,
    as if God were appealing through us.
We implore you on behalf of Christ,
    be reconciled to God.
For our sake he made him to be sin who did
        not know sin,
    so that we might become the righteousness
        of God in him.

Working together, then,
    we appeal to you not to receive the grace of
        God in vain.
For he says:

*In an acceptable time I heard you,
    and on the day of salvation I helped you.*

Behold, now is a very acceptable time;
    behold, now is the day of salvation.

Third Sunday of Lent, *March 15, 2009*

RESPONSORIAL PSALM
Ps 19:8, 9, 10, 11

R℣. (John 6:68c) Lord, you have the words of
everlasting life.

The law of the LORD is perfect,
    refreshing the soul;
the decree of the LORD is trustworthy,
    giving wisdom to the simple.

R℣. Lord, you have the words of everlasting life.

The precepts of the LORD are right,
    rejoicing the heart;
the command of the LORD is clear,
    enlightening the eye.

R℣. Lord, you have the words of everlasting life.

The fear of the LORD is pure,
    enduring forever;
the ordinances of the LORD are true,
    all of them just.

R℣. Lord, you have the words of everlasting life.

They are more precious than gold,
    than a heap of purest gold;
sweeter also than syrup
    or honey from the comb.

R℣. Lord, you have the words of everlasting life.

SECOND READING
1 Cor 1:22-25

Brothers and sisters:
Jews demand signs and Greeks look for
        wisdom,
    but we proclaim Christ crucified,
    a stumbling block to Jews and foolishness
        to Gentiles,
    but to those who are called, Jews and
        Greeks alike,
    Christ the power of God and the wisdom
        of God.
For the foolishness of God is wiser than
        human wisdom,
    and the weakness of God is stronger than
        human strength.

Gospel

John 4:5-42; L28A

Jesus came to a town of Samaria called Sychar,
    near the plot of land that Jacob had given to his son Joseph.
Jacob's well was there.
Jesus, tired from his journey, sat down there at the well.
It was about noon.

A woman of Samaria came to draw water.
Jesus said to her,
    "Give me a drink."
His disciples had gone into the town to buy food.
The Samaritan woman said to him,
    "How can you, a Jew, ask me, a Samaritan woman, for a drink?"
—For Jews use nothing in common with Samaritans.—
Jesus answered and said to her,
    "If you knew the gift of God
    and who is saying to you, 'Give me a drink,'
    you would have asked him
    and he would have given you living water."
The woman said to him,
    "Sir, you do not even have a bucket and the cistern is deep;
    where then can you get this living water?
Are you greater than our father Jacob,
    who gave us this cistern and drank from it himself
    with his children and his flocks?"
Jesus answered and said to her,
    "Everyone who drinks this water will be thirsty again;
    but whoever drinks the water I shall give will never thirst;
    the water I shall give will become in him
    a spring of water welling up to eternal life."
The woman said to him,
    "Sir, give me this water, so that I may not be thirsty
    or have to keep coming here to draw water."

Jesus said to her,
    "Go call your husband and come back."
The woman answered and said to him,
    "I do not have a husband."
Jesus answered her,
    "You are right in saying, 'I do not have a husband.'
For you have had five husbands,
    and the one you have now is not your husband.
What you have said is true."
The woman said to him,
    "Sir, I can see that you are a prophet.
Our ancestors worshiped on this mountain;
    but you people say that the place to worship is in Jerusalem."
Jesus said to her,
    "Believe me, woman, the hour is coming
    when you will worship the Father
    neither on this mountain nor in Jerusalem.
You people worship what you do not understand;
    we worship what we understand,
    because salvation is from the Jews.

But the hour is coming, and is now here,
    when true worshipers will worship the Father in Spirit and truth;
    and indeed the Father seeks such people to worship him.
God is Spirit, and those who worship him
    must worship in Spirit and truth."
The woman said to him,
    "I know that the Messiah is coming, the one called the Christ;
    when he comes, he will tell us everything."
Jesus said to her,
    "I am he, the one speaking with you."

At that moment his disciples returned,
    and were amazed that he was talking with a woman,
    but still no one said, "What are you looking for?"
    or "Why are you talking with her?"
The woman left her water jar
    and went into the town and said to the people,
    "Come see a man who told me everything I have done.
Could he possibly be the Christ?"
They went out of the town and came to him.
Meanwhile, the disciples urged him, "Rabbi, eat."
But he said to them,
    "I have food to eat of which you do not know."
So the disciples said to one another,
    "Could someone have brought him something to eat?"
Jesus said to them,
    "My food is to do the will of the one who sent me
    and to finish his work.
Do you not say, 'In four months the harvest will be here'?
I tell you, look up and see the fields ripe for the harvest.
The reaper is already receiving payment
    and gathering crops for eternal life,
    so that the sower and reaper can rejoice together.
For here the saying is verified that 'One sows and another reaps.'
I sent you to reap what you have not worked for;
    others have done the work,
    and you are sharing the fruits of their work."

Many of the Samaritans of that town began to believe in him
    because of the word of the woman who testified,
    "He told me everything I have done."
When the Samaritans came to him,
    they invited him to stay with them;
    and he stayed there two days.
Many more began to believe in him because of his word,
    and they said to the woman,
    "We no longer believe because of your word;
    for we have heard for ourselves,
    and we know that this is truly the savior of the world."

Gospel

John 4:5-15, 19b-26, 39a, 40-42; L28A

Jesus came to a town of Samaria called Sychar,
   near the plot of land that Jacob had given to his son Joseph.
Jacob's well was there.
Jesus, tired from his journey, sat down there at the well.
It was about noon.

A woman of Samaria came to draw water.
Jesus said to her,
   "Give me a drink."
His disciples had gone into the town to buy food.
The Samaritan woman said to him,
   "How can you, a Jew, ask me, a Samaritan woman, for a drink?"
—For Jews use nothing in common with Samaritans.—
Jesus answered and said to her,
   "If you knew the gift of God
   and who is saying to you, 'Give me a drink,'
   you would have asked him
   and he would have given you living water."
The woman said to him,
   "Sir, you do not even have a bucket and the cistern is deep;
   where then can you get this living water?
Are you greater than our father Jacob,
   who gave us this cistern and drank from it himself
   with his children and his flocks?"
Jesus answered and said to her,
   "Everyone who drinks this water will be thirsty again;
   but whoever drinks the water I shall give will never thirst;
   the water I shall give will become in him
   a spring of water welling up to eternal life."
The woman said to him,
   "Sir, give me this water, so that I may not be thirsty
   or have to keep coming here to draw water.

"I can see that you are a prophet.
Our ancestors worshiped on this mountain;
   but you people say that the place to worship is in Jerusalem."
Jesus said to her,
   "Believe me, woman, the hour is coming
   when you will worship the Father
   neither on this mountain nor in Jerusalem.
You people worship what you do not understand;
   we worship what we understand,
   because salvation is from the Jews.
But the hour is coming, and is now here,
   when true worshipers will worship the Father in Spirit and truth;
   and indeed the Father seeks such people to worship him.
God is Spirit, and those who worship him
   must worship in Spirit and truth."
The woman said to him,
   "I know that the Messiah is coming, the one called the Christ;
   when he comes, he will tell us everything."
Jesus said to her,
   "I am he, the one speaking with you."

Many of the Samaritans of that town began to believe in him.
When the Samaritans came to him,
   they invited him to stay with them;
   and he stayed there two days.
Many more began to believe in him because of his word,
   and they said to the woman,
   "We no longer believe because of your word;
   for we have heard for ourselves,
   and we know that this is truly the savior of the world."

FIRST READING
Exod 17:3-7

In those days, in their thirst for water,
  the people grumbled against Moses,
  saying, "Why did you ever make us leave
    Egypt?
Was it just to have us die here of thirst
  with our children and our livestock?"
So Moses cried out to the LORD,
  "What shall I do with this people?
A little more and they will stone me!"
The LORD answered Moses,
  "Go over there in front of the people,
  along with some of the elders of Israel,
  holding in your hand, as you go,
  the staff with which you struck the river.
I will be standing there in front of you on the
    rock in Horeb.
Strike the rock, and the water will flow from it
  for the people to drink."
This Moses did, in the presence of the elders
  of Israel.
The place was called Massah and Meribah,
  because the Israelites quarreled there
  and tested the LORD, saying,
  "Is the LORD in our midst or not?"

RESPONSORIAL PSALM
Ps 95:1-2, 6-7, 8-9

R̂. (8) If today you hear his voice, harden not
your hearts.

Come, let us sing joyfully to the LORD;
  let us acclaim the Rock of our salvation.
Let us come into his presence with
    thanksgiving;
  let us joyfully sing psalms to him.

R̂. If today you hear his voice, harden not
your hearts.

Come, let us bow down in worship;
  let us kneel before the LORD who made us.
For he is our God,
  and we are the people he shepherds, the
    flock he guides.

R̂. If today you hear his voice, harden not
your hearts.

Oh, that today you would hear his voice:
  "Harden not your hearts as at Meribah,
  as in the day of Massah in the desert,
where your fathers tempted me;
  they tested me though they had seen my
    works."

R̂. If today you hear his voice, harden not
your hearts.

SECOND READING
Rom 5:1-2, 5-8

Brothers and sisters:
Since we have been justified by faith,
  we have peace with God through our Lord
    Jesus Christ,
  through whom we have gained access by
    faith
  to this grace in which we stand,
  and we boast in hope of the glory of God.

And hope does not disappoint,
  because the love of God has been poured
    out into our hearts
  through the Holy Spirit who has been given
    to us.
For Christ, while we were still helpless,
  died at the appointed time for the ungodly.
Indeed, only with difficulty does one die for a
    just person,
  though perhaps for a good person one
    might even find courage to die.
But God proves his love for us
  in that while we were still sinners Christ
    died for us.

Gospel

Matt 1:16, 18-21, 24a; L543

Jacob was the father of Joseph, the husband of Mary.
Of her was born Jesus who is called the Christ.

Now this is how the birth of Jesus Christ came about.
When his mother Mary was betrothed to Joseph,
    but before they lived together,
    she was found with child through the Holy Spirit.
Joseph her husband, since he was a righteous man,
    yet unwilling to expose her to shame,
    decided to divorce her quietly.
Such was his intention when, behold,
    the angel of the Lord appeared to him in a dream and said,
    "Joseph, son of David,
    do not be afraid to take Mary your wife into your home.
For it is through the Holy Spirit
    that this child has been conceived in her.
She will bear a son and you are to name him Jesus,
    because he will save his people from their sins."
When Joseph awoke,
    he did as the angel of the Lord had commanded him
    and took his wife into his home.

FIRST READING

2 Sam 7:4-5a, 12-14a, 16

The LORD spoke to Nathan and said:
    "Go, tell my servant David,
    'When your time comes and you rest with
        your ancestors,
    I will raise up your heir after you, sprung
        from your loins,
    and I will make his kingdom firm.
It is he who shall build a house for my name.
And I will make his royal throne firm forever.
I will be a father to him,
    and he shall be a son to me.
Your house and your kingdom shall endure
    forever before me;
    your throne shall stand firm forever.'"

RESPONSORIAL PSALM

Ps 89:2-3, 4-5, 27 and 29

R̶. (37) The son of David will live forever.

The promises of the LORD I will sing forever,
    through all generations my mouth will
        proclaim your faithfulness,
For you have said, "My kindness is
    established forever";
    in heaven you have confirmed your
        faithfulness.

R̶. The son of David will live forever.

"I have made a covenant with my chosen one;
    I have sworn to David my servant:
Forever will I confirm your posterity
    and establish your throne for all
        generations."

R̶. The son of David will live forever.

"He shall say of me, 'You are my father,
    my God, the Rock, my savior.'
Forever I will maintain my kindness toward
    him,
    and my covenant with him stands firm."

R̶. The son of David will live forever.

SECOND READING

Rom 4:13, 16-18, 22

Brothers and sisters:
It was not through the law
    that the promise was made to Abraham
        and his descendants
    that he would inherit the world,
    but through the righteousness that comes
        from faith.
For this reason, it depends on faith,
    so that it may be a gift,
    and the promise may be guaranteed to all
        his descendants,
    not to those who only adhere to the law
    but to those who follow the faith of Abraham,
    who is the father of all of us, as it is written,
    I have made you father of many nations.
He is our father in the sight of God,
    in whom he believed, who gives life to the
        dead
    and calls into being what does not exist.
He believed, hoping against hope,
    that he would become *the father of many
        nations,*
    according to what was said, *Thus shall
        your descendants be.*
That is why *it was credited to him as
    righteousness.*

SECOND READING
Eph 2:4-10

Brothers and sisters:
God, who is rich in mercy,
 because of the great love he had for us,
 even when we were dead in our
  transgressions,
 brought us to life with Christ—by grace
  you have been saved—,
 raised us up with him,
 and seated us with him in the heavens in
  Christ Jesus,
 that in the ages to come
 he might show the immeasurable riches of
  his grace
 in his kindness to us in Christ Jesus.
For by grace you have been saved through
  faith,
 and this is not from you; it is the gift of
  God;
 it is not from works, so no one may boast.
For we are his handiwork, created in Christ
  Jesus for the good works
 that God has prepared in advance,
 that we should live in them.

FIRST READING
1 Sam 16:1b, 6-7, 10-13a

The LORD said to Samuel:
 "Fill your horn with oil, and be on your
  way.
I am sending you to Jesse of Bethlehem,
 for I have chosen my king from among his
  sons."
As Jesse and his sons came to the sacrifice,
 Samuel looked at Eliab and thought,
 "Surely the LORD's anointed is here before
  him."
But the LORD said to Samuel:
 "Do not judge from his appearance or from
  his lofty stature,
 because I have rejected him.
Not as man sees does God see,
 because man sees the appearance
 but the LORD looks into the heart."
In the same way Jesse presented seven sons
  before Samuel,
 but Samuel said to Jesse,
 "The LORD has not chosen any one of
  these."
Then Samuel asked Jesse,
 "Are these all the sons you have?"
Jesse replied,
 "There is still the youngest, who is tending
  the sheep."
Samuel said to Jesse,
 "Send for him;
 we will not begin the sacrificial banquet
  until he arrives here."
Jesse sent and had the young man brought to
  them.
He was ruddy, a youth handsome to behold
 and making a splendid appearance.
The LORD said,
 "There—anoint him, for this is the one!"
Then Samuel, with the horn of oil in hand,
 anointed David in the presence of his
  brothers;
 and from that day on, the spirit of the LORD
  rushed upon David.

RESPONSORIAL PSALM
Ps 23:1-3a, 3b-4, 5, 6

R̲̅. (1) The Lord is my shepherd; there is nothing I shall want.

The LORD is my shepherd; I shall not want.
 In verdant pastures he gives me repose;
beside restful waters he leads me;
 he refreshes my soul.

R̲̅. The Lord is my shepherd; there is nothing
I shall want.

He guides me in right paths
 for his name's sake.
Even though I walk in the dark valley
 I fear no evil; for you are at my side
with your rod and your staff
 that give me courage.

R̲̅. The Lord is my shepherd; there is nothing
I shall want.

You spread the table before me
 in the sight of my foes;
you anoint my head with oil;
 my cup overflows.

R̲̅. The Lord is my shepherd; there is nothing
I shall want.

Only goodness and kindness follow me
 all the days of my life;
and I shall dwell in the house of the LORD
 for years to come.

R̲̅. The Lord is my shepherd; there is nothing
I shall want.

SECOND READING
Eph 5:8-14

Brothers and sisters:
You were once darkness,
 but now you are light in the Lord.
Live as children of light,
 for light produces every kind of goodness
 and righteousness and truth.
Try to learn what is pleasing to the Lord.
Take no part in the fruitless works of
  darkness;
 rather expose them, for it is shameful even
  to mention
 the things done by them in secret;
 but everything exposed by the light
  becomes visible,
 for everything that becomes visible is light.
Therefore, it says:
 "Awake, O sleeper,
 and arise from the dead,
 and Christ will give you light."

Gospel

John 9:1-41; L31A

As Jesus passed by he saw a man blind from birth.
His disciples asked him,
    "Rabbi, who sinned, this man or his parents,
    that he was born blind?"
Jesus answered,
    "Neither he nor his parents sinned;
    it is so that the works of God might be made visible through him.
We have to do the works of the one who sent me while it is day.
Night is coming when no one can work.
While I am in the world, I am the light of the world."
When he had said this, he spat on the ground
    and made clay with the saliva,
    and smeared the clay on his eyes, and said to him,
    "Go wash in the Pool of Siloam"—which means Sent—.
So he went and washed, and came back able to see.

His neighbors and those who had seen him earlier as a beggar said,
    "Isn't this the one who used to sit and beg?"
Some said, "It is,"
    but others said, "No, he just looks like him."
He said, "I am."
So they said to him, "How were your eyes opened?"
He replied,
    "The man called Jesus made clay and anointed my eyes
    and told me, 'Go to Siloam and wash.'
So I went there and washed and was able to see."
And they said to him, "Where is he?"
He said, "I don't know."

They brought the one who was once blind to the Pharisees.
Now Jesus had made clay and opened his eyes on a sabbath.
So then the Pharisees also asked him how he was able to see.
He said to them,
    "He put clay on my eyes, and I washed, and now I can see."
So some of the Pharisees said,
    "This man is not from God,
    because he does not keep the sabbath."
But others said,
    "How can a sinful man do such signs?"
And there was a division among them.
So they said to the blind man again,
    "What do you have to say about him,
    since he opened your eyes?"
He said, "He is a prophet."

Now the Jews did not believe
    that he had been blind and gained his sight
    until they summoned the parents of the one who had gained his
        sight.
They asked them,
    "Is this your son, who you say was born blind?
How does he now see?"
His parents answered and said,
    "We know that this is our son and that he was born blind.
We do not know how he sees now,
    nor do we know who opened his eyes.
Ask him, he is of age;
    he can speak for himself."

His parents said this because they were afraid
    of the Jews, for the Jews had already agreed
    that if anyone acknowledged him as the Christ,
    he would be expelled from the synagogue.
For this reason his parents said,
    "He is of age; question him."

So a second time they called the man who had been blind
    and said to him, "Give God the praise!
We know that this man is a sinner."
He replied,
    "If he is a sinner, I do not know.
One thing I do know is that I was blind and now I see."
So they said to him,
    "What did he do to you?
    How did he open your eyes?"
He answered them,
    "I told you already and you did not listen.
Why do you want to hear it again?
Do you want to become his disciples, too?"
They ridiculed him and said,
    "You are that man's disciple;
    we are disciples of Moses!
We know that God spoke to Moses,
    but we do not know where this one is from."
The man answered and said to them,
    "This is what is so amazing,
    that you do not know where he is from, yet he opened my eyes.
We know that God does not listen to sinners,
    but if one is devout and does his will, he listens to him.
It is unheard of that anyone ever opened the eyes of a person born
        blind.
If this man were not from God,
    he would not be able to do anything."
They answered and said to him,
    "You were born totally in sin,
    and are you trying to teach us?"
Then they threw him out.

When Jesus heard that they had thrown him out,
    he found him and said, "Do you believe in the Son of Man?"
He answered and said,
    "Who is he, sir, that I may believe in him?"
Jesus said to him,
    "You have seen him,
    and the one speaking with you is he."
He said,
    "I do believe, Lord," and he worshiped him.
Then Jesus said,
    "I came into this world for judgment,
    so that those who do not see might see,
    and those who do see might become blind."

Some of the Pharisees who were with him heard this
    and said to him, "Surely we are not also blind, are we?"
Jesus said to them,
    "If you were blind, you would have no sin;
    but now you are saying, 'We see,' so your sin remains."

Fourth Sunday of Lent, *March 22, 2009*

Gospel

John 9:1, 6-9, 13-17, 34-38; L31A

As Jesus passed by he saw a man blind from birth.
He spat on the ground and made clay with the saliva,
    and smeared the clay on his eyes, and said to him,
    "Go wash in the Pool of Siloam"—which means Sent—.
So he went and washed, and came back able to see.

His neighbors and those who had seen him earlier as a beggar said,
    "Isn't this the one who used to sit and beg?"
Some said, "It is,"
    but others said, "No, he just looks like him."
He said, "I am."

They brought the one who was once blind to the Pharisees.
Now Jesus had made clay and opened his eyes on a sabbath.
So then the Pharisees also asked him how he was able to see.
He said to them,
    "He put clay on my eyes, and I washed, and now I can see."
So some of the Pharisees said,
    "This man is not from God,
    because he does not keep the sabbath."
But others said,
    "How can a sinful man do such signs?"

And there was a division among them.
So they said to the blind man again,
    "What do you have to say about him,
    since he opened your eyes?"
He said, "He is a prophet."

They answered and said to him,
    "You were born totally in sin,
    and are you trying to teach us?"
Then they threw him out.

When Jesus heard that they had thrown him out,
    he found him and said, "Do you believe in the Son of Man?"
He answered and said,
    "Who is he, sir, that I may believe in him?"
Jesus said to him,
    "You have seen him,
    and the one speaking with you is he."
He said,
    "I do believe, Lord," and he worshiped him.

The Annunciation of the Lord, *March 25, 2009*

FIRST READING

Isa 7:10-14; 8:10

The Lord spoke to Ahaz, saying:
Ask for a sign from the Lord, your God;
    let it be deep as the nether world, or high
        as the sky!
But Ahaz answered,
    "I will not ask! I will not tempt the Lord!"
Then Isaiah said:
    Listen, O house of David!
Is it not enough for you to weary people,
    must you also weary my God?
Therefore the Lord himself will give you this
        sign:
    the virgin shall conceive, and bear a son,
    and shall name him Emmanuel,
    which means "God is with us!"

RESPONSORIAL PSALM

Ps 40:7-8a, 8b-9, 10, 11

℟. (8a and 9a) Here I am, Lord; I come to do
your will.

Sacrifice or offering you wished not,
    but ears open to obedience you gave me.
Holocausts and sin-offerings you sought not;
    then said I, "Behold, I come";

℟. Here I am, Lord; I come to do your will.

"In the written scroll it is prescribed for me,
To do your will, O God, is my delight,
    and your law is within my heart!"

℟. Here I am, Lord; I come to do your will.

I announced your justice in the vast assembly;
    I did not restrain my lips, as you, O Lord,
        know.

℟. Here I am, Lord; I come to do your will.

Your justice I kept not hid within my heart;
    your faithfulness and your salvation I have
        spoken of;
I have made no secret of your kindness and
        your truth
        in the vast assembly.

℟. Here I am, Lord; I come to do your will.

SECOND READING

Heb 10:4-10

Brothers and sisters:
It is impossible that the blood of bulls and
        goats
    takes away sins.
For this reason, when Christ came into the
        world, he said:
    "Sacrifice and offering you did not desire,
        but a body you prepared for me;
    in holocausts and sin offerings you took no
        delight.
    Then I said, 'As is written of me in the scroll,
        behold, I come to do your will, O God.'"

First Christ says, "Sacrifices and offerings,
    holocausts and sin offerings,
    you neither desired nor delighted in."
These are offered according to the law.
Then he says, "Behold, I come to do your will."
He takes away the first to establish the
        second.
By this "will," we have been consecrated
    through the offering of the body of Jesus
        Christ once for all.

Gospel (cont.)
John 12:20-33; L35B

The crowd there heard it and said it was thunder;
> but others said, "An angel has spoken to him."

Jesus answered and said,
> "This voice did not come for my sake but for yours.

Now is the time of judgment on this world;
> now the ruler of this world will be driven out.

And when I am lifted up from the earth,
> I will draw everyone to myself."

He said this indicating the kind of death he would die.

FIRST READING
Ezek 37:12-14

Thus says the Lord GOD:
> O my people, I will open your graves
> and have you rise from them,
> and bring you back to the land of Israel.

Then you shall know that I am the LORD,
> when I open your graves and have you rise
> > from them,
> O my people!

I will put my spirit in you that you may live,
> and I will settle you upon your land;
> thus you shall know that I am the LORD.

I have promised, and I will do it, says the
> LORD.

RESPONSORIAL PSALM
Ps 130:1-2, 3-4, 5-6, 7-8

R⁄. (7) With the Lord there is mercy and fullness of redemption.

Out of the depths I cry to you, O LORD;
> LORD, hear my voice!

Let your ears be attentive
> to my voice in supplication.

R⁄. With the Lord there is mercy and fullness of redemption.

If you, O LORD, mark iniquities,
> LORD, who can stand?

But with you is forgiveness,
> that you may be revered.

R⁄. With the Lord there is mercy and fullness of redemption.

I trust in the LORD;
> my soul trusts in his word.

More than sentinels wait for the dawn,
> let Israel wait for the LORD.

R⁄. With the Lord there is mercy and fullness of redemption.

For with the LORD is kindness
> and with him is plenteous redemption;

and he will redeem Israel
> from all their iniquities.

R⁄. With the Lord there is mercy and fullness of redemption.

SECOND READING
Rom 8:8-11

Brothers and sisters:
Those who are in the flesh cannot please God.
But you are not in the flesh;
> on the contrary, you are in the spirit,
> if only the Spirit of God dwells in you.

Whoever does not have the Spirit of Christ
> does not belong to him.

But if Christ is in you,
> although the body is dead because of sin,
> the spirit is alive because of righteousness.

If the Spirit of the One who raised Jesus from
> the dead dwells in you,
> the One who raised Christ from the dead
> will give life to your mortal bodies also,
> through his Spirit dwelling in you.

Gospel

John 11:1-45; L34A

Now a man was ill, Lazarus from Bethany,
  the village of Mary and her sister Martha.
Mary was the one who had anointed the Lord with perfumed oil
  and dried his feet with her hair;
  it was her brother Lazarus who was ill.
So the sisters sent word to Jesus saying,
  "Master, the one you love is ill."
When Jesus heard this he said,
  "This illness is not to end in death,
  but is for the glory of God,
  that the Son of God may be glorified through it."
Now Jesus loved Martha and her sister and Lazarus.
So when he heard that he was ill,
  he remained for two days in the place where he was.
Then after this he said to his disciples,
  "Let us go back to Judea."
The disciples said to him,
  "Rabbi, the Jews were just trying to stone you,
  and you want to go back there?"
Jesus answered,
  "Are there not twelve hours in a day?
If one walks during the day, he does not stumble,
  because he sees the light of this world.
But if one walks at night, he stumbles,
  because the light is not in him."
He said this, and then told them,
  "Our friend Lazarus is asleep,
  but I am going to awaken him."
So the disciples said to him,
  "Master, if he is asleep, he will be saved."
But Jesus was talking about his death,
  while they thought that he meant ordinary sleep.
So then Jesus said to them clearly,
  "Lazarus has died.
And I am glad for you that I was not there,
  that you may believe.
Let us go to him."
So Thomas, called Didymus, said to his fellow disciples,
  "Let us also go to die with him."

When Jesus arrived, he found that Lazarus
  had already been in the tomb for four days.
Now Bethany was near Jerusalem, only about two miles away.
And many of the Jews had come to Martha and Mary
  to comfort them about their brother.
When Martha heard that Jesus was coming,
  she went to meet him;
  but Mary sat at home.
Martha said to Jesus,
  "Lord, if you had been here,
  my brother would not have died.
But even now I know that whatever you ask of God,
  God will give you."
Jesus said to her,
  "Your brother will rise."
Martha said to him,
  "I know he will rise,
  in the resurrection on the last day."
Jesus told her,

"I am the resurrection and the life;
  whoever believes in me, even if he dies, will live,
  and everyone who lives and believes in me will never die.
Do you believe this?"
She said to him, "Yes, Lord.
I have come to believe that you are the Christ, the Son of God,
  the one who is coming into the world."

When she had said this,
  she went and called her sister Mary secretly, saying,
  "The teacher is here and is asking for you."
As soon as she heard this,
  she rose quickly and went to him.
For Jesus had not yet come into the village,
  but was still where Martha had met him.
So when the Jews who were with her in the house comforting her
  saw Mary get up quickly and go out,
  they followed her,
  presuming that she was going to the tomb to weep there.
When Mary came to where Jesus was and saw him,
  she fell at his feet and said to him,
  "Lord, if you had been here,
  my brother would not have died."
When Jesus saw her weeping and the Jews who had come with her
      weeping,
  he became perturbed and deeply troubled, and said,
  "Where have you laid him?"
They said to him, "Sir, come and see."
And Jesus wept.
So the Jews said, "See how he loved him."
But some of them said,
  "Could not the one who opened the eyes of the blind man
  have done something so that this man would not have died?"

So Jesus, perturbed again, came to the tomb.
It was a cave, and a stone lay across it.
Jesus said, "Take away the stone."
Martha, the dead man's sister, said to him,
  "Lord, by now there will be a stench;
  he has been dead for four days."
Jesus said to her,
  "Did I not tell you that if you believe
  you will see the glory of God?"
So they took away the stone.
And Jesus raised his eyes and said,
  "Father, I thank you for hearing me.
I know that you always hear me;
  but because of the crowd here I have said this,
  that they may believe that you sent me."
And when he had said this,
  he cried out in a loud voice,
  "Lazarus, come out!"
The dead man came out,
  tied hand and foot with burial bands,
  and his face was wrapped in a cloth.
So Jesus said to them,
  "Untie him and let him go."

Now many of the Jews who had come to Mary
  and seen what he had done began to believe in him.

Fifth Sunday of Lent, *March 29, 2009*

Gospel
John 11:3-7, 17, 20-27, 33b-45; L34A

The sisters of Lazarus sent word to Jesus saying,
    "Master, the one you love is ill."
When Jesus heard this he said,
    "This illness is not to end in death,
    but is for the glory of God,
    that the Son of God may be glorified through it."
Now Jesus loved Martha and her sister and Lazarus.
So when he heard that he was ill,
    he remained for two days in the place where he was.
Then after this he said to his disciples,
    "Let us go back to Judea."

When Jesus arrived, he found that Lazarus
    had already been in the tomb for four days.
When Martha heard that Jesus was coming,
    she went to meet him;
    but Mary sat at home.
Martha said to Jesus,
    "Lord, if you had been here,
    my brother would not have died.
But even now I know that whatever you ask of God,
    God will give you."
Jesus said to her,
    "Your brother will rise."
Martha said,
    "I know he will rise,
    in the resurrection on the last day."
Jesus told her,
    "I am the resurrection and the life;
    whoever believes in me, even if he dies, will live,
    and everyone who lives and believes in me will never die.
Do you believe this?"
She said to him, "Yes, Lord.
I have come to believe that you are the Christ, the Son of God,
    the one who is coming into the world."

He became perturbed and deeply troubled, and said,
    "Where have you laid him?"
They said to him, "Sir, come and see."
And Jesus wept.
So the Jews said, "See how he loved him."
But some of them said,
    "Could not the one who opened the eyes of the blind man
    have done something so that this man would not have died?"

So Jesus, perturbed again, came to the tomb.
It was a cave, and a stone lay across it.
Jesus said, "Take away the stone."
Martha, the dead man's sister, said to him,
    "Lord, by now there will be a stench;
    he has been dead for four days."
Jesus said to her,
    "Did I not tell you that if you believe
    you will see the glory of God?"
So they took away the stone.
And Jesus raised his eyes and said,
    "Father, I thank you for hearing me.
I know that you always hear me;
    but because of the crowd here I have said this,
    that they may believe that you sent me."
And when he had said this,
    he cried out in a loud voice,
    "Lazarus, come out!"
The dead man came out,
    tied hand and foot with burial bands,
    and his face was wrapped in a cloth.
So Jesus said to them,
    "Untie him and let him go."

Now many of the Jews who had come to Mary
    and seen what he had done began to believe in him.

Gospel at Mass
Mark 14:1–15:47; L38B

The Passover and the Feast of Unleavened Bread
   were to take place in two days' time.
So the chief priests and the scribes were seeking a way
   to arrest him by treachery and put him to death.
They said, "Not during the festival,
   for fear that there may be a riot among the people."

When he was in Bethany reclining at table
   in the house of Simon the leper,
   a woman came with an alabaster jar of perfumed oil,
   costly genuine spikenard.
She broke the alabaster jar and poured it on his head.
There were some who were indignant.
"Why has there been this waste of perfumed oil?
It could have been sold for more than three hundred days' wages
   and the money given to the poor."
They were infuriated with her.
Jesus said, "Let her alone.
Why do you make trouble for her?
She has done a good thing for me.
The poor you will always have with you,
   and whenever you wish you can do good to them,
   but you will not always have me.
She has done what she could.
She has anticipated anointing my body for burial.
Amen, I say to you,
   wherever the gospel is proclaimed to the whole world,
   what she has done will be told in memory of her."

Then Judas Iscariot, one of the Twelve,
   went off to the chief priests to hand him over to them.
When they heard him they were pleased and promised to pay him
       money.
Then he looked for an opportunity to hand him over.

On the first day of the Feast of Unleavened Bread,
   when they sacrificed the Passover lamb,
   his disciples said to him,
   "Where do you want us to go
   and prepare for you to eat the Passover?"
He sent two of his disciples and said to them,
   "Go into the city and a man will meet you,
   carrying a jar of water.
Follow him.
Wherever he enters, say to the master of the house,
   'The Teacher says, "Where is my guest room
   where I may eat the Passover with my disciples?"'
Then he will show you a large upper room furnished and ready.
Make the preparations for us there."
The disciples then went off, entered the city,
   and found it just as he had told them;
   and they prepared the Passover.

When it was evening, he came with the Twelve.
And as they reclined at table and were eating, Jesus said,
   "Amen, I say to you, one of you will betray me,
   one who is eating with me."
They began to be distressed and to say to him, one by one,
   "Surely it is not I?"

He said to them,
   "One of the Twelve, the one who dips with me into the dish.
For the Son of Man indeed goes, as it is written of him,
   but woe to that man by whom the Son of Man is betrayed.
It would be better for that man if he had never been born."

While they were eating,
   he took bread, said the blessing,
   broke it, and gave it to them, and said,
   "Take it; this is my body."
Then he took a cup, gave thanks, and gave it to them,
   and they all drank from it.
He said to them,
   "This is my blood of the covenant,
   which will be shed for many.
Amen, I say to you,
   I shall not drink again the fruit of the vine
   until the day when I drink it new in the kingdom of God."
Then, after singing a hymn,
   they went out to the Mount of Olives.

Then Jesus said to them,
   "All of you will have your faith shaken, for it is written:
      I will strike the shepherd,
         and the sheep will be dispersed.
But after I have been raised up,
   I shall go before you to Galilee."
Peter said to him,
   "Even though all should have their faith shaken,
   mine will not be."
Then Jesus said to him,
   "Amen, I say to you,
   this very night before the cock crows twice
   you will deny me three times."
But he vehemently replied,
   "Even though I should have to die with you,
   I will not deny you."
And they all spoke similarly.

Then they came to a place named Gethsemane,
   and he said to his disciples,
   "Sit here while I pray."
He took with him Peter, James, and John,
   and began to be troubled and distressed.
Then he said to them, "My soul is sorrowful even to death.
Remain here and keep watch."
He advanced a little and fell to the ground and prayed
   that if it were possible the hour might pass by him;
   he said, "Abba, Father, all things are possible to you.
Take this cup away from me,
   but not what I will but what you will."
When he returned he found them asleep.
He said to Peter, "Simon, are you asleep?
Could you not keep watch for one hour?
Watch and pray that you may not undergo the test.
The spirit is willing but the flesh is weak."
Withdrawing again, he prayed, saying the same thing.
Then he returned once more and found them asleep,
   for they could not keep their eyes open
   and did not know what to answer him.

He returned a third time and said to them,
   "Are you still sleeping and taking your rest?
It is enough. The hour has come.
Behold, the Son of Man is to be handed over to sinners.
Get up, let us go.
See, my betrayer is at hand."

Then, while he was still speaking,
   Judas, one of the Twelve, arrived,
     accompanied by a crowd with swords and clubs
     who had come from the chief priests,
     the scribes, and the elders.
His betrayer had arranged a signal with them, saying,
   "The man I shall kiss is the one;
   arrest him and lead him away securely."
He came and immediately went over to him and said,
   "Rabbi." And he kissed him.
At this they laid hands on him and arrested him.
One of the bystanders drew his sword,
   struck the high priest's servant, and cut off his ear.
Jesus said to them in reply,
   "Have you come out as against a robber,
   with swords and clubs, to seize me?
Day after day I was with you teaching in the temple area,
   yet you did not arrest me;
   but that the Scriptures may be fulfilled."
And they all left him and fled.
Now a young man followed him
   wearing nothing but a linen cloth about his body.
They seized him,
   but he left the cloth behind and ran off naked.

They led Jesus away to the high priest,
   and all the chief priests and the elders and the scribes came together.
Peter followed him at a distance into the high priest's courtyard
   and was seated with the guards, warming himself at the fire.
The chief priests and the entire Sanhedrin
   kept trying to obtain testimony against Jesus
   in order to put him to death, but they found none.
Many gave false witness against him,
   but their testimony did not agree.
Some took the stand and testified falsely against him,
   alleging, "We heard him say,
   'I will destroy this temple made with hands
   and within three days I will build another
   not made with hands.'"
Even so their testimony did not agree.
The high priest rose before the assembly and questioned Jesus,
   saying, "Have you no answer?
What are these men testifying against you?"
But he was silent and answered nothing.
Again the high priest asked him and said to him,
   "Are you the Christ, the son of the Blessed One?"
Then Jesus answered, "I am;
   and 'you will see the Son of Man
     seated at the right hand of the Power
     and coming with the clouds of heaven.'"
At that the high priest tore his garments and said,
   "What further need have we of witnesses?
You have heard the blasphemy.
What do you think?"
They all condemned him as deserving to die.

Some began to spit on him.
They blindfolded him and struck him and said to him, "Prophesy!"
And the guards greeted him with blows.

While Peter was below in the courtyard,
   one of the high priest's maids came along.
Seeing Peter warming himself,
   she looked intently at him and said,
   "You too were with the Nazarene, Jesus."
But he denied it saying,
   "I neither know nor understand what you are talking about."
So he went out into the outer court.
Then the cock crowed.
The maid saw him and began again to say to the bystanders,
   "This man is one of them."
Once again he denied it.
A little later the bystanders said to Peter once more,
   "Surely you are one of them; for you too are a Galilean."
He began to curse and to swear,
   "I do not know this man about whom you are talking."
And immediately a cock crowed a second time.
Then Peter remembered the word that Jesus had said to him,
   "Before the cock crows twice you will deny me three times."
He broke down and wept.

As soon as morning came,
   the chief priests with the elders and the scribes,
   that is, the whole Sanhedrin, held a council.
They bound Jesus, led him away, and handed him over to Pilate.
Pilate questioned him,
   "Are you the king of the Jews?"
He said to him in reply, "You say so."
The chief priests accused him of many things.
Again Pilate questioned him,
   "Have you no answer?
See how many things they accuse you of."
Jesus gave him no further answer, so that Pilate was amazed.

Now on the occasion of the feast he used to release to them
   one prisoner whom they requested.
A man called Barabbas was then in prison
   along with the rebels who had committed murder in a rebellion.
The crowd came forward and began to ask him
   to do for them as he was accustomed.
Pilate answered,
   "Do you want me to release to you the king of the Jews?"
For he knew that it was out of envy
   that the chief priests had handed him over.
But the chief priests stirred up the crowd
   to have him release Barabbas for them instead.
Pilate again said to them in reply,
   "Then what do you want me to do
   with the man you call the king of the Jews?"
They shouted again, "Crucify him."
Pilate said to them, "Why? What evil has he done?"
They only shouted the louder, "Crucify him."
So Pilate, wishing to satisfy the crowd,
   released Barabbas to them and, after he had Jesus scourged,
   handed him over to be crucified.

The soldiers led him away inside the palace,
   that is, the praetorium, and assembled the whole cohort.

They clothed him in purple and,
  weaving a crown of thorns, placed it on him.
They began to salute him with, "Hail, King of the Jews!"
  and kept striking his head with a reed and spitting upon him.
They knelt before him in homage.
And when they had mocked him,
  they stripped him of the purple cloak,
  dressed him in his own clothes,
  and led him out to crucify him.

They pressed into service a passer-by, Simon,
  a Cyrenian, who was coming in from the country,
  the father of Alexander and Rufus,
  to carry his cross.

They brought him to the place of Golgotha
  —which is translated Place of the Skull—.
They gave him wine drugged with myrrh,
  but he did not take it.
Then they crucified him and divided his garments
  by casting lots for them to see what each should take.
It was nine o'clock in the morning when they crucified him.
The inscription of the charge against him read,
  "The King of the Jews."
With him they crucified two revolutionaries,
  one on his right and one on his left.
Those passing by reviled him,
  shaking their heads and saying,
  "Aha! You who would destroy the temple
  and rebuild it in three days,
  save yourself by coming down from the cross."
Likewise the chief priests, with the scribes,
  mocked him among themselves and said,
  "He saved others; he cannot save himself.
Let the Christ, the King of Israel,
  come down now from the cross
  that we may see and believe."
Those who were crucified with him also kept abusing him.
At noon darkness came over the whole land
  until three in the afternoon.
And at three o'clock Jesus cried out in a loud voice,
  "Eloi, Eloi, lema sabachthani?"
  which is translated,
  "My God, my God, why have you forsaken me?"
Some of the bystanders who heard it said,
  "Look, he is calling Elijah."
One of them ran, soaked a sponge with wine, put it on a reed
  and gave it to him to drink saying,
  "Wait, let us see if Elijah comes to take him down."
Jesus gave a loud cry and breathed his last.

Here all kneel and pause for a short time.

The veil of the sanctuary was torn in two from top to bottom.
When the centurion who stood facing him
  saw how he breathed his last he said,
  "Truly this man was the Son of God!"
There were also women looking on from a distance.
Among them were Mary Magdalene,
  Mary the mother of the younger James and of Joses,
  and Salome.

These women had followed him when he was in Galilee
  and ministered to him.
There were also many other women
  who had come up with him to Jerusalem.

When it was already evening,
  since it was the day of preparation,
  the day before the sabbath, Joseph of Arimathea,
  a distinguished member of the council,
  who was himself awaiting the kingdom of God,
  came and courageously went to Pilate
  and asked for the body of Jesus.
Pilate was amazed that he was already dead.
He summoned the centurion
  and asked him if Jesus had already died.
And when he learned of it from the centurion,
  he gave the body to Joseph.
Having bought a linen cloth, he took him down,
  wrapped him in the linen cloth,
  and laid him in a tomb that had been hewn out of the rock.
Then he rolled a stone against the entrance to the tomb.
Mary Magdalene and Mary the mother of Joses
  watched where he was laid.

or Mark 15:1-39; L38B

As soon as morning came,
  the chief priests with the elders and the scribes,
  that is, the whole Sanhedrin, held a council.
They bound Jesus, led him away, and handed him over to Pilate.
Pilate questioned him,
  "Are you the king of the Jews?"
He said to him in reply, "You say so."
The chief priests accused him of many things.
Again Pilate questioned him,
  "Have you no answer?
See how many things they accuse you of."
Jesus gave him no further answer, so that Pilate was amazed.

Now on the occasion of the feast he used to release to them
  one prisoner whom they requested.
A man called Barabbas was then in prison
  along with the rebels who had committed murder in a rebellion.
The crowd came forward and began to ask him
  to do for them as he was accustomed.
Pilate answered,
  "Do you want me to release to you the king of the Jews?"
For he knew that it was out of envy
  that the chief priests had handed him over.
But the chief priests stirred up the crowd
  to have him release Barabbas for them instead.
Pilate again said to them in reply,
  "Then what do you want me to do
  with the man you call the king of the Jews?"
They shouted again, "Crucify him."
Pilate said to them, "Why? What evil has he done?"
They only shouted the louder, "Crucify him."
So Pilate, wishing to satisfy the crowd,
  released Barabbas to them and, after he had Jesus scourged,
  handed him over to be crucified.

The soldiers led him away inside the palace,
   that is, the praetorium, and assembled the whole cohort.
They clothed him in purple and,
   weaving a crown of thorns, placed it on him.
They began to salute him with, "Hail, King of the Jews!"
   and kept striking his head with a reed and spitting upon him.
They knelt before him in homage.
And when they had mocked him,
   they stripped him of the purple cloak,
   dressed him in his own clothes,
   and led him out to crucify him.

They pressed into service a passer-by, Simon,
   a Cyrenian, who was coming in from the country,
   the father of Alexander and Rufus,
   to carry his cross.

They brought him to the place of Golgotha
   —which is translated Place of the Skull—.
They gave him wine drugged with myrrh,
   but he did not take it.
Then they crucified him and divided his garments
   by casting lots for them to see what each should take.
It was nine o'clock in the morning when they crucified him.
The inscription of the charge against him read,
   "The King of the Jews."
With him they crucified two revolutionaries,
   one on his right and one on his left.
Those passing by reviled him,
   shaking their heads and saying,

"Aha! You who would destroy the temple
   and rebuild it in three days,
   save yourself by coming down from the cross."
Likewise the chief priests, with the scribes,
   mocked him among themselves and said,
   "He saved others; he cannot save himself.
Let the Christ, the King of Israel,
   come down now from the cross
   that we may see and believe."
Those who were crucified with him also kept abusing him.

At noon darkness came over the whole land
   until three in the afternoon.
And at three o'clock Jesus cried out in a loud voice,
   "Eloi, Eloi, lema sabachthani?"
   which is translated,
   "My God, my God, why have you forsaken me?"
Some of the bystanders who heard it said,
   "Look, he is calling Elijah."
One of them ran, soaked a sponge with wine, put it on a reed
   and gave it to him to drink saying,
   "Wait, let us see if Elijah comes to take him down."
Jesus gave a loud cry and breathed his last.

   Here all kneel and pause for a short time.

The veil of the sanctuary was torn in two from top to bottom.
When the centurion who stood facing him
   saw how he breathed his last he said,
   "Truly this man was the Son of God!"

Gospel (cont.)
John 13:1-15; L39ABC

So when he had washed their feet
and put his garments back on and reclined at table again,
he said to them, "Do you realize what I have done for you?
You call me 'teacher' and 'master,' and rightly so, for indeed I am.
If I, therefore, the master and teacher, have washed your feet,
you ought to wash one another's feet.
I have given you a model to follow,
so that as I have done for you, you should also do."

FIRST READING
Exod 12:1-8, 11-14

The LORD said to Moses and Aaron in the land
of Egypt,
"This month shall stand at the head of
your calendar;
you shall reckon it the first month of the
year.
Tell the whole community of Israel:
On the tenth of this month every one of
your families
must procure for itself a lamb, one apiece
for each household.
If a family is too small for a whole lamb,
it shall join the nearest household in
procuring one
and shall share in the lamb
in proportion to the number of persons
who partake of it.
The lamb must be a year-old male and
without blemish.
You may take it from either the sheep or the
goats.
You shall keep it until the fourteenth day of
this month,
and then, with the whole assembly of Israel
present,
it shall be slaughtered during the evening
twilight.
They shall take some of its blood
and apply it to the two doorposts and the
lintel
of every house in which they partake of
the lamb.
That same night they shall eat its roasted
flesh
with unleavened bread and bitter herbs.

"This is how you are to eat it:
with your loins girt, sandals on your feet
and your staff in hand,
you shall eat like those who are in flight.
It is the Passover of the LORD.
For on this same night I will go through Egypt,
striking down every firstborn of the land,
both man and beast,
and executing judgment on all the gods of
Egypt—I, the LORD!
But the blood will mark the houses where you
are.
Seeing the blood, I will pass over you;
thus, when I strike the land of Egypt,
no destructive blow will come upon you.

"This day shall be a memorial feast for you,
which all your generations shall celebrate
with pilgrimage to the LORD, as a perpetual
institution."

RESPONSORIAL PSALM
Ps 116:12-13, 15-16bc, 17-18

R/. (cf. 1 Cor 10:16) Our blessing-cup is a communion with the Blood of Christ.

How shall I make a return to the LORD
for all the good he has done for me?
The cup of salvation I will take up,
and I will call upon the name of the LORD.

R/. Our blessing-cup is a communion with the Blood of Christ.

Precious in the eyes of the LORD
is the death of his faithful ones.
I am your servant, the son of your handmaid;
you have loosed my bonds.

R/. Our blessing-cup is a communion with the Blood of Christ.

To you will I offer sacrifice of thanksgiving,
and I will call upon the name of the LORD.
My vows to the LORD I will pay
in the presence of all his people.

R/. Our blessing-cup is a communion with the Blood of Christ.

SECOND READING
1 Cor 11:23-26

Brothers and sisters:
I received from the Lord what I also handed
on to you,
that the Lord Jesus, on the night he was
handed over,
took bread, and, after he had given thanks,
broke it and said, "This is my body that is
for you.
Do this in remembrance of me."
In the same way also the cup, after supper,
saying,
"This cup is the new covenant in my blood.
Do this, as often as you drink it, in
remembrance of me."
For as often as you eat this bread and drink
the cup,
you proclaim the death of the Lord until he
comes.

Gospel (cont.)

John 18:1–19:42; L40ABC

So the band of soldiers, the tribune, and the Jewish guards seized Jesus,
    bound him, and brought him to Annas first.
He was the father-in-law of Caiaphas,
    who was high priest that year.
It was Caiaphas who had counseled the Jews
    that it was better that one man should die rather than the people.

Simon Peter and another disciple followed Jesus.
Now the other disciple was known to the high priest,
    and he entered the courtyard of the high priest with Jesus.
But Peter stood at the gate outside.
So the other disciple, the acquaintance of the high priest,
    went out and spoke to the gatekeeper and brought Peter in.
Then the maid who was the gatekeeper said to Peter,
    "You are not one of this man's disciples, are you?"
He said, "I am not."
Now the slaves and the guards were standing around a charcoal fire
    that they had made, because it was cold,
    and were warming themselves.
Peter was also standing there keeping warm.

The high priest questioned Jesus
    about his disciples and about his doctrine.
Jesus answered him,
    "I have spoken publicly to the world.
I have always taught in a synagogue
    or in the temple area where all the Jews gather,
    and in secret I have said nothing. Why ask me?
Ask those who heard me what I said to them.
They know what I said."
When he had said this,
    one of the temple guards standing there struck Jesus and said,
    "Is this the way you answer the high priest?"
Jesus answered him,
    "If I have spoken wrongly, testify to the wrong;
    but if I have spoken rightly, why do you strike me?"
Then Annas sent him bound to Caiaphas the high priest.

Now Simon Peter was standing there keeping warm.
And they said to him,
    "You are not one of his disciples, are you?"
He denied it and said,
    "I am not."
One of the slaves of the high priest,
    a relative of the one whose ear Peter had cut off, said,
    "Didn't I see you in the garden with him?"
Again Peter denied it.
And immediately the cock crowed.

Then they brought Jesus from Caiaphas to the praetorium.
It was morning.
And they themselves did not enter the praetorium,
    in order not to be defiled so that they could eat the Passover.
So Pilate came out to them and said,
    "What charge do you bring against this man?"
They answered and said to him,
    "If he were not a criminal,
    we would not have handed him over to you."
At this, Pilate said to them,
    "Take him yourselves, and judge him according to your law."

The Jews answered him,
    "We do not have the right to execute anyone,"
    in order that the word of Jesus might be fulfilled
    that he said indicating the kind of death he would die.
So Pilate went back into the praetorium
    and summoned Jesus and said to him,
    "Are you the King of the Jews?"
Jesus answered,
    "Do you say this on your own
    or have others told you about me?"
Pilate answered,
    "I am not a Jew, am I?
Your own nation and the chief priests handed you over to me.
What have you done?"
Jesus answered,
    "My kingdom does not belong to this world.
If my kingdom did belong to this world,
    my attendants would be fighting
    to keep me from being handed over to the Jews.
But as it is, my kingdom is not here."
So Pilate said to him,
    "Then you are a king?"
Jesus answered,
    "You say I am a king.
For this I was born and for this I came into the world,
    to testify to the truth.
Everyone who belongs to the truth listens to my voice."
Pilate said to him, "What is truth?"

When he had said this,
    he again went out to the Jews and said to them,
    "I find no guilt in him.
But you have a custom that I release one prisoner to you at Passover.
Do you want me to release to you the King of the Jews?"
They cried out again,
    "Not this one but Barabbas!"
Now Barabbas was a revolutionary.

Then Pilate took Jesus and had him scourged.
And the soldiers wove a crown out of thorns and placed it on his head,
    and clothed him in a purple cloak,
    and they came to him and said,
    "Hail, King of the Jews!"
And they struck him repeatedly.
Once more Pilate went out and said to them,
    "Look, I am bringing him out to you,
    so that you may know that I find no guilt in him."
So Jesus came out,
    wearing the crown of thorns and the purple cloak.
And he said to them, "Behold, the man!"
When the chief priests and the guards saw him they cried out,
    "Crucify him, crucify him!"
Pilate said to them,
    "Take him yourselves and crucify him.
I find no guilt in him."
The Jews answered,
    "We have a law, and according to that law he ought to die,
    because he made himself the Son of God."

Now when Pilate heard this statement,
he became even more afraid,
and went back into the praetorium and said to Jesus,
"Where are you from?"
Jesus did not answer him.
So Pilate said to him,
"Do you not speak to me?
Do you not know that I have power to release you
and I have power to crucify you?"
Jesus answered him,
"You would have no power over me
if it had not been given to you from above.
For this reason the one who handed me over to you
has the greater sin."
Consequently, Pilate tried to release him; but the Jews cried out,
"If you release him, you are not a Friend of Caesar.
Everyone who makes himself a king opposes Caesar."

When Pilate heard these words he brought Jesus out
and seated him on the judge's bench
in the place called Stone Pavement, in Hebrew, Gabbatha.
It was preparation day for Passover, and it was about noon.
And he said to the Jews,
"Behold, your king!"
They cried out,
"Take him away, take him away! Crucify him!"
Pilate said to them,
"Shall I crucify your king?"
The chief priests answered,
"We have no king but Caesar."
Then he handed him over to them to be crucified.

So they took Jesus, and, carrying the cross himself,
he went out to what is called the Place of the Skull,
in Hebrew, Golgotha.
There they crucified him, and with him two others,
one on either side, with Jesus in the middle.
Pilate also had an inscription written and put on the cross.
It read,
"Jesus the Nazorean, the King of the Jews."
Now many of the Jews read this inscription,
because the place where Jesus was crucified was near the city;
and it was written in Hebrew, Latin, and Greek.
So the chief priests of the Jews said to Pilate,
"Do not write 'The King of the Jews,'
but that he said, 'I am the King of the Jews.'"
Pilate answered,
"What I have written, I have written."

When the soldiers had crucified Jesus,
they took his clothes and divided them into four shares,
a share for each soldier.
They also took his tunic, but the tunic was seamless,
woven in one piece from the top down.
So they said to one another,
"Let's not tear it, but cast lots for it to see whose it will be,"
in order that the passage of Scripture might be fulfilled that says:
They divided my garments among them,
and for my vesture they cast lots.

This is what the soldiers did.
Standing by the cross of Jesus were his mother
and his mother's sister, Mary the wife of Clopas,
and Mary of Magdala.
When Jesus saw his mother and the disciple there whom he loved
he said to his mother, "Woman, behold, your son."
Then he said to the disciple,
"Behold, your mother."
And from that hour the disciple took her into his home.

After this, aware that everything was now finished,
in order that the Scripture might be fulfilled,
Jesus said, "I thirst."
There was a vessel filled with common wine.
So they put a sponge soaked in wine on a sprig of hyssop
and put it up to his mouth.
When Jesus had taken the wine, he said,
"It is finished."
And bowing his head, he handed over the spirit.

Here all kneel and pause for a short time.

Now since it was preparation day,
in order that the bodies might not remain
on the cross on the sabbath,
for the sabbath day of that week was a solemn one,
the Jews asked Pilate that their legs be broken
and that they be taken down.
So the soldiers came and broke the legs of the first
and then of the other one who was crucified with Jesus.
But when they came to Jesus and saw that he was already dead,
they did not break his legs,
but one soldier thrust his lance into his side,
and immediately blood and water flowed out.
An eyewitness has testified, and his testimony is true;
he knows that he is speaking the truth,
so that you also may come to believe.
For this happened so that the Scripture passage might be fulfilled:
Not a bone of it will be broken.
And again another passage says:
They will look upon him whom they have pierced.

After this, Joseph of Arimathea,
secretly a disciple of Jesus for fear of the Jews,
asked Pilate if he could remove the body of Jesus.
And Pilate permitted it.
So he came and took his body.
Nicodemus, the one who had first come to him at night,
also came bringing a mixture of myrrh and aloes
weighing about one hundred pounds.
They took the body of Jesus
and bound it with burial cloths along with the spices,
according to the Jewish burial custom.
Now in the place where he had been crucified there was a garden,
and in the garden a new tomb, in which no one had yet been
buried.
So they laid Jesus there because of the Jewish preparation day;
for the tomb was close by.

FIRST READING

Isa 52:13–53:12

See, my servant shall prosper,
  he shall be raised high and greatly exalted.
Even as many were amazed at him—
  so marred was his look beyond human
    semblance
  and his appearance beyond that of the sons
    of man—
so shall he startle many nations,
  because of him kings shall stand speechless;
for those who have not been told shall see,
  those who have not heard shall ponder it.

Who would believe what we have heard?
  To whom has the arm of the LORD been
    revealed?
He grew up like a sapling before him,
  like a shoot from the parched earth;
there was in him no stately bearing to make
    us look at him,
  nor appearance that would attract us to him.
He was spurned and avoided by people,
  a man of suffering, accustomed to infirmity,
one of those from whom people hide their faces,
  spurned, and we held him in no esteem.

Yet it was our infirmities that he bore,
  our sufferings that he endured,
while we thought of him as stricken,
  as one smitten by God and afflicted.
But he was pierced for our offenses,
  crushed for our sins;
upon him was the chastisement that makes
    us whole,
  by his stripes we were healed.
We had all gone astray like sheep,
  each following his own way;
but the LORD laid upon him
  the guilt of us all.

Though he was harshly treated, he submitted
  and opened not his mouth;
like a lamb led to the slaughter
  or a sheep before the shearers,
  he was silent and opened not his mouth.
Oppressed and condemned, he was taken away,
  and who would have thought any more of
    his destiny?
When he was cut off from the land of the living,
  and smitten for the sin of his people,
a grave was assigned him among the wicked
  and a burial place with evildoers,
though he had done no wrong
  nor spoken any falsehood.
But the LORD was pleased
  to crush him in infirmity.

If he gives his life as an offering for sin,
  he shall see his descendants in a long life,
  and the will of the LORD shall be
    accomplished through him.

Because of his affliction
  he shall see the light
    in fullness of days;
through his suffering, my servant shall justify
    many,
  and their guilt he shall bear.
Therefore I will give him his portion among
    the great,
  and he shall divide the spoils with the
    mighty,
because he surrendered himself to death
  and was counted among the wicked;
and he shall take away the sins of many,
  and win pardon for their offenses.

RESPONSORIAL PSALM

Ps 31:2, 6, 12-13, 15-16, 17, 25

R̸. (Luke 23:46) Father, into your hands I
commend my spirit.

In you, O LORD, I take refuge;
  let me never be put to shame.
In your justice rescue me.
Into your hands I commend my spirit;
  you will redeem me, O LORD, O faithful God.

R̸. Father, into your hands I commend my
spirit.

For all my foes I am an object of reproach,
  a laughingstock to my neighbors, and a
    dread to my friends;
  they who see me abroad flee from me.
I am forgotten like the unremembered dead;
  I am like a dish that is broken.

R̸. Father, into your hands I commend my
spirit.

But my trust is in you, O LORD;
  I say, "You are my God.
In your hands is my destiny; rescue me
  from the clutches of my enemies and my
    persecutors."

R̸. Father, into your hands I commend my
spirit.

Let your face shine upon your servant;
  save me in your kindness.
Take courage and be stouthearted,
  all you who hope in the LORD.

R̸. Father, into your hands I commend my
spirit.

SECOND READING

Heb 4:14-16; 5:7-9

Brothers and sisters:
Since we have a great high priest who has
    passed through the heavens,
  Jesus, the Son of God,
  let us hold fast to our confession.
For we do not have a high priest
  who is unable to sympathize with our
    weaknesses,
  but one who has similarly been tested in
    every way,
  yet without sin.
So let us confidently approach the throne of
    grace
  to receive mercy and to find grace for
    timely help.

In the days when Christ was in the flesh,
  he offered prayers and supplications with
    loud cries and tears
  to the one who was able to save him from
    death,
  and he was heard because of his reverence.
Son though he was, he learned obedience
  from what he suffered;
  and when he was made perfect,
  he became the source of eternal salvation
    for all who obey him.

287

FIRST READING
Gen 1:1–2:2

In the beginning, when God created the
    heavens and the earth,
    the earth was a formless wasteland, and
        darkness covered the abyss,
    while a mighty wind swept over the waters.

Then God said,
    "Let there be light," and there was light.
God saw how good the light was.
God then separated the light from the darkness.
God called the light "day," and the darkness
    he called "night."
Thus evening came, and morning followed—
    the first day.

Then God said,
    "Let there be a dome in the middle of the
        waters,
    to separate one body of water from the
        other."
And so it happened:
    God made the dome,
    and it separated the water above the dome
        from the water below it.
God called the dome "the sky."
Evening came, and morning followed—the
    second day.

Then God said,
    "Let the water under the sky be gathered
        into a single basin,
    so that the dry land may appear."
And so it happened:
    the water under the sky was gathered into
        its basin,
    and the dry land appeared.
God called the dry land "the earth,"
    and the basin of the water he called "the
        sea."
God saw how good it was.
Then God said,
    "Let the earth bring forth vegetation:
    every kind of plant that bears seed
    and every kind of fruit tree on earth
    that bears fruit with its seed in it."
And so it happened:
    the earth brought forth every kind of plant
        that bears seed
    and every kind of fruit tree on earth
    that bears fruit with its seed in it.
God saw how good it was.
Evening came, and morning followed—the
    third day.

Then God said:
    "Let there be lights in the dome of the sky,
    to separate day from night.
Let them mark the fixed times, the days and
    the years,

and serve as luminaries in the dome of the
    sky,
    to shed light upon the earth."
And so it happened:
    God made the two great lights,
    the greater one to govern the day,
    and the lesser one to govern the night;
    and he made the stars.
God set them in the dome of the sky,
    to shed light upon the earth,
    to govern the day and the night,
    and to separate the light from the darkness.
God saw how good it was.
Evening came, and morning followed—the
    fourth day.

Then God said,
    "Let the water teem with an abundance of
        living creatures,
    and on the earth let birds fly beneath the
        dome of the sky."
And so it happened:
    God created the great sea monsters
    and all kinds of swimming creatures with
        which the water teems,
    and all kinds of winged birds.
God saw how good it was, and God blessed
    them, saying,
    "Be fertile, multiply, and fill the water of
        the seas;
    and let the birds multiply on the earth."
Evening came, and morning followed—the
    fifth day.

Then God said,
    "Let the earth bring forth all kinds of
        living creatures:
    cattle, creeping things, and wild animals of
        all kinds."
And so it happened:
    God made all kinds of wild animals, all
        kinds of cattle,
    and all kinds of creeping things of the earth.
God saw how good it was.
Then God said:
    "Let us make man in our image, after our
        likeness.
Let them have dominion over the fish of the sea,
    the birds of the air, and the cattle,
    and over all the wild animals
    and all the creatures that crawl on the
        ground."
God created man in his image;
        in the image of God he created him;
        male and female he created them.
God blessed them, saying:
    "Be fertile and multiply;
    fill the earth and subdue it.
Have dominion over the fish of the sea, the
    birds of the air,

and all the living things that move on the
    earth."
God also said:
    "See, I give you every seed-bearing plant all
        over the earth
    and every tree that has seed-bearing fruit
        on it to be your food;
    and to all the animals of the land, all the
        birds of the air,
    and all the living creatures that crawl on
        the ground,
    I give all the green plants for food."
And so it happened.
God looked at everything he had made, and
    he found it very good.
Evening came, and morning followed—the
    sixth day.

Thus the heavens and the earth and all their
    array were completed.
Since on the seventh day God was finished
    with the work he had been doing,
    he rested on the seventh day from all the
        work he had undertaken.

or

Gen 1:1, 26-31a

In the beginning, when God created the
    heavens and the earth,
    God said: "Let us make man in our image,
        after our likeness.
Let them have dominion over the fish of the sea,
    the birds of the air, and the cattle,
    and over all the wild animals
    and all the creatures that crawl on the
        ground."
God created man in his image;
        in the image of God he created him;
        male and female he created them.
God blessed them, saying:
    "Be fertile and multiply;
    fill the earth and subdue it.
Have dominion over the fish of the sea, the
    birds of the air,
    and all the living things that move on the
        earth."
God also said:
    "See, I give you every seed-bearing plant all
        over the earth
    and every tree that has seed-bearing fruit
        on it to be your food;
    and to all the animals of the land, all the
        birds of the air,
    and all the living creatures that crawl on
        the ground,
    I give all the green plants for food."
And so it happened.
God looked at everything he had made, and
    found it very good.

RESPONSORIAL PSALM

Ps 104:1-2, 5-6, 10, 12, 13-14, 24, 35

R̸. (30) Lord, send out your Spirit, and renew the face of the earth.

Bless the LORD, O my soul!
  O LORD, my God, you are great indeed!
You are clothed with majesty and glory,
  robed in light as with a cloak.

R̸. Lord, send out your Spirit, and renew the face of the earth.

You fixed the earth upon its foundation,
  not to be moved forever;
with the ocean, as with a garment, you
    covered it;
  above the mountains the waters stood.

R̸. Lord, send out your Spirit, and renew the face of the earth.

You send forth springs into the watercourses
  that wind among the mountains.
Beside them the birds of heaven dwell;
  from among the branches they send forth
    their song.

R̸. Lord, send out your Spirit, and renew the face of the earth.

You water the mountains from your palace;
  the earth is replete with the fruit of your
    works.
You raise grass for the cattle,
  and vegetation for man's use,
producing bread from the earth.

R̸. Lord, send out your Spirit, and renew the face of the earth.

How manifold are your works, O LORD!
  In wisdom you have wrought them all—
  the earth is full of your creatures.
Bless the LORD, O my soul!

R̸. Lord, send out your Spirit, and renew the face of the earth.

or

Ps 33:4-5, 6-7, 12-13, 20 and 22

R̸. (5b) The earth is full of the goodness of the Lord.

Upright is the word of the LORD,
  and all his works are trustworthy.
He loves justice and right;
  of the kindness of the LORD the earth is full.

R̸. The earth is full of the goodness of the Lord.

By the word of the LORD the heavens were
    made;
  by the breath of his mouth all their host.
He gathers the waters of the sea as in a
    flask;
  in cellars he confines the deep.

R̸. The earth is full of the goodness of the Lord.

Blessed the nation whose God is the LORD,
  the people he has chosen for his own
    inheritance.
From heaven the LORD looks down;
  he sees all mankind.

R̸. The earth is full of the goodness of the Lord.

Our soul waits for the LORD,
  who is our help and our shield.
May your kindness, O LORD, be upon us
  who have put our hope in you.

R̸. The earth is full of the goodness of the Lord.

SECOND READING

Gen 22:1-18

God put Abraham to the test.
He called to him, "Abraham!"
"Here I am," he replied.
Then God said:
  "Take your son Isaac, your only one, whom
    you love,
  and go to the land of Moriah.
There you shall offer him up as a holocaust
  on a height that I will point out to you."
Early the next morning Abraham saddled his
    donkey,
  took with him his son Isaac and two of his
    servants as well,
  and with the wood that he had cut for the
    holocaust,
  set out for the place of which God had told
    him.

On the third day Abraham got sight of the
    place from afar.
Then he said to his servants:
  "Both of you stay here with the donkey,
  while the boy and I go on over yonder.
We will worship and then come back to you."
Thereupon Abraham took the wood for the
    holocaust
  and laid it on his son Isaac's shoulders,
  while he himself carried the fire and the
    knife.
As the two walked on together, Isaac spoke to
    his father Abraham:
  "Father!" Isaac said.
"Yes, son," he replied.
Isaac continued, "Here are the fire and the
    wood,
  but where is the sheep for the holocaust?"
"Son," Abraham answered,
  "God himself will provide the sheep for the
    holocaust."
Then the two continued going forward.

When they came to the place of which God
    had told him,

Abraham built an altar there and arranged
    the wood on it.
Next he tied up his son Isaac,
  and put him on top of the wood on the altar.
Then he reached out and took the knife to
    slaughter his son.
But the LORD's messenger called to him from
    heaven,
  "Abraham, Abraham!"
"Here I am," he answered.
"Do not lay your hand on the boy," said the
    messenger.
"Do not do the least thing to him.
I know now how devoted you are to God,
  since you did not withhold from me your
    own beloved son."
As Abraham looked about,
  he spied a ram caught by its horns in the
    thicket.
So he went and took the ram
  and offered it up as a holocaust in place of
    his son.
Abraham named the site Yahweh-yireh;
  hence people now say, "On the mountain
  the LORD will see."

Again the LORD's messenger called to
    Abraham from heaven and said:
  "I swear by myself, declares the LORD,
  that because you acted as you did
  in not withholding from me your beloved
    son,
  I will bless you abundantly
  and make your descendants as countless
  as the stars of the sky and the sands of the
    seashore;
  your descendants shall take possession
  of the gates of their enemies,
  and in your descendants all the nations of
    the earth
    shall find blessing—
  all this because you obeyed my
    command."

or

Gen 22:1-2, 9a, 10-13, 15-18

God put Abraham to the test.
He called to him, "Abraham!"
"Here I am," he replied.
Then God said:
  "Take your son Isaac, your only one, whom
    you love,
  and go to the land of Moriah.
There you shall offer him up as a holocaust
  on a height that I will point out to you."

When they came to the place of which God
    had told him,
  Abraham built an altar there and arranged
    the wood on it.

Then he reached out and took the knife to
 slaughter his son.
But the LORD's messenger called to him from
 heaven,
 "Abraham, Abraham!"
"Here I am," he answered.
"Do not lay your hand on the boy," said the
 messenger.
"Do not do the least thing to him.
I know now how devoted you are to God,
 since you did not withhold from me your
 own beloved son."
As Abraham looked about,
 he spied a ram caught by its horns in the
 thicket.
So he went and took the ram
 and offered it up as a holocaust in place of
 his son.

Again the LORD's messenger called to
 Abraham from heaven and said:
 "I swear by myself, declares the LORD,
 that because you acted as you did
 in not withholding from me your beloved son,
 I will bless you abundantly
 and make your descendants as countless
 as the stars of the sky and the sands of the
 seashore;
 your descendants shall take possession
 of the gates of their enemies,
 and in your descendants all the nations of
 the earth
 shall find blessing—
 all this because you obeyed my command."

RESPONSORIAL PSALM
Ps 16:5, 8, 9-10, 11

℟. (1) You are my inheritance, O Lord.

O LORD, my allotted portion and my cup,
 you it is who hold fast my lot.
I set the LORD ever before me;
 with him at my right hand I shall not be
 disturbed.

℟. You are my inheritance, O Lord.

Therefore my heart is glad and my soul rejoices,
 my body, too, abides in confidence;
because you will not abandon my soul to the
 netherworld,
 nor will you suffer your faithful one to
 undergo corruption.

℟. You are my inheritance, O Lord.

You will show me the path to life,
 fullness of joys in your presence,
 the delights at your right hand forever.

℟. You are my inheritance, O Lord.

THIRD READING
Exod 14:15–15:1

The LORD said to Moses, "Why are you crying
 out to me?
Tell the Israelites to go forward.
And you, lift up your staff and, with hand
 outstretched over the sea,
 split the sea in two,
 that the Israelites may pass through it on
 dry land.
But I will make the Egyptians so obstinate
 that they will go in after them.
Then I will receive glory through Pharaoh
 and all his army,
 his chariots and charioteers.
The Egyptians shall know that I am the LORD,
 when I receive glory through Pharaoh
 and his chariots and charioteers."

The angel of God, who had been leading
 Israel's camp,
 now moved and went around behind them.
The column of cloud also, leaving the front,
 took up its place behind them,
 so that it came between the camp of the
 Egyptians
 and that of Israel.
But the cloud now became dark, and thus the
 night passed
 without the rival camps coming any closer
 together all night long.
Then Moses stretched out his hand over the
 sea,
 and the LORD swept the sea
 with a strong east wind throughout the night
 and so turned it into dry land.
When the water was thus divided,
 the Israelites marched into the midst of the
 sea on dry land,
 with the water like a wall to their right and
 to their left.

The Egyptians followed in pursuit;
 all Pharaoh's horses and chariots and
 charioteers went after them
 right into the midst of the sea.
In the night watch just before dawn
 the LORD cast through the column of the
 fiery cloud
 upon the Egyptian force a glance that
 threw it into a panic;
 and he so clogged their chariot wheels
 that they could hardly drive.
With that the Egyptians sounded the retreat
 before Israel,
 because the LORD was fighting for them
 against the Egyptians.

Then the LORD told Moses, "Stretch out your
 hand over the sea,
 that the water may flow back upon the
 Egyptians,
 upon their chariots and their charioteers."
So Moses stretched out his hand over the sea,
 and at dawn the sea flowed back to its
 normal depth.
The Egyptians were fleeing head on toward
 the sea,
 when the LORD hurled them into its midst.
As the water flowed back,
 it covered the chariots and the charioteers
 of Pharaoh's whole army
 which had followed the Israelites into the sea.
Not a single one of them escaped.
But the Israelites had marched on dry land
 through the midst of the sea,
 with the water like a wall to their right and
 to their left.
Thus the LORD saved Israel on that day
 from the power of the Egyptians.
When Israel saw the Egyptians lying dead on
 the seashore
 and beheld the great power that the LORD
 had shown against the Egyptians,
 they feared the LORD and believed in him
 and in his servant Moses.

Then Moses and the Israelites sang this song
 to the LORD:
 I will sing to the LORD, for he is gloriously
 triumphant;
 horse and chariot he has cast into the sea.

RESPONSORIAL PSALM
Exod 15:1-2, 3-4, 5-6, 17-18

℟. (1b) Let us sing to the Lord; he has covered
himself in glory.

I will sing to the LORD, for he is gloriously
 triumphant;
 horse and chariot he has cast into the sea.
My strength and my courage is the LORD,
 and he has been my savior.
He is my God, I praise him;
 the God of my father, I extol him.

℟. Let us sing to the Lord; he has covered
himself in glory.

The LORD is a warrior,
 LORD is his name!
Pharaoh's chariots and army he hurled into
 the sea;
 the elite of his officers were submerged in
 the Red Sea.

℟. Let us sing to the Lord; he has covered
himself in glory.

The flood waters covered them,
  they sank into the depths like a stone.
Your right hand, O Lord, magnificent in
  power,
  your right hand, O Lord, has shattered the
  enemy.

R∫. Let us sing to the Lord; he has covered
himself in glory.

You brought in the people you redeemed
  and planted them on the mountain of your
  inheritance—
the place where you made your seat, O Lord,
  the sanctuary, Lord, which your hands
  established.
The Lord shall reign forever and ever.

R∫. Let us sing to the Lord; he has covered
himself in glory.

FOURTH READING
Isa 54:5-14

The One who has become your husband is
  your Maker;
  his name is the Lord of hosts;
your redeemer is the Holy One of Israel,
  called God of all the earth.
The Lord calls you back,
  like a wife forsaken and grieved in spirit,
  a wife married in youth and then cast off,
  says your God.
For a brief moment I abandoned you,
  but with great tenderness I will take you
  back.
In an outburst of wrath, for a moment
  I hid my face from you;
but with enduring love I take pity on you,
  says the Lord, your redeemer.
This is for me like the days of Noah,
  when I swore that the waters of Noah
  should never again deluge the earth;
so I have sworn not to be angry with you,
  or to rebuke you.
Though the mountains leave their place
  and the hills be shaken,
my love shall never leave you
  nor my covenant of peace be shaken,
  says the Lord, who has mercy on you.
O afflicted one, storm-battered and
  unconsoled,
  I lay your pavements in carnelians,
  and your foundations in sapphires;
I will make your battlements of rubies,
  your gates of carbuncles,
  and all your walls of precious stones.
All your children shall be taught by the Lord,
  and great shall be the peace of your children.

In justice shall you be established,
  far from the fear of oppression,
  where destruction cannot come near you.

RESPONSORIAL PSALM
Ps 30:2, 4, 5-6, 11-12, 13

R∫. (2a) I will praise you, Lord, for you have
rescued me.

I will extol you, O Lord, for you drew me
  clear
  and did not let my enemies rejoice over me.
O Lord, you brought me up from the
  netherworld;
  you preserved me from among those going
  down into the pit.

R∫. I will praise you, Lord, for you have
rescued me.

Sing praise to the Lord, you his faithful ones,
  and give thanks to his holy name.
For his anger lasts but a moment;
  a lifetime, his good will.
At nightfall, weeping enters in,
  but with the dawn, rejoicing.

R∫. I will praise you, Lord, for you have
rescued me.

Hear, O Lord, and have pity on me;
  O Lord, be my helper.
You changed my mourning into dancing;
  O Lord, my God, forever will I give you
  thanks.

R∫. I will praise you, Lord, for you have
rescued me.

FIFTH READING
Isa 55:1-11

Thus says the Lord:
All you who are thirsty,
  come to the water!
You who have no money,
  come, receive grain and eat;
come, without paying and without cost,
  drink wine and milk!
Why spend your money for what is not bread,
  your wages for what fails to satisfy?
Heed me, and you shall eat well,
  you shall delight in rich fare.
Come to me heedfully,
  listen, that you may have life.
I will renew with you the everlasting
  covenant,
  the benefits assured to David.
As I made him a witness to the peoples,
  a leader and commander of nations,
so shall you summon a nation you knew not,

and nations that knew you not shall run
  to you,
because of the Lord, your God,
  the Holy One of Israel, who has glorified you.

Seek the Lord while he may be found,
  call him while he is near.
Let the scoundrel forsake his way,
  and the wicked man his thoughts;
let him turn to the Lord for mercy;
  to our God, who is generous in forgiving.
For my thoughts are not your thoughts,
  nor are your ways my ways, says the Lord.
As high as the heavens are above the earth,
  so high are my ways above your ways
  and my thoughts above your thoughts.

For just as from the heavens
  the rain and snow come down
and do not return there
  till they have watered the earth,
  making it fertile and fruitful,
giving seed to the one who sows
  and bread to the one who eats,
so shall my word be
  that goes forth from my mouth;
my word shall not return to me void,
  but shall do my will,
  achieving the end for which I sent it.

RESPONSORIAL PSALM
Isa 12:2-3, 4, 5-6

R∫. (3) You will draw water joyfully from the
springs of salvation.

God indeed is my savior;
  I am confident and unafraid.
My strength and my courage is the Lord,
  and he has been my savior.
With joy you will draw water
  at the fountain of salvation.

R∫. You will draw water joyfully from the
springs of salvation.

Give thanks to the Lord, acclaim his name;
  among the nations make known his deeds,
  proclaim how exalted is his name.

R∫. You will draw water joyfully from the
springs of salvation.

Sing praise to the Lord for his glorious
  achievement;
  let this be known throughout all the earth.
Shout with exultation, O city of Zion,
  for great in your midst
  is the Holy One of Israel!

R∫. You will draw water joyfully from the
springs of salvation.

SIXTH READING
Bar 3:9-15, 32–4:4

Hear, O Israel, the commandments of life:
  listen, and know prudence!
How is it, Israel,
  that you are in the land of your foes,
  grown old in a foreign land,
defiled with the dead,
  accounted with those destined for the
    netherworld?
You have forsaken the fountain of wisdom!
  Had you walked in the way of God,
  you would have dwelt in enduring peace.
Learn where prudence is,
  where strength, where understanding;
that you may know also
  where are length of days, and life,
  where light of the eyes, and peace.
Who has found the place of wisdom,
  who has entered into her treasuries?

The One who knows all things knows her;
  he has probed her by his knowledge—
the One who established the earth for all
    time,
  and filled it with four-footed beasts;
he who dismisses the light, and it departs,
  calls it, and it obeys him trembling;
before whom the stars at their posts
  shine and rejoice;
when he calls them, they answer, "Here we
    are!"
  shining with joy for their Maker.
Such is our God;
  no other is to be compared to him:
he has traced out the whole way of
    understanding,
  and has given her to Jacob, his servant,
  to Israel, his beloved son.

Since then she has appeared on earth,
  and moved among people.
She is the book of the precepts of God,
  the law that endures forever;
all who cling to her will live,
  but those will die who forsake her.
Turn, O Jacob, and receive her:
  walk by her light toward splendor.
Give not your glory to another,
  your privileges to an alien race.
Blessed are we, O Israel;
  for what pleases God is known to us!

RESPONSORIAL PSALM
Ps 19:8, 9, 10, 11

R̷. (John 6:68c) Lord, you have the words of
everlasting life.

The law of the LORD is perfect,
  refreshing the soul;

the decree of the LORD is trustworthy,
  giving wisdom to the simple.

R̷. Lord, you have the words of everlasting life.

The precepts of the LORD are right,
  rejoicing the heart;
the command of the LORD is clear,
  enlightening the eye.

R̷. Lord, you have the words of everlasting life.

The fear of the LORD is pure,
  enduring forever;
the ordinances of the LORD are true,
  all of them just.

R̷. Lord, you have the words of everlasting life.

They are more precious than gold,
  than a heap of purest gold;
sweeter also than syrup
  or honey from the comb.

R̷. Lord, you have the words of everlasting life.

SEVENTH READING
Ezek 36:16-17a, 18-28

The word of the LORD came to me, saying:
  Son of man, when the house of Israel lived
    in their land,
  they defiled it by their conduct and deeds.
Therefore I poured out my fury upon them
  because of the blood that they poured out
    on the ground,
  and because they defiled it with idols.
I scattered them among the nations,
  dispersing them over foreign lands;
  according to their conduct and deeds I
    judged them.
But when they came among the nations
    wherever they came,
  they served to profane my holy name,
  because it was said of them: "These are the
    people of the LORD,
  yet they had to leave their land."
So I have relented because of my holy name
  which the house of Israel profaned
  among the nations where they came.
Therefore say to the house of Israel: Thus
    says the Lord GOD:
  Not for your sakes do I act, house of Israel,
  but for the sake of my holy name,
  which you profaned among the nations to
    which you came.
I will prove the holiness of my great name,
  profaned among the nations,
  in whose midst you have profaned it.
Thus the nations shall know that I am the
    LORD, says the Lord GOD,
  when in their sight I prove my holiness
    through you.
For I will take you away from among the
    nations,

gather you from all the foreign lands,
  and bring you back to your own land.
I will sprinkle clean water upon you
  to cleanse you from all your impurities,
  and from all your idols I will cleanse you.
I will give you a new heart and place a new
    spirit within you,
  taking from your bodies your stony hearts
  and giving you natural hearts.
I will put my spirit within you and make you
    live by my statutes,
  careful to observe my decrees.
You shall live in the land I gave your fathers;
  you shall be my people, and I will be your
    God.

RESPONSORIAL PSALM
Ps 42:3, 5; 43:3, 4

R̷. (42:2) Like a deer that longs for running
streams, my soul longs for you, my God.

Athirst is my soul for God, the living God.
  When shall I go and behold the face of God?

R̷. Like a deer that longs for running streams,
my soul longs for you, my God.

I went with the throng
  and led them in procession to the house of
    God,
amid loud cries of joy and thanksgiving,
  with the multitude keeping festival.

R̷. Like a deer that longs for running streams,
my soul longs for you, my God.

Send forth your light and your fidelity;
  they shall lead me on
and bring me to your holy mountain,
  to your dwelling-place.

R̷. Like a deer that longs for running streams,
my soul longs for you, my God.

Then will I go in to the altar of God,
  the God of my gladness and joy;
then will I give you thanks upon the harp,
  O God, my God!

R̷. Like a deer that longs for running streams,
my soul longs for you, my God.

or

Isa 12:2-3, 4bcd, 5-6

R̷. (3) You will draw water joyfully from the
springs of salvation.

God indeed is my savior;
  I am confident and unafraid.
My strength and my courage is the LORD,
  and he has been my savior.
With joy you will draw water
  at the fountain of salvation.

R̷. You will draw water joyfully from the
springs of salvation.

Give thanks to the LORD, acclaim his name;
    among the nations make known his deeds,
    proclaim how exalted is his name.

R̸. You will draw water joyfully from the springs of salvation.

Sing praise to the LORD for his glorious achievement;
    let this be known throughout all the earth.
Shout with exultation, O city of Zion,
    for great in your midst
    is the Holy One of Israel!

R̸. You will draw water joyfully from the springs of salvation.

or

Ps 51:12-13, 14-15, 18-19

R̸. (12a) Create a clean heart in me, O God.

A clean heart create for me, O God,
    and a steadfast spirit renew within me.
Cast me not out from your presence,
    and your Holy Spirit take not from me.

R̸. Create a clean heart in me, O God.

Give me back the joy of your salvation,
    and a willing spirit sustain in me.
I will teach transgressors your ways,
    and sinners shall return to you.

R̸. Create a clean heart in me, O God.

For you are not pleased with sacrifices;
    should I offer a holocaust, you would not accept it.
My sacrifice, O God, is a contrite spirit;
    a heart contrite and humbled, O God, you will not spurn.

R̸. Create a clean heart in me, O God.

EPISTLE

Rom 6:3-11

Brothers and sisters:
Are you unaware that we who were baptized
    into Christ Jesus
    were baptized into his death?
We were indeed buried with him through
    baptism into death,
    so that, just as Christ was raised from the dead
    by the glory of the Father,
    we too might live in newness of life.

For if we have grown into union with him
    through a death like his,
    we shall also be united with him in the resurrection.
We know that our old self was crucified with him,
    so that our sinful body might be done away with,
    that we might no longer be in slavery to sin.
For a dead person has been absolved from sin.
If, then, we have died with Christ,
    we believe that we shall also live with him.
We know that Christ, raised from the dead,
    dies no more;
    death no longer has power over him.
As to his death, he died to sin once and for all;
    as to his life, he lives for God.
Consequently, you too must think of
    yourselves as being dead to sin
    and living for God in Christ Jesus.

RESPONSORIAL PSALM

Ps 118:1-2, 16-17, 22-23

R̸. Alleluia, alleluia, alleluia.

Give thanks to the LORD, for he is good,
    for his mercy endures forever.
Let the house of Israel say,
    "His mercy endures forever."

R̸. Alleluia, alleluia, alleluia.

"The right hand of the LORD has struck with power;
    the right hand of the LORD is exalted.
I shall not die, but live,
    and declare the works of the LORD."

R̸. Alleluia, alleluia, alleluia.

The stone which the builders rejected
    has become the cornerstone.
By the LORD has this been done;
    it is wonderful in our eyes.

R̸. Alleluia, alleluia, alleluia.

Gospel
Mark 16:1-7; L41B

When the sabbath was over,
   Mary Magdalene, Mary, the mother of James, and Salome
   bought spices so that they might go and anoint him.
Very early when the sun had risen,
   on the first day of the week, they came to the tomb.
They were saying to one another,
   "Who will roll back the stone for us
   from the entrance to the tomb?"
When they looked up,
   they saw that the stone had been rolled back;
   it was very large.

On entering the tomb they saw a young man
   sitting on the right side, clothed in a white robe,
   and they were utterly amazed.
He said to them, "Do not be amazed!
You seek Jesus of Nazareth, the crucified.
He has been raised; he is not here.
Behold the place where they laid him.
But go and tell his disciples and Peter,
   'He is going before you to Galilee;
   there you will see him, as he told you.'"

or, at an afternoon or evening Mass

Gospel
Luke 24:13-35; L46

That very day, the first day of the week,
   two of Jesus' disciples were going
   to a village seven miles from Jerusalem called Emmaus,
   and they were conversing about all the things that had occurred.
And it happened that while they were conversing and debating,
   Jesus himself drew near and walked with them,
   but their eyes were prevented from recognizing him.
He asked them,
   "What are you discussing as you walk along?"
They stopped, looking downcast.
One of them, named Cleopas, said to him in reply,
   "Are you the only visitor to Jerusalem
   who does not know of the things
   that have taken place there in these days?"
And he replied to them, "What sort of things?"
They said to him,
   "The things that happened to Jesus the Nazarene,
   who was a prophet mighty in deed and word
   before God and all the people,
   how our chief priests and rulers both handed him over
   to a sentence of death and crucified him.
But we were hoping that he would be the one to redeem Israel;
   and besides all this,
   it is now the third day since this took place.
Some women from our group, however, have astounded us:
   they were at the tomb early in the morning
   and did not find his body;
   they came back and reported
   that they had indeed seen a vision of angels
   who announced that he was alive.
Then some of those with us went to the tomb
   and found things just as the women had described,
   but him they did not see."

And he said to them, "Oh, how foolish you are!
How slow of heart to believe all that the prophets spoke!
Was it not necessary that the Christ should suffer these things
   and enter into his glory?"
Then beginning with Moses and all the prophets,
   he interpreted to them what referred to him
   in all the Scriptures.
As they approached the village to which they were going,
   he gave the impression that he was going on farther.
But they urged him, "Stay with us,
   for it is nearly evening and the day is almost over."
So he went in to stay with them.
And it happened that, while he was with them at table,
   he took bread, said the blessing,
   broke it, and gave it to them.
With that their eyes were opened and they recognized him,
   but he vanished from their sight.
Then they said to each other,
   "Were not our hearts burning within us
   while he spoke to us on the way and opened the Scriptures to us?"
So they set out at once and returned to Jerusalem
   where they found gathered together
   the eleven and those with them who were saying,
   "The Lord has truly been raised and has appeared to Simon!"
Then the two recounted
   what had taken place on the way
   and how he was made known to them in the breaking of bread.

FIRST READING
Acts 10:34a, 37-43

Peter proceeded to speak and said:
    "You know what has happened all over
        Judea,
    beginning in Galilee after the baptism
    that John preached,
    how God anointed Jesus of Nazareth
    with the Holy Spirit and power.
He went about doing good
    and healing all those oppressed by the devil,
    for God was with him.
We are witnesses of all that he did
    both in the country of the Jews and in
        Jerusalem.
They put him to death by hanging him on a
        tree.
This man God raised on the third day and
        granted that he be visible,
    not to all the people, but to us,
    the witnesses chosen by God in advance,
    who ate and drank with him after he rose
        from the dead.
He commissioned us to preach to the people
    and testify that he is the one appointed by
        God
    as judge of the living and the dead.
To him all the prophets bear witness,
    that everyone who believes in him
    will receive forgiveness of sins through his
        name."

RESPONSORIAL PSALM
Ps 118:1-2, 16-17, 22-23

R⫾. (24) This is the day the Lord has made; let
us rejoice and be glad.
        or:
R⫾. Alleluia.

Give thanks to the LORD, for he is good,
    for his mercy endures forever.
Let the house of Israel say,
    "His mercy endures forever."

R⫾. This is the day the Lord has made; let us
rejoice and be glad.
        or:
R⫾. Alleluia.

"The right hand of the LORD has struck with
        power;
    the right hand of the LORD is exalted.
I shall not die, but live,
    and declare the works of the LORD."

R⫾. This is the day the Lord has made; let us
rejoice and be glad.
        or:
R⫾. Alleluia.

The stone which the builders rejected
    has become the cornerstone.
By the LORD has this been done;
    it is wonderful in our eyes.

R⫾. This is the day the Lord has made; let us
rejoice and be glad.
        or:
R⫾. Alleluia.

SECOND READING
1 Cor 5:6b-8

Brothers and sisters:
Do you not know that a little yeast leavens all
        the dough?
Clear out the old yeast,
    so that you may become a fresh batch of
        dough,
    inasmuch as you are unleavened.
For our paschal lamb, Christ, has been
        sacrificed.
Therefore, let us celebrate the feast,
    not with the old yeast, the yeast of malice
        and wickedness,
    but with the unleavened bread of sincerity
        and truth.

or

Col 3:1-4

Brothers and sisters:
If then you were raised with Christ, seek what
        is above,
    where Christ is seated at the right hand of
        God.
Think of what is above, not of what is on earth.
For you have died, and your life is hidden
        with Christ in God.
When Christ your life appears,
    then you too will appear with him in glory.

SEQUENCE
Victimae paschali laudes

Christians, to the Paschal Victim
    Offer your thankful praises!
A Lamb the sheep redeems;
    Christ, who only is sinless,
    Reconciles sinners to the Father.
Death and life have contended in that combat
        stupendous:
    The Prince of life, who died, reigns
        immortal.
Speak, Mary, declaring
    What you saw, wayfaring.
"The tomb of Christ, who is living,
    The glory of Jesus' resurrection;
Bright angels attesting,
    The shroud and napkin resting.
Yes, Christ my hope is arisen;
    To Galilee he goes before you."
Christ indeed from death is risen, our new life
        obtaining.
    Have mercy, victor King, ever reigning!
    Amen. Alleluia.

Gospel (cont.)
John 20:19-31; L44B

Then he said to Thomas, "Put your finger here and see my hands,
and bring your hand and put it into my side,
and do not be unbelieving, but believe."
Thomas answered and said to him, "My Lord and my God!"
Jesus said to him, "Have you come to believe because you have seen
me?
Blessed are those who have not seen and have believed."

Now Jesus did many other signs in the presence of his disciples
that are not written in this book.
But these are written that you may come to believe
that Jesus is the Christ, the Son of God,
and that through this belief you may have life in his name.

The Ascension of the Lord, *May 21, 2009 (Thursday) or May 24, 2009*

SECOND READING
Eph 1:17-23

Brothers and sisters:
May the God of our Lord Jesus Christ, the
Father of glory,
give you a Spirit of wisdom and revelation
resulting in knowledge of him.
May the eyes of your hearts be enlightened,
that you may know what is the hope that
belongs to his call,
what are the riches of glory
in his inheritance among the holy ones,
and what is the surpassing greatness of
his power
for us who believe,
in accord with the exercise of his great
might,
which he worked in Christ,
raising him from the dead
and seating him at his right hand in the
heavens,
far above every principality, authority,
power, and dominion,
and every name that is named
not only in this age but also in the one to
come.
And he put all things beneath his feet
and gave him as head over all things to the
church,
which is his body,
the fullness of the one who fills all things
in every way.

or

Eph 4:1-13

Brothers and sisters,
I, a prisoner for the Lord,
urge you to live in a manner worthy of the
call you have received,
with all humility and gentleness, with
patience,
bearing with one another through love,
striving to preserve the unity of the spirit
through the bond of peace:
one body and one Spirit,
as you were also called to the one hope of
your call;
one Lord, one faith, one baptism;
one God and Father of all,
who is over all and through all and in all.

But grace was given to each of us
according to the measure of Christ's gift.
Therefore, it says:
*He ascended on high and took prisoners
captive;
he gave gifts to men.*
What does "he ascended" mean except that he
also descended
into the lower regions of the earth?
The one who descended is also the one who
ascended
far above all the heavens,
that he might fill all things.

And he gave some as apostles, others as
prophets,
others as evangelists, others as pastors and
teachers,
to equip the holy ones for the work of
ministry,

for building up the body of Christ,
until we all attain the unity of faith
and knowledge of the Son of God, to
mature manhood,
to the extent of the full stature of Christ.

or

Eph 4:1-7, 11-13

Brothers and sisters,
I, a prisoner for the Lord,
urge you to live in a manner worthy of the
call you have received,
with all humility and gentleness, with
patience,
bearing with one another through love,
striving to preserve the unity of the Spirit
through the bond of peace:
one body and one Spirit,
as you were also called to the one hope of
your call;
one Lord, one faith, one baptism;
one God and Father of all,
who is over all and through all and in all.

But grace was given to each of us
according to the measure of Christ's gift.

And he gave some as apostles, others as
prophets,
others as evangelists, others as pastors and
teachers,
to equip the holy ones for the work of
ministry,
for building up the body of Christ,
until we all attain the unity of faith
and knowledge of the Son of God, to
mature manhood,
to the extent of the full stature of Christ.

SECOND READING

1 Cor 12:3b-7, 12-13

Brothers and sisters:
No one can say, "Jesus is Lord," except by the
Holy Spirit.

There are different kinds of spiritual gifts but
the same Spirit;
there are different forms of service but the
same Lord;
there are different workings but the same God
who produces all of them in everyone.
To each individual the manifestation of the
Spirit
is given for some benefit.

As a body is one though it has many parts,
and all the parts of the body, though many,
are one body,
so also Christ.
For in one Spirit we were all baptized into one
body,
whether Jews or Greeks, slaves or free
persons,
and we were all given to drink of one Spirit.

or

Gal 5:16-25

Brothers and sisters, live by the Spirit
and you will certainly not gratify the desire
of the flesh.
For the flesh has desires against the Spirit,
and the Spirit against the flesh;
these are opposed to each other,
so that you may not do what you want.
But if you are guided by the Spirit, you are
not under the law.
Now the works of the flesh are obvious:
immorality, impurity, lust, idolatry,
sorcery, hatreds, rivalry, jealousy,
outbursts of fury, acts of selfishness,
dissensions, factions, occasions of envy,
drinking bouts, orgies, and the like.
I warn you, as I warned you before,
that those who do such things will not
inherit the kingdom of God.
In contrast, the fruit of the Spirit is love, joy,
peace,
patience, kindness, generosity,
faithfulness, gentleness, self-control.
Against such there is no law.
Now those who belong to Christ Jesus have
crucified their flesh
with its passions and desires.
If we live in the Spirit, let us also follow the
Spirit.

SEQUENCE

Veni, Sancte Spiritus

Come, Holy Spirit, come!
And from your celestial home
Shed a ray of light divine!
Come, Father of the poor!
Come, source of all our store!
Come, within our bosoms shine.
You, of comforters the best;
You, the soul's most welcome guest;
Sweet refreshment here below;
In our labor, rest most sweet;
Grateful coolness in the heat;
Solace in the midst of woe.
O most blessed Light divine,
Shine within these hearts of yours,
And our inmost being fill!
Where you are not, we have naught,
Nothing good in deed or thought,
Nothing free from taint of ill.
Heal our wounds, our strength renew;
On our dryness pour your dew;
Wash the stains of guilt away:
Bend the stubborn heart and will;
Melt the frozen, warm the chill;
Guide the steps that go astray.
On the faithful, who adore
And confess you, evermore
In your sevenfold gift descend;
Give them virtue's sure reward;
Give them your salvation, Lord;
Give them joys that never end. Amen.
Alleluia.

SECOND READING

Heb 9:11-15

Brothers and sisters:
When Christ came as high priest
　of the good things that have come to be,
　passing through the greater and more
　　perfect tabernacle
　not made by hands, that is, not belonging
　　to this creation,
　he entered once for all into the sanctuary,
　not with the blood of goats and calves
　but with his own blood, thus obtaining
　　eternal redemption.
For if the blood of goats and bulls
　and the sprinkling of a heifer's ashes
　can sanctify those who are defiled
　so that their flesh is cleansed,
　how much more will the blood of Christ,
　who through the eternal Spirit offered
　　himself unblemished to God,
　cleanse our consciences from dead works
　to worship the living God.

For this reason he is mediator of a new
　　covenant:
　since a death has taken place for
　　deliverance
　from transgressions under the first
　　covenant,
　those who are called may receive the
　　promised eternal inheritance.

OPTIONAL SEQUENCE

Lauda Sion

Laud, O Zion, your salvation,
Laud with hymns of exultation,
　Christ, your king and shepherd true:

Bring him all the praise you know,
He is more than you bestow.
　Never can you reach his due.

Special theme for glad thanksgiving
Is the quick'ning and the living
　Bread today before you set:

From his hands of old partaken,
As we know, by faith unshaken,
　Where the Twelve at supper met.

Full and clear ring out your chanting,
Joy nor sweetest grace be wanting,
　From your heart let praises burst:

For today the feast is holden,
When the institution olden
　Of that supper was rehearsed.

Here the new law's new oblation,
By the new king's revelation,
　Ends the form of ancient rite:

Now the new the old effaces,
Truth away the shadow chases,
　Light dispels the gloom of night.

What he did at supper seated,
Christ ordained to be repeated,
　His memorial ne'er to cease:

And his rule for guidance taking,
Bread and wine we hallow, making
　Thus our sacrifice of peace.

This the truth each Christian learns,
Bread into his flesh he turns,
　To his precious blood the wine:

Sight has fail'd, nor thought conceives,
But a dauntless faith believes,
　Resting on a pow'r divine.

Here beneath these signs are hidden
Priceless things to sense forbidden;
　Signs, not things are all we see:

Blood is poured and flesh is broken,
Yet in either wondrous token
　Christ entire we know to be.

Whoso of this food partakes,
Does not rend the Lord nor breaks;
　Christ is whole to all that taste:

Thousands are, as one, receivers,
One, as thousands of believers,
　Eats of him who cannot waste.

Bad and good the feast are sharing,
Of what divers dooms preparing,
　Endless death, or endless life.

Life to these, to those damnation,
See how like participation
　Is with unlike issues rife.

When the sacrament is broken,
Doubt not, but believe 'tis spoken,
　That each sever'd outward token
　　doth the very whole contain.

Nought the precious gift divides,
Breaking but the sign betides
　Jesus still the same abides,
　　still unbroken does remain.

The shorter form of the sequence begins here.

Lo! the angel's food is given
To the pilgrim who has striven;
　See the children's bread from heaven,
　　which on dogs may not be spent.

Truth the ancient types fulfilling,
Isaac bound, a victim willing,
　Paschal lamb, its lifeblood spilling,
　　manna to the fathers sent.

Very bread, good shepherd, tend us,
Jesu, of your love befriend us,
　You refresh us, you defend us,
　Your eternal goodness send us
In the land of life to see.

You who all things can and know,
Who on earth such food bestow,
　Grant us with your saints, though lowest,
　Where the heav'nly feast you show,
Fellow heirs and guests to be. Amen. Alleluia.

The Solemnity of the Most Sacred Heart of Jesus, *June 19, 2009*

FIRST READING
Hos 11:1, 3-4, 8c-9

Thus says the LORD:
When Israel was a child I loved him,
  out of Egypt I called my son.
Yet it was I who taught Ephraim to walk,
  who took them in my arms;
I drew them with human cords,
  with bands of love;
I fostered them like one
  who raises an infant to his cheeks;
yet, though I stooped to feed my child,
  they did not know that I was their healer.

My heart is overwhelmed,
  my pity is stirred.
I will not give vent to my blazing anger,
  I will not destroy Ephraim again;
for I am God and not a man,
  the Holy One present among you;
  I will not let the flames consume you.

RESPONSORIAL PSALM
Isa 12:2-3, 4, 5-6

R̹. (3)You will draw water joyfully from the springs of salvation.

God indeed is my savior;
  I am confident and unafraid.
My strength and my courage is the LORD,
  and he has been my savior.
With joy you will draw water
  at the fountain of salvation.

R̹. You will draw water joyfully from the springs of salvation.

Give thanks to the LORD, acclaim his name;
  among the nations make known his deeds,
  proclaim how exalted is his name.

R̹. You will draw water joyfully from the springs of salvation.

Sing praise to the LORD for his glorious
    achievement;
  let this be known throughout all the earth.
Shout with exultation, O city of Zion,
  for great in your midst
  is the Holy One of Israel!

R̹. You will draw water joyfully from the springs of salvation.

SECOND READING
Eph 3:8-12, 14-19

Brothers and sisters:
To me, the very least of all the holy ones, this
    grace was given,
  to preach to the Gentiles the inscrutable
    riches of Christ,
  and to bring to light for all what is the plan
    of the mystery
  hidden from ages past in God who created
    all things,
  so that the manifold wisdom of God
  might now be made known through the
    church
  to the principalities and authorities in the
    heavens.
This was according to the eternal purpose
  that he accomplished in Christ Jesus our
    Lord,
  in whom we have boldness of speech
  and confidence of access through faith in
    him.

For this reason I kneel before the Father,
  from whom every family in heaven and on
    earth is named,
  that he may grant you in accord with the
    riches of his glory
  to be strengthened with power through his
    Spirit in the inner self,
  and that Christ may dwell in your hearts
    through faith;
  that you, rooted and grounded in love,
  may have strength to comprehend with all
    the holy ones
  what is the breadth and length and height
    and depth,
  and to know the love of Christ which
    surpasses knowledge,
  so that you may be filled with all the
    fullness of God.

FIRST READING
Isa 49:1-6

Hear me, O coastlands,
  listen, O distant peoples.
The Lord called me from birth,
  from my mother's womb he gave me my
    name.
He made of me a sharp-edged sword
  and concealed me in the shadow of his arm.
He made me a polished arrow,
  in his quiver he hid me.
You are my servant, he said to me,
  Israel, through whom I show my glory.

Though I thought I had toiled in vain,
  and for nothing, uselessly, spent my strength,
yet my reward is with the Lord,
  my recompense is with my God.
For now the Lord has spoken
  who formed me as his servant from the
    womb,
that Jacob may be brought back to him
  and Israel gathered to him;
and I am made glorious in the sight of the
    Lord,
  and my God is now my strength!
It is too little, he says, for you to be my servant,
  to raise up the tribes of Jacob,
  and restore the survivors of Israel;
I will make you a light to the nations,
  that my salvation may reach to the ends of
    the earth.

RESPONSORIAL PSALM
Ps 139:1b-3, 13-14ab, 14c-15

R℣. (14a) I praise you, for I am wonderfully
made.

O Lord you have probed me and you know
    me:
  you know when I sit and when I stand;
  you understand my thoughts from afar.
My journeys and my rest you scrutinize,
  with all my ways you are familiar.

R℣. I praise you, for I am wonderfully made.

Truly you have formed my inmost being;
  you knit me in my mother's womb.
I give you thanks that I am fearfully,
    wonderfully made;
  wonderful are your works.

R℣. I praise you, for I am wonderfully made.

My soul also you knew full well;
  nor was my frame unknown to you
when I was made in secret,
  when I was fashioned in the depths of the
    earth.

R℣. I praise you, for I am wonderfully made.

SECOND READING
Acts 13:22-26

In those days, Paul said:
"God raised up David as king;
  of him God testified,
  I have found David, son of Jesse, a man
    after my own heart;
  he will carry out my every wish.
From this man's descendants God, according
    to his promise,
  has brought to Israel a savior, Jesus.
John heralded his coming by proclaiming a
    baptism of repentance
  to all the people of Israel;
  and as John was completing his course, he
    would say,
  'What do you suppose that I am? I am not he.
Behold, one is coming after me;
  I am not worthy to unfasten the sandals of
    his feet.'

"My brothers, sons of the family of Abraham,
  and those others among you who are God-
    fearing,
  to us this word of salvation has been sent."

Gospel (cont.)
Mark 5:21-43; L98B

And he looked around to see who had done it.
The woman, realizing what had happened to her,
    approached in fear and trembling.
She fell down before Jesus and told him the whole truth.
He said to her, "Daughter, your faith has saved you.
Go in peace and be cured of your affliction."

While he was still speaking,
    people from the synagogue official's house arrived and said,
    "Your daughter has died; why trouble the teacher any longer?"
Disregarding the message that was reported,
    Jesus said to the synagogue official,
    "Do not be afraid; just have faith."
He did not allow anyone to accompany him inside
    except Peter, James, and John, the brother of James.
When they arrived at the house of the synagogue official,
    he caught sight of a commotion,
    people weeping and wailing loudly.
So he went in and said to them,
    "Why this commotion and weeping?
The child is not dead but asleep."
And they ridiculed him.
Then he put them all out.
He took along the child's father and mother
    and those who were with him
    and entered the room where the child was.
He took the child by the hand and said to her, *"Talitha koum,"*
    which means, "Little girl, I say to you, arise!"
The girl, a child of twelve, arose immediately and walked around.
At that they were utterly astounded.
He gave strict orders that no one should know this
    and said that she should be given something to eat.

or Mark 5:21-24, 35b-43; L98B

When Jesus had crossed again in the boat
    to the other side,
    a large crowd gathered around him, and he stayed close to the sea.
One of the synagogue officials, named Jairus, came forward.
Seeing him he fell at his feet and pleaded earnestly with him, saying,
    "My daughter is at the point of death.
Please, come lay your hands on her
    that she may get well and live."
He went off with him,
    and a large crowd followed him and pressed upon him.

While he was still speaking, people from the synagogue official's house
    arrived and said,
    "Your daughter has died; why trouble the teacher any longer?"
Disregarding the message that was reported,
    Jesus said to the synagogue official,
    "Do not be afraid; just have faith."
He did not allow anyone to accompany him inside
    except Peter, James, and John, the brother of James.
When they arrived at the house of the synagogue official,
    he caught sight of a commotion,
    people weeping and wailing loudly.
So he went in and said to them,
    "Why this commotion and weeping?
The child is not dead but asleep."
And they ridiculed him.
Then he put them all out.
He took along the child's father and mother
    and those who were with him
    and entered the room where the child was.
He took the child by the hand and said to her, *"Talitha koum,"*
    which means, "Little girl, I say to you, arise!"
The girl, a child of twelve, arose immediately and walked around.
At that they were utterly astounded.
He gave strict orders that no one should know this
    and said that she should be given something to eat.

SS. Peter and Paul, Apostles, *June 29, 2009*

FIRST READING
Acts 12:1-11

In those days, King Herod laid hands upon
        some members of the church to harm
        them.
He had James, the brother of John, killed by
        the sword,
    and when he saw that this was pleasing to
        the Jews
    he proceeded to arrest Peter also.
—It was the feast of Unleavened Bread.—
He had him taken into custody and put in
        prison
    under the guard of four squads of four
        soldiers each.
He intended to bring him before the people
        after Passover.
Peter thus was being kept in prison,
    but prayer by the church was fervently
        being made
    to God on his behalf.

On the very night before Herod was to bring
        him to trial,
    Peter, secured by double chains,
    was sleeping between two soldiers,
    while outside the door guards kept watch
        on the prison.
Suddenly the angel of the Lord stood by him,
    and a light shone in the cell.
He tapped Peter on the side and awakened
        him, saying,
    "Get up quickly."
The chains fell from his wrists.
The angel said to him, "Put on your belt and
        your sandals."
He did so.
Then he said to him, "Put on your cloak and
        follow me."

So he followed him out,
    not realizing that what was happening
        through the angel was real;
    he thought he was seeing a vision.
They passed the first guard, then the second,
    and came to the iron gate leading out to
        the city,
    which opened for them by itself.
They emerged and made their way down an
        alley,
    and suddenly the angel left him.
Then Peter recovered his senses and said,
    "Now I know for certain
    that the Lord sent his angel
    and rescued me from the hand of Herod
    and from all that the Jewish people had
        been expecting."

RESPONSORIAL PSALM
Ps 34:2-3, 4-5, 6-7, 8-9

R̸. (5) The angel of the Lord will rescue those
who fear him.

I will bless the LORD at all times;
    his praise shall be ever in my mouth.
Let my soul glory in the LORD;
    the lowly will hear me and be glad.

R̸. The angel of the Lord will rescue those
who fear him.

Glorify the LORD with me,
    let us together extol his name.
I sought the LORD, and he answered me
    and delivered me from all my fears.

R̸. The angel of the Lord will rescue those
who fear him.

Look to him that you may be radiant with joy,
    and your faces may not blush with shame.

When the poor one called out, the LORD heard,
    and from all his distress he saved him.

R̸. The angel of the Lord will rescue those
who fear him.

The angel of the LORD encamps
    around those who fear him, and delivers
        them.
Taste and see how good the LORD is;
    blessed the man who takes refuge in him.

R̸. The angel of the Lord will rescue those
who fear him.

SECOND READING
2 Tim 4:6-8, 17-18

I, Paul, am already being poured out like a
        libation,
    and the time of my departure is at hand.
I have competed well; I have finished the race;
    I have kept the faith.
From now on the crown of righteousness
        awaits me,
    which the Lord, the just judge,
    will award to me on that day, and not only
        to me,
    but to all who have longed for his
        appearance.

The Lord stood by me and gave me strength,
    so that through me the proclamation might
        be completed
    and all the Gentiles might hear it.
And I was rescued from the lion's mouth.
The Lord will rescue me from every evil
        threat
    and will bring me safe to his heavenly
        Kingdom.
To him be glory forever and ever. Amen.

Fifteenth Sunday in Ordinary Time, *July 12, 2009*

SECOND READING
Eph 1:3-10

Blessed be the God and Father of our Lord
        Jesus Christ,
    who has blessed us in Christ
    with every spiritual blessing in the
        heavens,
    as he chose us in him, before the foundation
        of the world,
    to be holy and without blemish before him.
In love he destined us for adoption to himself
        through Jesus Christ,
    in accord with the favor of his will,
    for the praise of the glory of his grace
    that he granted us in the beloved.

In him we have redemption by his blood,
    the forgiveness of transgressions,
    in accord with the riches of his grace that
        he lavished upon us.
In all wisdom and insight, he has made
        known to us
    the mystery of his will in accord with his
        favor
    that he set forth in him as a plan for the
        fullness of times,
    to sum up all things in Christ, in heaven
        and on earth.

Seventeenth Sunday in Ordinary Time, *July 26, 2009*

Gospel (cont.)
John 6:1-15; L110B

Then Jesus took the loaves, gave thanks,
    and distributed them to those who were reclining,
    and also as much of the fish as they wanted.
When they had had their fill, he said to his disciples,
    "Gather the fragments left over,
    so that nothing will be wasted."
So they collected them,
    and filled twelve wicker baskets with fragments
    from the five barley loaves
    that had been more than they could eat.
When the people saw the sign he had done, they said,
    "This is truly the Prophet, the one who is to come into the world."
Since Jesus knew that they were going to come and carry him off
    to make him king,
    he withdrew again to the mountain alone.

Eighteenth Sunday in Ordinary Time, *August 2, 2009*

Gospel (cont.)
John 6:24-35; L113B

So Jesus said to them,
    "Amen, amen, I say to you,
    it was not Moses who gave the bread from heaven;
    my Father gives you the true bread from heaven.
For the bread of God is that which comes down from heaven
    and gives life to the world."

So they said to him,
    "Sir, give us this bread always."
Jesus said to them,
    "I am the bread of life;
    whoever comes to me will never hunger,
    and whoever believes in me will never thirst."

Assumption of the Blessed Virgin Mary, *August 15, 2009*

Gospel (cont.)
Luke 1:39-56; L622

He has cast down the mighty from their thrones,
    and has lifted up the lowly.
He has filled the hungry with good things,
    and the rich he has sent away empty.
He has come to the help of his servant Israel
    for he has remembered his promise of mercy,
    the promise he made to our fathers,
    to Abraham and his children forever."

Mary remained with her about three months
    and then returned to her home.

FIRST READING
Rev 11:19a; 12:1-6a, 10ab

God's temple in heaven was opened,
    and the ark of his covenant could be seen in the temple.

A great sign appeared in the sky, a woman clothed with the sun,
    with the moon under her feet,
    and on her head a crown of twelve stars.
She was with child and wailed aloud in pain as she labored to give
        birth.
Then another sign appeared in the sky;
    it was a huge red dragon, with seven heads and ten horns,
    and on its heads were seven diadems.
Its tail swept away a third of the stars in the sky
    and hurled them down to the earth.
Then the dragon stood before the woman about to give birth,
    to devour her child when she gave birth.
She gave birth to a son, a male child,
    destined to rule all the nations with an iron rod.
Her child was caught up to God and his throne.
The woman herself fled into the desert
    where she had a place prepared by God.

Then I heard a loud voice in heaven say:
    "Now have salvation and power come,
        and the Kingdom of our God
        and the authority of his Anointed One."

Assumption of the Blessed Virgin Mary, August 15, 2009

RESPONSORIAL PSALM
Ps 45:10, 11, 12, 16

℟. (10bc) The queen stands at your right
hand, arrayed in gold.

The queen takes her place at your right hand
    in gold of Ophir.

℟. The queen stands at your right hand,
arrayed in gold.

Hear, O daughter, and see; turn your ear,
    forget your people and your father's house.

℟. The queen stands at your right hand,
arrayed in gold.

So shall the king desire your beauty;
    for he is your lord.

℟. The queen stands at your right hand,
arrayed in gold.

They are borne in with gladness and joy;
    they enter the palace of the king.

℟. The queen stands at your right hand,
arrayed in gold.

SECOND READING
1 Cor 15:20-27

Brothers and sisters:
Christ has been raised from the dead,
    the firstfruits of those who have fallen
      asleep.
For since death came through man,
    the resurrection of the dead came also
      through man.
For just as in Adam all die,
    so too in Christ shall all be brought to life,
    but each one in proper order:

Christ the firstfruits;
    then, at his coming, those who belong to
      Christ;
then comes the end,
    when he hands over the Kingdom to his
      God and Father,
    when he has destroyed every sovereignty
    and every authority and power.
For he must reign until he has put all his
    enemies under his feet.
The last enemy to be destroyed is death,
    for "he subjected everything under his feet."

Twenty-First Sunday in Ordinary Time, August 23, 2009

SECOND READING

or Eph 5:2a, 25-32

Brothers and sisters:
Live in love, as Christ loved us.
Husbands, love your wives,
    even as Christ loved the church
    and handed himself over for her to sanctify
      her,
    cleansing her by the bath of water with the
      word,
    that he might present to himself the church
      in splendor,
    without spot or wrinkle or any such thing,
    that she might be holy and without
      blemish.

So also husbands should love their wives as
    their own bodies.
He who loves his wife loves himself.
For no one hates his own flesh
    but rather nourishes and cherishes it,
    even as Christ does the church,
    because we are members of his body.
For this reason a man shall leave his father
    and his mother and be joined to his wife,
    and the two shall become one flesh.
This is a great mystery,
    but I speak in reference to Christ and the
      church.

Twenty-Second Sunday in Ordinary Time, August 30, 2009

Gospel (cont.)
Mark 7:1-8, 14-15, 21-23; L125B

You disregard God's commandment but cling to human tradition."

He summoned the crowd again and said to them,
    "Hear me, all of you, and understand.
Nothing that enters one from outside can defile that person;
    but the things that come out from within are what defile.

"From within people, from their hearts,
    come evil thoughts, unchastity, theft, murder,
    adultery, greed, malice, deceit,
    licentiousness, envy, blasphemy, arrogance, folly.
All these evils come from within and they defile."

Twenty-Seventh Sunday in Ordinary Time, *October 4, 2009*

Gospel (cont.)

Mark 10:2-16; L140B

And people were bringing children to him that he might touch them,
  but the disciples rebuked them.

When Jesus saw this he became indignant and said to them,
  "Let the children come to me;
    do not prevent them, for the kingdom of God belongs to such as
      these.
Amen, I say to you,
  whoever does not accept the kingdom of God like a child
    will not enter it."
Then he embraced them and blessed them,
  placing his hands on them.

or Mark 10:2-12; L140B

The Pharisees approached Jesus and asked,
  "Is it lawful for a husband to divorce his wife?"
They were testing him.
He said to them in reply, "What did Moses command you?"
They replied,
  "Moses permitted a husband to write a bill of divorce
    and dismiss her."
But Jesus told them,
  "Because of the hardness of your hearts
    he wrote you this commandment.
But from the beginning of creation, *God made them male and female.*
For this reason a man shall leave his father and mother
  and be joined to his wife,
    and the two shall become one flesh.
So they are no longer two but one flesh.
Therefore what God has joined together,
  no human being must separate."
In the house the disciples again questioned Jesus about this.
He said to them,
  "Whoever divorces his wife and marries another
    commits adultery against her;
      and if she divorces her husband and marries another,
        she commits adultery."

Twenty-Eighth Sunday in Ordinary Time, *October 11, 2009*

Gospel (cont.)

Mark 10:17-30; L143B

They were exceedingly astonished and said among themselves,
  "Then who can be saved?"
Jesus looked at them and said,
  "For human beings it is impossible, but not for God.
All things are possible for God."
Peter began to say to him,
  "We have given up everything and followed you."
Jesus said, "Amen, I say to you,
  there is no one who has given up house or brothers or sisters
    or mother or father or children or lands
    for my sake and for the sake of the gospel
  who will not receive a hundred times more now in this present age:
    houses and brothers and sisters
    and mothers and children and lands,
    with persecutions, and eternal life in the age to come."

or Mark 10:17-27

As Jesus was setting out on a journey, a man ran up,
  knelt down before him, and asked him,
    "Good teacher, what must I do to inherit eternal life?"
Jesus answered him, "Why do you call me good?
No one is good but God alone.

You know the commandments: *You shall not kill;*
  you shall not commit adultery;
    you shall not steal;
    you shall not bear false witness;
    you shall not defraud;
    honor your father and your mother."
He replied and said to him,
  "Teacher, all of these I have observed from my youth."
Jesus, looking at him, loved him and said to him,
  "You are lacking in one thing.
Go, sell what you have, and give to the poor
  and you will have treasure in heaven; then come, follow me."
At that statement his face fell,
  and he went away sad, for he had many possessions.

Jesus looked around and said to his disciples,
  "How hard it is for those who have wealth
    to enter the kingdom of God!"
The disciples were amazed at his words.
So Jesus again said to them in reply,
  "Children, how hard it is to enter the kingdom of God!
It is easier for a camel to pass through the eye of a needle
  than for one who is rich to enter the kingdom of God."
They were exceedingly astonished and said among themselves,
  "Then who can be saved?"
Jesus looked at them and said,
  "For human beings it is impossible, but not for God.
All things are possible for God."

Twenty-Ninth Sunday in Ordinary Time, *October 18, 2009*

Gospel

Mark 10:42-45; L146B

Jesus summoned them and said to them,
  "You know that those who are recognized as rulers over the Gentiles
  lord it over them,
  and their great ones make their authority over them felt.
But it shall not be so among you.
Rather, whoever wishes to be great among you will be your servant;
  whoever wishes to be first among you will be the slave of all.
For the Son of Man did not come to be served
  but to serve and to give his life as a ransom for many."

All Souls, *November 2, 2009*

FIRST READING

Dan 12:1-3; L1011.7

In those days, I, Daniel, mourned
  and heard this word of the Lord:
At that time there shall arise
  Michael, the great prince,
  guardian of your people;
It shall be a time unsurpassed in distress
  since nations began until that time.
At that time your people shall escape,
  everyone who is found written in the book.

Many of those who sleep in the dust of the
    earth shall awake;
Some shall live forever,
  others shall be an everlasting horror and
    disgrace.
But the wise shall shine brightly
  like the splendor of the firmament,
And those who lead the many to justice
  shall be like the stars forever.

RESPONSORIAL PSALM

Ps 27:1, 4, 7, and 8b, and 9a, 13-14

R℣. (1a) The Lord is my light and my
salvation.
  or:
R℣. (13) I believe that I shall see the good things
of the Lord in the land of the living.

The LORD is my light and my salvation;
  whom should I fear?
The LORD is my life's refuge;
  of whom should I be afraid?

R℣. The Lord is my light and my salvation.
  or:
R℣. I believe that I shall see the good things of
the Lord in the land of the living.

One thing I ask of the LORD;
  this I seek:
To dwell in the house of the LORD
  all the days of my life,
That I may gaze on the loveliness of the LORD
  and contemplate his temple.

R℣. The Lord is my light and my salvation.
  or:
R℣. I believe that I shall see the good things of
the Lord in the land of the living.

Hear, O LORD, the sound of my call;
  have pity on me and answer me.
Your presence, O LORD, I seek.
  Hide not your face from me.

R℣. The Lord is my light and my salvation.
  or:
R℣. I believe that I shall see the good things of
the Lord in the land of the living.

I believe that I shall see the bounty of the
    LORD
  in the land of the living.
Wait for the LORD with courage;
  be stouthearted, and wait for the LORD!

R℣. The Lord is my light and my salvation.
  or:
R℣. I believe that I shall see the good things of
the Lord in the land of the living.

SECOND READING

Rom 6:3-9; L1014.3

Brothers and sisters:
Are you unaware that we who were baptized
    into Christ Jesus
  were baptized into his death?
We were indeed buried with him through
    baptism into death,
  so that, just as Christ was raised from the
    dead
  by the glory of the Father,
  we too might live in newness of life.

For if we have grown into union with him
    through a death like his,
  we shall also be united with him in the
    resurrection.
We know that our old self was crucified with
    him,
  so that our sinful body might be done away
    with,
  that we might no longer be in slavery to
    sin.
For a dead person has been absolved from sin.
If, then, we have died with Christ,
  we believe that we shall also live with him.
We know that Christ, raised from the dead,
    dies no more;
  death no longer has power over him.

Thirty-Second Sunday in Ordinary Time, *November 8, 2009*

Gospel

Mark 12:41-44; L155B

Jesus sat down opposite the treasury
    and observed how the crowd put money into the treasury.
Many rich people put in large sums.
A poor widow also came and put in two small coins worth a few cents.
Calling his disciples to himself, he said to them,
    "Amen, I say to you, this poor widow put in more
    than all the other contributors to the treasury.
For they have all contributed from their surplus wealth,
    but she, from her poverty, has contributed all she had,
    her whole livelihood."

Thanksgiving Day, *November 26, 2009*

FIRST READING

Sir 50:22-24; L943.2

And now, bless the God of all,
    who has done wondrous things on earth;
Who fosters people's growth from their
        mother's womb,
    and fashions them according to his will!
May he grant you joy of heart
    and may peace abide among you;
May his goodness toward us endure in Israel
    to deliver us in our days.

RESPONSORIAL PSALM

Ps 67:2-3, 5, 7-8; L919.1

R℣. (7) The earth has yielded its fruit, the Lord our God has blessed us.
    or:
R℣. (4) O God, let all the nations praise you!

May God have pity on us and bless us;
    may he let his face shine upon us.
So may your way be known upon earth;
    among all nations, your salvation.

R℣. The earth has yielded its fruit, the Lord our God has blessed us.
    or:
R℣. O God, let all the nations praise you!

May the nations be glad and exult
    because you rule the peoples in equity;
    the nations on the earth you guide.

R℣. The earth has yielded its fruit, the Lord our God has blessed us.
    or:
R℣. O God, let all the nations praise you!

The earth has yielded its fruits;
    God, our God, has blessed us.
May God bless us,
    and may all the ends of the earth fear him!

R℣. The earth has yielded its fruit, the Lord our God has blessed us.
    or:
R℣. O God, let all the nations praise you!

SECOND READING

1 Cor 1:3-9; L944.1

Brothers and sisters:
Grace to you and peace from God our Father
    and the Lord Jesus Christ.

I give thanks to my God always on your
        account
    for the grace of God bestowed on you in
        Christ Jesus,
    that in him you were enriched in every way,
    with all discourse and all knowledge,
    as the testimony to Christ was confirmed
        among you,
    so that you are not lacking in any spiritual
        gift
    as you wait for the revelation of our Lord
        Jesus Christ.
He will keep you firm to the end,
    irreproachable on the day of our Lord Jesus
        Christ.
God is faithful,
    and by him you were called to fellowship
        with his Son, Jesus Christ our Lord.

Choral Settings for the General Intercessions

Purchasers of this volume may reproduce these choral arrangements for use in their parish or community. The music must be reproduced as given below, with composer's name and copyright line.

ADVENT

Music: Kathleen Harmon, SNDdeN, ©1999, Institute for Liturgical Ministry, 4960 Salem Avenue, Dayton OH 45416. All rights reserved.

CHRISTMAS and EASTER

Music: Kathleen Harmon, SNDdeN, ©1999, Institute for Liturgical Ministry, 4960 Salem Avenue, Dayton OH 45416. All rights reserved.

LENT

Music: Kathleen Harmon, SNDdeN, ©1999, Institute for Liturgical Ministry, 4960 Salem Avenue, Dayton OH 45416. All rights reserved.

SOLEMNITIES

Music: Kathleen Harmon, SNDdeN, ©1999, Institute for Liturgical Ministry, 4960 Salem Avenue, Dayton OH 45416. All rights reserved.

ORDINARY TIME, WEEKS 2-7

Cantor:

we pray to the Lord,

SATB Response:

Descant

Lord,_____ hear our prayer.

Lord,_____ hear our prayer.

ORDINARY TIME, WEEKS 12-23

Cantor:

we pray to the Lord,

SATB Response:

3

Lord, hear_____ our prayer.

3

ORDINARY TIME, WEEKS 24-33

Cantor:

we pray____ to the Lord,

SATB Response:

Lord, hear our prayer.

Lectionary Pronunciation Guide

Lectionary Word	Pronunciation
Aaron	EHR-uhn
Abana	AB-uh-nuh
Abednego	uh-BEHD-nee-go
Abel-Keramin	AY-b'l-KEHR-uh-mihn
Abel-meholah	AY-b'l-mee-HO-lah
Abiathar	uh-BAI-uh-ther
Abiel	AY-bee-ehl
Abiezrite	ay-bai-EHZ-rait
Abijah	uh-BAI-dzhuh
Abilene	ab-uh-LEE-neh
Abishai	uh-BIHSH-ay-ai
Abiud	uh-BAI-uhd
Abner	AHB-ner
Abraham	AY-bruh-ham
Abram	AY-br'm
Achaia	uh-KAY-yuh
Achim	AY-kihm
Aeneas	uh-NEE-uhs
Aenon	AY-nuhn
Agrippa	uh-GRIH-puh
Ahaz	AY-haz
Ahijah	uh-HAI-dzhuh
Ai	AY-ee
Alexandria	al-ehg-ZAN-dree-uh
Alexandrian	al-ehg-ZAN-dree-uhn
Alpha	AHL-fuh
Alphaeus	AL-fee-uhs
Amalek	AM-uh-lehk
Amaziah	am-uh-ZAI-uh
Amminadab	ah-MIHN-uh-dab
Ammonites	AM-uh-naitz
Amorites	AM-uh-raits
Amos	AY-muhs
Amoz	AY-muhz
Ampliatus	am-plee-AY-tuhs
Ananias	an-uh-NAI-uhs
Andronicus	an-draw-NAI-kuhs
Annas	AN-uhs
Antioch	AN-tih-ahk
Antiochus	an-TAI-uh-kuhs
Aphiah	uh-FAI-uh
Apollos	uh-PAH-luhs
Appius	AP-ee-uhs
Aquila	uh-KWIHL-uh
Arabah	EHR-uh-buh
Aram	AY-ram
Arameans	ehr-uh-MEE-uhnz
Areopagus	ehr-ee-AH-puh-guhs
Arimathea	ehr-uh-muh-THEE-uh
Aroer	uh-RO-er
Asaph	AY-saf
Asher	ASH-er
Ashpenaz	ASH-pee-naz
Assyria	a-SIHR-ee-uh
Astarte	as-TAHR-tee
Attalia	at-TAH-lee-uh
Augustus	uh-GUHS-tuhs
Azariah	az-uh-RAI-uh
Azor	AY-sawr
Azotus	uh-ZO-tus
Baal-shalishah	BAY-uhl-shuh-LAI-shuh
Baal-Zephon	BAY-uhl-ZEE-fuhn
Babel	BAY-bl
Babylon	BAB-ih-luhn
Babylonian	bab-ih-LO-nih-uhn
Balaam	BAY-lm
Barabbas	beh-REH-buhs
Barak	BEHR-ak
Barnabas	BAHR-nuh-buhs
Barsabbas	BAHR-suh-buhs
Bartholomew	bar-THAHL-uh-myoo
Bartimaeus	bar-tih-MEE-uhs
Baruch	BEHR-ook
Bashan	BAY-shan
Becorath	bee-KO-rath
Beelzebul	bee-EHL-zee-buhl
Beer-sheba	BEE-er-SHEE-buh
Belshazzar	behl-SHAZ-er
Benjamin	BEHN-dzhuh-mihn
Beor	BEE-awr
Bethany	BEHTH-uh-nee
Bethel	BETH-el
Bethesda	beh-THEHZ-duh
Bethlehem	BEHTH-leh-hehm
Bethphage	BEHTH-fuh-dzhee
Bethsaida	behth-SAY-ih-duh
Beth-zur	behth-ZER
Bildad	BIHL-dad
Bithynia	bih-THIHN-ih-uh
Boanerges	bo-uh-NER-dzheez
Boaz	BO-az
Caesar	SEE-zer
Caesarea	zeh-suh-REE-uh
Caiaphas	KAY-uh-fuhs
Cain	kayn
Cana	KAY-nuh
Canaan	KAY-nuhn
Canaanite	KAY-nuh-nait
Canaanites	KAY-nuh-naits
Candace	kan-DAY-see
Capernaum	kuh-PERR-nay-uhm
Cappadocia	kap-ih-DO-shee-u
Carmel	KAHR-muhl
Carnelians	kahr-NEEL-yuhnz
Cenchreae	SEHN-kree-ay
Cephas	SEE-fuhs
Chaldeans	kal-DEE-uhnz
Chemosh	KEE-mahsh
Cherubim	TSHEHR-oo-bihm
Chislev	KIHS-lehv
Chloe	KLO-ee
Chorazin	kor-AY-sihn
Cilicia	sih-LIHSH-ee-uh
Cleopas	KLEE-o-pas
Clopas	KLO-pas
Corinth	KAWR-ihnth
Corinthians	kawr-IHN-thee-uhnz
Cornelius	kawr-NEE-lee-uhs
Crete	kreet
Crispus	KRIHS-puhs
Cushite	CUHSH-ait
Cypriot	SIH-pree-at
Cyrene	sai-REE-nee
Cyreneans	sai-REE-nih-uhnz
Cyrenian	sai-REE-nih-uhn
Cyrenians	sai-REE-nih-uhnz
Cyrus	SAI-ruhs
Damaris	DAM-uh-rihs
Damascus	duh-MAS-kuhs
Danites	DAN-aits
Decapolis	duh-KAP-o-lis
Derbe	DER-bee
Deuteronomy	dyoo-ter-AH-num-mee
Didymus	DID-I-mus
Dionysius	dai-o-NIHSH-ih-uhs
Dioscuri	dai-O-sky-ri
Dorcas	DAWR-kuhs
Dothan	DO-thuhn
dromedaries	DRAH-muh-dher-eez
Ebed-melech	EE-behd-MEE-lehk
Eden	EE-dn
Edom	EE-duhm
Elamites	EE-luh-maitz
Eldad	EHL-dad
Eleazar	ehl-ee-AY-zer
Eli	EE-lai
Eli Eli Lema Sabachthani	AY-lee AY-lee luh-MAH sah-BAHK-tah-nee

Lectionary Word	Pronunciation	Lectionary Word	Pronunciation	Lectionary Word	Pronunciation
Eliab	ee-LAI-ab	Gilead	GIHL-ee-uhd	Joppa	DZHAH-puh
Eliakim	ee-LAI-uh-kihm	Gilgal	GIHL-gal	Joram	DZHO-ram
Eliezer	ehl-ih-EE-zer	Golgotha	GAHL-guh-thuh	Jordan	DZHAWR-dn
Elihu	ee-LAI-hyoo	Gomorrah	guh-MAWR-uh	Joseph	DZHO-zf
Elijah	ee-LAI-dzhuh	Goshen	GO-shuhn	Joses	DZHO-seez
Elim	EE-lihm	Habakkuk	huh-BAK-uhk	Joshua	DZHAH-shou-ah
Elimelech	ee-LIHM-eh-lehk	Hadadrimmon	hay-dad-RIHM-uhn	Josiah	dzho-SAI-uh
Elisha	ee-LAI-shuh	Hades	HAY-deez	Jotham	DZHO-thuhm
Eliud	ee-LAI-uhd	Hagar	HAH-gar	Judah	DZHOU-duh
Elizabeth	ee-LIHZ-uh-bth	Hananiah	han-uh-NAI-uh	Judas	DZHOU-duhs
Elkanah	el-KAY-nuh	Hannah	HAN-uh	Judea	dzhou-DEE-uh
Eloi Eloi Lama	AY-lo-ee AY-lo-ee	Haran	HAY-ruhn	Judean	dzhou-DEE-uhn
Sabechthani	LAH-mah sah-	Hebron	HEE-bruhn	Junia	dzhou-nih-uh
	BAHK-tah-nee	Hermes	HER-meez	Justus	DZHUHS-tuhs
Elymais	ehl-ih-MAY-ihs	Herod	HEHR-uhd	Kephas	KEF-uhs
Emmanuel	eh-MAN-yoo-ehl	Herodians	hehr-O-dee-uhnz	Kidron	KIHD-ruhn
Emmaus	eh-MAY-uhs	Herodias	hehr-O-dee-uhs	Kiriatharba	kihr-ee-ath-AHR-buh
Epaenetus	ee-PEE-nee-tuhs	Hezekiah	heh-zeh-KAI-uh	Kish	kihsh
Epaphras	EH-puh-fras	Hezron	HEHZ-ruhn	Laodicea	lay-o-dih-SEE-uh
ephah	EE-fuh	Hilkiah	hihl-KAI-uh	Lateran	LAT-er-uhn
Ephah	EE-fuh	Hittite	HIH-tait	Lazarus	LAZ-er-uhs
Ephesians	eh-FEE-zhuhnz	Hivites	HAI-vaitz	Leah	LEE-uh
Ephesus	EH-fuh-suhs	Hophni	HAHF-nai	Lebanon	LEH-buh-nuhn
Ephphatha	EHF-uh-thuh	Hor	HAWR	Levi	LEE-vai
Ephraim	EE-fray-ihm	Horeb	HAWR-ehb	Levite	LEE-vait
Ephrathah	EHF-ruh-thuh	Hosea	ho-ZEE-uh	Levites	LEE-vaits
Ephron	EE-frawn	Hur	her	Leviticus	leh-VIH-tih-kous
Epiphanes	eh-PIHF-uh-neez	hyssop	HIH-suhp	Lucius	LOO-shih-uhs
Erastus	ee-RAS-tuhs	Iconium	ai-KO-nih-uhm	Lud	luhd
Esau	EE-saw	Isaac	AI-zuhk	Luke	look
Esther	EHS-ter	Isaiah	ai-ZAY-uh	Luz	luhz
Ethanim	EHTH-uh-nihm	Iscariot	ihs-KEHR-ee-uht	Lycaonian	lihk-ay-O-nih-uhn
Ethiopian	ee-thee-O-pee-uhn	Ishmael	ISH-may-ehl	Lydda	LIH-duh
Euphrates	yoo-FRAY-teez	Ishmaelites	ISH-mayehl-aits	Lydia	LIH-dih-uh
Exodus	EHK-so-duhs	Israel	IHZ-ray-ehl	Lysanias	lai-SAY-nih-uhs
Ezekiel	eh-ZEE-kee-uhl	Ituraea	ih-TSHOOR-ree-uh	Lystra	LIHS-truh
Ezra	EHZ-ruh	Jaar	DZHAY-ahr	Maccabees	MAK-uh-beez
frankincense	FRANGK-ihn-sehns	Jabbok	DZHAB-uhk	Macedonia	mas-eh-DO-nih-uh
Gabbatha	GAB-uh-thuh	Jacob	DZHAY-kuhb	Macedonian	mas-eh-DO-nih-uhn
Gabriel	GAY-bree-ul	Jairus	DZH-hr-uhs	Machir	MAY-kih
Gadarenes	GAD-uh-reenz	Javan	DZHAY-van	Machpelah	mak-PEE-luh
Galatian	guh-LAY-shih-uhn	Jebusites	DZHEHB-oo-zaits	Magdala	MAG-duh-luh
Galatians	guh-LAY-shih-uhnz	Jechoniah	dzhehk-o-NAI-uh	Magdalene	MAG-duh-lehn
Galilee	GAL-ih-lee	Jehoiakim	dzhee-HOI-uh-kihm	magi	MAY-dzhai
Gallio	GAL-ih-o	Jehoshaphat	dzhee-HAHSH-uh-fat	Malachi	MAL-uh-kai
Gamaliel	guh-MAY-lih-ehl	Jephthah	DZHEHF-thuh	Malchiah	mal-KAI-uh
Gaza	GAH-zuh	Jeremiah	dzhehr-eh-MAI-uh	Malchus	MAL-kuhz
Gehazi	gee-HAY-zai	Jericho	DZHEHR-ih-ko	Mamre	MAM-ree
Gehenna	geh-HEHN-uh	Jeroham	dzhehr-RO-ham	Manaen	MAN-uh-ehn
Genesis	DZHEHN-uh-sihs	Jerusalem	dzheh-ROU-suh-lehm	Manasseh	man-AS-eh
Gennesaret	gehn-NEHS-uh-reht	Jesse	DZHEH-see	Manoah	muh-NO-uh
Gentiles	DZHEHN-tailz	Jethro	DZHEHTH-ro	Mark	mahrk
Gerasenes	DZHEHR-uh-seenz	Joakim	DZHO-uh-kihm	Mary	MEHR-ee
Gethsemane	gehth-SEHM-uh-ne	Job	DZHOB	Massah	MAH-suh
Gideon	GIHD-ee-uhn	Jonah	DZHO-nuh	Mattathias	mat-uh-THAI-uhs

Lectionary Word	Pronunciation	Lectionary Word	Pronunciation	Lectionary Word	Pronunciation
Matthan	MAT-than	Parmenas	PAHR-mee-nas	Sabbath	SAB-uhth
Matthew	MATH-yoo	Parthians	PAHR-thee-uhnz	Sadducees	SAD-dzhoo-seez
Matthias	muh-THAI-uhs	Patmos	PAT-mos	Salem	SAY-lehm
Medad	MEE-dad	Peninnah	pee-NIHN-uh	Salim	SAY-lim
Mede	meed	Pentecost	PEHN-tee-kawst	Salmon	SAL-muhn
Medes	meedz	Penuel	pee-NYOO-ehl	Salome	suh-LO-mee
Megiddo	mee-GIH-do	Perez	PEE-rehz	Salu	SAYL-yoo
Melchizedek	mehl-KIHZ-eh-dehk	Perga	PER-guh	Samaria	suh-MEHR-ih-uh
Mene	MEE-nee	Perizzites	PEHR-ih-zaits	Samaritan	suh-MEHR-ih-tuhn
Meribah	MEHR-ih-bah	Persia	PER-zhuh	Samothrace	SAM-o-thrays
Meshach	MEE-shak	Peter	PEE-ter	Samson	SAM-s'n
Mespotamia	mehs-o-po-TAY-mih-uh	Phanuel	FAN-yoo-ehl	Samuel	SAM-yoo-uhl
		Pharaoh	FEHR-o	Sanhedrin	san-HEE-drihn
Micah	MAI-kuh	Pharisees	FEHR-ih-seez	Sarah	SEHR-uh
Midian	MIH-dih-uhn	Pharpar	FAHR-pahr	Sarai	SAY-rai
Milcom	MIHL-kahm	Philemon	fih-LEE-muhn	saraph	SAY-raf
Miletus	mai-LEE-tuhs	Philippi	fil-LIH-pai	Sardis	SAHR-dihs
Minnith	MIHN-ihth	Philippians	fih-LIHP-ih-uhnz	Saul	sawl
Mishael	MIHSH-ay-ehl	Philistines	fih-LIHS-tihnz	Scythian	SIH-thee-uihn
Mizpah	MIHZ-puh	Phinehas	FEHN-ee-uhs	Seba	SEE-buh
Moreh	MO-reh	Phoenicia	fee-NIHSH-ih-uh	Seth	sehth
Moriah	maw-RAI-uh	Phrygia	FRIH-dzhih-uh	Shaalim	SHAY-uh-lihm
Mosoch	MAH-sahk	Phrygian	FRIH-dzhih-uhn	Shadrach	SHAY-drak
myrrh	mer	phylacteries	fih-LAK-ter-eez	Shalishah	shuh-LEE-shuh
Mysia	MIH-shih-uh	Pi-Hahiroth	pai-huh-HAI-rahth	Shaphat	Shay-fat
Naaman	NAY-uh-muhn	Pilate	PAI-luht	Sharon	SHEHR-uhn
Nahshon	NAY-shuhn	Pisidia	pih-SIH-dih-uh	Shealtiel	shee-AL-tih-ehl
Naomi	NAY-o-mai	Pithom	PAI-thahm	Sheba	SHEE-buh
Naphtali	NAF-tuh-lai	Pontius	PAHN-shus	Shebna	SHEB-nuh
Nathan	NAY-thuhn	Pontus	PAHN-tus	Shechem	SHEE-kehm
Nathanael	nuh-THAN-ay-ehl	Praetorium	pray-TAWR-ih-uhm	shekel	SHEHK-uhl
Nazarene	NAZ-awr-een	Priscilla	PRIHS-kill-uh	Shiloh	SHAI-lo
Nazareth	NAZ-uh-rehth	Prochorus	PRAH-kaw-ruhs	Shinar	SHAI-nahr
nazirite	NAZ-uh-rait	Psalm	Sahm	Shittim	sheh-TEEM
Nazorean	naz-aw-REE-uhn	Put	puht	Shuhite	SHOO-ait
Neapolis	nee-AP-o-lihs	Puteoli	pyoo-TEE-o-lai	Shunammite	SHOO-nam-ait
Nebuchadnezzar	neh-byoo-kuhd-NEHZ-er	Qoheleth	ko-HEHL-ehth	Shunem	SHOO-nehm
		qorban	KAWR-bahn	Sidon	SAI-duhn
Negeb	NEH-gehb	Quartus	KWAR-tuhs	Silas	SAI-luhs
Nehemiah	nee-hee-MAI-uh	Quirinius	kwai-RIHN-ih-uhs	Siloam	sih-LO-uhm
Ner	ner	Raamses	ray-AM-seez	Silvanus	sihl-VAY-nuhs
Nicanor	nai-KAY-nawr	Rabbi	RAB-ai	Simeon	SIHM-ee-uhn
Nicodemus	nih-ko-DEE-muhs	Rabbouni	ra-BO-nai	Simon	SAI-muhn
Niger	NAI-dzher	Rahab	RAY-hab	Sin (desert)	sihn
Nineveh	NIHN-eh-veh	Ram	ram	Sinai	SAI-nai
Noah	NO-uh	Ramah	RAY-muh	Sirach	SAI-rak
Nun	nuhn	Ramathaim	ray-muh-THAY-ihm	Sodom	SAH-duhm
Obed	O-behd	Raqa	RA-kuh	Solomon	SAH-lo-muhn
Olivet	AH-lih-veht	Rebekah	ree-BEHK-uh	Sosthenes	SAHS-thee-neez
Omega	o-MEE-guh	Rehoboam	ree-ho-BO-am	Stachys	STAY-kihs
Onesimus	o-NEH-sih-muhs	Rephidim	REHF-ih-dihm	Succoth	SUHK-ahth
Ophir	O-fer	Reuben	ROO-b'n	Sychar	SI-kar
Orpah	AWR-puh	Revelation	reh-veh-LAY-shuhn	Syene	sai-EE-nee
Pamphylia	pam-FIHL-ih-uh	Rhegium	REE-dzhee-uhm	Symeon	SIHM-ee-uhn
Paphos	PAY-fuhs	Rufus	ROO-fuhs	synagogues	SIHN-uh-gahgz

Lectionary Word	Pronunciation	Lectionary Word	Pronunciation	Lectionary Word	Pronunciation
Syrophoenician	SIHR-o fee-NIHSH-ih-uhn	Timon	TAI-muhn	Zebedee	ZEH-beh-dee
Tabitha	TAB-ih-thuh	Titus	TAI-tuhs	Zebulun	ZEH-byoo-luhn
Talitha koum	TAL-ih-thuh-KOOM	Tohu	TO-hyoo	Zechariah	zeh-kuh-RAI-uh
Tamar	TAY-mer	Trachonitis	trak-o-NAI-tis	Zedekiah	zeh-duh-KAI-uh
Tarshish	TAHR-shihsh	Troas	TRO-ahs	Zephaniah	zeh-fuh-NAI-uh
Tarsus	TAHR-suhs	Tubal	TYOO-b'l	Zerah	ZEE-ruh
Tekel	TEH-keel	Tyre	TAI-er	Zeror	ZEE-rawr
Terebinth	TEHR-ee-bihnth	Ur	er	Zerubbabel	zeh-RUH-buh-behl
Thaddeus	THAD-dee-uhs	Urbanus	er-BAY-nuhs	Zeus	zyoos
Theophilus	thee-AH-fih-luhs	Uriah	you-RAI-uh	Zimri	ZIHM-rai
Thessalonians	theh-suh-LO-nih-uhnz	Uzziah	yoo-ZAI-uh	Zion	ZAI-uhn
Theudas	THU-duhs	Wadi	WAH-dee	Ziph	zihf
Thyatira	thai-uh-TAI-ruh	Yahweh-yireh	YAH-weh-yer-AY	Zoar	ZO-er
Tiberias	tai-BIHR-ih-uhs	Zacchaeus	zak-KEE-uhs	Zorah	ZAWR-uh
Timaeus	tai-MEE-uhs	Zadok	ZAY-dahk	Zuphite	ZUHR-ait
		Zarephath	ZEHR-ee-fath		